NATURE
OF BRITAIN

NATURE
OF BRITAIN

DK

LONDON, NEW YORK, MELBOURNE,
MUNICH AND DELHI

Senior editor Paula Regan
Project art editor Anna Hall

Managing editor Debra Wolter
Managing art editor Karen Self

Production editor Maria Elia
Production controller Linda Dare

Managing cartographer David Roberts
Cartographer Paul Eames
Regional Directory maps
Encompass Graphics Ltd

Art director Bryn Walls
Publisher Jonathan Metcalf
Associate Publisher Liz Wheeler

Produced for Dorling Kindersley by

cobaltid

The Stables, Wood Farm, Deopham Road,
Attleborough, Norfolk NR17 1AJ
www.cobaltid.co.uk

Editors Louise Abbott, Kati Dye, Maddy King,
Sarah Tomley, Marek Walisiewicz

Designers Darren Bland, Claire Dale,
Rebecca Johns, Paul Reid, Lloyd Tilbury

This edition published in 2009
First published in Great Britain in 2009 as
RSPB Where to go Wild in Britain
by Dorling Kindersley Limited
80 Strand, London WC2R 0RL
A Penguin company
Copyright © 2009 Dorling Kindersley Limited

2 4 6 8 10 9 7 5 3 1

A CIP catalogue record for this book is available from the
British Library

ISBN 978-1-4053-4772-3

Printed and bound in Singapore by Star Standard

Every effort has been made to ensure that this book is as up-to-date as possible at
the time of going to press. Some details, however, such as telephone numbers,
opening hours, and travel information are liable to change. The publishers cannot
accept responsibility for any consequences arising from the use of this book, nor for
any material on the third-party websites, and cannot guarantee that any website
address in this book will be a suitable source of travel information.

Discover more at
www.dk.com

CONTENTS

Remember to always follow the
Countryside Code, available at
www.countrysideaccess.gov.uk

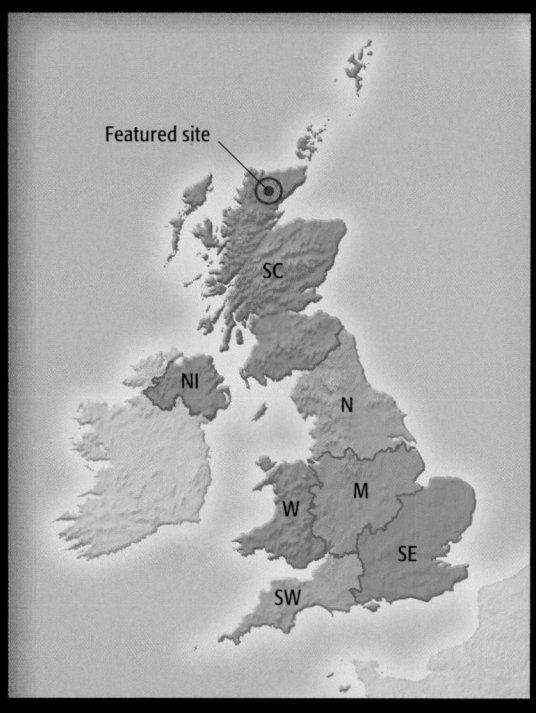

Featured site

HOW TO USE THE MAPS
The location of each featured site is marked
on the maps by a red dot. The UK is divided
into seven areas which correspond with the
Regional Directory on pages 312–328, in which
details of all the sites, including those listed in
the "Where Else To See" panels, are given:

SC – Scotland
N – Northern England
NI – Northern Ireland
M – Midlands
W – Wales
SE – Southeast England
SW – Southwest England

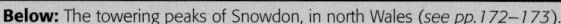

Below: The towering peaks of Snowdon, in north Wales (see pp.172–173).

FOREWORD

LET'S START WITH SOME INCONTROVERTIBLE FACTS: a walk in the countryside to look for wildlife is cheap, healthy for the mind and body, and great fun. However, I am often surprised by how few people I bump into when admiring a blaze of orchids in a summer meadow, or flocks of wading birds over an estuary in winter. So why are many of our finest nature locations still woefully under-visited? Well, part of the reason may be down to the fact that the Great British public needs more of a guiding hand when deciding where to go and when to visit.

Irrespective of where you live, or when you take your holiday, every page of this book is brimming with ideas about where to go each month to see the very best of our wildlife. You'll discover where to find the most glorious bluebell woodlands in spring, the finest seabird colonies in summer, the most impressive red deer rut in autumn, and the greatest high-tide winter wader roosts. I am lucky enough to spend most of the year filming the best wildlife Britain has to offer, but I was astonished by the abundance of new ideas for future filming trips.

Britain may not have the awe-inspiring great game spectacles of the east African plains, or the immense biological diversity of the Amazon rainforest, but our islands do possess an astonishing mosaic of habitats, which, as the seasons shift, play host to a constantly changing cast of characters. In my adopted city of Bristol, for example, I am no more than an hour's drive (or train ride) away from ancient woodland, rolling grassland, vast estuaries, and primeval wetland; all of which reveal a multitude of differing wildlife treats depending on the month visited.

Only by making the most of Britain's unique wildlife heritage will our most precious sites be ultimately cherished, conserved, and protected for future generations. All you need to do now is pack your camera, your binoculars, and this book, put your walking boots on, and get out there and enjoy!

MIKE DILGER

WHEN WAS THE LAST TIME NATURE TAPPED YOU ON THE SHOULDER? You know, one of those moments where you have a connection with something wild that changes the course of your whole day?

Moments like those are the reason the RSPB exists. From the surprise and delight you feel when a robin, bold as you like, lands on the handle of your garden spade, to the sense of awe and humility that grips you when you're confronted with an ancient landscape, we're here to protect the things that have the greatest power to move us. We have a million members speaking out for birds and wildlife – people like you, who nature enchants, tickles, relaxes, inspires, and rewards.

So often these days, wildlife is an afterthought, and sometimes not thought of at all. At the RSPB, we believe that the environment should be at the top of the agenda when people plan where to build houses, put up wind farms, handle transport problems, put out fishing boats, or educate our children. We're there to be a voice for nature, never giving up, getting things done, changing things for the better – for wildlife and for you.

To be enchanted by nature, you really need to experience it firsthand, and that is what this book is all about. It picks a selection of the finest places and most extraordinary sights the British Isles have to offer, whether on RSPB land or elsewhere. Some, like roosting gulls, boxing hares, dancing grebes, or purple heather moorlands, are found in many places. Others are truly rare, but all are special.

Our nature reserves punctuate the landscape, but our campaigning voice speaks up for wildlife wherever it lives. The whole nature conservation movement wants you to share enjoyable moments with wildlife. Nature is amazing – please help us to keep it that way.

MARK BOYD
www.rspb.org.uk

JANUARY

Where to Go: **January**

January is a stepping-stone to the rest of the year – but what a start! The cold weather and bare landscapes present a unique opportunity to see the barren bones of the world around us, especially among the woods and hedgerows, and to appreciate what lies beneath the best wildlife places, before they are smothered in the green growth of spring. Birds are abundant in lowland areas, especially near the coast: flocks of ducks and geese feed on the mudflats of our estuaries, which provide such a vital refuge from bitter winter weather farther north and east. Inland, floods and reservoirs provide opportunities to see swans, ducks, and gulls, and you might, with luck, come across a water vole, or a couple of resting brown hares. Higher up, on the northern

INLETS AND ESTUARIES

DEE ESTUARY View across the Dee estuary from Hilbre Island.

WETLANDS

OUSE WASHES Bewick's swans at dawn over the Ouse Washes.

WILD IN THE CITY

LONDON WETLAND CENTRE Look for the endangered water vole.

DEE ESTUARY
CHESHIRE/NORTH WALES [N]

This wide, shallow estuary divides Wales from England, and is a great place to watch waders and ducks in the water, while short-eared owls hunt overhead.
See pp.14–15

CHICHESTER HARBOUR
WEST SUSSEX [SE]

Watch wading birds probe the mudflats for food at low tide, and then, as the tide comes in, move on to their roosting sites to huddle in their thousands.
See pp.14–15

At low tide, the Dee estuary reveals swathes of golden sand interspersed with sinuous channels of water, lazily making their way to the sea.

OUSE WASHES
CAMBRIDGESHIRE [SE]

Come here to see the largest concentration of Bewick and whooper swans in the country, swooping in groups of thousands across the water.
See pp.22–23

COTSWOLD WATER PARK
GLOUCESTERSHIRE [SE]

Thousands of birds spend the winter on the 140 man-made lakes that make up the site, while up to 25 hobbies hunt over their waters.
See pp.26–27

ATTENBOROUGH GRAVEL PITS
NOTTINGHAMSHIRE [SE]

Reclaimed land that has been imaginatively landscaped and managed to provide a range of wildlife habitats for birds, animals, and plants.
See pp.26–27

This wetland centre is a green oasis surrounded by urban sprawl – a true wildlife haven, just a stone's throw from central London.

LONDON WETLAND CENTRE
LONDON [SE]

This award-winning site is ideal for a tranquil walk in search of shy bitterns and water voles, but also organizes plenty of family activities, both indoors and out.
See pp.16–17

WINNALL MOORS
HAMPSHIRE [SW]

The River Itchen flows right through this reserve, just 1km (½ mile) from Winchester city centre, attracting all the wildlife associated with chalk streams.
See pp.16–17

FAL ESTUARY
FALMOUTH, CORNWALL [SW]

One of southwest England's most beautiful estuaries, with pale, gleaming mudflats, rockpools to explore, and "meadows" of eelgrass amongst which scuttle crabs and cuttlefish.
See pp.20–21

EXE ESTUARY
EXETER, DEVON [SW]

Over 20,000 birds winter here, including avocets, glossy ibises, lapwings, redshanks, and ducks. Harvest mice, otters, and water shrews live around the shore.
See pp.14–15

LEE VALLEY PARK
ESSEX/HERTFORDSHIRE [SE]

This huge country park, a "green lung" for Greater London, is the perfect, wildlife-rich getaway for city-dwellers.
See pp.26–27

BOUGH BEECH RESERVOIR
SEVENOAKS, KENT [SE]

A great location for ducks; there are also bird feeders that allow close-up views of shy species such as brambling and great spotted woodpecker.
See pp.16–17

BURRY INLET
GOWER PENINSULA, SOUTH WALES [W]

Thousands of birds live on these mudflats and saltmarshes. Little egrets, great crested grebes, grey herons, and brent geese can all be seen in January.
See pp.14–15

Up to one-tenth of the British wintering population of bitterns can be found in the Lee Valley Park

NEWPORT WETLANDS
GWENT, SOUTH WALES [W]

This is a great place to see otters and also fantastic starling roosts – huge "swarms" of birds that fill the sky as the day ends.
See pp.16–17

STAINES RESERVOIR
MIDDLESEX [SE]

Nestling below the flight path of Heathrow this reserve attracts plenty of birds, including peregrine falcons, which like to scan for prey from the pylons.
See pp.16–17

Previous page: A winter greeting between two brown hares.

moors, mountain hares will be clad in their thick white winter coat. In mainland Scotland, and around the Hebridean islands, you can more easily see beautiful red deer.

Woodland birds gather into nomadic mixed flocks, roaming through the trees in search of food; you'll normally hear them first as they noisily give themselves away. Suddenly there are more birds than you can watch all at once – and then they all fly off, leaving the woods eerily quiet. On the coast, you might still see grey and common seals, and have fun poking about in the rockpools left by the outgoing tide. It is, however, the birds that dominate even here by the sea, with turnstones, oystercatchers, and purple sandpipers among the winter gems.

COAST

DRURIDGE BAY The long, wind-blown sand dunes fill with birds.

HEATH AND MOOR

GELTSDALE Both red and black grouse make their homes here.

ISLANDS

ISLAY Seals can be found in bays around the island.

DRURIDGE BAY
NORTHUMBERLAND [N]

Druridge Bay is the longest beach in Northumberland; thousands of wintering birds live on its sand dunes and lagoons in January, including geese, swans, and ducks.
See pp.20–21

PAGHAM HARBOUR
SIDLESHAM, WEST SUSSEX [SE]

The shingle spits that border this harbour are filled with dark-bellied brent geese, wigeons, black-tailed godwits, knots, and avocets.
See pp.20–21

THE NORTH YORK MOORS
YORKSHIRE [N]

Red grouse, golden plovers, and curlews brave the northern winter here, along with merlins – the UK's smallest birds of prey.
See pp.24–25

ISLAY
INNER HEBRIDES [SC]

The southernmost Hebridean island, with something for everyone: seals, deer, otters, wintering seabirds, and birds of prey including the magnificent golden eagle.
See pp.12–13

In winter, hen harriers hunt over the lower Islay moors, and you just might have a once-in-a-lifetime encounter with a golden eagle.

LINDISFARNE
NORTHUMBERLAND [N]

The extensive sand dunes and long sandy beaches of this tidal island sparkle in winter sunshine, while rock pools shelter all manner of sea creatures.
See pp.20–21

YNYS-HIR
POWYS, SOUTH WALES [W]

The bracken-covered slopes of this reserve are hunting grounds for birds of prey. Polecats and badgers also live here.
See pp.18–19

GELTSDALE
BRAMPTON, CUMBRIA [N]

This forbidding landscape is home to red and black grouse, and birds of prey, including hen harriers, buzzards, and short-eared owls.
See pp.24–25

ISLE OF SKYE
INNER HEBRIDES [SC]

A dramatic place to see eagles, red and roe deer, seals, otters, dolphins, whales, porpoises, and thousands of seabirds.
See pp.12–13

HOLKHAM
NORTH NORFOLK [SE]

The sight of some 150,000 birds that winter on the mudflats, nearly all pink-footed geese from the Arctic, is unmissable. The pinewoods and the beach are beautiful too.
See pp.18–19

The blanket bogs, heath, and woods stretch out before you in a glorious wilderness; the short, crisp days are perfect for walking.

ISLE OF MULL
INNER HEBRIDES [SC]

A mountainous isle lying just off the Scottish mainland, this is perhaps the most beautiful place to watch the white-tailed sea eagle and golden eagle commanding the skies.
See pp.12–13

ST CATHERINE'S POINT
ISLE OF WIGHT [SE]

Winters can be mild on this south coast island, with beautiful cliff downlands and headlands from which to watch for seabirds.
See pp.20–21

MINSMERE
SUFFOLK [SE]

This is a great time to look for birds of prey hunting over the heathland, and flocks of tits and finches among the trees, as well as enjoying the water birds.
See pp.26–27

ISLE OF ARRAN
NORTH AYRSHIRE [SC]

Three species of striking diving ducks winter here. The last berries on the unique Arran whitebeam provide welcome food for hungry perching birds.
See pp.12–13

NORTH UIST
OUTER HEBRIDES [SC]

This unspoilt Western Isle is home to the rare corncrake, along with wheeling Arctic terns and noisy gannets.
See pp.12–13

WHERE
Islay, Argyll and Bute, Scotland.

CONTACT
RSPB Loch Gruinart Reserve, Bushmills Cottage, Gruinart, Bridgend, Isle of Islay, Argyll and Bute PA44 7PR, Scotland; tel: 01496 850505; loch.gruinart@rspb.org.uk

GETTING THERE
Ferries leave from Kennacraig three or four times a day on weekdays and Saturdays, and twice on Sundays. The Loch Gruinart reserve is signed from the A847 Bridgend to Bruichladdich Road, 4.8km (3 miles) from the turn-off. The nearest bus stop to the reserve is at this turn-off.

ACCESS AND FACILITIES
The RSPB reserve has good access to viewing points and one hide is specially adapted for wheelchair users (access by car can be arranged). The centre has full-access toilets for all abilities, parking, and refreshments, and is pushchair friendly. The woodland trail is not suitable for wheelchairs.

OPENING TIMES
The reserve is open at all times. The visitor centre is open daily from 10am to 5pm.

CHARGES
None.

Legend of the goose

Barnacle geese are not named for a fondness for barnacles – their preferred food is leaves, stems, roots, and seeds – but gain their name from old English folklore. The belief was that they spent the summer developing underwater in the form of barnacles, only to emerge in winter in bird form (thus explaining the sudden arrival of the birds in winter). This convenient legend permitted Catholics to see these birds as sea life, and so eat their flesh during Lent, when believers were supposed to abstain from meat and poultry.

Above (left to right): A golden eagle; the Mull of Oa; the beach near Kidalton, on the south shore of the island.
Main: Cliffs overlooking the Mull of Oa, Islay.

HEBRIDEAN HIGHLIGHT

SLAY IS THE SOUTHERNMOST ISLAND OF THE INNER HEBRIDES, lying at the entrance to the Firth of Lorn. Its vast range of habitats supports a terrific variety of wildlife. In winter, hen harriers hunt over the lower moors and you just might have a once-in-a-lifetime encounter with a golden eagle, especially in the rugged south of the island towards the Oa peninsula. Look out, too, for red-billed choughs on the tidelines of the sandy bays, feeding on insects found in the seaweed.

Islay has 130 miles of indented coastline, with sand and shingle beach, mudflats, and cliffs. Loch Indaal and Loch Gruinart, both with mudflats and smooth green marsh at the head of enclosed bays, are marvellous places for wintering waders, divers, grebes, and sea ducks such as eiders and scaups. But it is the extraordinary population of geese that everyone comes to see in winter: around 37,000 barnacle geese and 13,000 white-fronted geese inhabit the island from autumn until April, creating a magnificent sight and sound. The barnacle geese from Greenland are indistinguishable from barnacle geese breeding in Spitsbergen (which spend the winter on the Solway Firth), while the orange-billed, white-fronted geese are darker than the much more numerous pink-billed ones from Siberia, and form a distinct race. You can see both species around the head of Loch Gruinart.

Look out too, for the shyer island inhabitants, like the red, fallow, and roe deer, and the secretive otters. Common and grey seals can be found around the coast, in places such as Killinallan Point, east of Loch Gruinart. The Rhinns in the north and the Oa in the south are good for birds of prey, including golden eagles, buzzards, hen harriers, peregrines, merlins, and kestrels; while common and black guillemots, razorbills, kittiwakes, fulmars, and shags fly around the cliffs. The blue-grey rock doves, truly wild and untainted by domestic stock, feed on cliff-top grasslands and nest around the seacliffs.

Islay's many offshore islets, particularly in the south, provide perfect places for grey and common seals to haul out of the water and bask in any winter sun.

Inset: Common seals with their thick, insulating layer of winter blubber.
Below (left to right): Barnacle geese in flight; white-fronted geese foraging.

JAN

WHERE ELSE TO SEE
ROCKY ISLANDS

There are hundreds of islands around the Scottish coast, many of which are uninhabited by people, but are home to thousands of birds. They can be reached by special boat trips, or by ferry, in some cases.

The **Isle of Skye** is the largest island of the Inner Hebrides. Its northern tip provides a dramatic backdrop for seabirds, including fulmars, kittiwakes, and shags, while Broadford Bay in the south is good for seeing rarer migrants. [SC]

The **Isle of Mull** (see pp.226–227), another Inner Hebridean island, is well known both for its seabirds and its birds of prey, which hunt over the moors and fish over the lochs and sea. [SC]

The **Isle of Arran** (see pp.42–43), has two distinct halves: a moutainous northern half, and moorlands in the south. Its large bird population lives alongside otters, red deer, and red squirrels. [SC]

North Uist (see pp.108–109) has rocky shores, freshwater lochans, sea lochs on the east of the island, and machair habitat along the west coast. There is an RSPB reserve at Balranald where you can see corncrakes. [SC]

THROUGH THE YEAR
ISLAY

In **spring** Islay comes alive with the songs of lapwings, redshanks, and curlews, and the drumming displays of snipe. All the birds can be easily seen at the RSPB reserve at Loch Gruinart.

A special **summer** bird is the corncrake, whose rasping notes can be heard in May and June, mostly at night. Common terns and ringed plovers nest on the beaches.

In **autumn** the geese return, and many wintering ducks including wigeons, teals, and scaups. Fieldfares and redwings pass through in autumn. Look for purple sandpipers and rock pipits along the shore.

Below: Corncrakes nest on undisturbed farmland.

FEB
MAR
APR
MAY
JUN
JUL
AUG
SEP
OCT
NOV
DEC

WHERE
The Dee Estuary lies between Thurstaston, Wirral CH61 0, England, and the Point of Ayr CH8 9, North Wales; www.deeestuary.co.uk

CONTACT
Wirral Country Park: 0151 6484371/3884; Hilbre Island Nature Reserve: 0151 6324455; Wirral Rangers: coastalpark@wirral.gov.uk RSPB Dee Estuary: 0151 3367681.

GETTING THERE
There are several access points along the estuary. From Chester take the A55 towards Queensferry, then you can either take the A548 along the Welsh side, to reach places such as Talacre and Point of Ayr; or take the A540 to visit places on the English side such as Parkgate and West Kirby. There is a bus to the RSPB reserve at Gayton Sands, Parkgate, every hour from Neston, which is the nearest rail connection, at 3km (2 miles) away. To walk to the islands, start from the Dee Lane Slipway at West Kirby.

ACCESS AND FACILITIES
There are public toilets at the Dee Lane Slipway. The most easily accessible viewing points are the sea wall at the Point of Ayr, and Parkgate promenade or Parkgate Old Baths car park, near The Boathouse pub.

CHARGES
None.

Chinese mitten crab

In 2006, an Asian species of crab, the Chinese mitten crab, was found to have invaded the Dee Estuary. They had colonized other rivers in the south coast of England, where they caused both environmental problems – by burrowing into the riverbanks, causing them to collapse – and health problems, as they carry a parasitic flatworm called a lung fluke. The crab's identifying features are the dense patches of hairs on its white-tipped claws, from which it acquired its unusual name.

Above (top to bottom): Brent geese look out from an island on the Dee Estuary; a dunlin forages in the water.

Below: Weaver fish hide just under the sand, and their poisonous spines impart a vicious sting – if stung, apply hot flannels to the wound for at least 15 minutes.

Right panel (top and bottom): Bright-billed oystercatchers search for cockles, their favourite food; the Dee Estuary divides Wales from England.

Main: Oystercatchers and cormorants roosting on Little Eye after the high tide forces them inland – Hilbre Island is visible in the distance.

ACROSS THE SANDS OF DEE

IT'S NOT SURPRISING THAT SO MANY ARTISTS HAVE BEEN INSPIRED by the Dee Estuary. At low tide, the vast mouth of the estuary reveals swathes of golden sand interspersed with sinuous channels of water, lazily making their way to the sea. The wide, shallow estuary divides North Wales from northwest England, covering approximately 150sq km (58 sq miles). It is one of the best places to see large numbers of breeding, wintering, and migrating birds, and it is internationally recognized for its wealth of habitats, which support an amazing variety of wildlife. There are tidal rivers, mud and sand flats, lagoons, sand dunes, saltmarshes, and even cliffs.

The seemingly endless marshlands of Parkgate and Burton, lying fairly far inland on the English side, are good places to watch short-eared owls hunt, or seabirds and waders start to rise up in flocks as the tide pushes them inland. Travelling along the Welsh side you can really appreciate how the estuary moves from being a

Looking out from the dunes at the Point of Ayr, you begin to see why the estuary is home to 130,000 waders and wildfowl in winter.

Above: The main channel of the Dee Estuary at low tide.

THROUGH THE YEAR
DEE ESTUARY

The Dee Estuary is an important breeding site for little and common terns, which both start nesting in May. **Spring** is a busy breeding time for many other birds within the estuary, including oystercatchers, redshanks, and skylarks, and also for the scarce natterjack toad, which breeds in the dunes at Talacre.

There is a large colony of grey seals that haul up on West Hoyle bank, just south of Hilbre island in **summer**. During August you can see up to 500 seals; although many leave during the winter months, non-breeders stay, so you usually see seals all year round. The summering flock of non-breeding black-tailed godwits is one of the largest in the UK. Botanists will enjoy seeking out specialities like the rare petalwort and sea spleenwort; there is also a subspecies of rock sea-lavender here that is found in only a few other places in in Europe.

Thousands of waders fly in to the estuary in **autumn** to feed on the mudflats. Large flocks of ducks can be seen escaping the rough open seas. The berried bushes of Thurstaston Country Park provide welcome food for fieldfares and redwings, while Greenfield welcomes many elegant great crested grebes.

WHERE ELSE TO SEE
ESTUARY WILDLIFE

Britain is lucky to have many other estuary sites that are renowned for birds and other wildlife.

Visit **Chichester Harbour**, West Sussex, in autumn or winter to see many different waders and wildfowl, including curlews, whimbrels, godwits, oystercatchers, snipe, and grey plovers. [SE]

The **Exe Estuary** (see pp.286–287), in Devon, is one of the best places to see waders and wildfowl, including wintering avocets and brent geese. [SW]

Burry Inlet, Gower (see pp.122–123), supports thousands of birds on its mudflats and saltmarshes. Little egrets, great crested grebes, grey herons, and brent geese can all be seen in winter. [W]

Slimbridge (see pp.34–35), on the Severn estuary, is excellent for wild ducks, swans, and geese. [M]

freshwater river to a salty sea mouth. At Connah's Quay the ducks can still enjoy freshwater and salt-water habitats; about half way along the estuary, at Greenfield, the mudbanks are exposed at low tide, encouraging waders and shelducks. Walk out to the shingle spit at the Point of Ayr, protuding right out to sea, and you'll see wondrous numbers of roosting waders, including knots, oystercatchers, curlews, and bar-tailed and black-tailed godwits.

Rising out of the sands towards the mouth of the estuary lie three sandstone islands: Middle Eye, Little Eye, and Hilbre Island. At low tide you can walk to Hilbre: check the tides before you go, as you can easily become cut off. The shoreline here has fascinating inhabitants: red beadlet anenomes, dog whelks, and winkles hide among the rocks; sea spleenwort grows on the cliff faces; and sabellaria reef worms live in the sandy seabed. But watch out for weaver fish, which can hide just under the sand at low tide, exposing their venomous dorsal spines. There's also an unwelcome visitor to the Dee Estuary, the Chinese mitten crab, which probably arrived in ships' ballast water. While striking in looks, it is causing environmental problems (see box, left).

JAN
FEB
MAR
APR
MAY
JUN
JUL
AUG
SEP
OCT
NOV
DEC

WHERE
London Wetland Centre, Barnes, London
SW13 9WT; www.wwt.org.uk

CONTACT
London Wetland Centre, tel: 020 8409 4400;
info.london@wwt.org.uk

GETTING THERE
By car, turn off the A306 (the South Circular)
at Barnes and follow signs to the centre.
By train, travel to Barnes or Barnes Bridge.
The nearest London Underground station is
Hammersmith. A bus runs from here directly
to the centre: Duck bus no. 283 (stand K).
Bus nos. 33, 72, and 209 all stop nearby.
By cycle, follow the Sustrans Cycle Route.

ACCESS AND FACILITIES
There is a free car park, and extensive
facilities including multi-storey hides, a
viewing tower, and a discovery centre. There
are mini-beast safaris and pond-dipping
sessions for children. The site is wheelchair
friendly, with good paths, access to heated
hides, and lifts to the tower and restaurant.

OPENING TIMES
All year round; 9.30am–9pm in summer;
9.30am–6pm in winter.

CHARGES
Yes, for non-WWT members (all children
under 4 go free).

Bats galore

The London Wetland Centre is one of the most
popular sites in the UK for seeing bats – six
different species have been recorded here,
including the large noctule, the tiny pipistrelle,
and Daubenton's bat (*shown below, catching
fish*). The bats hibernate through the winter,
but the centre lays on guided evening bat walks
during the spring and summer, where special bat
detectors are provided, to help visitors hear and
see the bats more clearly.

Left: The three-storey Peacock Tower hide gives amazing views over the whole centre.

Right (left to right): A colony of water voles live at the centre; pochard ducks visit in winter; around 200 moorhens forage for food; the kingfisher is often seen around water within the reserve.

Main: The vast expanse of the London Wetland Centre is a welcome sight to inflying migrant birds. **Far right:** Grey heron with water vole.

CITY WILDERNESS

THE LONDON WETLAND CENTRE IS A LARGE SPLASH OF GREEN surrounded by urban sprawl. The result of a huge project by the Wildfowl & Wetlands Trust to turn a Victorian reservoir complex by the Thames into a true wetland wildlife haven, just a stone's throw from central London, it has been a huge success since it opened to the public in May 2000. Today, lagoons, reedbeds, grazing marsh, and small wooded areas cover over 40 hectares (100 acres), and attract a wide range of birds. Visit in January and you'll see both wild ducks and those captive in the various enclosures at their best, having moulted into their breeding plumage. The World Wetlands Walk takes you through the natural habitat sets of various countries around the world, and features representative species of captive wildfowl. Out on the lagoons – which can be viewed from the comfort of various hides – wildfowl include gadwalls, teals, wigeons, shovelers, pintails, and the two commoner diving ducks: the tufted duck and pochard.

Above: An eye-catching female wasp spider – the males are simply brown.

JAN

FEB

MAR

APR

MAY

JUN

JUL

AUG

SEP

OCT

NOV

DEC

Like feathered commuters, globetrotting birds flock to this city sanctuary to join the resident wildlife.

THROUGH THE YEAR
LONDON WETLAND CENTRE

In **spring**, many migrant birds visit the centre. These often include hobbys, garganeys, yellow wagtails, and various species of wader.

Little ringed plovers, reed and sedge warblers, kingfishers, and sand martins are some of the avian highlights in **summer**. Look out for reptiles: grass snakes, common lizards, and slow-worms populate the wilder areas. Butterflies abound in specially planted areas, and dragonflies are numerous. If you like bugs, follow the sounds of grasshoppers and crickets, and you might see a wasp spider, which weaves intricate webs to catch its prey.

Migrant birds arrive in **autumn**, along with visiting winter birds. Visitors can help to harvest blueberries, cranberries, primroses, and nettles – and learn ways in which to use them. Autumn is often the best time to see owls flying over these wetlands, and occasionally a soaring peregrine or hovering kestrel.

WHERE ELSE TO SEE
URBAN WETLANDS

Some cities have nature reserves within a few kilometres of their centre, boosting the numbers of birds and butterflies within the area as a whole.

Staines Reservoir in Middlesex nestles below the flight path of Heathrow and attracts plenty of wintering wildfowl. In spring and autumn it has a large number of passage waders and terns. [SE]

Bough Beech Reservoir, in Kent, is a great location for ducks in winter. The surrounding woodland is rich in birdlife, and an orchard feeding station offers close-up views of shy species such as brambling and great spotted woodpecker. [SE]

Newport Wetlands, in Wales, has an excellent mix of habitats, including reedbeds, saline lagoons, wet grassland, and scrub. It's a great place for birds, orchids, butterflies, dragonflies, and otters. [W]

Winnall Moors nature reserve is 1km (½ mile) from Winchester city centre. The River Itchen flows right through it, attracting all the wildlife associated with chalk streams. [SE]

Numbers of wildfowl and waders on the reserve at any one time can depend on the state of the tide, as some species – such as teal – often leave the reserve to feed on the Thames at low tide. Bitterns sometimes overwinter here, and January is one of the best months in which to spot this normally shy species. Look along the edge of reedbeds and stay alert for movement, as they are superbly camouflaged. Peregrine falcons hunt over the reserve and can cause mayhem when on the attack. A typical winter visit will give you views of stonechats, Cetti's warblers, meadow pipits, and siskins feeding in the alders. Both fieldfares and redwings can often be seen along the trails. If you hear a call similar to a piglet squealing, it is probably a water rail; look for it quickly – it's so shy that you'll only get the fleetest of views before it darts for cover. There are more than 20 water rails here in winter, and they soon establish their winter feeding territories.

On a cold day it's sometimes hard to leave the warmth of the centre's cafe, but climb up the Peacock Tower hide – or take the lift – and you'll get a great view of the whole reserve. Then it's impossible to resist the network of paths beckoning you down to explore the wildlife.

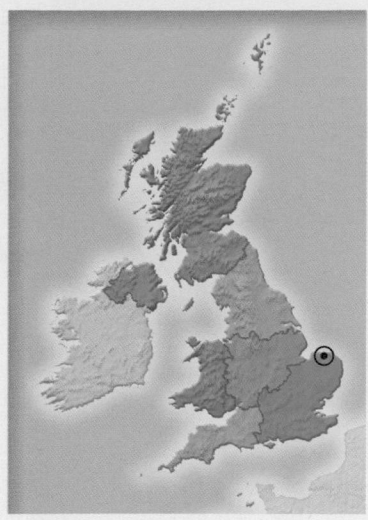

WHERE
Holkham Nature Reserve, Holkham,
Wells-next-the-Sea, Norfolk, NR23 1AD;
www.naturalengland.org.uk

CONTACT
Natural England, tel: 01328 711183;
enquiries.east@naturalengland.org.uk

GETTING THERE
The reserve is 4.8km (3 miles) west of
Wells-next-the-Sea on the A149. By rail, travel
to either King's Lynn (closest) or Sheringham.
By bus, catch the hourly Norfolk Coasthopper,
which stops at the entrance. By cycle, take
the National Cycle Network Route no.1.

ACCESS AND FACILITIES
There are three access points, at Burnham
Overy, Wells Beach Road, and Lady Ann's
Drive. The Norfolk Coastal path links the car
parks. At Lady Ann's Drive, opposite Holkham
Hall, there are no facilities but there is a pub
and café at the park entrance. Wells car park
has public toilets. This site is not easy for
wheelchair or pushchair users due to the
soft sandy tracks.

OPENING TIMES
Open all year round.

CHARGES
None, except for car parking charges at Lady
Ann's Drive and Wells Beach Road.

WINTERING GEESE

THE SOUND OF A WILD GOOSE FLOCK IS ONE OF THE DELIGHTS of a short winter day on the coast. Variously barking, yelping, murmuring, or honking geese, according to species, migrate to Britain for the winter from a huge swathe of the Arctic, from Canada to Siberia. On the north Norfolk coast, most numerous is the pink-footed goose, where in recent years the total population has reached around 150,000. And it is still increasing, helped by the availability of their favoured foods: spilt grain among stubble and sugar-beet tops.

The pink-footed geese roost on the mudflats and shallow waters of The Wash and Scolt Head Island, and fly to and from these at dusk and dawn to their feeding grounds. As they move around to forage for food, it can be difficult to predict where they will be during the day, although at one site – the grazing marshes at Holkham – the availability of marshland grass is sufficiently constant to make this a reliable location. Park in Lady Ann's Drive,

Almost half of the world's pink-footed geese spend their winter on the north Norfolk coast.

Introduced species

Distinction is drawn in goose populations between the wild and the not-so-wild. Most of our greylags (*pictured*) and Canada geese, and all our Egyptian geese, are derived from birds once kept for ornamental purposes that have escaped. Increases in the numbers of these birds are of concern because they stir up mud and produce producing copious droppings, which have a detrimental effect on water quality. This has led to attempts to control their numbers by egg-pricking and direct culling.

JAN

FEB

MAR

APR

MAY

JUN

JUL

AUG

SEP

OCT

NOV

DEC

scan the fields, and there they will be, often with up to 500 European white-fronted geese and a few thousand wigeons. Continue down to the beach, across the dunes, and you have a good chance of finding a flock of snow buntings and perhaps a few Lapland buntings and shore larks feeding along the strandline. The marshes also hold flocks of dark-bellied brent geese, a smaller and more compact visitor from Siberia that's often best seen from the nearby Wells Beach Road.

Careful examination of goose flocks can reveal much rarer vagrants within them. A Ross's goose or two, largely white and black, may be among the pink-feet, while the brents could be hiding a North-American black brant. Add to these the resident feral greylags, Canada geese, and Egyptian geese, and a few barnacle geese of uncertain origin, and you have the chance to see almost any goose on the British list. Whether feeding in a tight flock, or flying over in successive V-formations, the sight and sounds of wild geese in these huge skies adds drama to any winter day at Holkham.

WHERE ELSE TO SEE
WINTERING GEESE

Greenland and Icelandic geese winter in huge numbers in northwest Europe, and particularly in the UK. They are generally found around the coasts, but can be seen at a few sites further inland.

Slimbridge in Gloucestershire (*see pp.34–35*) is one of the most important wintering sites in the UK for white-fronted geese. You might also see taiga, bean, and pink-footed geese, or a rare lesser white-fronted goose. [M]

Look for Greenland white-fronted geese at **Ynys-hir** (*see pp.106–107*) near Machynlleth, Wales. There is a winter flock of pale-bellied brent geese on **Anglesey** in North Wales, which is sometimes joined by black brant, or the Pacific brent goose. [W]

The **Ken-Dee Marshes**, near the Solway Firth in Dumfries and Galloway, are home to migrant white-fronted geese. **Mersehead** and **Caerlaverock** on the north Solway shore have barnacle geese, which can also be seen on a number of Hebridean islands, such as **Tiree**. [SC]

Above: Brent geese flying in formation.

Main: Thousands of geese winter at Holkham.

Left panel (top to bottom): Both pink-footed and greylag geese have pink legs, but pink-footed geese have short necks, and almost-black heads; Egyptian goose.

Below: The white-fronted goose is white on its bill, not – as you might expect – on its chest.

THROUGH THE YEAR
HOLKHAM BAY

As **spring** approaches, the geese depart from Holkham, their calls replaced with the territorial piping of redshanks and oystercatchers. Marsh harriers settle into their reedbed breeding territories, alongside a few hen harriers lingering from the winter. In the pine plantations on the dunes there may be crossbills nesting as early as February.

In **summer**, the sand dunes burst into flower, with sea-holly, pyramidal orchid, and the vile-smelling hound's-tongue. Where pools have formed, look for marsh helleborines and southern marsh orchids, and breeding natterjack toads.

Attention turns to the pines in **autumn**, which are a magnet for migrant songbirds such as goldcrests, and even, after northeasterly winds, rarities like Pallas's warblers and olive-backed pipits. Fungi spring up in their many and varied forms: look out for earth-stars, fly agaric, and the sweet-smelling dune stinkhorn.

Below: Holkham Bay is perfect for tranquil walks in summer.

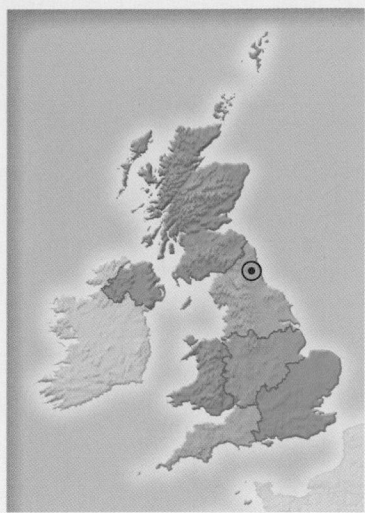

WHERE
Druridge Bay Country Park, Red Row,
Morpeth, Northumberland NE61 5BX;
www.northumberland.gov.uk

CONTACT
Druridge Bay Country Park Visitor Centre,
tel: 01670 760968;
druridgebay@northumberland.gov.uk
Northumberland Wildlife Trust,
tel: 0191 2846884; mail@northwt.org.uk

GETTING THERE
Druridge Bay Country Park is off the A1068,
near Amble. By rail, travel to Widdrington.
By bus, take the 518 bus between Morpeth
and Alnwick, which stops at Hadston, a
15-minute walk from the bay.

ACCESS AND FACILITIES
The nearest facilities are at the Druridge Bay
Country Park's wheelchair-friendly visitor
centre, which includes a café, shop, toilets,
play areas, parking, and access to one part
of the beach by wheelchair. Hauxley Nature
Reserve, at the other end of the bay from the
country park, also has ample car parking, an
information centre, and full-access toilets.

OPENING TIMES
Access to the bay all year round.

CHARGES
None.

Strutting sanderlings

Sanderlings are small, pale sandpipers known for
enjoying themselves on the beach: they are often
seen in flocks chasing the receding waves, and
then running up the beach again as the waves
come up behind them. In fact, this comical
behaviour has a purpose: the birds are rushing in
to pick up invertebrates stranded in the sand as
the waves recede, and probe around in the wet
sand for other food. Some non-breeding adults
stay in their winter home all year round.

Above (top and bottom): Flocks of sanderlings gather
at the shoreline to forage; Coquet Island, a bird
sanctuary, is just 1.6km (1 mile) off the coast at Amble.

Below: Grey herons are often seen feeding on the eels
of Druridge's freshwater pools.

Right (top and bottom): The pintail duck favours
intertidal habitats; snow buntings can be seen around
Druridge Bay through the winter, taking off for their high
Arctic breeding grounds in April.

Main: Druridge Bay is the longest uninterrupted stretch of beach and dune habitat in Northumberland.

A BRACING BEACH WALK

S TRETCHING FROM AMBLE IN THE NORTH TO CRESSWELL IN THE SOUTH, the 9.6km (6 mile) sweep of
Druridge Bay takes in some of the finest birdwatching locations in the northeast of England. Parts of the bay
are under ownership of the National Trust, while other sections are protected as nature reserves.

The bay can be a cold place in January, but the great birdwatching on offer will soon make you forget the
weather. The bay is defined by a long sandy beach behind which are sand dunes, scrub, hedgerows, and a series of
lagoons – formed through the landscaping of former open-cast coal-mining sites. At the southern end of the bay,
Cresswell Pond is a brackish lagoon fringed by reeds and marsh, where wintering waterfowl are the main
attraction in January, and at dusk the pond is sometimes used by roosting pink-footed geese and whooper swans.
The pink-footed geese feed in the large fields at the back of the bay and can often be seen on the larger lagoons, or

Above: Little stints are sometimes seen probing the sands for food.

THROUGH THE YEAR
DRURIDGE BAY

Large numbers of birds pass through the area on passage in **spring**, most notably little gulls, black terns, kittiwakes, and garganeys. Waders may include greenshanks, whimbrels, sandpipers, and little stints.

Breeding birds around the area in **summer** include various warblers, particularly the grasshopper warbler, which can be heard "reeling" (singing) in the scrub in the dunes and around the pools. On the beach, gulls and terns regularly sit in flocks and you may see some roseate terns, which breed on nearby Coquet Island.

In **autumn** you can see many returning waders, including the pectoral sandpiper, and passage seabirds including terns and skuas. Look out also for smaller birds such as wheatears, whinchats, redstarts, and pied flycatchers. You've also got a good chance of seeing some rare birds.

Viewed from below, the pretty snow bunting looks completely white, giving it the fond nickname of "snowflake".

WHERE ELSE TO SEE
SAND DUNES

Sand dunes are a nationally declining habitat, but many are actively managed to encourage wildlife.

Lindisfarne, Northumberland (*see pp.274–275*), offers extensive sand dunes, long, sandy beaches, and vast areas of tidal mudflats swarming with birds in winter. **Seal Sands**, on Teesmouth, East Yorkshire (*see pp.304–305*), offers great winter birdwatching, right in the middle of an industrial heartland. [N]

The red-breasted merganser can be seen on the **Fal Estuary**, Cornwall, which leads to the Carrick Roads – a deep waterway served by the River Truro. [SW]

Pagham Harbour in West Sussex is bordered by shingle spits, and is a great place to see passage waders in autumn. St Catherine's Point, on the **Isle of Wight** (*see pp.224–225*) is a good place to see many of the Druridge birds. [SE]

Kenfig Reserve in South Wales regularly sees bitterns, shovelers, ruddy ducks, smews, merlins, and peregrines. At ground level, look out for the endangered fen orchid in June and July. [W]

flying overhead. If you walk in a northerly direction away from Cresswell, you come to Druridge pools. These large lagoons are surrounded by scrub and reeds, and bordered by sand dunes to the east and farmland to the west. There's always a great variety of birds here, though those on the lagoons can be quite distant, so bring a telescope if you can. Red-breasted mergansers are regular visitors, and you might see smews in January. Walk through the dunes to the beach and scan for waders: both the bar-tailed godwit and the sanderling prefer sandy areas to mud. Offshore, divers, grebes, and sea ducks such as scoter and long-tailed duck are possibilities.

On the beach itself you may find snow buntings, easily identified by their twittering call and flash of under-wing white while flying. Venturing further north you reach East Chevington, where pools and reedbeds attract wildfowl and rare birds. At the northern end of the bay, Hauxley Nature Reserve has hides overlooking a freshwater pool, which attracts wintering ducks such as pintails, scaups, wigeons, and sometimes long-tailed ducks and smews. The berry-laden hedgerows and bushes at the reserve are popular with wintering thrushes, redwings, and fieldfares.

JAN

FEB

MAR

APR

MAY

JUN

JUL

AUG

SEP

OCT

NOV

DEC

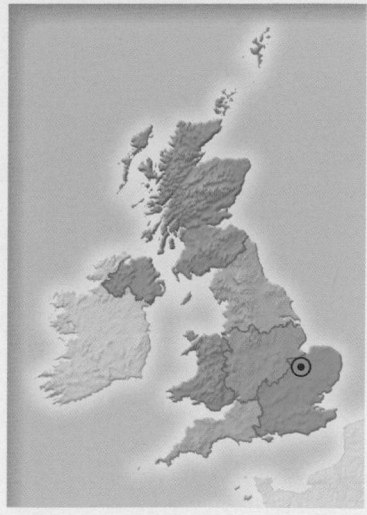

WINTERING SWANS

WILD SWANS MAKE ONE OF THE FINEST WILDLIFE SIGHTS IN THE UK, and the Ouse Washes are home to the largest concentration of Bewick and whooper swans in the country. The site forms a spectacular setting for the tens of thousands of swans, geese, gulls, and ducks that make their home here in winter, when the floodwater rises, forming temporary lakes that run in dead-straight lines for over 32km (20 miles) across the Cambridgeshire countryside. Don't wait for a clear, sunny day – these majestic birds are best seen on a misty day when all looks soft, grey, and mysterious, and the breathy whistle of the swans' wings takes on an ethereal charm.

Two or three decades ago the great majority of the swans were Bewick's swans from northern Siberia. These smaller swans, around two-thirds the size of the familiar all-year-round mute swan, are still big, dramatic birds, which are completely white except for their black and yellow bills. Now, whooper swans from Iceland have

WHERE
RSPB Ouse Washes, Welches Dam, Manea, March, Cambridgeshire PE15 0NF; www.rspb.org.uk

CONTACT
RSPB Ouse Washes, tel: 01354 680212; ouse.washes@rspb.org.uk

GETTING THERE
By car, leave the village of Manea and turn right at the T-junction, then left opposite the Rose and Crown pub. Turn left at the next T-junction towards Welches Dam, continuing to the signposted car park. The bus stops in Manea, which is 4km (2½ miles) from the reserve. Manea Station is 5km (3 miles) from the reserve.

ACCESS AND FACILITIES
The visitor centre is wheelchair friendly with car parking, toilets, refreshments, picnic tables, and accessible hides. There are 10 hides in total and one short nature trail.

OPENING TIMES
The birdwatching hides are open at all times. The visitor centre is open 9am–5pm every day except Christmas and Boxing Day.

CHARGES
None, but the RSPB welcomes donations.

Above (top to bottom): Black-tailed godwits from northern Europe take refuge from harsher winters on the Ouse Washes; a cormorant drying its wings.

Main: Bewick's swans at dawn on the Ouse Washes.

Below (left to right): The Ouse Washes attract many wintering birds of prey, such as this short-eared owl. Washland ditches were created in the 17th century to retain flood waters, so preventing farmland from flooding; mute swans live in the UK all year round; whoopers are winter visitors from Iceland.

Family affairs

Bewick's and whooper swans are much wilder than our regular mute swans. They can seem deceptively tame when seen in spectacular close-up from the Ouse Washes hides, especially when they are being fed. But find them away from here – grazing on nearby farmland, for instance, or on a small lake or a riverside meadow – and they will be quick to fly off. They are much more vocal too, and to hear their quiet, bubbling conversation softly through a thick mist is extra-special.

become almost as numerous at times, especially on the more northerly washes, where swans are fed daily with barrows of grain. The whoopers are as big as mute swans, but they look more like Bewick's, with black and yellow colouring on the face and beak. Bewick's have more irregular but essentially rounded yellow patches against the black, while whoopers have longer, more wedge-shaped bills with a narrow, triangular wedge of yellow on each side.

Adult swans can be identified individually by their face patterns, which remain fixed. Studies have shown that they mate for life, and at the Ouse Washes you can often see mother and father together with one, two, three, or more dull-grey youngsters, depending on the success of the breeding season in the far northern tundra. Families stick together and perform frequent greeting ceremonies, and interact with other groups, leaning forward with stretched necks and raised wings and calling in concert.

WHERE ELSE TO SEE
WINTERING SWANS

Mute swans live in the UK all year round, and they are joined from October to March by migratory colonies of Bewick's swans from Siberia and whoopers from Iceland.

A little further north on the Washes, the Wildfowl & Wetland Trust's **Welney** reserve is also a prime site for wintering swans. [SE] Visit the Trust's reserve at **Slimbridge** (see pp.34–35), Gloucestershire, to see Bewick's swans and flocks of wild ducks around the collections of captive ones. Around 250 Bewick's arrive at Slimbridge from Siberia every winter. [M]

Loch of Strathbeg, Scotland, is the UK's largest dune loch – a loch entirely surrounded by sands – which becomes home to thousands of wild geese, swans, and ducks in the winter. These migrating birds also gather in large numbers around **Mersehead** and **Caerlaverock**, both of which lie on the north shore of Scotland's Solway Firth. [SC]

Another great place to see large gatherings of swans is **Lindisfarne Island** (see pp.274–275), situated off the coast of Northumberland. [N]

THROUGH THE YEAR
OUSE WASHES

In **spring**, search drier areas for migrating flocks of ruffs, often showing off their spectacular breeding plumage, and black-tailed godwits. Watch out for dramatic snipe and lapwing displays.

Avocets and marsh harriers can often be seen in the **summer**, unless flash floods have forced them to leave. Foxes are often seen here and you may be lucky enough to catch a glimpse of an otter; more likely sightings are of stoats.

Autumn is a good time to see migrant wading birds, terns, and gulls. Look out for tree sparrows and finch flocks along the tideline of the floods, as they search for washed-up seeds. Cormorants like to roost on overhead wires and you can often find short-eared and barn owls, merlins, hen harriers, and sparrowhawks hunting over the embankments.

Below: Bewick's swans are a familiar sight on the Ouse Washes.

JAN
FEB
MAR
APR
MAY
JUN
JUL
AUG
SEP
OCT
NOV
DEC

Left: Geltsdale is famous for its black grouse.

Right (left to right): Geltsdale is part of the Pennine Area of Outstanding Natural Beauty; brown hares winter on the moor; red foxes prey on smaller animals in winter.

Right, below: Buzzards live in large numbers at Geltsdale – listen out for their distinctive, challenging "mew" call.

WHERE
RSPB Geltsdale, Stagsike Cottages, Hallbankgate, Brampton, Cumbria CA8 2PW; www.rspb.org.uk

CONTACT
Reserve Information Point, tel: 01697 746717; northernengland@rspb.org.uk

GETTING THERE
From the A69 near Brampton, take the A689 to Hallbankgate and Alston. At Hallbankgate, take the minor road that runs in front of the "Belted Will" pub. By train, Brampton Junction is around 3.2km (2 miles) away. The nearest bus stop is at Hallbankgate.

ACCESS AND FACILITIES
The small car park is in Hallbankgate. There are full-access toilets, a picnic area, and a live camera. There are several trails, of varying lengths. Wheelchair access over the moor is difficult due to the terrain, but it can be pre-arranged by contacting the Reserve Information Point (*see above*). The tarn viewpoint will soon be fully accessible.

OPENING TIMES
Trails are open all day, and the Reserve Information Point is open from 9am to 5pm.

CHARGES
None.

Stoat in ermine

In January, look out for the stoat. This sharp-eyed predator is red-brown on top and creamy-white beneath, with a bushy black-tipped tail. In the north in winter, some become white except for the tail tip. Known as ermines, these are familiar as the black-spotted white furs of ceremonial robes. Stoats keep to cover but are apt to run over open ground, even along drystone walls, and are incurably curious. If a stoat dives out of sight, keep still and quiet and it will often reappear.

Main: Geltsdale is a walker's paradise in winter, providing stunning views, such as this one from the summit of Talkin Fell.

NEW YEAR ON THE MOORS

THE NORTH PENNINES ARE AT THEIR MOST BLEAKLY DRAMATIC IN WINTER; on Geltsdale, the blanket bogs, heath, upland farmland, and woods stretch out before you in a glorious wilderness, and the short, crisp days are perfect for walking, with only the occasional bird of prey for company.

This is a harsh, challenging environment and few birds and mammals are equipped to cope with it. It is, however, one of the UK's few sites for nesting hen harriers, and they wheel above the forbidding landscape all year round, joined by hunting buzzards and short-eared owls. Smews occasionally visit the glistening tarns, making the most of their seclusion, which will disappear when the lapwings, redshanks, snipe, and curlews arrive early in spring. In hidden little gullies with thickets of thorns, fieldfares and redwings feed on the berries in late autumn, but even they have to move out on to open pastures below the moor in winter.

Above: Cattle grazing on the RSPB Geltsdale reserve in summer.

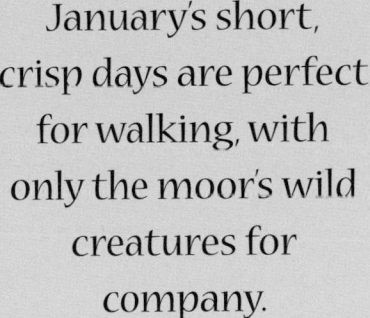

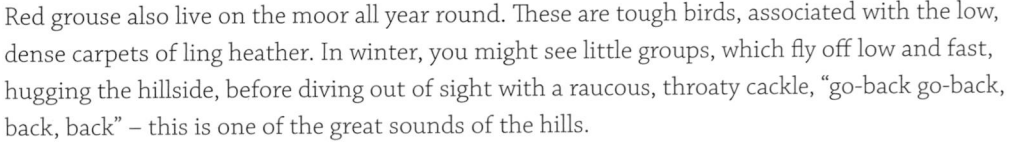

January's short, crisp days are perfect for walking, with only the moor's wild creatures for company.

THROUGH THE YEAR
GELTSDALE

Lapwings, redshanks, snipe, and curlews arrive early in **spring** and can be seen on the fields around the moor before dispersing to their territories. The hum of drumming snipe overhead and the rippling, bubbling songs of curlews are typical of the wetter parts of the moor. Take the woodland Bruthwaite Trail to look for warblers and redstarts.

In **summer**, meadow pipits, swallows, and stonechats are evident. Barn owls and short-eared owls hunt in the evenings. Breeding birds include golden plovers, curlews, ring ouzels, merlins, and short-eared owls. Stoats are raising their young, which will be fully independent and able to hunt their own prey by the end of the season.

Fieldfare and redwing flocks arrive in **autumn**, when black grouse become more visible around the reserve trails.

WHERE ELSE TO SEE
PENNINE WILDLIFE

Many of the animals and birds at Geltsdale can be found around the UK, in similar environments. However, some, such as the red grouse, are virtually restricted to heather moorland. Golden plovers, merlins, and hen harriers breed mainly on moorland.

The **North York Moors** (*see pp.232–233*) have many of the birds and flowers of Geltsdale. They are good for finding red grouse and have a few golden plovers and curlews. A colony of stoats lives in the ruins of **Mount Grace Priory**, North Yorkshire. [N]

Stoats are widespread in many habitats but are always rather unpredictable. They can be seen hunting along the estuary track at **Conwy** (*see pp.278–279*) in North Wales. [W]

Hen harriers can be seen in the summer in Scotland on **Islay** (*see pp.12–13*) and **Orkney** [SC]. In winter they can be found around the **Solway Firth**; for example at Campfield Marsh RSPB reserve, on the English side [N].

Red grouse also live on the moor all year round. These are tough birds, associated with the low, dense carpets of ling heather. In winter, you might see little groups, which fly off low and fast, hugging the hillside, before diving out of sight with a raucous, throaty cackle, "go-back go-back, back, back" – this is one of the great sounds of the hills.

Geltsdale is famous for its black grouse, too: bigger birds with a much greater difference between the sexes. Females are grey-brown, but the males are stunningly blue-black, with white wingbars, a white puffball under the tail, and red fleshy wattles over the eyes. When they wish to mate, these males will gather on open spaces to display, calling and mock-fighting in a spectacle known as the "lek", designed to impress the watching hens (*see pp. 102–103*).

The extensive blanket bogs of the moorland are characterized by multicoloured sphagnum mosses, which form a natural sponge, holding water in the hills and forming deep deposits of peat. These areas, often drained and eroded, are being restored through reducing grazing by sheep and heather-burning, and the blocking of artificial moorland drains.

JAN

FEB

MAR

APR

MAY

JUN

JUL

AUG

SEP

OCT

NOV

DEC

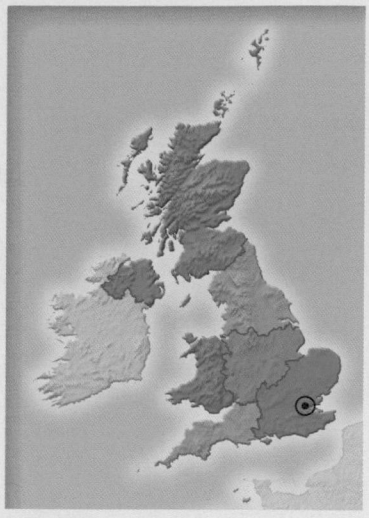

WHERE
Lee Valley Park, Essex and Herts;
www.leevalleypark.org.uk

CONTACT
Lee Valley Regional Park Visitor Centre, tel:
01992 702200; info@leevalleypark.org.uk

GETTING THERE
The park extends from Ware in Hertfordshire to Leyton in London, stretching for 42km (26 miles) on both sides of the River Lee. The Regional Park Visitor Centre at Fisher's Green is signposted from the B195 just north of Waltham Abbey (M25 junction 26). By train, travel to Waltham Cross for the south of the park; Cheshunt for the central park; and Broxbourne for the north. By bus, nos. 211, 212, 213, 240, 250, 251, and 505 all serve the park area.

ACCESS AND FACILITIES
The bittern watchpoint is at Fisher's Green, Stubbins Hall Lane, EN9 2EF. Parking is free. Access to disabled toilets is with key only. There are various facilities across the valley; contact the Lee Valley Regional Park Visitor Centre or visit the park's website for details.

OPENING TIMES
Open all year round.

CHARGES
None.

East Anglian bitterns

While many of Britain's overwintering bitterns are believed to be refugees from frozen wetlands on the continent, ringing and radio-tracking studies have demonstrated that at least some of the Lee Valley birds move between the park and several established breeding sites in East Anglia. Work is under way to extend and improve the reedbed habitat within the Lee Valley, both to safeguard the bitterns' winter haunts and to encourage them eventually to stay and breed.

LEE VALLEY PARK

FORMING THE BOUNDARY BETWEEN ESSEX AND HERTFORDSHIRE, the River Lee lies within a broad valley that penetrates to the very heart of London. It has been hugely modified by human activities, but our influence has been far from negative. Our need for drinking water and construction aggregates has resulted in the creation of a complex series of reservoirs and gravel pits that together form a wetland of international significance.

The best place to start is the Lee Valley Regional Park Authority's visitor centre at Fisher's Green, near Waltham Abbey. From here it is a short walk to Seventy Acres Lake, one of the flooded gravel pits, which is overlooked by a series of hides, including the renowned

Walthamstow Marsh nature reserve is an important part of the Lee Valley Park, together with Coppermill Fields and Leyton Marsh – remnants of London's once widespread river valley grasslands.

bittern watchpoint. Up to one-tenth of the British wintering population of bitterns can be found in the Lee Valley, and the small reedbed in front of the watchpoint often holds one or more. Be patient and you may well be rewarded with close views as a reclusive bittern stalks out of the reeds and starts to fish in the cleared channels.

While you are waiting, listen out for the squeals of water rails, and scan the waterfowl on the lake. Among the mallards, coots, and Canada geese you should find gadwalls and shovelers, tufted ducks and, if there has been hard weather on the continent, a few smews. Most will be "redheads" – brownish females and young birds – but you might see an adult male, stunningly white with a tracery of black, which makes for effective camouflage against sunlit ripples. There may be a few goosanders, which are equally attractive but much larger.

A midwinter walk around Fisher's Green, or any of the other nature reserves in the valley, including Amwell and Rye Meads, will be enlivened by flocks of small birds. Roving bands of blue, great, and long-tailed tits often include an overwintering chiffchaff, and the alder trees on the margins of the lakes could reveal a twittering group of redpolls and siskins.

Main: Lee Valley Park covers 405 hectares (1,000 acres) of land across Essex and Hertfordshire.
Below (left to right): An acrobatic siskin in an alder tree; a goosander lands on water; the striking adult male smew.
Inset: Walthamstow Marsh Nature Reserve provides a restful respite from the city on a winter's day.

JAN
FEB
MAR
APR
MAY
JUN
JUL
AUG
SEP
OCT
NOV
DEC

Above: A mute swan cygnet on the River Lee in spring.

WILDLIFE CALENDAR
LEE VALLEY PARK

Spring is a good time to try to find one of the small local otter population: try Rye Meads, in the early morning. Bird breeding is under way, including grey herons in the alders at Waltham Abbey (now called Gunpowder Mills). Herons, swans, cormorants, and nowadays a few little egrets also breed around Walthamstow Reservoirs.

During the **summer**, the wetlands come alive with insect life, especially dragonflies and damselflies. One part of the valley, Cornmill Meadows (*see pp.210–211*), is managed especially for this fascinating group of insects, but they can be seen anywhere. At least 17 species are known to breed here, including such scarce species as hairy dragonfly and ruddy darter. An evening visit will reveal several species of bats, including Daubenton's bat, typically skimming low over water in search of food.

Waterbird numbers build up rapidly from late summer into the **autumn**. Tufted ducks and pochards arrive to moult; and as they become flightless, they favour the middle of the larger lakes, well out of the way of ground predators.

WHERE ELSE TO SEE
MAN-MADE WETLANDS

There are many places where wildfowl and other waterbirds have moved onto wetlands created over the past century, which began their lives as reservoirs.

The **Cotswold Water Park**, Gloucestershire, consists of more than 140 lakes, where thousands of birds spend the winter. Look out for pochards, gadwalls, goosanders, smews, Caspian gulls, yellow-legged gulls, and little egrets. [M]

Also in the Midlands, **Attenborough Gravel Pits**, Nottingham, has a good selection of waterbirds, as does **Rutland Water** reservoir in Rutland. [M]

Pensthorpe wildlife reserve near Norwich, has many waterbirds, and **Abberton Reservoir**, Colchester, hosts 30,000 or more in the early winter. Look for bitterns along the coast, at **Minsmere** (*see pp.100–101*) and **Walberswick** in Suffolk. [SE]

FEBRUARY

Where to Go: **February**

Winter fades out gradually and rather uncertainly to spring: February is an in-between month, and global warming has made the weather quite unpredictable. There are few signs of the wildlife of warmer months, which remain hidden or abroad. Birds and seals bring life to our coasts and offshore islands, and in the north and west of the country, you might come across an otter.

Inland, the wetlands – lakes, reservoirs, and marshes – have ducks, coots, and swans, but there are many other birds, too, from great crested and little grebes, coots, and moorhens, to beautiful jewel-like kingfishers and delicate, dancing grey wagtails. If they all suddenly take off in panic, look around for a sparrowhawk, or, if you're really lucky, a peregrine falcon.

ISLANDS

ARRAN The Kilbrannan Sound and the Mull of Kintyre.

WETLANDS

SLAPTON LEY The rare Cetti's warbler hides in the reeds here.

WOODLANDS

SHERWOOD FOREST An historic royal hunting forest and ancient woodland.

FARNE ISLANDS
NORTHUMBERLAND [N]

Visit Farne to see 100,000 pairs of wintering seabirds, including puffins and guillemots, and to watch the antics of one of Europe's largest grey seal populations.
See pp.42–43

BROWNSEA ISLAND
POOLE HARBOUR, DORSET [SW]

Black-tailed godwits can be seen here, along with large numbers of native red squirrels.
See pp.38–39

SLAPTON LEY
KINGSBRIDGE, DEVON [SW]

The largest freshwater lake in southwest England supports around 75,000 birds in winter. The starling roost is spectacular.
See pp.40–41

KINGLEY VALE
WEST SUSSEX [SE]

The yews of the ancient forest here are among the oldest living things in Britain. Their dark majesty is highlighted by the bareness of the winter scene.
See pp.36–37

ISLE OF ARRAN
NORTH AYRSHIRE [SC]

Red squirrels live in the south of the island, while the resident ducks are joined by goldeneyes, teals, and wigeons in February.
See pp.42–43

The Isle of Arran is known as "Scotland in miniature" for its dramatic, rugged mountains, carved valleys, and aged woodlands.

SLIMBRIDGE
GLOUCESTERSHIRE [SE]

There's plenty to do and see at the original site for the Wildfowl & Wetlands Trust; in winter, it shelters hundreds of Bewick's swans and other water birds.
See pp.34–35

STODMARSH
STOUR VALLEY, KENT [SE]

A wonderful place too see birds, including hen harriers and ducks in winter, as well as rarities. Look for the insect-eating greater bladderwort plant in the dykes.
See pp.46–47

WINDSOR GREAT PARK
WINDSOR, BERKSHIRE [SE]

This royal park has several woodlands, and in winter you can see many of its roe deer. Little owls and tawny owls look for prey at night.
See pp.36–37

ISLE OF SKYE
INNER HEBRIDES [SC]

The largest island of the Inner Hebrides provides a dramatic backdrop for seabirds, including fulmars, kittiwakes, and shags.
See pp.42–43

HICKLING BROAD
NORFOLK [SE]

The largest of the Broads shelters thousands of birds, including reedbed specialities, such as bitterns and water rails.
See pp.46–47

It is clear from its 1790 description that the Major Oak – Sherwood's oldest tree – has been hollow for at least two centuries.

SHERWOOD FOREST
NOTTINGHAM [N]

One of Britain's oldest trees lives in the famous Sherwood Forest; it may be 1,000 years old.
See pp.36–37

ISLE OF MULL
INNER HEBRIDES [SC]

The island is well known both for its seabirds and for its birds of prey, which hunt over the moors and fish over the lochs and sea.
See pp.42–43

SOMERSET LEVELS
SOMERSET [SW]

This great network of ditches, grazing marshes, and peatland, has wading birds and otters among its varied wildlife.
See pp.46–47

WISTMAN'S WOOD
DEVON [SW]

This ancient wood grows at high altitude, and its dwarf oak trees grow tangled and twisted among moss-carpeted boulders, like a fairy-tale forest.
See pp.36–37

EPPING FOREST
ESSEX [SE]

Enjoy the largest public open space in the London area and the wildlife that makes its home here. The woods contain many venerable trees.
See pp.36–37

Previous page: Dunadoon Point, on the Isle of Arran.

Flocks of birds come together at dusk to roost: tens of thousands of starlings take up perches in trees and reeds, and hundreds, sometimes thousands, of woodpigeons, stock doves, rooks, and jackdaws descend in noisy, tumbling flocks into the dark shelter of the woods. Bands of fieldfares and redwings roam the fields by day, but they too come together to roost in trees and thickets each night, seeking out warmth and safety in numbers in the still-short, cold winter days. By the end of the month, however, there are inklings of spring, and the landscape begins to show flecks of colour and life. Look out for cascades of yellow hazel catkins, golden early celandines, and the flat orange flowerheads of coltsfoot – all signs that the seasons are changing.

HEATH AND MOOR

EXMOOR Home to Britain's most famous wild ponies.

UPLANDS

GIGRIN FARM Hundreds of red kites feed here daily.

INLETS AND ESTUARIES

POOLE HARBOUR Witness huge flocks of birds on the Dorset coast.

EXMOOR
DEVON AND SOMERSET [SW]

Enjoy the dramatic beauty of the moor without the crowds, but look in the gentler, wooded valleys, too, for snowdrops and other harbingers of spring.
See pp.44–45

Small, stocky goats survive on Exmoor in winter with the help of a layer of fine hair – cashmere – next to their skin, which keeps out the cold.

THE NEW FOREST
HAMPSHIRE [SW]

At this time of year, while the trees are still bare, seeing deer is easier: see if you can identify all three of our native species – red, roe, and fallow deer.
See pp.36–37

DARTMOOR
DEVON [SW]

The biggest, wildest area of open country in England offers shelter to deer, foxes, otters, badgers, grey squirrels, and hares in the winter.
See pp.44–45

WESTHAY MOOR
SOMERSET LEVELS {SW}

The moor hosts a huge starling roost – in some years it can include up to 8 million birds.
See pp.40–41

GIGRIN FARM
RHAYADER, MID WALES [W]

This wildlife-friendly farm offers unparalleled views of red kites – at "feeding time", up to 400 of these spectacular raptors gather in one field.
See pp.32–33

LOCH KEN
SOUTHERN UPLAND WAY [SC]

In February you can see birds of prey, including red kites, peregrines, and barn owls here, together with the rare Greenland white-fronted geese.
See pp.32–33

BLACK MOUNTAIN
BRECON BEACONS [W]

Escape to the wide-open spaces of this National Park, where red grouse hide among the upland moorlands and birds of prey, such as red kites, fly overhead.
See pp.44–45

The Brecon Beacons landscape is extraordinary, with fantastic waterfalls, amazing caves, and the highest mountains in southern Britain.

SYMONDS YAT
WYE VALLEY [M]

This famous viewpoint is a superb vantage point for watching birds of prey – ospreys, honey buzzards, goshawks and, if you're lucky, red kites.
See pp.32–33

WIDEWATER LAGOON
SHOREHAM, WEST SUSSEX [SE]

The sea filters in during high tides, making this the perfect home for herons, mute swans, oystercatchers, and redshanks.
See pp.38–39

POOLE HARBOUR
DORSET [SW]

This vast natural harbour is full of wintering birds, including the elegant, black-tailed godwits, scarce grebes, curlews, grey plovers, knots, and dunlins.
See pp.48–49

LANGSTONE HARBOUR
HAVANT, HANTS [SE]

Thousands of waders and brent geese migrate from the Arctic to feed and roost in safety here.
See pp.48–49

PAGHAM HARBOUR
WEST SUSSEX [SE]

Shelter in one of the hides to watch waders, or take a walk out to Pagham Spit where, especially at high tide, you can see seaducks, divers, and grebes.
See pp.48–49

BELFAST LOUGH
ANTRIM [NI]

See black-tailed and sometimes bar-tailed godwits at incredibly close quarters from the RSPB's cosy observation room here.
See pp.38–39

WHERE
Gigrin Farm, South Street, Rhayader, Powys, LD6 5BL, Wales.

CONTACT
Gigrin Farm information, tel: 01597 810243; lena@gigrin.co.uk

GETTING THERE
Gigrin Farm is on the A470, 1km (½ mile) south of the town of Rhayader. Network trains are available to Llandrindod.

ACCESS AND FACILITIES
The farm is wheelchair friendly, and three of the hides have ramps. Facilities are good, with toilets, a shop, and refreshments. Feeding takes place at 3pm in summer and 2pm in winter.

OPENING TIMES
Open every day, except Christmas Day.

CHARGES
Yes, except for children 4 years and under.

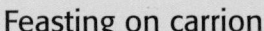

Feasting on carrion

Red kites are opportunists, feeding mainly on carrion and scavenging any handouts they encounter. They take only small live prey, such as young pigeons, rabbits, and invertebrates. Sheep carrion is a favourite, but because of their relatively weak bills, they rely on ravens, buzzards, foxes, or cats to open carcases for them. Recent legislation has meant fallen animals have to be removed and incinerated, which has eliminated one of the kites' best potential food sources.

Above (top to bottom): Birdwatchers take in the spectacle at feeding time; the kites must defend their meal from opportunistic crows, ravens, and buzzards.

Right panel (top and bottom): The sky fills with birds just before feeding time; the pale grey head of the kite features pin-sharp, hooded amber eyes.

Below: Red kites often feed in mid-air, once safely away from other birds, who might steal the food.

Main: With its massive wingspan, the majestic red kite effortlessly soars and glides through the air.

RED KITES FEEDING

THE FIRST THING YOU NOTICE ABOUT A RED KITE is its extraordinary wingspan, stretching nearly 2m (5½ft); it is so wide in comparison to its light bodyweight that this bird can stay in the air for hours with hardly a beat of its wings. You might notice its distinctive forked tail, and the beautiful autumnal colours of its body, before realising, as you watch it in an aerobatic display, that this is also a bird of incredible agility.

Gigrin Farm in Wales offers unparalleled views of these spectacular raptors – at times more than 400 kites assemble for a daily offering, and in some weeks more than 250kg (around a quarter of a ton) of meat is thrown to the kites. Feeding takes place each day in the early afternoon, which makes the food effectively a "top up", as kites wake up hungry and hunt for food in the early morning. As an official feeding station for these birds since 1992, Gigrin Farm has helped draw people away from the nesting sites – which suffered badly from egg thefts – and

THROUGH THE YEAR
GIGRIN FARM

Red kites, common buzzards, and ravens all come to the farm to feed in **spring**. Other possibilities include peregrines, goshawks, merlins, and barn owls. Polecats live around the area, but are rarely seen. You might be luckier with the water voles, and there are a few badger setts within the surrounding woods.

Gigrin Farm is set in a landscape of open heather and grass moorland that's wonderful in **summer**. The ancient oakwoods are full of pied flycatchers, redstarts, and wood warblers, and there is also a 2km (1½ mile) nature trail around the farm that links it to the RSPB's Dyffyn Reserve, attracting gadwalls and herons.

The feeding station is still busy in the **autumn**, with hundreds of raptors visiting the farm. If you are accompanying children, you might enjoy visiting the farm animals, too, including ponies, donkeys, goats, ducks, chickens, and even a peacock.

WHERE ELSE TO SEE
RED KITES

Away from mid Wales there are a few locations in Britain where you can see reintroduced red kites.

Red kites fly around Symonds Yat in the **Wye Valley** (*see pp.80–81*), together with goshawks, hobbies, ospreys, and honey buzzards. Afternoon is the best time to visit. [M]

Loch Ken, on the Black Isle in the north of Scotland, is a collection of marshes centred around a loch. In winter you'll see a good collection of birds of prey, including red kites, peregrines, and barn owls, and also Greenland white-fronted geese. Red kites were reintroduced to the Black Isle in the late 1980s, and Scotland now has 122 breeding pairs. [SC]

More than 90 red kites were released into Gateshead's **Lower Derwent Valley** between 2004 and 2006, and they are most easily seen between Burnopfield and Rowlands Gill. [N]

As feeding time draws near, tension starts to build, as both birds and spectators wait for the show to begin.

guaranteed food for the hungry young kites, many of whom were dying over the winter. Although, when times are hard, kites will take a range of live prey that even stretches to earthworms, at Gigrin Farm they are fed beef, fit for human consumption.

As you sit in the hides just before feeding time, the tension starts to build as kites start arriving; some alight in nearby trees, while others glide high above the hills. Crows and common buzzards join them, also waiting for the food to arrive. The deep "rronk, rronk" of ravens builds in the background. Once the meat has been thrown out, crows are quick to try to snatch a scrap but immediately the kites rush in, rarely if ever landing – they pluck the food in their talons from the ground, or – cheekily – from the crows' claws. They twist and turn, dive and climb, and there are so many of them it becomes a maelstrom of spectacular aerobatics.

Visit Gigrin Farm in February and you may be lucky enough to see kite pairs in a courtship flight, or rival males grappling each other by their talons, spinning and spiralling towards earth. By the end of the month these fearsome birds can be seen avidly nest-building.

Above: Red kites hatch in tree nests during April and May.

JAN

FEB

MAR

APR

MAY

JUN

JUL

AUG

SEP

OCT

NOV

DEC

WILDFOWL AT SLIMBRIDGE

FLOWING IN A GREAT ARC FROM MID WALES THROUGH SHROPSHIRE, the mighty Severn river reaches the sea in a huge estuary. Where the river broadens into the sand and mudflats, there are green, watery pastures on the east side, including the New Grounds at Slimbridge. Here the Wildfowl & Wetlands Trust was founded by Sir Peter Scott, a great conservationist, after he watched several thousand white-fronted geese spending the winter here. With warmer winters, geese no longer come in such numbers – 7,000 declining to just 550–750 in recent years. Most now need fly no farther than the Low Countries on their annual migrations from Russia.

The other famous winter birds at Slimbridge, Bewick's swans, have also declined in number, but you can still see around 200, and often they fly to the pools beside the visitor centre to give exceptional views. There, too, you can see pochards, wigeons, shovelers, and pintails, as the wild ducks mingle with the Trust's captive species.

WHERE
Wildfowl & Wetlands Trust, Slimbridge, Gloucestershire, GL2 7BT;
www.wwt.org.uk

CONTACT
Tel: 01453 891900;
enquiries@wwt.org.uk

GETTING THERE
By car, leave the M5 at either junctions 13 or 14 between Gloucester and Bristol, then follow the brown duck signs. The nearest train station is 6.4km (4 miles) away at Cam and Dursley Station. Cyclists should take the Sustrans route 41.

ACCESS AND FACILITIES
Of the 15 hides, 12 are accessible by wheelchair and buggy. There's also free electric scooter and manual wheelchair loan. The wheelchair-friendly centre has toilets, baby-changing facilities, restaurant, gallery, shop, and parking. The centre offers 4WD "safaris", visits to the crane school, and guided walks around the reserve.

OPENING TIMES
Winter (November–March) 9.30am to 5pm. Summer (April–October) 9.30am to 5.30pm.

CHARGES
Yes, for non-WWT members.

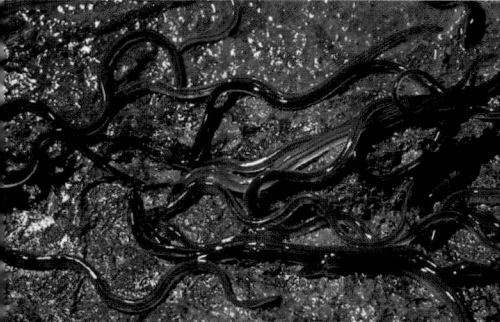

Long-distance traveller

Eels have long been a part of the River Severn's history, and elver fishers still trawl for them in the river at night. Mysteriously, no one has ever seen an eel spawn – because it takes place at 100–150 fathoms deep, in the Sargasso Sea 6,400km (4,000 miles) away from Britain. The elvers grow as they swim towards Europe, arriving when they are around three years old. They either stay in tidal lagoons or, like the elvers of the Severn, make their way up rivers to live in fresh water.

Main: One of the many bustling pools at Slimbridge that allow the public to see wildlife at close range.

Left: Bewick's swans enjoy a greeting ceremony between families.

Right (left to right): European eels live in the waters of the Severn; the spectacular view from Sloane Tower.

Right panel (top and bottom): Wigeon gather at Slimbridge; the Severn Bore, a large tidal wave that sweeps up the river, brings food for the waterfowl.

Bewick's swans are especially dramatic under the evening floodlights, but the geese attract most birdwatchers; it's fun to pick out bean, barnacle, and pink-footed geese mixed up with so many white-fronts from continental Europe. In some years there are even very rare lesser white-fronted geese. You can search for these strangers in comfort from Sloane Tower, which provides panoramic views across the entire reserve. On the pastures the scene is dominated by flocks of wigeons, which advance on foot across the fields, grazing sweet grasses and shoots. Rich-brown females set off the blue-grey-bodied, pink-breasted males, each with a blaze of palest primrose on the forehead. Few ducks match the wigeons for visual appeal, or for their wild chorus of whistles if they are disturbed into flight. Out on the estuary, thousands of gulls gather to roost. Those that feed inland fly out in the evening and, when this coincides with the high-tide roost of diners from the beaches, 10,000 black-headed gulls and 7,000 lesser black-backed gulls create an amazing spectacle.

WHERE ELSE TO SEE
BIRDS AT CLOSE QUARTERS

Slimbridge is the perfect wildlife reserve for accessibility: it has a large, educational visitor centre, walkways that bisect the habitat areas, and lots of hides. It's possible to see many of the animals at close range, and to feed the captive birds. Several other well-managed sites in the UK also aim to make the wildlife experience more accessible.

Welney is one of the UK's most popular wildlife sites, with around 30,000 visitors during the winter swan season. Its observatories, heated hides, and guided tours are among the easiest ways to see the Ouse Washes, and increase your knowledge. [SE]

The **London Wetland Centre** (*see pp.16–17*) may just be the best urban wetland centre in Europe. It has a unique "bird airport" observatory, six hides, and an adventure area where children can enjoy mini-beast safaris and pond-dipping sessions. [SE]

Llanelli is the national wetland centre for Wales, and it has some fun ways to see wildlife, including canoe safaris and bike trails (you can hire the bikes). On a wet day, the indoor interactive Millennium Discovery Centre brings you closer to the wildlife. [W]

Slimbridge occupies 365 hectares (900 acres) of water meadows, bordering the mud flats of the Severn.

THROUGH THE YEAR
SLIMBRIDGE

Spring sees the movement of wading birds such as lapwings, dunlins, redshanks, and curlews, as well as swallows and sand martins. Listen for the noisy call of sedge warblers, and for whitethroats in the hedgerows and thickets.

In **summer**, you might see shelducks on the marsh, and there is a chance of a kingfisher. Slimbridge is the only place in Europe where you can see, among the exotic captive birds, all six species of flamingo.

Autumn is good for returning wading birds of many kinds – look in the enclosures for water rails. Starling numbers increase and large flocks can be seen swirling overhead in dramatic shapes before settling to roost.

Below: Flamingo chicks are a popular sight in summer at Slimbridge.

JAN

FEB

MAR

APR

MAY

JUN

JUL

AUG

SEP

OCT

NOV

DEC

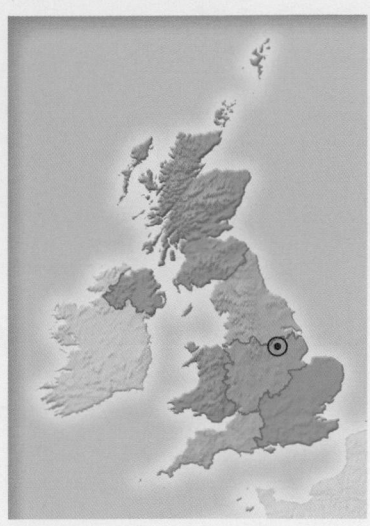

VETERAN TREES

FOREVER LINKED WITH THE NAME OF ROBIN HOOD, the legendary medieval outlaw, Sherwood Forest was one of the royal hunting forests created by King William I after his victory over the English in 1066. It was never a continuous tract of woodland, but a "wood pasture", with areas of grassland, sandy heath, and oakwood.

Astoundingly, some of its trees are almost as old. The Major Oak in Birklands Wood – the only surviving large area of woodland in Sherwood – was a huge, ancient tree when it was first described by Major Hayman Rooke in 1790, and the trunk's immense 10m (33ft) girth has barely increased since. Tree girth is one of the best indicators of age, and it suggests

Surviving for 500 or even 1,000 years, some of the ancient trees of Sherwood are among the oldest living organisms on Earth. Their hollow trunks form refuges for all manner of of woodland animals, especially in winter.

that the tree is between 800 and 1,000 years old. Such a lifespan seems almost incredibly long, but trees can live longer. Some Californian bristlecone pines are known to be nearly 5,000 years old, and several British churchyard yew trees may be well over 2,000 years old.

The Major Oak certainly looks ancient, with its hollow trunk and lower branches supported by steel poles. These signs of decay might seem to threaten its imminent demise, but it is clear from the 1790 description that it has been in this state for at least two centuries. In fact, the fungi that eat out the dead wood at the heart of a hollow tree leave the outer wood and bark as a living shell, and since a broad, hollow trunk is stronger than slender, solid trunk of the same weight, such trees often survive storms that destroy much younger trees.

They may also save energy by dying back at the crown, creating the "stag-headed" effect that reduces the tree's vulnerability. Ancient forestry practice played a part, as many trees had their branches lopped to encourage new growth, in a technique called "pollarding". This prolonged the life of the tree by lowering its centre of gravity, making it less likely to blow over. These ancient pollards are best seen in winter, when there is no foliage to obscure their shape. Such veteran trees are among the national monuments of Britain.

Main: A gnarled ancient yew tree in the forest. Some yews in the UK are believed to be over 2,000 years old.
Below (left to right): At home in the trees: a noctule bat; a great spotted woodpecker; a tawny owl.
Inset: Sherwood Forest covers 180 hectares (450 acres), with its spectacular ancient oaks still guarding Birklands Wood.

Forest parasite

Forever associated with Christmas, mistletoe is seen on the branches of deciduous trees in the forest – especially ash, hawthorn, and lime. This evergreen is a semi-parasite, taking nutrients from its host tree, but photosynthesizing to make its own carbohydrates. Its seeds are eaten by birds, passing intact through their digestive systems, before being deposited on the branch of another tree; "mistletoe" is derived from the Anglo-Saxon words, *mistel* (dung) and *tan* (twig).

JAN

FEB

MAR

APR

MAY

JUN

JUL

AUG

SEP

OCT

NOV

DEC

Above: "Chicken of the woods" fungus is mostly found on oak trees.

THROUGH THE YEAR
SHERWOOD FOREST

In **spring**, the woodlands around the Major Oak are full of birdsong as woodland birds – including many returned migrants – claim their breeding territories. The abundant insect life provides plenty of food for their nestlings, but these conscientious parents must be wary of sparrowhawks, which also have young mouths to feed.

In **summer**, the forest is a good place to look for woodland butterflies such as the speckled wood, ringlet, and white admiral. At dusk, nightjars can often be heard giving their strange, mechanical "churring" call from patches of heathland within the reserve.

Autumn brings a flush of autumn colour and a host of fungi, including several that live on the veteran trees. Over 200 different species have been recorded growing on the trees and the woodland floor.

WHERE ELSE TO SEE
ANCIENT TREES

Veteran trees are a speciality of Britain, and especially England. In continental Europe it is rare to find a tree more than 200 years old, but in England trees twice this age are common, especially in churchyards, old parkland, and ancient woodlands. Many grow in hedgerows, where they mark medieval boundaries.

The oldest-known trees are yews. Those of **Kingley Vale** in West Sussex (*see pp.310–311*) are at least 500 years old, and many churchyard yews may be much older. [SE]

The yew in **Much Marcle** churchyard, Herefordshire, is at least 1,000 years old. [M]

There are many ancient oaks in **Windsor Great Park**, Berkshire (*see pp.258–259*), and **The New Forest** in Hampshire (*see pp.174–175*). **Epping Forest**, on the borders of London and Essex, contains many venerable trees, most of which were pollarded in the past. [SE]

Wistman's Wood in Devon (*see pp.160–161*) dates back to prehistoric times. [SW]

WHERE
Belfast Lough RSPB Reserve, Belvoir Park Forest, Belfast, Antrim, Northern Ireland BT8 7QT.

CONTACT
RSPB Belfast Lough, tel: 02891 479009; belfast.lough@rspb.org.uk

GETTING THERE
The reserve is in Belfast Harbour Estate (10 minutes from central Belfast). Two entrances are signposted along the A2 (Belfast to Holywood road). From the Dee Street entrance the reserve car park is a further 3.2km (2 miles) and from the Tillysburn entrance it is 1.6km (1 mile).

ACCESS AND FACILITIES
The reserve has two hides and a cosy observation room. The observation room and one hide have good access for wheelchair users. Facilities include a car park, full-access toilets, and an information centre.

OPENING TIMES
The two outdoor hides are always open. The observation room is open Tuesday–Sunday, from 9am–5pm.

CHARGES
None.

The black-tailed godwit

The black-tailed godwits that spend the winter on the reserve come all the way from Iceland. They rarely breed in the UK, where there are fewer than 40 pairs. Many waders can be tricky to identify, but black-tailed godwits are easier than most: the black tail of their name is only really visible when they fly, but you can always spot their long straight bills, stilt-length legs, and – in February – pretty grey plumage. In spring and summer they sport beautiful deep-red underparts.

Left: A ring-billed gull makes its distinctive call: a shrill "ooooww" followed by a series of short "a-a-as".

Right (left to right): The red-breasted merganser diving duck; a common tern stretches its wings; a teal on the waters of the Lough; a view of Belfast Lough RSPB reserve, which is a sheltered lagoon off the main lough.

Main: Seals on their way along the coast rest on the islets of Belfast Lough. **Far right:** Oblivious to passing ships, herons, gulls, and black-tailed godwits mingle at the reserve.

LIFE AT THE CITY LIMITS

BELFAST LOUGH IS AN OASIS OF CALM just outside Belfast city centre. In February, the first thing you notice might be a gentle group of light-bellied brent geese floating gracefully on the water, or the bobbing heads and somnolent silhouettes of harbour seals. At high tide, however, the deeper water teems with birds: great northern and red-throated divers, grebes, and large numbers of sea ducks – long-tailed ducks, scaups, goldeneyes, eiders, scoters, and the tufty-headed, red-breasted mergansers. Scaups seem to love the lough, and sometimes you can see more than 500 in February, the white stripes around their bodies looking like wide bandages.

On one side of the lough, the RSPB manages a reserve, the centrepiece of which is a large brackish lagoon. Wildfowls and waders gather on the lagoon at high tide, and the star species in February are the leggy black-tailed godwits, which poke about the mudflats with their long, fine bills, looking for worms and molluscs. They come

JAN

FEB

MAR

APR

MAY

JUN

JUL

AUG

SEP

OCT

NOV

DEC

Above: Swifts fly over the Lough constantly in spring.

Over 180 different species of birds can be found on the 13-hectare (32-acre) RSPB reserve beside Belfast Lough.

THROUGH THE YEAR
BELFAST LOUGH

Passage waders in **spring** include greenshanks, common sandpipers, and whimbrels, as well as the much loved black-tailed godwits. You may be lucky and chance upon a garganey. Swallows and swifts hawk over the lagoon, while the common terns are busily courting. Look out for young foxes – there is a managed population of this predator at the Lough.

In **summer**, the common and Arctic terns breed on the reserve – head to one of the hides for close-up views of them raising their young. The observation room also brings wonderful views of reed buntings, linnets, and greenfinches.

Every **autumn** migrant flocks arrive to take advantage of the easy food-pickings at Belfast Lough. The black-tailed godwits are joined by overstcatchers, redshanks, dunlins, and, curlews with their elegant, long, curved bills.

WHERE ELSE TO SEE
WETLAND LAGOONS

There are a number of wildlife areas in the UK that feature lagoons and their associated wildlife.

Widewater Lagoon, Shoreham, West Sussex, is an area of brackish water landlocked by a shingle bank and home to herons, swans, oystercatchers, and redshanks. **Titchfield Haven** in Hampshire, behind the Solent, also has a large population of black-tailed godwits and a few bitterns. [SE]

Black-tailed godwits can be seen along the **Exe Estuary**, Devon (*see pp.286–287*), and on **Brownsea Island**, Dorset (*see pp.56–57*). [SW]

Blithfield Reservoir, just outside Burton upon Trent, Staffordshire, has many of the same winter birds as Belfast Lough, and occasionally rarer grebes, scaups, and smews. You need to apply for permits to access the better, northern half of the reserve; otherwise take binoculars to the causeway. [M]

incredibly close to the heated observation room overlooking the reserve in winter, and there is no better site in Britain for seeing this otherwise rarely seen species. The wetland formed when the area was enclosed from the sea and used for dumping silt dredged from the lough. Birds soon spotted its potential and started to use it, until eventually the lagoon was actively developed into a natural habitat more attractive to a wide range of birds and animals. Today it is considered to be one of the richest bird reserves in Ireland.

Wigeons, teals, and shovelers may be joined by vagrants such as the North American green-winged teal, which sometimes overwinters here. This estuarine habitat attracts many species to feed, and the numbers of birds present on the reserve's lagoon tends to be tide-dependent. At high tide, large numbers of gulls come in to roost; look among them for the rarer "white-winged" gulls such as the glaucous and Iceland gull. The younger birds appear to be all-white – they have no black in their wings – which is why they are collectively referred to as "white-winged". Look even closer, and you may spot one or two rare ring-billed gulls from North America hiding among them.

WINTER STARLING ROOSTS

SOME WILDLIFE EXPERIENCES ARE SO EXTRAORDINARY that they defy comprehension. A broad swathe of wild flowers may dazzle the eye, or the leap of a migrating salmon make your heart skip a beat, but you can understand why or how these things arise. The aerial ballet of starlings going to roost is of a quite different order. It is both dazzling and even heart-stopping but, for most of us, it is above all a joyous, defiant mystery.

Some winter starling roosts are colossal, with more than a million birds gathering to spend the night together for warmth and safety in numbers. But small can be beautiful too, and all over Britain, local starlings put on performances that draw the crowds. One of the best is to be seen over Slapton Ley on the south Devon coast, where the reedbeds attract up to 75,000 birds each night outside the breeding season. In February the nights draw in early, so you need to arrive by about 4pm to catch the first flocks arriving, shortly before dusk.

WHERE
Slapton Ley National Nature Reserve, Slapton, Kingsbridge, Devon TQ7 2QP; www.slnnr.org.uk

CONTACT
Slapton Ley Field Centre, tel: 01548 580466; enquiries.sl@field-studies-council.org

GETTING THERE
By car, the reserve is accessed via minor roads from the A379, 30km (18 miles) east of Plymouth, 15km (9 miles) south of Totnes, and 10km (6¼ miles) east of Kingsbridge. The nearest train stations are in Totnes and Plymouth. A bus service runs from Plymouth.

ACCESS AND FACILITIES
The car park near Torcross has toilets and a hide adapted for disabled access. There are hides and a 2.5km (1½ mile) nature trail; guided walks are organized by the Field Centre. The starlings roost happens in the Ireland Bay reedbed. The nearest refreshments are at Slapton and Torcross, 0.5 km (⅓ mile) away. There are toilets and picnic sites at the A379 car parks.

OPENING TIMES
Open all year round.

CHARGES
None.

> Vast flocks, several thousand strong, swirl through the night air in a breathtaking aerial dance.

Dwindling populations

The spectacle of starlings swirling overhead in what is poetically known as a "murmuration" was once common in towns and cities. Yet breeding populations have drastically declined, especially in urban areas, largely because starling nest sites in roof spaces are being eliminated by modern roofing techniques. However, most of the birds that roost in rural areas in winter are seasonal migrants from Europe, attracted by the mild winter climate, so their aerial displays should continue to amaze us well into the future.

Main: A roosting starling flock is a breathtaking sight.

Panel (above left): The view across Slapton Sands.

Left: The vast, open skies of Slapton Ley.

Right (left to right): A starling flock roosting in trees; the winter plumage of a male adult starling; a roosting flock can often look like a shoal of fish.

As the flock gathers over the reedbeeds, other flocks arrive to join it, swelling its numbers until there are several thousand starlings flying in tight formation. And then it begins. From being a mass of birds, the flock is transformed into an immense super-organism in which each individual becomes subordinated to some instinctive choreography of the air. They swirl through the sky in looping, fluid shapes, like a vast shoal of fish in a tropical sea.

The flock can tighten to a knot, then expand in a split second to apparently fill the air, surging overhead with a crackling hiss of massed wings. Sometimes a sparrowhawk or peregrine appears, but often seems mesmerized by the spectacle and unable to latch onto a target. Then suddenly it all ends. As if sucked down a drain, part of the flock pours out of air into the reedbed, disappearing in an instant. The rest billow up and drop down again to allow more to cascade into the roost. Bit by bit the airborne flock dwindles until the last group dives for cover. They are gone.

WHERE ELSE TO SEE
STARLING ROOSTS

Despite recent serious population declines, starlings are still common throughout the British Isles, and their aerial performances are a regular feature of the winter scene. They usually occur over woodlands, shelter belts, and reedbeds, but the birds may also roost on pylons and in derelict buildings.

The largest starling roost is the reedbed at **Westhay Moor** on the Somerset Levels, which in some years attracts up to eight million birds. The area is a nature reserve, but its popularity with visitors at roosting time means that the site can get overcrowded. [SW]

One of best-known roosting sites is the ruined West Pier at **Brighton** in East Sussex. Here the birds often swirl against the backdrop of the sun setting over the sea, creating an unforgettable spectacle. [SE]

There is a large reedbed starling roost near the Wildfowl & Wetland Trust site at **Slimbridge** (*see pp.34–35*) in Gloucestershire. The reserve at **Marazion Marsh** in Cornwall also includes a large reedbed that attracts thousands of starlings on winter evenings. [SW]

THROUGH THE YEAR
SLAPTON LEY

In **spring** Slapton Ley reserve welcomes thousands of migrant birds from further south. They may include rare vagrants such as golden orioles as well as passage migrants that drop in to feed before continuing their journey. April also sees the mass spawning of fish in the channel of Slapton Ley itself.

An evening walk through the reserve in **summer** is likely to be rewarded by the sight of glow worms in the grassy banks. By day the insect life includes a wide variety of butterflies, some attracted by the maritime plants that bloom on the shingle ridge.

On dark **autumn** nights thousands of eels leave the Ley via the weir at Torcross on their way to the tropical Atlantic to breed. The water also provides a hunting ground for ospreys, while the reedbeds shelter big flocks of pied wagtails.

Below: Peregrine falcons are often found around starling roosts.

JAN
FEB
MAR
APR
MAY
JUN
JUL
AUG
SEP
OCT
NOV
DEC

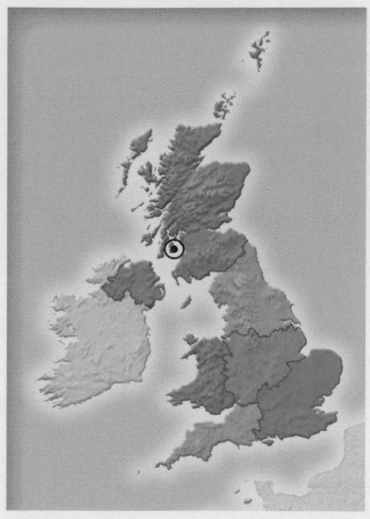

WHERE
Isle of Arran, Scotland;
www.ayrshire-arran.com

CONTACT
Countryside Ranger Service, Brodick Castle and Country Park, Isle of Arran, tel: 01770 302462. Ayrshire and Arran Tourist Board, tel: 0845 2255121; info@ayrshire-arran.com

GETTING THERE
There's a daily ferry service from Ardrossan (North Ayrshire) to Brodick, which takes 55 minutes, and another service from Claonaig to Lochranza. For details of all ferry services contact www.calmac.co.uk Regular buses connect from the ferries around the island, contact Stagecoach on Arran, tel: 0141 3326811.

ACCESS AND FACILITIES
Contact individual sites for access details, and the Arran Tourist board for specific information (details above). Brodick Castle (www.nts.org.uk) has facilities and some access for wheelchair users (notably Wilma's Walk).

OPENING TIMES
Contact individual sites for details.

CHARGES
Admission fee to Brodick Castle (free to NTS members).

Island divers

Arran has become one of the best places in the UK to see three different species of divers, or loons as they are sometimes called, because of their yodelling breeding calls. In winter you can see red-throated (*shown below*), black-throated, and great northern divers as they come and shelter on inland and coastal lochs. Although these elegant birds may not be in their smart breeding plumages at this time of year, they are still a delight to watch.

SCOTLAND IN MINIATURE

OF ALL THE BRITISH ISLANDS, ARRAN MUST BE THE MOST SPECTACULAR destination for nature lovers. Whether you're an animal, plant, or geology enthusiast, Arran will never fail to disappoint. It is one of the many islands in the Firth of Clyde between Ayrshire and Kintyre, which are Scotland's most southerly isles, but still retain many aspects of Scotland's highlands and lowlands. You can understand why this stunning island is known as "Scotland in Miniature". It has a vast wealth of habitats, from dramatic, rugged mountains in the north to gently rolling hills, carved valleys, and woodlands in the south. A trip here at any time of the year is wonderful, but winter is especially rewarding.

Scanning the wide skies above may reward you with spectacular views of soaring golden eagles, which practise their impressive display flights in February.

The Gulf Stream ensures that winters are usually mild, making the north's wild, mountainous glens surprisingly busy in February. You may catch fleeting views of white ptarmigan and red grouse across the moors, while the awesome golden eagles soar overhead. Red deer roam in large herds and you've got a good chance of spotting them just north of the String Road, which cuts across the island from Brodick on the east coast. In extremely bad weather deer sometimes wander through villages.

The many lochs and tarns are a welcome home for birds. Mallard, shelduck, goosander, and eider are a few of the resident species, and these are joined in winter by many others, including goldeneye, teal, and wigeon. The larger areas of moorland support a large population of hen harriers; Machrie Moor is a good place to see them with other moorland birds. In the leafy woodlands on the south of the island, you may spot a red squirrel. Grey squirrels have never been brought to the island, so the rare red species thrives on Arran. One of the best places to look is in the grounds of Brodick Castle. Otters can sometimes be seen down on the shoreline, especially in February, when the young are born. Although they readily hunt in salt water, they are not sea otters, as commonly misidentified.

Main: The calm, western bays of Arran are sheltered by the Kilbrannan Sound and the Mull of Kintyre.
Below (left to right): Rock ptarmigans are white in winter and brown in summer; otters feed on fish around the west coast; the mountain Cir Mhor, meaning "big comb", in reference to its likeness to a cockscomb. **Inset:** A golden eagle.

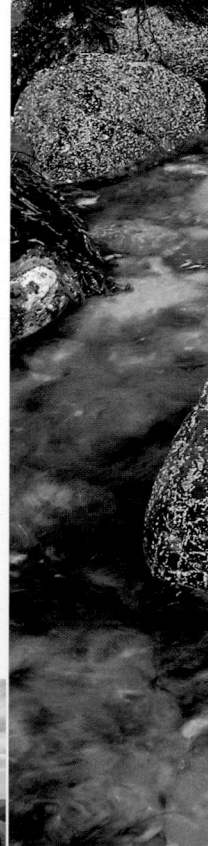

JAN
FEB
MAR
APR
MAY
JUN
JUL
AUG
SEP
OCT
NOV
DEC

Above: *Allium ursinum* – wild garlic – carpets the woodland in spring.

THROUGH THE YEAR
ISLE OF ARRAN

Some of the first flowers in **spring** to appear are wood anemone and golden saxifrage; later, many woodland floors are covered in ramsons, bluebells, and bugle.

In **summer** Arran's damp meadows are alive with stands of purple loosestrife, meadowsweet, valerian, and hemp agrimony. The unusual Arran whitebeam is a tree species unique to the island.

The **autumn** brings chances of sighting migrating ospreys, and it is worth visiting the Cock of Arran, just north of Lochranza, where basking sharks can sometimes be seen offshore.

WHERE ELSE TO SEE
ISLAND WILDLIFE

All of the islands off the British coasts have much to offer – they are often dramatic landscapes with unusual and changing wildlife.

The **Farne Islands** (*see pp.126–127*) have around 100,000 pairs of wintering seabirds, including puffins and guillemots, and one of Europe's largest grey seal populations. [N]

The **Isle of Skye** is the largest island of the Inner Hebrides. Its northern tip provides a dramatic backdrop for seabirds, including fulmars, kittiwakes, and shags, and its waters are home to Britain's largest jellyfish, the moon jellyfish. [SC]

The **Isle of Mull** (*see pp.226–227*), another Inner Hebridean island, is well known both for its seabirds and its birds of prey, which hunt over the moors and fish over the lochs and sea. A particular attraction are the breeding pairs of reintroduced white-tailed sea eagles. [SC]

WHERE
Exmoor National Park, Devon/Somerset;
www.exmoor-nationalpark.gov.uk

CONTACT
National Park Authority, Exmoor House,
Dulverton, TA22 9HL, tel: 01398 323665;
info@exmoor-nationalpark.gov.uk; Dulverton
Visitor Centre, tel: 01398 323841;

GETTING THERE
Exmoor is easily accessible by road from the
M5, junction 27. There is also a bus network
through the park (www.travelinesw.com or
tel: 0871 2002233). The nearest train
stations are at Barnstaple, Taunton, and
Tiverton Parkway.

ACCESS AND FACILITIES
There are visitor centres with facilities at
Cross Street, Combe Martin, EX34 0DH;
Dunster Steep, Dunster, TA24 6SG; Fore
Street, Dulverton, TA22 9EX; Blackmoor Gate,
Lynmouth, EX35 6EQ; and the Old School,
High Street, Porlock, TA24 8QD. For
information on opening times, events, and
on wheelchair access throughout the park,
visit www.exmoor-nationalpark.gov.uk

OPENING TIMES
Open all year round.

CHARGES
None.

The Dartmoor pony

Dartmoor (*see also pp.244–245*) has its own
native breed of ponies, which have lived there
for many centuries. They are around the same
size as Exmoors, and are equally tough, but they
are good-tempered and approachable. They
can be almost any colour and many have white
"blazes" on their foreheads giving them a less
distinctive look, although their stocky build,
deep bodies, thick neck, long manes, and
short legs make them instantly recognizable.

Left (left to right): Wild
goats at the Valley of the
Rocks, Lynton; a buzzard
in the snow.

Right (left to right):
A stream in full winter
spate at Watersmeet,
on Exmoor; pony grazing
on the Exmoor hills.

Main and far right: A pair of Exmoor ponies on a fog-shrouded moor.

WILD EXMOOR

PONIES LIVE WILD IN SEVERAL AREAS OF BRITAIN, but the rolling heather moorlands and stark coastal
cliffs of Exmoor provide their most dramatic habitat. Here they are essential parts of the moorland landscape,
where their grazing and browsing have played an important part in the ecosystem for thousands of years.

The Exmoor pony is the most primitive of the UK's native ponies, and its oldest breed – predating the
arrival of the Romans in Britain. It is an extremely hardy little pony, resistant to disease and with great powers
of endurance, and its long survival on the cold, wet – but beautiful – moor with little food or shelter is testimony
to its strength. In February you can really see how the pony has evolved to survive: it grows a soft, woolly
undercoat, topped by a longer, oily, water-repellent outer coat. Look for the broad fan of hair at the base of
the tail – known as the "ice tail" or "snow chute" – that helps channel cold rain away from the body.

JAN

FEB

MAR

APR

MAY

JUN

JUL

AUG

SEP

OCT

NOV

DEC

Above: Looking from the heather-clad moor over the Devon countryside.

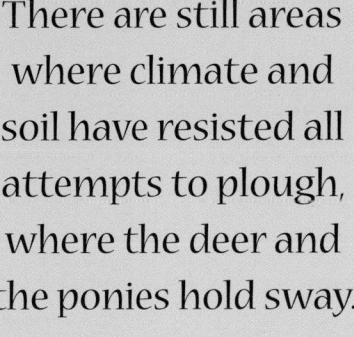

There are still areas where climate and soil have resisted all attempts to plough, where the deer and the ponies hold sway.

THROUGH THE YEAR
EXMOOR

Exmoor was designated a National Park in 1954, and covers a 692 sq km (267 sq mile) area that falls within Devon and Somerset. Its mixture of woodland, scrub, bracken, grassland, bog, and upland heath makes it home to many rare plants and animals.

In **spring** the moor's seven rare species of whitebeam – none found outside Britain – are covered with clusters of white flowers. Look for them in old coastal oakwoods such as Watersmeet, Woody Bay, and Culbone. Look out for stonechats, whinchats, wheatears, and rare birds of prey such as the merlin.

Exmoor's native red deer are most easily found on higher ground, among the heather, during the **summer**. The smaller roe deer and fallow deer usually hide in darker woodland areas. Look out for some of Britain's rarest butterflies: the heath, marsh, and high brown fritillary butterflies.

The majestic red deer start mating in **autumn**, and the sound of clashing antlers fills the woodlands. The woodlands burst into glorious colour, and their floors are peppered with rare fungi, such as the sandy stilt puffball and ballerina waxcap fungus.

WHERE ELSE TO SEE
WILD PONIES

The national parks of the **New Forest** (see pp.174–175), Hampshire [SE], and **Dartmoor**, Devon [SW], are home to thousands of wild ponies.

You can see wild ponies at several sites in Wales: **Black Mountain**, in the Brecon Beacons National Park; the great raised bog of **Cors Caron** at Tregaron (see pp.190–191); and on the saltmarshes of the **Burry Inlet**, on the north shore of the **Gower Peninsula** (see pp.122–123). The rare Carneddau ponies can be found on the hills of **Snowdonia** (see pp.172–173). [W]

The hills of the **Lake District** have provided habitat for rare fell herds for around 2,000 years. These stocky ponies are predominantly black, with full manes and tails, and "feathering" on the legs. [N]

Always some shade of brown or bay, the pony's distinctive appearance comes from its wide forehead with large, pale-ringed eyes, its mealy nose, strong, thick neck, broad back, and sturdy, short legs. The pale rings around the eyes ("hooded" or "toad" eyes) are actually thick fleshy surrounds to protect the eyes against the frequent rain that lashes the moor in winter. Their teeth are also unusually suited to the environment – an extra molar ensures they can easily chew coarse, thorny plants. Even the nose and ears have evolved efficiently: small ears keep heat loss to a minimum, while large nasal passages help to warm the freezing air before it reaches the lungs.

Exmoor was used as a training ground during World War II, and great numbers of ponies were killed: only some 50 survived. Local people rescued the remaining herds but numbers remained low until the early 1980s. The total now stands at between 1,000 and 2,000; these are caught once a year and branded for conservation reasons. However gently they nuzzle their young, the ponies you see today are direct descendants of those that once pulled mighty chariots for the fearsome Celts. The ponies are approachable, but can kick, so stand well clear of their hind legs.

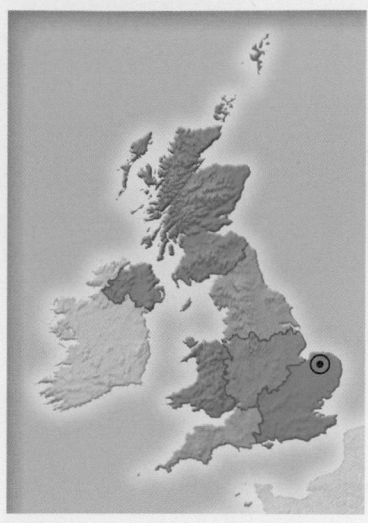

THE HEART OF BROADLAND

THE NORFOLK BROADS ARE JUSTLY FAMOUS both for the beauty of their landscape, with their intricate system of waterways graced by sailing boats, motor cruisers, and windmills, and their abundant wildlife. Hickling is the largest of the broads, stretching over 200 hectares (500 acres); like the other broads, it is thought to have been formed by peat and clay-digging and is only around 1.5m (5ft) deep with a gravel bottom. It includes one of the largest areas of open water in the whole of East Anglia, fringing marshes, reedbeds, sedge beds, and patches of scrub, sprinkled with tracts of wet alder, willow, and birch "carr" woodland. Hickling offers the best birdwatching in the whole of the Broads, including reedbed specialities such as bearded tits, bitterns, and water rails – all resident breeders – and a very wide range of spring and autumn migrants. The winter landscape may seem empty by comparison, but you just need to look more carefully: the quality is wonderful.

WHERE
Hickling Broad National Nature Reserve, Stubb Road, Hickling, Norwich NR12 0BW; www.norfolkwildlifetrust.org.uk

CONTACT
Norfolk Wildlife Trust, tel: 01603 625540; wild@norfolkwildlifetrust.org.uk

GETTING THERE
Hickling Broad is 6.5km (4 miles) south of Stalham, off the A149 Stalham to Caister-on-Sea road, Norfolk. From Hickling village follow the "brown badger" tourist signs. Buses from both Norwich and Cromer stop in Hickling village; the reserve is a 20-minute walk away.

ACCESS AND FACILITIES
There are hides overlooking pools and a boardwalk trail suitable for pushchairs and wheelchairs. At this time of year, the nearest public toilets are in Hickling village. The reserve's visitor centre has full-access toilets and refreshments.

OPENING TIMES
The nature reserve is open all year round, 10am–5pm. The visitor centre opens 10am–5pm, April–September.

CHARGES
Small charge for entry, except for children and NWT members.

Hickling Broad is the largest of the Norfolk Broads, with over 200 hectares (500 acres) of open water, and 485 hectares (1,200 acres) of wildlife-friendly land.

Return of the cranes

Much of the UK breeding population of the common crane (*Grus grus*) can be seen wintering around Hickling Broad. Cranes recolonized the Norfolk Broads in the 1980s after an absence of around 400 years. Today, reintroduction programmes are in progress, aimed at boosting their population in East Anglia by rearing eggs imported from wild birds in Germany. The elevated watchpoint at Stubb Mill provides excellent views of the birds.

Wildfowl include whooper and Bewick's swans, pink-footed geese, goldeneyes, smews, and goosanders, and if you head over to the special viewing area by Stubb Mill around mid-afternoon, you'll get some superb views of birds of prey as they fly in to their roost sites. Marsh harriers are guaranteed, with over 40 birds often recorded, while hen harriers, sparrowhawks, and merlins are likely. An even greater thrill comes from seeing the huge common cranes: despite their name, they are very rare in Britain, and this is the best place to see them. Standing 1m (3ft) tall, with broad wings spanning as much as 2.2m (over 7ft), they are even bigger than the grey herons.

The grazing of hardy eastern European ponies, cattle, and sheep at Hickling Broad is a key tool in managing the site and keeping the restored areas of the reserve clear of invasive vegetation. Reed and sedge beds are regularly mown and water levels maintained at optimum for the wading and breeding birds.

WHERE ELSE TO SEE
FENS AND REEDBEDS

Fens and large areas of reeds are a scarce and threatened habitat throughout Europe. Britain does have a significant proportion of the total, but there are few very large reedbeds.

Strumpshaw Fen RSPB Reserve, in the Broads nearer Norwich (see pp.152–153), and **Wicken Fen** Reserve in Cambridgeshire (see pp.204–205) both contain rich collections of wetland plants and animals, many of them rare. [SE]

Stodmarsh National Nature Reserve in the Stour Valley, Kent, is a wonderful place for seeing birds, including hen harriers and ducks in winter, as well as rarities. Look for the insect-eating greater bladderwort plant in the dykes. [SE]

The **Somerset Levels**, extending from Bridgwater Bay into the heart of Somerset, include many wildlife reserves protecting the great network of ditches, grazing marshes, and peatland, where you can see masses of wildflowers, dragonflies, wading birds, and otters, among much other wildlife. [SW]

THROUGH THE YEAR
HICKLING BROAD

Spring bird migrants range from Temminck's stints and other rare waders to scarce black terns, little gulls, spoonbills, and ospreys. From March onwards, the golden yellow flowers of marsh marigolds appear on the site, with early marsh orchids and water violets joining them in May.

In **summer**, you can enjoy the yellow iris flowers lighting up the banks of the broad and look for swallowtail butterflies between mid-May and June (with smaller numbers in August) along the Weaver's Way path. You may also find the equally striking green-and-black caterpillars feeding on the forked leaves of milk parsley plants.

Summer visitors that stay to nest include handsome little garganey ducks, common and little terns, and reed, sedge, and grasshopper warblers. As well as being a good time for checking out migrant birds, **autumn** sees the gradual build-up of birds of prey and cranes at the roost site, from October onwards.

Main: Hickling Broad is a medieval man-made lake.

Above (top and bottom): A marsh harrier in flight; a golden plover in winter plumage forages for food.

Left panel (top and bottom): Lapwings can be seen year-round, but are most abundant in winter; the barn owl has a distinctive heart-shaped face.

Below: Large pike are to be found in Hickling's waters.

Below: The southern hawker dragonfly lays its eggs in pond vegetation.

JAN
FEB
MAR
APR
MAY
JUN
JUL
AUG
SEP
OCT
NOV
DEC

WHERE
Poole Harbour, Dorset;
www.pooletourism.com

CONTACT
Poole Welcome Centre, Poole Quay, Poole,
Dorset, BH15 1HJ; tel: 01202 253253;
info@pooletourism.com
Dorset Wildlife Trust, tel: 01305 264620;
mail@dorsetwildlife.co.uk

GETTING THERE
By car, take the A31 or A352 to Poole
Harbour. Travel to Wareham by train or coach.

ACCESS AND FACILITIES
The best way to see the wintering birds in
the Harbour is by boat: the RSPB run cruises
from Poole Quay about every six weeks in
winter; book early via Brownsea Ferries
(01929 462383). There are many places to
enjoy general facilities around the harbour.
Visit www.pooletourism.com for information
on parking, including blue-badgeholder-
reserved spaces. For Brownsea Island and
Arne, see pages 56–57 and138–139.

OPENING TIMES
The many wildlife sites have varying opening
times. No vehicular access to Poole Park
6am–10am Monday to Saturday.

CHARGES
Charges may be levied at some reserves.

Home to egret chicks

The thriving colony of little egrets on Brownsea
Island is a recent arrival. These beautiful white
herons were once only very rare visitors to Britain,
with a mere nine birds recorded up to 1950. After
a gradual increase, there was a dramatic influx
starting in 1989. By 1996 the first pair bred in
England, at Brownsea Island, and subsequently
spread to other parts of southern England, East
Anglia, and the south coast of Ireland. They feed
along muddy creeks and river channels, and roost
in trees or along the saltmarsh.

Above (left to right): The shingle beach of Poole Harbour; oystercatchers feed in the intertidal zone; avocets winter around the harbour.
Main: The wildlife has the whole of Poole Harbour virtually to itself at dawn.

SAFE HARBOUR FOR BIRDS

ONE OF THE WORLD'S LARGEST NATURAL HARBOURS, Poole Harbour's great sweep encloses 96km (60 miles) of coastline and contains several islands. The wealth of habitats includes huge areas of intertidal sand flats and mud flats, saltmarsh, reedbeds, and woodlands. Many thousands of birds from the far north seek the shelter of the harbour in winter, including waders such as the elegant black-tailed godwits – in internationally important numbers – curlews, grey plovers, knots, and dunlins; wildfowl, such as brent geese and red-breasted mergansers; and scarce grebes. By the shipping entrance to the harbour, the seaward side of the peninsula at Sandbanks can be a good place to see sea-ducks, particularly eiders and common scoters, divers, grebes, and auks. On the western and southern shores of the peninsula known as the Isle of Purbeck, two reserves protect outstanding lowland heath: RSPB Arne (*see pp.138–139*) and the National Nature Reserve of Studland and Godlingston Heath. Their birdlife is particularly rich.

Poole Park, just behind the quay, is a major winter site for Canada geese, tufted ducks, and pochards, and, especially in cold weather, other scarcer ducks such as scaups, goosanders, red-breasted mergansers, smews, and goldeneyes. Look on the boating lake for these scarcer species, and for occasional grebes and divers. The many common species of gulls sometimes include much scarcer species, such as yellow-legged, glaucous, or Iceland gulls. It's worth visiting some of the harbour's eight islands: three of them, including Brownsea (*see pp.56–57*), are home to the beleaguered red squirrel. Head for the four hides on Brownsea that overlook the brackish mud and water of the lagoon, where you can see one of the largest groupings of avocets in Britain: over 1,000 of these graceful black-and-white birds roost here. In the trees nearby, grey herons nest colonially, along with increasing numbers of pristine white little egrets.

You can't help noticing the beautiful little egrets: the black of their legs contrasts so sharply with the bright yellow of their feet, as if they had been dipped in paint.

Inset: Little egrets grace the harbour in winter.
Below (left to right): A preening red-breasted merganser; dunlins take flight.

JAN

FEB

MAR

APR

MAY

JUN

JUL

AUG

SEP

OCT

NOV

DEC

WHERE ELSE TO SEE
ESTUARY WILDLIFE

Britain contains many other estuary sites that are renowned for birds and other wildlife, including several near to Poole that you might like to visit on a journey along England's south coast.

Langstone and **Chichester** harbours, farther east on the Hampshire/West Sussex border, also have a huge area of mudflats and saltmarshes. A winter visit will guarantee sightings of many different waders and wildfowl, as well as little egrets. [SE]

Pagham Harbour, a little farther east along the West Sussex coast, has shingle spits, wet grassland, mud, and pools, and is a notable site for migrant birds in spring and autumn. [SE]

Travelling west from Poole, the **Exe Estuary** (*see pp.286–287*) in Devon is one of the best places to see waders and wildfowl, including flocks of wintering avocets and brent geese. [SW]

THROUGH THE YEAR
POOLE HARBOUR

Spring is a good time to visit the reserves at Arne and Studland, where sprightly little Dartford warblers sing from the tops of gorse bushes before modestly diving out of sight. At Brownsea, the little egrets are at their most splendid from May to June, sporting long, delicate plumes hanging down from the nape.

During **summer** you can enjoy watching the sandwich and common terns that breed on artificial nesting rafts in the lagoon on Brownsea Island. Just after dusk on the heaths, nightjars sing their strange churring song, and snap up beetles in their huge gapes. Take a wildlife-watching boat trip that ventures beyond the harbour, and you may see a few puffins among the breeding seabirds on the Purbeck cliffs.

In **autumn**, the wintering birds begin to return to the shelter of the harbour. It's also a good time to look for red squirrels among Brownsea's pinewoods, less shy as they search out extra food for the winter.

Below: Dorset supports 80 per cent of the south coast's puffins.

MARCH

Where to Go: **March**

The onset of spring cannot be denied now, though there may be many false dawns before the days of frost and grey fog are behind us. Frogs and toads gather in shallow ponds in a frenzy of mating and spawning. On the open fields, brown hares box each other's ears as males and females get to know each other more intimately. A sudden rash of molehills reveals unseen activity below ground.

In undisturbed woods, grey herons are nesting. They build great platforms of thick sticks and lay eggs very early in spring: by late March, many have noisy youngsters and the heronries become busy, lively places. Down on the woodland floor, lesser celandines, primroses, and wood anemones add colour to the well-rotted leafmould, in which hungry woodcocks probe deeply for worms.

WETLANDS

RADIPOLE LAKE The rich reedbeds of Radipole reawaken in spring.

PARKS AND GRASSLANDS

LYME PARK Boxing hares perform courtship rituals in March.

WOODLANDS

RANNOCH Woodland, lochs, and moor can be seen at the Black Wood.

RADIPOLE LAKE
WEYMOUTH, DORSET [SW]

This classic urban nature reserve is the place to hear the explosive song of the Cetti's warbler.
See pp.60–61

LYME PARK
STOCKPORT, CHESHIRE [N]

Watch "mad March hares" boxing in the grounds of a magnificent Tudor house.
See pp.62–63

The estate's real charm lies in the rough grassland of the surrounding medieval deer park, where brown hares court in the spring.

KIELDER FOREST
NORTHUMBERLAND [N]

The huge reservoir of Kielder Water lies at the heart of this forest, where you can see sparrowhawks and red squirrels.
See pp.66–67

SOMERSET LEVELS
LANGPORT, SOMERSET

Head for Swell Wood in the West Sedgemoor RSPB reserve to see not only nesting herons but also dainty little egrets; look down to see primroses and other early flowers.
See pp.54–55

REGENT'S PARK
LONDON [SE]

Reed warblers, mistle thrushes, and pied wagtails chatter in the trees in spring, while around 20 herons can be seen nesting by the boating lake.
See pp.54–55

BLACK WOOD OF RANNOCH
PERTH AND KINROSS [SC]

The open woodlands of aspen, holly, and juniper are home to many rare animals and flowers, including capercaillies and the carnivorous Scottish wood ant.
See pp.66–67

Glossy black capercaillies perform dramatic displays, strutting about and leaping in the air while uttering bizarre sounds.

BLACKTOFT SANDS
HUMBERSIDE [N]

Set off early – not only are there water birds to be seen, but the dawn chorus here is rightly famous: reed and sedge warblers, reed buntings, and bearded tits all greet the new day.
See pp.60–61

NORTHWARD HILL
HOO, KENT [SE]

Kent's Hoo peninsula is alive with the noisy calls of herons, as spring dawns in the UK's largest heronry at Northward Hill.
See pp.54–55

SALFORD FOREST PARK
GREATER MANCHESTER [N]

The lakes and riversides here provide a breath of fresh air for city-dwellers.
See pp.54–55

BRECKLAND
NORFOLK/SUFFOLK [SE]

Forest birds here include rare and elusive golden pheasant, goshawks, hobbies, woodcocks, and woodlarks.
See pp.66–67

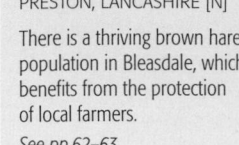

BLEASDALE
PRESTON, LANCASHIRE [N]

There is a thriving brown hare population in Bleasdale, which benefits from the protection of local farmers.
See pp.62–63

KINGLEY VALE
WEST SUSSEX [SE]

This ancient woodland is one of the finest yew forests in Europe, and has trees that are more than 2,000 years old.
See pp.66–67

LESNES ABBEY WOODS
LONDON [SE]

The 12th-century ruins of Lesnes Abbey are surrounded by an ancient forest filled with daffodils and bluebells in spring.
See pp.58–59

Previous page: A red squirrel foraging for food – perhaps an overlooked cache of nuts from the autumn.

Even though snow may still fall thick and soft in the northern hills, golden eagles, peregrines, and ravens are nesting, and often squabbling above their respective cliffs, being uneasy neighbours; all are spectacular to watch, especially during their electric courtship display flights. Look, too, for red deer moving up to the hills, and the roe deer, still in their dark winter brown coats, but beginning to show a hint of the rusty-red coat that comes with summer. In lowland Britain the sudden appearance, on a mild sunny day, of a bright, pale yellow spot dancing through the garden or along a hedgerow marks the brimstone butterfly, generally the earliest butterfly to emerge from hibernation. The land is warming, and the animals are awakening.

COAST

BRAUNTON BURROWS Britain's first UNESCO biosphere reserve.

UPLANDS

FARNDALE MOOR A daffodil delight in early spring.

ISLANDS

JERSEY The seas around Jersey hide wonders like the cuckoo wrasse.

HAVERGATE ISLAND
ORFORD, SUFFOLK [SE]

Famous for its breeding avocets and terns, this reserve also has a flourishing brown hare population, which is most evident – and entertaining – during their March courtships.
See pp.62–63

THE GOLDEN TRIANGLE
GLOUCESTERSHIRE [SE]

The area around Newent and Dymock used to be served by a "daffodil train" from London, and is still famous for these and other spring flowers.
See pp.58–59

JERSEY
CHANNEL ISLANDS [SW]

Spring is an ideal time to enjoy Jersey's mild climate. This island offers a huge number of wildlife habitats in a small area – or, suit up to explore the fascinating waters around its shores.
See pp.64–65

BRAUNTON BURROWS
DEVON [SW]

Shelter in the dunes of Braunton Burrows, which are studded with miniature flowers in spring, including sand mouse-ear, spring sandwort, and dune pansies.
See pp.68–69

GRASMERE
CUMBRIA [N]

The Lake District has so many beautiful landscapes, but at this time of year, the one that inspired the poet William Wordsworth is a must.
See pp.58–59

SCILLY ISLES
OFF LAND'S END [SW]

Colourful and unusual plants are matched by the birdlife: golden orioles, hoopoes, and woodchat shrikes are among the many spring migrants here. Seals and dolphins swim offshore.
See pp.64–65

THE LIZARD
CORNWALL [SW]

This frost-free habitat has many rare plants that cannot survive elsewhere, including the Cornish heath, and breeding choughs have made a welcome return.
See pp.65–66

FARNDALE MOOR
HUTTON-LE-HOLE, YORKSHIRE [N]

Here on the southern flanks of the North York Moors, a walk alongside the pretty River Dove will reveal that spring is slowly vanquishing winter.
See pp.58–59

The heather-clad hills of the North York Moors hide red grouse, meadow pipits, wheatears, and adders, basking in the warm spring sunlight.

BROWNSEA ISLAND
POOLE HARBOUR, DORSET [SW]

One of the last strongholds of the red squirrel in southern Britain; courting pairs leap from branch to branch among the pine woods in March.
See pp.56–57

One of the largest shingle and sand dune bars in Britain, Culbin Sands sees huge flocks of knots, bar-tailed godwits, and oystercatchers.

CULBIN SANDS
MORAY FIRTH [SC]

The sand dunes here line the Moray Firth, and in spring they host migrating birds such as sandwich terns. Dolphins play in the waters of the Firth.
See pp.68–69

QUEEN ELIZABETH FOREST PARK
STIRLING, SCOTLAND [SC]

Ospreys, kestrels, peregrines, and golden eagles quarter the skies here, while badgers come out to forage at night.
See pp.56–57

SCOLT HEAD ISLAND
NORTH NORFOLK [SE]

Resident birds are joined by many migrants in spring, including flycatchers, warblers, and chats. The saltmarshes are considered to be the UK's finest.
See pp.68–69

LINDISFARNE
NORTHUMBERLAND [N]

Stunning beaches, lots of birds, and rockpools filled with delights such as anemones, starfish, and sponges.
See pp.68–69

WHERE
Northward Hill RSPB Reserve, High Halstow, Kent ME3 8DS.

CONTACT
RSPB North Kent Marshes, tel: 01634 222480; northkentmarshes@rspb.org.uk

GETTING THERE
By car, leave the M2 at junction 1 and take the A228 towards Grain, then turn left to High Halstow. Two RSPB car parks are signposted at the T-junction in the village. By train, travel to Strood; trains run every hour from London. Buses run from Strood to High Halstow village (every 30 minutes), from where it is a short walk to the Woodland car park.

ACCESS AND FACILITIES
There are full-access toilets at the Bromhey Farm car park. There are four trails varying in length from 0.8–6.5km ($\frac{1}{2}$–4 miles). The site is not easily accessible for wheelchair users as the tracks are unimproved paths.

OPENING TIMES
Open at all times.

CHARGES
None.

Striking a pose

Grey herons nest colonially, usually in trees, but in more exposed areas of the UK they sometimes nest in bush tops or, rarely, on the ground. Breeding pairs greet each other and respond to others close by using very deliberate postures, such as a "stretch" display (*above*), where the wings are outstretched, and the head and bill point skywards. Aggression is indicated by an arched neck, raised crest, and erect body plumes. Look out for these postures at Northward Hill in March, as the herons begin the breeding season.

Above (left to right): A little egret tests the water; a sparrowhawk searches for prey; the Northward Hill reserve.
Main: A breeding pair of grey herons.

HERONS AT HOME

JUST NORTH OF HIGH HALSTOW, ON KENT'S HOO PENINSULA, there is a ridge with the most wonderful view across the Thames Estuary marshes. This is the home of a splendid RSPB nature reserve – Northward Hill – a huge area of grazing marsh, woodland, and farmland. If you can follow one of the two circular routes through the wood, you'll hear some particularly weird and wonderful noises in March: the sharp, barking calls and rattling bills of courting and nesting grey herons.

This is the UK's largest heronry, with 100–150 pairs. In recent years the herons have been joined by one of the largest colonies of little egrets in the UK, which first nested here in 2000, but now number more than 100 pairs. Watch over the sanctuary area and you'll see herons flying in and performing their ritual greeting and courtship displays at their big treetop nests. These large birds can look surprisingly pale against the dark woodland canopy at this time of year, while the smaller egrets are almost startlingly white. In March, the shrubs and trees are still largely leafless,

Herons fly with remarkable grace for such large, long-legged birds, as their 1.5m (5ft) wingspan takes them wooping through the air.

giving you a better chance to see Northward's songbirds, although the migrant warblers will not yet have arrived. The dawn chorus here is an unforgettable experience, with blackbirds, song thrushes, robins, wrens, dunnocks, great tits, and woodpigeons. Nightingales sing from the denser undergrowth later in spring, when the open parts of the wood are carpeted in bluebells.

The longest trail leads out to three new marshes, recently recreated from arable farmland by raising water levels. They have made an immediate impact, with avocets nesting on islands in the newly created lagoons, while lapwings and redshanks breed close by. Marsh harriers hunt over the open countryside, and in March you could see a merlin or peregrine, too, or even a sparrowhawk displaying over its nesting woods. Look out for its unusually slow, rhythmic wingbeats, which precede a series of steep switchbacks and a sudden dive.

Inset: The huge grey heron in flight.
Below (left to right): A heron fishing; these heavy birds need large nests.

WHERE ELSE TO SEE
HERONS

Herons love water – you may see them in wetland marshes, reservoirs, estuaries, lakes, or rivers. If you have an ornamental fish pond, you might even be lucky enough to attract one into your garden!

Grey herons nest in a few easily seen places, including **Regent's Park** in London. [SE]

Herons are often seen beside urban lakes and riversides, including **Salford Forest Park**, in Greater Manchester. In the spring you can see them nesting at **Muncaster Castle**, in the Lake District, Cumbria, and the **Waterton Countryside Discovery Centre**, Wakefield, Yorkshire. [N]

West Sedgemoor RSPB Reserve in the Somerset Levels has one of the largest heronries in the UK in Swell Wood. In spring they can be seen building large nests from sticks in the woodland trees. [SW]

The Quoile Pondage nature reserve at **Strangford Lough** (*see pp.288–289*) in Northern Ireland has a freshwater lagoon overlooked by hides where you can see herons, cormorants, and grebes all year. [NI]

THROUGH THE YEAR
NORTHWARD HILL

In **summer,** hobbies hunt dragonflies over the marsh. You could see the rare white-letter hairstreak butterfly in the woodland, where its caterpillars rely on elms, and perhaps turtle doves on overhead wires.

In **autumn,** swallows gather around farm buildings and on wires before migration and you should see jays flying over the woods with their stores of acorns.

The marshes are full of wildfowl in **winter,** including teals, shovelers, wigeons, and pintails. Hen harriers, kestrels, merlins, and peregrines hunt over the estuary. Wintering thrushes, finches, and buntings – especially redwings and fieldfares – are often seen in the orchards below the wood. One spectacular feature at Northward Hill is the gathering of up to 4,000 rooks as they come to roost in the woodland.

Below: Grey heron chicks hatch in late spring.

JAN
FEB
MAR
APR
MAY
JUN
JUL
AUG
SEP
OCT
NOV
DEC

WHERE
Brownsea Island, Poole Harbour, Dorset
BH13 7EE; www.nationaltrust.org.uk

CONTACT
National Trust, tel: 01202 707744;
brownseaisland@nationaltrust.org.uk

GETTING THERE
Ferries operate from Poole Quay, Sandbanks
Jetty, Bournemouth Pier, and Swanage.
Contact Brownsea Island Ferries (tel: 01929
462383, www.brownseaislandferries.com),
Dorset Cruises (tel: 01202 558550;
www.dorsetcruises.co.uk), or Greenslade
Pleasure Boats (tel: 01202 631828,
www.greensladepleasureboats.co.uk).

ACCESS AND FACILITIES
The island has full-access toilets at the visitor
reception, visitor centre, and the Baden-
Powell Outdoor Centre. There is a shop and
café, both accessible by wheelchair. Tracks on
the island can be rough in places, but tractor
trailer trails are available for the less mobile.

OPENING TIMES
The island is open from March to November.
Booked groups only during the winter.

CHARGES
Yes.

Grey invader

Red squirrels favour conifer woodland, where
they enjoy a mixed diet. However, oaks are the
predominant tree in lowland Britain, and this
suits grey squirrels, because they can live on a
diet of acorns alone. This has enabled the greys
to build up their numbers to the point where
they eat most of the available nut crop in autumn,
leaving little for the reds, who then starve. Further
north there are more pines and fewer oaks,
giving red squirrels the edge they need to survive.

Left (left to right): Poole
Harbour; maritime pine
trees on Brownsea Island.

Right (left to right): A carpet
of pine cones gnawed by
squirrels; a red squirrel
feeding on hoarded nuts.

Panel (below right):
Squirrels can not only climb
but descend trees at speed.

Main: Squirrels are active for most of the day, and have few natural predators, so are easy to spot.

RED SQUIRREL STRONGHOLD

I N THE WAKE OF THE LAST ICE AGE, SOME 8,000 YEARS AGO, the rising sea levels that created the North Sea
and English Channel also flooded a network of low-lying river valleys in southern England to form the broad
expanse of Poole Harbour. In the process, a sandstone hill rising above the valleys was cut off, to become
Brownsea Island, and among the animals that found themselves isolated on the island was a recent arrival from
Europe, the red squirrel. A few thousand years later this was to prove a blessing, because when the American grey
squirrel was introduced to the UK at the turn of the 20th century – with disastrous consequences for its smaller,
less aggressive relative – the island was one of the few places in England that it could not colonize. As a result,
Brownsea is now one of the last strongholds of the red squirrel in southern Britain. But as you approach Brownsea
on the ferry on a bright March morning, the narrow strip of glittering water that separates it from the mainland

Above: A red squirrel shelters under its tail.

Brownsea provides a refuge for 200 to 250 red squirrels – just enough to form a self-sufficient population.

WHERE ELSE TO SEE
RED SQUIRRELS

Competition from the grey squirrel has driven the red squirrel out of most of England and Wales, and on the British mainland it now lives mainly in Scotland, where it is still fairly common. However, there are a few scattered colonies further south, and it is also widespread in Ireland.

There is a red squirrel colony in **Parkhurst Forest** on the Isle of Wight (see pp.224–225), where – as on Brownsea – the island location prevented a grey squirrel invasion. The forest welcomes visitors, and has a red squirrel viewing hide and safari trail. [SE]

Red squirrels also survive in good numbers on the island of **Anglesey**, off North Wales. [W]

Red squirrels are still doing well in parts of northern England, such as the **Lake District** and the **Formby Pinewoods** Red Squirrel Sanctuary, near Ainsdale Dunes (see pp.88–89), Merseyside. [N]

A good place to see red squirrels in Scotland is the **Queen Elizabeth Forest Park**, Stirling. [SC]

THROUGH THE YEAR
BROWNSEA ISLAND

In **summer** the open heaths of Brownsea are bright with flowers that attract butterflies such as the small copper, the common blue, the silver-studded blue, and the green hairstreak. Big-jawed green tiger beetles can also be seen hunting other insects.

In **autumn** the red squirrels are very active gathering nuts and other food to fatten up for the winter. Treecreepers and nuthatches forage over the tree trunks while goldcrests and coal tits feed higher up in the pines.

Winter is the time to come to see avocets, black-tailed godwits, and other waders that feed in the lagoon to the northeast of the island. There is a birdwatching hide close to the landing stage. There is also a large heronry to the north, which attracts breeding herons in February and March.

seems a flimsy defence against invasion, and at first you may get little sense of the uniqueness of the place. Head west, away from the landing area, and you will soon find yourself surrounded by pine woodland. Before long you may come across signs of squirrel activity, such as the gnawed cores of pine cones, surrounded by the woody scales that the squirrels bite off to get at the seeds, or the shattered shell fragments of hastily eaten hazelnuts.

In the hot summer months such clues may be all you see, but in March the squirrels are much more active, and a commotion in a Scots pine may well herald the appearance of a courting pair chasing through the treetops. The squirrels prefer a "closed canopy" where they can leap from tree to tree without coming to ground, and they display amazing agility and speed as they jump and scramble through the branches, using their long bushy tails for balance. Their sharp claws enable them to cling to the bark with just one foot, and they frequently run headfirst down trees. With their chestnut fur and long ear tufts they are irresistibly attractive, the more so when they pick up food with their forepaws so they can gnaw at it in comfort.

JAN

FEB

MAR

APR

MAY

JUN

JUL

AUG

SEP

OCT

NOV

DEC

Daffodils under threat

The true wild daffodil is a plant of delicate beauty, but it is at risk, mainly from genetic pollution. Well-meaning but misguided attempts to brighten the countryside sometimes result in people planting daffodils – very often garden varieties (*as below*) – which look out of place in the wild. The rule for wild daffodils is: don't pick them, don't dig them up, and don't try to add to them. Simply enjoy nature at its purest and best.

GOLDEN DAFFODILS

EVERYBODY LOVES A DAFFODIL, AND BETTER STILL A MASS OF THEM, brightening up a dull March day with the promise of spring. There can be barely a garden in the country that doesn't have daffodils, but these are often large, vivid, blowsy flowers, very different to our genuine native form, with its dainty flowers and long, narrow trumpets.

In areas where wild daffodils are a feature in the landscape, they are valued and celebrated by local people and visitors alike. In the beautiful, deep valley of Farndale, on the southern flanks of the North York Moors, you are greeted in March by the astonishing sight of daffodils everywhere – broadly lining the 5km-long (3 mile) daffodil walk.

Until the mid-19th century, wild daffodils – *Narcissus pseudonarcissus* – bloomed prolifically all around Britain, carpeting the riverbanks, woodlands, and meadows of every county in spring.

The walk starts from the tiny post office at Farndale's Low Mill, from which you follow the well-trodden footpath down to the tranquil River Dove. It is here that you realize what a phenomenon this is – the wide banks of the river, the meadows, and the open woodland are awash with thousands of yellow, swaying flowerheads. The walk remains interesting throughout the season: as spring progresses, so a range of other spring plants appear, including yellow primrose, lesser celandine, and patches of the starry white flowerheads of wild garlic. As the trees and bushes burst into leaf, the flowers of bird cherry, blackthorn, and goat willow start to attract insects on sunny days – bumblebees, peacock butterflies, and others, looking for food after their long hibernation. The first chiffchaffs are likely to be singing in the alders, while grey wagtails and dippers feed along the river bank. In April, listen out for male redstarts delivering their short, melancholy song from the tree tops.

If you want a more challenging walk, look for waymarked paths from the daffodil walk onto the open moorland above. The heather-clad hills may look rather weatherbeaten at this time of year, but red grouse, meadow pipits, and the first wheatears can be found, while adders bask alongside the paths, especially early in the morning on a sunny day.

Main: The banks of the River Dove, Farndale, are lined with wild daffodils.
Below (left to right): Primroses follow the daffodil season; the goat willow ("pussy willow") has catkins in March; lesser celandine.
Inset: Wild daffodils have paler petals than garden varieties, and a narrower trumpet.

Above: The view across the moor in winter.

JAN

FEB

MAR

APR

MAY

JUN

JUL

AUG

SEP

OCT

NOV

DEC

THROUGH THE YEAR
FARNDALE MOOR

As spring gives way to **summer**, Farndale fills up with summer birds – spotted flycatchers, willow warblers, wood warblers, and redstarts in the riverside woods. Tree pipits deliver their beautiful song in flights from isolated trees. At the same time, the damp grassland bursts into flower, with marsh marigold giving way to meadowsweet, common valerian, and wild angelica as the season progresses.

By **autumn**, the surrounding moorland comes into its own, the purple haze of common heather, or ling, becoming home to noisy groups of red grouse before the winter chill descends. In **midwinter**, look at the alders by the river – with a little patience, you should find parties of lesser redpolls and siskins feeding on the seeds in the treetops, alongside roving parties of tits and other small birds.

WHERE ELSE TO SEE
WILD DAFFODILS

Wild daffodils are found over much of England and Wales, but especially in the west and around the valleys of the uplands.

The Lake District village of **Grasmere** is famous for its daffodils, descendants of those that inspired William Wordsworth's famous poem. [N]

The "golden triangle" around the villages of **Newent** and **Dymock** in Gloucestershire, and **Ross-on-Wye** in Herefordshire, is so well known for its daffodils that it was once served by a "daffodil train" from London. [M]

The valleys of **Dartmoor** and **Exmoor** (*see pp.44–45*) provide many opportunities to see daffodils at their best, often extending out of the valley bottoms onto the bracken-clad hillsides. [SW]

Even the London area has its share of wild daffodils – try **Lesnes Abbey Woods** in Bexley. [SE]

Left: Cattle graze on the urban marshland.

Right (left to right): The timid Cetti's warbler is a rare resident; a bird's-eye view of the RSPB Radipole reserve.

Below right (top and bottom): The snipe is a regular winter visitor to the reserve; a grey heron keeps watch among the reeds.

WHERE
RSPB Radipole Lake, Weymouth, Dorset
DT4 7TZ; www.rspb.org.uk

CONTACT
Radipole Lake Visitor Centre,
tel: 01305 778313;
weymouth.reserves@rspb.org.uk

GETTING THERE
By road, head for the Swannery car park, off the A354 in Weymouth; the reserve is next door. By train, Weymouth Station is less than 400m (350 yards) from the reserve.

ACCESS AND FACILITIES
Parking is available in the council-run Swannery pay-and-display car park. The nearest parking to the centre is 10m (30ft) from the entrance. The centre is wheelchair friendly, and so are some of the trails and hides. Refreshments include snacks and drinks; there's also an RSPB shop. There are two trails, of 1.5km (¾ mile) and 2km (1¼ miles).

OPENING TIMES
The visitor centre is open daily 9am–5pm (closes 4pm in winter); the hide is open 8.30am–4.30pm.

CHARGES
There is a charge for parking and for non-RSPB members to use the hide.

Reed management

Radipole has over 200 plant species, and the largest reedbed in southwest England. Sections of the reedbed are cut back between autumn and spring to promote new growth, which will give rise to better quality seed heads the following autumn. This process ensures a food supply for wintering birds, especially the bearded tits, while the new reedbed growth provides a home for insects that the birds eat in spring, and then plenty of seeds for the birds to eat in winter.

Main: Extensive reedbeds at Radipole are the largest in the southwest of England.

GO WILD IN WEYMOUTH

R ADIPOLE LAKE IS A CLASSIC URBAN NATURE RESERVE, where a river has backed up behind a coastal sandbar to create a wet marsh. It is served by excellent footpaths and hides, but turn away from the housing to the west and look instead along the reedbeds and pools – you might be on a much wilder stretch of coast.

The first thing to remember when you arrive at the reserve, which is close to the middle of Weymouth, is not to neglect the car park. In March, there are often gulls scattered across the tarmac, some of which may be quite rare, such as the Mediterranean gull. Check in the visitor centre to find out what's about.

Then take the path across the bridge to the Buddleia Walk. The buddleias are not out in March, but the bushes alongside the path have one special bird, one of a handful of warblers that stay over winter in the UK: Cetti's warbler. It is small, rather dark, reddish-brown above and pale below, with a noticeable grey tinge, and has

Radipole Lake is an urban oasis for people and wildlife – providing peace and security within wide open spaces.

Above: A small tortoiseshell on the reserve's Buddleia Walk.

THROUGH THE YEAR
RADIPOLE LAKE

In the **summer**, Radipole is alive with birds over the water and reeds, including swallows and house martins; even secretive water rails feed in the reeds. Reed, sedge, and willow warblers create a wonderful early morning chorus. Butterflies are busy on the flowering shrubs along the Buddleia Walk and in the reserve's flower-rich meadows, including migrants such as painted ladies and clouded yellows, whose numbers vary greatly from year to year.

In **autumn** (as in spring), the unpredictable nature of bird migration is likely to throw in unexpected species. Go early in the morning, before the trails are too disturbed, and you may see some rarities. Bearded tits are easiest to find in autumn, as are hobbies (swift-flying falcons) – which are out hunting dragonflies and martins.

Radipole Lake is at its best for wildfowl in **winter.** Pochards, shovelers, and teals spend the winter on the lake, and shy water rails come out of hiding. Patience may be rewarded by a rare sighting of the elusive bittern among the reedbeds.

WHERE ELSE TO SEE
URBAN WILDFOWL

Urban reedbeds are few and far between, but they are worth seeking out for a locally based day out.

Cardiff in Wales boasts a great town centre park with good lakes, but **Conwy** (see pp.278–279) on the North Wales coast is a reserve that combines accessibility with even more wildlife interest. [W]

London has a number of large parks, but not that many feature the rarer forms of wildfowl. The **London Wetlands Centre** in Barnes, south west London (see pp.16–17), is an exception. [SE]

Southport on Merseyside is a good wildlife town, but the best place for viewing birds also seen at Radipole is probably **Blacktoft Sands** in East Yorkshire (see pp.158–159), on the Humber estuary. [N]

JAN
FEB
MAR
APR
MAY
JUN
JUL
AUG
SEP
OCT
NOV
DEC

a pale line over the eye. A broad, rounded tail helps distinguish it from other possibilities, but in early spring before the reed and sedge warblers arrive, there is little to confuse it with. Listen for its sharp, sudden "quilp" calls. Much more distinctive, once it gets going in spring, is its song: a sudden, loud outburst of rich, fast, musical notes. March is a good time to enjoy this bird and its sweet song, as there is little aural competition, and the vegetation is still relatively sparse; later in the year this secretive warbler can be particularly hard to spot.

Radipole's birds are not all so difficult. From the bridge you can often see a wide variety of cormorants – developing quite handsome spring colours in March – with gulls, moorhens, and ducks of several kinds, including tufted ducks and pochards. Walk on until you reach the shelter and the farthest hide, where you can often see grey herons and wading birds, including snipe and perhaps a kingfisher if you are lucky. Look out for little egrets, especially in the evening when they come to roost. Even bearded tits have been known to put in an appearance in this remarkable sanctuary, compressed between Weymouth's suburbs, railway, roads, and the town centre.

WHERE
Lyme Park, Disley, Stockport, Cheshire,
SK12 2NR;
www.nationaltrust.org.uk/main/w-lymepark

CONTACT
Lyme Park, tel: 01663 762023. National
Trust infoline, tel: 01663 766492;
lymepark@nationaltrust.org.uk

GETTING THERE
By road, the entrance is on the A6, 10.5km
(7 miles) southeast of Stockport, 9.3km
(12 miles) northwest of Buxton. The house
and car park is 1.6km (1 mile) from the
entrance. By train, Disley is 0.8km
(0.5 miles) from the park entrance. The
TrentBarton no. 199 Buxton–Manchester
Airport bus stops at the park entrance.

ACCESS AND FACILITIES
There's a licensed restaurant and café in The
Timber Yard and a refreshment kiosk in the
main car park. There are full-access toilets
throughout the site and wheelchair access
to the buildings and parts of the grounds, but
there are steep slopes and uneven ground.

OPENING TIMES
The park is open all year round; the house
is open March–November.

CHARGES
Yes, for non-National Trust members.

High-speed hares

Unlike rabbits, which bolt for their burrows at
the first hint of danger, long-legged hares rely
on their speed to escape attack. A brown hare
can accelerate to 45mph (72kph) on level
ground, and is so light that it can easily turn
in its tracks and dart off in a different direction
to outwit a heavier pursuer. For centuries, pitting
greyhounds against each other in pursuit of hares
was a popular sport. Since 2004, "hare coursing"
has been banned in Britain, but illegal coursing
is still a problem in some regions.

Above (top and bottom): The Cage observation
tower overlooking Lyme Park, an ideal place to spot
hares; some of the park's red deer hinds.

Below: A tree clings to a rocky outcrop at Lyme Park's
West Park gate.

Far right (top and bottom): An alert hare checks
for danger; another keeps a low profile in a hollow,
or "form", in an arable field.

Main: Boxing hares are not – as was once thought – two competitive males, but a female fending off a potential suitor.

BOXING HARES

SET IN OPEN COUNTRYSIDE A FEW MILES SOUTHEAST OF STOCKPORT, and overlooked by the brooding
mass of Derbyshire's High Peak, Lyme Park is one of the most magnificent buildings in Cheshire. Originally
a Tudor country house, its exterior was remodelled in the 18th century to create a grand Palladian facade,
complete with a huge neo-classical portico and superb formal gardens. For many, however, the estate's real
charm lies in the rough grassland of the surrounding medieval deer park, because in spring this is an ideal place
to watch one of the most bizarre of all natural spectacles: the stand-up boxing matches of the wild brown hares.

Immortalized by Lewis Carroll in *Alice's Adventures in Wonderland*, the "mad March hare" has mystified
wildlife watchers for centuries. Unlike smaller, less agile rabbits, brown hares spend their lives above ground in
open country, and in spring when the grass is short their extraordinary courtship rituals are conducted in full

Above: Red deer in winter at Lyme Park.

THROUGH THE YEAR
LYME PARK

In **summer** the moors and woodlands of Lyme Park are good places to look for insects, and especially butterflies and moths. The hares are still active, but harder to see in the long grass.

Autumn sees the annual rut of Lyme Park's resident herds of fallow and red deer. Watch and marvel at the dramatic spectacle, but don't venture too close because the rutting stags can turn on intruders. The park is a great place to go fungi-spotting; it often has a great show of the almost-fluorescent red *Hygrocybe splendidissima* – the splendid waxcap.

Lyme Park tends to get a dusting of snow in **winter**, providing excellent conditions for tracking animals that come out mainly at night. Look for the trails of foxes, with their characteristic single lines of prints. Sometimes a fox trail shadows that of a rabbit, with its pattern of short fore-prints and long hind-prints. Following a trail may lead you to the site of a kill.

Bounding, leaping, sparring, dancing – the hares' mad display signals the dawn of spring.

WHERE ELSE TO SEE
BROWN HARES

Although introduced to Ireland, the brown hare is native to mainland Britain – or has been since Roman times. It is most numerous on open fields and pasture, but it may use nearby woodlands as refuges, especially in cold weather. Since it is largely nocturnal it is rarely seen in broad daylight. It is also easiest to see in spring before crops and grasses grow too tall.

Hares are particularly common on the broad fields and fenlands of East Anglia, but are so wide-ranging that spotting them is a matter of luck. **Havergate Island** in Suffolk – an RSPB reserve more famous for its breeding avocets and terns – has a flourishing hare population. [SE]

There is a thriving brown hare population at **Bleasdale** near Preston, Lancashire, where the animals are encouraged by local farmers. [N]

JAN · FEB · MAR · APR · MAY · JUN · JUL · AUG · SEP · OCT · NOV · DEC

view. If you want to witness these extravagant rituals at Lyme Park, one of the best places is The Cage, an ornate 18th-century hunting lodge that offers a vast panorama of the Cheshire Plain and even the foothills of Snowdonia, and provides a fine vantage point for hare-watching.

Arrive as early as possible: brown hares are most active at dawn and dusk, but you will need the morning light. If hares are about, you will see groups out in the open, clearly visible through binoculars. Males and females look alike, but if one dashes off, chased by several others, she will be a female in breeding condition. Her pursuers are males, each intent on mating with as many females as possible. One may shadow her more closely than the others, even driving them away, but the common belief that boxing hares are rival males is wrong. A female frequently becomes so irritated by an ardent suitor that she turns and delivers a swift punch. He retaliates, and the two may rear up on their long hind legs to exchange a flurry of blows. No damage is done, and quite often the wild chase resumes almost immediately. Eventually his persistence may pay off, and she will allow him to mate – after which he immediately starts looking for another female.

SPRINGTIME ON JERSEY

THE LARGEST OF THE CHANNEL ISLANDS, JERSEY IS THE SOUTHERNMOST outpost of the British Isles, lying some 160km (100 miles) off the south coast of England. Spring arrives early this far south, so a March visit is guaranteed to provide wildlife, and there's a good chance of fine weather. Apart from the specialities not found elsewhere in Britain, or only sparingly, the beauty of Jersey is that it offers a wide range of habitats within a compact area; it is easy to travel around, and its clear, rich seas add a further dimension to the natural scenes.

Broadly speaking, the coastline is cliffed in the north and southwest, with sandy bays, dunes, and wetlands on the west and south coast. The extensive clifftops are a good place to start, as the heaths, gorse, and heather combine to provide an ideal home for Dartford warblers, which are more obvious in March because of their towering song-flights. Stonechats are ever-present, together with rock pipits foraging from the cliffs below.

WHERE
Jersey, Channel Islands;
www.nationaltrustjersey.org.je

CONTACT
National Trust for Jersey, The Elms, La Chève Rue, St Mary, JE3 3EN, Jersey;
tel: 01534 483193;
enquiries@nationaltrustjersey.org.je

GETTING THERE
You can sail from Poole or Weymouth by ferry and be in Jersey in less than four hours. There are regular flights from London – about 12 a day – and around 25 other airports in the UK fly to the island.

ACCESS AND FACILITIES
Jersey welcomes all disabled visitors and has a website with helpful information:
www.jersey.com/English/aboutjersey/disabledinformation

CHARGES
There are charges for non-members for some National Trust reserves on the island.

Above: Offshore islets.

Main: The view over Plemont Bay from the clifftop.

Below: Two of Jersey's more unusual sea creatures, the beautiful cuckoo wrasse fish (*above*), and the short snouted seahorse (*below*).

Far right (top to bottom): The dunes are home to many interesting miniature plants; Jersey is the only natural home of the western green lizard; the lesser white-toothed shrew; the short-toed treecreeper is unique to Jersey within the British Isles.

Moving house

One of Jersey's more unusual mammals is the lesser white-toothed shrew. Within the British Isles, this species is found only on Jersey, Sark, and the Scilly Isles. The shrews produce 4–5 litters each year, each of which consist of 1–6 young. If the nest is disturbed, the mother leads her young to a new nest site by "caravanning": the little shrews follow her in a long line, each shrew holding on to the tail of the shrew in front of it. Adult shrews scent their new territory by dragging their bellies along the ground.

Prostrate broom may be just beginning to flower, though it will be a couple of months before the mosaic of sea campion, thrift, and ox-eye daisy completes the picture. A careful search could reveal some of the most sought-after flowers, such as sand crocus and spotted rock-rose, though the crocus closes in dull weather and the rock-rose drops its petals by about noon on the day it opens. Look out for green lizards on the heaths and dunes of the southwest. This is the largest lizard species in Britain, at up to 40cm (16in) long, and the male tranforms in the breeding season: his green body becomes stippled with black, and his throat turns a beautiful shade of blue.

The dunes, best seen at Les Blanches Banques, are also well worth a spring visit. Small plants are at the peak of their flowering, including the early sand-grass and the dwarf pansy, only seen on the Channel and Scilly islands. Wander further inland, and you'll find woodlands that are home to red squirrels, and a few stony banks with populations of the delicate Jersey fern.

WHERE ELSE TO SEE
MARITIME HEATHS

Some of the unusual features of Jersey's maritime heath can be found on other British islands, and even on the mainland.

The Lizard in Cornwall (*see pp.116–117*) and other parts of the southwest peninsula have similar ranges of habitats, including maritime heathland, but the unique geology of the Lizard ensures that it has a good range of additional rare plants that can't survive the frosts elsewhere. [SW]

The **Scilly Isles** are less dramatic scenically than Jersey, but they share some of its special species and a similarly rich marine environment. [SW]

Extensive maritime heaths, interspersed with dunes and sandy bays, can be found along the Welsh coast. There are some magnificent stretches in **Gower** (*see pp.122–123*) and the Pembrokeshire Coast (from Tenby to Cardigan), and some on the **Lleyn Peninsula** and **Anglesey** in the north. [W]

THROUGH THE YEAR
JERSEY

Summer on Jersey is the best time to seek out its special reptiles: the green lizard and the wall lizard, basking on rocks and walls. Although now rather scarce on the island, the Jersey (or "lax-flowered") orchid grows nowhere else naturally, and it flowers in early summer. In **August**, look along the large dune systems for the impressive and rare lizard orchid.

The sea is warmest in early **autumn**, and its meadows of eel-grass hide short-snouted sea-horses; boulders and seaweeds provide niches for ormers and spider-crabs. There's a wide range of fish, including the dragonet, tub gurnard, and the beautifully coloured cuckoo wrasse. Look too for bottlenose dolphins, basking sharks, and grey seals.

Winter is generally short and mild. Visit the eel-grass beds to see feeding brent geese of two distinct races: most are dark-bellied Siberian birds, but a fair proportion are pale-bellied birds from the east Canadian high Arctic population.

Below: The Jersey tiger moth has a wingspan of 42–52mm (1½–2in).

JAN

FEB

MAR

APR

MAY

JUN

JUL

AUG

SEP

OCT

NOV

DEC

WHERE
Black Wood of Rannoch, Kinloch Rannoch,
Perth and Kinross, Scotland;
www.perthshire.co.uk

CONTACT
Rannoch Moor Visitor Centre, Rannoch
Station, Perth and Kinross PH17 2QA;
tel: 01796 472215.

GETTING THERE
The Black Wood lies on the southern shores
of Loch Rannoch. It is part of the Caledonian
Forest Reserve, which is part of the Tay Forest
Park, west of Dall. Kinloch Rannoch, off the
B846, is the nearest town or village. Black
Wood is 3.2km (2 miles) west of Kinloch
Rannoch, on South Loch Rannoch road.
Rannoch Station lies on the West Highland
Line, between Glasgow and Fort William.

ACCESS AND FACILITIES
There are no facilities in the wood; access is
from an unclassified road running south of
Loch Rannoch. The nearest facilities (and
tearoom) are at the Rannoch Moor Visitor
Centre in Rannoch railway station.

OPENING TIMES
Trails open all year round. The visitor centre
is open March–October, 10am–5pm.

CHARGES
None.

Rare insect life

In the Black Wood of Rannoch there are many
ancient moss- and lichen-festooned birches
intermixed with the pines. The living trees and
the deadwood combine to make a rare habitat
uniquely supportive of insects: two rare species
of moths take their common names from the
place: the Rannoch looper, and the Rannoch
sprawler (*shown above*). The wood is also one
of the few places to see the UK's timberman
beetle, the larvae of which bore into the rotting
wood of fallen pine trunks and stumps.

Above: The Scottish crossbill (*far right*) is very similar to the common crossbill (*centre*) and parrot crossbill (*left*).
Main: Red deer roam free in the wood.

IN THE BLACK WOOD

A WALK THROUGH A CALEDONIAN FOREST is a very different experience to visiting to an old-style, mature pine plantation, where the gloom cast by the serried ranks of conifers and the carpet of tough dead needles on the ground make for relatively little wildlife. It is far more open, with the pines interspersed with birch, rowan, alder, bird cherry, and willow. This allows the development of an understorey of shrubs such as aspen, holly, hazel, and juniper; while the acidic soil gives rise to a rich ground layer of plants, such as bell heather, crowberry, and bilberry (called "blaeberry" in Scotland). Rare wildflowers such as the lesser twayblade and creeping lady's-tresses orchids grow here, along with one-flowered wintergreen and twinflower, as well as many fungi.

This special habitat supports many uncommon or rare species of animals, from hoverflies and beetles, to red squirrels, rare wildcats, and pine martens, and several birds that live only or mainly here. The crested tit is a Caledonian forest bird, along with the Scottish crossbill, whose name refers to the crossed tip of the bill, an adaptation for extracting seeds from conifer cones. Recent estimates suggest there may be fewer than 2,000 of these remarkable birds left. Another Black Wood inhabitant lies at the other end of the size scale from these two songbirds: the capercaillie. The glossy black males are the size of a turkey, and perform dramatic displays to attract females at communal "leks" or displays, strutting about and leaping in the air while uttering bizarre sounds.

The wood is home to many rare moths and insects, including the Scottish wood ant, which makes large conical nests from the pine needles. These carnivorous ants tend and protect the greenfly aphids, which are prevalent in pine forests, in return for the honeydew they produce. But the ants themselves often fall prey to the green woodpecker, which digs its long beak into their nests, and scoops up the ants with its long sticky tongue.

One of the most special birds of the Black Wood is the lively crested tit, named for its jaunty black-and-white crest. It excavates its nests in old, rotten pine stumps.

Inset: Crested tits are found only in the Scottish Highlands.
Below: Rannoch Moor is dotted with lakes, including Loch Tulla.

WHERE ELSE TO SEE
CONIFER FORESTS

Although they lack the special features of the Caledonian forests, some mature conifer plantations in Scotland and other parts of Britain are also rich in wildlife. Apart from the lofty, red-barked Scots pine, Britain's only two other native conifers are the yew and the juniper.

Kielder Forest in Northumberland is one of the largest areas of planted forest in Europe. You can look for a wide range of birds among the conifers, including crossbills and that powerful and elusive relative of the sparrowhawk, the goshawk. [N]

Breckland, on the border between Norfolk and Suffolk, contains plantations of mature Scots pine and other trees, where forest birds include rare and elusive golden pheasants, goshawks, hobbies, woodcocks, and woodlarks. [SE]

Large areas of ancient yew woodland are rare, but in **Kingley Vale** in West Sussex (*see pp.310–311*), some of the trees may be over 2,000 years old. Their twisted and gnarled, glowing, deep-red trunks contrast with the almost blackish-green foliage. [SE]

THROUGH THE YEAR
BLACK WOOD OF RANNOCH

Early **summer** is a good time to see – and hear – breeding songbirds such as crested tits, tree pipits, and siskins. Wildflowers are in bloom, and insects are active. Do not try to watch capercaillies at their display grounds; a better site for this is the Osprey Centre at the RSPB's Loch Garten reserve (*see pp.86–87*), where it is possible to watch the birds without disturbing them.

Autumn can be a good time to see capercaillies, as more birds are about after breeding. They are less disturbed by vehicles than an approach on foot, but the best chance of an encounter is to book a trip with a reputable wildlife-watching company.

From autumn and through **winter**, crested tits start to group together in small roving flocks, often with other songbirds such as coal tits and goldcrests. Listen for the Crested tit's distinctive call: a purring trill.

Below: The capercaillie's song includes a sound like wine being uncorked.

JAN

FEB

MAR

APR

MAY

JUN

JUL

AUG

SEP

OCT

NOV

DEC

Left: Looking south along Saunton Sands beach, backed by Braunton Burrows.

Right (left to right): Sand cat's-tail; the dune-carpeting moss *Tortula ruraliformis*; sea mouse-ear.

Right, below: The diminutive dune pansy, instantly recognizable by its resemblance to showier garden pansies and violas.

WHERE
Braunton Burrows, Heddon Mill, Braunton, Devon EX33 2NQ.

CONTACT
Braunton Tourist Information Centre, The Bakehouse Centre, Caen Street, Braunton, Devon EX33 1AA; tel: 01271 816400.

GETTING THERE
From Braunton take the B3231 for 1.6km (1 mile), and turn left at Sandy Lane. Access is via the Coast Path/Tarka Trail. From Barnstaple, take A361 towards Braunton, and just before you reach the village take the left turn signposted to Crow Point. Follow this lane straight to Sandy Lane car park in the centre of the dunes, or turn left down the toll road to Broad Sands car park, near Crow point.

ACCESS AND FACILITIES
There are no facilities. The nearest are in Braunton. Caution: the Ministry of Defence still use a part of the dunes as a training area and if there is to be any live firing it will be indicated with red flags.

OPENING TIMES
Open all year round.

CHARGES
None.

The Burrows biosphere

Braunton Burrows is a UNESCO Biosphere Reserve. This means it is considered a "living laboratory" for testing integrated management of land, water, and biodiversity. Biosphere Reserves must demonstrate the conservation of biodiversity together with sustainable use. The unique collection of wildlife habitats at Braunton Burrows is recognized as owing much to the long-standing use of traditional farming and fishing practices within the area.

Main: The dunes at Braunton Burrows are dominated by marram grass, the roots of which form a three-dimensional anchoring mesh in the sand.

JEWELS IN THE DUNES

LIFE ON SAND IS STRESSFUL FOR PLANTS. Blown into dunes, sand is inhospitable, mobile, and very prone to drought in the summer. But the plants that can tolerate the dry conditions are immensely useful – they help to stabilize the sand, helping it to grow into dunes, sometimes forming extensive systems. This is the situation at Braunton Burrows, where dunes up to 30m (100ft) high dominate the mouth of the Taw-Torridge estuary.

At the start of spring, it might seem surprising to find botanists exploring the windswept dunes. They are there because some plants are already flowering, miniature delights that really repay a closer look. The turf is studded with the tiny bright-blue flowers of early forget-me-not; white stars of sand mouse-ear, whitlow-grass, and spring sandwort; the yellow or purple (or both) faces of dune pansy; and grasses like the diminutive sand cat's-tail and dune fescue. This kaleidoscope of colour forms a turf rarely more than a few centimetres tall.

JAN

FEB

MAR

APR

MAY

JUN

JUL

AUG

SEP

OCT

NOV

DEC

Above: The vivid spikes of viper's bugloss.

Braunton Burrows is the largest sand-dune system in England; it is significant at an international level.

THROUGH THE YEAR
BRAUNTON BURROWS

In **summer**, Braunton Burrows features many interesting plants, from the attractive blue viper's bugloss and pink sea bindweed, to scarce species such as sea stock and some very rare flora: the round-headed club-rush is found at only a handful of British sites. There are nesting birds too – wheatears and shelducks breed in rabbit holes on the dunes.

Autumn brings migrating songbirds, attracted especially by the berries and shelter provided by sea buckthorn. The low turf landward of the main dunes supports a number of brightly coloured waxcap fungi.

The windswept dunes have few birds in **winter**, with skylarks and meadow pipits making up the majority. But viewing from the southern tip, Crow Point, at low tide should reveal large numbers of wading birds, including curlews, golden plovers, and lapwings, and perhaps also seals at high water.

WHERE ELSE TO SEE
SAND DUNES

Sand dunes may form wherever there is a supply of wind-blown sand, and where the angle of the coast means that winds are predominantly onshore.

South Wales used to have an almost unbroken dune system from the river Ogmore to the Gower peninsula; much has now been lost, but a magnificent remnant can be found at **Kenfig**, near Port Talbot. On Anglesey, there are two large systems, **Newborough Warren** (see pp.142–143) and **Aberffraw**. [W]

On the east coast, **Scolt Head Island** in Norfolk is accessible by boat trips from the quay at Burnham Overy Staithe, off the A149 coast road. [SE]

Much of **Lindisfarne**, (see pp.274–275) in Northumberland, is made up of dunes. [N]

In Scotland, **Culbin Sands** on the Moray Firth still has areas of open sand dune, although much of the area has now been planted with conifer trees. [SC]

The factor that links these plants is timing – they flower early in the season to survive the high summer stress as relatively drought-tolerant seeds. In fact many are winter annuals: plants that germinate in the autumn, grow slowly through the winter, flower, set seed, and die before the drought bites. Their whole life-cycle is adapted to avoiding the heat of summer.

Search carefully at ground level among the low-lying dune slacks and you might just find one of Braunton's rarest inhabitants, the internationally protected liverwort *Petalophyllum ralfsii*. Take a look, too, at the incredibly diverse mosses and lichens that grow here. Cushions of sandhill screw-moss are bright green, the silvery hair points on their leaves spreading like tiny stars – unless, that is, the last few weeks have been dry, in which case the moss is blackened and screwed up, waiting for the next rains, when it will rehydrate and carry on unperturbed. The carpets of grey lichens towards the back of the dunes, mostly of *Cladonia* species, have such an intriguing array of forms – from flat plates to branched bushlets to tiny cups – to be fascinating to novice and specialist alike.

APRIL

Where to Go: April

Showers and storms notwithstanding, April brings real, warm, delicious spring at last, and with it the great migrations of summer-visiting birds from southern Europe and Africa. As fieldfares, redwings, and tens of thousands of ducks and wading birds leave for the north and east, so we see warblers, chats, swallows, and martins arriving everywhere. Willow warblers have the most delicate spring song, but nightingales, perhaps, have the most mesmerizing and varied. Blackcaps and garden warblers compete to be the most musical, but even the lisping, slurred twitter of a newly arrived swallow is welcome to our ears. Woodlands become awash with bluebells, one of the great glories of Britain, and flowers are suddenly everywhere, multi-coloured

WOODLANDS

NORSEY WOOD Oaks, sweet chestnuts, hornbeams, birches, and alders.

WETLANDS

LEIGHTON MOSS The elusive bittern takes to the skies.

PARKS AND GRASSLANDS

CRICKLADE MEADOW The nodding heads of snakeshead fritillaries.

NORSEY WOOD
BILLERICAY, ESSEX [SE]

This 400-year-old deer park is utterly magical in late April, when it is full of bluebells, wood anemones, lily-of-the-valley, dog violets, and stitchwort.
See pp.84–85

WOOLSTON EYES
WARRINGTON, CHESHIRE [N]

A young reserve, created in 1980, this has over 220 bird species, including the elegant black-necked grebe. Watch out for the sharp features of inquisitive stoats.
See pp.76–77

CRICKLADE MEADOW
CRICKLADE, WILTSHIRE [SE]

This damp meadow has one of the few significant fritillary colonies left in Britain – several million fritillaries burst into flower here in April.
See pp.74–75

PERIVALE WOOD
LONDON [SE]

Don't miss a visit to this London woodland, which is only open to the public this month so that visitors may admire its glorious bluebells.
See pp.84–85

LEIGHTON MOSS
CARNFORTH, LANCASHIRE [N]

If you want to hear bitterns booming, visit the secret world of Leighton Moss in April. Courting pairs of marsh harriers fly overhead.
See pp.78–79

Few wild flowers can match the delicate beauty and poise of the snakeshead fritillary; its chequered blooms nod over slender, arched stems.

SALISBURY PLAIN
WILTSHIRE [SW]

Stone curlews, quails, whinchats, stonechats, and grasshopper warblers all live around this vast area of chalk grassland.
See pp.92–93

RYTON WOOD
WARWICKSHIRE [M]

The spring bluebells within this ancient oak woodland sit beneath chattering spring birds: six species of warblers live here, and woodpeckers and nightingales breed among its trees.
See pp.84–85

LOCHWINNOCH
PAISLEY, RENFREWSHIRE [SC]

Watch the entrancing dance of the great crested grebes, as they fan out their feathers, dive, and perform the "ghostly penguin" and "weed ceremony".
See pp.82–83

GRAFHAM WATER
CAMBRIDGESHIRE [SE]

Great grested grebes dance in courtship rituals around the lagoons. Flocks of waders fly overhead, and hobbies look for easy prey.
See pp.82–83

LEE VALLEY PARK
ESSEX/HERTFORDSHIRE [M]

This huge park is a great place to see spring migrating birds, such as terns and warblers, as well as foxes, and even otters, at Fisher's Green.
See pp.78–79

The ancient Caledonian forests still guard their red squirrels, roe deer, and rare crossbills within a rich ecosystem dating back to the Ice Age.

LOCH AN EILEIN
ROTHIEMURCHUS [SC]

This beautiful loch is surrounded by the magnificent pines of Rothiemurchus Forest, which provides shelter for red squirrels, capercaillies, and rare Scottish crossbills.
See pp.86–87

RUTLAND WATER
RUTLAND [M]

Ospreys and grebes breed here in April. A hide overlooking a badger sett is open to small guided groups from mid-April.
See pp.82–83

MAGDALEN COLLEGE MEADOW
OXFORD [M]

Beautiful fritillaries cover half the meadow here in April, uninterrupted by other flowers. The college grove is also home to fallow and muntjac deer.
See pp.74–75

Previous page: Fresh green foliage and a carpet of bluebells make woodlands vibrant with colour.

and hugely varied in form, demanding more of our time to inspect, identify, and enjoy them. Exciting rarities, such as fritillaries and pasque flower, can be found in a few treasured places, but in mild areas, even a quiet roadside verge can suddenly offer a long list, from early purple orchids to stitchworts and violets, creating a glorious swathe of colour.

Butterflies are beginning to appear, and fish such as chub and bream are spawning in our rivers, often rolling in the shallows in the ecstasy of their mysterious rituals. Everything seems to be seized with the urgency of spring. Riversides are great places in April, with kingfishers, dippers, common sandpipers, and sand martins all making the most of the warmer weather.

COAST

PORTLAND BILL Pulpit Rock welcomes migrating birds.

HEATH AND MOOR

WEETING HEATH A grassy heathland reserve with pine plantations.

LAKES AND WATERWAYS

WYE VALLEY A famous fishing ground for the brown trout.

PORTLAND BILL
DORSET [SW]

One of the UK's hotspots for the spring migration: thousands of birds pass through in April and May, sometimes including rarities such as the dark-eyed junco.
See pp.90–91

AINSDALE DUNES
SEFTON COAST, MERSEYSIDE [N]

These coastal dunes host sand lizards, great crested newts, and natterjack toads, which breed in the shallow dune pools in April.
See pp.88–89

By April the natterjack breeding season is in full swing, as the males gather around the pools to enchant the females with their ratcheting calls.

WINTERTON DUNES
NORFOLK [SE]

These dunes near Great Yarmouth have a flourishing colony of natterjack toads, as well as a large population of birds, and several adders. You can often see seals swimming just offshore.
See pp.88–89

DUNGENESS
LYDD, KENT [SE]

Pools behind the expanse of shingle attract interesting birds, including black-necked grebes, little egrets, marsh harriers, and avocets. Listen, too, for the call of marsh frogs.
See pp.90–91

CORRIMONY
HIGHLAND [SC]

Set in stunning moorland and Caledonian forest, this beautiful reserve is a real discovery for anyone who loves birds. Black grouse may be displaying; take care not to disturb them.
See pp.86–87

MAIDSCROSS HILL
LAKENHEATH, SUFFOLK [SE]

This dry Breck grassland provides the perfect habitat for Breckland birds and specialist plants, such as Breckland wild thyme.
See pp.92–93

WEETING HEATH
NORFOLK [SE]

Weeting Heath is recognized as the best place in the UK to see stone curlew, and hear its banshee-like call. Look out for wheatears and tree pipits among the pine trees.
See pp.92–93

The Breckland heath provides the perfect breeding ground for the yellow-eyed stone curlew, whose eerie call haunts the Brecks at night.

THE LODGE
SANDY, BEDFORDSHIRE [SE]

The reserve that surrounds the RSPB's headquarters will, when fully restored, form the largest stretch of heathland in this county.
See pp.82–83

THE WYE VALLEY
HEREFORDSHIRE [M]

The River Wye, rich in salmon, chub, and brown trout, lies below Symonds Yat – where peregrines can be seen diving from tremendous heights.
See pp.80–81

LOCH GARTEN
HIGHLANDS [SC]

The Abernethy native pine forest sits around this vast loch, and is home to ospreys, capercaillies, black grouse, buzzards, red and roe deer, and red squirrels.
See pp.86–87

CROMFORD CANAL NATURE RESERVE
PEAK DISTRICT, DERBYSHIRE [N]

This rich, freshwater habitat provides a home for kingfishers, herons, and little grebes, alongside water voles.
See pp.94–95

LLANGOLLEN CANAL
NORTH WALES [W]

Witness the electric-blue flash of a hunting kingfisher over these restored waterways. The birds are feeding their young in April.
See pp.94–95

FIELDS OF GLORY

FEW WILD FLOWERS CAN MATCH THE DELICATE BEAUTY AND POISE of the snakeshead fritillary. For most of the year it is invisible, but for a few short weeks in April and May whole meadows are flushed with a garnet glow of delicate reddish purple as hundreds of thousands of fritillaries flower at once, their extraordinary chequered blooms nodding in the breeze on slender, arched stems.

Yet this abundance is an illusion, for nationally the plant is extremely rare. It now grows wild on just a few damp meadows – so few that there are only about 30 significant fritillary colonies left in Britain. To see one in its full glory is a rare privilege, and in late April one of the best places to go for just this sight is North Meadow, Cricklade, on the banks of the upper Thames. A century ago the floral richness of North Meadow would have been less remarkable, for it was one of thousands of riverside flood meadows set aside for a hay crop that was cut and dried in the sun in July, after most of its wild flowers had bloomed and set seed. This was not deliberate

WHERE
North Meadow, Cricklade NNR, Cricklade, Wiltshire, SN6 6HA; www.naturalengland.org.uk

CONTACT
Natural England Wiltshire, tel: 01380 726344; wiltshire@naturalengland.org.uk

GETTING THERE
Cricklade is off the A419 linking junction 15 of the M4 and Cirencester, with Cricklade roughly halfway between the two. The nearest railway station is Swindon, with a bus link to Cricklade. There is some roadside parking within 300m (330 yards) of the reserve. A bus service that runs through Cricklade stops at the meadow.

ACCESS AND FACILITIES
There is a small car park at the top end of Cricklade High Street. From the bottom end, a 20-minute walk along the Thames Path leads to the meadow. You must keep to the public footpaths as these delicate flowers are easily damaged. There is a disabled access gate at the site, although access is not advised in very wet conditions.

OPENING TIMES
Open all year round.

CHARGES
None.

Rare white fritillaries

The flowers of the snakeshead fritillary are typically dusky purple, but on many sites, including North Meadow, the drifts of purple are dotted with white, thanks to a white form of the flower that grows alongside the typical form. Delicately veined with green, this is a natural variation of the same species, caused by "recessive" genes that produce white flowers only if both parent plants are white too.

Main and far right: The bell-like flowers have curiously angled petals that are mottled like snakeskin.

Left (left to right): The cuckoo flower grows on the river banks; the early marsh orchid also enjoys the damp conditions in North Meadow.

Right (left to right): A brimstone butterfly; a tiny field vole forages in the short sward.

conservation, but a timetable dictated by the relatively short period when the meadows were dry after winter flooding. On most farms flooding is now prevented and the grass is harvested much earlier, but on the ancient common land of North Meadow the old regime is still followed, as it has been for at least eight centuries. The annual timetable of haymaking and winter grazing has allowed the grassland flowers to flourish and multiply, creating one of the best examples of a lowland hay meadow in Europe.

In particular it has provided ideal conditions for the fritillaries, which need damp, undisturbed ground where river silt deposited by floodwater provides nutrients essential to plant growth, but not so many that more vigorous plants outgrow and overwhelm them. The result is the breathtaking sight that greets any visitor to the site in spring, when in a good year there may be several million fritillaries in flower, dusky and mysterious on an overcast day, but gleaming like stained glass when the sun shines through their petals.

> This single meadow contains an astonishing 80 per cent of Britain's wild snakeshead fritillaries.

WHERE ELSE TO SEE
FRITILLARY MEADOWS

There were many fritillary meadows at the beginning of the 20th century, but they have gradually disappeared as the land has been drained or treated with fertilizers, which encourages other plants to grow at the fritillaries' expense. All those that remain are in the lowlands of southern and central England, where the plant originally grew in damp woodland clearings.

The most celebrated fritillary site after North Meadow is **Magdalen College Meadow** in Oxford. Here fritillaries cover roughly half the meadow in April, and they grow more or less alone, without other showy flowers such as dandelions to distract the eye. There is another site just outside Oxford in **Iffley**. [SE]

Another colony survives in flood meadows by the River Windrush in **Ducklington**, Oxfordshire, and is only open once a year on "Fritillary Sunday". [SE]

A colony at **Fox Meadow** in Suffolk was almost destroyed in the late 1960s, but survived by a fluke. As with the Ducklington meadow, this is open to visitors on just one day of the year. [SE]

THROUGH THE YEAR
NORTH MEADOW

As the fritillaries on North Meadow go to seed and die back in **summer**, their place is taken by a kaleidoscope of meadow flowers: meadow buttercup, ragged robin, ox-eye daisy, red clover, meadowsweet, and devil's-bit scabious. The flowers attract a host of butterflies, and skylarks sing overhead while swallows, house martins, and sand martins dart through the air.

By **autumn** the hay crop has been cut and the meadow is used for grazing animals such as cattle and horses. Many of the birds leave for the tropics, while others retreat to nearby hedgerows to feast on berries and seeds.

Though the Thames flows across the southwest corner of North Meadow, it is usually the River Churn, on the northwest side, that floods the meadow in **winter**, as it has done for centuries, attracting waterfowl and waders such as snipe.

Below: A skylark soars above the meadow in June.

JAN
FEB
MAR
APR
MAY
JUN
JUL
AUG
SEP
OCT
NOV
DEC

WHERE
Woolston Eyes, Weir Lane, Woolston, Warrington, Cheshire WA1 4QQ; www.woolstoneyes.co.uk

CONTACT
Apply via the Woolston Eyes Conservation Group at www.woolstoneyes.co.uk

GETTING THERE
There are several possible entrances, but the best route by car is to leave the M6 at junction 21 and take the A57 signposted to Warrington. After about 200m (220 yards), turn left down Weir Lane and park by Woolston Weir. The bus to Weir Lane (to access the reserve from the north side) along the A57 is the no. 3 from Warrington.

ACCESS AND FACILITIES
There is a public footpath from the end of Weir Lane along the west side of no. 2 bed and the north side of the canal to Thelwall Lane. You need a permit to access the rest of the reserve. There is parking at the top of Weir Lane, or in the dedicated car park at the end of Thelwall Lane. There are no facilities.

OPENING TIMES
Open all year round.

CHARGES
Parts of the reserve are free, but there's a fee for the areas requiring permit access.

A haven for newts

Woolston Eyes is home to quite a collection of reptiles and amphibians, including snakes, frogs, toads, and newts. Both the great crested newt and the smooth newt (*shown below*) can be found on the site – look for them around the water edges. On land, they eat insects and worms, catching them with their minute teeth; in the water they flick out their long tongues to capture insects, worms, and water snails. They emerge from hibernation in March.

Left: An alert weasel uses a well-decayed log as a lookout point.

Right (left to right): a pair of black-necked grebes mating; unhatched chicks make "peeping" noises to tell their parents that the eggs need turning or incubating more; for the first week after hatching, the grebe chicks are carried through the water on their mother's back.

Main: The Woolston Eyes reserve. **Far right:** Black-necked grebe sitting on nest.

WATERFOWL AT WOOLSTON

A N AMAZING ONE-THIRD OF THE TOTAL UK POPULATION of the stunning black-necked grebe can be found at Woolston Eyes. This young wetland reserve was only created in 1980 as a by-product of the Manchester Ship Canal, which lies right beside it, and which made use of the site as a dumping ground for its dredgings. The word "Eyes" comes from the Saxon "Ees", meaning "land near a looping river", which describes the area well. Over time the land has been used for grazing meadows, factories (during the Industrial Revolution), and then extensive canal building. Now it is a wonderful mosaic of man-made wetland habitats, with reedbeds and a network of islands.

This diverse habitat is an important breeding site for one of the UK's most attractive birds; some might argue, *the* most attractive of our birds. The black-necked grebe in breeding plumage is truly magnificent. It has a fiery red eye and bright golden tufts sweeping off either side of its face, which contrast dramatically against the

JAN

FEB

MAR

APR

MAY

JUN

JUL

AUG

SEP

OCT

NOV

DEC

Above: Look for the black darter dragonfly in summer.

THROUGH THE YEAR
WOOLSTON EYES

Grasshopper warblers, common warblers, chiffchaffs, willow warblers, blackcaps, and common whitethroats breed around Woolston Eyes in **summer**. You can usually see nesting gulls from bed no. 3, and grebes from the centre. Plant life includes lots of orchids, including the southern marsh, common spotted, and bee orchid, and also the rare broad-leaved helleborine.

By the beginning of **October,** incoming wintering birds include fieldfares and redwings. There are often large numbers of skylarks and meadow pipits. Long-eared owls can sometimes be seen in the trees around the south bank in **autumn**.

Wintering wildfowl numbers build to a peak in January and February, and this is the best time to catch sight of the water rail. Try the feeders to the east of the Frank Linley hide for a sighting of the uncommon willow tit. Scaups and smews can be seen in the weir pool in **winter**.

Grebes are almost entirely aquatic, spending around 15 per cent of their time under the water, in search of prey.

WHERE ELSE TO SEE
BLACK-NECKED GREBES

Black-necked grebes like reservoirs, gravel pits, and estuaries. There are around 60 breeding pairs scattered around England and Scotland, with occasional birds spotted in Anglesey, Wales.

On the Kent coast, **Dungeness** (*see pp.162–163*) is teeming with interesting birds, including black-necked grebes, little egrets, marsh harriers, and avocets. [SE]

The Fal Estuary, Cornwall, and **Poole Harbour**, Dorset (*see pp.48–49*) are good places to look for grebes in April. There is a great selection of wild ducks and geese, including brent geese, on the **River Exe**, especially around the estuary in winter (*see pp.286–287*). [SW]

Slimbridge (*see pp.34–35*) in Gloucestershire, on the Severn estuary, is excellent for wild ducks, swans, and geese. [M]

black of its neck and back. The birds spend the winter at sea or on larger lakes, but in the spring they start to return to their favourite breeding sites, such as Woolston Eyes. Here they find the all-important undisturbed, invertebrate-rich habitat they need for successful breeding – sometimes even producing two broods in one season.

There are four main wetland areas at the reserve, referred to as beds; each one is numbered. If you haven't seen the elusive water rail for some time, head to bed no. 3 (ensuring that you have first secured a permit). When the water levels are low, in periods of drought, you can get some really good views. This bed is also a reliable place to see large numbers of grebes: black-necked, little, and great crested grebes can all be seen in the water here, and the great crested grebes put on elaborate courtships displays in spring.

This lush reserve has over 220 bird species, as well as many other animals that you notice as you wander around its quiet paths in April, including the very rare great crested newt, the much-loved dormouse, and the adder – freshly emerged from hibernation and feeling peckish.

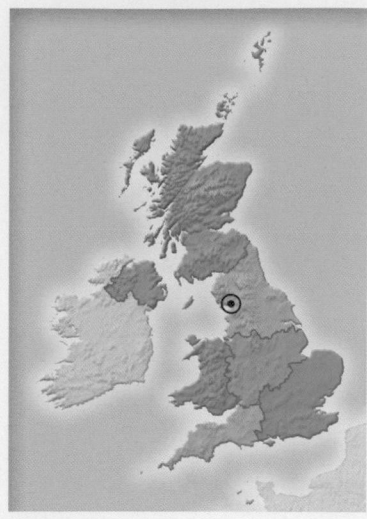

WHERE
RSPB Leighton Moss Reserve, Storrs Lane, Silverdale, Carnforth, Lancashire LA5 0SW.

CONTACT
Tel: 01524 701601;
leighton.moss@rspb.org.uk

GETTING THERE
The reserve lies on the outskirts of Silverdale, 6km (4 miles) north of Carnforth. From the M6, take the A6 north from junction 35. Brown signs direct you off the A6 to the reserve. Silverdale station is 150m (165 yards) from the reserve; the Silverdale shuttle bus stops just opposite its entrance.

ACCESS AND FACILITIES
The car park has bicycle racks. The wheelchair-friendly visitor centre has a café, shop, full-access toilets, and baby changing facilities. There are 8km (5 miles) of trails, some suitable for wheel-chairs and pushchairs. One wheelchair available for loan.

OPENING TIMES
Open all year round (except 25 December), 9am–dusk. Visitor centre open 9.30am–5pm (9.30am–4.30pm in winter).

CHARGES
Charges for admission to hides and nature trails, except for RSPB members and those who come by public transport or bike.

Masters of camouflage
Bitterns are relatively sluggish and slow in flight, so rely heavily on camouflage to avoid predators. If a bittern detects a threat, it will raise its bill to the sky, showing a vertically streaked brown breast that is virtually indistinguishable from the surrounding reeds. It may even sway slowly to match the movement of the vegetation in the wind. The bird is not defenceless – its sharp bill and claws are a strong deterrent and it will puff out its feathers to make its body appear bigger to a potential attacker.

Above (left to right): The reedbed wetland at Leighton Moss; bittern chicks in a nest made from reed stems close to the water-level.
Main: Bitterns remain motionless as part of their camouflage, but occasionally need to stretch their wings.

Above: A bittern drinks and washes its bill, knee-deep in water.

BOOMING BITTERNS

TURN LEFT FROM THE RAILWAY STATION AND LEFT AGAIN, to the visitor centre, and you hardly know you are near water: Leighton Moss is a wonderful, secret world in a quiet valley close to the Lancashire coast. Running through it is a series of clean, sparkling lagoons, thickly surrounded by reed. Bitterns need this intricate mix of water and reed: they must catch fish, so open water is vital, but they won't come into the open, so they have to find areas where water penetrates the reedbed. A series of narrow ditches through reeds standing in quite deep water make ideal bittern habitat. Unfortunately, this means that they are exceptionally difficult to see, especially as their streaked tawny-brown plumage matches the dead, upright stems of reeds to perfection.

Instead, you must listen for them – and luckily, this is not a difficult thing to do: when a bittern booms, it is hard not to notice. To see one, you'll need to sit quietly in one of Leighton Moss's hides overlooking the lagoons with your fingers crossed; but to hear one, just stop and

It's easy to see that a bittern is a member of the heron family when you see one in flight; its feet trail beyond the tail, and its head is hunched into the shoulders.

listen: the sound of a bittern's boom carries right across the valley. Only the male booms; the sound is his territorial song, saying "Here I am, this is my patch. If you are male, keep away. If you're a female, I'm over here."

Bittern numbers are measured according to "booming males". Each "boom" is as individual as a fingerprint, making it possible to count the bitterns on a site. But all you need do is listen for the boom: an eerie sound, especially at dawn or dusk, or in the hours of darkness. If you are close, you might hear a short note, almost like an intake of breath, before a deep, booming, almost (but not quite) musical "whooomp!" It has been likened to the bellow of a bull, or the boom of a distant foghorn, or even the sound you can make by blowing across the top of a large, empty bottle. However you hear it, you are unlikely to mistake this amazing "boom" from the reedbeds of Leighton Moss for anything else.

Inset: A bittern in flight shows its broad wingspan.
Below (left to right): Lucky visitors to the reserve may see an otter; a bearded tit.

WHERE ELSE TO SEE
BITTERNS

Bitterns can be seen all year round, but they are more visible in winter, and their numbers are higher. However, their booming mating call is most often heard in spring, so head for a place where they are known to breed, and listen out for their distinctive call.

East Anglia provides a home for around two-thirds of the UK's bittern population. **Minsmere** in Suffolk is a favourite place for watching bitterns, but the **Norfolk Broads** also have a scattering of bittern pairs. You might see one in the reedbeds along the north Norfolk coast. **Ely Pits and Meadows** in Cambridgeshire is an important inland site. [SE]

Male bitterns have recently been heard again around the **Humber** estuary in Lincolnshire, within the **Far Ings** reserve near Barton on Humber. [N]

The **Lee Valley** regional park's Bittern Watchpoint at Fishers Green, Hertfordshire, is a popular place to see bitterns near London. It supports approximately 10 per cent of the UK winter population. [SE]

THROUGH THE YEAR
LEIGHTON MOSS

In spring and **summer**, the lakes, marshes, and trees of Leighton Moss are especially good for reed warblers and sedge warblers, as well as common woodland birds. Bearded tits breed and may be seen or heard, especially on calmer days; look for them at a "birdtable" set up on the central causeway public footpath. Watch out, too, for the spectacular aerial courtship of the marsh harriers.

In summer and **autumn**, listen for water rails in the reeds and watch for them on sheltered muddy patches beside the reedbeds. Autumn is often good for seeing roosting swallows.

Through the **winter**, Leighton Moss is excellent for ducks, including many gadwalls, teals, and pochards, and a few shovelers and pintails. You should also see a good-sized starling roost, with flocks performing fantastic aerobatics over the reeds at dusk.

JAN
FEB
MAR
APR
MAY
JUN
JUL
AUG
SEP
OCT
NOV
DEC

WHERE
The Wye Valley, Herefordshire;
www.visitwyevalley.com

CONTACT
Forestry Commission, tel: 0845 3673787;
Symonds Yat information assistant,
tel: 07736 792511

GETTING THERE
To reach Symonds Yat Rock, follow the brown
tourist signs on the B4432 to Symonds Yat
from Coleford, Forest of Dean. The viewpoint
is approximately 250m (270 yards) from the
car park; just follow the "peregrine viewing"
signs. There are also buses that run from
Coleford Bus Station.

ACCESS AND FACILITIES
There is an information point at Symonds Yat
Rock run by the RSPB and Forest Enterprise
who fund telescopes to help visitors see the
peregrines. There are toilets and a café on
site, and both are wheelchair friendly. A
refreshment kiosk is open daily during the
summer, from 10am to 4pm.

OPENING TIMES
Open all year round. Car park and toilets are
open 10 am to 8.30 pm, or dusk if sooner.

CHARGES
Free access, but car-parking charges apply.

Wild boars in the forest

Wild boars disappeared from the UK around 300
years ago, largely due to being over-hunted. The
Forest of Dean, in the Wye Valley, was one of the
boars' last homes, and it seems they are staging
a comeback. A large group of boars – the perfect
mixture of males, sows, and juveniles – escaped
from local farms in 2004 and started breeding in
the forest. There are now around 50 or so living
wild. Look out for exposed plant roots and turned
earth, which are signs of boar rooting – but if
you spot the boars themselves, keep well away.

Above (left to right): Jackdaws roost in the forest, and in the crevices of Symonds Yat; the woodlands cover 10,900 hectares (27,000 acres).

VIBRANT VALLEY LIFE

THE WYE VALLEY IS JUSTLY DESIGNATED an area of outstanding natural beauty. It is divided into two areas: the Lower Wye Gorge – between Chepstow and Symonds Yat, with dramatic limestone cliffs and a narrow floodplain far below; and the gentler Herefordshire lowlands – lying north of Ross on Wye, where the river meanders across red sandstone. Both offer some of the most beautiful views in Britain, and have been attracting visitors since the 18th century.

In the Wye Gorge, the river runs between small earth cliffs – in which kingfishers and sand martins nest – and mud banks, over which the river flows to flood the plain each year. Woods line the length of the gorge, and the area buzzes with wildlife. Dragonflies and damselflies fill the air in spring, and six different types of mussel live in the river among the extraordinary number of fish: more than 30 species have been recorded here. In the right conditions, you stand a chance of seeing brown trout, chub, perch, roach, and eels as you walk along the river banks. In spring, the many migratory species include salmon, sea and river lampreys, and Wye specialities such as the allis and twaite shad, all coming upstream from the sea to spawn.

For a really dramatic viewpoint on to the valley and a close-up of its most famous inhabitants – the peregrine falcons – visit the limestone cliffs of Yat Rock, a scenic viewpoint towering 120m (400ft) above the Wye on the Gloucestershire side. From April onwards you can witness the aerial displays of these fascinating birds of prey, demonstrating their incredible speed and control.

Down on the ground, the night draws out a few wary foxes and badgers, and there have been sightings of polecats, recently returned to the valley after an absence of more than a century. Otters have also returned to play along the tributary streams, while 15 different species of bats swoop through the air above them.

Kingfishers, peregrines, grey herons, and and martins are among the many birds hunting in and over the wildlife-rich River Wye.

Main: The Wye river in its lush valley, as seen from Yat Rock.
Inset: Kingfishers are a common sight over the river.
Below (left to right): The Wye rapids at Symonds Yat; a brown trout.

WHERE ELSE TO SEE
VALLEY WILDLIFE

The Wye Valley is home to a unique collection of wildlife, but many of its inhabitants can be found at other sites around Britain.

Peregrines are found on rocky sea cliffs in the breeding season, and on marshes along the east coast – particularly Suffolk and Norfolk – in winter. They are also found nesting in cities, including **Chichester** (see pp.134–135). [SE]

The **River Avon** in Hampshire has a large fish population, which can be viewed from the bank at several popular beauty spots and small wildlife reserves. Visit Hampshire County Council's website – www3.hants.gov.uk – or livingriver.co.uk for details of the Avon Valley Path. [SE]

The Dove river, in **Dovedale** on the Staffordshire/ Derbyshire border, moves through valleys and gorges, and woods and meadows, and is home to a rich mix of wildlife. [M]

THROUGH THE YEAR
THE WYE VALLEY

There are grass snakes around the valley in **summer**, together with a number of dragonflies and butterflies, including holly blue butterflies. Hummingbird hawkmoths can sometimes be seen darting between flowers around the Symonds Yat Rock viewpoint during the summer. Look for chub, brown trout, and salmon in the River Wye, kingfishers along its banks, and otters in the tributary streams.

In **autumn** watch for buzzards, and keep an eye out at any time for peregrines. You should also see swallows and martins moving south through the valley and the appearance of a great variety of fungi in the woods.

The mild valley is good for seeing migrating **winter** birds such as redwings, fieldfares, and finches. Keep an eye out for foxes and fallow deer early in the morning and at dusk.

JAN
FEB
MAR
APR
MAY
JUN
JUL
AUG
SEP
OCT
NOV
DEC

Below: Peregrines have nested at Symonds Yat every year since 1982.

WHERE
RSPB Lochwinnoch, near Paisley,
Renfrewshire, Scotland PA12 4JF;
www.rspb.org.uk

CONTACT
RSPB Lochwinnoch, tel: 01505 842663;
lochwinnoch@rspb.org.uk

GETTING THERE
The reserve is 29km (18 miles) southwest of
Glasgow, beside the A760 Largs Road, which
is off the A737 Irvine Road (easily reached
from the M8 at Junction 28A). Lochwinnoch
railway station is 400m (440yds) from the
visitor centre. National Cycle Route 7 runs
through the reserve, adjacent to the A737.

ACCESS AND FACILITIES
Parking is free at the visitor centre, which has
toilets, snack- and drinks- vending machines,
and a picnic area. Both nature trails are
suitable for wheelchairs and pushchairs; the
two hides have adapted viewing positions for
wheelchair users. One wheelchair is available
for loan. Dogs are allowed on all footpaths,
but must be kept on a lead.

OPENING TIMES
Open daily, 10am to 5pm (except 25–26
December and 1–2 January).

CHARGES
Yes, for non-RSPB members.

Nesting time

Once a clutch of eggs is laid, both parents take
turns to sit on the nest. While they are superb
swimmers and divers, grebes are awkward birds
out of water: their legs are set right back by the
tiny tail and they have broadly lobed toes,
useless for walking. As soon as the eggs hatch
the birds gladly return to the water, carrying the
striped chicks on their backs. Grebes feed their
own downy breast feathers to their chicks, to
prevent fish bones penetrating their stomachs.

Main: To the observer, male and female grebes look identical, heightening the symmetry of the courtship performance. **Far right:** the "weed ceremony".

THE DANCE OF THE GREBES

ONE OF THE LAST AND BEST WETLANDS IN SOUTHWESTERN SCOTLAND, Lochwinnoch is a perfect place
to see water birds on the open loch. This watery haven is home to all manner of ducks, geese, and swans,
but it is the great crested grebes that catch the eye with their intriguing performances in spring. Take the nature
trail to the Aird Meadow Loch on a sparkling April day, keep quiet and still, and you should get good views.

In spring, the grebe's head is adorned with a short, black, two-horned crest, and a broad fan of very fine
chestnut and black feathers, normally lying flat, on each cheek. In their courtship displays, the grebes raise
these fans and horns to create a broad, saucer-like facial disc. You never can tell which is the female and which
is the male; even when mating they take turns to be on top. Their courtship displays are instinctive and strictly
ritualized, following an almost automatic, regimented sequence. Loud, growling calls initiate the ceremony.

Left (left to right): Aird Meadow Loch; coots fight over their prospective mates; Bar Loch, on the Lochwinnoch reserve.

Right (left to right): A grebe makes a streamlined approach to its partner, low in the water; bold eye markings combined with erect horns and ruff give the grebe an exotic, almost tribal look.

Watch until the pair come together, almost beak-to-beak, in a perfect, mirrored sequence of movements.

WHERE ELSE TO SEE
GREAT CRESTED GREBES

Great crested grebes can be seen on rivers, pools, and reservoirs throughout England and Wales but only locally in southern Scotland: from autumn to late winter, look for them on sheltered coastal bays.

Grafham Water (*see pp.302–303*) and the flooded gravel workings at **Little Paxton**, both in Cambridgeshire, have great crested grebes. [SE]

Grebes can be seen at both **Blithfield Reservoir** in Staffordshire and **Rutland Water** in Rutland. **Cotswold Water Park** in Gloucestershire has an important breeding population, together with other star wetland wildlife including otters and bitterns. [M]

Llangorse Lake in the Brecon Beacons National Park is a good place for seeing grebes (try the Llangasty hide). [W]

THROUGH THE YEAR
LOCHWINNOCH

A rich diversity of wetland wildlife can be seen at Lochwinnoch year-round. Watch for other wetland birds and an excellent range of warblers, from grasshopper warblers in rough grassy areas to sedge warblers in the bushy swamps and chiffchaffs, willow warblers, blackcaps, and whitethroats in trees, scrub and hedgerows. Listen for the shrill whistle and "plop" of a diving kingfisher or the pig-like squealing of a water rail in the reeds.

Lochwinnoch is great in winter, with whooper swans from **October** to **March**, a good variety of ducks including rather grebe-like goosanders, and greylag geese. If you are lucky, you might see a smew, a rare relative of the goosander.

Summer is the time to watch baby ducklings and cygnets, as well as many kinds of butterflies and damselflies: but try a visit at dusk, keep quiet and still, and you might see an otter.

Autumn is the time to watch roosting flocks: first of swallows and house martins, and later, of fieldfares, newly arrived from the continent.

JAN
FEB
MAR
APR
MAY
JUN
JUL
AUG
SEP
OCT
NOV
DEC

One bird dives underwater, then resurfaces with just its head visible, swimming towards its mate, leaving a V-shaped wake (the "ripple approach"). The other raises itself from the water, with part-open wings, in the "cat display". The diving bird emerges with its back to its partner, rising up vertically but with its head bowed stiffly down, in the "ghostly-penguin" performance. It then rotates to face its mate, and the two begin the most easily seen part of the display, the ritual "head-shaking". In spring, this part of the ritual continues over a far longer period than any of the other actions. Both birds spread their crests, raise their heads, open their bills, and waggle their heads from side to side, making quiet "ticking" calls. This subsides into a silent, side-to-side waggle with closed beaks, and then they pretend to preen their wing and back feathers with an exaggerated sweep of the beak.

You might, if you are particularly lucky, witness the remarkable "weed ceremony", in which one or both birds carry weed in the beak and the two rise breast to breast in the weed dance: a beautiful performance to celebrate the pair's "engagement".

Below: A water rail forages in the shallows.

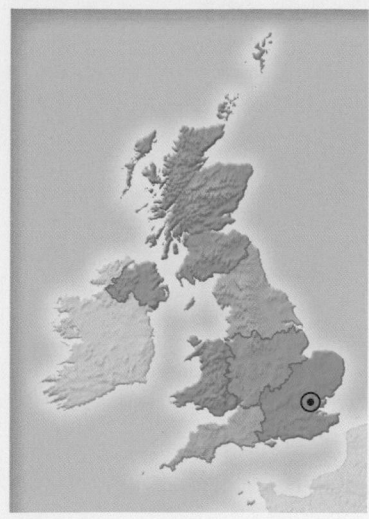

A HAZE OF BLUEBELLS

IF THERE IS ONE FLOWER THAT SYMBOLIZES THE GLORY OF SPRINGTIME IN BRITAIN, it is the bluebell. Insignificant in itself, this slender wild hyacinth flowers by the million to create one of the most dazzling, yet ephemeral of all floral displays – a shimmering, fragrant haze of purest blue. This is a uniquely British spectacle, for only in Britain's mild, moist climate do bluebells flourish in such profusion. In the wetter regions of the west and north they may grow in the open, but over most of Britain the massed flowers appear in open broad-leaved woodlands like Norsey Wood, Essex – a 400-year-old deer park that becomes utterly magical in late April.

Bluebells thrive here because their life-cycle is adapted to fit in with that of deciduous woodland. They sprout in January when the trees are bare, and as spring sunlight floods the woodland floor they put on a spurt of growth that climaxes with a mass flowering just as the leaves begin to unfurl on the trees. Within a few days the

WHERE
Norsey Wood Nature Reserve, Outwood Common Road, Billericay, Essex CM11 1HA; www.norseywood.org.uk

CONTACT
Norsey Wood Information Centre, tel: 01277 624553; or Basildon Council Countryside services, tel: 01268 550088; nws@stones.com

GETTING THERE
Norsey Wood lies just northeast of Billericay. From the A127, take the A176; take the right fork at the far end of Billericay High Street (Norsey Road), then turn right on to Outwood Common Road. From the B1007, turn left at the roundabout after entering Billericay. At the end of the road, turn left, then right into Outwood Common Rd. By public transport: from Billericay Rail Station, take the 102NB bus.

ACCESS AND FACILITIES
Visitor centre with toilets and picnic area opens Saturdays and Sundays but closes if the ranger is needed at other sites. Access for wheelchairs is limited, but there is an easy-access trail and a mobility vehicle on site.

OPENING TIMES
The woods can be accessed all day.

CHARGES
None.

A native bluebell – *Hyacinthoides non-scripta* – takes seven years to grow from seed, and extends its range by only a modest 50m (165ft) in 35 years.

Spanish invaders
The native bluebell has a close relative, the Spanish bluebell, introduced to Britain long ago and discovered growing in the wild in 1909. Bigger, tougher, and with a spire of broader flowers, it interbreeds with the native species to produce vigorous fertile hybrids. These are now found in around one in six of the UK's woodlands. They threaten the survival of the more delicate native bluebell, as do milder winters: when trees spread their leaves earlier, they shade out the woodland flowers before they have set seed.

flowers fade to swollen seedheads, disappearing as the spreading tree canopy favours other plants that are able to cope with deep shade. For the rest of the year they stockpile food in their bulbs. This cycle evolved in natural oakwoods, and in the drier south and east of England bluebells are an indicator of ancient woodland. Norsey Wood is certainly ancient, but while it does have tall oaks, most of its hornbeam and sweet chestnut trees have been coppiced to make new shoots. This yields a renewable harvest of "underwood", traditionally used for making products such as woven hurdles. At Norsey the process is repeated in different areas of the wood each year, letting in light to encourage bluebells along with other spring flowers – wood anemones, lily-of-the-valley, dog violets, and stitchwort. These attract nectar-feeding butterflies such as brimstones, orange-tips, and speckled woods, while the spring flush of leaf-eating caterpillars is exploited by breeding wrens, blackcaps, and other birds, whose jubilant songs celebrate one of the finest wildlife shows of the year.

Main: Norsey Wood is an ancient mix of oak, sweet chestnut, hornbeam, birch, and alder.

Left panel (top to bottom): Norsey Wood's bluebells are the true native species; a badger snuffles along.

Above: Razor-strop fungus, also known as polypore fungus, lives on the bark of the birch trees.

Below: Tawny owls hunt in the woods after dusk.

WHERE ELSE TO SEE
BLUEBELLS

Bluebells – often known as wild hyacinths in Scotland – grow throughout most of the British Isles except Orkney and Shetland. They need moist soil, so in most regions they grow in damp, broad-leaved woodland, with tall oaks and ashes and shorter, often coppiced hazel or chestnut. They also grow along hedgerows – often a sign of vanished ancient woodland – and on open grasslands and coastal cliffs in the north and west.

Bluebell woods are still numerous throughout Britain, and some even survive in city parks and suburbs. These include **Perivale Wood**, London, normally closed but open to visitors at bluebell time, and the woods around Queen Charlotte's Cottage in **Kew Gardens** in Surrey. There are wonderful bluebells in the ancient woodland of the RSPB reserve at **Northward Hill**, Kent (*see pp.54–55*). [SE]

Ryton Wood, Warwickshire, is famous for bluebells, as is **Dole Wood** in Lincolnshire. [M]

In Scotland, head for **Carstramon Wood** near Gatehouse of Fleet, Dumfries and Galloway. [SC]

THROUGH THE YEAR
NORSEY WOOD

Most of the woodland flowers vanish in **summer**, shaded out by the trees, but the verges of the main ride and the well-named Butterfly Ride are bright with flowers and nectar-feeding insects. Visit the ponds in the northeastern corner of the wood to see a colourful variety of dragonflies and damselflies.

In **autumn** the wood glows with the russets and yellows of autumn colour while a wide variety of fungi push up through the gathering carpet of fallen leaves. Nocturnal dormice feed on nuts, seeds, and berries to fatten up for their winter sleep.

The bare branches can often provide good views of resident birds like the great spotted woodpecker in **winter**, while a dusting of snow illuminates the wood and may reveal the occasional prowling fox.

Below: The spiny casings of sweet chestnut.

JAN
FEB
MAR
APR
MAY
JUN
JUL
AUG
SEP
OCT
NOV
DEC

WHERE
RSPB Loch Garten, Tulloch, Nethy Bridge, Highland PH25 3EF, Scotland; www.rspb.org.uk

CONTACT
Tel: 01479 831476; abernethy@rspb.org.uk

GETTING THERE
The reserve lies off the A95. By rail, go to Aviemore: 16km (10 miles) from the reserve. By bus, take the no. 34 from Aviemore to Grantown on Spey (ask for Raebreck junction). From here a footpath leads to the Osprey Centre (2km/1.6 miles). The reserve is on Route 7 of the National Cycle Network.

ACCESS AND FACILITIES
The site is wheelchair friendly with access to viewing hides. The visitor centre is pushchair friendly with full-access toilets, baby-changing facilities, and a live camera on the osprey nest. Cold drinks and snacks are available.

OPENING TIMES
Open daily 10am–6pm from April–August, with last entry at 5pm. The centre is also open earlier in April and May to watch for capercaillies (check times before visiting).

CHARGES
Yes, for non-RSPB members.

Curious nests

Here and there in the forest you'll notice big, grey mounds of pine needles. If you look closely, you'll see that these mounds are alive with wood ants – Britain's largest ants – who collect the pine needles to make their dome-shaped nests. The needles are carefully placed to shed water very efficiently, keeping the nest dry. The ants' activity is crucial to the forest's ecosystem as they clear large areas of dropped pine needles that would otherwise smother the ground.

HIGHLAND ESCAPE

NOWHERE IN BRITAIN HAS SUCH A MARVELLOUS STRETCH of native pine forest as the western edge of the Cairngorms, including Abernethy and Rothiemurchus. These pinewoods are a world away from the more familiar uniform plantations found across the UK. They are light and airy, richly green, and bright with the orange of Scots pine bark. Situated around the vast and peaceful waters of Loch Garten, the Abernethy forest also has its own blue pools with grassy islands and busy wildlife. For centuries this has been a famous region for naturalists, "collectors", shooting parties, and stalkers, and some birds all but disappeared. But the capercaillie, gone by the 18th century, was reintroduced in 1837 and in spring you

> The capercaillies are a joy to watch in April, during their mating display. Holding their wings down, they fan out their tail feathers, then emit an extraordinary sequence of noises, including gurgles, wheezes, and intermittent popping sounds.

can see these highly active and feisty birds – occasionally a "rogue" male will even attack people or vehicles. The RSPB's Osprey Centre lies in the heart of the forest, and CCTV cameras around the site mean that you can catch every second of their nesting habits, thrilling flying displays, and prodigious hunting skills. As you walk the trails, you're also likely to see buzzards, black grouse, crested tits, crossbills, and siskins, and perhaps the shyer red and roe deer. Red squirrels are busy in the forest, their tails fading to pale cream in late spring. Pine martens are much more difficult to see, but keep your eyes open – even the very rare wildcats, Britain's most threatened wild mammals, live among these pines.

Abernethy is extraordinarily rich in insects and rare spiders, including 400 kinds of beetle. The forest is full of possibility: one recently discovered fly was new to science. You may see Scotch argus and dark green fritillary butterflies, and rare dragonflies such as the northern damselfly, which breed in the forest bogs and lochans. Rare wild flowers include intermediate and serrated wintergreen, and the lovely little twinflower. Abernethy is the only place in Britain to see nine species of microfungi, and there are many others that only grow in this habitat. These old Scots pines and juniper trees hide a multitude of plants, mammals, and insects.

Main: The hides of the RSPB Osprey Centre lie close to the shores of beautiful Loch Garten.
Below (left to right): Red squirrels climb in the Scots pines; ospreys catch trout from the freshwater loch.
Inset: In April, capercaillies move into more open woodland to "lek" – display – for prospective female partners.

JAN

FEB

MAR

APR

MAY

JUN

JUL

AUG

SEP

OCT

NOV

DEC

Above: Osprey in nest with young.

THROUGH THE YEAR
LOCH GARTEN

In **summer**, watch the ospreys, tree pipits, redstarts, and crested tits. The woods are enlivened by lilac-pink heather, and the shiny greens of bilberry and cowberry.

Autumn sees most birds moving away but crested tits remain, as do the red squirrels, and there is a chance of a scarce migrant from the north such as a great grey shrike. Red kites wander widely at this time.

Pink-footed and greylag geese come to roost on Loch Garten in **winter**, and you should also see whooper swans, goldeneyes, and goosanders. Keep a look out for both red and roe deer.

WHERE ELSE TO SEE
PINE FOREST WILDLIFE

The UK's large native pine forests are all in Scotland. Pinewoods do not support a large diversity of plants and animals, but those that can survive in this habitat are generally rare, and well worth a visit.

Trails around **Loch an Eilean** in Rothiemurchus are good for crossbills, crested tits, and red squirrels, but please avoid searching for capercaillies, especially in spring and summer. They are rare birds, and it is illegal to disturb them when they are nesting. [SC]

Corrimony, west of Loch Ness, has black grouse, but not capercaillies. **Glen Affric** is a wonderful area with splendid patches of "Caledonian" forest and you can also see some of these native pinewoods around **Loch Maree** and **Beinn Eighe** (see pp.202–203) in Wester Ross. [SC]

Naturally there are no Scottish pinewoods in southern Britain, but you can see crossbills in the established Scots pines of **Breckland** in Norfolk. [SE]

Elsewhere in southern England, red squirrels can be found among the pine trees on **Brownsea Island**, Dorset (see pp.56–57). [SW]

Left (left to right): The dunes at Ainsdale on the Sefton Coast; a sand lizard.

Right (left to right): Toads breed in pools within the dune slacks; the male toad clasps the female as she lays her eggs; the female spawns a double-strand string of eggs.

Panel (below right): A natterjack's mottled brown skin provides camouflage.

WHERE
Ainsdale Dunes, Sefton Sands, Formby, Liverpool L37 1LJ; www.seftoncoast.org.uk

CONTACT
Natural England, site manager, tel: 01704 578774; northwest@naturalengland.org.uk

GETTING THERE
The reserve is between Ainsdale, 2km (1¼ miles) to the north, and Freshfield, near Formby, 2km (1¼ miles) to the south. All three towns are on the A565. By car, access to the reserve is via minor roads from the A565. The nearest train station is Ainsdale, a 20-minute walk from the site. The reserve is on the National Cycle Network, Route no. 62.

ACCESS AND FACILITIES
Access to the site is by permit only, which visitors need to apply for. Contact the site manager (tel: 01704 578774) for details. Three major trails pass through or near the reserve while public footpaths follow the perimeter of the reserve. The main path through the reserve is suitable for cycling and wheelchairs. The nearest toilets and refreshments are in local towns.

OPENING TIMES
Open all year round.

CHARGES
None.

New breeding pools

The natterjacks of the Sefton Coast owe their success to a dune conservation strategy developed in 1996 as part of the Sefton Coast Life Project. Scrub was cleared from the dunes, and grazing animals were introduced to prevent its return. Meanwhile more breeding pools were created, and within two years there were greater numbers of spawning natterjacks. Today they are flourishing all along the Sefton Coast, as are similar species such as the sand lizard.

Main: Natterjack toads are stocky and short-legged, with a body length of around 20cm (8in).

NATTERJACK CHORUS

COASTAL SAND DUNES ARE AMONG THE MOST EPHEMERAL of wildlife habitats. They can be literally here today and gone tomorrow, if there is a big storm overnight. If they escape this fate they tend to stabilize, sprout dune grasses, and evolve into scrubland. But as fast as this happens, new dunes tend to form, providing a mosaic of habitats for the often rare plants and animals that live among them.

The most extensive coastal dunes in Britain lie along the Sefton Coast near Merseyside. There are several good sites, but one of the best is Ainsdale Dunes. The whole "succession" of dune habitats exists here, including mobile dunes, fixed dunes, damp dune slacks, and scrub. Rare species such as sand lizards and great crested newts live in the dunes, and the extensive pinewoods support a thriving population of red squirrels. But in April the prime attraction for any wildlife watcher is the ringing chorus of the natterjack toads that breed in the shallow dune pools.

> The massed chorus of up to 1,000 male natterjacks is so loud that it can be heard from well over 2km (1.2 miles) away.

WHERE ELSE TO SEE
NATTERJACK TOADS

In Britain the natterjack is restricted to warm, sandy habitats, usually within 100m (330ft) of sea level. It was once numerous on the sandy heaths and coasts of southern and eastern England, but its main strongholds are now in the northwest, from Merseyside to the Solway Firth.

Apart from the Sefton Coast, the main area for natterjacks in England is Cumbria. Try the vast sand-dune systems of the **Ravenglass Estuary**. [N]

A flourishing East Anglian natterjack colony breeds among the coastal dunes at **Winterton**, Norfolk, north of Great Yarmouth. The nature reserve also supports adders, many birds, and, later in the year, orchids and dragonflies. **Holme Dunes** National Nature Reserve near Hunstanton is another Norfolk natterjack refuge. **The Lodge**, in Bedfordshire – the RSPB's UK headquarters – also has a population. [SE]

Natterjacks also flourish on coastal dunes on the Scottish shores of the Solway Firth. They are most abundant on the saltmarsh margins of **Caerlaverock** National Nature Reserve, south of Dumfries. [SC]

THROUGH THE YEAR
AINSDALE DUNES

In **summer** the dune slacks are bright with flowers, including a number of rare species such as the dune helleborine, a type of orchid. Rare sand lizards also hunt among the dunes, and both adults and young lizards can be seen basking in the sun to warm up on August mornings.

The cooler weather in **autumn** makes lizards and natterjacks slip into hibernation, but it also sees the arrival of masses of migrant waders that feed along the tidal shores of the estuaries.

Winter can be a good time to look for the red squirrels that live in the pinewoods backing the dune systems. The area supports one of the main surviving red squirrel populations in England.

The natterjack is among the rarest of British amphibians, partly because it is on the edge of its habitable range in Britain – it thrives only in lowland heaths and dunes where it can find plenty of insect prey and burrow easily to escape the summer sun. Smaller and more agile than the common toad, with a distinctive yellow stripe down its back, it spawns in warm, shallow pools that are too brackish and short-lived to attract predators such as newts and diving beetles.

By April the breeding season at Ainsdale is in full swing, with hundreds of male natterjacks gathering around the pools and singing to attract females. You need to arrive near dusk to catch their post-sunset performance. The call is a racheting "rrrrRRP" that lasts for about a second but, multiplied many times over, creates a continuous trilling that can be astonishingly loud. Flick on a torch and you may see a male in mid-call, the vocal sac beneath his throat inflated to amplify the sound. Males and females pair up at random, each female slipping into a pool to lay long strings of eggs that the male fertilizes while clinging to her back. By dawn the whole process is over, and the natterjacks retreat to their burrows to prepare for a repeat performance the following night.

Below: A common lizard on the dunes along the Sefton Coast.

JAN
FEB
MAR
APR
MAY
JUN
JUL
AUG
SEP
OCT
NOV
DEC

PASSAGE THROUGH PORTLAND

I MAGINE YOU'RE A BIRD RETURNING NORTH to breed from your warm wintering home in southern Europe or Africa. You're exhausted, dropping closer and closer to the sea, when you chance upon Portland, jutting 10km (6 miles) out from the Dorset coast into the English Channel. Here you can rest and prepare yourself for the next stage of your journey. It's no wonder Portland Bill is such a birding hotspot for watching the spring migration. The "Bill" refers to Portland's most southerly point, so it tends to be the first stretch of land birds see. Migrants start returning in early March but the peak months are April and May, when thousands of birds pass through.

Certain factors can increase your chances of seeing more birds: ideally, you want strong southerly winds, bringing cloud and light rain overnight; and fog, which will naturally force birds to ground, and prevent the morning sun from moving them on too early. The earlier you can arrive, the more migrants you're likely to see.

WHERE
Portland Bill, Portland, Dorset DT5 2JT; www.portlandbirdobs.org.uk

CONTACT
Portland Bird Observatory and Field Centre, tel: 01305 820553; obs@btinternet.com; Tourist Information Centre, tel: 01305 861233; portlandtic@weymouth.gov.uk

GETTING THERE
Portland Bill is joined to the mainland of Weymouth by Chesil Beach and a road bridge. By car from Weymouth, follow the signposts to Portland (along the A354) and then to Portland Bill. The nearest train station is in Weymouth, 14.4km (9 miles) away. There is also a regular bus service to Portland from Weymouth.

ACCESS AND FACILITIES
There is free parking at the Portland Bird Observatory and lighthouse. The Portland Tourist Information Centre is based at the lighthouse and there is a visitor centre there too. The area is not suitable for wheelchairs.

OPENING TIMES
The observatory is open all year round, the lighthouse from July to September.

CHARGES
Small entry charge for the lighthouse.

Portland spurge

Portland spurge is a low-growing, sprawling plant, restricted to coastal regions in southwest Britain, the Channel Islands, and of course, Portland. You may come across it either on sandy dunes or rocky ledges; its red-tinted flowers and red stems distinguish it from its close relative, sea spurge. As with all spurges, it has fleshy leaves, excellent for storing water, with a waxy coating that reduces evaporation by drying winds, The leaves and stems contain a white latex, which rabbits and other herbivores find unpalatable.

Left: Common whitethroat.

Right (left to right): The serin is a rare visitor to our shores; rock samphire on the cliff-top; a blue-headed wagtail.

Right panel (top and bottom): A hoopoe is an exotic sight; signs of quarrying are everywhere at the Bill – Portland stone was used in the building of both St Paul's Cathedral, London, and the Cobb at Lyme Regis.

Some of the regular migrants you can expect to see (sometimes in their hundreds) are chiffchaffs, willow warblers, pipits, wheatears, pied and spotted flycatchers, common redstarts, ring ouzels, and hirundines. If you're lucky you might see hoopoes, golden orioles, and honey buzzards; but, as every birdwatcher knows, migrations can produce spectacular rarities. Some of the Bill's very rare species include dark-eyed junco, northern water thrush, and Allen's gallinule.

Take extra care on the Bill if it's stormy. Wet conditions make the sea-level ledges very slippery, and large waves can easily wash you away if you are too close to the sea. Visit the Portland Bird Observatory at the Old Lower Lighthouse if you have time, as the logbook will tell you what's around, and bushes in the gardens provide good cover for birds. You might also enjoy visiting Portland's famous limestone quarries. Take care not to lose your footing when clambering through disused quarries. They can be fantastically atmospheric, and sometimes downright eerie.

The wheatear is the harbinger of spring at Portland – it's the first bird to return from wintering in Africa.

WHERE ELSE TO SEE
SPRING MIGRATION

As spring approaches, birdwatchers start licking their index fingers to "test" the all important wind direction. As birds return northwards from Europe and Africa, any winds that push birds towards the UK are welcomed. Most of the spring migration hotspots tend to be on promontories or islands.

Lizard Point (see pp.116–117), in Cornwall, is a long peninsula that exhausted birds home in on. Visitors include swallows, swifts, warblers, and flycatchers. From early March, firecrests and redstarts start arriving, followed by chiffchaffs, short-eared owls, wheatears, and swallows, swifts, and warblers. [SW]

Much of the east coast welcomes migrating birds, including **Dungeness** (see pp.162–163), Kent, and **Blakeney Point** (see pp.214–215), Norfolk. [SE]

Flamborough Head (see pp.252–253), Yorkshire, is another east-coast destination for migrants. [N]

The **Isles of Scilly**, off Land's End, Cornwall, are good for unusual birds, with regular sightings of golden orioles, hoopoes, and woodchat shrikes. [SW]

THROUGH THE YEAR
PORTLAND BILL

If you visit Portland in May and June, you're likely to see seabirds, such as fulmars, kittiwakes, and even a few puffins, breeding on the West Cliffs. Dolphins, basking sharks, and seals can be seen swimming around the Bill. Portland also has some impressive plant species: during the **summer** months, bee orchids and pyramidal orchids grow in the disused quarries. In early summer, you can see one of Portland's rarest plants – the beautiful early gentian. Look out for rare wall lizards basking in the sunshine on the rocks.

The birds that arrived in spring start to leave again as early as July, carrying on until the end of October. But even as the skylarks and pipits leave, there are new **autumn** arrivals, such as the continental warblers.

During **winter**, the harbour is a great place to look for divers, grebes, mergansers, and even eider ducks.

Below: Migrant butterflies like this painted lady also stop off here.

JAN

FEB

MAR

APR

MAY

JUN

JUL

AUG

SEP

OCT

NOV

DEC

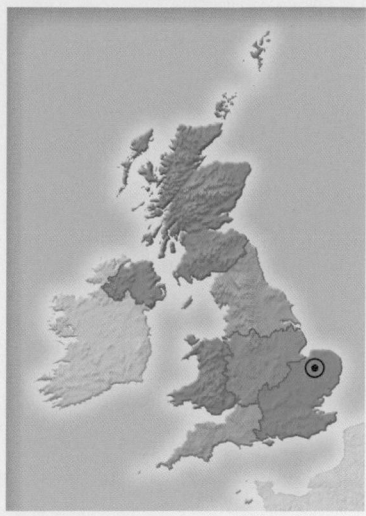

WHERE
Weeting Heath Reserve, Hockwold Road, Weeting, nr Brandon, Norfolk IP26 4NQ.

CONTACT
Norfolk Wildlife Trust, tel: 01842 827615; www.norfolkwildlifetrust.org.uk

GETTING THERE
Weeting Heath Reserve is just west of Brandon; take the A1065 to Mundford; turn left to Weeting village and once there, turn left to Hockwold cum Wilton. The car park and visitor centre are signed 2.5km (1½ miles) west of Weeting. The nearest train station is Brandon. Buses from Brandon stop a short walk from the nature reserve.

ACCESS AND FACILITIES
The visitor centre has interpretive displays, information boards, and car parking. There are several hides on the reserve. The reserve is wheelchair friendly, with full-access toilets.

OPENING TIMES
The visitor centre and nature reserve are open April–September, 7am to dusk.

CHARGES
A small entry charge for adult non-members of Norfolk Wildlife Trust; children go free.

Stone curlew protection

Through concerted action under the Biodiversity Action Plan, stone curlew numbers in Britain have grown from around 170 pairs to more than 300 in the past decade. Nest site protection and targeted agri-environment schemes have played a major role, as has a better understanding of its habitat management needs. At Weeting Heath, a healthy rabbit population is crucial in maintaining the short grassy sward that supports high densities of the curlews' favoured insect prey — including this localized stripe-winged grasshopper.

Above (top to bottom): Weeting Heath visitor centre; the grazing of rabbits, seen in their dozens in the early morning, keeps the grasslands short and rich.

Below: Several rare speedwells grow at Weeting, including the Breckland speedwell, shown here.

Right panel (top and bottom): A woodlark finds the perfect perch for a song; a breeding pair of stone curlews, with their distinctive yellow eyes.

Main: The stone curlew uses a distraction display to lure an intruder away from its nest site.

GUARDIAN OF THE HEATH

THE BRECKLAND OF NORFOLK AND SUFFOLK IS A VAST AREA of wind-blown glacial sand, overlying chalk at variable depths. Infertile, freely-draining, and in the driest part of the country, it was colonized by Neolithic man, cleared of its sparse forest cover, and grazing stock were brought in. This is how the Breckland heaths were created, and they are more akin to the steppes of eastern Europe than anywhere else in Britain.

Unfortunately, the once-continuous heathlands have now been highly fragmented by the planting of conifers and the onset of intensive agriculture, causing the loss of some of its iconic birds, including the great bustard. However, some species have weathered the changes, such as the stone curlew, whose eerie nocturnal calls remain an integral part of the Breckland soundscape. This rare, strange-looking bird visits the UK in summer to breed, in very vulnerable nests on the ground. It is hard to see during the day, when it remains

WEETING HEATH NORFOLK　93

JAN

FEB

MAR

APR

MAY

JUN

JUL

AUG

SEP

OCT

NOV

DEC

Above: Lapwings wintering in the Brecks.

THROUGH THE YEAR
WEETING HEATH

During the **summer**, the Breckland heaths continue to reveal their botanical delights, such as spiked speedwell and maiden pink. Ground-dwelling insects proliferate, especially grasshoppers, including the stripe-winged grasshopper, a speciality of this area. At dusk, listen to nightjars churring and watch the woodcocks' dusk "roding" flights (*see p.119*).

In **autumn**, deer become more obvious, as the red and fallow deer move out from the forestry plantations to embark upon the rutting season. Roe deer and muntjac deer, however, generally remain in dense cover – as secretive as ever.

Winter sometimes sees the arrival of a great grey shrike or two, and in some years there can be quite large numbers of crossbills in the conifers, breeding as early as February. Groups of bramblings or a few hawfinches may be found in favoured places, such as among beech or hornbeam trees.

The stone curlew is a secretive bird, but quick to defend its breeding territory on the close-cropped heathland of the Brecks.

WHERE ELSE TO SEE
BRECKLAND HEATH WILDLIFE

Breckland's climate is almost continental: high summer temperatures, low rainfall, and frequent frosts. Its chalk substrata, thinly covered by sand, makes it a unique habitat.

Breckland specialities can be found in many of the heathland reserves of East Anglia, including **East Wretham**, **Brettenham**, and **Cavenham Heaths**, but access may be restricted during the breeding season. **Maidscross Hill**, Lakenheath, and **Barnham Cross Common**, Thetford, are two sites where access is possible at all times. The **Suffolk Sandlings** (heathland between Lowestoft and Ipswich) has a small population of stone curlews. [SE]

Stone curlews are otherwise found mainly on **Salisbury Plain** [SW] and **Porton Down** in Wiltshire [SE], although much of these areas are out of bounds for military reasons.

largely inactive; your best chance is to visit the hides at the Norfolk Wildlife Trust's Weeting Heath reserve at dawn or dusk. You'll need to scan the ground very carefully to see these well-camouflaged birds, with their staring yellow eyes and stocky yellow legs, but wardens are on hand throughout the season to help you.

Other spring visitors to look out for are the wheatear – usually associated with the uplands, but here breeding in lowland rabbit burrows – and the tree pipit, which you usually hear before you see it, delivering its fluty song in flight or from the top of an isolated tree. The descending "lu–lu–lu" of the woodlarks can be heard too, adding to the uplifting spring melody.

One field on the reserve is managed as an arable field for rare plants. Here you can find three rare annual speedwells – spring, fingered, and Breckland – which grow only at a few sites in East Anglia, and are recognizable by their small, bright-blue flowers. As spring turns to summer, the delicate flowers of Spanish catchfly appears, along with field wormwood. All are specialities of the region, together helping to make the Brecks a unique botanical delight.

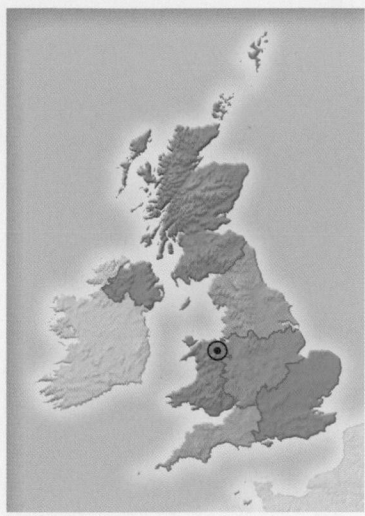

WHERE
Llangollen Canal, Llangollen, Wales LL20.

CONTACT
British Waterways, tel: 01606 723800;
enquiries.wbc@britishwaterways.co.uk

GETTING THERE
The nearest towns are Llangollen in the
south and Nantwich in the north, and the
aqueduct is located near Cefn-Mawr. For
Llangollen, take Junction 10A of the M6
for the M54 and Shrewsbury and continue
along the M54 until it meets the A5, which
takes you to Llangollen. For the Nantwich
end, where the Llangollen Canal leaves
the Shropshire Union Canal at Hurleston
Junction, leave the M6 at junction 16.

ACCESS AND FACILITIES
There are no facilities on the canal towpaths,
but there are plenty in nearby towns along
the canal. Wheelchair access is variable,
depending on which trail you take, but some
towpaths are paved. You can take circular
walks along Colemere and the Ellesmere
Canal towpath.

OPENING TIMES
Open all year round.

CHARGES
None.

Ice-fishing

Kingfishers prefer to hunt in still or slow-flowing
waters, making canals good habitats. However,
canals freeze over more readily than do
fast-flowing streams and rivers, which can make
winter feeding a challenge – especially given that
a kingfisher must eat at least its own bodyweight
of fish every day. Birds may feed through holes
in the ice or move away from their breeding
habitats in winter. Some settle by nearby open
water but others migrate to tidal estuaries or
even sheltered coasts.

Above (left to right): Llangollen Canal; a kingfisher brings food to its young at a nesthole in a sandbank.
Main: A kingfisher leaving the water with its catch.

KINGFISHERS ON THE CANAL

ONCE VITAL ARTERIES OF COMMERCE, PULSING WITH TRAFFIC delivering the raw materials and products of heavy industry, the canals of Britain have undergone a dramatic transformation into refuges for wetland wildlife. Even restored canals carry so little traffic now that they remain tranquil havens for shyer animals. Waterways such as the Llangollen Canal on the North Wales border offer many opportunities for watching these more elusive animals, both from the towpath and from the slow-moving narrowboats that can be hired along the route. April is perfect, as there are few other boats on the water. If you sit quietly on a moving boat, animals will often allow you to get surprisingly close, providing memorably intimate views.

One of the most dazzling sights on the canal – almost literally – is the electric-blue flash of a hunting kingfisher. Often this flash is all you see, as the bird zips low over the water with a shrill whistle and disappears around a bend. But if you check the overhanging vegetation carefully you may spot one on its fishing perch, watching the water intently for prey. It can be surprisingly hard to pick out, despite its bright blue and orange plumage, because the brilliant streak down its back is often obscured until it flies. With luck, it will spot a likely target, and plunge into the calm, clear water with a splash, before reappearing with a small fish in its bill. Returning to its perch, it often beats its luckless victim against something hard before juggling it around in its long, stout bill to swallow it head-first.

Spring is the busiest time for kingfishers because they have extra mouths to feed. Each pair may have up to seven chicks, and each chick needs 12–18 fish a day. The birds nest in burrows in the bank, which are often identifiable by the white streak of droppings below the tunnel entrance. There is a regular nesting site on Blake Mere, one of several quiet lakes or "meres" flanking the canal near Ellesmere in Shropshire, which were formed by melting ice at the end of the last Ice Age. This is one of the best places to explore the canal on foot, providing access not only to the canal and wildlife-rich meres but also to the nearby Wood Lane Reserve: a quarry with a flourishing colony of sand martins. These smaller, browner relatives of house martins are among the earliest migrant birds to return to their nesting sites in spring, and by April the colony is bustling with birds bringing food to their young – a truly wonderful place to watch and marvel at the sheer exuberance of nature.

WHERE ELSE TO SEE
KINGFISHERS

Kingfishers are widespread throughout the British Isles, but favour lowland habitats where there are more slow-flowing rivers and canals. They generally remain near their breeding sites throughout the year unless forced to move by winter ice. They like water that has a lot of overhanging vegetation, so disused or quiet canals are ideal.

The **Basingstoke Canal** in Surrey and Hampshire is partly disused, making it an excellent place to search for kingfishers, who enjoy its tranquility. The **Lee Valley** country park (*see pp.26–27*), near Waltham Abbey on the northern outskirts of London, has a number of wetlands as well as the River Lee itself, offering plenty of potential fishing sites for hungry kingfishers. [SE]

The **Cromford Canal** Nature Reserve in the Peak District of Derbyshire is a rich freshwater habitat, with kingfishers as well as other water birds such as herons and little grebes. The canal is also one of the last strongholds of the declining water vole. [M]

THROUGH THE YEAR
LLANGOLLEN CANAL

In **summer** the canal develops luxuriant marginal vegetation, which is bright with the glinting wings of insects. By day these attract insect-eating birds, such as warblers, while at dusk you may see low-flying Daubenton's bats hunting over the water.

Many of the plants start to die down in **autumn**, and the water becomes dotted with autumn leaves that have fallen from overhanging trees. But many larger insects will still be flying, such as the brown hawker dragonfly, which has distinctive amber wings.

Many birds, such as herons and kingfishers, are easier to spot in **winter** – although they can see you more easily too. Watch especially for the elusive water rail, a colourful relative of the moorhen, which has a strange pig-like, squealing call.

JAN

FEB

MAR

APR

MAY

JUN

JUL

AUG

SEP

OCT

NOV

DEC

Below (left to right): The electric blue of a kingfisher's back; during courtship, a male, with his entirely black beak, offers fish to the female.

Below: The Llangollen Canal aqueduct in winter.

MAY

Where to Go: May

On the finest, sunniest days and long, lingering evenings, May is a match for any month in the countryside: it is a joyous time, when the trees, hedgerows, and meadows are at their glorious best. The intense purple-black of the rooks at their treetop nests contrasts most beautifully with the brilliance of the fresh, green spring leaves; the great spotted woodpecker in the wood is wonderfully contrasted against the fresh foliage. Bird song is evident everywhere and challenges us to test our powers of discrimination and identification. On the coast, seabirds collect in huge colonies at places such as Bempton Cliffs, where numbers need to be seen to be believed. Heathlands welcome back their rare reptiles and more widespread but elusive ones,

ISLANDS

NORTH UIST Wildflowers flourish on the dunes of North Uist.

HEATH AND MOOR

RUABON MOOR One of the UK's great wildernesses.

COAST

BEMPTON CLIFFS Nesting gannets cover the cliff tops.

NORTH UIST
OUTER HEBRIDES [SC]

The unique habitat of the machair, a shell-sand soil, gives rise to a vibrant coastal grassland in spring and a multitude of unusual flowers.
See pp.108–109

RUABON MOOR
WREXHAM, NORTH WALES [W]

Visit The World's End, below the limestone ride of Maesyrychen Mountain, to watch the amazing "lek" display of the black grouse. Birds of prey keep watch.
See pp.102–103

STUDLAND HEATH
DORSET [SW]

This heathland is one of the last refuges of the rare, threatened sand lizard and the smooth snake, which live alongside healthy populations of common lizards and adders.
See pp.128–129

BEMPTON CLIFFS
BRIDLINGTON, YORKSHIRE [N]

The cliffs are famous for their seabirds: more than 200,000 make their home here between May and August.
See pp.104–105

PAPA WESTRAY
ORKNEY ISLANDS [SC]

The meadows at the green southern end of the island are alive with corncrakes and twite, while the rocky cliffs of the north act as a summer home for puffins, razorbills, and kittiwakes.
See pp.112–113

Our native reptiles come to life in the increasing warmth of the sun; watch out for them basking on paths on the heath.

GOWER PENINSULA
SOUTH WALES [W]

A mix of estuary, saltmarshes, sand dunes, woods, reedbeds, and beaches, Gower is home to all manner of creatures, and rich in coastal wildflowers.
See pp.122–123

COQUET ISLAND
NORTHUMBERLAND [N]

More than 18,000 pairs of puffins breed on this tiny island, which is most important for its tern colony, which includes the rare and endangered roseate tern.
See pp.126–127

THURSLEY COMMON
SURREY [SE]

Lying just outside Guildford, the sandy heaths of Thursley Common are alive with reptiles: common and sand lizards, adders, grass snakes, and smooth snakes all bask and slither.
See pp.128–129

RATHLIN ISLAND
COUNTY ANTRIM [NI]

A favourite spot for seabird enthusiasts in Northern Ireland; you can also see many birds of prey here. Grey and common seals bask on the rocks; dolphins swim offshore.
See pp.104–105

LIZARD POINT
LIZARD, CORNWALL [SW]

The frost-free environment of The Lizard means that many rare plants can survive here that would die anywhere else in the UK. Stars include the pygmy rush.
See pp.116–117

THE FARNE ISLANDS
NORTHUMBERLAND [N]

These uninhabited islands provide a dramatic backdrop for watching thousands of seabirds.
See pp.126–127

WESTHAY MOOR
SOMERSET LEVELS [SW]

Otters live along the riverbanks of the moorland, which are rich in sundew plants – a red, moss-like plant that digests unsuspecting insects.
See pp.120–121

BASS ROCK
FIRTH OF FORTH [SC]

So many gannets live on the rock that it looks as though it has been covered in icing. These, and other seabirds, breed here in spring.
See pp.104–105

Previous page: Puffins on the Farne Islands.

such as adders, which start to venture back into the sun. The heathland birds are suddenly everywhere, including one of the most mysterious and remarkable of all – the strange nightjar – which appears at dusk to sing and snatch moths in mid-flight. Butterflies, dragonflies, bumblebees, and hornets make this a good month for insects, and the nectar-feeders among them have an abundance of spring flowers to exploit. You can discover strange and colourful orchids in our chalk grasslands and dunes, and a veritable rock garden blooming on the cropped grassland of western clifftops. Islands offshore are sometimes swamped in bluebells and red campion, making a stunning backdrop to colonies of nesting gulls.

PARKS AND GRASSLANDS

HAMPSTEAD HEATH Home of London's finest dawn chorus.

HAMPSTEAD HEATH
HAMPSTEAD, LONDON [SE]

The woodlands, scrub, and grasslands of the heath fill with songbirds in May, and the dawn chorus is tremendous.
See pp.110–111

The longer, warmer evenings provide opportunities to observe a whole new cast of creatures that become active at night.

BERRY HEAD
TORBAY, DEVON [SW]

Stride out on this lovely headland, but pause, too, to admire its beautiful wild flowers, including the rare white rock rose. Bats throng the air in the evenings.
See pp.116–117

CLUMBER PARK
NOTTINGHAMSHIRE [M]

Interesting by day, but fascinating at dusk, when the large populations of nightjars and woodcocks mark out their territories.
See pp.118–119

KILLYKEEGHAN
COUNTY FERMANAGH [NI]

The cuckoo sings loudly here in May, above the largest limestone grassland in Northern Ireland. Peacock butterflies enjoy insects lured by its rare pink thyme.
See pp.114–115

WETLANDS

SHAPWICK HEATH Otters play on wetland once covered by the sea.

SHAPWICK HEATH
SOMERSET [SW]

The otters are the biggest draw here, but you can also see birds of prey, including more than 30 hobbies, and the rare garganey duck.
See pp.120–121

FINGRINGHOE WICK
ESSEX [SE]

The wetlands here overlook the tidal estuary, but the star attraction in spring is the liquid song of nightingales among the trees.
See pp.124–125

CLEY-NEXT-THE-SEA
NORTH NORFOLK [SE]

The large reedbeds and scrapes at this reserve are served by well-placed hides, bringing birds in their hundreds into easy view.
See pp.100–101

MINSMERE
SUFFOLK [SE]

The RSPB's flagship reserve, on the beautiful Suffolk coast. It lays on an extensive programme of guided walks and family-based activities.
See pp.100–101

UPLANDS

YNIS-HIR This colourful reserve lies at the head of the Dyfi estuary.

YNIS-HIR
POWYS [W]

One of the country's most stunning reserves in spring, the woodlands here feature a special trio of birds: the redstart, wood warbler, and pied flycatcher.
See pp.106–107

There is life at last in the huge flat fields where the lapwings breed, while the superb old oakwoods wake up to the calls of a myriad birds.

ORTON FELLS
CUMBRIA [N]

The rolling upland farmlands of this site are rich in limestone, with specialized plants such as rigid-buckler fern, limestone fern, and Solomon's seal.
See pp.114–115

UPPER TEESDALE
COUNTY DURHAM [N]

This unique fragment of the Ice Age contains three large waterfalls, attracting wagtails, dippers, and sandpipers. Botanical delights in May include the mountain pansy.
See pp.114–115

CORRIMONY
HIGHLAND [SC]

Take part in an RSPB minibus safari to watch black grouse in their extraordinary mating displays close to the track at this reserve in May.
See pp.102–103

Left: In 1971, the only pair of surviving marsh harriers in the UK lived at Minsmere.

Right (left to right): A view over the marshes of Minsmere; the man-made islands of the Scrape; in 1947 only 4 pairs of bearded tits survived in the UK – all at Minsmere.

Right, below: There are around 100 breeding pairs of avocets at the reserve today.

WHERE
RSPB Minsmere, Westleton, Saxmundham, Suffolk IP17 3BY; www.rspb.org.uk

CONTACT
Tel: 01728 648281;
minsmere@rspb.org.uk

GETTING THERE
By car, follow the brown tourist signs from the A12. By rail, go to Darsham station; by bus, travel to Leiston. Demand-responsive Coastlink buses will meet buses and trains if booked in advance (01728 833526). By cycle, national cycle route 1 links with regional route 42 (Suffolk Coast Cycle route).

ACCESS AND FACILITIES
The large car park has bike racks. There's an information centre, toilets with baby-changing facilities, RSPB shop, restaurant, and tearoom. There is good wheelchair access throughout the reserve, including the visitor centre.

OPENING TIMES
Reserve open daily from 9am to dusk. Visitor centre open daily 9am to 5pm (closes 4pm 1 November–31 January).

CHARGES
Yes, for non-RSPB members.

Viewing at the Scrape

Of Minsmere's seven birdwatching hides, four – plus a viewing platform – overlook the Scrape. This is the home of the waders, including the avocets, spotted redshanks, spoonbills, black terns, and even the scarce Temminck's stint. The Scrape also has 416 species of invertebrates, or "mini-beasts", many of which live on the margins of the saline lagoons. The abundance of these creatures is what draws in the hungry birds, making viewing at the Scrape a must.

Main: A dunlin flock flies over the shallow lagoons that dominate the Minsmere reserve.

SUFFOLK SANCTUARY

DURING WORLD WAR II, COASTAL AREAS OF SUFFOLK were flooded as a defence against invasion. Luckily the military invasion never occurred, but a wildlife invasion was almost instant – even the avocet, absent from England as a breeding bird for decades, returned to the Suffolk shores. One of the RSPB's flagship reserves, Minsmere's importance was quickly recognized, and today its breeding-bird list approaches 100. Many of these birds can be seen on what is fondly known as "the Scrape", an extensive area close to the coast that has been scraped clear of vegetation and is subject to controlled flooding around a number of small artificial islands.

One hundred pairs of avocets nest on these islands, feeding in the surrounding shallows that are just salty enough for their favourite shrimps. They share the islands with black-headed gulls, lapwings, and common terns, as well as non-breeding migrant waders. Black-tailed godwits and spotted redshanks linger all summer long.

Above: Red deer stags are at their most majestic during the October rut.

JAN
FEB
MAR
APR
MAY
JUN
JUL
AUG
SEP
OCT
NOV
DEC

THROUGH THE YEAR
MINSMERE

In **summer**, watch for butterflies and dragonflies, which attract hobbies. Yellow horned poppies flower on the beach-side shingle, where there is also sea kale, and you can find marsh mallow along the trails. Little terns nest on the beach.

The woods have a fine population of red deer, best seen, and especially heard, during the **autumn** rut in October, when the great stags are "roaring" and fighting over the hinds.

Winter wildfowl include wigeons and Bewick's swans and usually a few wild geese; shelducks, gadwalls, and shovelers are seen all year. Look for red-throated divers on the sea.

Minsmere has saved many birds from extinction, including the bittern, the avocet, and the marsh harrier.

WHERE ELSE TO SEE
REEDBED BIRDS

Minsmere has a large diversity of habitats, attracting hundreds of different kinds of birds – many of which can be found at other sites along the east coast.

You can find large reedbeds and "scrapes" at **Cley-next-the-sea**, North Norfolk, and avocets now breed in a string of English east-coast nature reserves including **Elmley Marshes** in Kent (*see pp.306–307*). Marsh harriers are best seen in coastal reserves along the east coast, but can also be spotted above the **Norfolk Broads**. [SE]

Minsmere's migrant waders can be seen at other coastal lagoons, including **Saltholme** on Teesside. Avocets breed as far afield as **RSPB Marshside**, near Southport, Lancashire. [N]

After the harsh winter of 1947, bearded tits could only be found at Minsmere. But today you can see them at many places around the east and south coasts; there are breeding pairs at **Blacktoft Sands** (*see pp.158–159*) on the Humber estuary, between Lincolnshire and East Yorkshire. [N]

Minsmere has much more than the Scrape, though: it is surrounded by a fine reedbed, where you can hear bitterns and stand a good chance of seeing one flying overhead in May. Marsh harriers are guaranteed, and on a calm day when the reeds are still, you would be unlucky not to see a bearded tit. These are the three reedbed specials: but the lagoons also have great crested grebes, a good selection of ducks, and water voles – with a chance of an otter as well.

Minsmere's balance of salty lagoon and freshwater reed swamp is vulnerable to rising sea levels due to global warming, and there are fears for this very special mix of wildlife habitats. The wet meadows nearer the beach are full of wild flowers, including colourful southern marsh orchids, while the surrounding woodlands are excellent for butterflies and birds, including singing nightingales, and they are awash with nodding bluebells in May. There is heathland, too, and a chance to see an adder if you are sharp-eyed and stealthy enough; at dusk, watch out for glow-worms and nightjars. A few Dartford warblers and scolding stonechats live around the heaths, and in May show their concern for young chicks by calling at you from bush-tops if you get too close.

WHERE
The best starting point for Ruabon Moors is the Coed Llandegla Forest Visitor Centre, Ruthin Road, Llandegla, Wrexham LL11 3AA.

CONTACT
Coed Llandegla Forest Visitor Centre, tel: 01978 751656; info@coedllandegla.com

GETTING THERE
Coed Llandegla Forest is located on the A525, 11km (7 miles) west of Wrexham; from Wrexham, follow the signs from the road. By train, travel to Wrexham; buses run from Wrexham to within 1.5km (1 mile) of the forest – catch the X50 service to Denby.

ACCESS AND FACILITIES
There is a café in the Coed Llandegla visitor centre, with full-access toilet facilities. From here you can take various walks or mountain bike routes. The well-marked Black Grouse Walking Route takes you to the RSPB bird hide overlooking Ruabon Moors. It takes around 2.5 hours and is 11km (7 miles) long. The walkers' trails are uneven, and may prove difficult for wheelchairs and pushchairs.

OPENING TIMES
The centre is open every day except Mondays, 10am–5.30pm.

CHARGES
Free access to moors walks.

Do not disturb

Approach a black grouse lek only in a vehicle and not on foot; human presence usually causes serious disturbance, whereas the birds take little notice of stationary vehicles. Make sure you arrive and switch off the engine before it is light, and park no nearer than 100m (330ft) away. Don't start the car engine again until activity has wound down, typically about two hours after dawn. Make sure you keep to footpaths to avoid disturbing nesting females and young and leave your dog at home if going to watch the grouse.

THE BLACK GROUSE "LEK"

ALTHOUGH FEMALE BLACK GROUSE (OR GREYHENS) ARE QUITE SIMILAR to female red grouse, the males – blackcocks – are very distinctive. They are spectacularly plumaged birds: glossy black with white wingbars, and white beneath the lyre-shaped tail. They prefer the areas close to the edge of coniferous forests, where they can find a greater range of food, including buds, catkins, and the fruits of bilberries and crowberries. But their main appeal is their remarkable ritualized mating display, at communal display grounds, called "leks".

Ruabon Moors in North Wales, with its good access by road, is one of the best sites to watch these extraordinary performances. The World's End area below the great limestone ridge of Maesyrychen Mountain is a prime site, while another is on the moorland at Coed Llandegla. A dawn visit in spring is essential, since much of the activity occurs in the half-light, and April and May see the peak of activity.

Left: Ruabon Moors are bounded by mountains to the north and south: Minera and Esclusham in the north; and Ruabon and Eglwyseg to the south.

Right: Lekking males jump vertically during their elaborate display.

Right panel (top and bottom): A female black grouse; a lekking male lets out a characteristic, wide-beaked "rookooing" call.

Wait patiently and safely (*see box, below left*), and you will be rewarded by one of the world's most unforgettable wildlife experiences. The dapper males, looking like gentlemen in evening dress with a glowing-red, fleshy comb above each eye, advance on one another in the twilight, spreading and raising their tails to reveal the fluffed-out white undersides, drooping their wings, and inflating their neck feathers. This is accompanied by a rhythmic dove-like cooing, known as "rookooing", rising and falling in pitch, interspersed with harsh explosive hissing sounds and the barking calls of the watching females. Males are promiscuous, but the females make just one choice.

In the early 1900s, Ruabon Moors was a popular shooting venue, but today a recovery project is underway to save the black grouse, including improvement of the habitat and control of the grouse's major predators: crows, foxes, and stoats. Fortunately, this seems already to be bearing fruit, as numbers of grouse have begun to flourish within the forest.

WHERE ELSE TO SEE
BLACK GROUSE

Black grouse are far less common in Britain than the more familiar red grouse, for which large areas of heather moorland in northern England and Scotland are set aside for shooting. Black grouse are most numerous and widespread in Scotland but also breed in northern England and parts of Wales.

The population of black grouse in England is concentrated largely in the North Pennines. Good places to see them include the RSPB reserve at **Geltsdale** (*see pp.24–25*) in the Lake District; **Upper Teesdale** in County Durham (*see pp.114–115*); and **Durham**, where there is a large national nature reserve. [N]

Corrimony RSPB reserve, near Glen Affric, to the southwest of Inverness in Scotland, is one of the most beautiful, remote, and easy sites to see black grouse. Take part in an RSPB minibus "safari" to watch the birds display close to the track at their lek in April and May. [SC]

Half the black grouse population of Wales lives and breeds on this wild heather moorland.

THROUGH THE YEAR
RUABON MOORS

The moorland is at its most beautiful between June and August when the heather is in bloom. **Summer** is also a good time to look for breeding birds, including peregrines, merlins, hen harriers, and goshawks. There's plenty of other wildlife – look for the common lizards and adders (take care!), which like to bask in the sun, especially around the old grouse-shooting butts or on the paths. Scarce wildflowers growing on limestone outcrops include dark red helleborine orchids and rigid buckler-fern.

Young black grouse become independent of their parents at about three months old, so you may be lucky enough to see some of them in **autumn**.

Winter can be bleak up on the moors, and at an altitude of up to about 500m (over 1,500ft) the roads can be treacherous or even impassable due to snow and ice. Blackcocks spend much of their time in groups together. Avoid looking for grouse after heavy snowfall, when the birds may be stressed.

Below: Ring ouzels are scarce spring passage migrants.

JAN

FEB

MAR

APR

MAY

JUN

JUL

AUG

SEP

OCT

NOV

DEC

WHERE
RSPB Bempton Cliffs, Cliff Lane, Bempton, Bridlington, East Yorkshire YO15 1JD; www.rspb.org.uk

CONTACT
RSPB Bempton, tel: 01262 851179; bempton.cliffs@rspb.org.uk

GETTING THERE
By road, the reserve is on the cliff road from the village of Bempton, on the B1229 Flamborough to Filey road. The nearest bus stop is in Bempton village, 1.5km (1 mile) from the reserve. It's about 15 minutes on foot from the White Horse Pub. Bempton train station is south of the village about 20 minutes on foot from the reserve.

ACCESS AND FACILITIES
The RSPB visitor centre is wheelchair friendly, with specially created cliff-top viewpoints. There's also a café, information centre, toilets, car park, picnic areas, and pushchair-friendly trails. A bird feeding station is easily accessed, as it is only 50m (54 yards) from the car park.

OPENING TIMES
The reserve is open all year; the visitor centre is open daily March–October 10am–5pm, November–February 9.30am–4pm.

CHARGES
Yes, for non-RSPB members.

Cormorant or shag?
The cormorant and shag are very similar birds – their long necks and bodies give them a primitive, almost reptilian look. The birds will often stand with wings outstretched, in a very imposing stance; they have a similar outline, though the shag is smaller and slimmer, and its plumage – which can at times look black – is actually a deep, glossy green. They are most easily differentiated by the narrow crest that pops up on the top of the shag's head during the breeding season.

Above (left to right): Bempton Cliffs; a gannet plunge-diving; a puffin perches on the cliff face.
Main: Tiers of gannets nesting on the cliff face at Bempton.

HIGH-RISE SEABIRD CITY

BEMPTON CLIFFS RISE SHEER FROM THE WAVES of the North Sea. At 120m (400ft), the cliff-top is no place for anyone scared of heights, but for those brave enough to venture near the edge, the site provides an awe-inspiring view onto one of the UK's largest seabird colonies. In fact, there are perfectly safe footpaths that run along the cliffs, and specially constructed viewpoints, so you can enjoy incredible sights without any danger.

Bempton has always been famous for its seabirds: kittiwakes and guillemots have long been abundant here, and they form the majority of the 200,000 or so seabirds that you might see around the cliffs between mid-March and early August. As you walk from the car park through the small visitor centre, nothing can prepare you for the sight, sound, and smell awaiting you at the edge of the cliff. Tiny guillemots and smart razorbills buzz around the cliff face, while the more graceful kittiwakes screech for attention like children in a playground, their black wing-tips looking as thought they've been dipped in ink. As your eyes travel up and down the cliff face you'll notice herring gulls and fulmars; look away from the rock, and you'll see shags and cormorants flying close by, over the sea. There are hundreds of seabirds everywhere you look.

In recent decades the cliffs have become famous for gannets: for years there was a small colony to the north, until numbers reached a certain critical point and the colony took off – now the path south of the entry point gives the best views. But there is one bird that everyone looks for: the puffin. Small numbers nest here, and, with patience and the use of binoculars, you should not be disappointed. They typically stand beside holes in the cliff, under boulders, or in steep cliff-top turf, and are much smaller than most people expect, but real gems nevertheless.

Nothing really beats the noise and action of a great seabird colony. These birds spend the winter far out at sea and it is almost miraculous that, from a cold, windswept wave-top, way out of sight of land, they can unerringly return to a favourite nesting ledge each spring. They have to come to land to breed, but they are ill-equipped to do much more than stand on their ledges, being so superbly adapted to live over, on, and – when they are feeding – under the sea. Whether you stay on the cliffs, or take a boat trip from nearby Bridlington, there is no denying the immense pleasure to be had from watching the guillemots and razorbills duck under the surface and swim down deep, using their short, slender wings to "fly" underwater.

Below (left to right): Similar to the cormorant, the razorbill is more heavily built with white underparts; a cormorant in flight.

WHERE ELSE TO SEE
SEABIRD COLONIES

Large colonies of seabirds tend to be found further north in the UK, though there are interesting smaller colonies to the west and south.

In Scotland, there are thriving seabird colonies on the **Mull of Galloway**, Dumfries and Galloway; at **Fowlsheugh**, south of Aberdeen; **Noss Head**, near Wick; and on several islands in **Orkney** and **Shetland**. The **Bass Rock** (*see pp.168–169*) near North Berwick, in the Firth of Forth, is by far the largest accessible gannet colony, but there is another on the mainland at **Troup Head** near Banff. [SC]

Rathlin Island, County Antrim, is a favourite spot for seabird enthusiasts in Northern Ireland. [NI]

Large numbers of seabirds can be seen on **Skomer** (*see pp.150–151*) and **Ramsey** (*see pp.182–183*), two Pembrokeshire islands. A smaller colony is found on **South Stack**, near Holyhead on Anglesey. [W]

In the south of England, the largest seabird colony can be seen at the **Berry Head** nature reserve in Devon, either from the cliffs or from kayaks. [SW]

THROUGH THE YEAR
BEMPTON CLIFFS

At any time, look out for tree sparrows near the visitor centre, and rock pipits along the cliffs. The pigeons here are feral pigeons – domestic birds turned wild – not, sadly, true rock doves.

The sea beneath the colony is dotted with resting and bathing birds all **summer**, although they feed much farther out. This is the time to watch baby birds taking their first tentative flights.

By August many of the birds have moved on, except the gannets, which stay until September, but you can see interesting seabirds, including skuas and shearwaters, offshore in **autumn**, as well as the chance of many migrant birds along the cliff-top path.

Bempton Cliffs are rather bleak in **winter**, but adjacent farmland is good for finding various birds from flocks of finches to hunting short-eared owls, as well as occasional roe deer and brown hares.

JAN

FEB

MAR

APR

MAY

JUN

JUL

AUG

SEP

OCT

NOV

DEC

Below: A guillemot, a bird that winters out at sea, with its chick.

Left: A wood warbler tends to its young in the nest.

Right (left to right): An oak tree at Ynys-hir; a male redstart; the view over grassland to the woods at Ynys-hir.

Below right: A male great spotted woodpecker.

WHERE
Ynys-hir RSPB reserve, Eglwys-fach, Machynlleth, Powys, Wales SY20 8TA; www.rspb.org.uk

CONTACT
RSPB Ynys-hir, tel: 01654 700222; ynys-hir@rspb.org.uk

GETTING THERE
By road, the reserve is between Machynlleth and Aberystwyth. Turn off the A487 in the village of Eglwys-fach and proceed for 1.6km (1 mile) to the car park. The nearest train station is Machynlleth. There is a regular bus service between Machynlleth and Aberystwyth that stops in Eglwys-fach. By bike, the reserve is on National Cycle Network Route no. 8.

ACCESS AND FACILITIES
This is a rugged reserve unsuitable for wheelchairs. Access to the visitor centre and toilets is via steps or a steep slope. There are seven hides, two viewpoints, and a 1.2m (4ft) birdfeeder outside the visitor centre.

OPENING TIMES
The reserve is open daily 9am–9pm, or dusk if earlier. The visitor centre is open 9am–5pm, April to October, and 10am–4pm, November to March (closed Mondays and Tuesdays).

CHARGES
None.

Range recovery

Ynys-hir is in a good area for polecats, but this ferret-like creature is remarkably elusive. They were once widespread across Britain, but heavy persecution by gamekeepers and farmers took its toll, and by 1915 the polecat's range was restricted to just mid Wales. Today the species is staging a recovery, but its range is still restricted to Wales, the Midlands, Cumbria, parts of the south coast, and a few other isolated areas.

Main: The view towards Foel Fawr Dyfi Estuary, on the RSPB reserve at Ynys-hir.

VIEWS ACROSS THE VALLEY

I N THE WEST OF WALES, LYING DEEP BETWEEN BEAUTIFUL WOODED HILLS and exposed moor and pasture on the Cardiganshire coast, Ynys-hir is a real gem. It is a big reserve, and one of the RSPB's most beautiful, with a varied habitat that allows it to support a huge variety of wildlife all through the year.

In spring, attention focuses on the lagoons to the east, where wading birds, including snipe and redshanks, breed. In the west, the huge flat fields managed especially for breeding lapwings are showing signs of life; while the superb old oakwoods wake up to the calls of a wide variety of birds. Set yourself an identification challenge: the trees house both marsh tits and the slightly scruffier willow tits – with the minutest of differences between them. This is when the wheatears, chiffchaffs, cuckoos, and blackcaps begin to arrive, and the meadow pipits return to the moors. Grey wagtails and common sandpipers take to the streams, where dippers can be found all

JAN
FEB
MAR
APR
MAY
JUN
JUL
AUG
SEP
OCT
NOV
DEC

Above: The saltmarsh and River Dovey at Ynys-hir.

THROUGH THE YEAR
YNYS-HIR

In **summer** the woods are quiet but lapwings flock and redshanks gather around the reserve pools. Keep an eye on the horizon for peregrines, red kites, and buzzards practising their aerial displays.

By early **autumn** there are flocks of meadow pipits and other signs of migration getting under way, and by late autumn the reserve sees the arrival of redwings and fieldfares.

In **winter** the lagoons and flat areas of closely cropped grass have dense flocks of teals and wigeons. A special visitor is the white-fronted goose: Ynys-hir is one of the very few British overwintering homes for the Greenland race. Look out also for lapwings, golden plovers, and birds of prey.

In the spring, green-veined white and speckled wood butterflies fly over woodland carpets of bluebells.

WHERE ELSE TO SEE
OAKWOOD BIRDS

British oak woodlands are considered internationally important because of the extensive diversity of their plant and animal communities. These complete ecosystems are worth seeing in several forms.

Oakwood birds can be found in many parts of Wales, including secluded valleys of **Snowdonia** (*see pp.172–173*), and the woodlands around the **Elan Valley** and the **Llangollen Canal** (*see pp.94–95*), which runs from Shropshire into North Wales. [W]

Visit Nagshead in the **Forest of Dean**, Gloucestershire, for the oakwood songbirds and birds of prey. [M]

Redstarts and wood warblers breed in the **New Forest** (*see pp.174–175*), Hampshire. [SE]

In **Coombes Valley**, North Staffordshire, you are almost guaranteed to see pied flycatchers, redstarts, and wood warblers. [M]

year round. Several trails cut through the woods, and a spacious hide lets you look through the canopy of the trees to watch birds at eye level. These western-UK oakwoods have a trio of special birds, which are harder to see in the east: redstarts, wood warblers, and pied flycatchers.

Redstarts and flycatchers nest in holes, or nestboxes, while the wood warbler nests among the dead leaves on the ground. All sing in the canopy, or from open branches just beneath, and this trio are well worth seeking out for their elegance of colour and design: the male redstart, especially, is a jewel. You are also likely to hear the sharp calls of great spotted woodpeckers, the boyish whistles of nuthatches, and the peevish calls of treecreepers before you see them, but they are all there for the patient watcher to find. The dawn chorus in these woods is a real delight.

Beyond the woods the reserve fades into grassland, saltmarsh, and muddy estuary. Look back at the woods and you might see buzzards and even a red kite or a goshawk. Look again at the estuary and you could find little egrets, shelducks, and oystercatchers. If you spot a spiky-headed duck, it's likely to be one of the red-breasted mergansers that nest here and feed on the river.

WHERE
North Uist, Outer Hebrides, Scotland.

CONTACT
RSPB Balranald, tel: 01463 715000;
nsro@rspb.org.uk

GETTING THERE
North Uist is an island in the Outer Hebrides, so you can reach it by boat or plane. It is also linked by causeways to Benbecula and South Uist. By boat, catch a car/people ferry from Uig on Skye to Lochmaddy, or from Oban to Lochboisdale on South Uist. Fly to Benbecula from Glasgow. To reach Balranald RSPB reserve, turn west off the A865 towards Hougharry, 5km (3 miles) north of Bayhead.

ACCESS AND FACILITIES
The visitor centre at the RSPB reserve has an information centre and toilets with baby-changing facilities. Guided walks are offered, but note that the nature trails are unsuitable for wheelchairs. The circular nature trail through the croft land of the reserve is 4.5km (3 miles) long.

OPENING TIMES
The reserve and visitor centre are both open at all times.

CHARGES
None, but donations help the RSPB to continue their invaluable work here.

Shelly sands

Machair is a distinctive sand-dune formation that is found only on the north and west coasts of Scotland, and in western Ireland. It incorporates siliceous sand from glacial sediments, and calcareous sand from the shells of sea animals, making it unusually rich for a sand-dune system. Even more unusually, it has long been an important agricultural resource. Ancient cultivation practices, such as shallow ploughing, have allowed harvesting without destruction of the machair plants.

Above and below: Listen out for the rasping call of the corncrake; North Uist has some of the highest densities of nesting waders to be found anywhere in Britain, including the dunlin, shown here nesting.

Right panel: Ragged robin (*top*) and yellow iris (*bottom*) are among the moisture-loving plants that grow in the wet, marshy areas (*centre*) that lie behind the well-drained sandy shoreline and are threaded by small channels.

Main: Classic machair flora on the shore of North Uist, which measures around 29km (18 miles) from east to west, and 19km (12 miles) from north to south.

MACHAIR IN BLOOM

PERCHED ON THE WESTERN EDGE OF EUROPE, North Uist lies within the Outer Hebrides, a chain of islands running from north to south off the west coast of Scotland. Essentially treeless, the island is exposed to the full force of Atlantic storms in winter, while in summer it can bask in more sunshine than most of the mainland. Long, white, sandy beaches on the west coast contrast with a rugged, rocky coast on the eastern side. From May through to July the island's west coast becomes bathed in colour, courtesy of one of Europe's rarest habitats: machair. Wind-blown sand and broken shells from the beach give the soil of this habitat a calcium-rich start, which is enhanced by the addition of the underlying peat to create a vibrant coastal grassland, with a multitude of flowers. Vetches, clovers, corn marigolds, crane's bills, and orchids all thrive here. Ragged robin and yellow iris beds run riot in the wetter areas, whose hollows are ablaze with the yellow of marsh marigolds.

Above: The stone circle of Pobull Fhinn ("Finn's People"), North Uist.

THROUGH THE YEAR
NORTH UIST

Flowers are in bloom on the machair through to August. In **summer**, breeding birds include oystercatchers, golden and ringed plovers, lapwings, dunlins, snipe, curlews, and redshanks. Red grouse and Arctic skuas breed on the moors, while some lochs have nesting mute and whooper swans. Ducks and terns breed on the dunes and beaches.

In the **autumn**, a few Manx shearwaters may be passing offshore, and there's a chance of seeing the rarer sooty shearwater. Look out for raptors – hen harriers, buzzards, kestrels, merlins, peregrine falcons, and even golden eagles hunt from North Uist's skies.

The island has spectacular **winter** storms. It is an important winter haven for both passage and overwintering birds, including pink-footed and white-fronted geese, pintails, scaups, and waders such as whimbrels and ruffs.

WHERE ELSE TO SEE
MACHAIR FLORA AND BIRDS

"Machair" is used to describe coastal grassy plains that are formed of wind-blown, shell-derived sands. These habitats develop in places with a damp and windy climate, as found on the northwest coasts of Scotland and Ireland.

Machair is a rare habitat, but can be found extensively on **South Uist** and **Benbecula**, and on smaller stretches of the island of **Harris**. It can also be found on some parts of the Inner Hebrides. On **Tiree**, for example, it covers almost half the island. [SC]

The corncrake likes hay meadows and damp pasture, and it is occasionally seen around the southwest, including **Portland** (see pp.90–91), **Land's End**, Cornwall and **Hengistbury Head** in Dorset. [SW]

Corn buntings are becoming increasingly rare, and their brown colouring makes them hard to see. Sites such as **East Fleetham** in Northumberland and **Swinefleet** in East Yorkshire are good places to look for them. [N]

Some of the best examples of uncultivated machair and its associated wildlife can be found on the Balranald RSPB reserve. This is one of the best places in Britain to see a corncrake, and May is ideal, as the flora is low enough to expose this notoriously secretive bird. The corn bunting, so rare on the mainland, is still found here, where it sits on fence posts singing its distinctive jingly song. The machair supports high densities of breeding waders, including snipe, lapwings, redshanks, and oystercatchers. Important populations of dunlins and ringed plovers nest here, but they have been badly hit by the introduction of hedgehogs in 1974; these animals roam across the machair at night, eating eggs and chicks.

Otters inhabit North Uist's coasts but are rarely seen. You may be luckier with red-throated divers, which are often seen just offshore in May – listen out for their distinctive quacking notes as they fly back to breeding lochs on the moorland. Roadside fence posts are favourite perching places for cuckoos and short-eared owls in May, and twites are commonly seen along the roadside. This northern bird, confined to Scotland and the north Pennines, is a relative of the linnet.

JAN
FEB
MAR
APR
MAY
JUN
JUL
AUG
SEP
OCT
NOV
DEC

DAWN CHORUS IN THE CITY

HAMPSTEAD HEATH IS ONE OF THE UK'S BEST CITY LOCATIONS to see and hear birds. Despite the fact that this big park – one of the capital's largest – is surrounded by main roads and houses, it is an oasis of green with a variety of habitats, including woodland, grassland, scrub, and over 30 ponds and lakes. It hosts a wide range of breeding birds and acts as a magnet to migrant birds, too. Evidence for this is provided every morning, especially in spring and early summer, as the dawn chorus strikes up.

You'll have to be up early, but one bonus of being out on the heath around dawn is that there are few people around to disturb the birds, and you can spot both the resident and passing migrant birds more easily. Some of the passage birds take part in the "avian orchestra", and you can test your skill by listening for their songs among the more familiar sounds of resident song thrushes, robins, blackbirds, and great tits.

WHERE
Hampstead Heath, North London;
www.cityoflondon.gov.uk/hampstead

CONTACT
London Borough of Camden:
tel: 020 7332 3322;
hampstead.heath@cityoflondon.gov.uk

GETTING THERE
The nearest London Underground stations are Hampstead Heath, Golders Green, and Kentish Town (all Northern Line); nearest overland train stations are Gospel Oak and Hampstead. The following buses stop at the park: 268, 46, 168, 24, C11, 210. By car, from central London take the A502, heading northwest via Chalk Farm and Belsize Park.

ACCESS AND FACILITIES
The park has many paths and rides, which are accessible to cycles, pushchairs, and wheelchairs. There are several car parks, and full-access public toilets in most areas.

OPENING TIMES
Open all year round. Dawn chorus meetings and walks are held in May, between 4 and 5am. Access-controlled areas open at various times around 8.30am and tend to shut at dusk.

CHARGES
None.

Urban foxes

It is estimated that up to 30,000 foxes now live in Britain's urban areas, with London being home to around 10,000 of these elusive creatures. They colonized cities in the 1930s, when houses in city suburbs were given larger gardens, making them attractive places to find food and shelter. If you're in a city park at dawn, you may see one of these beautiful animals – or even hear it barking along with the dawn chorus. Fox litters are born in March, and by May they are ready to leave the den, so watch out for playful cubs, too.

Left: Hampstead Heath offers birds a valuable mix of habitats.

Right (left to right): The female robin has her own feeding territory, so sings the dawn chorus as well as the male; in early May, wrens start singing especially vigorously.

Right panel (top and bottom): The blackbird sings like a flute, and then breaks into a babble, before pausing to begin again; look for spring migrants around the heath's lakes and ponds.

Singing is most intense around dawn because sound travels more easily then. On the whole, it is only male birds that sing the dawn chorus, although there are some exceptions: both male and female robins sing. The main purpose of the males' performance is to convey two messages – to rival males it says, "Go away, this is my territory", and to receptive females, "Come here, I want to mate". Gaps between bursts of song allow males to listen for replies from other males and gauge the strength of the opposition. They can pinpoint the direction from which the sound is coming and direct their vocal efforts accordingly, concentrating on males on the edge of their territory, or within it, that are attempting to take over. The mate-attracting versions of songs are often longer and more intricate than the territorial bouts. Singing uses up a good deal of energy and after a night with no food, a male capable of producing a loud, complex song is likely to be a strong and healthy one; it has been shown that females prefer such males and judge them on the quality of their songs.

WHERE ELSE TO HEAR
THE DAWN CHORUS

Woodlands are generally the best places to hear the dawn chorus, but city parks throughout Britain also resound with the calls of birds as the sun rises. If you can't make it at dawn, try listening to the dusk chorus; it's less spectacular, but still heart-lifting.

London is one of the world's greenest cities, and as such has many other parks that are great for wildlife, including **South Norwood Country Park** in the southeast, and **Kew Gardens** and **Richmond Park** to the southwest of the city. [SE]

Many of the RSPB's nature reserves around the UK have superb areas of woodland where the dawn chorus is particularly good. Organized walks are arranged where you can learn to identify birds and their songs with the help of experts. Visit www.rspb.org.uk for details.

Forestry Commission sites, National Nature Reserves (NNRs), and local nature reserves run by Wildlife Trusts are all worth investigating for local possibilities.

> Birdsong is the perfect medium for communicating over long distances, in every direction at once.

THROUGH THE YEAR
HAMPSTEAD HEATH

The dawn chorus is at its most intense in spring and early **summer**, when male birds are establishing or defending a breeding territory or trying to attract a mate. In high summer, you can also enjoy watching breeding kingfishers at the special artificial sandbank built for them by the reserve pond, and look out for equally brilliant dragonflies.

Autumn is the time to look for a wide variety of fungi. Mammals that can be seen include foxes, weasels, badgers, and little muntjac deer.

There is still much of interest to be seen on the heath in **winter**, although few birds are singing apart from robins, which sing almost all year round. As well as grey herons, cormorants, and tufted ducks at the ponds, you can watch great spotted woodpeckers on the trees. Look out, too, for winter visitors such as redwings, siskins, and redpolls.

Below: Autumnal colour on Hampstead Heath.

JAN

FEB

MAR

APR

MAY

JUN

JUL

AUG

SEP

OCT

NOV

DEC

ALL AT SEA

KNOWN LOCALLY AS PAPAY, Papa Westray is one of the most northerly of the Orkney islands. It's home to only around 65 people, but a fabulous population of birds. Its southern end is green and cultivated, with sandy bays and islets, and flowery meadows, where corncrakes and twites sing. The northern half of the island widens into a broad heathery moor, fringed with quite low, rusty-brown cliffs and dramatic offshore rocks.

The throng of seabirds here, with their chorus of calls and constant movements to and from the sea, are a sight to behold. The low cliffs afford superb close views; the combination of the thriving colony, surging sea, and rough cliff scenery is incomparable.

This is one of Orkney's smallest islands, with a human population of less than 100, yet it easily accommodates thousands upon thousands of summer visitors – in the shape of breeding seabirds.

It was here, at Fowl Craig, that the last great auk was shot in 1813, ensuring the extinction of the species. Today the seabirds are protected, and the cliffs provide a summer home for guillemots, razorbills, puffins, and kittiwakes, while the moorland is filled with exciting Arctic and great skuas, and Arctic terns. What you see depends on the food supply for these seabirds: in recent years the terns and kittiwakes have all but given up, leaving early in the season because sand eels have become so scarce as a consequence of rising sea temperatures.

Many of the seabirds arrive at the cliffs in mid-March, with the terns being the last to arrive in mid May. Terns and kittiwakes can be seen flying towards the cliffs to feed their chicks, carrying fish in their beaks– only to have the hard-earned food stolen by the skuas. Great skuas are big and bold enough to actually dip a gannet into the sea to steal its fish, but the hundred or more pairs of smaller Arctic skuas depend on their supreme acrobatics and persistence, chasing gulls and terns until they are forced to drop their catch – only to see the skua snatching it up before it hits the ground. Skuas are said to be halfway between a gull and a bird of prey – they will eat whatever is available, whether this is fish, carrion, or even the chicks of other birds. In the air they are among the UK's most beautifully streamlined birds.

Main: Papa Westray is one of Orkney's smallest isles, at just 6km (4 miles) long by 1.6km (1 mile) wide.
Below (left to right): A razorbill rests on a nesting ledge with its chick; kittiwakes nesting on the cliffs; a great skua.
Inset: The wide sandy bays of Papa Westray.

Scottish primrose

The Scottish primrose, *Primula scotica*, is on the edge of extinction, and lives wild in only two places in the world: Caithness and Orkney. It grows on Papa Westray within the North Hill Reserve, which provides the plant's ideal habitat: moist, well-drained grassland near the coast. The primrose has two flowering periods: a few plants flower in late April–May, but the main season is July–August, when they all burst into flower.

JAN

FEB

MAR

APR

MAY

JUN

JUL

AUG

SEP

OCT

NOV

DEC

Above: Orcas have been spotted just off the coast of Papa Westray.

THROUGH THE YEAR
PAPA WESTRAY

In **summer** the seabird colonies are in full swing and you can see oystercatchers, ringed plovers, curlews, purple sandpipers, and turnstones.

In **autumn**, watch for whales offshore on calm days, with orcas – killer whales – a possibility. You may also be lucky enough to see seals and seal pups. Watch the skies at night: the spectacular natural light show known as the aurora borealis, or "northern lights", occurs in September and October.

Winter days are short, with the sun barely leaving the horizon, but fulmars return to the cliffs and you can see grey and common seals hauled up on the rocky shore or surfing in the waves.

WHERE ELSE TO SEE
SEABIRD COLONIES

Many Orkney and Shetland islands have seabird colonies and skuas, but the birds are also seen on the east coast of England during spring.

Fair Isle, **Fetlar**, **and Hoy** are all wonderful places for seabird colonies. You can see skuas, too, on **Handa Island** off the Sutherland coast. Whales are often spotted from **Sumburgh Head** at the southern tip of Shetland's mainland. On mainland Scotland, visit **Duncansby Head**, just east of John O'Groats, for cliff-nesting seabirds and spectacular costal scenery. [SC]

Breeding terns can be seen on the **Farne Islands** in Northumberland (*see pp.126–127*). [N]

The coastlines of Norfolk, Suffolk, and Essex often plays host to migrating skuas and terns. **Blakeney Point**, on the north Norfolk coast (*see pp.214–215*), has a large breeding tern population that can be seen up close from seal-watching boat trips. [SE]

A JOURNEY UP RIVER

UPPER TEESDALE IS A UNIQUE FRAGMENT OF OUR POST-GLACIAL LANDSCAPE, situated in the north Pennines. As a result of the extreme upland climate, its wildlife and landscape hark back to times just after the retreat of the last Ice Age. Start at Middleton, and follow the course of the River Tees upstream: the tumbling river descends over rocky rapids and waterfalls: Low Force, High Force (a magnificent 21m/70ft cascade over the Whin Sill), and Cauldron Snout. Grey wagtails, dippers, and common sandpipers flitter around the river fringes, using a bobbing action for camouflage. The yellow-flowered shrubby cinquefoil – native only here and in Cumbria – grow along the banks. Around High Force, take a wander through the juniper forest; this head-high woodland teems with willow warblers. The valley meadows are full of botanical delights, especially in May, when great burnet, globe-flower, northern bedstraw, wood crane's-bill, and melancholy thistle are bursting into flower.

WHERE
Moor House Upper Teesdale National Nature Reserve, Widdybank Farm, Langdon Beck, Forest in Teesdale, Barnard Castle, Co Durham; www.naturalengland.org.uk

CONTACT
Natural England: 0845 6003078; enquiries@naturalengland.org.uk

GETTING THERE
The Upper Teesdale side of the nature reserve can be reached by car from the B6277 Middleton-in-Teesdale to Alston road. By bus, there's a limited service from Middleton-in-Teesdale to Langdon Beck (and Cow Green on request). However, there's no bus service to the Moor House side of the reserve. By cycle, follow National Cycle Network Route no. 68. The Pennine Cycleway, the Eden Valley Cycleway, and the C2C all run close to the Moor House side of the reserve.

ACCESS AND FACILITIES
Car parking is available at Cow Green Reservoir, High Force, Hanging Shaw, and Bowlees. The reserve's tracks are unsuitable for wheelchair access.

OPENING TIMES
Open all year round.

Spring gentian

The spring gentian is a true Arctic-alpine plant, found in the higher mountain ranges of Europe and at lower altitudes in cold northerly regions. Elsewhere in the British Isles it is known only from the extensive limestone region of the Burren in western Ireland, near Galway Bay, where it can be seen right down to sea level. Along with other mountain plants it is at risk, mainly from climate change and overgrazing – it bloomed magnificently after livestock reductions following foot-and-mouth disease.

Main: Low Force falls, Upper Teesdale.

Left: Shrubby cinquefoil.

Right (left to right): Mountain pansy; yellow saxifrage; Cronkley Fell, home to many delicate botanical gems; lapwing bathing in a moorland stream.

Right, above: Upper Teesdale's attractive landscape can be an easy walk in summer.

JAN
FEB
MAR
APR

MAY

JUN
JUL
AUG
SEP
OCT
NOV
DEC

Further upstream, around Cow Green Reservoir, you'll reach Cronkley Fell and Widdybank Fell. Their crumbly, crystalline sugar limestone provides a refuge for Arctic-alpine plants of extraordinary and fragile beauty: the mountain pansy, yellow or purple, shot through with fine inky-black veins; the slender alpine bistort; the fluffy pink cat's-foot; and the spring sandwort. All of these are dotted among the flowers of the area's iconic species – the indigo-blue spring gentian. There's yet more on the slopes: the subtle alpine bartsia, the delicate flower-globes of bird's-eye primrose, and twinkling yellow saxifrage. And everywhere, the sounds of breeding birds: golden plovers and dunlins on the high tops; redshanks, oystercatchers, lapwings, curlews, and snipe in the damp fields; ring ouzels and wheatears around the stone walls. Black grouse are numerous, and a large lek (*see pp.102–103*) is often visible from the road that crosses to St John's Chapel in Weardale to the north. Upper Teesdale is rightly considered a place of pilgrimage for wildlife enthusiasts.

WHERE ELSE TO SEE
LIMESTONE FLORA

The sugar limestone habitat of Upper Teesdale is extremely rare, but there are many interesting limestone pavements and grasslands to explore within northern England and Wales.

On **Orton Fells**, Cumbria, you can find the very rare rigid-buckler fern, limestone fern, and angular Solomon's seal. The grassland around the pavement gives rise to blue moor grass, bird's-foot trefoil, fairy flax, limestone bedstraw, and autumn gentian. [N]

The best-known limestone pavement in the UK is above **Malham Cove** in the Yorkshire Dales. [N]

Craig-y-Cilau nature reserve in Crickhowell, Wales, is part of a massive limestone escarpment with some very rare plants, including several species of whitebeam – one unique to this site. [W]

Killykeeghan and Crossmurrin Nature Reserve is the most extensive area of limestone grassland in Northern Ireland, and its grey limestone supports thyme, harebell, and yellow bird's-foot trefoil, as food for its common blue and peacock butterflies. [NI]

THROUGH THE YEAR
UPPER TEESDALE

As **summer** progresses, the Teesdale meadows provide an ever-changing mosaic of colour, and the chicks of the breeding waders hatch and grow. At least nine species of lady's mantle grow here, many not found anywhere else in the UK.

In late summer and **autumn**, a purple haze of heather blankets the hills, and the fruits of rowan trees ripen red and attract feeding thrushes. Look for giant bellflowers on river banks and woodland edges, harebells in short grassland turf, and the ivory-white flowers of grass-of-Parnassus in damp places.

By **winter** most birds have departed from the higher tops: only meadow pipits are numerous, forming the main prey of a few roving merlins. The upland reservoirs attract a few ducks; mainly mallards, teals, and wigeons. Don't let the lack of wildlife put you off – a frosty morning offers atmospheric landscapes.

The flowers of Upper Teesdale are not only Ice-Age survivors – they are lustrous botanical jewels.

Below: The graceful spires of the greater bellflower.

WHERE
Lizard Point, Lizard, Cornwall, TR12 7NT;
www.lizard-peninsula.co.uk

CONTACT
Lizard Countryside Office,
tel: 01326 561407;
lizard@nationaltrust.org.uk

GETTING THERE
By car, from the M5 at Exeter, take the A38
via Plymouth, or the A30 over Bodmin Moor.

ACCESS AND FACILITIES
Parking is very limited at the Point; it's best
to park in Lizard town or at the Lizard
Lighthouse. The paths to viewpoints
overlooking Lizard Point are wheelchair-
friendly but other areas are unsuitable due to
steep slopes. There are full-access toilets next
to the car park at the Lizard. There's ground-
level access for wheelchairs at the lighthouse
and also a café at the Point.

OPENING TIMES
There is year-round access to countryside
paths and to external views of the lighthouse.

CHARGES
Only to look round the lighthouse.

The Hottentot fig

The Lizard's unique nature may be due to its
frost-free climate, but this could also be its
undoing. Many invasive frost-sensitive plants
have become established here, and some are
encroaching very significantly into the wild.
Perhaps worst of all is the Hottentot fig, a South
African succulent with prostrate stems and large
yellow or pink flowers. Without frosts to keep it in
check, physical removal is the only real option to
give native plants the space they need to survive.

Above (top and bottom): Grey seals and dolphins can
be seen in the sea around the Lizard; low-growing thrift.

Right: Early purple orchids grow on the Lizard's
heathland. **Inset:** The chough – Cornwall's symbol,
and according to legend, home to King Arthur's spirit
when he died.

Below: The rare long-headed clover, which until
recently was only found on the Lizard.

Main: The unusual rock formations of the Lizard are altered peridotite – part of the Earth's mantle, normally 30–200km (18–125 miles) below ground.

LIFE ON THE LIZARD

FORMING THE SOUTHERNMOST EXTREMITY OF MAINLAND BRITAIN, Lizard Point is a unique location for
wildlife. Its highly oceanic climate – wet and warm, with rarely any frost – coupled with its complex and
varied geology, based mainly on serpentine rocks, make this the premier site for rare plants in Britain.

If you start in the heart of the village, on Lizard Green, you are already among the rarities. Even around the
parked cars, the low turf has patches of fringed rupturewort, a mat-forming plant that grows nowhere else in the
country. A short walk brings you to the coastal path and its swathes of thrift, with added splashes of yellow from
bird's-foot trefoil and kidney vetch, and white sea campion just starting to flower. Around here you can start
looking for more of the Lizard's specialities: the south-facing slopes above Caerthilian Cove have an amazing
collection of rare clovers, including twin-headed, upright, long-headed, and western varieties. And if you're

Above: Look for convolvulus hawk-moths in autumn.

Choughs returned to the Lizard in 2001, breeding the following year for the first time in England in 50 years.

THROUGH THE YEAR
THE LIZARD

The dramatic, pink-spiked Cornish heath is abundant across the serpentine heaths that form the heart of the Lizard; at its best in July, it has been described as the commonest rare plant in Britain, on account of its local abundance. The wet heaths in **summer** have bog asphodel, cotton-grass, black bog-rush, and sundew in flower.

Into the **autumn**, the cliff-top grasslands are still blooming, with wild carrot, sea aster, rock samphire, harebell, and sheep's-bit scabious. Increasingly large areas are becoming orange, under the invasive, albeit attractive, monbretia. The Lizard is good for migrant songbirds in autumn, while seabirds and dolphins linger offshore. It is especially renowned for its moths and butterflies: hummingbird hawk-moths by day, convolvulus hawk-moths by night, and many, many more when the winds are from the south.

Winter never really arrives on the Lizard. Frost and snow are so infrequent that there are always plants in flower. The first cultivated daffodils, for instance, are usually ready to be cut in January.

WHERE ELSE TO SEE
COASTAL HEATH PLANTS

Many of the Lizard's plants are unique to this one area, so while there are similar habitats, none are a precise match.

Some heaths, such as those at **Arne**, Dorset (*see pp.138–139*), lack the species that dominates the Lizard – the Cornish heath – but do have plenty of interesting plants, and are especially dramatic in autumn. **Prawle Point** in Devon is an interesting area of cliff-top grassland. [SW]

The **Gower Peninsula** (*see pp.122–123*) and **St David's Head** in Wales have maritime and cliff-top grassland that echo the Lizard in plantlife. [W]

For a different kind of maritime grassland, try the limestone of **Berry Head** in Torbay, Devon, which is home to several very rare plants, including white rock rose – found at only two places in the UK. [SW]

interested in miniature plants, search out the shallow, damp depressions: they will reveal an array of diminutive stars, including pygmy rush and yellow centaury. The exposure to wind and salt spray on the cliff slopes is so severe that several plants have adopted prostrate growth forms to cope with it. The wild asparagus is a trailing plant closely related to the upright garden asparagus; but others are simply horizontal forms of a common species, such as the prostrate broom – here low and arching, but extremely dramatic in flower.

Such are the botanical riches that you might find yourself looking down and ignoring the rest of the landscape and wildlife. So it is perhaps lucky that the "star" bird, the chough, so noisily cries out its name. Having settled here as a breeding bird as recently as 2002, these cheeky black birds can be seen anywhere in the area, but the vicinity of Lizard Point is a good place to try, especially as there is a manned watchpoint here during the nesting season. With luck, their numbers will increase, and they will become a familiar sight on the Lizard, probing their slender red bills into the turf for food, and sky-dancing like wind-blown sprites on the air currents.

JAN
FEB
MAR
APR
MAY
JUN
JUL
AUG
SEP
OCT
NOV
DEC

BIRDS IN THE DUSK

OUR LONG, LINGERING TWILIGHT IS A WONDERFUL, MYSTERIOUS TIME. You might notice Venus, brilliant above the western horizon, or the silver light of a full moon gaining power as dusk falls. As it gets really shady, on bushy heaths or around the edges of old, wild woods, you sometimes hear one of the strangest wildlife sounds of all: the churring of a nightjar. Now and then it changes pitch abruptly, but this low, drill-like call is otherwise unchanging, perhaps for minutes on end, never seemingly pausing for breath.

Clumber Park is full of wildlife action at night, but it's huge – 1,500 hectares (3,800 acres) – and to hear nightjars, it's a good idea to do a bit of reconnaissance in daylight. Look for the heathy spots, with scattered pines and high, dead branches, which make ideal nightjar perches. At night, listen for the churring; as it stops, the bird launches itself with a few wing-claps, then sets off in pursuit of moths, or a rival. Like moths, it flies silently,

WHERE
Clumber Park, Worksop, Nottinghamshire S80 3AZ.

CONTACT
The Estate Office, tel: 01909 544917;
Infoline, tel: 01909 476592;
clumberpark@nationaltrust.org.uk

GETTING THERE
The park lies between Worksop and Retford, 1.6km (1 mile) from the A1/A57 and 18km (11 miles) from the M1. By rail, travel to Worksop or Retford; by bus, travel to Carburton which is 1km (½ mile) away.

ACCESS AND FACILITIES
Parking is available throughout the park, with the main car park only 180m (200 yards) from wheelchair-friendly visitor facilities with full-access toilets, baby-changing facilities, kiosk, restaurant, and child carriers/buggies for hire. Dogs are allowed on the lead.

OPENING TIMES
Open all year round (except 16 August and 25 December). The shop and restaurant is open all year round but the times do vary throughout the year, so check before visiting.

CHARGES
Vehicle entry charge, and to visit Clumber Park's traditional walled kitchen garden.

Above: The nightjar "gapes" with its extraordinarily wide mouth to scare off intruders.

Main: Look for the nightjar's striking silhouette at dusk.

Right (top to bottom): Woodcock "roding"; it is almost impossible to spot this woodcock nesting among dead leaves; the woodcock's eyes are unusually close to the top of its head, giving excellent peripheral vision.

Below: A nightjar in flight.

Finding a nightjar

You will probably hear a nightjar before you see it, because its mottled grey-brown colouring camouflages it well against the forest floor (where it nests) or the brown bark of branches. Scan the trees with binoculars (the bigger the lenses, the more light they gather) and you should see its low, big-headed, blackbird-sized form on a branch. Unusually, the nightjar tends to perch lengthwise along branches, and this distinctive "gravy-boat" silhouette (*see above and main picture*) is a useful identifier.

guided by large eyes that enable it to see in very low light-levels. In the air, it is a fantastic bird, a wraith; wonderfully acrobatic, twisting and spinning, its long wings equalled by a long, broad tail. It makes a new call in flight: a deep, vibrant "goo-ik" that floats eerily through the darkness.

Another call note may draw your attention to a quite different night bird: a woodcock in its circuitous, territorial flight, called "roding". Alternately it calls a sharp, thin "tswick" and a deep, guttural, repeated "croak"; sometimes the croak is heard first, sometimes the whistle. The woodcock lives by day on the woodland floor, but its colours camouflage it so effectively against the fallen leaves that you're unlikely to see it unless you accidentally disturb it, at which it will dash away, swerving from side to side. It feeds at night in soft, muddy ditches and drains, and your only real hope of catching a glimpse is when it flies over the treetops at dusk – a sharp-winged, fat-bodied, long-billed silhouette, zigzagging through the air.

WHERE ELSE TO SEE
BIRDS ACTIVE AT NIGHT

Nightjars breed mainly in southern England, but scatterings of these birds are found further north as far as central Scotland.

Heathland with nightjars, woodlarks, stonechats, linnets, and meadow pipits can be found on the **Surrey Heaths**, in and around the **New Forest** (*see pp.174–175*) in Hampshire, which has Dartford warblers, too. [SE]

The **Suffolk Sandlings**, a string of heathlands close to the coast, has nightjars, woodlarks, and linnets, and they can also be heard on **Chobham Common** and other heathland in Surrey. In the **Breckland** on the Norfolk–Suffolk border (*see also* **Weeting Heath**, *pp.92–93*), nightjars are often in areas of recently clear-felled plantation. Woodcocks can be seen in similar areas, but more often over denser woodland. [SE]

Cannock Chase in Staffordshire has scattered heathlands with nightjars, and woodcocks over its conifer plantations. [M]

THROUGH THE YEAR
CLUMBER PARK

Clumber Park has rich broadleaved woodland, farmland, and open, grassy parks as well as heaths, so birds are varied all year.

Watch for buzzards and sparrowhawks displaying over the woods in **summer**, and listen for drumming great spotted woodpeckers. Nuthatches are noisy, with loud trills and whistles.

In **autumn**, fieldfares arrive in nomadic flocks, feeding in hedges until the berries are finished and then moving on to open pastures. Fallow deer are frequent and you might come across a fox or, with real luck, a badger.

In **winter**, you might find flocks of siskins, redpolls, and goldfinches feeding in alders, taking seeds from the dark cones. Treecreepers, long-tailed tits, and goldcrests are easier to see with no leaves on the deciduous trees.

Below: Clumber Park is a feast of colour in autumn.

JAN
FEB
MAR
APR
MAY
JUN
JUL
AUG
SEP
OCT
NOV
DEC

Left: Surface water drains, or "rhyns", act as wet fences.

Right (left to right): Roe deer are born in May and June; look out for the marbled white butterfly in the rough grassland; hobbies can be spotted in the air from April to October; the UK's largest grasshopper, the large marsh grasshopper, can be seen in Shapwick's meadows.

WHERE
Shapwick Heath, Shapwick, near Glastonbury, Somerset BA6 9TT; www.naturalengland.org.uk

CONTACT
Natural England, tel: 01458 860120; somerset@naturalengland.org.uk

GETTING THERE
The heath is 1km (¾ mile) north of Shapwick village and 7km (4¼ miles) west of Glastonbury. By car, access is from the A39 and B3151. The nearest train station is Castle Cary, 25km (15½ miles) away. Buses run between Castle Cary, Glastonbury, and Shapwick village. The reserve is near Route 3 of the National Cycle Network.

ACCESS AND FACILITIES
There is a car park at the Peat Moors Centre, not far from the reserve's main entrance, as well as a second car park at the other end of the reserve. There are also cycle racks at the site's entrance. There are no toilets or refreshments on site, however wheelchair access to hides is good, especially to the Mere Heath Hide, and there is also an easy-access boardwalk.

OPENING TIMES
Open all year round.

CHARGES
None.

A rarely seen dabbler
One of the rarer birds that you may be lucky to spot at Shapwick Heath, the garganey breeds in the UK during the spring and winters in Africa. It is a dabbling duck, like the shovelers, meaning that it feeds by filtering small particles from water passing through its bill, rather than by diving into the water. Garganeys take off from water swiftly and easily, using a fast twisting motion. Despite their secretive nature, if you do see one it is easily identified by the white stripe over the eyes.

Main and far right: Shapwick Heath was once completely covered by the sea; today, otters play in the river shallows.

THRIVING WETLANDS

SCAN THE SKY ABOVE SHAPWICK HEATH ON A SUNNY DAY IN MAY and you have a strong chance of spotting a hobby. In fact, you may see a flock of 30 or more of these small falcons hawking for dragonflies, as the locally breeding birds are joined this month by their migrant cousins at this large, historic nature reserve.

Lying in the heart of the Somerset Levels, Shapwick Heath was a bare peat-working just a few years ago, but it is now one of the finest examples of wetland flora and fauna in the UK. The star attractions are the river otters, which have around four territories within the reserve. The best time to see them is at dawn or dusk, from one of the Shapwick hides; but be patient and quiet – if alarmed, otters dive into water and swim off, and you'll just catch a glimpse of their sleek, glossy fur shimmering away under the surface. The real rarities here are the lesser silver diving beetles – an endangered species that is particularly fond of the still, peat-rich waters of this reserve. Large

Above: Visit at dusk in winter to witness the huge starling roost.

Shapwick Heath's many habitats – from reedbed and fen to meadow and woodland – make it a wildlife wonderland.

THROUGH THE YEAR
SHAPWICK HEATH

Dragonflies, butterflies, and breeding birds are the main attractions in **summer**. Look for the beautiful white admiral butterfly in a woodland glade off the pathway to the Mere Heath Hide.

Passage waders and an autumn roost of little egrets are among the best sights in **autumn**.

Visit in **winter** for one of the greatest avian spectacles in Europe. At dusk each day starlings in their hundreds of thousands and sometimes millions (six million have been counted) descend on the reserve to roost. A wide variety of wildfowl can also be seen during winter.

WHERE ELSE TO SEE
PEAT-WORKINGS

Old peat-workings make excellent nature reserves, once the peat extraction has stopped, because peat only forms in wetlands – so under conservational management, the wetlands revert to a perfect habitat for many different kinds of animals and flora.

Westhay Moor nature reserve, near Shapwick, is an old peat-working with remnants of a raised bog that is now managed for wildlife. Its resident plants and animals are similar to those at Shapwick, but it also features carnivorous sundew plants, which are unusual and fun. [SW]

Catcott Lows, Somerset, is grassland in summer, but flooded during the winter, making it a great place to see wintering wildfowl between November and April. [SW]

The **Humberhead Peatlands**, South Yorkshire, is a peatland remnant of moor, bog, and fen that once surrounded the head of the Humber estuary. [N]

marsh grasshoppers live in the sphagnum moss bogs, and the reed- and carr-fringed pools play host to a bird that can only be found in the UK during the summer: the small garganey duck, which lives in the northern tropics of Africa for the rest of the year. Other summer migrants include various common warblers, which come to the woodland and fen of the reserve to join the resident Cetti's warblers, water rails, and reed buntings. If you're walking the tracks in the early morning or around dusk, you may catch sight of a roe deer as it slips quietly across a path or hovers on a woodland edge, or see barn owls hunting over the grassland.

The wide range of habitats here allows for a rich flora and wide diversity of insects. The hay meadows are traditionally managed by rare breeds of cattle and sheep, and are covered in wild flowers, including the southern marsh orchids. The flowers draw in butterflies and dragonflies, such as the hairy dragonfly and marbled white butterfly. Even the drains that act as "wet fences" support life, harbouring greater water dock, yellow flag iris, purple loosestrife, and the beautiful frogbit – a tiny waterlily that floats on the surface, protecting the tadpoles and fish hiding beneath.

JAN FEB MAR APR MAY JUN JUL AUG SEP OCT NOV DEC

THE WILD PENINSULA

A RECTANGULAR SLAB OF PALE LIMESTONE TOPPED by sandstone hills, all but detached from the south coast of Wales, the Gower Peninsula is a wonderful destination for the geologist, geographer, archaeologist, and wildlife enthusiast, with its big estuary, extensive saltmarshes, sand dunes, beaches, woods, moors, and reedbeds. Not least among its charms are the limestone cliffs and clifftop grasslands that run along its southern coast, from Mumbles Head to the magnificent Worm's Head, reaching far out into Carmarthen Bay. Beautiful panoramas extend across the Bristol Channel to Exmoor, Ilfracombe, Hartland Point, and Lundy.

The mild climate and south-facing prospect ensure a long, early growing season. In May, look out for the yellow whitlow-grass that grows on cliffs such as Pwll Du Head, and at Pennard Castle – it grows nowhere else in the UK. The open grassland above the cliff is at its finest at this time of year: ungrazed areas with deeper soils,

WHERE
Gower Peninsula, Swansea, South Wales;
www.welshwildlife.org
www.the-gower.com

CONTACT
Wildlife Trust of South and West Wales,
tel: 01656 724100;
info@welshwildlife.org

GETTING THERE
By car, follow the M4. You can access Gower from a number of different junctions. For South Gower and Mumbles, take junction 42, which will take you on the Swansea Bay road. For North Gower, take junction 47. By bus, National Express coaches run from London Victoria, Gatwick, and Heathrow airports, and stops around Yorkshire and the Midlands to Swansea bus station.

ACCESS AND FACILITIES
The peninsula covers 181 sq km (70 square miles) and is home to 19 nature reserves, most well served by rural businesses. At Rhossili and Llanmadoc there are pubs and cafés with full access for wheelchairs and pushchairs, plus car parking.

CHARGES
You are free to roam on much of the peninsula, while respecting private property; there may be charges for some reserves.

Wild ponies

Llanrhidian, a small, remote village on the north Gower coast, has spectacular views over the estuary. It is the least populated part of the peninsula, and has become a haven for wildlife, including wild marsh ponies, which graze among the rare wildfowl on the sweet marsh grasses, marsh mallow, and sea lavender that grows around the saltmarshes. The north Gower marshes extend for 13 km (8 miles) from Llanrhidian to Carmarthen Bay, and are designated internationally important wetlands.

Main: The limestone cliffs of the Gower Peninsula.

Left: Bladder wrack seaweed.

Right (left to right): Worm's Head, Gower; burnet roses grow on the sand dunes at Nicholaston Burrows; a fulmar calling.

Right panel (top and bottom): Visit Worm's Head for seabirds, such as this shag; bluebells flower on Gower's clifftops.

such as Long Hole Cliff and Overton Cliff, are thick with heath, gorse, hawthorn, blackthorn, and juniper thickets. On the poorer soils and well-trodden areas you're more likely to find typical limestone plants such as early purple orchids, shocking-pink splashes of bloody cranesbill, and the yellow carline thistle. Bird's-foot trefoil and kidney vetch abound, and there are whorls of the rare, green, Portland spurge. Look out for salt-tolerant plants, such as sea campion, golden samphire, rock sea-lavender, scurvygrass, sea beet, spring squill, and thrift, and the only maritime fern – sea spleenwort. Rarities include hoary rockrose, goldilocks aster, and wild asparagus, which has been greatly reduced by collectors and, like any rarity, should be left alone.

Over the sea there's a good chance of seeing passing Manx shearwaters and gannets, and the clifftops have ravens, jackdaws, choughs, stonechats, linnets, and yellowhammers. Buzzards are common on Gower, while Oxwich Marsh has reed and sedge warblers, herons, and kingfishers.

WHERE ELSE TO SEE
LIMESTONE CLIFFS

Hard cliffs – made up of granite, sandstone, or limestone – occur mainly in the south of England; northwest and southwest Wales; west and north Scotland; and the north coast of Northern Ireland.

Limestone cliffs and their associated flora and insect life can be enjoyed on the Dorset coast at **Portland** (see pp.90–91). **Durlston Head** near Swanage, Dorset, has Adonis blue butterflies and the extremely localized Lulworth skipper, while the cliffs west of **Hope's Nose** in Devon are great for limestone grassland flowers. [SW]

North Wales has areas of limestone grassland above cliffs at the Great Orme, **Conwy** (see pp.278–279). On Anglesey, maritime heathland around **South Stack** and **Penrhosfeilw** has flowers and butterflies as well as choughs, ravens, and stonechats. [W]

The great cliffs of **Bempton** (see pp.104–105) and **Flamborough Head** (see pp.252–253) in Yorkshire are limestone; areas of grassland between fields and along the cliff remain good for wildlife. [N]

MAY

With its estuary, saltmarshes, sand dunes, beaches, woods, moors, and reedbeds, Gower has everything.

THROUGH THE YEAR
GOWER PENINSULA

In **summer**, watch for gannets, shearwaters, and fulmars offshore, and, from Worm's Head, large flocks of common scoters. Listen for the distinct, summery warble of the many species of grasshopper and cricket resident on Gower. Check the stony, grassy clearings on the slopes above Mumbles Head for grayling, common and small blue, brown argus, and dark green fritillary butterflies, among the showy plants of red valerian, yellow-wort, common centaury, and pyramidal orchids.

The majestic oak and ash woodland of Parkwood, west of Swansea, is a great place to enjoy the rich colours of **autumn**, along with buzzards, woodpeckers, horseshoe bats, and a wealth of archaeological treasures dating back 14,000 years.

The cliffs are bleak in **winter**, but look for ravens and peregrines, and purple sandpipers and turnstones on the shore below.

Below: Gower has 16 species of grasshopper and cricket.

JAN
FEB
MAR
APR
JUN
JUL
AUG
SEP
OCT
NOV
DEC

Left (left to right):
Fingringhoe Wick; the River Colne estuary looking towards Brightlingsea, Essex.

Right (left to right):
Nightingale eggs in a nest; a female sitting on her nest with a grub in her beak.

Panel (below right):
Look for chestnut-brown tail feathers to identify a nightingale.

WHERE
Fingringhoe Wick, South Green Road, Fingringhoe, Essex, CO5 7DN; www.essexwt.org.uk

CONTACT
Essex Wildlife Trust, tel: 01206 729678; fingringhoe@essexwt.org.uk

GETTING THERE
The reserve lies 4.8km (3 miles) southeast of Colchester. Follow the B1025 from Colchester to Mersea for 4.8km (3 miles). Cross the Roman River bridge; immediately turn left, and then follow the brown signs to the nature reserve.

ACCESS AND FACILITIES
At the visitor centre there are refreshments, a gift shop, toilets, and baby-changing facilities. There is a free car park with some disabled parking. Out on the reserve you will find a picnic area, a short nature trail suitable for people in wheelchairs, and bird hides (some easy access). There is also a viewing tower and observation room with panoramic views.

OPENING TIMES
Open daily, 9am–5pm.

CHARGES
None, but the Essex Wildlife Trust does invite donations.

Birdsong at night
A songbird singing in the night is not bound to be a nightingale. Blackbirds and song thrushes both regularly sing after nightfall, as do sedge warblers. In cities, robins reacting to street lights may sing in the dead of night, and a robin may have been the original "nightingale" that sang in Berkeley Square. During the day, the beautiful warbling of a blackcap can be mistaken for a nightingale, although it lacks the latter's distinctive staccato, measured delivery, and startling variety.

Main: A nightingale singing in a hawthorn hedge.

NIGHTINGALES SINGING

A FEW KILOMETRES TO THE SOUTH OF COLCHESTER IN EAST ANGLIA lies the estuary of the River Colne: a wild expanse of saltmarsh and mudflats flanking winding tidal creeks. Fifty years ago much of its western shore, near Fingringhoe, was a barren landscape created by industrial gravel extraction, and hardly an obvious haven for wildlife. But the Essex Wildlife Trust had a vision of what it could become, and in 1961 it acquired the site and set about turning it into a nature reserve.

Thanks to the Trust's careful management, Fingringhoe Wick has now matured into a rich mixture of habitats including ponds, reedbeds, grassland, gorse heathland, dense scrub, and woodland, all overlooking the tidal estuary. Bright with flowers and teeming with insect life, it is a magnet for migrant birds, including that most famous and charismatic of summer visitors: the nightingale.

Above: Nightingale chicks demanding food.

JAN

FEB

MAR

APR

MAY

JUN

JUL

AUG

SEP

OCT

NOV

DEC

The nightingale has tremendous stamina: many fly home to West Africa from the UK in one non-stop flight.

THROUGH THE YEAR
FINGRINGHOE WICK

Summer is the best time to see the more colourful wild flowers at Fingringhoe Wick, including dog roses and sea-lavender on the saltmarsh. Dragonflies and damselflies can also be seen, along with butterflies and other insects, basking snakes, and lizards.

In **autumn** the summer migrants leave for warmer climes, including the nightingales and their fledged broods, but other birds arrive from further north to spend the winter on the reserve and the nearby estuary. They include masses of waders and wildfowl, especially avocets and large flocks of brent geese.

The shorebirds are the highlight of **winter**, but the reserve can also be a good place to watch for brown hares, foxes, stoats, and weasels. You may also see common seals in the estuary.

WHERE ELSE TO SEE
NIGHTINGALES

Nightingales are summer migrants from Africa that arrive in April and leave in September. They do not penetrate very far north, rarely straying beyond a line drawn from the Severn to the Humber, and the main breeding populations are in Kent and Essex.

Many nightingales can be heard in the ancient oak woodland at **Northward Hill** reserve in north Kent (*see pp.54–55*). There is a carpet of bluebells in early May when the nightingales are in full voice. [SE]

Wolves Wood near Hadleigh in Suffolk is another ancient woodland managed by the RSPB. The nightingales sing most sweetly in early morning. [SE]

The evening nightingale walks at Paxton Pits Nature Reserve in **Little Paxton**, Cambridgeshire, attract hundreds of visitors every year. [SE]

Sussex Wildlife Trust organizes evening nightingale walks at its reserve at **Woods Mill**, near Henfield, West Sussex. You can also hear nightingales at the nearby RSPB reserve at Pulborough Brooks. [SE]

Each spring the Wick attracts around 30 nesting pairs, and by May the males are in full song as they compete for the best breeding territories. Their wonderfully exuberant, inventive song is justly celebrated, and few people can fail to be amazed by its rich variety of clear, mellow, fluting notes, staccato phrases, trills, and strange croaks and chuckles, especially when delivered on a warm, still night when it is often the only bird singing. And here the birds' territories are so close together that they almost sing in chorus – an unforgettable experience.

If anything, the magical quality of the nightingale's song is enhanced by the bird's secretive, skulking nature. It nearly always sings from dense cover – by day and by night – and a typical "view" of a nightingale consists of little more than a dark shape in thick scrub. You may see one flit from bush to bush, revealing itself as a rather drab brown bird, slightly larger than a robin, but with a distinctive chestnut tail. That glimpse of chestnut is often all you get, but just occasionally a nightingale may forget itself and emerge to perch in full view, open its beak, and perform. At such times disbelief soon fades into simple joy at the wonder of natural creation.

WHERE
The Farne Islands lie 2.5–7.5km (1½–5 miles) off the Northumberland coast.

CONTACT
National Trust, tel: 01665 720651 (general enquiries); farneislands@nationaltrust.org.uk For boat trips, tel: 01665 721099 (Infoline); enquiries@farne-islands.com

GETTING THERE
Boat trips run every day from Seahouses harbour (weather permitting) in spring and summer; some include a landing on Staple Island. The nearest rail station to Seahouses is Chathill, 6km (4 miles) away. The closest bus services – nos. 401 and 501 – run to Dunstanburgh Castle and Seahouses.

ACCESS AND FACILITIES
You can park in Seahouses opposite the harbour. On Inner Farne there's a wheelchair-friendly walkway round the island. Staple Island is rocky and not recommended for disabled visitors. There are full-access toilets on Inner Farne and near the harbour in the centre of Seahouses.

OPENING TIMES
Daily trips in summer to Staple Island (morning) and Inner Farne (afternoon).

CHARGES
There are charges for the boat trips.

Sightseeing by boat
On your boat trip around the Farne Islands you're likely to see rafts of birds – especially guillemots, razorbills, and puffins – resting and feeding on the surface of the water. Inner Farne is the largest of the islands, and you can go ashore here, subject to a small landing charge. If you're looking for sandwich terns, head for the centre of the island. These birds are more sensitive to human disturbance than those on the rocks, so tread quietly, and you may be rewarded with a stunning display of courtship dancing.

Above (left to right): Arctic terns courting; shags mating; the male eider's black-and-white plumage is quite different to the female's brown.
Main: The bird sanctuary and breeding colony of Staple Island, one of the Farne Islands.

FARNE HORIZONS

LYING JUST OFF THE NORTHUMBRIAN COAST, the Farne Islands number 15 to 28, depending on the tide. Uninhabited by people, they provide a haven for thousands of breeding seabirds; mainly puffins, guillemots, and Arctic terns, but also shags, razorbills, kittiwakes, eiders, and several other species. What sets the Farnes apart from other great birdwatching islands is just how close you can be to the birds. You can see everything from the regular boat trips that run out of Seahouses, but for an overwhelming experience, take a boat with landing rights, and step ashore.

The National Trust opens two of the main islands of the archipelago – Staple Island and Inner Farne – for half of each day during the breeding season (May–July), in the morning and afternoon respectively. As you stand on the islands, the birds are everywhere – at close range, on the cliffs, on rocks and grassy slopes, and wheeling in the air around you. Puffins hurtle past, often with beaks bursting with sand eels, heading for the burrows in the turf in which they breed. Arctic terns defend their patch noisily and with physical force. Be warned, a hat is essential – terns are quite adept at drawing blood! Otherwise your needs are rather few: binoculars are hardly necessary, but make sure you are armed with plenty of camera memory or film – there are photo opportunities at every step. And the wild seabirds, going about their daily business, seem oblivious to human presence.

Up to 55,000 pairs of puffins – that comical, instantly recognizable, and beloved seabird – nest in turf burrows on Northumberland's Farne Islands.

Birds thrive here for several reasons: their protection and careful management by the National Trust, their isolation, and the abundant food supply in the surrounding waters. A healthy population of some 6,000 grey seals and regular sightings of harbour porpoises demonstrate the richness of the seas. Scuba-diving trips are also available for those who want to see the underwater world at first hand, exploring the wildlife of the rocks, reefs, and shipwrecks.

Inset: Puffins rub their beaks together when "billing" as part of courtship.
Below (left to right): The pinnacles of Staple Island; an eider nesting.

WHERE ELSE TO SEE
ISLAND SEABIRDS

Islands around our coastline often harbour important seabird breeding populations, especially those that are free of predators, such as rats. All those mentioned here are easily accessible by wildlife-watching boat trips, and often include a period of time on the island itself.

In Scotland, at the mouth of the **Firth of Forth** (see pp.296–297) and farther out, on the **Isle of May** and **Bass Rock** (see pp.168–169) there is a similar range of species. Bass Rock also has 40,000 pairs of gannets, whose presence makes it look as though it has snowed. The western isles of Scotland provide numerous seabird spectacles – try the Treshnish Isles off **Mull** (see pp.226–227). [SC]

Coquet Island, off the coast of Northumberland, is especially important for terns, including the rare roseate tern. [N]

Lundy [SW], **Skomer** (see pp.150–151), and **Skokholm** [W] in the Bristol Channel are renowned for puffins and Manx shearwaters.

THROUGH THE YEAR
THE FARNE ISLANDS

In **summer** the breeding season is in full swing, and the islands are covered in birds and their young. If you're including a trip to Lindisfarne, be sure to look for the delicate creamy-yellow flowers of the Lindisfarne helleborine on the dunes in July–August.

As the bird breeding season draws to a close in **autumn**, the focus shifts to the grey seals, who use the islands as pupping grounds. Watch the skies over the sea for a constant stream of passing seabirds, including terns and skuas in autumn and little auks after northerly winter gales. Boat trips to the islands stop at the end of September.

The islands are home to wintering flocks of pale-bellied brent geese, wigeons, and other wildfowl. Budle Bay, near Lindisfarne, is an especially good birdwatching spot in **winter**.

Below: The young Arctic tern is well protected by its fierce parents.

JAN
FEB
MAR
APR
MAY
JUN
JUL
AUG
SEP
OCT
NOV
DEC

Left (left to right): The heather and gorse of Thursley Common; young bell heather springs up following a fire on the heath the previous year.

Right (left to right): The long, shiny, grey-brown body of the slow-worm, which is in fact a legless lizard; common lizards are in abundance at Thursley.

WHERE
Thursley Common, near Godalming, Surrey GU8 6LW; www.naturalengland.org.uk

CONTACT
Natural England Sussex, tel: 01273 476595; sussex.surrey@naturalengland.org.uk

GETTING THERE
The reserve is north of the village of Thursley, 5km (3 miles) southwest of Milford and 8km (5 miles) southwest of Godalming. By car, access is either via the A3, which runs to the east of the reserve; the Thursley village road to the south; or the Thursley to Elstead road to the west. The nearest train station is in Milford. A regular bus service runs from Godalming to Thursley via Milford.

ACCESS AND FACILITIES
The Moat car park, to the northwest of the reserve and accessed via the Elstead road, has picnic tables and limited disabled access to parts of the reserve. There's limited parking in Thursley village. The nearest facilities are in the village or at the National Trust's Whitley Visitor Centre, 3km (1¾ miles) to the east, on the opposite side of the A3.

OPENING TIMES
Open all year round.

CHARGES
None.

Nesting and laying

Grass snakes are easily identified by the distinctive yellow-and-black collar behind the head. Towards the end of May, they are busy looking for nest sites. Their favourite places are patches of rotting vegetation, where the process of decomposition generates the warmth they need. The female will lay between 10 and 40 cream-coloured, leathery eggs, which hatch in early autumn. The young chip themselves out of the shell with the help of their "egg-tooth".

Main: Britain's only venomous snake, the adder, favours heathland, such as Thursley. **Right, above:** The sand lizard is a rare sight in the UK.

HEATHLAND REPTILES

THE SANDY HEATHS OF SURREY ARE WONDERFULLY WILD LANDSCAPES in the heart of commuter country. Just a few miles southwest of Guildford lies one of the most rewarding – Thursley Common – a broad expanse of heather, gorse, birch, and scattered pine surrounding a peat bog dotted with dark bog pools, cotton grass, bog asphodel, and insectivorous sundew plants. In May it is a prime location for reptiles: on cool mornings at least five species can be seen basking in the spring sun, warming up for a day's hunting.

Reptiles are notoriously elusive, slipping into cover at the slightest hint of danger, but at Thursley they can be quite bold. When you step on to the boardwalk leading east over the boggy ground from the Moat Pond, watch where you walk. The older boards are favourite basking sites for common lizards – small, sleek, brown or greenish-brown reptiles with dark stripes down their backs. There are lots of these small lizards, but if you are very lucky

Above: A grass snake shedding its skin.

THROUGH THE YEAR
THURSLEY COMMON

Throughout the **summer** Thursley Common is alive with the shimmering wings of dragonflies. At least 26 species have been recorded here – a record number for southern England. You may also see their predators over the Common; hobbies – swift-flying falcons – are agile enough to catch and eat dragonflies in mid-air.

Dragonflies keep flying until the first frosts of **autumn**, and some may fall victim to the great grey shrikes that arrive to spend winter here. Hen harriers and merlins can be seen hunting over the heathland.

Winter is a hard time for the resident Dartford warblers, which suffer badly in cold weather because, unlike most other insect-eating warblers, they do not migrate to the tropics. Large flocks of redwings and fieldfares may arrive to roost on the boggy ground in winter.

Adders are not aggressive to people, but will bite if threatened. The bite is painful and needs medical attention.

WHERE ELSE TO SEE
NATIVE REPTILES

The adder, grass snake, common lizard, and slow-worm are widespread in mainland Britain.

The Dorset heaths at **Studland** and **Arne** (*see pp.138–139*) are among the last refuges of the rare sand lizard and smooth snake, and have healthy populations of common lizards and adders. **Shapwick Heath** (*see pp.120–121*) on the Somerset Levels is another excellent spot for reptiles. [SW]

The heaths of the **New Forest** (*see pp.174–175*) in Hampshire are good places to look for reptiles. If you can't find them, visit the **Holiday Hill Reptiliary** near Lyndhurst, which has all six native species. Many reptiles live in woodlands, grasslands, and, in the case of grass snakes, wetlands. Watch out for them in locations such as **Bookham Commons** (*see pp.170–171*), in Kent. [SE]

you may see the much rarer sand lizard – a chunkier reptile with dark blotches and, on males, emerald-green flanks that are at their most vivid in spring. The males display these breeding colours to intimidate each other, and they fight fiercely over the browner females.

Even more spectacular are the contests between rival male adders, which rear up and "dance" together as each tries to force the other to the ground. Britain's only venomous snake, the adder preys on small mammals, which it seizes and swallows whole. It favours lowland heaths, such as Thursley, where you may spot one coiled on a clump of heather soaking up the sun, recognizable by its copper eyes and the dark zigzag down its back. The much rarer smooth snake has the same basking habit and can look similar, but has dark spots rather than a continuous zigzag. It preys on other lizards, including the snake-like slow-worm that is also found at Thursley, subduing them by constriction. The much bigger grass snake targets frogs, and is semi-aquatic – a ripple in one of the peaty bog pools could betray one swimming across it like an eel, holding its head clear of the water so it can test the air for the scent of prey with its flickering forked tongue.

JAN
FEB
MAR
APR
MAY
JUN
JUL
AUG
SEP
OCT
NOV
DEC

JUNE

Where to Go: June

As midsummer nears, in the far north, nights are so short that it barely gets dark: the Shetland Islands' "simmer dim" is a remarkable experience, where the sun barely dips below the horizon. In the south the evenings are long and bright; badgers emerge well before dark, and even barn owls, working hard to find enough food for growing families, must hunt by day.

Fields are ablaze with scarlet poppies, the most obvious and common arable field "weeds"; most wildflower populations have dwindled to a few, specially protected meadows. These are worth seeking out, not only for their almost-forgotten flowers and scent, but also to see and hear the wonderful abundance of insects that go with them. A traditional flowery meadow is a

WILD IN THE CITY

CHICHESTER CATHEDRAL Peregrine-watching in the city.

PARKS AND GRASSLANDS

ARNE A great block of lowland with swirls of reed swamps.

WOODLANDS

ROCKINGHAM FOREST Fallow deer live in the forest.

CHICHESTER CATHEDRAL
WEST SUSSEX [SE]

A 14th-century church may seem like an unlikely bird-nesting place, but Chichester Cathedral was chosen by a pair of peregrines as the perfect place to breed.
See pp.134–135

The soaring cathedral structure defies both gravity and belief, in much the same way as the peregrines during their awesome displays.

ARNE
ISLE OF PURBECK [SW]

One of the best places to see the Dartford warbler, this rich heathland also shelters grass snakes, adders, and the rarer smooth snakes.
See pp.138–139

ROCKINGHAM FOREST
NORTHAMPTONSHIRE [N]

One of the few places you might see hawfinches and the scarce hazel dormouse, treading carefully among foxes, badgers, polecats, stoats, and deer.
See pp.140–141

CREEKSIDE NATURE CONSERVATION CENTRE
LONDON [SE]

Witness the marvel of mini nature reserves on the "green roofs" of large industrial buildings, here dedicated to preserving the endangered black redstart.
See pp.156–157

The Downs tumble in steep, emerald-green, grassy slopes to scattered hawthorn and bramble brakes, where they melt into peaceful valleys.

WYE DOWNS
WYE, KENT [SE]

Twenty-one species of orchid can be found on these chalklands, in turn attracting countless butterflies.
See pp.148–149

HALDON FOREST
EXETER, DEVON [SW]

Wandering among the broad-leaved trees of this forest, you're likely to see one of our rarest breeding raptors: the honey buzzard.
See pp.144–145

OLD MOOR AND FAIRBURN INGS
YORKSHIRE [N]

These wonderful nature reserves were formed on brownfield sites as a result of mining subsidence; they are now rich in birds, wildflowers, insects, and other wildlife.
See pp.156–157

TATE MODERN
LONDON [SE]

One of the most accessible peregrine nesting sites is on the old power station that houses this art gallery, with telescopes for close-up views.
See pp.134–135

ASTON ROWANT
THE CHILTERNS, OXFORDSHIRE [SE]

These chalk downs overflow with fragrant orchids and wild herbs in the summer months.
See pp.148–149

WISTMAN'S WOOD
DEVON [SW]

Pedunculate oaks dwarfed into tiny twisted trees to make this small, ancient wood, where they grow among gigantic, moss-covered granite boulders to eerie, magical effect.
See pp.160–161

The wood's vast, trackless expanses of heather and shattered granite have an air of savage mystery that is both hostile and exhilarating.

CANVEY WICK
CANVEY ISLAND, ESSEX [SE]

This ex-oil refinery site is now a hotbed of biodiversity, with lizards, snakes, badgers, water voles, songbirds, and the rare shrill carder-bee.
see pp.156–157

WEST PENTIRE
CORNWALL [SW]

The poppies and corn marigolds are in full colour here in June, where they live alongside the rare Venus's looking glass and the lesser snapdragon.
See pp.136–137

CANNOCK CHASE
STAFFORDSHIRE [N]

You can see the rare Dartford warbler here, together with nightjars and woodlarks in June. Green tiger beetles burrow into the ground to make nests.
See pp.138–139

THE WOOD OF CREE
DUMFRIES & GALLOWAY [SC]

This ancient forest in southern Scotland has a large population of kestrels, sparrowhawks, hen harriers, buzzards, merlins, and even golden eagles.
See pp.144–145

Previous page: Field poppies.

tremendous eye-opener, and a reminder of what we have lost elsewhere. Chalk downs are great places for walking among flowers and the butterflies that feed on their nectar, including the iridescent common blue, strong-flying dark green fritillary, and the pretty, white-speckled marbled white. These chalklands represent an entirely different world to the intensive farmland that surrounds them and are worth seeking out in summer, when you can enjoy them at their very best. But there is also wildlife to be found in the most unexpected places: fast-flying, dynamic peregrines, for example, will be nesting and breeding on tall buildings in many of our busiest cities, from London and Chichester to Birmingham, Manchester, and Glasgow.

UPLANDS

WHITBARROW Butterflies seek out the limestone's wildflowers.

WETLANDS

STRUMPSHAW FEN Booming bitterns hide in these reedbeds.

COAST

NEWBOROUGH WARREN Botanical treasures grow among the dunes.

WHITBARROW
CUMBRIA [N]

Britain's most extraordinary limestone pavement bursts into colour in June, as fritillaries, wild thyme, and wild strawberries grow from its fissures.
See pp.146 147

CWM CLYDACH
SWANSEA [W]

The woodland of Cwm Clydach grows on steep slopes down to the Clydach gorge, where you can see spectacular waterfalls and a great variety of butterflies, fungi, and woodland birds.
See pp.154–155

STRUMPSHAW FEN
NORFOLK [SE]

Bird, plant, and butterfly enthusiasts will find plenty to see in June, including the magnificent swallowtail butterfly.
See pp.152–153

NEWBOROUGH WARREN
ANGLESEY [W]

The dune slacks hide the Warren's best treasures: dune helleborines and many wild orchids grow up through the silver-leaved creeping willow.
See pp.142–143

GAIT BARROWS
CARNFORTH, LANCASHIRE [N]

Over 800 different species of moth fly above these limestone pavements, among damselflies, dragonflies, butterflies – including the rare Duke of Burgundy – and tuneful woodland birds.
See pp.146–147

BLACKTOFT SANDS
YORKSHIRE [N]

The largest tidal reedbeds in England are visited by many breeding birds, including the rare corn bunting and the tree sparrow. Many animals depend upon its shallow waters.
See pp.158–159

DUNGENESS
KENT [SE]

The stark shingle landscape of Dungeness is softened by salt- and wind-tolerant plants, whose flowers attract the Sussex emerald moth and the brown-banded carder-bee.
See pp.162–163

THE SOUTH DOWNS
WEST SUSSEX [SE]

Nearly half of Britain's orchid species can be found here, including musk and bee orchids, among other rare wild flowers. You can also see foxes, badgers, deer, and rabbits.
See pp.136–137

LAKE VYRNWY
POWYS [W]

This long, fork-tipped reservoir is a manmade wonder, made even more special by the birdsong that rings through its surrounding woodlands.
See pp.154–155

> While away a summer's day amid the shining network of gentle waterways that form the Norfolk Broads.

THE LONDON WETLAND CENTRE
LONDON [SE]

A wonderful wetland in the heart of the capital, with a huge range of waterfowl to be seen. Dragonflies and damselflies hover over the waters.
See pp.152–153

SKOMER ISLAND
WEST WALES [W]

Take a 20-minute boat trip from the coast to see the thousands of sea birds that come here to breed in summer, including that comical bird, the puffin.
See pp.150–151

CHESIL BEACH
DORSET [SW]

This long, wild, and windswept shingle beach has been colonized by a host of species, from breeding birds to rare flora; the famous Abbotsbury swannery is nearby.
See pp.162–163

RANWORTH BROAD
NORFOLK [SE]

Wildflowers such as marsh valerian and marsh fern attract butterflies and dragonflies here in June. Cetti's warblers hide in low bushes and great crested grebes swim elegantly on the water.
See pp.152–153

WHERE
Chichester Cathedral, St Richards Walk,
Chichester, West Sussex, PO19 1QB;
www.rspb.org.uk

CONTACT
RSPB Regional Office, tel: 01273 775333.
Webcam footage and news of the birds is at
www.chichester.co.uk and www.rspb.org.uk

GETTING THERE
By car, take the A27 exit from the M27, then
follow signs for the city centre. By rail or bus,
travel to Chichester; on coming out of the
station, turn immediately left and walk across
the Cathedral Green.

ACCESS AND FACILITIES
The RSPB peregrine viewpoint is in the
grounds of the Cloisters Café, where there
are telescopes; footage from the nest
camera runs in the cathedral's restaurant,
accessible for wheelchairs and buggies.
Full-access toilets are available in the
cathedral restaurant, and there are disabled
parking spaces nearby, on West Street.

OPENING TIMES
The grounds are open at all times; the RSPB
camera and manned viewpoint operate April
to June, 10am–5pm (4pm on Sundays).

CHARGES
Only for car parking in the city centre.

Breeding success

During the 1960s the peregrine population in
Britain was almost wiped out by crop pesticides.
The birds accumulated the poisons in their
bodies by taking seed-eating prey such as
pigeons, with the result that their eggshells
thinned and collapsed during incubation. In 1972,
DDT was banned, and the birds started to return
to areas they had deserted. The breeding success
of the Chichester peregrines marks a real
turn-around in the fortunes of the species.

Above (top and bottom): Peregrine in flight;
Chichester cathedral offers many vantage points.

Below: An adult female peregrine feeds two juveniles
on wood pigeon. When the peregrines are very young,
they are known as "eyases".

Right panel (top and bottom): A peregrine adult
and juvenile play, mid-air – this is how the adult falcon
teaches its young to hunt; the cathedral spire.

Main: The fastest animal on Earth, the peregrine is about the size and weight of a crow. **Inset:** Juvenile peregrine.

CHICHESTER'S HIGH FLIERS

THE MEDIEVAL CATHEDRALS OF BRITAIN ARE AMONG THE NATION'S most breathtaking buildings – soaring
structures of stone and glass that defy both gravity and belief. Chichester Cathedral in West Sussex is a fine
example, largely 14th century, but with a spire that, owing to its unfortunate collapse in 1861, was rebuilt by the
Victorian architect George Gilbert Scott. An enthusiast for the Gothic revival, he ornamented it with a splendid
array of battlements and pinnacles, and in 1994 these caught the eye of an airborne visitor – a peregrine falcon.

The peregrine is the ultimate bird of prey. Eagles are bigger, ospreys more spectacular, but nothing is faster
or more thrilling than the bird-hunting peregrine. Big, burly, long-winged, it patrols high in the sky, singles out an
airborne victim such as a pigeon, then dives in a high-speed "stoop" on half-folded wings to collide with its target
at shattering speeds of up to 290 kph (180 mph), killing it on impact.

Above: Peregrines like to roost on ledges, at great heights.

JAN
FEB
MAR
APR
MAY
JUN
JUL
AUG
SEP
OCT
NOV
DEC

Peregrines are bird hunters, taking a vast range of species – from a thrush to a mallard – but pigeons are a favourite prey.

WHERE ELSE TO SEE
URBAN PEREGRINES

The peregrine is a bird of mountains and cliffs, so its strongholds in the wild are the uplands and rocky coasts of the north and west of the British Isles. However, it has recently started using tall buildings as both roosting and nesting sites. The events below are part of the RSPB's "Aren't birds brilliant!" project, and details may change depending on access to the sites and the presence of breeding birds.

One of the most accessible peregrine nesting sites is in London, on the old power station that houses the **Tate Modern** art gallery. The RSPB organizes a peregrine-watching event in June with telescopes set up to give superb views of the birds. [SE]

A similar event is run by the RSPB in the city centre of **Manchester**, where peregrines have a regular nesting site on a tower block. [N]

A pair of peregrines has taken to nesting in the Clock Tower of the city hall in **Cardiff**, and live pictures of them are shown on screens within the nearby National Museum of Cardiff. [SW]

THROUGH THE YEAR
CHICHESTER'S PEREGRINES

The peregrine family remains on or around the cathedral spire until **autumn**, when the female and young birds disperse to hunt over the nearby tidal estuaries of Chichester and Pagham Harbours.

Even in **winter** the nest site is not deserted, because the male peregrine usually roosts on the spire throughout the season. Like the other peregrines he hunts over the nearby estuaries, but may also target starlings near the cathedral.

The female peregrine returns to the nest in **spring**, when the peregrines can be seen performing spectacular aerial displays together. The female lays her clutch of four eggs, but does not start incubating until all the eggs are laid. All of the nestlings hatch at once about a month later.

The male peregrine sizing up Chichester Cathedral in the winter of late 1994 was not hunting. It was looking for a secure roost for the night. Before long, a female was attracted to the spire. A nestbox was provided, but nothing happened. It was only when the Sussex Ornithological Society installed an improved nestbox in 2001 that the female – now accompanied by a new male – laid four eggs. These proved infertile, but the following spring the pair hatched four chicks. Since then the same birds have raised three or four young every year.

In 1994 the RSPB installed a camera overlooking the nest, giving intimate views of the nestlings and their parents. These can be shared by anyone visiting the cathedral from early April to June, when telescopes are set up in the cathedral grounds to provide stunning close-ups of the young peregrines as they perch on the pinnacles and play in the air around the spire. You may even see a parent bird returning with prey, and while the nestlings are in the nest you can watch on live TV as their mother carefully tears up the food and feeds them one by one. It is a riveting insight into the private life of this extraordinary, iconic bird.

WHERE
West Pentire, Crantock, Cornwall, TR7 1PJ;
www.cornwallwildlifetrust.org.uk

CONTACT
Cornwall Wildlife Trust, tel: 01872 273939;
info@cornwt.demon.co.uk

GETTING THERE
West Pentire is an exposed headland
1.6km (1 mile) from Crantock, Cornwall,
just south of Newquay off the A3075.
Follow the road through Crantock to West
Pentire. The nearest train station is 8.8km
(5½ miles) away in Newquay. You can get
a bus from Newquay to Crantock, but not
out to the headland.

ACCESS AND FACILITIES
There is a pub in West Pentire village; the
nearest shops are in Crantock, where you'll
also find public toilets and a café. There are
also toilets in nearby Cubert. Wheelchair
access is limited as there are no made-up
paths at West Pentire.

OPENING TIMES
Open all year round.

CHARGES
None.

The harvest mouse

Managed habitats like this one that focus on
farmland or "agricultural weeds" are valuable
homes for the harvest mouse, which is in serious
decline in Britain. Much of its ideal habitat has
been lost to housing or large-scale agriculture,
and the increase in early harvesting means that
the mouse's wheatfield nest sites are destroyed.
The mouse is so tiny that you're unlikely to see
one, but look out for its cosy nests.

Above (left to right): The beach and sea at Pentire Point offer a range of habitats; a wild cornflower; the low-growing scarlet pimpernel.
Main: Poppies stretch away to the horizon at West Pentire.

CORNISH DREAM

FARMLAND WILD FLOWERS HAVE FOUND IT HARD TO SURVIVE in recent decades. It is easy to draw attention to the decline of farmland birds, such as lapwings, skylarks, and corn buntings, but the huge loss of once-common countryside flowers is at least as dramatic. Sadly, many of them grew in the "wrong place" – amongst crops – so they were classed as weeds. They have suffered from both indiscriminate and more selective weedkillers in the intensified farming system that still grows most of our food. Flower identification guides may still call some of these plants "common", but they can be remarkably hard to find.

At West Pentire in Cornwall, on a wonderful coastal walk south of Newquay, you can enjoy a marvellous array of these colourful and thoroughly enjoyable "weeds" each summer. They are a breath of fresh air and a link to times long since gone. Some of the fields at West Pentire are specially managed for their flowers and have stunning shows, especially in June and July when the poppies and corn marigolds are in full colour. You'll also spot the bell-shaped flowers of Venus's looking-glass, the delicate white shepherd's needle, the sticky stems of the small-flowered catchfly, and "weasel's snout" or lesser snapdragon. All of these are now rare in the UK, unlike the familiar red or common poppy, which fills whole fields at Pentire. This is a classic farmland weed, with a cycle that fits in well with cereal crops, as it can flower and set seed before the corn is harvested.

As well as the flowers of the fields, there are lovely flowers of lime-rich, sandy grassland here, too, including the conical purple-pink spikes of pyramidal orchids and the strange, "dead" straw-and-gold flowers of carline thistle, which never show any hint of purple or pink. If you find yourself anywhere in the UK with sandy soils, chalk, or limestone, take a look around for wild flowers – any still growing tend to be remarkably rich and colourful.

Native plants and wildlife have co-evolved, so that plants meet the exact food and shelter needs of wildlife. If one side dies out, the other's existence becomes threatened.

Inset: A corn bunting, perched on barley.
Below (left to right): A lapwing on its nest; a brown hare on the alert.

WHERE ELSE TO SEE
WILD FLOWERS

Poppy fields are apt to crop up almost anywhere in arable farmland in summer, but can be unpredictable. Wild flowers will grow wherever conditions are right; you may find delightful varieties very close to home.

Martin Down, west of Salisbury in Wiltshire, is a superlative chalk downland site that has fields red with poppies close by. Both Martin Down and West Pentire are wonderful for orchids and butterflies. [SW]

The South Downs, in West Sussex, have good poppy fields, and a wide spread of wild flowers, as do the **Cotswolds**, in Gloucestershire. [SW]

The **Chilterns** includes many areas of wild flowers, right up to the south Bedfordshire downs near Luton and Dunstable. **Aston Rowant** (*see pp.222–223*), near Oxford, also features a wide range of wild herbs and orchids. [SE]

THROUGH THE YEAR
WEST PENTIRE

Autumn brings visiting birds including occasional Lapland and snow buntings to the West Pentire fields. Look for fulmars around the cliff area from November to late summer, and buzzards at any time. Grey seals breed here, and often haul themselves up on to rocks – you'll be able to view them very closely if you are still and quiet. Scan Holywell Bay in good weather for basking sharks, porpoises, and dolphins.

A thin crop of barley is sown at West Pentire to provide food for seed-eating birds in **winter**. This means you're likely to see the ever-rarer grey partridge, and some corn buntings, among the winter visitors.

In **spring**, look for cowslips on open grassy meadows and primroses and lesser celandines in shady hedge banks.

Below: View from West Pentire in the winter season.

JAN
FEB
MAR
APR
MAY
JUN
JUL
AUG
SEP
OCT
NOV
DEC

DORSET HEATHLAND

ONE OF THE GREAT NATURAL HARBOURS OF THE WORLD, Poole Harbour lies between the urban mass of Poole, Sandbanks, and Bournemouth to the east, and the Arne and Studland peninsulas to the west. Arne is a great block of low land – its central heathland fringed by reed swamps, saltmarsh, and bogs. Immortalized by the novelist and poet Thomas Hardy, such heaths used to be widespread, but forestry, neglect, and changing economic realities led to their decline. Heathland wildlife dwindled too, so remnants such as Arne are of exceptional value.

In June, it is a sunny, bright, colourful place, sweet with the coconut scent of millions of gorse blooms. Look closely and you'll find the ground is a rich tapestry of colour and texture. This is formed by the many lichens, mosses, and flowering plants, all seemingly in miniature on this exposed, demanding habitat, with its thin, acid soils and wet, boggy flushes. And yet it was here that one of Britain's scarcest birds, the Dartford warbler, found a

WHERE
RSPB Arne, Arne Road, Arne, Wareham, Dorset BH20 5BJ; www.rspb.org.uk

CONTACT
RSPB Arne, tel: 01929 553360; arne@rspb.org.uk

GETTING THERE
By car, from Wareham town centre, head south over the causeway to Stoborough. Arne is signposted from here. The nearest railway station is 6.5km (4 miles) away at Wareham. Buses stop at Stoborough village, 5km (3 miles) from the reserve.

ACCESS AND FACILITIES
There is an information centre, car park, toilets, and picnic area, however, the site is unsuitable for wheelchair users. You will find the car park just as you enter the village of Arne. There are a series of trails around the reserve – approx 6.5km (4 miles) in total – with views over Poole Harbour and a double-decker bird hide with views of the saltmarsh and mudflats of Arne Bay.

OPENING TIMES
The trails are open at all times; the car park is locked at dusk.

CHARGES
For non-RSPB members.

Constant management

Heathland, left to its own devices, quickly becomes woodland. It was first established in southern Britain when people cleared forests for agriculture; on land with poor, stony soils, there was little choice but to use it for grazing animals, harvesting gorse for fuel and the heather and bracken for livestock bedding. Grazing, cutting, and frequent fires kept the heathland open, but gradually these practices stopped and heathland suffered centuries of neglect. Today, tree saplings are removed to maintain these open tracts.

Main: The Shipstal trail on the RSPB Arne reserve, with a view of Poole Harbour.

Left: A stonechat in spring.

Right (left to right): A marsh gentian in flower; nightjar on the ground in the heather; heathland merges into saltmarsh on the Arne Peninsula.

Right panel (top to bottom): A female silver-studded blue butterfly; Britain's rarest reptile – the smooth snake; Shipstal beach.

last refuge after the devastating 1963 winter wiped out all but a handful of this species. You can look for them today in the gorse and tall heather: they may scold you from a bush top, cocking their long, slim tails above their backs, before diving out of sight. At dusk, the nightjars appear. You'll hear their strange churring songs, which may last unbroken for several minutes. Look against the evening sky for their long-winged, long-tailed silhouettes as they catch moths in flight.

Grass snakes and adders are both here, but the smooth snake is the great prize. A very small, slender reptile, it is confined in the UK to a few of these southern heathlands. While common lizards are widespread, the sand lizard, bigger and often brighter green, is another rare speciality of the area. Add rare wild flowers, such as the strikingly blue marsh gentian, butterflies like the stunning silver-studded blues in June and July, and a host of dragonflies and damselflies, and Arne is a real national treasure, as well as a beautiful and relaxing place to unwind.

WHERE ELSE TO SEE
HEATHLAND WILDLIFE

The combination of huge open heathland and old oak woodland found at Arne is rare in Britain, giving rise to an unusual combination of inhabitants. However, some of its rarer forms of wildlife can be found in other parts of Britain.

New Forest (*see pp.174–175*) heaths, close to Arne, have many of its wildlife specialities but they are elusive, and harder to find in the forest's 370 sq km (144 sq mile) area. [SE]

Many of Arne's birds, dragonflies, and flowers are found on heathland in Surrey, particularly **Thursley Common** (*see pp.128–129*), which also has British native reptiles. Dartford warblers live on the heaths of the Suffolk coast, such as **Dunwich**. [SE]

Cannock Chase in Staffordshire has a precious few Dartford warblers, and some nightjars (in summer), but not the rarer reptiles. [M]

THROUGH THE YEAR
ARNE

There is much more to Arne than the heath: it is a great place for estuary birds, too. Watch for egrets at any time, and for avocets feeding in the tidal shallows.

In **autumn**, keep your eyes open for ospreys, which fish in the harbour area while making their relaxed southward journey to West Africa.

Some of the scarcer migrating birds visit Arne Bay in **winter**, such as black-necked grebes and scaups. Hen harriers and marsh harriers set up temporary home around the Middlebere area. Winter is a great time to watch flocks of wading birds.

In **spring**, the swallows, martins, cuckoos, willow warblers, and blackcaps return. Listen out for lesser spotted woodpeckers, which are most vocal at this time of year.

Below: Purple heather replaces the yellow gorse in late summer.

JAN

FEB

MAR

APR

MAY

JUN

JUL

AUG

SEP

OCT

NOV

DEC

WHERE
Rockingham Forest, Rockingham, near Corby
Northamptonshire NN17 3BB;
www.forestrycommission.gov.uk

CONTACT
Forestry Commission Northants, tel: 01780
444920; northants@forestry.gsi.gov.uk

GETTING THERE
Fineshade Woods, within the forest, has an
RSPB visitor centre, shop, and café at Top
Lodge, which is signposted from the A43,
14.4km (9 miles) northeast of Corby, and
9.6km (6 miles) southwest of Stamford.

ACCESS AND FACILITIES
Rockingham Forest has more than 400km
(250 miles) of walks, and includes Wakerley
Great Wood, Fermyn Wood, Southey Wood,
Fineshade Wood, and Bedford Purlieus
nature reserve. The RSPB's visitor centre at
Fineshade has refreshment facilities and is
wheelchair friendly. Some of the trails are
not suitable for wheelchairs.

OPENING TIMES
The woods are open all year round; the
visitor centre opens from 10am to 5pm.

CHARGES
None, except to park at the Top Lodge
car park, Fineshade.

Identifying hairstreaks

Distinguishing the four hairstreak butterflies can
be tricky. They rarely open their wings except in
flight, and even then they usually fly too high up
for the upperwings to be seen. Use binoculars to
look at the underwings: the brown hindwings of
the black hairstreak (*above*) have a broader,
brighter orange band bearing tapering black dots,
while the inner white band lacks the "W"-shaped
kink of the white-letter species; those of the brown
hairstreak are paler and mainly golden- brown,
and the purple hairstreak's are pale silvery grey.

Above (left to right): Fallow deer; a long-eared owl; badger cubs foraging.
Main: Ancient woodland at Wakerley Great Wood, part of Rockingham Forest.

HISTORIC WOODLANDS

LIKE THE NEW FOREST, ROCKINGHAM WAS AN IMPORTANT ROYAL FOREST during medieval times, reserved by William the Conqueror during the 11th century for hunting deer and wild boar. It consists of a mosaic of wooded areas and more open country, with farmland and small villages, beautiful historic buildings of local stone, and two extremely rare Bronze Age cairns. Only about half the ancient woodland remains – of ash, field maple, and oak, interspersed with rarer trees such as the wild service tree and the small-leaved lime.

For centuries the woods were managed by coppicing. The many branches this produced had a myriad of uses, from fencing and house-building to providing firewood or producing charcoal. Today, this traditional management is still carried out to encourage wildlife, and one bird that benefits particularly is the nightingale. Hazel dormice, scarce in much of the country, thrive here in the coppiced woodland and overgrown hedgerows, which provide them with essential food and shelter. Other mammals include foxes, badgers, polecats, stoats, fallow deer, and muntjac deer. The forest has an understorey of hawthorn, blackthorn, and hazel, and the ground layer is exceptionally rich in plant life. Bluebells and wood anemones abound, but there are also rarer plants, including various species of orchids, toothwort, and stinking hellebore.

Birdlife includes tawny and long-eared owls, all three species of British woodpeckers, marsh and willow tits, and hawfinches – whose huge bills are capable of cracking cherry stones. Most famous are the magnificent red kites that were introduced here in the 1990s, and have since built up a thriving self-sustaining population. Over 20 butterfly species breed here; look for the rare black hairstreak butterfly among mature stands of blackthorn bushes, especially in the sunny glades and woodland margins sheltered from the wind. Its caterpillars feed mainly on the blackthorn leaves. This is a very localized species – just 30 colonies remain, all in the woods of the East Midlands forest belt. Seeing this elusive little butterfly will give you a great sense of privilege: its flight period is very brief, from mid-June to mid-July, and it spends much of its time feeding on aphid honeydew in the tops of the larger trees. Three other species of hairstreaks can also be seen in Rockingham; try the nature reserve at Bedford Purlieus for the rarest one, the brown hairstreak, whose caterpillars feed on blackthorn. Those of the commoner purple hairstreak eat oak leaves, while the caterpillars of the white-letter hairstreak prefer elm.

Below (left to right): Red kites build untidy nests in trees; the tawny owl – the largest of the UK's native owls – is another forest breeder.

WHERE ELSE TO SEE
ANCIENT WOODLANDS

The ancient woodlands of England and Wales are those in which the trees have grown continuously since 1600 or earlier, and in Scotland since at least 1750. Although over half the ancient broadleaved woodland has been cleared or planted with conifers since the 1930s, valuable areas remain.

The best known and richest in wildlife of all is the **New Forest** (*see pp.174–175*). It is home to five species of deer, and an extraordinarily rich variety of fungi, wildflowers, dragonflies, reptiles, and rare birds. [SE]

Over 20 per cent of England's ancient woodlands are in the southwest. Two superb examples are on Dartmoor: **Wistman's Wood** (*see pp.160–161*) is a strange world of wind-dwarfed oaks growing among granite boulders, while **Black Tor Copse** is an exceptional site for lichens and woodland birds. [SW]

There are patches of ancient woodland within Greater London. **Highgate Wood** and **Queen's Wood** in north London are examples, while nearby **Epping Forest** is renowned for fungi, woodland birds, and insects, including 1,400 species of beetles. [SE]

THROUGH THE YEAR
ROCKINGHAM FOREST

Autumn is the time to seek out toadstools, from the bracket fungi that protrude from tree trunks, such as dryad's saddle, to the spectacular poisonous devil's bolete, found under oaks. Bedford Purlieus nature reserve, near Peterborough, is a great place to see the golden lime trees contrasting with dark-green conifers and blue-black sloes on blackthorn bushes.

By **winter**, many of the juvenile red kites have left and the adults form large roosts. There may be a total of up to 400 kites throughout the forest. Other winter birds include crossbills, siskins, and redpolls.

The greatest diversity of wildlife is in spring and summer, when the birds are breeding, and reptiles and insects are most active. **Spring** brings a swelling chorus of songbirds: listen for the newly arrived male nightingales in areas with dense coppice and brambles. Speckled wood butterflies are among the earliest on the wing.

JAN

FEB

MAR

APR

MAY

JUN

JUL

AUG

SEP

OCT

NOV

DEC

Below: Wildflowers carpet the floor of the woodland glades in spring.

SHIFTING SANDS

FOR ITS SIZE, THE ISLAND OF ANGLESEY HAS A REMARKABLE DIVERSITY of landscapes, from mountain to marsh, and cliff to mudflat. The sand dunes of its southern coast are internationally renowned, and the greatest of these is Newborough Warren (Niwbwrch in Welsh). The area stretches over 15 sq km (6 sq miles), and almost half of this was planted with Corsican and Scots pine in the last century. As you walk through the forest on your way to the Warren, listen and watch out for goldcrests and coal tits, and even red squirrels – the greys have been eradicated here, and the native reds reintroduced with considerable success.

Out of the forest and on to the open dunes, you are enveloped by an undulating sea of sand, clothed in the stiff waxy leaves of marram grass. The size of the Warren is such that the area's natural dynamism is still taking place – the dunes are mobile, and occasionally blow out, right down to the water table, forming a pool, or dune

WHERE
Newborough Warren, Isle of Anglesey (Ynys Môn in the Welsh language), LL61, Wales.

CONTACT
Tel: 01248 672500 (Warden), or 0845 1306229 (Countryside Council for Wales enquiry line); info@wales.info

GETTING THERE
From the Menai Bridge on the A5, take the A4080 south to Newborough village (Niwbwrch). Follow the signs to Newborough Warren and Llanddwyn (this is a Forestry Commission road and subject to a toll/parking fee). Llanddwyn Island is accessible on foot at low tide.

ACCESS AND FACILITIES
There is disabled access just off the main car park in Newborough Forest; there are also toilets here. There is an accessible bird hide by Llyn Rhos-Ddu.

OPENING TIMES
Open all year round.

CHARGES
Parking fee at Llanddwyn car park.

Marram grass

As with dunes worldwide, Newborough Warren's are dominated by marram. Indeed, the dunes' existence is due to the presence of this grass: its unique, almost unlimited ability to grow upwards and sideways through bare sand creates a three-dimensional mesh that helps stabilize the sand; as more sand is blown onshore, so the marram skeleton extends to build the dune. It is stabilization by marram that then allows a whole range of other plants to colonize and thrive on the dunes.

Left (left to right): Sea holly – an important nectar source for the dune's butterflies; marsh helleborine.

Right (left to right): Grass-of-Parnassus; the grayling butterfly seeks out open areas in which to bask in the sun – it can only fly when warm.

Right panel (top and bottom): Ravens live in the cliffs behind the dunes; the disused lighthouse at Porth Twr Mawr is Newborough Warren's main landmark.

JAN
FEB
MAR
APR
MAY
JUN
JUL
AUG
SEP
OCT
NOV
DEC

slack. These slacks harbour many of the Warren's botanical treasures. Often the dominant plant, creeping willow, is in fruit in June, the cotton-wool of its wind-dispersed seeds erupting from a silvery-leaved shrub barely knee-high. Growing through it are orchids: bee, northern marsh, and early marsh (in its distinctive red-flowered dune form), among marsh and dune helleborines. The latter is the least attractive – with greenish flowers on drooping spikes – but arguably the most important: it is only known to grow here and on the dunes of the Lancashire coast. Bog pimpernel, butterwort, yellow bird's-nest, and round-leaved wintergreen all add to the spectacle.

If you can drag yourself away from the microcosm of the slacks, visit Llanddwyn Island, an exposed section of the volcanic rocks that run under the Warren. The lichens are spectacular: look out for the rare and extremely beautiful golden hair-lichen which has recently been discovered here. And look up from the rocks: cormorants and shags can be seen nesting on the cliffs and rocky islets.

WHERE ELSE TO SEE
SAND DUNES

Most of our larger sand-dune systems show the development of dune slacks. One feature of many of these sites is that they support the dune-loving natterjack toad.

Just a few kilometres west of Newborough, **Abberffraw** dunes are a little more compact, though lacking in some of the structural diversity. [W]

Some of the best dune slacks, including around half of the creeping willow scrub in Britain, can be found at **Ainsdale** (*see pp.88–89*) and other sites on the Sefton Coast on Merseyside. [N]

The dune systems at **Saltfleetby-Theddlethorpe** in Lincolnshire have a good slack system. [M]

Magilligan, near Londonderry, comprises almost all of the dune slack habitat of Northern Ireland. [NI]

In the southwest of England, good examples include **Braunton Burrows** (*see pp.68–69*) and **Dawlish Warren** in Devon, and **Studland Bay**, Dorset. [SW]

As dusk falls, a huge flock of around 800 ravens flies in to roost, in the largest gathering of ravens worldwide.

THROUGH THE YEAR
NEWBOROUGH WARREN

As the summer slips into **autumn**, flowers keep coming: the beautiful pearly-white single flowers of the grass of Parnassus spring up in the slacks, and autumn lady's-tresses emerge from the turf. This is a small orchid, with spiralling spikes of white flowers.

In **winter**, ravens and choughs move down from the mountains and cliff-nesting areas to find food. Pintails are a particular feature of the mudflats, along with wigeons, teals, and redshanks. Purple sandpipers and turnstones feed around seaweed-covered rocks.

Spring sees the return of the breeding birds, both noisy, piping oystercatchers and the cliff-nesting cormorants and shags. The maritime turf becomes bedecked with the flowers of thrift, and – especially where there is a little shelter – bluebells. In early spring, the open dunes are busy with botanists, hunting for one of our rarest plants: the extremely minuscule early sand-grass.

Below: the sandy beach is about 1.6km (1 mile) in length.

REALM OF THE RAPTORS

PERCHED ON A RIDGE 260M (850FT) HIGH, Haldon Forest lies at the southeastern edge of the Great Haldon ridge in Devon. Stand at any of its viewpoints for a thrilling view down and over the Exe Estuary and beyond. The forest is a mosaic of coniferous and broadleaved trees, dotted with woodland rides and glades.

It is worth a visit at any season, but in summer it is one of the best sites in Britain for watching one of our rarest breeding raptors: the honey buzzard. And there's more – the skies here are home to common buzzards, sparrowhawks, and even peregrine falcons. The goshawk, so difficult to see in the UK, can be spotted here most frequently between April and June, when they rise high into the sky to display. Hobbies hawk overhead for insect prey or the occasional hapless swallow or house martin. In both spring and autumn migrating raptors are around the forest, and in early June you may still see an osprey, heading north to breed.

WHERE
Haldon Forest Park, Kennford, Exeter, EX6 7XR; www.forestry.gov.uk/haldonforestpark

CONTACT
Haldon Forest Park Ranger, tel: 01392 834251; haldon.rangers@forestry.gsi.gov.uk

GETTING THERE
By car, take the Exeter Racecourse turning off the A38. From the A380, follow the brown tourist signs for Haldon Belvedere. By bus, catch the no. 360 to Belvedere Tower and join the trails through the woods from the lay-by. By cycle, follow the A38 Cycle Way, (part of the National Cycle Network). Turn off at the racecourse and follow the signs for Haldon Forest Park.

ACCESS AND FACILITIES
There are two all-ability trails and a "secret path" to follow. There is a picnic area and food van, and plans to open a permanent restaurant. Cycles can be hired from "the hub" near the ranger's office, near Gateway car park. The main car park has full-access toilets, and disabled parking bays.

OPENING TIMES
Haldon Forest Park is open all year round. The car park is open from 8.30am–5pm.

CHARGES
There is a small car parking charge.

Honey buzzard

Few sites in Britain can match Haldon Forest for views of honey buzzards. Primarily insect eaters, they relish the larvae and pupae of social wasps and bees, and will dig out a nest using their strong legs and blunt claws. The best chance of seeing a honey buzzard is to spend time in June at the bird of prey viewpoint. A bright sunny day will produce plenty of thermals – currents of warm air that rise up from the forest – and it is these thermals that the buzzards will use to soar effortlessly into the sky.

If you can drag your eyes away from the excitement overhead, Haldon Forest has more to offer on the ground. An impressive 34 species of butterfly live in the forest, including the rare and very beautiful pearl-bordered and silver-washed fritillaries. Take the butterfly trail from the Haldon Gateway, which will give you stunning views across the Teign Valley as well as the chance to see butterflies. Halfway through the walk you'll come to a pond that's home to large numbers of dragonflies and damselflies, including the golden-ringed dragonfly and the beautiful demoiselle damselfly. A multitude of small mammals call the forest home, including dormice – which spend three-quarters of their time asleep and so readily use the nestboxes put up for them. At dusk in June, head for a clear-fell area and you may hear the distinctive churring song of a nightjar. Follow the sound, and you may be rewarded with seeing them display or feed on the wing around the clearings and along the woodland rides of this huge and exciting forest.

WHERE ELSE TO SEE
BIRDS OF PREY

Seeing birds of prey in a woodland setting can be a challenge; keep your eyes and ears open, and look along rides and in glades.

Thetford Forest in Norfolk shares many of Haldon's birds, including goshawks and nightjars, and also offers a chance of seeing the rare firecrest. Roe deer are abundant. [SE]

Kielder Forest in Northumberland is England's largest forest, and is home to some spectacular wildlife, including goshawks, kestrels, and buzzards – and the very rare red squirrel. [N]

The wildlife of the **New Forest** (*see pp.174–175*) has been protected since 1079, and includes many birds of prey, including the honey buzzard. [SE]

The Wood of Cree, an ancient forest in southern Scotland, has a large population of kestrels, sparrowhawks, and buzzards. Hen harriers, merlins, and golden eagles are occasionally seen. [SC]

THROUGH THE YEAR
HALDON FOREST

Watch for migrant birds of prey from the viewpoint in **autumn**. Look for discarded hazelnuts with a small neat round hole nibbled in one side, which is a sure sign of a dormouse.

Crossbills may be in the conifers in **winter**. Look for dippers along the streams, and keep an eye out for goshawks from the bird of prey viewpoint.

Haldon Forest comes alive in **spring** with the first butterflies of the year on the wing. Arriving migrants include nightjars. Honey buzzards and goshawks will be displaying.

JAN
FEB
MAR
APR
MAY
JUN
JUL
AUG
SEP
OCT
NOV
DEC

Main: Honey buzzards breed in the UK in June.

Left (top to bottom): Haldon Forest; a goshawk landing; the peregrine falcon is always alert.

Above: A sparrowhawk perches on a post – these birds particularly like the larch trees of Haldon Forest.

Below: A pearl-bordered fritillary can feed only on violet-coloured plants.

Below: A view across the estuary of the River Exe.

LIMESTONE LANDSCAPE

ALL LANDSCAPES ARE DEFINED BY THEIR GEOLOGY. The nature of the rock gives the land its form and character, and is reflected in the wild plants that colonize it. This is true of all types of rock, but few display their influence quite so dramatically as limestone. For although every rock has its unique qualities, limestone is special. At Whitbarrow National Nature Reserve in southern Cumbria you can see this even from a distance: as you approach from the village of Witherslack, the hill looming above you is castellated with an imposing rampart of pale, bare rock rising high above the trees on the lower slopes. Yet this is nothing compared to the view that starts to open out as you climb through the trees to the top.

WHERE
Whitbarrow, Howe, near Kendal, Cumbria.

CONTACT
Natural England, tel: 0845 600 3078; enquiries@naturalengland.org.uk Cumbria Wildlife Trust, tel: 01539 816300; mail@cumbriawildlifetrust.org.uk

GETTING THERE
Whitbarrow National Nature Reserve is 8km (5 miles) southwest of Kendal. By car, follow signs to the A590; take the road signposted to Witherslack; drive through the village then turn right at Witherslack Hall into the reserve. By train, travel to Kendal on the TransPennine Express, or Grange-over-Sands with Northern Rail.

ACCESS AND FACILITIES
There are no facilities on site; the nearest are in Grange-over-Sands. The nature reserve is not suitable for wheelchair users. There is no formal car park, but you can leave your car by the side of the road on the western side of the reserve.

OPENING TIMES
Open all year round.

CHARGES
None.

The fissures of a limestone pavement act as portholes for rainwater. It trickles down to a network of caves and streams beneath the rock – festooned with calcite curtains, hanging stalactites, and rising stalagmites.

As the trees thin out, you emerge into a different world. In summer it is a place of dazzling colour and fragrance, with the bright wings of common blue butterflies or bigger, more spectacular dark green fritillaries flitting between the flowers of wild strawberry, wild thyme, and common rock-rose. In many places, especially along the eastern side of the reserve, these plants sprout from a complex network of fissures and crevices between blocks of bare limestone – the weird, almost alien terrain of a limestone pavement.

Rainwater runs down through the fissures, or "grikes", in the limestone, leaving the rock surface itself dry and largely barren. But over the years pockets of soil have formed in the grikes, which soak up water draining off the limestone blocks, or "clints", to provide a moist roothold for lime-loving plants such as limestone oak fern, hart's-tongue fern, meadow cranesbill, and even trees – such as juniper, ash, and rowan. Every crevice contains its own community of plants, which flourish in the sheltered, damp, but perfectly drained microclimate. So making your way across the limestone pavement can be a slow process as you are distracted by each floral delight. But don't forget to look up, because the view over the fells of southern Lakeland from the summit is nothing short of stupendous.

Main: The clints and grikes of Whitbarrow's limestone pavement.
Below (left to right): Meadow cranesbill; a common blue butterfly; limestone reflects the sun, helping to ripen wild strawberries.
Inset: Golden-leaved *Sedum acre*, commonly known as wall pepper, likes the wet, alkaline conditions of the pavement.

Remnants of the Ice Age

This weird landscape is unique to limestone regions that were covered by moving ice some 14,000 years ago, and regularly deluged by heavy rain ever since. The grinding glaciers scoured the landscape clean, allowing rainwater – naturally slightly acid – to seep gradually into cracks and erode the rock, creating deep fissures. The glacier that moved over Whitbarrow also deposited the stray boulders now seen on the surface, which it had picked up earlier in its course.

JAN

FEB

MAR

APR

MAY

JUN

JUL

AUG

SEP

OCT

NOV

DEC

Above: Ash is a tree associated with limestone habitats.

WHERE ELSE TO SEE
LIMESTONE PAVEMENT

In mainland Britain, the best examples of limestone pavement lie in northern England and north Wales.

The most famous limestone pavements in England lie in the southern Yorkshire Dales around **Ingleton** and **Malham**. **Scales Moor** above Chapel-le-Dale is a magnificent expanse of bare limestone dotted with boulders – "glacial erratics" – dropped by the Ice-Age glaciers as they melted away some 13,000 years ago. [N]

Gait Barrows National Nature Reserve and nearby **Arnside Knott** near Carnforth, in Lancashire, have extensive areas of limestone pavement, with a wonderful variety of plant life, including several species of orchid. [N]

There is a superb stretch of limestone pavement on **Great Orme's Head** in North Wales, which offers the bonus of a dramatic coastal backdrop. [W]

THROUGH THE YEAR
WHITBARROW

In September and October the path that leads up through woodland to the top of Whitbarrow glows with **autumn** colour, and the scent of fungi hangs in the air. Watch for birds gathering berries from the trees and shrubs.

Ice, snow, and even rain in **winter** can make the limestone pavements especially hazardous, so it is probably best to avoid them at such times. If you do decide to risk it, the panorama of lakeland from the summit – Lord's Seat – can make the climb worthwhile on a clear frosty day.

In **spring** skylarks hover above the rocky summit, pouring out their silvery stream of song. Wheatears are often to be seen searching for insects, and if you watch carefully you may see one taking food to a brood of young in a nest among the rocks.

WHERE
Wye Downs National Nature Reserve,
Wye, Ashford, Kent TN25 5HE;
www.naturalengland.org.uk

CONTACT
Natural England, Kent, tel: 01233 812525
or 0845 600 3078 (local rate);
enquiries@naturalengland.org.uk

GETTING THERE
The nature reserve is 2km (3¼ miles)
southeast of Wye and 6km (9½ miles)
northeast of Ashford, Kent. By car, follow
minor roads from the A28, about 1.5km
(1 mile) southeast of Wye. The reserve's
eastern boundary is marked by a road from
Wye to Hastingleigh; here you'll find a car
park. The nearest train station is in Wye. The
reserve lies on the Sustrans National Cycle
Network, Route 18.

ACCESS AND FACILITIES
Parking is available at the reserve. There are
no toilets and the 4km (6½ miles) of nature
trails are unsuitable for wheelchairs. Picnic
tables are available.

OPENING TIMES
Open all year round.

CHARGES
None.

Mimicry in orchids

Bee orchids only flower in June and July, and
can be difficult to find – if you're not a male bee.
The flowers are a delicate pink and brown, with
a furry, bee-like "body" designed to attract male
bees. The flowers release counterfeit bee sex
pheromones to further encourage the bees, who
attempt to copulate with the flower, so convinced
are they by the flower's disguise. They depart
frustrated, but carrying the flower's pollen, which
they then deposit on another flower, so fertilizing
the orchids.

Above (left to right): Some of the orchids found in the Wye Downs – the burnt orchid; military orchid; and frog orchid.
Main: A bee orchid, with flowers that mimic the shape of a bee to achieve pollination.

CHALKLAND ORCHIDS

TAKE TO THE NORTH DOWNS NEAR ASHFORD IN KENT, and you'll come across the outstanding chalkland reserve of Wye Downs. You'll first be struck by the magnificent views – west over Romney Marsh and the Weald, and east over the Channel coast. Then you notice the unusual plants – chalk and limestone allow for many specialized wild flowers.

The Wye Downs tumble in steep, emerald-green, grassy slopes to scattered hawthorn and bramble brakes, sweeping down into quiet valleys with patches of broadleaved woodland. It is all irresistibly beautiful, but if you want to hunt out the area's special prize – its orchids – head to the chalk grassland. Here you'll find as many as 21 species of orchid, including lady orchid, burnt orchid, fly orchid, the rare late and early spider orchids, and man orchid. Be careful where you walk, as many of these plants are inconspicuous, and you need to develop a slow, systematic searching technique to see the best of them. Or you can let nature lead you, and just take a simple walk along the footpaths, which is a delight in summer when an abundance of colourful flowers and butterflies can be seen with ease. The grassland is grazed to prevent the encroachment of trees and bushes, and it's an outstanding mixture of elegant grasses and flowers in summer. Notice the pale yellow of horseshoe vetch and cowslips, and the rare, diminutive but vivid Kentish milkwort.

Butterflies abound, and usually include a range of the more common ones, such as small coppers, meadow browns, gatekeepers, and common blues, plus a much rarer one: the brown-and-orange chequered Duke of Burgundy. Look for the butterflies on the flowering brambles, where they seek out nectar on sunny days. If you walk quietly, especially on a warm summer morning before it gets too hot, you might also find an adder or two, a grass snake, a slow-worm, or a common lizard winding across your path.

The grasslands of the Wye Downs contain up to 40 plant species in one square metre (10 sq ft). This reserve is home to around 4,000 different plant species in all.

Inset: The common spotted orchid.
Below (left to right): The slopes of the Wye Downs; cattle grazing controls scrub.

WHERE ELSE TO SEE
CHALKLAND FLORA

Chalklands exist across the country, both on the coast and inland. Orchids can be found in many places across Britain, although some species can only grow in very specific conditions. Alkaline soils suit a wide variety of orchids, while acid soils can only support a few.

Chalk downs can be enjoyed at **Ivinghoe Beacon**, Buckinghamshire, and **Dunstable Downs**, Bedfordshire; orchids can be seen at reserves with grassland in the Chilterns, including **Aston Rowant** (*see pp.222–223*), Oxfordshire, and the excellent **Warburg** reserve near Henley-on-Thames. [SE]

Martin Down, Salisbury, is a magnificent stretch of grassland, rich in flowers and butterflies. [SE]

Orchids and butterflies can be found on sand dune habitats such as the Kenfig reserve near Bridgend in Wales. [W]

Folkestone Warren, at the end of the chalk downs on the Kent coast, has chalk plants and butterflies including the vivid Adonis blue. [SE]

THROUGH THE YEAR
WYE DOWNS

Flowers and butterflies appear in sequence from April to September, so these downs are well worth visiting through the **summer** and **autumn**. Look out especially for the subtle, purplish-blue flowers of autumn gentian. Various migrant birds, such as redwings, can be seen from October onwards.

In **winter**, there are stonechats, linnets, yellowhammers, and a few birds of prey. Farmers leave areas of stubble in the fields to provide a feeding place for the birds.

By **spring** the birds are looking for breeding grounds, so some fields are left fallow for birds such as skylarks, which like to nest in open fields. Brimstones and orange-tip butterflies, and early flowers including cowslips, lady's smock, primroses, violets, and celandines start to appear.

Below: Kestrels hunt over the Wye Downs.

JAN
FEB
MAR
APR
MAY
JUN
JUL
AUG
SEP
OCT
NOV
DEC

WHERE
Skomer Island, South West Wales, SA62 3BE;
www.welshwildlife.org

CONTACT
The Wildlife Trust South and West Wales,
tel: 01656 724100; info@welshwildlife.org

GETTING THERE
The island is reached by boat from Martin's
Haven, a small cove 3.2km (2 miles) from
the village of Marloes, which is off the B4327
from Haverfordwest towards Dale. Pass
through the village and turn left for Martin's
Haven. Boat trips, which take 20 minutes,
depart between 10am–noon and return
between 3pm–4pm. The boatman will
advise on the day.

ACCESS AND FACILITIES
There's a National Trust car park at Martin's
Haven. There are no refreshments, so take
a picnic and plenty to drink. There are toilets
situated in the centre of the island beside the
old farmhouse. Wheelchair users should check
with The Wildlife Trust (www.welshwildlife.org)
before visiting.

OPENING TIMES
Boat trips run from Easter to the end of
October, weather permitting.

CHARGES
Yes, for car parking and the boat trip.

Nesting burrows

There are around 6,000 breeding pairs of puffins
on Skomer during the spring and summer. They
build nests of grass, sea campion, and bluebell
stems in burrows on the slopes or rocky cliffs,
and the female puffin lays a single egg. After an
incubation of 39–45 days, the fluffy grey "puffling"
hatches out. At the end of July the young puffins
begin to leave the island – at night – to escape
predatory gulls. They stay at sea for two years,
before returning to the colony.

Left (left to right): Skomer
Island is home to around
500,000 seabirds; the
Skomer vole is larger and
paler than mainland voles.

Right (left to right): A puffin
takes off from the sea; puffins
are also known as "sea
clowns", for good reason!

Panel (below right): Puffins
can carry around 10 sand eels
in their beaks at any one time.

Main: Skomer's puffin population returns faithfully to this tiny island to breed each year.

THE CLOWNS OF THE SEA

THE ISLANDS OFF THE WEST OF WALES – Bardsey in the north, Ramsey, Skokholm, Skomer, and Grassholm
in the south – all have a special character and charm. Skomer, one of the largest and most appealing in spring
and summer, is full of interest and excitement. The boat that takes you to the island drops off at "The Neck", a thin
strip of land where the main island is almost severed from its smaller eastern extension by the sea. You can
explore the main section on well-used footpaths, from which you soon see that thousands of handsome herring
and lesser black-backed gulls populate the middle of the island.

You'll also notice that the island is riddled with holes. These are the homes of tens of thousands of rabbits
and Manx shearwaters, but some of them – such as the burrows on the steep grassy slopes above the sea cliffs –
contain puffins. Puffins are smaller than you probably think, barely as big as a town pigeon, but always comical

> Puffins use their wings not only to fly but also to propel themselves through water, in long dives chasing fish.

THROUGH THE YEAR
SKOMER ISLAND

Autumn is a great time to see migrant birds, including thousands of swallows; tree pipits, meadow pipits, and various warblers; occasional Lapland buntings; and black redstarts and ring ouzels. Islands are often good sites for finding rarities, and it is worth exploring the adjacent headlands in September and October. Ravens can sometimes be seen in scores. Watch the sea for dolphins and even sunfish.

The island's mallards are joined in **winter** by wigeons, teals, and a small flock of barnacle geese. Choughs fly around the mainland cliffs near St David's, and peregrines can be seen chasing pigeons.

The white flowers of scurvy grass announce **spring** on Skomer. The gulls look stunning standing in dense swathes of tall bluebells and red campion, while the puffin pairs can be seen busily courting and reinforcing their long-lasting pair bonds. Offshore, watch for gannets, dolphins, porpoises, and seals. Choughs cavort around the coastal cliffs.

WHERE ELSE TO SEE
PUFFINS

Very few puffins breed on the British mainland, but there are many colonies on the offshore islands dotted around the coast.

Puffins can be enjoyed in very small numbers at **South Stack**, Anglesey. [W]

There is a large puffin colony at **Farne Islands** (see pp.126–127), Northumberland, and a smaller one at **Bempton Cliffs** (see pp.104–105) in Yorkshire. [N]

Northerly seabird colonies in Scotland often include puffins, try **Fowlsheugh**, south of Aberdeen, **Troup Head** on the Moray Firth (see pp.220–221), and the great cliffs of Caithness including those near **Berriedale**, **Wick**, **Duncansby Head,** and **Dunnet Head**. A popular place to see them remarkably closely is Lunga, one of the **Treshnish Islands**, off Mull (see pp.226–227). [SC]

Below: Skomer Island during winter.

JAN
FEB
MAR
APR
MAY
JUN
JUL
AUG
SEP
OCT
NOV
DEC

and fun to watch, even from a distance: their inky-black backs, sparkling white undersides, and orange legs often catch the eye before the famously colourful beak. When several get together they seem incurably nosy, poking their red, yellow, and blue beaks into other puffins' business and not infrequently getting fiercely pecked for their trouble. You can sometimes see puffins locked in fairly harmless combat, rolling down a slope until they fall off the cliff and take flight.

What is truly amazing about puffins is that they live all winter in the most savage conditions, far out in the Atlantic – certainly entirely out of sight of land – but, every spring, driven by mysterious instincts and helped by even more remarkable means of navigation, they fly back to their very own burrow, and probably meet up once again with their own familiar mate.

The puffins of Grassholm, farther out to sea, died out long ago when their burrowing simply eroded all the soil from that small island, and they scratched and scraped themselves out of house and home. There is no such problem here on Skomer, but southern puffin colonies are generally declining, possibly because rising sea temperatures are affecting the marine food chain.

WHERE
RSPB Strumpshaw Fen, Brundall, Norfolk
NR13 4HS; www.rspb.org.uk

CONTACT
RSPB Strumpshaw Fen, tel: 01603 715191;
strumpshaw@rspb.org.uk

GETTING THERE
The reserve is just beyond the village of
Brundall, which lies east of Norwich off
the A47. From the A47 roundabout, drive
through Brundall and continue on the same
road towards Strumpshaw. Turn right into
Stone Road, then follow RSPB signs. The
closest train station is Brundall, which is on
the Norwich–Lowestoft line. An hourly bus
service from Norwich stops 1.1km (¾ mile)
from the reserve on the Brundall to
Strumpshaw road at the junction of Long
Lane and Stone Road (except Sundays).

ACCESS AND FACILITIES
The information centre is wheelchair friendly.
Some trails are accessible by wheelchair and
there is an accessible viewing platform. The
two circular walks through fenland and
woodland are not advisable by wheelchair.

OPENING TIMES
Open from dawn until dusk every day.

CHARGES
For non-RSPB members.

Harriers gain ground

The marsh harrier used to nest in large numbers
in the UK, but egg theft and the drainage of
wetlands left only one breeding pair in 1971.
Protection of its favourite nesting sites – dense
reedbeds – has resulted in numbers of breeding
females rising to around 350. With luck, you'll
see fledgling harriers over the reedbeds at
Strumpshaw in summer, as around a dozen
birds breed there.

Above (left to right): A swallowtail caterpillar eating milk-parsley; reed warbler; barn owls can be seen during the day in summer.
Main: Strumpshaw Fen is part of the Mid Yare Reserve in the Norfolk Broads.

SUMMER ON THE BROADS

T HE NORFOLK BROADS ARE A MAGNIFICENT AREA OF WILDERNESS in the heart of
Norfolk, combining shallow freshwater lakes, rivers and canals, and low-lying pastureland,
reedbeds, and swamp. The flat landscapes create a huge feeling of open space, and the area is as
famous for its enormous, dramatic skies as for its teeming wildlife.

Strumpshaw Fen is a relatively small, accessible, and manageable area from which to begin
exploring the Broads. It is loved by birdwatchers and butterfly fans, offering plenty to see all
summer. Butterfly enthusiasts travel here in June to see the spectacular swallowtail butterfly   it
is Britain's largest butterfly, and one of the rarest. Its caterpillars feed on milk-parsley, which used
to grow in sedge fens in several places in eastern England, but now grows only on the Norfolk
Broads. The adult butterfly flies strongly over the fens, seeking out milk-parsley on which to lay
eggs, but feeding eagerly from pink or mauve flowers, such as ragged robin and creeping thistle.

In June you'll also see marsh harriers, the males
perhaps still performing their spectacular displays high
overhead. The marsh is alive with the songs of sedge
and reed warblers, cuckoos, grasshopper warblers, and
whitethroats. Look for lesser spotted woodpeckers in
surrounding woodland: this is not a bird you are often
likely to come across, as it is declining almost everywhere.

Linger in the meadow, where you can enjoy a rich
display of wild flowers, including six species of orchids.
There are around 20 kinds of dragonfly here, including
the rare Norfolk hawker. Dragonflies in turn attract
hobbies, those small, agile falcons that specialize in
catching large flying insects in summer, and small birds
later in the autumn. Add this to the year-long treats
that the fen has to offer – including kingfishers, Cetti's
warblers, and even bitterns – and you begin to see why
the Broads are one of Britain's favourite wildlife haunts.

On warm sunny days,
Strumpshaw Fen is alive
with the flutter of wings,
as butterflies,
dragonflies, and
damselflies take flight.

Inset: Bitterns hide in the Strumpshaw Fen reedbeds.
Below (left to right): A tufted duck; the rare swallowtail butterfly.

WHERE ELSE TO SEE
REEDBED WILDLIFE

Britain's reedbeds are a relic of what existed before
the drainage of our wetlands. They are evocative
places, filled with the sounds of unseen birds and
insects, and harbour the diversity of life you would
expect at the boundary between water and land.

Ranworth Broad in Norfolk has swallowtail
butterflies in June, a large variety of dragonflies,
and wild flowers including marsh valerian, royal
fern, and marsh fern. Look for Cetti's warblers in
the low bushes and reeds, redpolls and siskins
in the alders, and cormorants and great crested
grebes on the open water. [SE]

The **London Wetlands Centre**, in Barnes
(see pp.16–17) is a good urban reserve for seeing
hobbies and peregrine falcons, and some of the
more unusual butterflies and damselflies, such as
the painted lady and the blue-tailed damselfly. [SE]

THROUGH THE YEAR
STRUMPSHAW FEN

In **autumn**, you'll see wading birds and water rails
on muddy patches if the water level is low. Marsh
harriers gather in groups to roost. In early autumn,
ospreys are regularly seen fishing, as they linger
on their southward migration.

Hundreds of ducks, including teals, gadwalls, and
shovelers, feed in the reedbed pools during the
winter. In some winters, thousands of starlings
also roost in the reeds, attracting sparrowhawks,
peregrines, and merlins. Shy Chinese water deer
are often spotted early and late in the day.

In **spring**, listen out for booming bitterns and the
drumming of woodpeckers. Swallows and swifts
flit across the pools where great crested grebes
build their nests.

Summer dawn choruses are great experiences, with
the songs of woodland birds mingling with sedge
and reed warblers. Marsh harriers nest and you
may see bearded tits and kingfishers.

Below: In winter, the fen offers a welcome home to migrating birds.

JAN

FEB

MAR

APR

MAY

JUN

JUL

AUG

SEP

OCT

NOV

DEC

A WESTERLY HAVEN

LAKE VYRNWY, IN THE HEART OF WALES, IS A MAN-MADE WONDER. The long, fork-tipped reservoir that lies so serenely in the Berwyn Mountains was actually created by flooding a valley in the 1880s, to store water for the city of Liverpool. The beautiful wildlife reserve around the lake has many habitats, many favoured by birds of prey: cliffs with peregrines and ravens; conifer forest with goshawks, sparrowhawks, and buzzards; and moorland with merlins, hen harriers, and kestrels. But it also contains one of the wildlife glories of Wales – old, gnarled oak woods, filled with the sound and activity of delightful small woodland birds.

A narrow road runs around the reservoir, starting at the Victorian stone dam at the southern end; much of it runs through dense conifer plantations, but in hidden dips and valleys you suddenly come across patches of oakwood. Seek these out in early summer, before the foliage becomes too dense, and before the birds stop singing.

WHERE
Lake Vyrnwy, Bryn Awel, Llanwddyn, Powys, Wales SY10 0LZ; www.rspb.org.uk

CONTACT
RSPB Lake Vyrnwy Reserve, tel: 01691 870278; vyrnwy@rspb.org.uk

GETTING THERE
Lake Vyrnwy lies just west of the village of Llanfyllin. By car from Llanfyllin, take the B4393 to Llanwddyn and continue along this road until you reach the dam. Turn left here, then left again at the end of the dam. The RSPB visitor centre is on the right. The reserve is difficult to reach by public transport. By train, travel to Welshpool, 32km (20 miles) away. There is an infrequent bus service to the Vyrnwy dam.

ACCESS AND FACILITIES
The reserve has a visitor centre with information, refreshments, shop, toilets, baby-changing facilities, picnic area, and wheelchair/pushchair-friendly trails.

OPENING TIMES
Open daily from 1 April to 24 December, 10.30am–5.30pm (closing at 4.30pm in winter). Open weekends only from 1 January to 31 March.

CHARGES
None.

Food for life
It is difficult to know why the redstart, wood warbler, and pied flycatcher have such a westerly distribution in the UK. Perhaps it is because these long-distance migrants from Africa all like an open woodland floor, and a dense canopy full of foliage brimming with caterpillars – exactly the conditions supplied by these lush Welsh woodlands. The fortunes of all breeding birds are strongly linked to the variable numbers of moth caterpillars in the oak leaves in spring – which are reliably high at Lake Vyrnwy in most years.

Main: Clear, still days provide magnificent views over the lake.

Left: A grey wagtail sings his right to territory and calls for a mate.

Right (left to right): A family of treecreepers huddles together on a tree trunk; a brightly coloured chaffinch flies down towards a woodland drinking pool; a pied flycatcher patiently waits for its insect prey.

Right panel (above and below): More than 30 streams splash down through the woods into the lake; a seedling oak.

Three new arrivals make this time of year really special in these western woods: redstarts, wood warblers, and pied flycatchers. All spend the winter in Africa; the males return as early as they dare to carve out a breeding territory, defending it against all comers with their song, while the females return a few days later. Males that fail to find a mate may sing for weeks; successful birds settle to a less punishing schedule of singing, but have more work to do rearing a family.

See if you can find all three of these determined songsters. The male redstart is a dandy: blue-grey above, rich-orange below, with a striking white forehead and inky-black bib. Wood warblers are sleek birds, with a pale-green, white, and soft-yellow plumage. It is easiest to find a male by his song: a hesitant, thin, metallic ticking sound that accelerates into a silvery, shivery trill. Pied flycatchers do as they promise: they catch flies and the males, at least, are black and white, with an upright, short-legged, long-winged shape that helps them dart from a perch to a fly in a "snap"!

The pure air, spectacular mountain scenery, and large, languid lake here are reminiscent of the Alps.

WHERE ELSE TO SEE
OAKWOOD BIRDS

Loss of woodland around the country has led to a decline in oakwood birds, and it's thought that lack of management of the remaining woodlands has exacerbated the problem – overcrowding of trees leads to canopy closure, loss of open space, and a shaded understorey.

The ancient oak woodland of **Strid Wood**, at Bolton Abbey in the Yorkshire Dales, has a similar range of bird species to those at Lake Vyrnwy, including dippers. [N]

Coombes Valley Nature Reserve in Staffordshire is a peaceful oak woodland where you're likely to see redstarts, pied flycatchers, woodcocks, and great spotted woodpeckers. [M]

The woodland of **Cwm Clydach** in South Wales grows on steep slopes down to the Clydach gorge. There are spectacular waterfalls and a great variety of butterfly, fungi, and woodland birds. **Ynys-hir** (see pp.106–107) on the Dyfi estuary near Machynlleth also has superb oakwood birds, including the westerly trio of redstarts, wood warblers, and pied flycatchers. [W]

THROUGH THE YEAR
LAKE VYRNWY

Spring is a good time to watch for birds of prey hunting across open land and water. Great crested grebes display on the lake, and you stand a good chance of seeing goosanders on the water too.

Autumn is a quiet time, but you may still find some butterflies, such as the pearl-bordered fritillaries, haunting the woodland glades. This is a good area for polecats and otters too, but both are quick to hide, and hard to find. The fairytale fly agaric fungi, bright red with white spots, grows in the woodlands.

Winter sees large flocks of redwings and fieldfares around the lake. Siskins join the tits and other finches at the bird feeders by the visitor centre. Look for treecreepers in the woods, and dippers by the streams. There are teals, goosanders, and little grebes to be found, and ravens begin their tumbling displays.

Below: Goshawks fly down from the woodlands to catch prey.

JAN

FEB

MAR

APR

MAY

JUN

JUL

AUG

SEP

OCT

NOV

DEC

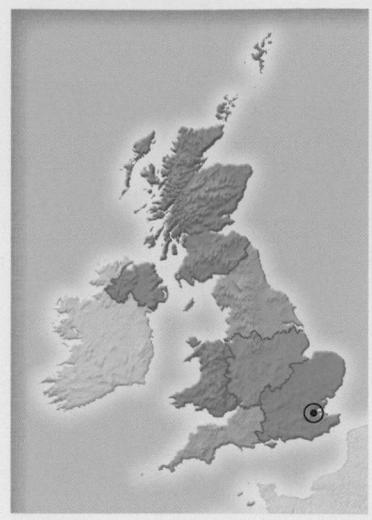

WHERE
Canvey Wick, Canvey Island, Essex SS8 0PT;
www.naturalengland.org.uk

CONTACT
Natural England, tel: 0845 6003078;
enquiries@naturalengland.org.uk

GETTING THERE
By car, take the A130 as far as the B1014.
The nearest train station is Benfleet. From
there you can take a bus to the Canvey
Island supermarket on Northwick Road,
next to the reserve's entrance.

ACCESS AND FACILITIES
As yet there are no facilities on site and
wheelchair access is problematic.

CHARGES
None.

NEW LIFE AT CANVEY WICK

TAKE ONE TRACT OF ESSEX GRAZING MARSH, add hundreds of truckloads of sand and silt, build an oil refinery, knock it down, then apply a liberal dose of informal recreation. Let it stand for 30 years, and what do you get? A nationally important wildlife site.

This is the story of Canvey Wick, an area of some 80 hectares (200 acres) that forms the southwestern portion of Canvey Island, and is now recognized as a hotbed of biodiversity. As a result of its history, climate, and use, Canvey Wick is home to an incredible array of plants and animals. It supports hundreds of types of insects, many of which are locally or nationally rare, including some that have long been believed to be extinct in Britain, and

> Canvey Wick was the first brownfield site to be protected specifically for its invertebrates – among them the shrill and brown-banded carder-bees, the five-banded weevil wasp, and the scarce emerald damselfly.

others that have never before been found in this country. Perhaps most significantly, it has a thriving population of the shrill carder-bee, once widespread across England, but now, with most of its flower-rich habitats destroyed, on the verge of extinction. At Canvey Wick it forages from a range of plants, both natives (like the narrow-leaved bird's-foot trefoil) and aliens, such as goat's-rue and the broad-leaved everlasting pea. In June it buzzes among the Wick's beautiful butterflies, including the marbled white, common blue, and Essex skipper.

Other protected species live here too, such as common lizards, adders, badgers, and water voles. There are thriving populations of the songbirds that are in decline throughout Britain's countryside, and swathes of attractive flowers, including four species of orchid and spectacular yellow splashes of biting stonecrop.

With more rare insects than any other English site of its size, Canvey Wick is unique. But then, so is every brownfield site such as this – each is the product of its singular geography, geology, and history, and each offers a uniquely developed habitat. Any such previously developed site has the potential to be a haven for wildlife. The message is clear – don't overlook the wildlife on your doorstep in your quest for the best spots to go wild.

Main: Canvey Wick is swathed in orchids, including the beautiful southern marsh orchid, which flowers in June.
Below (left to right): The marbled white butterfly; the everlasting pea, a favourite food plant of carder-bees; the bee orchid.
Inset: Canvey Wick has the most important population of the shrill carder-bee in the Thames region, and possibly the UK.

A return to nature

"Brownfield" simply means land that has been developed in the past. There are numerous examples – like Canvey Wick – of areas where nature has reasserted itself after development, but arguably the most surprising are the Norfolk Broads (*pictured below*). Now an internationally important wetland site, the origins of the Broads lie in medieval peat diggings, which were left to fill with water. The resulting rivers, dykes, and cuts allowed wildlife to flourish undisturbed.

Above: Adders can be seen around Canvey Wick in spring and summer.

JAN

FEB

MAR

APR

MAY

JUN

JUL

AUG

SEP

OCT

NOV

DEC

THROUGH THE YEAR
CANVEY WICK

As the flowers and insects fade away at the end of **summer**, the fruits and berries of sea buckthorn and other bushes attract feeding birds, such as the resident blackbirds and immigrant redwings. Bullfinches, always present but hard to see, become more obvious among the bare trees of autumn.

All is quiet on Canvey Wick in the **winter**, except perhaps for a burst of song from a Cetti's warbler on a warm day, or a snipe rising from a winter-wet puddle. But take a look over the sea wall: at low tide, Holehaven Creek is home to internationally important numbers of black-tailed godwits, and you may see a peregrine hunting smaller waders like dunlin over the mudflats.

Spring brings a resumption of reptile activity, with common lizards, grass snakes, and adders basking in any early warmth, while great crested newts return to their breeding ponds and ditches. The blackthorn bursts into a profusion of white flowers, which, along with the pollen from goat willow, forms a vital source of energy and food for early emerging queen bumblebees.

WHERE ELSE TO SEE
BROWNFIELD RESERVES

Nature reserves are one of the more ingenious ways to reuse old brownfield sites, bringing animals and flora back into otherwise barren areas.

The **Old Moor and Fairburn Ings** nature reserves in Yorkshire were formed as a result of mining subsidence. The alkaline slag heaps of **Nob End**, near Bolton, Lancashire, have had a new lease of life and been colonized by thousands of orchids. [N]

The **Cotswold Water Park** in Gloucestershire is a huge collection of gravel pits that is now of immense value to wildlife and recreational interests alike. [M]

"Green roofs" are miniature, artificial brownfield sites that use the roofs of large industrial buildings as nature reserves, such as the **Creekside Nature Conservation Centre** in Deptford, London, which is dedicated to preserving the black redstart. [SE]

REEDBED WILDLIFE

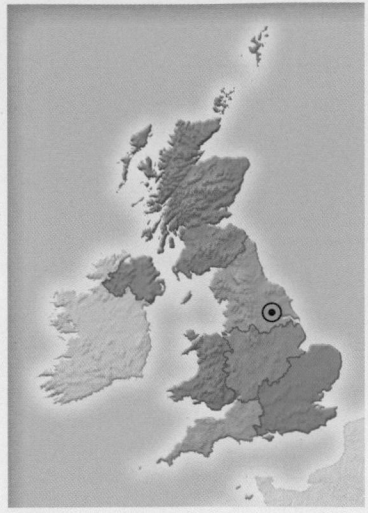

BLACKTOFT SANDS LIES ON THE INNER HUMBER ESTUARY, out of sight of the main river, in an area of extraordinary calm. It is a vast expanse of tidal reedbeds – the largest in England – dotted with artificial lagoons and dykes. The reserve appeals to a huge range of breeding birds, including several of the classic, rare reedbed specialities that are more often associated with East Anglia. Even the elusive bitterns arrive; they are easiest to see in June, as they often fly over the reedbeds carrying fish to their chicks.

Marsh harriers, big birds that hunt on the wing, fly low over the reed tops and lagoon edges, or across neighbouring fields. You'll know them by their long, up-tilted wings. In June the male does the hunting, bringing food back for his mate and young. As he arrives he calls to the female, who flies from the nest to receive the food in a mid-air "food pass", rolling over beneath the male, mid-air, to take the prey from his outstretched feet.

WHERE
Blacktoft Sands RSPB reserve, near Goole, East Yorkshire; www.rspb.org.uk

CONTACT
RSPB Blacktoft Sands, tel: 01405 704665; blacktoftsands@rspb.org.uk

GETTING THERE
From Goole, take the A161 to Swinefleet, turn left at the mini-roundabout in Swinefleet, then right at the next T-junction and follow the minor road for the next 8km (5 miles) through Reedness, Whitgift, and Ousefleet. About 0.5km (⅓ mile) past Ousefleet, heading towards Adlingfleet, turn left into the reserve's car park.

ACCESS AND FACILITIES
The car park has disabled parking, an information centre, picnic area, and toilets. A 1.2km (¾ mile) trail links all six of the reserve's hides. There is firm, level path leading to five of the hides, and all have wheelchair access. The path to Ousefleet hide is rough in places.

OPENING TIMES
Open daily 9am–9pm, or dusk if earlier.

CHARGES
For non-RSPB members.

Hunting out treasure

It can be hard to believe that sweeping a bill through mud or silt can yield a nutritious meal for a bird. However, mud is packed with living organisms and organic material and different species have evolved their own ways to find these foods. Birds with long bills, such as curlews and godwits go deep to pull out worms, while shorter-beaked coots, dunlins, and sanderlings pick off insects from the surface, and avocets have upturned bills, which are ideal for filtering food from fine mud and silt.

Main: The vast expanses of tidal reedbeds at Blacktoft Sands.

Left: A greenshank in flight.

Right (left to right): A brown hare drinks at the water's edge; a bearded tit feeds on insects amongst the reeds.

Right panel (top and bottom): A male marsh harrier passes food to a female in flight; the black-tailed godwit.

Many visitors come to see the owls: short-eared owls hunt during the day, and barn owls – who prefer the dark – may join them when they have young to feed. Equally important are the bearded tits: listen out for their sharp, metallic "pinging" calls. With patience, a bit of luck, and some good weather, you should see them frollicking around in the reedbeds.

From the main central hide you can see avocets nesting, and in the ditches just in front of you, the furry water voles: rare little creatures, with appealing short, fat faces, stub noses, and dainty forefeet, which they use to manipulate their food. There's an abundance of butterflies, including painted ladies, red admirals, and peacocks. Walk one way into the reserve, pausing at the various hides, then return to the centre and go on in the other direction to repeat the process. The sun swings around behind you, so the light over the reserve is extraordinarily good – and in this wide coastal landscape, the cloudscapes add magnificently to the scene.

Blacktoft is in the perfect place for coastal migrants. Over 200 bird species have been recorded here.

WHERE ELSE TO SEE
REEDBEDS AND LAGOONS

The reedbed and coastal lagoon combination is found at a number of sites, mainly in East Anglia – the classic home for reedbed birds.

Norfolk coastal sites, from **Holme** and **Cley-next-the-sea** to **Breydon Water**, are wonderful places to see reedbed birds, as are those further south, along the Suffolk coast, such as **Walberswick** and **Minsmere** (*see pp.100–101*). **Fingringhoe Wick** (*see pp.124–125*), in Essex, also sees an influx of wildfowl. [SE]

Many of the waders and wildfowl seen at Blacktoft can also be seen around Kent, at **Elmley Marshes** (*see pp.306–307*), **Dungeness** (*see pp.162–163*), and **Cliffe Pools**. [SE]

More westerly sites are home to some of the birds seen at Blacktoft, but not the full coastal lagoon and reedbed range. These include **Radipole Lake** (*see pp.60–61*) and **Lodmoor** in Dorset; and **Chew Valley Lake** and **Ham Wall** in Somerset. [SW]

THROUGH THE YEAR
BLACKTOFT SANDS

Autumn brings large numbers of greenshanks, ruffs, black-tailed godwits, spotted redshanks, and dunlins, as well as water rails, which like to run around the lagoon edges. Stay late to witness the roosting flocks of swallows and martins.

The best time for hen harriers and merlins roosting in the reeds at dusk is in **winter**; marsh harriers return from mid-February. Teals and wigeons are common, but check for shovelers, pintails, gadwalls, and other ducks from the Ousefleet Hide. Look out, too, for tree sparrows and barn owls.

In **spring** the reserve is alive with reed, sedge, and willow warblers, blackcaps, and whitethroats. The marsh harriers begin their stunning aerial courtship displays, while the eery sound of bitterns booming can be heard at dawn and dusk.

Below: The barn owl prefers hunting at night.

JAN

FEB

MAR

APR

MAY

JUN

JUL

AUG

SEP

OCT

NOV

DEC

WHERE
Wistman's Wood National Nature Reserve, Two Bridges, Devon PL20 6SW; www.naturalengland.org.uk

CONTACT
Natural England Devon, tel: 0300 0601110; devon@english-nature.org.uk; Wistman's Wood site manager, tel: 01626 832330.

GETTING THERE
Wistman's Wood is near the centre of the Dartmoor National Park. By car it's 2km (1¼ miles) north of Princetown at the junction of the B3357 and B3212 between Tavistock and Ashburton. The nearest train station is 25km (15½ miles) away at Newton Abbot.

ACCESS AND FACILITIES
There are no facilities on site and no car park nearby. There is no wheelchair access. The nearest car park is at the old quarry in Two Bridges. In Princetown you will find The High Moorland Visitor Centre, which is wheelchair friendly and has toilets. The site is approx. 2km (1¼ miles) north of Princetown – about 25 minutes on foot.

OPENING TIMES
Open all year round.

CHARGES
None.

Rare lichens and ferns

Despite its small size, Wistman's Wood has an astonishing diversity of life. It is home to 119 species of lichens and 47 species of mosses and liverworts, including one of the rarest lichens in Britain, *Bryoria smithii*. There are also two rare species of filmy ferns: Wilson's, and Tunbridge (*shown below*) – which have fronds just one cell thick. They can survive only in places with constantly damp conditions – like the dark, wet, and ancient rocks of Wistman's Wood.

Left (left to right): A view of Wistman's Wood, showing the low profile of its dwarf oaks; the migrant whinchat returns to the wood to breed in spring.

Right (left to right): Beard lichen, just one of the many varieties found in the wood; an emperor moth.

Panel (below right): The common polypody fern growing on an oak trunk.

Main: The oak trees of Wistman's Wood are likely to have grown here in prehistoric times.

IN THE WILD WOOD

FEW PLACES IN BRITAIN CAN EVOKE SUCH A SENSE OF WILDERNESS AS DARTMOOR. Even in June, beneath a blue sky, its vast, trackless expanses of heather and shattered granite have an air of savage mystery that is both hostile and exhilarating. For many people, the almost mystical power of the place is most intensely felt in a small area in the very heart of the moor, in the green shade of Wistman's Wood.

It is a tiny woodland, little more than a dab of green on a large-scale map, and as you approach it along the valley of the West Dart River it looks like barely more than a thicket clinging to the eastern slope of the valley. But when you walk into the wood you realize that this is no mere patch of scrub. The trees are pedunculate oaks, exactly like those that grace the parks and hedgerows of middle England, but here stunted by hardship into dwarf, elfin forms barely twice the height of a man, with gnarled and twisted limbs that are smothered with luxuriant

Above: Bilberry grows among the mosses and ferns within the wood.

> Sunlight filters through the green canopy, creating a magical, almost luminous atmosphere.

THROUGH THE YEAR
WISTMAN'S WOOD

In **autumn** the dwarf oaks lose their leaves, letting more light through to the rocky ground below and revealing the contorted shapes of the trees. Meanwhile, heavy rain can turn the nearby West Dart River into a turbulent torrent.

As **winter** tightens its grip on the moor, the weather can be harsh, encouraging small birds to take refuge among the trees. A dusting of snow on the ground creates a completely different atmosphere within the wood, reflecting sunlight up into the branches.

Migrant whinchats and wheatears return to breed alongside resident stonechats on the surrounding moorland and within the wood itself during the **spring**. Wet patches of ground become flushed with colour as acid-loving plants burst into bloom.

WHERE ELSE TO SEE
ANCIENT WOODS

Few woodlands have such an atmosphere of antiquity as Wistman's Wood, because most have undergone centuries of management. Despite this, old woodlands have a distinct appeal, and boast a rich diversity of plant species.

One woodland with the same magical air as Wistman's Wood is **Kingley Vale** (see pp.310–311) in West Sussex: a grove of ancient yew trees that lies at the heart of one of Europe's finest yew forests. [SE]

Bradfield Woods, in Suffolk, has been under continuous management since the 13th century, and many of the trees there are still coppiced in the traditional way. [SE]

Birklands Wood, situated in Sherwood Forest, Nottinghamshire (see p.36–37), contains a great number of veteran oak trees that have been allowed to mature naturally. [M]

The **Black Wood of Rannoch** (see pp.66–67) is one of the last patches of the Caledonian pine forest that covered most of Scotland. [SC]

lichens. They sprout from a tumbled mass of granite boulders, themselves thickly felted with mosses, which combines with the pervading smell of earthy antiquity to create a supremely eerie, magical effect. Small wonder that the place is associated with legends of ghosts, fairies, and druids. Luckily the days are long in June, for you might not want to stay here after dusk has fallen.

Even in broad daylight the trees look as if they have been here for ever, and in a sense this may be true. Fossil pollen preserved in the moorland peat shows that until about 7,000 years ago much of Dartmoor was wooded, but then the pollen record shows a sudden increase in bracken and grasses, almost certainly because the woodland was being cleared by people, probably by burning. Remains of their settlements can be seen near Wistman's Wood, and indeed all over Dartmoor. Eventually nearly all the trees were destroyed, but for some reason – probably the boulders – Wistman's Wood seems to have been left uncleared. If so, this means that the trees are descended from the last surviving fragment of primeval wildwood on Dartmoor. If you visit it, you will not doubt this for a second.

JAN

FEB

MAR

APR

MAY

JUN

JUL

AUG

SEP

OCT

NOV

DEC

SHINGLE WILDERNESS

NOTHING REALLY PREPARES YOU FOR THE MAGICAL DESOLATION OF DUNGENESS. The shark-fin-shaped promontory sticks out into the Straits of Dover, in a huge, wide-open, flat expanse that stretches for miles and miles, occasionally punctured with low patches of vegetation and artistically scattered flotsam and jetsam.

Natural England classes Dungeness as a desert, but in fact it is one of the largest shingle landscapes in the world. Although it may look deserted, there's a lot going on here. Not only are there two nuclear power stations (only one is active), but there are two lighthouses, a visitor centre, a bird observatory, a miniature railway, and an RSPB reserve. However large these man-made edifices may be, they are dwarfed by the vast landscape, which has a unique ecosystem. The shingle supports a specialized plant community, which in turn encourages rare insects and lichens. The brown-banded carder bee (almost extinct in the UK), is doing well here. Some of the shingle

WHERE
Dungeness, Dungeness Rd, Lydd, Kent
TN29 9PN.

CONTACT
RSPB Dungeness Nature Reserve,
tel: 01797 320588; dungeness@rspb.org.uk

GETTING THERE
By car take the Dungeness road out of Lydd
and after 1.5km (1 mile) turn right. The
RSPB visitor centre and car park are one mile
along the entrance track. The nearest train
station is Rye; take the no.711 bus to Lydd,
then change to the no.12. A popular way to
arrive is via the miniature railway that runs to
Dungeness from Hythe; visit www.rhdr.org.uk
for details. Dungeness lies on Route 2 on the
Sustrans National Cycle Network.

ACCESS AND FACILITIES
The RSPB visitor centre has full-access toilets,
and hot and cold drinks and snacks. The car
park for the RSPB Hanson ARC site, with
short, accessible trails to birdwatching hides,
is opposite the reserve main entrance on the
left of the Dungeness Road.

OPENING TIMES
Year-round. The visitor centre is open from
10am–5pm (or 4pm November–February).

CHARGES
Parking charges for non-RSPB members.

The medicinal leech

The shallow muddy pools at Dungeness are the
perfect habitat for the medicinal leech. These
blood-sucking, worm-like creatures grow to
20cm (8 in) long, and were nearly used
to extinction by doctors in the 18th century.
Leeches only have to feed every six months,
and never take more than they need. They have
strong suckers on both ends of their bodies –
one for biting, and one for latching on to a host,
which may be a bird, fish, or frog.

Main and far right:
Boardwalks protect the shingle
habitat; the black-and-white
lighthouse is a landmark.

Left (left to right): The very
rare great crested newt; the
view across the lagoons
managed by the RSPB.

Right (left to right): Wild
carrot; viper's bugloss; the
Nottingham catchfly, with insects
caught by its sticky glands.

speciality include the fragrant Nottingham catchfly. This nectar-rich plant flowers at night, attracting moths such as the rare Sussex emerald. Dense clusters of white-flowering sea kale hug the outer shingle ridges and dotted around the numerous pools of water you can see swathes of viper's bugloss, short-stemmed foxgloves, and wild carrot – perfect food for the Sussex emerald caterpillar. In the areas of undisturbed shingle you'll find lichen-rich communities supporting myriad species, including the very rare pygmy footman moth. Lichens are also useful in that they help build up the soil content in the shingle, encouraging other plants to grow.

Towards the interior of the promontory lies the RSPB reserve: a vast network of gravel pits, reedbeds, and shingle that attracts seabirds and wintering wildfowl. Look out too for the great crested newt and the enormous green medicinal leech. The promontory itself is one of the best places in the UK to watch the spring and autumn migration.

> The stark beauty of Dungeness belies its rich wildlife: over 60 bird species and 600 plant types thrive here.

THROUGH THE YEAR
DUNGENESS

In **autumn** there are always lots of migrating birds in passage, such as redstarts and wheatears. The goldeneyes arrive in October, but you'll need to wait until November to be in with a chance of seeing smews, goosanders, and hen harriers.

Although an amazing variety of duck species spend the **winter** on the lagoons at Dungeness, you can also see wild swans and white-fronted geese. There's a pretty good chance of seeing merlins and peregrines, and – spectacularly – flocks of up to 6,000 lapwings.

As the winter migrants leave in **spring**, a new wave of birds arrive, some passing through Dungeness, while others stay to breed. You'll see an increase in warblers; sedge warblers, reed warblers, and whitethroats all nest on the reserve. As the waters warm up in the lakes and ditches, great crested newts start returning to still water to breed. Listen out for the raucous chuckle of male marsh frogs as they start calling for mates in early spring.

WHERE ELSE TO SEE
SHINGLE HABITATS

There are three other major shingle habitats in Britain, although none as large as Dungeness.

On the Suffolk coast, **Orford Ness** is a 15km (9 mile) shingle spit. Like Dungeness it also has a variety of specialized flora, including sea pea and false oat-grass. [SE]

The long, wild, and windswept **Chesil Beach** (*see pp.180–181*) in Dorset is another fine example of shingle habitat. This storm beach has been colonized by a host of species, ranging from breeding birds to rare flora. [S]

The **Culbin Shingle Bar** on the coast of Scotland's Moray Firth (*see pp.220–221*) is the most northerly shingle habitat. The bar is roughly 7km (4 miles) long and is a pristine remnant of a much larger shingle habitat. [SC]

JAN
FEB
MAR
APR
MAY
JUN
JUL
AUG
SEP
OCT
NOV
DEC

Below: Sea kale, dwarfed by the onshore winds, in flower.

JULY

Where to Go: July

Summer continues unabated: but already we see the freshness of the green woods and hedges begin to fade a fraction, and the brightest greens turn just a touch darker. Butterflies, bees, and grasshoppers are at their peak, and dragonflies and damselflies are still increasing in number as the summer progresses. Common blue, chalkhill blue and, in rare places, Adonis blue butterflies can be seen on short, cropped grassland, while other splendid butterflies – purple emperors, white admirals, silver-washed fritillaries and purple hairstreaks – can be seen in some of our mature woods. The birds, those great indicators of the state of the world around us, are already signalling that the best of the summer might have gone. The woods are quieter: only on the

COAST

ABBOTTS HALL The marshes are covered in wildflowers in summer.

ABBOTTS HALL FARM
COLCHESTER, ESSEX [SE]

Conservationists here are experimenting with letting the sea reclaim the land, resulting in a botanical feast on the saltmarshes.
See pp.192–193

CHESIL BEACH
DORSET [SW]

An elemental place, with the world's largest tombolo, or shingle bank. Massive cliffs and coastal shingle allow only the hardiest of plants to grow.
See pp.180–181

ORFORD NESS
ORFORD, SUFFOLK [SE]

Europe's largest shingle spit is a truly wild and remote location, harbouring rare shingle flora. Winter flooding encourages large numbers of wildfowl and waders.
See pp.180–181

SOUTH STACK
ANGLESEY, NORTH WALES [W]

The cliffs contain some of Wales' oldest rocks, and are home to over 8,000 nesting birds in summer. Adders bask around the cliff tops.
See pp.182–183

ISLANDS

RAMSEY ISLAND Choughs perform aerial displays around the cliffs.

RAMSEY ISLAND
PEMBROKESHIRE, WALES [W]

Grey seals offshore, and whole families of choughs cavorting around the cliffs. Peregrines hunt in the air above them.
See pp.182–183

Look for groups of gannets plunge-diving: the huge white birds enter the ocean like darts, their wings closing just a second before entry.

RATHLIN ISLAND
COUNTY ANTRIM [NI]

The windswept rocks, cliffs, and grasslands of Rathlin Island are a haven for wildlife. In summer the island is vibrant with pinks and purples from the abundant flora.
See pp.182–183

AILSA CRAIG
FIRTH OF CLYDE [SC]

This isolated granite island has high, dramatic seacliffs, which make the perfect home for breeding seabirds in summer.
See pp.168–169

BASS ROCK
EAST LOTHIAN [SC]

This volcanic rock towers out of the ocean, covered in nesting seabirds – especially gannets – during the summer.
See pp.168–169

NOSS
SHETLAND [SC]

The rugged, uninhabited island of Noss might be one of the best places in the UK to watch seabirds, but in summer the ungrazed, high moors are awash with colourful wildflowers.
See pp.168–169

PARKS AND GRASSLAND

WIMBLEDON COMMON Rival male stag beetles show off their prowess.

WIMBLEDON COMMON
LONDON [SE]

The deadwood around the common provides the perfect arena for pitched battles between stag beetles; duck to avoid their clumsy flights.
See pp.188–189

FARTHING DOWNS AND HAPPY VALLEY
LONDON [SE]

These North Downs chalklands are a stretch of green within the M25. By day, look for wildflowers and butterflies; by night, watch for the light of the glow worm.
See pp.176–177

RODBOROUGH COMMON
GLOUCESTERSHIRE [M]

Some of our rarest grassland butterflies live on this Cotswold common in summer, including the beautiful Adonis blue, which can be seen among the grasses.
See pp.194–195

An area of rolling hills and broad views, the Cotswolds are blessed with a building stone the colour of honey that suffuses every one of the villages.

OLD WINCHESTER HILL
HAMPSHIRE [SE]

A reserve for lovers of wild flowers, with rare round-headed rampions, several types of unusual orchids, as well as some archaeological features.
See pp.176–177

heaths and commons does the yellowhammer keep going, singing all day, every day, all summer long. Swifts zoom around in screaming parties around the houses, already thinking of heading south. At reservoir edges and marshes, green sandpipers appear, having come back south from Scandinavia, and flocks of lapwings begin to decorate the shorelines. For them it is already autumn.

This is a wonderful time to visit an island, where the seabirds are still busy, and you might have the chance of a great day watching the aerial displays of peregrines or choughs. Stay overnight on Skomer or Skokholm to experience the magic of the Manx shearwaters, flying towards their nesting burrows with a great caterwauling chorus, under the cover of darkness.

UPLANDS

YORKSHIRE DALES One of the UK's last remaining hay meadows.

YORKSHIRE DALES
YORKSHIRE [N]

The valley meadows of The Dales are transformed into dazzling displays of floral diversity during the summer, as wildflowers grow among the grass before haymaking.
See pp.184–185

WEARDALE
COUNTY DURHAM [N]

One of the richest grassland habitats in Britain, this site overflows with wildflowers, and breeding waders can be seen foraging in the springy moist soil.
See pp.184–185

CHEDDAR GORGE
SOMERSET [SW]

The highest inland cliffs in the UK are spectacular; deep beneath, Cheddar's caves provide a refuge for bats, including the very rare lesser horseshoe bat.
See pp.186–187

Two of the largest caves in Cheddar are said to have inspired JRR Tolkien's trilogy, *The Lord of the Rings*, after his honeymoon visit to the gorge.

GORDALE SCAR
MALHAM, NORTH YORKSHIRE [N]

This awesome and dramatic gorge slices through the limestone cliffs of Malham, creating a unique wildlife habitat for rare flora. Peregrine falcons nest on the cliffs.
See pp.186–187

CORS CARON
CEREDIGION, MID WALES [W]

A glorious mosaic of colourful vegetation, the bog pools buzz with dragonflies, while red kites, merlins, and peregrines soar high in the skies above.
See pp.190–191

WOODLAND

NEW FOREST The perfect place for animal-oriented summer walks.

BOOKHAM COMMONS
LEATHERHEAD, SURREY [SE]

Two of our most magnificent butterflies – the silver-washed fritillary and rare purple emperor – can be found here.
See pp.170–171

THE NEW FOREST
HAMPSHIRE [SW]

This royal hunting ground is ablaze with yellow gorse and purple heather in summer. Ponies, deer, and squirrels roam in the ancient woodland.
See pp.174–175

KIELDER FOREST
NORTHUMBERLAND [N]

England's biggest forest also has the largest area of blanket bog. The many forest ponds teem with insect life, including the rare lesser Emperor dragonfly and the southern hawker.
See pp.170–171

BLEAN WOODS
FAVERSHAM, KENT [SE]

A huge, ancient broadleaved woodland that shelters nightingales and nightjars in summer. Look out, too, for the heath fritillary butterfly.
See pp.170–171

MOUNTAINS

SNOWDON Polecats hide among the mountains.

SNOWDON
GWYNEDD, NORTH WALES [W]

This enormous national park is full of wildlife and rare flowers, such as the Snowdon lily. Jackdaws, choughs, and ravens fly around the mountain.
See pp.172–173

The dramatic and varied landscapes of Snowdonia have all the grandeur of the Scottish Highlands, even though the scale is somewhat smaller.

INVERPOLLY
HIGHLAND [SC]

This vast and remote area of heather and grass moorland has divers and ducks on the lochs in summer; wheatears and ring ouzels breed on the slopes.
See pp.178–179

WINNATS PASS
CASTLETON, DERBYSHIRE [M]

The massive power of nature can be experienced at these towering, awesome crags. The fossilized coral reef limestone is rich with crinoids, ammonites, and brachiopods.
See pp.186–187

THE CAIRNGORMS
ABERDEENSHIRE [SC]

A true British wilderness hides our most sought-after wildlife, including reindeer, ptarmigans, snow buntings, and dotterel.
See pp.178–179

GLASLYN ESTUARY
PORTHMADOG, NORTH WALES [W]

This deep and dramatic ravine provides a harsh, rocky habitat for wildlife. Look to the skies for red kites, merlins, and peregrines.
See pp.172–173

WHERE
Bass Rock lies in the Firth of Forth, 1.6km (1 mile) off the coast of North Berwick, Scotland.

CONTACT
The Scottish Seabird Centre, The Harbour, North Berwick EH39 4SS, Scotland, tel: 01620 890202; www.seabird.org

GETTING THERE
The Scottish Seabird Centre at North Berwick runs wildlife-watching boat trips around the islands of Bass Rock and Craigleith, and to Fidra. The island of Fidra is an RSPB reserve (www.rspb.org.uk).

ACCESS AND FACILITIES
Access is by boat only; there are no facilities on the island. Visitors may need to use ladders to access the boat and the island.

OPENING TIMES
Boat trips generally run from April to October, from North Berwick, but only certain operators have landing rights for the island, so check before you book.

CHARGES
Boat trip charges vary.

Sky-pointing

The gannet is one of the most studied seabirds in the world. Ornithologists have noted that gannets exhibit ritualized behavior that communicates specific actions to their mate, possibly due to living in such a crowded colony. For example, when one of the pair is about to leave the nest, it will "sky-point" to indicate that it is about to fly off, by pointing its bill upwards and dropping its wings slightly. It holds this position for a few seconds before lifting off.

Above: Razorbills are found among the cliffs of Cable Gulley and around the inner landing.

Below (top to bottom): Seals can often be seen around the base of Bass Rock; a black-legged kittiwake.

Right panel (top and bottom): The birds nest in very close proximity to one another – just beyond pecking distance; the spectacular plunge-dive of the gannet.

Main: The gannet colony at Bass Rock was described by Sir David Attenborough as "one of the wildlife wonders of the world".

GANNETS ON BASS ROCK

R ESEMBLING A WHITE ICED BUN FROM A DISTANCE, it is only when you approach Bass Rock by boat that you realize that the "icing" is a living mass of gannets. Deriving their species name *Morus bassana* from Bass Rock, the gannet reigns supreme here, with 75,000 pairs covering almost every square inch of ground and accessible cliff. As you reach the rock, you'll be struck by two more things: the overpowering smell of guano, and the sheer noise coming from this enormous colony of seabirds. This is truly an extravagance of birds.

Perched in the Firth of Forth and easily seen from the shore at North Berwick, the rock is a volcanic plug of phonolite standing over 100m (330ft) high, with a circumference of 1.6km (1 mile). Up close, "the Bass" towers out of the ocean; clouds of creamy-white gannets circle its cliffs and nearly every available space on land is taken by the nesting birds. These are the largest seabirds in the northern hemisphere, with a wingspan of

Above: Both the male and female gannets provide food for the chicks.

WHERE ELSE TO SEE
GANNETS

Gannets nest in dense colonies on cliffs, rocks, grassy coastal slopes and flat-topped islands around the UK.

Ailsa Craig, a large rock off the west coast of Scotland in the Firth of Clyde, is home to a thriving gannet colony. [SC]

Bempton Cliffs RSPB Reserve in Yorkshire (*see pp.104–105*) is perhaps Britain's most accessible gannet colony. [N]

Hermaness and **Noss** in Shetland both have impressive colonies of gannets along with a suite of other seabirds. [SC]

St Kilda is home to one of our best known gannet colonies – tens of thousands nest on the sea stacks here – but access is tricky and only by boat from the Scottish west coast. [SC]

Gannets are made for high-speed diving: they have skulls as thick as crash helmets, and throat sacs that instantly swell with air.

THROUGH THE YEAR
BASS ROCK

Gannets and other breeding seabirds will still be present on the rock in early **autumn**, as the gannet chicks prepare to leave for Africa, but weather dictates whether boat trips will run.

The first gannets start to return in February but the rock is inaccessible to humans at this time of year. The Scottish Seabird Centre at North Berwick has a live show of the birds, with images beamed from cameras around the rock; you can also watch the birds of nearby Fidra island. Look around just offshore from North Berwick too: a few sea ducks, divers, and grebes may be present in the Firth of Forth, and along the rocky shoreline look out for purple sandpipers.

Seabird breeding starts in the **spring**, and will be in full swing by May.

180cm (70in), and while they are ungainly on land, they glide low over the sea with extraordinary grace. Look out too, for groups plunge-diving: the birds enter the ocean like white darts, their wings closing just a second before entry, hitting the water at 100kph (60mph) in search of fish.

Other birds do breed here, too, where they can find space: guillemots, razorbills, eider ducks, gulls, and even a few comical puffins can be seen. A pair of peregrine falcons have taken up partial residence as they breed nearby – there is certainly no shortage of food for these fast raptors. Grey seals languish in the sun on the exposed rocks at the base of the rock, and if you're lucky, you might see porpoises and dolphins in the seas around the rock.

Looking at Bass Rock today, it is almost inconceivable to imagine that humans once inhabited it; even the lighthouse is now unmanned. But the Bass has a long and varied history stretching back more than a thousand years. Ruins of a pre-Reformation chapel, built around 1490, still stand halfway up the rock, and its isolated position has led to its use as both a fortress and a prison in the past – but the true owners have always been the hundreds of thousands of birds.

JAN

FEB

MAR

APR

MAY

JUN

JUL

AUG

SEP

OCT

NOV

DEC

WOODLAND BUTTERFLIES

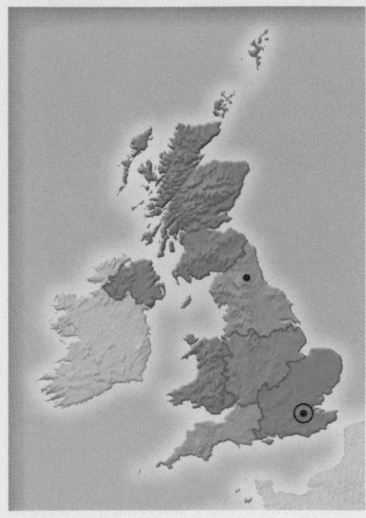

WOODLAND IS NOT THE FIRST HABITAT YOU MIGHT ASSOCIATE with butterflies, yet woodlands have their sunny spots, at their edges and in clearings, and these often support a rich variety of flowering plants and shrubs that provide both nectar for adult butterflies and food for their caterpillars. Most of Britain's breeding species are regularly found in woodlands, and many rarely occur anywhere else. They include two of our most magnificent butterflies – the large silver-washed fritillary and the rare purple emperor – both among the most beautiful in Europe, and both of which can be found at Bookham Commons in Surrey. Donated to the National Trust in the 1920s, these three adjacent areas of common land on

WHERE
Bookham Commons, Leatherhead, North Downs, Surrey KT22.

CONTACT
The National Trust North Downs Countryside Office, tel: 01372 220641; bookham@nationaltrust.org.uk
Natural England Surrey, tel: 01483 568121.

GETTING THERE
The Commons are on the North Downs on the A246 between Leatherhead and Guildford. The nearest train station and bus stop is Bookham Station, from where you can walk to the Commons via a footbridge.

ACCESS AND FACILITIES
There are three parking areas, but no facilities of any sort on the Commons – the nearest are at Great Bookham. Wheelchair access is limited. The London Natural History Society (www.lnhs.org.uk) holds monthly meetings on the Commons as part of their ongoing ecological survey of the site, and will also host Field Study days for interested visitors, by prior arrangement.

OPENING TIMES
Open all year round.

CHARGES
None.

The comma butterfly is among more than 300 species of butterflies and moths that have been recorded at Bookham Commons – as well as 17 species of dragonfly, 611 different species of beetles, and 1,140 true flies.

the North Downs are dominated by oak woodland, one of the richest of all Britain's wildlife habitats. Visit them on a sunny day in July, and you are sure to see a good range of butterflies. The first you come across may be a speckled wood – a chocolate-brown, cream-spotted insect that enjoys basking in patches of sunlight. The males adopt these as territories, vigorously defending them against rival males but welcoming any visiting females.

The rarer, but far more spectacular silver-washed fritillary has a similar taste for sunny clearings with dense undergrowth (such as brambles), so if you see a suitable site, investigate it. The butterfly is unmistakable because of its size – it is by far the largest British species – and the striking silvery-green of its underwings. Another woodland specialist is the white admiral, a largely black butterfly with striking white wing-bands. But the real prize is the white admiral's close relative, the purple emperor, which spends its time high in the treetops sipping the sugary honeydew produced by aphids. The female looks like a larger version of the white admiral, but the wings of the male have an iridescent purple sheen, visible only at certain angles. Its treetop habits make it a rare sight, but occasionally the males fly down to the woodland floor to drink, and if you happen to be watching, you will not be disappointed.

Main: A pearl-bordered fritillary, feeding on foxglove.
Below (left to right): Speckled wood butterfly; a brimstone butterfly; the purple emperor.
Inset: The comma butterfly is easily identified by its ragged wings.

Strange tastes

The purple emperor is notoriously elusive, but the iridescent males do flutter to the ground for several minutes to sip at what we would consider disgusting sources – such as muddy puddles, the decaying remains of dead animals, and even fresh dung. They do this to obtain sodium and other minerals that are essential for the healthy function of their reproductive systems. Females do not need these mineral supplements, so they normally stay high in the treetops.

Above: A trail through Bookham Commons, crossing a wooden bridge.

JAN

FEB

MAR

APR

MAY

JUN

JUL

AUG

SEP

OCT

NOV

DEC

THROUGH THE YEAR
BOOKHAM COMMONS

All woodlands are glorious places to visit in **autumn**, and those of Bookham Commons are no exception. A few butterflies may still be on the wing, especially species that hibernate as adults, such as the comma and the brimstone. There may also be some late dragonflies patrolling the paths and clearings.

In **winter** the bare branches allow light through to the woodland floor, and provide good views of woodland birds. This is a good place to look for the massive-billed hawfinch, a typically elusive bird that becomes more visible when feeding in flocks at this time of year.

Spring sees the return of migrant breeding birds, notably the nightingale, which sings among patches of scrub on the site. The first butterfly to appear is nearly always the yellow-winged brimstone.

WHERE ELSE TO SEE
WOODLAND BUTTERFLIES

The best butterfly woods are old, species-rich, broadleaved woodlands with plenty of open spaces, so low-growing plants – the perfect caterpillar food – can flourish. Coppicing creates ideal woodland butterfly habitat, so the best sites are ancient woodlands that are coppiced for nature conservation.

The rare heath fritillary can be found in **Blean Woods** near Faversham, Kent, and **Thrift Wood** and **Hockley Woods** in Essex. [SE]

Bernwood Forest, near Oxford, is a good site for the purple emperor and silver-washed fritillary, as well as the smaller black, brown, and purple hairstreaks, which are also woodland specialists. [SE]

Kielder Forest, Northumberland, is home to the small pearl-bordered fritillary, large heath fritillary, and dark green fritillary. [N]

WHERE
Snowdon/Yr Wyddfa, Snowdonia National Park, Gwynedd, Wales; www.eryri-npa.gov.uk

CONTACT
Snowdonia National Park Authority, National Park Office, Penrhyndeudraeth, Gwynedd LL48 6LF, tel: 01766 770274; parc@snowdonia-npa.gov.uk

GETTING THERE
Llanberis is the nearest town to Snowdon. By car, leave the A55 at J11, and follow signs for the B4366 towards Bethesda until you see signs for Llanberis. By rail, travel to Bangor, then take a bus either to Llanberis, or go to Pen-y-pas, 359m (1,117ft) above sea level – getting a walk off to a good start.

ACCESS AND FACILITIES
The local council runs a Sherpa "hop on, hop off" bus service that stops at many places within Snowdonia, including Snowdon. You can also catch a train right to the top of Snowdon (www.snowdonrailway.co.uk) from Llanberis. The visitor centres at Llanberis and at the top of the mountain are wheelchair friendly, with refreshments and toilets.

OPENING TIMES
Open all year round (weather dependent).

CHARGES
For car parking.

An Ice-Age fish
Llyn Tegid lake, in the Snowdonia National Park, is home to the very rare gwyniad fish, which was trapped in the lake at the end of the last Ice Age – around 10,000 years ago – and does not exist anywhere else. A combination of deteriorating water quality and competition from an introduced fish, the ruffe, in the 1980s, means that the gwyniad could face extinction. Conservationists are moving its eggs to safer sites in the hope of starting a new population elsewhere.

Above (top and bottom): Rainbow leaf beetles mating; the rare Snowdon lily grows from crevices.

Below: There are around 1,000 goats in Snowdonia, which winter up in the mountains, but can be seen further down, among the lakes, in summer.

Right panel (top and bottom): A raven parent feeds its one-week-old chicks in their nest; Snowdonia is one of the main strongholds for polecats in the UK.

Main: Walking at an average rate, it takes a little over 3 hours to climb up one of the easier paths to the summit of Snowdon.

MOUNTAIN MAJESTY

SNOWDONIA'S RICH WILDLIFE IS PROTECTED within the Snowdonia National Park, which stretches for a breathtaking 2,131 sq km (823 sq miles). The dramatic and varied landscapes have all the grandeur of the Scottish Highlands, even though the scale is reduced – in fact, the smaller area seems to make the mountains look even more dramatic. The biggest of all is, at 1,085 m (3,560 ft), the highest British mountain outside Scotland. This is Snowdon, known in Welsh as *Yr Wyddfa*, meaning "The Burial Place" – legend has it that the cairn at the top of the mountain marks the grave of a local giant.

Situated almost at the centre of Snowdonia, Snowdon's pyramid-shaped peak is particularly imposing, as it stands apart from the many other surrounding mountains and can be seen from afar. Much of the mountain is a Site of Special Scientific Interest, and it is home to rare wildlife. Among the hardy alpine wildflowers that survive

Above: Snowdon makes treacherous climbing in winter.

Snowdonia is especially significant for the polecat, as it spread from this refuge to recolonize most of Wales and the English Midlands.

THROUGH THE YEAR
SNOWDON

Fine weather in **autumn** can make a walk up Snowdon very enjoyable. Remember, though, that snow can fall any time from October. The colours of oaks, larches, and other trees, and of the bracken are spectacular. This is a good time to look for birds of prey, including merlins, hen harriers, and red kites, while winter-visiting wildfowl, such as goldeneyes and goosanders, arrive from September onwards.

Winter requires special care on the slopes. The weather is especially variable, and may change from sunshine to driving rain and back within an hour. Winter also brings extremely harsh weather, making it a challenging time even for the tough mountain sheep and feral goats. Ravens rely a great deal on sheep carrion for survival during this season.

Spring may come late and snow can linger until late May or even early June. Ring ouzels, which look like blackbirds but have a white crescent on the chest, return from the Mediterranean region to breed in remote gulleys. Smaller, black-and-white-tailed wheatears are more common. Purple saxifrage is one of the first wildflowers to appear as the snow melts.

WHERE ELSE TO SEE
MOUNTAIN WILDLIFE

There are well over 100 other fine mountains to explore in Snowdonia. The Welsh name for the region, *Eryri*, means "Land of the Eagle", and while there are no eagles, there are other birds of prey, such as kestrels, merlins, peregrines, and buzzards.

At **Glaslyn Estuary**, Porthmadog, on the north west corner of Snowdonia National Park, you can get great views of Wales's only pair of breeding ospreys. [W]

Other good areas for mountain wildlife, geology, and scenery include the **Lake District** and **Pennines** in northern England. [N]

The most extreme conditions in all Britain's mountain regions are to be found in the **Cairngorms** (see pp.178–179), where the high tops are the nearest thing we have to Arctic landscapes. This is the land of golden eagles and Britain's only herd of reindeer. [SC]

there, the Snowdon lily has pride of place, because in Britain it occurs at only a few sites, and these are all in Snowdonia. The lily grows here among inaccessible patches of poor soil on sheer north- and north east facing cliffs. Other alpines include several saxifrages, among them mossy saxifrage, which produces drifts of nodding white flowers in late spring and summer, and moss campion, whose pink summer flowers rise above cushions of tiny pointed leaves. There are also scarce species of clubmosses and many rare lichens.

Rare insects include the dwarf willow-feeding sawfly, which feed on the shrub whose name it bears, and two beetles very rare in Britain: the dull-coloured ground beetle *Nebria nivalis*, which lives among the frost-shattered boulders at the top of Snowdon; and the striped rainbow leaf beetle, which is found only on Snowdon and nearby Cwm Idwal, on the leaves of wild thyme. Jackdaws, carrion crows, and ravens can be seen, as well as their scarcer relative the chough, its black plumage contrasting with bright red legs and feet, and a bright-red, downcurved bill. There are lots of herring gulls, too, and if a group of them suddenly scatters, look for a peregrine.

JAN
FEB
MAR
APR
MAY
JUN
JUL
AUG
SEP
OCT
NOV
DEC

WHERE
The New Forest, Hampshire, SO40 2LR;
www.thenewforest.co.uk

CONTACT
Lyndhurst Visitor Information Centre,
tel: 02380 282269;
Lymington Visitor Information Centre,
tel: 01590 689000;
Ringwood Visitor Information Centre,
tel: 01425 470896.

GETTING THERE
There are three main routes in to the
New Forest: from the M27 J1, the A35
from Southampton, and the A31 from
Bournemouth. Trains stop at Ashurst,
Beaulieu Road, Brockenhurst, and Sway.

ACCESS AND FACILITIES
The New Forest National Park is well
equipped for visitors; car parking, toilets, and
picnic areas are plentiful. Ranger-led walks
can all be booked via the website. There are
three access-friendly trails for wheelchairs
and pushchairs. The New Forest can be very
boggy in winter, so keep to the gravel tracks.

OPENING TIMES
Open all year round.

CHARGES
None.

Singing cicadas

One of the more unusual creatures to be found in
the New Forest is the New Forest cicada – the only
cicada that lives in Britain. At this time of year, in
open, sunny woodland rides and clearings
bordered by scrub, the males can be heard singing
with a high-pitched ringing buzz more reminiscent
of the Mediterranean than an English woodland.
The adults do not live long after breeding, but
their young live underground for up to 10 years,
feeding on the root sap of plants, before emerging
as adults to sing and breed in their turn.

Above (left to right): A sundew, one of the native carnivorous plants; a smooth snake, Britain's rarest reptile, basks in the sunshine.
Main: Wild ponies browse on New Forest heathland.

Above: Beechwood in autumn colour.

A ROYAL PRESERVE

D ESPITE ITS NAME, THE "NEW" FOREST is one of the most ancient landscapes in lowland Britain, where archaic forest laws have conserved an internationally important patchwork of unenclosed pasture, heathland, and ancient woodland. The New Forest was created by King William I in 1079 and the local people were given grazing rights for their animals but not permitted to fence their land; as a result cattle, pigs, and ponies still roam freely with the wild deer. In medieval times a "forest" was simply an area set aside for hunting – less than half of the New Forest Heritage Area is broadleaved woodland, while the remainder is open heath, rough grassland, and bog.

July is high season on the heathlands, which become the most dramatic features of the New Forest, with great tracts of heather and gorse extending to the horizon. The gorse, blazing with coconut-scented yellow flowers and with seedpods cracking audibly in the heat, offers a thorny refuge for the secretive Dartford warbler – a small, red-eyed songbird with a buzzy call.

The New Forest's ancient woodlands and wilderness heath have remained largely unchanged over the past 1,000 years.

Far more conspicuous are the stonechats that perch high on the bushes giving their loud "chack-chack" alarm calls, and the dragonflies that flash through the air on rattling wings. These beautiful insects breed in the dark, peaty water of the mires and valley bogs – such as the one at Wilverley between Brockenhurst and Burley – which also support unusual plants such as insectivorous sundews, bog asphodel, and the rare marsh gentian.

The extensive beech and oak woodlands contain flourishing populations of fallow, roe, and red deer. These can be elusive, but at dawn – a magical time in the forest – they emerge onto the grassy, mossy clearings or "lawns" to feed. Deeper into the woods, squirrels and woodland birds provide prey for the magnificent goshawk, a powerful ambush hunter that has started to breed again in the wild, having been driven to extinction in Britain by 1900. Several pairs now nest high in the treetops of the New Forest.

Inset: The New Forest has the highest concentration of veteran trees in western Europe.
Below (left to right): Fallow deer; a Dartford warbler perches on gorse.

THROUGH THE YEAR
THE NEW FOREST

As summer turns to **autumn** the heather begins to glow with purple flowers, creating a rich tapestry of colour, and the deciduous trees in the woodlands turn shades of brown, yellow, and even red.

Bare trees in **winter** make woodland wildlife such as deer and foxes much easier to see, provided you stay downwind and keep very still.

In **spring** the woodlands erupt with song as breeding birds claim their territories, and heathland reptiles such as adders and lizards emerge from hibernation to warm themselves in the sun.

The Reptiliary near Lyndhurst, open all year round, is an ideal place for a guaranteed sighting of snakes, natterjack toads, sand lizards, and other reptiles.

WHERE ELSE TO SEE
HEATH AND WOODLAND

The variety of habitats that make up the New Forest make it an excellent destination for wildlife watchers, but similar habitats can be visited elsewhere in Britain.

Ashdown Forest in East Sussex and **Thursley Common** (*see pp.128–129*) in Surrey feature lowland heath similar to that of the New Forest, with many of the same species occupying boggy areas as well as large expanses of heather and gorse. The beechwoods of the **Chilterns** are also magnificent in autumn. [SE]

For long walks in large tracts of broadleaved woodland visit the **Forest of Dean**, Gloucestershire, or **Sherwood Forest**, Nottinghamshire. Like the New Forest, these woodlands have a long history of management, but this has only enhanced their value as wildlife habitats. [M]

Arne (*see pp.138–139*) in Dorset is a wonderful expanse of heathland and old oak woodland. Both the Dartford warbler and several native reptiles can be heard and seen on the open heath. [SW]

JAN
FEB
MAR
APR
MAY
JUN
JUL
AUG
SEP
OCT
NOV
DEC

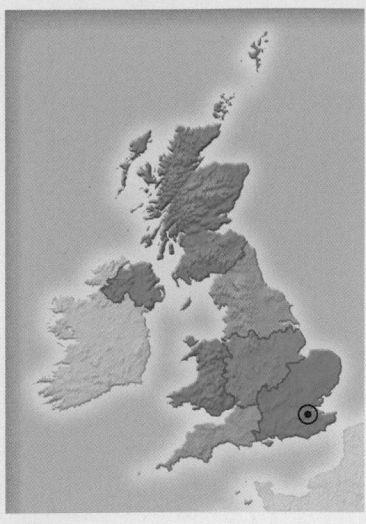

WHERE
Farthing Downs and Happy Valley, Ditches Lane, Coulsdon, Surrey CR5 3EA; www.croydon.gov.uk

CONTACT
Merlewood Estate Office, tel: 020 8660 8533
Croydon Tourist Information Centre, tel: 020 8253 1000

GETTING THERE
The site is very close to Coulsdon South train station, 30 minutes from London Charing Cross and 26 minutes from London Victoria. By car, take the A23 east, turning off at the B276 junction (Marlpit Lane), then take the second right into Downs Road, and left into Ditches Lane where you will find a car park.

ACCESS AND FACILITIES
The only facilities are the car park and toilets in Ditches Lane.

CHARGES
There are no charges for entry to the downs, but car-parking fees may apply.

The Roman snail

Roman snails are very rare in the UK, where they are found only on the downlands of southern England. The snail's shell measures around 5cm (2 in) across, so is very distinctive, but no fossils of this animal have ever been found, leading experts to believe that the snail was introduced to Britain possibly by the Romans (hence its name). The snails mate on cool, damp nights, when you might see them "kissing" one another, by joining their tentacles.

Above: The purple blooms of round-headed rampion.

Right panel (top and bottom): The pretty chalkhill blue butterfly lives on the horseshoe vetch that grows on the chalk grasslands; the greater yellow-rattle, which weakens grass and opens up the grassland, allowing other plants to grow and creating a species-rich area.

Below: Dropwort in flower.

Main: The "unimproved" grasslands of Farthing Downs and Happy Valley provide the perfect habitat for hundreds of rare wild plants.

GLORIOUS GRASSLANDS

THANK GOODNESS FOR PLACES LIKE FARTHING DOWNS AND HAPPY VALLEY. The hill and valley are part of the North Downs, a chalkland that sits within the bounds of the M25 on the doorstep of millions of people, acting like a green lung for the metropolis. The City of London Corporation manages it precisely for this purpose, along with other major open spaces such as Hampstead Heath and Epping Forest.

But it is far from being a glorified country park. Its downland habitats are so rich in wildlife that they would merit an honourable mention in any setting. The chalk grassland supports a colourful range of plants: round-headed rampion, dropwort, several species of orchids including the man orchid, and the greater yellow-rattle, a nationally rare and protected species. You might also find the yellow-flowered horseshoe vetch, which acts as a foodplant for the caterpillars of one of the site's many butterflies, the chalkhill blue. Other insects

JAN
FEB
MAR
APR
MAY
JUN
JUL
AUG
SEP
OCT
NOV
DEC

Above: Redwings rely on winter berries for food during the colder months.

One of Britain's rarest plants, the greater yellow-rattle, thrives on these grasslands within the bounds of its largest city.

THROUGH THE YEAR
FARTHING DOWNS

The fruits of **autumn** appear all over the downs: spindle and hawthorn berries brighten the scrub areas; yew and guelder-rose add colour in the woodland. As they ripen, the fruits are devoured by birds, particularly thrushes such as blackbirds and winter-visiting redwings; in some years you may even spot a flock of colourful waxwings.

The last berries to form and to ripen are those on ivy, which become an essential food resource for birds and field mice in **winter**, especially in severe weather. Wintering flocks of starlings roost in the denser scrub, and long-eared owls roost and nest in the older, taller thickets.

As **spring** progresses, look for butterflies emerging from hibernation, especially brimstones. Skylarks are in song, setting up territories, and in April the summer migrants arrive – willow warblers, chiffchaffs, and whitethroats adding their voices to the chorus. And take a walk into the woods: where the ground is not shaded by yew trees, bluebells and greater stitchwort are bursting into flower.

WHERE ELSE TO SEE
CHALK DOWNLANDS

Chalk downland habitats can be found in all major chalk regions, although they have become fragmented as a result of modern agriculture.

Elsewhere on the North Downs, **Box Hill**, Surrey, is characterized by the abundance of its eponymous shrub, and around **Down House**, near Bromley, Kent, you can experience the environment that inspired Charles Darwin's evolutionary theories. [SE]

On the South Downs in Sussex, **Kingley Vale** (*see pp.310–311*), **Seven Sisters**, and **Old Winchester Hill** are among the numerous nature reserves, while Chilterns chalklands can be visited at **Aston Rowant** (*see pp.222–223*). [SE]

Two chalkland reserves that have survived in the north are **Red Hill** in Lincolnshire [M] and **Millington Pastures**, Pocklington, Yorkshire [N].

include the glow worm (*see pp.222–223*), despite the level of nocturnal light pollution, which can upset the breeding behaviour of this snail-eating beetle. And while rambling across the Downs, you are likely to come across the golfball-sized shells of the Roman snail, some, especially after rain, still with their equally impressive occupants. Over much of the site, there is a constant battle with invasive scrub; a combination of cutting and goat-browsing is used to tackle established areas, after which mowing and grazing – by sheep and cattle – continue the good work.

Areas of ancient ash and oak woodland, such as Devilsden Wood, which have an understorey of hazel and yew, have developed on the valley slopes. The yew casts such dense shade that few plants can survive under it, but where the canopy is more open, the white-flowered sweet woodruff and fast-spreading yellow archangel are typical late spring indicators of the antiquity of the woodland. You may come across two more orchids – white helleborine and bird's-nest orchid – around the scattered stands of beech. Both flower in summer despite the gloomy conditions under a mature beech tree.

UP AMONG THE CLOUDS

THE CAIRNGORMS NATIONAL PARK IS HOME TO SOME OF OUR MOST SOUGHT-AFTER WILDLIFE. It is a huge area of real wilderness – its mountains, moorlands, forests, rivers, lochs, and glens cover 3,800 sq km (1,400 sq miles) – and endures some of Britain's toughest weather conditions. The mountains are the UK's highest and largest, with peaks rising above 1,000m (3,280ft). The highest – Ben Macdui – rises to 1,310m (4,300ft). The stunning scenery of this national park lures climbers and serious walkers even in winter, with its thick layer of tempting snow, but it is June and July when the mountains are at their easiest and safest to explore.

In summer the Arctic-alpine flora is at its best; in July the corries offer shelter to roseroot and mountain sorrel, while the rock walls are covered in purple saxifrage. There are a huge number of walks through the park, but whichever one you take, it will be brightened by moss campion, trailing azaleas, alpine lady's-mantle, and

WHERE
The Cairngorms National Park, Aviemore, Scottish Highlands.

CONTACT
Cairngorms National Park Authority, tel: 01479 873535; enquiries@cairngorms.co.uk Glenmore Visitor Centre, Glenmore Forest Park, Aviemore, Highland PH22 1QU, Scotland; tel: 01479 861220. The Reindeer Centre: 01479 861228; www.reindeer-company.demon.co.uk

GETTING THERE
By road, take the A9 to Aviemore, then follow signs to the Cairngorms National Park. By train, travel to Aviemore. By bus, take the no. 501 Heather Hopper, which connects Ballater and Grantown-on-Spey, and travels right through the centre of the National Park.

ACCESS AND FACILITIES
Wheelchair access is limited; contact the Park Authority (see details above) before arriving, as some access can be arranged. The visitor centre has parking and a full range of facilities. There is a funicular railway to the Ptarmigan Restaurant, which is the UK's highest restaurant. There is also a viewing platform giving views for miles around.

CHARGES
Car-parking charges only.

Role reversal

Dotterels are rarely seen in Britain outside Scotland, where they start to arrive on the high tops in early May. Unusually, it is the male not the female that has the dowdier plumage. When the brighter-looking female displays over her territory, it is a further indication of the way in which gender roles are reversed in this member of the plover family, with the male being left to incubate the eggs and rear the chicks. Dotterels can be extremely tame and will, if disturbed, often not fly up, but run off quickly in short, fast bursts.

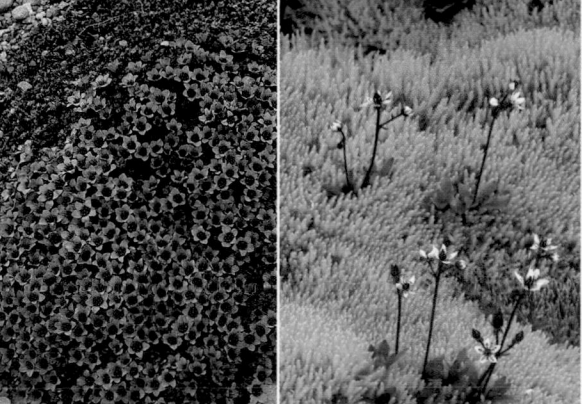

Left: Purple saxifrage growing on rocky ground in the summer; the long shoots of starry saxifrage.

Right (left to right): The snow bunting's summer plumage is monochrome – its white head sits above a black mantle and wing tips; ptarmigans can only be found in the Scottish highlands, where they live on the highest mountains.

starry saxifrage. This is also the best time to see the mountain birds that breed on the summits, such as the beautiful montane wader, the dotterel. Snow buntings and ptarmigans breed in this desolate landscape too, but they are harder to find. Ptarmigans are a very tame type of grouse; they spend all year at high altitudes, and are rarely seen, especially as their summer plumage of speckled grey camouflages them so remarkably well among the lichen-covered rocks.

The ptarmigan always keeps an eye directed towards the sky – as golden eagles patrol these mountains – and they breed in the more remote corners. Mountain hares are their favourite prey, and these animals have become particularly cautious, running away at the slightest sound. Red grouse and red deer live on the lower slopes in summer, the deer grazing on fresh, young shoots. A herd of around 150 Scandinavian reindeer roam around the foot of the Cairngorm Mountain, and guides are available to help you safely approach and even hand-feed these gentle creatures.

WHERE ELSE TO SEE
MOUNTAIN WILDLIFE

The wild northern tundra of the Cairngorms, coupled with its ancient Caledonian forests, makes the area unique. However, you can experience some of its wildlife and types of habitat elsewhere in Scotland.

The large reserve of **Inverpolly** on the northwest coast of Scotland is a mix of mountains, bogs, lochs, and rushing streams. The high tops are home to ptarmigans and golden eagles. [SC]

Pine forest and mountain tops support many Scottish Highland birds at **Beinn Eighe** (see pp.202–203), together with some beautiful montane flora. [SC]

Snowdonia (see pp.172–173) in North Wales has a similar mixture of mountains, forests, and rivers, but a very different climate. Its birds include peregrines and ring ouzels, and it has two unique species: the Snowdon lily and the rainbow leaf beetle. [W]

Main image: The granite walls of the Sticil, one of the most impressive cliffs in the Cairngorms, surround Loch Avon, sending streams tumbling down to the meadows and sands that sit close to the crystal blue water's edge.

Above and below: All reindeer – males and females alike – grow a new set of antlers every year; mountain hares are always alert to potential danger.

THROUGH THE YEAR
THE CAIRNGORMS

As summer turns to **autumn**, the dotterels leave the area, while the ptarmigans and mountain hares start to moult into their white winter plumage and coats. Flocks of snow buntings fly overhead, and otters can sometimes be seen swimming along the River Spey, hunting for food.

Winter is harsh on the Cairngorm plateaux. Ptarmigans and mountain hares favour the corries in winter but may be hard to see. Snow buntings take shelter around the ski car parks. The reindeer roam widely, still warm in their woollier winter coats.

As the snows melt in **spring**, life returns to the tops. Snow buntings start singing, while the ptarmigans get busy calling and displaying. Dotterels arrive in May. The rivers Dee, Don, and Spey are full of salmon and trout, while freshwater pearl mussels cling to the river floor, sadly in ever-declining numbers.

Below: The Cairngorm reindeer in their thick winter coats.

JAN
FEB
MAR
APR
MAY
JUN
JUL
AUG
SEP
OCT
NOV
DEC

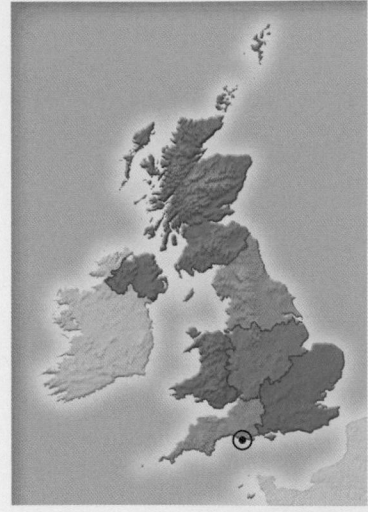

WHERE
Chesil Bank and Fleet Nature Reserve,
Portland Beach Road, Portland, Dorset
DT4 9XE; www.chesilbeach.org

CONTACT
Chesil Bank and Fleet Nature Reserve,
tel: 01305 760579;
reserve@chesil.fsworld.co.uk

GETTING THERE
The visitor centre is located off the A354
between Weymouth and Portland. Follow
signs to Portland. About 0.8km (½ mile)
after crossing Ferrybridge at Wyke Regis, you
will see the centre on the right-hand side of
the road. By public transport, take a bus to
Portland (1 or X1) and get off at Ferrybridge.

ACCESS AND FACILITIES
The visitor centre has a car park, toilets, and
a café as well as information boards and
telescopes. Access to the beach for disabled
visitors is possible at West Bexington,
Chiswell, and Abbotsbury.

OPENING TIMES
The beach and visitor centre are open all
year round.

CHARGES
Yes, for car parking only.

Abbotsbury swannery

This famous swannery was established by
Benedictine monks around 1040, who used to
farm the swans for food. It is now home to a
protected herd of around 800 wild mute swans
that feed on the eel-grass that grows extensively
around Chesil Beach. At the end of July, the birds
are unable to fly due to moulting their flight
feathers and are driven into the swannery using
canoes. Here they can be recorded and have
their health checked.

CHESIL BEACH

MOST PEOPLE'S IDEA OF A BEACH IS A COMFORTABLE CRESCENT of golden sand
within a sheltered bay that's perfect for a picnic. Chesil Beach is nothing like this.
It is a stupendous, elemental place, which you visit because it is a wonder of nature – a
colossal shingle bank or "tombolo" extending in a magnificent arc from the Dorset coast
to the Isle of Portland. It is the largest tombolo in the world, running for 29km (18 miles);
on a warm July day, the far end is often lost in the heat haze. For around half of its length
it is separated from the mainland by a shallow, salty lagoon called the Fleet, which is the
home of the Abbotsbury swannery and its flock of breeding mute swans.

Chesil Beach probably formed well
south of its current position around
12,000 years ago, at the end of the
last ice age. As the glaciers and ice
sheets melted, the sea levels rose,
and the waves pushed the beach
north to where it is today.

For an excellent view of the offhore section of Chesil Beach, stop on the heights of White Hill,
just west of Abbotsbury. Then go to either end of the bank: Burton Bradstock near Bridport,
or Ferrybridge near Portland – site of the Chesil Beach visitor centre – for a dramatically close
view. The Portland end is massive; its great ridge of shingle has been built up by winter
storms to reach up to 14m (46ft) high. Curiously, the pebbles that form the beach are also
bigger at this end, being roughly the size of hens' eggs, while those at Burton Bradstock are
pea-sized. They are graded, becoming progressively larger as you head east.

Mobile coastal shingle is a hostile plant habitat, but where it has stabilized on the
landward side of the bank it provides a roothold for plants such as sea campion, sea kale,
yellow horned poppy, the rare sea pea, and, in places, the spectacular sea holly. There are also
saltmarsh plants such as shrubby sea-blite and sea purslane on the fringes of the Fleet. Many
are in bloom in July, and land birds such as linnets, skylarks, and meadow pipits nest among
the vegetation. Chesil also provides a breeding site for the rare little tern, in a fenced-off area
in Ferrybridge. You can still see the birds, however, and marvel at the way such fragile-looking
creatures can flourish in such a windswept, dramatic place.

Main: The shingle ridge of Chesil Beach is unusual because it is no longer being actively formed.
Inset: The rocky outcrop of East Cliff, seen from West Bay harbour.
Below (left to right): Little tern chicks can be seen in summer; sea campion growing at the northwest end of the beach; sea holly.

Above: A gannet in flight.

JAN

FEB

MAR

APR

MAY

JUN

JUL

AUG

SEP

OCT

NOV

DEC

THROUGH THE YEAR
CHESIL BEACH

As summer fades into **autumn**, a lot of the beach flora dies back, and the breeding birds leave for warmer winter quarters. But the beach is still spectacular, and autumn is the best season for sea anglers looking to catch bass, cod, or plaice.

Winter can be a bleak season on Chesil Beach, which is notorious for its ferocious storm waves. Visit the beach during one of these storms and you will get a real idea of the power of the sea.

Chesil Beach is often the landfall for many migrant birds from southern Europe and Africa that stop off to feed and rest in **spring**, before flying north to their breeding grounds. This is also the best time to visit the swannery at Abbotsbury, when the swans are nesting and rearing their cygnets.

WHERE ELSE TO SEE
SHINGLE BEACHES

Shingle is nearly always formed of flints, which have been washed out of chalk cliffs and eroded into rounded shapes by the sea. This means that the shingle beaches of Britain are characteristic of the east and south coasts, rich in chalk and flint.

Dungeness in Kent (see pp.162–163) is a huge shingle beach, shaped into a triangular headland rather than a long bank. It is famous for its unusual migrant birds, huge variety of insects, and over 600 different plant species. [SE]

To see an elongated shingle bank that is still extending, through the process of longshore drift, visit **Orford Ness** in Suffolk. Some 15km (9 miles) long, it is the largest vegetated shingle spit in Europe. [SE]

Further north, a series of sand and shingle banks stretching across the Humber Estuary leads out to **Spurn Point** (see pp.264–265). The curving spit is only 50m (160ft) wide in places, but is held together by marram grass and sea buckthorn. [N]

RETURN OF THE CHOUGHS

THE JOYFUL, EXCITED CALL OF A CHOUGH ECHOES AROUND THE SEA CLIFFS above a wave-washed bay. Go to Ramsey Island and you will see the chough in its element, exploiting the air currents around the cliffs, soaring on fingered wings, diving down in fast, controlled swerves to disappear into sea caves, or simply bouncing around the sky for fun. A single chough, or a whole family group, will suddenly fold its wings back towards its tail, the tips still slightly separated into fingers for expert control, and see-saw through the air, head up one moment, tail up the next. Few birds express such apparent joy in their everyday actions.

Like most crows, choughs are black, but with an intense sheen of blue and purple. They have a special bonus feature: both the bill and the thick legs are bright red. That curved, sharp-pointed bill is used to probe beneath patches of soil and grass against the edge of a rock, between loose stones and firm earth, into the base

WHERE
Ramsey Island, Pembrokeshire, West Wales; www.rspb.org.uk

CONTACT
RSPB Ramsey Island, tel: 07836 535733; ramsey.island@rspb.org.uk

GETTING THERE
The island is only accessible by boat from St Justinians harbour. By car, follow the A487 from Haverfordwest to St Davids for 25.6km (16 miles). From Cross Square in St Davids, follow signs for St Justinians, which is 2.5km (1½ miles) away. A regular bus service runs between Haverfordwest and St Davids and a shuttle bus runs to St Justinians, which is also on National Cycle Network Route 4.

ACCESS AND FACILITIES
There is parking at St Justinians, while on the island there is an information centre serving hot drinks and snacks, toilets, and a picnic area. The trails are unsuitable for wheelchairs. The main trail is 5.6km (3½ miles), but this can be divided into two loops.

OPENING TIMES
The reserve is open from April to October, 10am–4pm.

CHARGES
For the boat crossing. Landing fees also apply for non-RSPB members.

Nesting and rearing

Choughs' bulky, scrappy nests are made from twigs and roots held together by mud and lined with wool or other soft materials. Rocky crevices and cliff ledges are their favourite nest sites. Both parents are involved in rearing young. While the female broods, the male often brings her food; the female feeds the young for the first few days, then the male joins in with the feeding until the young fledge. Choughs live in small, tight-knit family groups, but come breeding time, each couple will fiercely defend its territory.

Main: Sea pinks (thrift) on the cliffs of Ramsey Island.

Left (top to bottom): A grey seal swimming into one of the island's caves; a bird's-eye view of Ramsey Island; golden hair lichen.

Right (left to right): Sociable adult choughs feeding on the beach; chough in flight; choughs pair for life and use the same nesting site every year.

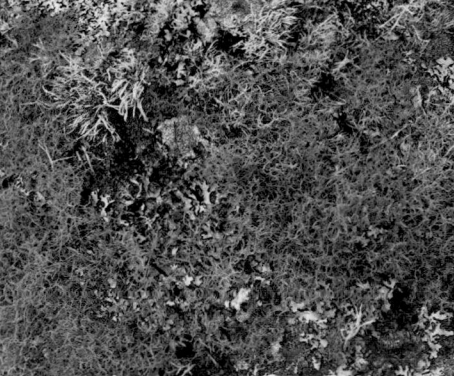

of a grass tussock, or even underneath a cowpat: anywhere that it can find some scurrying insect or other creepy-crawly to snap up. In winter, the chough also forages on wave-washed sandy beaches, looking for sandhoppers in the tideline tangle of seaweed and detritus.

Choughs pair for life. They first breed at three years old and raise just one brood each year, using the same nest site year after year. It is often on a ledge far inside a dark sea cave, or in a deep crevice on a cliff face; quarries or mineshafts are used inland. The bulky nests are made of sticks, heather stems, and wool, ready for the three mottled cream eggs. The female sits for 17–18 days and then cares for the chicks for the first 10 days or so, when the male begins to do his share.

British and Irish choughs are restricted to small areas on the coast and islands, and they number around 1,200 breeding pairs today. They stopped breeding in England in 1948, but returned to Cornwall in 2001, and now nest at Lizard Point (*see pp.116–117*) and Land's End.

Above: A soaring flock of choughs.

WHERE ELSE TO SEE
CHOUGHS

Following a long period of decline, chough populations in the UK have recently shown signs of recovery, though there are still only around 500 pairs of these birds in Britain.

Choughs can be seen on **Islay** (*see pp.12–13*) in the Inner Hebrides off western Scotland, especially at the south end of the island. [SC]

Rathlin Island, just off the coast of County Antrim, Northern Ireland, used to be a haven for choughs, but there are only a few pairs there today. [NI]

The beautiful cliffs of the **Isle of Man** (*see pp.300–301*) are home to seabirds and choughs, even quite close to Douglas. There are more on the **Calf of Man**, at the southern tip. [N]

You will see choughs easily at **South Stack** on Anglesey in Wales. Try cliffs along the **Lleyn Peninsula** in North Wales, and on the Cardiganshire and Pembrokeshire coastline as well. [W]

THROUGH THE YEAR
RAMSEY ISLAND

In the **autumn**, you can watch a colony of breeding grey seals. Look and listen for the females and their white pups on the beaches, and the large, dark males patrolling just offshore.

Choughs gather in large groups in the **winter**, which clearly have significance for this sociable bird. Ramsey Island is closed to visitors over the winter, but you might come across choughs in around the adjacent coastline footpaths.

In **spring** Ramsey becomes awash with colour as bluebells, red campion, sea pink (thrift), and purple heather take turns to dominate the scene. The cliff-top has a wild rock garden of sea campion, spring squill, and yellow rockroses. From the summit of Carn Llundain, look for displaying lapwings below, and keep an eye out for stonechats and wheatears.

JAN

FEB

MAR

APR

MAY

JUN

JUL

AUG

SEP

OCT

NOV

DEC

Left: Hay meadows are actively farmed and often privately owned, so always keep to footpaths when visiting.

Right (left to right): Pignut in flower; melancholy thistle.

Right panel (top to bottom): The striking yellow globeflower; a marbled white butterfly feeding on a field scabious flower.

WHERE
The Yorkshire Dales, Yorkshire.

CONTACT
Yorkshire Dales National Park Authority, tel: 01756 751600; info@yorkshiredales.org.uk
Dales Countryside Museum, Station Yard, Hawes, North Yorkshire DL8 3NT; tel: 01969 666220.

GETTING THERE
The Muker Meadows surround the Swaledale village of Muker, which lies on the B6270, just east of Thwaite. Upper Wensleydale is the area surrounding the town of Hawes, on the A684, where the Dales Countryside Museum (*see above*) is situated. The Yorkshire Dales National Park Authority is committed to encouraging the use of public transport to and within the area; visit its travel information site, www.traveldales.org.uk

ACCESS AND FACILITIES
The towns of Hawes, Aysgarth, and Leyburn offer full facilities, including parking and toilets. There are no facilities along walks within the Yorkshire Dales themselves. Always keep to the public rights of way.

OPENING TIMES
Open all year round.

CHARGES
None.

Reviving a tradition

Restoration projects are helping to recreate precious hay meadow habitat. The projects involve harvesting hay from ancient meadows and spreading it on selected sites so the seed falls naturally to the ground. The owners of the new sites then follow the traditional haymaking regime to encourage a variety of flowers. Grants cover any loss of income, but in any case the species-rich hay has a nutritive value for livestock that cannot be matched by grass alone.

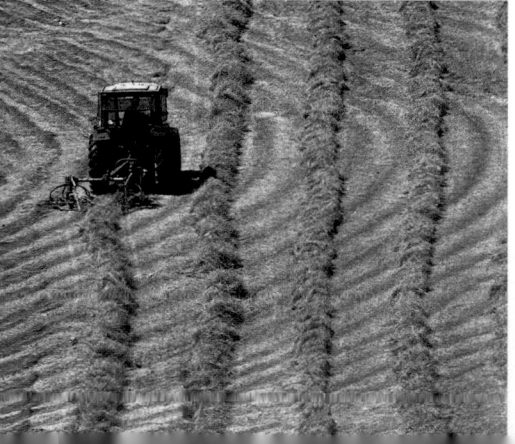

Main: A buttercup meadow near Muker, Swaledale.

TRADITIONAL HAY MEADOWS

THE YORKSHIRE DALES ARE AMONG THE MOST ICONIC OF ENGLISH LANDSCAPES. Their long, grassy valleys, etched with stone walls and dotted with isolated field barns, are part of everyone's vision of England at its best. Much of their charm is perennial, but for a few weeks in high summer some of the valley meadows are transformed into dazzling displays of floral diversity, as they burst into a mass of short-lived flower.

Hay meadows in the Dales are traditionally cleared of grazing animals in May, allowing grasses and plants to grow until late July or August. These are cut and left to dry before being baled. The land is then grazed by farm animals until winter closes in. The haymaking calendar gives the plants a chance to flower and set seed, and since the land is not fertilized, flowering plants are able to flourish without being overwhelmed by dense grass. The result is a spectacular tapestry of colour as whole meadows flower at once. The dominant yellow of meadow

Some hay meadows in the Yorkshire Dales can boast more than 80 wildflower species.

JAN

FEB

MAR

APR

MAY

JUN

JUL

AUG

SEP

OCT

NOV

DEC

WHERE ELSE TO SEE
UPLAND HAY MEADOWS

Traditional, flower-rich, upland hay meadow is one of the rarest types of grassland in Britain. It occurs mainly in the north of England – almost half the total occurs within the northern Pennines. In most areas the amount of hay meadow is shrinking rapidly.

The hay meadows of **Moor House** Nature Reserve in Upper Teesdale, Cumbria (*see pp.114–115*) lie at the highest altitude in Britain, and support several rare species of lady's-mantle and a flourishing population of globeflower. [N]

The hay meadows of **Weardale**, County Durham, provide excellent sightings of birds, such as lapwings and waders, which come for the moist soils that harbour plentiful worms. Common sandpipers, grey wagtails, redshanks, and curlews may all be seen in the area. [N]

To see fields of wild flowers, albeit in a different type of managed landscape, visit **West Pentire**, Cornwall (*scc pp. 136–137*), where areas of land have been dedicated to traditional cornfield wild flowers.

THROUGH THE YEAR
THE YORKSHIRE DALES

By **autumn** the hay has been cut and cattle and sheep graze where the flowers once stood. But clear, crisp air and the rich colours of the season create some of the best views of the year from the hills flanking the meadow valleys.

Winter snowfall transforms the Dales, with the network of stone walls forming an intricate web of lines across a white landscape. Many waterfalls are at their most spectacular as the snow starts to melt.

In **spring**, wading birds such as curlews, golden plovers, and oystercatchers return to breed on the hills, filling the air with their calls, while the pastures and woodlands become bright with wild flowers.

Below: The Yorkshire Dales in winter.

buttercup is punctuated by the deep pink of red clover, the delicate white sprays of pignut – a relative of cow parsley – and the rich reddish-purple of a real hay-meadow specialist, the wood cranesbill. On the oldest meadows, managed in this way for centuries, there may be more than 30 different plant species for every square metre (10 sq ft). All these flowers attract a host of butterflies, bees, and other nectar-feeding insects.

One of the best places to witness this celebration of biodiversity is Muker Meadows in Swaledale, where you can find specialist plants such as globeflower, lady's-mantle, eyebright, and melancholy thistle, and well as the more widespread species. And in Upper Wensleydale, beside the River Ure, below Askrigg or beyond Appersett, you can stroll past meadows full of blue cranesbill accompanied by the constant song of common sandpipers. There are also some superb hay meadows further south in Yorkshire alongside the River Wharfe in Upper Wharfedale, and in neighbouring Littondale. Like all these meadows, they also support the sweet vernal grass that imparts such a delicious fragrance to the hay when it is cut.

CLIFFS AND CAVES

SLICED THROUGH THE HEART OF THE BEAUTIFUL MENDIP HILLS lies the truly magnificent Cheddar Gorge, whose towering limestone walls are the highest inland cliffs in the UK. The gorge itself was formed over a million years ago by melting glaciers, and around 40,000 years ago our ancestors lived in these caves. Two of the largest caves here are called Gough's and Cox's, after their discoverers, and they are said to have inspired JRR Tolkien's trilogy, *The Lord of the Rings*, after his honeymoon visit to the gorge.

These days the caves are an important refuge for some of our rarest species of bats. The lesser horseshoe and the even rarer greater horseshoe bat regularly use these caves as roost sites. The bats hang upside-down in the caves during the day, leaving them by night to hunt for insects in the woodlands. They're easy to miss, but you'll almost certainly see one of the gentle giants of the spider world, *Meta menardi*, the photophobic cave spider.

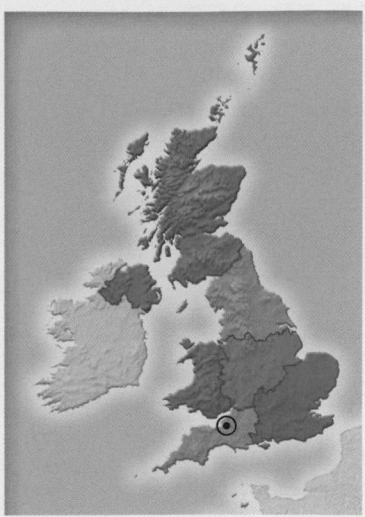

WHERE
Cheddar Gorge, Cheddar, Somerset
BS27 3QF; www.cheddarcaves.co.uk

CONTACT
Cheddar Caves, tel: 01934 742343;
caves@cheddarcaves.co.uk

GETTING THERE
Cheddar Gorge is southwest of Bristol, off the M4 motorway. Take the A38 out of Bristol to Axbridge, and follow the A371 for a short distance to the B3135, which is the actual road through the gorge itself.

ACCESS AND FACILITIES
The visitor centre features shops, cafes, and toilets, and is wheelchair friendly. The cliff-top walk is unsuitable for wheelchairs but there is good access to Gough's cave, and open-top bus rides offer a good overview of the gorge. Dormouse tours are available through the Mammal Society (tel: 01458 210345).

OPENING TIMES
The caves are open all year round (except Christmas Day), 10am–5.30pm in July and August, and 10.30am–5pm from September to June.

CHARGES
There are no charges for the walks, but entry to the caves is subject to charges. Parking is pay-and-display.

Above and below: Lesser horseshoe bats hang from roots in the caves; the caves of the gorge all feature both stalactites and stalagmites.

Main: Cheddar Gorge is 113m (371ft) at its deepest point, and has a near-vertical cliff face to the south.

Right panel (top and bottom): Feral goats around the gorge help keep the scrub in check; the limestone cliffs seen from Landslip Quarry.

Unique Cheddar plants

The Cheddar pink (*pictured above*) and Cheddar bedstraw are both examples of Britain's rarest plants. They are unique to Cheddar Gorge, where they thrive due to their fully protected status. Both flower around late spring and early summer, making this an ideal time to visit the gorge. The low-growing, bluish-grey leaves of the Cheddar pink, related to garden pinks, stay green all year round. Other nationally rare plant species growing around the gorge include little robin, slender tare, and rock stonecrop.

The crags and ledges throughout the gorge support numerous rare and specialized plant species, including the Cheddar pink and Cheddar bedstraw, both species unique to Cheddar. At the top of the gorge you'll find limestone plateaus covered in calciferous grasslands packed full of sweet-scented flowers. Summer is a great time to visit: not only is the air full of heady aromas from plants such as wild marjoram and thyme, but wild orchids will also be flowering.

On the lower slopes you can see areas of ancient woodland, thick with oak, hazel, whitebeam, and holly. Dormice live in the thick cover of hazel and oak coppice, and peregrine falcons fly overhead. A good way to get a feel for the area is to walk up the 274 steps of Jacob's Ladder. This route takes you up to Pavey's lookout tower, where you can take in the views across the Mendips and towards Exmoor. From there you can pick up the cliff-top gorge walk, a 5km (3 mile) circular route, where you just might be accompanied by feral goats and ravens.

Harebell, rockrose, and marjoram grow in the thin soil overlaying much of the rock, while lizards, adders, and grass snakes bask on warm, bare rock.

WHERE ELSE TO SEE
GORGES

Most of the gorges in the UK are found in limestone country, and although Cheddar is the largest, there are many others dotted around the UK.

Britain's second-largest gorge, **Winnats Pass**, is in Derbyshire. Its magnificent, towering limestone sides are home to a variety of wild flowers, including Jacob's ladder and bird's-foot trefoil. [M]

Near to the vast limestone cliff face of Malham Cove in North Yorkshire is the mighty **Gordale Scar**. This impressive gorge is 1km (½ mile) long with sides raising up to 80m (260ft) at its highest points. [N]

The **Avon Gorge** on the River Avon in Bristol is home to some spectacular wildlife, including breeding peregrine falcons and the rare Bristol rock-cress. [SW]

One of the most atmospheric gorges must be Wales's **Fairy Glen** in Snowdonia, which has been the inspiration for many artists and writers. Swallow Falls and Conwy Falls are not far away. [W]

THROUGH THE YEAR
CHEDDAR GORGE

From **autumn** onwards, Cheddar's dormice feast on nuts, seeds, and insects – they also enjoy blackberries – fattening themselves up to almost double their normal body weight to see them through their long winter nap.

The bats regularly use the caves as their **winter** roost sites, and although they spend periods of time between October to April hibernating, they can occasionally be quite active.

By late **spring**, the Cheddar pink will begin to flower. Look out for purple gromwell and starved wood-sedge in the woodlands around the gorge, and many species of mosses and lichens on the limestone rock itself. Peregrine falcons nest around the gorge in spring, and may be seen hunting or displaying.

Below: Hazel dormice sleeping.

JAN

FEB

MAR

APR

MAY

JUN

JUL

AUG

SEP

OCT

NOV

DEC

WHERE
Wimbledon Common, London SW19 5NR;
www.wpcc.org.uk

CONTACT
The Ranger's Office, Manor Cottage,
Windmill Road, Wimbledon Common, tel:
020 8788 7655; rangersoffice@wpcc.org.uk

GETTING THERE
By car, the A3 is the main route to
Wimbledon from the M25 Motorway. The
A219 runs through Wimbledon Hill Road.
The nearest train station is Wimbledon, with
regular trains from central London. The
nearest London Underground stations are
South Wimbledon on the Northern Line, and
Wimbledon on the District Line. Bus nos.
493, 93, 156, and 200 go through the area.

ACCESS AND FACILITIES
There's a car park and Information Centre at
the windmill – now a museum – on the
common, and both are wheelchair friendly.

OPENING TIMES
Open all year round.

CHARGES
None.

Long-lived larvae

Having suffered a sharp decline over recent
decades, the stag beetle is a protected species. It
breeds in old, rotting timber, but modern forestry
practice and tidy gardening have made breeding
sites harder to find. The larvae need to feed on
rotting wood for up to six years before crawling
out to burrow into the soil. Here they pupate,
while their bodies are rebuilt into adult form. The
beetles emerge from early summer, and spend
the last few weeks of their lives breeding.

Left (left to right):
Wimbledon Common has
many accessible paths;
fierce little shrews are
among the few small
predators that will take
on a male stag beetle.

Right (left to right): The
shorter jaws of the female
stag beetle can still deliver
a sharp nip; a stag beetle
spreads its wing-cases to
unfurl its wings.

Main and far right: Stag beetles fight for females – the "winner" is the beetle that turns the other one on its back.

BATTLING BEETLES

NOTHING CAN QUITE PREPARE YOU FOR YOUR FIRST ENCOUNTER with a flying male stag beetle on a
summer evening. Heralded by a gentle buzzing, a bizarre vision looms out of the twilight, with six
outstretched legs, flared wing-cases, and a pair of alarmingly long, spiked, antler-like jaws, hanging half upright
on apparently inadequate wings as it blunders towards you through the warm air.

Instinctively you duck, and possibly scream, because the whole experience feels like something out of a
science-fiction film. It is certainly not what you expect when you're out for an evening stroll in July, especially
somewhere such as Wimbledon Common. Yet this suburban parkland is a key site for these magnificent, if
disconcerting, insects. The females lay their eggs in decaying timber, preferably oak, and there is plenty of this
lying on the ground along the western side of the common. The woodland in this part of the common is very

The male stag beetle is the biggest British beetle, but despite its appearance it is quite harmless.

JAN

FEB

MAR

APR

MAY

JUN

JUL

AUG

SEP

OCT

NOV

DEC

WHERE ELSE TO SEE
STAG BEETLES

In Britain, stag beetles are confined to the southern counties of England, extending north to Norfolk and South Wales. Within this region they are associated with old woodlands, but they often turn up in suburban streets, where beetles flying by night are attracted to street lamps.

Several London parks besides Wimbledon Common have flourishing populations of stag beetles. They include **Richmond Park** (*see pp.276–277*), where their presence was one reason for the Park's designation as a National Nature Reserve. [SE]

Stag beetles are common in the **New Forest** (*see pp.174–175*) where they breed in decaying timber in the large areas of oak woodland. [SE]

Epping Forest is also a good place to find stag beetles. Since regular cutting of the larger forest trees stopped in 1878, a large quantity of dead wood has piled up on the forest floor, creating ideal conditions for stag beetles and a host of other insects. [SE]

THROUGH THE YEAR
WIMBLEDON COMMON

In early **autumn**, watch for bats fluttering through the dusk in pursuit of moths and flies. Six species are regularly seen over the common, including the biggest British bat, the noctule. Among the trees, look for the long-eared bat, which is able to pluck insects from their perches on leaves.

The shallow pools on the common attract a variety of ducks and geese in **winter**, including the spectacular mandarin duck. The male ducks are in their finest plumage at this time of year as they court the females before the spring breeding season.

Spring sees the emergence of innumerable caterpillars in the trees, which attract breeding songbirds that rely on the caterpillars as a food for their nestlings. You may also see sparrowhawks hunting to feed their own families.

carefully managed to help encourage wildlife, which includes leaving the dead timber where it falls. The big male beetles that waver through the dusk towards you across the common are, of course, in search of females, who are much smaller, far less inclined to fly, and do not have the enormous reddish jaws that make the males look so intimidating.

This is, in fact, their function, for the long mandibles are too weak to inflict anything more than a determined nip. Rival males flaunt them at each other and may use them to fight over females, gripping their opponents around the body and trying to toss them aside like miniature sumo wrestlers. The winner then mates with the female, enabling her to go off and lay clusters of large yellow eggs, which will take six years to grow into adults.

Having achieved this, the adults' job is done, and since they eat only a little sugary tree sap, they soon die. Most of a stag beetle's life is spent as a burrowing larva, slowly building up the resources that will fuel its meteoric career as a flying adult. If it thinks at all, it must be baffled by its astonishing, if short-lived, transformation.

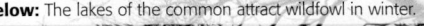

Below: The lakes of the common attract wildfowl in winter.

WHERE
Cors Caron National Nature Reserve,
Tregaron, Ceredigion, SY25 6AN Wales.

CONTACT
Tel: 0845 1306229; info@wales.info

GETTING THERE
The reserve is 3.2km (2 miles) to the
north of the village of Tregaron, which
lies on the A485 between Lampeter and
Aberystwyth. The main access to the reserve
is from the new car park on the B4343.
Cyclists and walkers can use the Ystwyth
Trail. There is a very limited bus service,
contact Traveline Cymru on 0870 6082608
or www.traveline-cymru.org.uk

ACCESS AND FACILITIES
The boardwalk to the viewing hide to the
south of the car park is wheelchair friendly,
although the hide 2km (1¼ miles) to the
north of the car park is not. There are toilets
in the car park. Just north of the reserve, in
the nearby town of Pontrhydfendigaid, there
are public toilets and two pubs.

OPENING TIMES
Open all year round.

CHARGES
None.

Preserving the peat

For centuries locals cut peat from the Welsh
boglands to burn on their hearths. Over the
years, the horticultural demand for peat grew,
so much so that by 1955 Cors Caron was
designated a National Nature Reserve in order to
save this precious habitat. Peat extraction has
become a major environmental issue. Most
multi-purpose composts for garden use will
contain between 70 and 100 per cent peat.
Many alternative products are widely available,
so look for products labelled as "peat-free".

Above (left to right): Sphagnum moss acidifies the water; bogbean grows around the pools; redshanks breed at Cors Caron in summer.
Main: The reserve at Cors Caron stretches over an area of 816 acres (330 hectares).

PEATLAND PARADISE

T HERE CAN BE FEW LANDSCAPES MORE TREACHEROUS THAN RAISED BOGS. These vast, quaking sponges of water-saturated peat and moss have a reputation as quagmires into which people disappear without trace, and while the reality is rarely quite so dramatic, they are still places to treat with respect. On the other hand, where people dare not go, wildlife can flourish – so they are exciting places to visit, provided you do not stray from the marked paths.

Cors Caron in mid Wales is one of the finest examples of a raised bog system in Britain, and one of the most accessible. In July it is a glorious mosaic of colourful vegetation, buzzing with dragonflies that breed in the bog pools. The bogs formed on the site of an ancient shallow lake that became gradually choked with aquatic plants until it turned into a marshy, wooded fen. Dead vegetation cannot decay properly in such waterlogged conditions, so the area began to build up thick layers of peat. These were colonized by sphagnum mosses – plants that can absorb many times their own weight of water and grow well above the groundwater level – forming great domes of moss and peat that overwhelm even the trees.

There are three of these domes at Cors Caron, interlocking to form a complex that demonstrates every stage of the bog's development over the last 12,000 years. The sphagnum moss creates an acidic environment that suits specialized plants such as cottongrass, bog asphodel, and insect-eating sundews. You can see these at close quarters from the boardwalk that runs for some 3.5km (2 miles) over the southeast bog, together with 16 different species of dragonfly and, occasionally, the beautiful large heath butterfly, which lays its eggs on the white-beaked sedge that lines the edges of the pools. Watch out for red kites, merlins, and peregrines soaring overhead, and be sure to visit the lake hide for a chance of seeing curlews, redshanks, otters, and polecats.

Cors Caron was the last stronghold for the magnificent red kite when it was hunted to near-extinction in Britain during the 16th–19th centuries.

Inset: A red kite in flight above the bogs.
Below (left to right): Fluffy cottongrass; an insectivorous sundew plant.

WHERE ELSE TO SEE
RAISED BOGS

Raised bogs develop in high-rainfall areas, often with hard, impermeable bedrock that impedes drainage. They are characteristic of northwest England, Wales, Scotland, and Ireland.

Whixall Moss is one of a complex of three raised bogs near the Llangollen Canal in Shropshire (see pp.94–95). They are among the most southerly raised bogs in Britain, which suffered acute damage from peat-cutting in the past, but have been restored to encourage a rich diversity of wildlife. [M]

Peatlands Park near Dungannon in Northern Ireland is a large raised bog that supports insectivorous plants, many species of dragonfly and a wide variety of birds. There is also a boggy woodland growing on drumlins – rounded heaps of debris created by moving ice during the last Ice Age. [NI]

Braehead Moss in south Lanarkshire, Scotland, consists of two linked, raised bogs with large areas of undisturbed bog vegetation that is home to breeding populations of red grouse and curlews. [SC]

THROUGH THE YEAR
CORS CARON

In **autumn** the bog attracts passage migrants, such as the green sandpiper, that stop off on their way south to their winter refuges. Waterfowl arrive to stay over winter. This includes whooper swans – the most southerly large wintering flock in Britain.

Winter is an excellent time to watch for raptors such as hen harriers, buzzards, and peregrines. In winter the local red kites are fed every day at Pont Einon overlooking the bog.

Highlights of **spring** include the return of many small migrant songbirds such as the sedge warbler and willow warbler, shadowed by the cuckoos that parasitize them by laying eggs in their nests. Check the bog pools for early dragonflies such as the four-spotted chaser and large red damselfly.

Below: Cors Caron provides excellent cover for migrant birds in autumn.

JAN
FEB
MAR
APR
MAY
JUN
JUL
AUG
SEP
OCT
NOV
DEC

WHERE
Abbotts Hall Farm, Great Wigborough, Colchester, Essex CO5 7RZ; www.essexwt.org.uk

CONTACT
Essex Wildlife Trust, tel: 01621 862960; admin@essexwt.org.uk

GETTING THERE
Take the B1026 from Colchester towards Peldon; about 3km (1¾ miles) south of the causeway across Abberton Reservoir, turn east. The entrance to Abbotts Hall Farm is about 1km (²/₃ mile) on the right.

ACCESS AND FACILITIES
Abbotts Hall Farm has not long been open to the public, so facilities are basic, but being developed all the time – the Essex Wildlife Trust has opened a new headquarters on the site. There is currently a car park and full-access toilets, but no refreshment facilities – the nearest are at Abberton Reservoir, 10 minutes away by car.

OPENING TIMES
Tuesday to Friday 9am–5pm.

CHARGES
None.

Working with nature

Managed realignment – allowing nature to reclaim areas that humans previously claimed from the sea – began in Essex in the 1980s, as an initiative to restore saltmarshes and create natural sea defences. Initial small-scale experiments were successful and led to much larger schemes. This principle, of working with nature rather than against it, is now accepted as a fundamental part of our efforts to manage the risks from both tidal and river flooding.

Above: The little tern hovers with flickering wings forming a characteristic "V" shape.

Right panel (top and bottom): Spotted redshanks are often early-returning migrants; painted lady butterflies enjoy the nectar of saltmarsh flowers.

Below (top and bottom): Around seven pairs of shelducks breed at Abbotts Hall Farm; sea aster, looking much like its garden relatives, flowers in summer.

Main: Abbotts Hall Farm marshes are covered by the delicate flowers of sea pinks and sea lavender in summer.

THE SALTMARSHES OF ESSEX

ESSEX SALTMARSHES ARE UNDER THREAT: THEY ARE SUFFERING EROSION as sea levels rise, which has been happening ever since the retreat of the last Ice Age but is now speeding up due to global warming. One possible response runs contrary to instinct: rather than shore up sea walls, why not breach them ourselves? Letting in the sea, and allowing the tides do some good by bringing in silt and seeds from saltmarshes beyond the old sea walls, recreates valuable saltmarsh without any further intervention. At Abbotts Hall Farm on the Blackwater Estuary, the Essex Wildlife Trust has done just this, returning, in 2002, 50 hectares (25 acres) of land to the influence of the tides. At the time, this was the largest example of managed realignment of the coastline in Britain. And with every year that passes, the new saltmarshes get bigger and better, increasingly coming to resemble the remaining marshes in the estuary as more plants colonize, creating a summertime wash of colour.

Above: Glassworts create a warm-toned carpet with their autumn colours.

JAN
FEB
MAR
APR
MAY
JUN
JUL
AUG
SEP
OCT
NOV
DEC

THROUGH THE YEAR
ABBOTTS HALL FARM

As summer gives way to **autumn**, more waders and other water birds arrive, some of which will remain for the winter, while others continue their migration as far south as Africa. The marshes adopt a range of hues from the glassworts, a group of succulent plant species differentiated by their autumn colours, which range from yellow to brown and purple.

During **winter**, the marshes are frequented by large flocks of dark-bellied brent geese from Siberia that add their soft, liquid cackle to the general sounds of an Essex winter. Short-eared owls and hen harriers hunt over the marshes, and flocks of buntings and finches, often including a few twites, feed on the seeds of saltmarsh plants such as sea-purslane.

The first sign of **spring** is the increase in territorial behaviour of those birds that remain to breed. Redshanks hover over the marshes, pairs of oystercatchers and ringed plovers set up territories on any sandy patch, and the songs of skylarks and meadow pipits fill the air in the spring sunshine.

Marine life around the saltmarshes includes shore crabs, jellyfish, lugworms, and shrimp, and fish such as sand smelt, herring, and goby.

WHERE ELSE TO SEE
SALTMARSHES

Saltmarshes are found on the coastline wherever there is a degree of shelter – allowing muddy sediments to be deposited. They also lie in the heart of estuaries such as the Thames, Medway, and Solent, and in the lee of barrier beaches.

Elsewhere in Essex, **Hamford Water** is a complex series of backwaters within a natural bay; further south on the remote **Dengie Marshes**, saltings extend out from the sea wall on the open coast. [SE]

On the north Norfolk coast, the best saltmarshes have developed behind the shelter of **Scolt Head Island** and **Blakeney Point** (*see pp.214–215*). [SE]

In the southwest, saltmarshes can be found at **Poole Harbour** in Dorset (*see pp.48–49*). [SW]

One of the first flowers to come to prominence in early summer is thrift, or sea pink, which has delicate shell-pink flowerheads. In July, swathes of flowers erupt: sea-lavender creates a serene purple haze, followed and topped by sea aster, whose Michaelmas daisy-like flowerheads are a magnet for nectar-feeding insects. Migrating butterflies such as red admirals and painted ladies take advantage of the refuelling stop as they arrive on our shores, before moving inland.

Amid this botanical palette there are, of course, birds, who find the habitat irresistible. Redshanks, incessantly piping alarm calls in their role as "warden of the marshes", breed on the upper saltmarsh, out of reach of all but the highest tides. They mingle with the first returning migrants from the north, perhaps a greenshank or a spotted redshank, often showing traces of its blackish breeding dress. Little terns from nearby beach colonies hover with rapidly beating wings over the shallow pools, plunge-diving to catch small fish. Little egrets stalk through the shallows after the same food, but by their own hunting method. Graceful, sweeping avocets and parties of shelducks, accompanied by their piebald chicks, feed on the innumerable tiny snails in the mud.

WHERE
Rodborough Common, Stroud,
Gloucestershire GL5 5DE;
www.nationaltrust.org.uk

CONTACT
The National Trust, tel: 0844 8001895;
enquiries@thenationaltrust.org.uk or
Gloucester Wildlife Trust, tel: 01452 383333;
info@gloucestershirewildlifetrust.co.uk

GETTING THERE
Exit the M5 at junction 13 for Stroud.
Rodborough Common lies between the A46
and the A419 south of Stroud. By train, travel
to Stroud railway station, then catch the
Cotswold Green bus, no. 28 (Stroud–
Cirencester). By bicycle, National Cycle
Network Route no. 45 runs within 1.5km
(1 mile) of the common.

ACCESS AND FACILITIES
There are two free car parks: The Fort and
The Sunken, which both display information
about the common. The nearest toilets are in
Minchinhampton or Stroud, and the nearest
refreshments can be found in the various
pubs that border the common.

OPENING TIMES
Open all year round.

CHARGES
None.

The Adonis blue returns

During the 1950s, many of the Cotswold
grasslands became overgrown and the Adonis
blue butterfly disappeared. But conservation
work has led to it recolonizing many of its former
sites, including Rodborough Common, where the
Jurassic limestone grasslands provide the perfect
habitat. Interestingly, the larvae are often cared
for by ants. This symbiotic relationship is good
for both species: the larvae are protected from
predators, and the ants feed on the secretions
provided by the obliging larvae.

Above (left to right): A burnet moth; cinnabar moth caterpillars on ragwort; a meadow brown butterfly.
Main: The enchanting chalkhill blue butterfly (this is a female) can be found at Rodborough from mid-July to mid-September.

GRASSLAND BUTTERFLIES

THE COTSWOLDS ARE THE QUINTESSENTIAL ENGLISH LANDSCAPE – a region of rolling hills and broad views, blessed with a local building stone the colour of pale honey that suffuses every village with a glorious golden glow. This Jurassic limestone forms a plateau that slopes towards the northwest, ending abruptly in a series of steep "edges" that overlook the Severn Vale. Around Stroud, five streams converge, to create a network of valleys with south-facing grassy slopes that support a wide variety of delicate, lime-loving plants. The combination of sunny conditions and floral diversity provides ideal conditions for some of our rarest grassland butterflies.

One of the best places to look for them is Rodborough Common, just to the south of Stroud, which is managed by the National Trust. On a sunny day in early July, the most conspicuous species is likely to be the marbled white, a striking butterfly with black-and-white wings that is easy to spot as it sips nectar from a scabious or knapweed flower. It will often share a perch with the far less showy meadow brown, which exists in large numbers around the grassland.

Both these butterflies lay their eggs on grasses, but the much smaller common blue relies on small vetches like bird's-foot trefoil, which flourish on these sunny slopes. The warmth is particularly important for the horseshoe vetch, a spreading, yellow-flowered plant that is essential to the rarer chalkhill blue and the very scarce Adonis blue (*see box, below left*), since it is the only plant that is eaten by their caterpillars. A male chalkhill blue butterfly has distinctive milky-blue wings bordered with dark brown, but it literally pales into insignificance if seen beside the brilliant sky blue of a male Adonis. The male will mate with a number of females on the first day of emerging, before bedding down in a communal roost, closing its wings to sleep in a rough pocket of grass.

The distinctive marbled white butterfly is widespread throughout the south of the UK, and has started to expand its range to the north and east in recent years.

Inset: The marbled white can be seen from mid-June to mid-August.
Below (left to right): The male chalkhill blue; a dark green fritillary butterfly.

WHERE ELSE TO SEE
GRASSLAND BUTTERFLIES

Some grassland butterflies, such as the meadow brown, are widespread, but others are very selective about where they live, because their caterpillars rely on certain foodplants. Grassland species were always uncommon, but now that so many wild grasslands have been ploughed up or "improved" by spreading fertilizers – which eliminate the natural flora – many species are now rare. The best places to look are warm, south-facing slopes with ancient grassland.

Prehistoric earthworks are ideal sites, since they have natural turf that is thousands of years old. Look in the sunny areas of places like **Old Winchester Hill** in Hampshire, or **Cissbury Ring** in West Sussex. [SE]

In the west of England, investigate the magnificent ramparts of **Maiden Castle**, near Dorchester in Dorset, where you might see some butterflies. [SW]

The **Aston Rowant** nature reserve (*see pp.222–223*) on the Chilterns in Oxfordshire is a prime site for the very rare silver-spotted skipper butterfly. [SE]

THROUGH THE YEAR
RODBOROUGH COMMON

In **autumn**, look for grassland fungi like the field mushroom, the imposing parasol mushroom, and the shaggy ink cap. Most of the butterflies will have gone, but you may see a few common blues and big species like the red admiral, peacock, and comma.

Cold days in **winter** can provide the most beautiful views over the Severn Vale, since all the moisture is frozen out of the air.

Spring is a glorious time to visit Rodborough Common, as it offers the chance to see the Duke of Burgundy, a very rare butterfly that flourishes here and flies in April and May. The site is also famous for its beautiful spring flowers, including the pasque flower, which blooms around Easter. At least 13 species of orchid flower on the grasslands in spring and summer.

Below: Riders enjoy a morning trek around Rodborough Common.

JAN FEB MAR APR MAY JUN JUL AUG SEP OCT NOV DEC

AUGUST

Where to Go: **August**

In Scotland you must contend with the midge: the one part of British wildlife that most of us would prefer to avoid. But you can be saved by even a moderate breeze, which will keep them off as you peer across moors and lochs for otters, deer, eagles, hen harriers, ospreys, and red and black grouse. Heading south, you'll find a different kind of wildlife, enjoying the all-too-rare heat; this is a good month on far southern heaths for searching out our scarcer smooth snakes and sand lizards, and watching dragonflies and the smaller damselflies. The trees are full of birds – such as Dartford warblers, families of woodlarks, and young buzzards – all calling to be fed. On the coast, look out to sea for Manx shearwaters, fulmars, gannets, and those seafaring

UPLANDS

BEINN EIGHE A cluster of rocky peaks in the northwest Highlands.

BEINN EIGHE
HIGHLAND [SC]

Britain's first National Nature Reserve is a wild and forbidding landscape.
See pp.202–203

> The Highlands are the British stronghold for a group of plants that evolved to cope with life on the freezing Arctic tundra.

MIGNEINT MOORS
NORTH WALES [W]

The river Conwy (Afon Conwy) rises on the great upland plateau of Migneint, where wild and open moorland abounds with wildlife.
See pp.216–217

ASTON ROWANT
THE CHILTERNS, OXFORDSHIRE [SE]

This downland turf has remained uncultivated for centuries, and its wildflowers conceal, until dusk, large numbers of the astonishing glow worm.
See pp.222–223

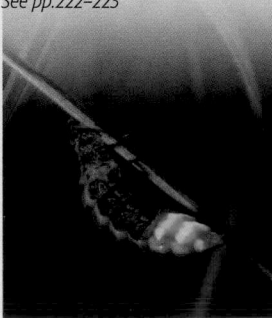

BEN NEVIS
FORT WILLIAM [SC]

The highest mountain in the UK; its specialities include the mountain ringlet butterfly and the magnificent golden eagle.
See pp.208–209

COAST

BLAKENEY POINT Seals love to bask on the shingle.

BLAKENEY POINT
NORTH NORFOLK [SE]

Around 500 seals – both common and grey – haul themselves on to Blakeney Point in the summer. There should be lots of pups at this time of year.
See pp.214–215

GIANT'S CAUSEWAY
COUNTY ANTRIM [NI]

Europe's largest lava plateau makes huge and wondrous shapes on this beach – walk out to sea on the stacks and try sitting on a "giant's boot".
See pp.208–209

FOWLSHEUGH
ABERDEENSHIRE [SC]

This coastal nature has high cliffs teeming with nesting seabirds. Seals, porpoises, and occasionally even minke whales visit its waters.
See pp.208–209

LYME BAY
DEVON/DORSET [SW]

As well as its Jurassic rocks, the bay is home to some of the best underwater wildlife in the UK, with reefs and rare sealife.
See pp.226–227

BAY OF BISCAY
NORTH ATLANTIC OCEAN

Take a sea voyage to the Bay to see marine mammals, such as whales and dolphins.
See pp.200–201

WETLANDS

FORSINARD One of our few remaining peatlands sparkles in summer.

ROSS LOUGH
COUNTY FERMANAGH [NI]

The open water, fen, and wet meadow here are home to many wetland plants, such as purple loosestrife, and an abundance of insects.
See pp.204–205

FORSINARD FLOWS
HIGHLAND [SC]

The immense peatland of the Flow Country is dotted with black pools and an army of carnivorous plants.
See pp.216–217

WICKEN FEN
ELY, CAMBRIDGESHIRE [SE]

Our most famous fenland has an astonishing wealth of wildlife – the shimmering wings of dragonflies seem to be absolutely everywhere.
See pp.204–205

CORNHILL MEADOWS
WALTHAM ABBEY, ESSEX [SE]

This dragonfly sanctuary within the Lee Valley Park shelters 21 species of damselflies and dragonflies, really challenging your identification skills.
See pp.210–211

HAM WALL
SOMERSET LEVELS [SW]

This newly created wetland provides a safe home for many rare species, including water voles and otters.
See pp.204–205

Previous page: A female otter surfaces from a wetland pool.

thieves, the skuas. Watch the waves for the rolling backs of cetaceans, large and small: porpoises and dolphins for sure, but also minke whales and killer whales if you have a real slice of luck. The tall, lazy fin of a gigantic basking shark is a possibility, too. Island life is full and busy in August: Mull is the place for otters and eagles, both golden and white-tailed, as well as familiar but beautiful birds such as oystercatchers and eiders, which stalk around the rocky shores. Wherever you are, you will notice little signs that summer is coming to an end: a dryness in the grass, a dullness in the leaves, the absence of some familiar birds, even berries appearing on the rowans and hedgerow shrubs. Autumn is coming.

INLETS AND ESTUARIES

MORAY FIRTH The best and easiest place to see bottlenose dolphins.

MORAY FIRTH
ROSS-SHIRE [SC]

Salmon return to the Firth in summer, pursued by over 130 bottlenose dolphins. Harbour porpoises are common, and a few minke whales coast around the outer bay.
See pp.220–221

DORNOCH FIRTH
ROSS-SHIRE [SC]

This is the northernmost firth on the east coast of Scotland. It has significant numbers of osprey, bar-tailed godwits, and curlew. Common seals give birth to pups here in August.
See pp.214–215

On the Moray Firth, with luck, dolphins will appear in front of you, surfacing and leaping clear of the water, just a little way from the shore.

ARDTORNISH
OBAN, ARGYLL [SC]

You can see families of otters around the shores of Loch Aline on this estate, where they hunt in daylight, catching fish and crabs at low tide.
See pp.206–207

CROMARTY FIRTH
ROSS-SHIRE [SC]

An inlet of the Moray Firth, the Cromarty Firth is a great place to see dolphins, seals, otters, and osprey.
See pp.220–221

LAKES AND WATERWAYS

FRIARS CRAG The still waters reflect the glorious landscape.

FRIARS CRAG
KESWICK, CUMBRIA [N]

This promontory juts out into Derwentwater, long considered one of the most beautiful scenes in Europe. Watch ospreys snatch fish straight from the lake.
See pp.212–213

TRENTHAM ESTATE
STOKE ON TRENT, STAFFORDSHIRE [N]

This is a great place to enjoy walks along the lakeside and in the woodlands. Good for ducks and grebes, it is also home to a large heronry.
See pp.212–213

BLASHFORD LAKES
NEW FOREST, HAMPSHIRE [SW]

Wetland birds, badgers, and deer make their homes around this series of tranquil man-made lakes surrounded by woodland, reeds, and grassland.
See pp.212–213

On the River Test on a still, summer evening, it's magical to watch flies tempting the trout to rise and take their prey with a noisy splash.

THE RIVER TEST
HAMPSHIRE [SW]

Our most famous trout stream travels through some of England's finest countryside. Brown trout, sea trout, chub, graylings, dace, and roach swim below the kingfishers.
See pp.218–219

ISLANDS

ISLE OF MULL Eagles swoop along the island's mountain slopes.

ISLE OF MULL
INNER HEBRIDES [SC]

Renowned for its otters, dolphins, and whales, Mull is also home to golden eagles and the very rare – and elegant – white-tailed sea eagles.
See pp.226–227

Sea eagles can be seen hunting over the lochs and rocky shores of Mull, or around their nesting site near Loch Frisa in early summer.

ISLE OF WIGHT
ENGLISH CHANNEL [SE]

Clouds of butterflies and moths, including the rare hummingbird moth, spill across the Channel to feed on the island's flowers.
See pp.224–225

ISLE OF SKYE
INNER HEBRIDES [SC]

Visit the otter centre on the Isle of Skye and watch otters hunt and play on the length of the shoreline.
See pp.206–207

ISLE OF MAY
FIRTH OF FORTH [SC]

This small island is owned by Scottish Natural Heritage, which protects its breeding birds including puffins, guillemots, and razorbills. Watch out for seals that swim offshore.
See pp.214–215

ISLE OF LEWIS
WESTERN ISLES [SC]

Seabirds live all around the coast; dolphins, porpoises, and sharks swim in its seas. Ancient stone circles add to the attractions inland, along with otters, eagles, and peregrine falcons.
See pp.216–217

GIANTS OF THE DEEP

KAIKOURA IN NEW ZEALAND, MONTEREY BAY IN CALIFORNIA, HERMANUS IN SOUTH AFRICA – these are names to conjure with on the trail of great whales. But there are places in the northeast Atlantic to rival any of these, and a ferry trip from Portsmouth or Plymouth to northern Spain will take you through some of the richest waters for cetaceans – whales, dolphins, and porpoises – anywhere in the world: the Bay of Biscay.

An evening sailing means you wake up rounding Finisterre, already into exciting waters. Relatively shallow and cool, these waters are likely to be harbouring minke whale, harbour porpoises, and bottlenose dolphins. A few hours later the real treats begin, as the ferry crosses the edge of the continental shelf and the water depth plunges rapidly from 200 to 4,000m (650–13,000ft). If sea conditions allow, the tall blows of large whales, mostly fin whales, should now start to appear, singly, or in small groups, sometimes more than a hundred on a single

WHERE
Sailing from the south coast of England to the Bay of Biscay, North Atlantic Ocean, off the coasts of France and Spain.

CONTACT
P&O Ferries, tel: 08716 645645; www.poferries.com; help@poferries.com or companies specialising in whale-watching cruises around the bay lasting several days.

GETTING THERE
Car ferries sail from Portsmouth to Bilbao and from Plymouth, Portsmouth, and Poole to Santander. Most of the specialist whale-watching cruise companies tend to depart from Plymouth or Portsmouth.

ACCESS AND FACILITIES
Ferries and sight-seeing boats generally have good wheelchair facilities and access.

CHARGES
These vary depending on the length of trip and time of year: check for prices with individual ferry and boat companies.

Whale-watching tips

Identifying whales and dolphins is quite an art. Although the larger boats and ferries are stable, they don't stop or steer nearer to the cetaceans, and some of the animals only surface for a few seconds at a time. Move between decks if you can: a lower deck will bring you a closer view, but upper decks allow you to see further. Take a good pair of binoculars, and a polarized lens for your camera if possible, as this will allow you to see the whale's body under the water. Start by scanning the sea for the misty blow of a whale.

Main: The deep-diving sperm whale surfaces for air for 8–10 minutes before diving again.

Left (left to right): A Cory's shearwater skims the waves of the bay; the ocean sunfish is the heaviest bony fish in the world.

Right: The distinctive dorsal fin of a fin whale, which may measure up to 24m (80ft) long.

Right panel (top and bottom): Great skuas; a minke whale.

voyage, and they often approach the ships very closely. The helicopter deck of the ferries provides an admirably stable and elevated viewing platform, and on many services expert guidance is on hand to point things out. Fin whales may predominate, but there are likely to be other species too: sperm whales, with their forward-directed, low, bushy spouts, and habit of raising their tail flukes out of the water as they dive deep in search of squid; schools of common and striped dolphins, sometimes riding the bow wave of the vessel; and – especially over the deep water canyons nearer the Spanish coast – small parties of the little-known Cuvier's beaked whale. You might also see ocean sunfish and basking sharks, along with numerous seabirds, especially just after stormy weather. Shearwater species – including great, Cory's, and the globally threatened Balearic – skim the waves. Gannets fly by in battalions, while storm petrels flitter over the surface of the water and skuas cause mayhem as they steal food from other seabirds.

> Over 30 species of whale and dolphin have been recorded in the Bay of Biscay.

THROUGH THE YEAR
BAY OF BISCAY

Whale-watching in Biscay is best in the summer and early **autumn**, though it's not clear whether this is because there are more whales then, or because the calmer seas make them easier to see. Sightings of female cetaceans with their young are frequent during June and July. Be sure to take a look around the boat itself: boats often provide a refuge for small birds migrating across the bay, and anything could turn up, from warblers and swallows to turtle doves and merlins. Likewise, migrating moths and butterflies often take advantage of the unexpected availability of "dry ground".

Numbers of fin whales in particular drop in **winter** and sightings become sporadic. The area is a regular wintering area for flocks of Sabine's gulls, little gulls, and kittiwakes, together with great skuas, fulmars, and possibly Leach's petrels.

In **spring**, whale sightings pick up from around April. By May, ferry passengers begin to see mother whales, dolphins, and harbour porpoises with their young, which tend to be about half the size of the adult cetaceans.

WHERE ELSE TO SEE
WHALES

Although you're likely to get the best view of cetaceans from boats, it is also possible to do some whale- or dolphin-watching from land.

The Inner and Outer **Hebrides** provide many opportunities to see larger cetaceans, particularly minke whales and sometimes killer whales during the summer. A trip from **Tobermory** on the **Isle of Mull** (*see pp.226–227*) should reveal whales, bottlenose dolphins, and basking sharks. Large whales are not a regular sight in the North Sea, although a few minkes turn up in the **Moray Firth** (*see pp.220–221*) from time to time. [SC]

For land-based observers, headlands in southwest England and Wales give the best chance of spotting whales. Try **Lands End** and **The Lizard** (*see pp.116–117*) in Cornwall. [SW]

Below: The white-headed Cuvier's beaked whale.

WHERE
Beinn Eighe National Nature Reserve, Torridon Mountains, Kinlochewe, Highland, Scotland.

CONTACT
Scottish National Heritage, Kinlochewe Office, IV22 2PD; tel: 01445 760254; Beinn Eighe Visitor Centre, tel: 01445 760254.

GETTING THERE
Beinn Eighe lies at the southeast end of Loch Maree, near the village of Kinlochewe. It can be reached from two roads: the A832 and the A896. The nearest train station is 30km (19 miles) away at Achnasheen. There is a limited bus service from Inverness.

ACCESS AND FACILITIES
The visitor centre is wheelchair friendly, and offers parking, toilets, a picnic area, cycle rack, and interpretive displays. There is also a basic camp site. Short wheelchair-friendly trails lead out from the visitor centre. For a more strenuous walk, with slopes and steps, take the mountain trail.

OPENING TIMES
The visitor centre is open April–October.

CHARGES
None.

Ancient forests

When you visit Beinn Eighe, make sure you have time to include the Scots pine woodland beside Loch Maree. Some of these trees are more than 350 years old, and they are part of a wood that has been growing here for over 8,000 years. The wood is one of the few surviving fragments of the original Caledonian pine forest, which spread north after the Ice-Age glaciers retreated and the climate gradually warmed up. Such pine trees once covered most of Scotland.

Above: A thin carpet of vegetation covers all but the highest peaks of this seemingly barren landscape.

Right panel (top and bottom): Unusual clubmosses cling to life in this harsh environment for plants; cowberry fruits.

Below (top and bottom): Heathers and other wiry shrubs bind the thin, rocky soil with their roots; the insect-eating butterwort grows in patches of wet soil lower down the slopes.

Main: The Beinn Eighe National Nature Reserve includes all of the Torridon Mountains.

LIFE AT THE TOP

THE SCOTTISH HIGHLANDS ARE THE MOST RUGGED, WILD, AND FORBIDDING landscapes in Britain. Even in August their climate can be bracing, to say the least, so it's no surprise that they are the British stronghold for a group of plants that evolved to cope with life on the Arctic tundra. These Arctic-alpines were widespread in southern Britain 20,000 years ago, during the last Ice Age, but as the climate warmed, they retreated to the highest, most northerly peaks, where the harsh growing conditions remain very like those at sea level on the polar fringes.

You can see this for yourself if you climb the slopes of Beinn Eighe, a great cluster of rocky peaks and ridges in the northwest Highlands, which was declared a National Nature Reserve as long ago as 1951. The peaks are capped with pale, glittering quartzite, which is all but barren, but many of the higher slopes are covered with a low-growing scrub of tough woody plants, such as dwarf willow and prostrate juniper, interspersed with blaeberry,

Beinn Eighe was
Britain's first
National Nature
Reserve – reflecting
its value to botanists,
naturalists, and
geologists.

WHERE ELSE TO SEE
MOUNTAIN PLANTS

By their nature, Arctic-alpines and other mountain plants are normally restricted to high mountains in Britain, although they grow at sea level in the Arctic. Many are commonly cultivated, but to see them growing wild, you need to visit the uplands – and especially the Scottish Highlands – in summer.

One of the best sites is **Ben Lawers**, near Loch Tay in the Breadalbane Hills of the southern Highlands. Its mica schist rocks have created lime-rich soils that support more than 60 per cent of the mountain plant species native to Britain. [SC]

The Cairngorms in the eastern Highlands (*see pp.178–179*) form a high plateau with large areas that rise above 1,100m (3,600ft). Although the rock is acid granite, the region can boast a wide variety of mountain plants. [SC]

In England, the sugar limestone habitat of **Upper Teesdale** (*see pp.114–115*) in the Pennines, Cumbria, supports rare mountain plants that have survived here since just after the last Ice Age. [N]

THROUGH THE YEAR
BEINN EIGHE

In **autumn** the mountain plants start to shut down for the winter, but there is still plenty to see on the lower slopes. Watch out for red squirrels and deer, and scan the ancient pine forest for Scottish crossbills using their modified beaks to extract seeds from pine cones.

The climate on Beinn Eighe in **winter** can be truly glacial, so you are unlikely to venture far up the mountain trail. But look out for mountain hares in their white winter coats on lower slopes and around Loch Maree, and if it has snowed, check the ground for footprints. Both pine martens and wildcats live on the reserve, and this offers the best chance of detecting them.

Spring sees a burst of plant growth on the mountain as the winter snows melt. Watch for ravens tumbling through the sky as they perform their aerial courtship displays. Black-throated divers start arriving to breed, and the white-tailed eagles begin nest building.

Below: Wildcats live and breed in the Caledonian forest.

cowberry, heather, clubmosses, and sedges. Aptly known to botanists as "dwarf shrub heath", this is almost exactly like the vegetation that covers vast areas of Arctic tundra. Standing here, you could be on the rocky, windswept fringes of Greenland.

The quartzite and sandstone of Beinn Eighe are hard, acid rocks that break down only reluctantly, so the soil here is poor in minerals and consists largely of acid peat. In some parts of the Highlands, however, outcrops of lime-rich rock provide nutrients that allow a wider diversity of plants to grow. An intriguing variety of microhabitats such as loose scree, wet flushes, and rock ledges are colonized by a range of Arctic-alpines such as alpine forget-me-not, moss campion, alpine saxifrage, mountain avens, and alpine gentian – many of which will be in flower in August.

The best places to find botanical rarities are the ungrazed crags and cliffs, so look up as well as down, and take a pair of binoculars. They can save a lot of fruitless and possibly dangerous exploration – and you will be very glad of them if a golden eagle or a white-tailed eagle soars into view around the flank of the mountain, or a cautious pine marten shows its heart-shaped face.

JAN
FEB
MAR
APR
MAY
JUN
JUL
AUG
SEP
OCT
NOV
DEC

WHERE
Wicken Fen, Lode Lane, Wicken, Ely,
Cambridgeshire, CB7 5XP;
www.wicken.org.uk

CONTACT
The National Trust, tel: 01353 720274;
wickenfen@nationaltrust.org.uk

GETTING THERE
Wicken Fen lies just south of the A1123 and
4.8km (3 miles) west of Soham, near the
town of Ely. The nearest train station is in Ely,
from where you can catch a bus to Soham or
Stretham. By cycle, the reserve is on Route
11 of the National Cycle Network.

ACCESS AND FACILITIES
Of the three trails, the boardwalk trail is the
easiest; it is ideal for wheelchairs and buggies
and has a specially adapted hide. The visitor
centre has a shop, toilets, and refreshments.
The café – next door to the visitor centre –
provides a wide range of hot and cold food.

OPENING TIMES
The visitor centre is open daily, 10am–5pm,
(Tuesdays–Sundays) all year except for
Christmas Day.

CHARGES
Small entry charge for non-National Trust
members.

Wind-pump drainage

The wind pump on Sedge Fen is now the only
working woodpump in the whole of the Fens,
though at one time there were around 700. In
the 17th century, landowners tried to reclaim
fenland by draining it, but the drying out of the
fens caused them to sink below river levels
– when it rained, excess rain could no longer
reach the river, so the fens flooded. Wind pumps
were then introduced to control the water levels.
The pump at Sedge Fen was last used to drain
the land for food production during World War II.

Above (left to right): The very rare great crested newt; marsh harriers specialize in hunting at low level over the wetlands; a water rail.
Main: Wicken Fen is a surviving fragment of the once huge fenland that stretched from Cambridge to The Wash.

A PATCH OF TRUE FENLAND

FOUR HUNDRED YEARS AGO A VAST AREA OF EASTERN ENGLAND to the south of The Wash was fenland – a waterlogged, peaty landscape of reeds, willow, and alder, dotted with meres of open water and teeming with animal life. From the 1620s onwards, the land was progressively drained to turn the fen peat into extremely fertile farmland, and today nearly all the wild fenland has disappeared. Just a few patches remain, and of these the most famous is certainly Wicken Fen.

One of the first nature reserves to be created in Britain, Wicken Fen was saved thanks to the foresight of Victorian naturalists who bought sections of the fen and presented them to the National Trust. Even then they could see that the site had an astonishing wealth of wildlife, considering its relatively small area. It is particularly rich in insects, something that becomes very clear if you visit the reserve in August. The shimmering wings of dragonflies are everywhere – 19 species breed in the ditches and ponds on the reserve – and every flower is alive with nectar-feeding butterflies, hoverflies, and beetles. And if you look down into the clear water you will see roach, rudd, and perch, and maybe a water vole or even a swimming grass snake. The nearby mere is a magnet for ducks, geese, and herons, and there is a good chance of seeing the magnificent marsh harrier.

Apart from the wonderful wildlife, the most intriguing thing about Wicken Fen is its relationship to the surrounding landscape. When the fenland peat was drained for agriculture it dried out, shrank, and started wasting away, to the point where some areas now lie more than 2.4m (8ft) below sea level. But Wicken Fen has never been drained, and it now stands high above the surrounding fields like a slice of rich, moist cake on a dry, almost empty, plate. Despite this, when you are in the middle of the fen itself, all that you see is the watery wilderness of a lost world. Wicken Fen is not just a nature reserve – it is a window into the past.

n amazing total of more than 8,000 species of lants, fungi, and animals have been recorded at Wicken Fen – including over 20 types of ragonfly and damselfly.

Inset: Look for the emperor dragonfly around the fen's lodes, or waterways.
Below (left to right): Grass snakes swim the ditches looking for frogs; a water vole.

WHERE ELSE TO SEE FENS

Nearly all – 99.9 per cent – of the once vast fens of eastern England is now arable farmland. Wicken Fen is one of just four surviving patches of wild fenland in the region. Other areas of fenland do exist elsewhere in Britain, but most fenland has been drained because, unlike the acid peat of upland bogs, the alkaline peat of fenland makes very fertile soil.

In the Fens proper, **Woodwalton Fen** near Huntingdon in north Cambridgeshire is a superb example of a near-natural wetland, rivalling Wicken Fen in biodiversity. The "Great Fen Project" aims to link Woodwalton with nearby **Holme Fen**, another good site. [SE]

Further east, there is plenty of fenland surviving in the Norfolk Broads. One of the best sites is **Strumpshaw Fen** (see pp.152–153), one of the last strongholds of the swallowtail butterfly. [SE]

Ham Wall nature reserve on the Somerset Levels is an extensive area of reedbed and fen recreated by wetland restoration. [SW]

Ross Lough nature reserve in County Fermanagh, Northern Ireland, is a mosaic of habitats including open water, swamp, and fen, supporting a rich variety of wildlife. [NI]

THROUGH THE YEAR WICKEN FEN

In **autumn**, winter migrants such as hen harriers and short-eared owls come here from the uplands to join the resident marsh harriers. The reserve also attracts large numbers of overwintering waterfowl.

Winter is a good time to look for resident mammals such as foxes, stoats, and weasels. Brown hares are regularly seen on Adventurer's Fen, and the site has started to attract visiting otters.

The reserve bursts into flower in **spring**, as colourful plants such as the yellow flag iris bloom along the waterways. Migrant songbirds such as blackcaps and reed warblers return to breed, and male bitterns can be heard booming in the reedbeds.

Below: Reed grows in the tall fen, which is flooded during the winter.

JAN

FEB

MAR

APR

MAY

JUN

JUL

AUG

SEP

OCT

NOV

DEC

WHERE
Ardtornish Estate, Morvern, near Oban, Argyll, Scotland, PA34 5UZ; www.ardtornish.co.uk

CONTACT
Ardtornish Estate Office, tel: 01967 421288; tourism@ardtornish.co.uk

GETTING THERE
Fort William is the nearest transport hub; the onward journey via the Corran Ferry to Ardtornish, at the southern end of the peninsula, is only practicable for the visitor by car. There is also a ferry between Lochaline to the Isle of Mull; a Caledonian MacBrayne ferry connects Mull with Oban on the Scottish mainland.

ACCESS AND FACILITIES
Although Ardtornish is a private estate there is open access for walkers to the sea lochs. The estate also includes and co-manages part of the Scottish Wildlife Trust's Rahoy Hills Reserve, most easily accessed from Acharn; you must contact the Ardtornish Estate office or the Trust (01463 714746) if you intend to enter the higher areas of the reserve.

OPENING TIMES
Open all year round.

CHARGES
For ferries, and to visit Ardtornish Gardens.

Breeding time

Otters are generally solitary, but when females are ready to breed – usually in spring – they attract males and indulge in an energetic courtship before mating. Two or three cubs are born two months later – between May and August – in an underground den, or holt. Their mother raises them alone, feeding them on her milk inside the den. At 10 weeks they venture outside to play, but do not enter the water until they are three months old, and it may be another six months before they can hunt and fend for themselves.

Main: A young otter dries off amidst the seaweed on the lochside.

LAND OF THE OTTER

L YING ON THE WEST COAST OF SCOTLAND, the Morvern Peninsula – separated from the Isle of Mull by only a narrow strip of water – is one of the most remote regions of Scotland. Few people live here, and its rugged landscape, with spectacular views and tranquil shores, has changed little over the centuries. But while it may not be among the most accessible of places, this is a magical destination for wildlife watchers. Its perfectly preserved habitats host a tremendous diversity of flowers, birds, and animals, and perhaps most excitingly, it is the home of one of the UK's most charismatic creatures: the otter.

Loch Aline, a quiet and sheltered sea loch on the Ardtornish Estate, is a wonderful otter-spotting area, and August is a great time to visit, when the climate is generally at its mildest, and when you are most likely to see families of otter cubs (*see box, left*). Otters are usually thought of as river animals, but the shores of western

Left (left to right): Loch Sunart separates the Morvern Peninsula from the Isle of Mull; a golden eagle soars overhead.

Right (top and bottom): A female otter catches a crab to take back to her cubs; their sleek, streamlined form makes otters the perfect swimming machines.

Above: The cubs stay together on their first open-air expeditions.

This remote peninsula is one of the very rare places in Britain where otters may regularly be seen during daylight.

WHERE ELSE TO SEE
OTTERS

After decades of decline, the otter population is recovering and is beginning to recolonize former haunts around Britain. River otters are more elusive than those that live on the coast, and are rarely seen; years of disturbance have made them wary and they nearly always hunt at night. Otters can usually be detected by the signs they leave – dark, oily, fish-scented droppings, their five-toed footprints in muddy river banks, and the chutes and slides they use to slip into the water.

The RSPB reserve at **Leighton Moss** in Lancashire (*see pp.78–79*) is home to several otters that can often be seen from the birdwatching hides. [N]

The **Somerset Levels** is ideal otter country, but good vantage points are scarce. Try the Mere Hide at **Shapwick Heath** reserve (*see pp.120–121*). [SW]

The Camel Valley, in Cornwall, has a healthy otter population. Bicycles can be hired at several points along the peaceful 27.3km (17 miles) Camel cycle trail. [SW]

The west coast of Scotland and the islands of the **Hebrides**, **Shetland**, and **Orkney** are among the best places to spot coastal otters, on quiet rocky shores and in sea lochs. There is an otter haven and hide on the **Isle of Skye**. [SC]

THROUGH THE YEAR
ARDTORNISH ESTATE

During the **summer**, the ferry trip from the Isle of Mull to the Morvern Peninsula may well offer sightings of minke whales and basking sharks.

Long-legged, spiny shore crabs may be seen at the margins of Loch Aline in **autumn**, just as young otters are learning to catch their own food. Lengthy chases often ensue.

In **winter** sea eagles and golden eagles may be seen ranging across the clear, cold skies. Pine martens become less cautious, venturing out from cover to forage for food. These creatures exist in very small numbers outside Scotland, and the Morvern Peninsula is one of the best places to spot them.

Scotland host one of the largest otter populations in Europe, and on the Ardtornish Estate the otters have been left to their own devices. Otters are much easier to see here than on inland rivers, partly because of their numbers but also because, unlike river otters, these coastal-dwelling animals routinely hunt in daylight. The summer nights are very short in this part of Scotland, so they have little option, but since they suffer so little disturbance, they also have no reason to hide away. Instead, the lives of coastal otters are governed by the tides, for they find it much easier to catch fish and crabs at low tide when the rich seaweed beds that lie just offshore are within easy reach of the surface.

Otters can often be seen eating small prey in the water, or hauling large fish such as eels or lumpsuckers ashore to devour at leisure among the weed-strewn rocks. Look out for the distinctive V-shaped wake of an otter swimming low in the water when they are out fishing for food. Otters spend a lot of time grooming their dense brown fur, which tends to become matted by the salty seawater, and if you move quietly, you may glimpse one resting in the seaweed on the lochside.

JAN

FEB

MAR

APR

MAY

JUN

JUL

AUG

SEP

OCT

NOV

DEC

WHERE
The Giant's Causeway, Bushmills, County Antrim, BT57 8SU Northern Ireland; www.northantrim.com/giantscauseway.htm

CONTACT
National Trust (Co. Antrim), tel: 028 20731582; giantscauseway@nationaltrust.org.uk

GETTING THERE
The Causeway is 3.2km (2 miles) east of Bushmills. Take the B17 from Coleraine to Bushmills, then the A2 until you see the Causeway Road signposted left. By rail, catch a train to Coleraine (16km/10 miles) or Portrush (13km/8 miles). Ulsterbus routes 172 and 177 run to the Causeway; in summer you can also catch the Causeway Rambler Bus (Ulsterbus no. 376).

ACCESS AND FACILITIES
The visitor centre has parking (including disabled-reserved), a cafe, and full-access toilets. There is a wheelchair- and pushchair-friendly bus that runs from the visitor centre to the Causeway. The site is partly accessible, but much of the area has uneven terrain that is difficult to negotiate.

OPENING TIMES
Open all year round.

CHARGES
None, but donations are welcome.

GIANT STEPPING STONES

MYTH AND LEGEND SURROUND THE BEAUTIFUL CAUSEWAY COAST. The star attraction – The Giant's Causeway – is a UNESCO World Heritage site consisting of 40,000 basalt columns along the coastline, which were formed at various stages from 60 million to 15,000 years ago, when lava from volcanic eruptions met the sea. The Causeway itself is a promontory made of columns, but there are many other interesting formations: follow the Finn MacCool Trail to visit them all, including The Wishing Chair and The Giant's Boot. The immense columns of The Giant's Organ and The Giant's Gate will tempt you to believe that these were the work of a giant's hand.

This part of the North Antrim coast has Ireland's most spectacular scenery: enormous cliffs, haunting basalt columns, secluded bays, and eerie, isolated ruins. While you're following the trail around the Causeway, keep an eye out for some interesting plants and birds, too. Black guillemots nest close by, and you might see

The Giant's Causeway is the largest lava plateau in Europe, covered with intriguing rock formations like the famous Giant's Boot.

Colour contrasts

As you walk along the Causeway, be sure to look closely at the rocks themselves, which are extremely colourful in places. Look out especially for places where the oldest, lowest layer of rock, known as "lower basalt" shows through – this has weathered to a deep red colour. Red rock pools may have a base of this ancient red basalt, or – on closer inspection – turn out to have a covering of rare red algae. A surrounding of green algae and black tar lichen (*as shown above*) usually suggests the "red" is living algae.

them just offshore: look out for their striking black-and-white breeding plumage. Buzzards, peregrines, and ravens nest on the cliffs, while rock pipits live among the rocks along the shore. Stonechats fly above the path that leads down from the visitor centre to the shore.

More than 200 species of plant occur around the Causeway, including some rarities such as Scots lovage and the waxy-leaved oyster plant, whose leaves actually taste like oysters. Devil's-bit scabious, thrift, and sea and bladder campion grow wherever they can, as do some beautiful orchids, including the heath spotted, early purple, and the very rare frog orchid. Down on the rocks, scrambled over by hundreds of people each day, there are some plants that are so inconspicuous they probably go unnoticed by most visitors, but take a closer look: the black stripes on the rocks are tar lichens. The rock pools hide winkles, limpets, and the aptly-strange sea anemones, which look like plants growing underwater, but are in fact meat-eating animals.

Main: Spectacular scenery combines with myth and legend to make The Giant's Causeway awe-inspring

Above and below: Oyster plants grows on the shingle near the sea; Scots lovage grows only in Scotland and here, in Northern Ireland.

Left panel (inset and below): The Giant's Boot, in legend cast off by the mythical Finn MacCool; the Chimney Stacks are a number of columns separated from the cliffs by erosion.

WHERE ELSE TO SEE
VOLCANIC LANDSCAPES

Volcanic activity during the Palaeozoic era, 425 million years ago, led to the creation of Scotland's Caledonian mountains. Volcanoes were still erupting in western Scotland, around Mull, Skye, and St Kilda, during the Tertiary period, 2.5–65 million years ago, when The Giant's Causeway was formed.

Fingal's Cave, on the Hebridean island of **Staffa**, is made of basalt columns like the Giant's Causeway, and was formed in the same way, at the same time. **St Abb's Head**, Berwickshire, is another complex coastline of cliffs and offshore stacks formed by volcanoes that has outstanding wildlife. [SC]

The sandstone cliffs of **Fowlsheugh**, Aberdeenshire, have green volcanic extrusions, and the cliffs themselves include sections of volcanic stone. The area is home to over 150,000 birds in summer. [SC]

The area around **Ben Nevis** in Scotland is a huge volcanic complex. Ben Nevis – itself a volcanic outcrop – rises from Loch Linnhe like a huge granite whale-back, to a height of 1,344m (4,406ft). The Nevis gorge, to its south, contains remnants of the ancient Caledonian pine forest. [SC]

THROUGH THE YEAR
GIANT'S CAUSEWAY

In **autumn**, look for the bobbing heads of grey seals offshore. Ravens, buzzards, and peregrines will be out looking for prey, while smaller birds will be trying to avoid them as they forage for food among the cliffs, seashore, and grasslands.

In many ways, the stones can be enjoyed at their best in **winter**, when the summer crowds have gone and huge waves crash over the stepped stones. If you're feeling brave, you might want to visit the Carrick-a-rede rope bridge, near Ballintoy, where you can cross from the mainland to the island of Carrick some 30m (100ft) above the crashing waves, amid steep and scary cliffs.

Seabirds return to the cliffs in **spring**, including black guillemots and fulmars. A pair of choughs – rarely seen in Northern Ireland – breeds at the site. Look for early spring flowers along the cliff paths, and emerging animals – Irish hares, foxes, badgers, rabbits, and stoats all live along this coast.

Below: Little rock pipits flit among the giant rocks of the Causeway.

JAN

FEB

MAR

APR

MAY

JUN

JUL

AUG

SEP

OCT

NOV

DEC

WHERE
Cornmill Meadows Dragonfly Sanctuary,
Abbey Gardens, Waltham Abbey,
Essex EN9 1XQ;
www.leevalleypark.org.uk

CONTACT
Lee Valley Park rangers, tel: 01992 717711;
info@leevalleypark.org.uk

GETTING THERE
By car, exit the M25 at junction 26 and join
the A121; go straight through several sets
of traffic lights, then turn left at the next
roundabout into the car park for Abbey
Gardens. By rail, travel to Waltham Cross,
Cheshunt, or Broxbourne. Bus numbers 211,
212, 213, 240, 250, 251, and 505 all stop
at Cornmill Meadows.

ACCESS AND FACILITIES
The sanctuary has full wheelchair and
pushchair access, and full-access toilets.
There is a picnic site, and guided tours
can be arranged. Dogs are welcome.

OPENING TIMES
Open all year round.

CHARGES
None.

Below the surface

Dragonflies and damselflies lay their eggs on
aquatic plants; these hatch into nymphs (*above*)
that live underwater for 1–3 years, feeding on
minnows, tadpoles, and aquatic insects. They are
ambush predators, hiding by underwater rocks
or leaves until prey swims close enough for the
nymph to grab it with its extendable jaws. When
it is ready to emerge, the nymph climbs up a leaf
from the water to the air, and waits until its outer
case dries and splits. The adult then emerges, and
gradually stretches out its glorious wings.

Above (left to right): Cornmill Meadows; brilliant emerald dragonfly.
Main: An emperor dragonfly laying its eggs.

DAZZLING DRAGONFLIES

NSECTS ARE EXTRAORDINARY CREATURES. For many people they are just pests, but once you start to look at them carefully, it's hard not to become fascinated by their sculptured bodies, iridescent colours, and weirdly mechanical movements. Some of the most dazzling are the dragonflies and their smaller relatives, the damselflies; and one of the best places to see them is the Cornmill Meadows Dragonfly Sanctuary in the River Lee Country Park in Essex. This mosaic of wetland habitats provides a home for 21 of the 38 species that regularly breed in Britain, and if you visit on a sunny day in August you stand a good chance of seeing most of them.

Seeing dragonflies is one thing, but identifying them is not always so easy. The bigger, more powerful "hawkers" move very fast, displaying amazing agility as they loop and swerve through the air in pursuit of small airborne insects. There is little chance of noting their more subtle distinguishing features unless they land in front of you, but luckily some are unmistakable,

Damselflies and dragonflies are expert fliers, able to swerve, dive, and change direction instantly in order to catch other, slower, flying insects.

like the magnificent male emperor dragonfly with its kingfisher-blue body, and the brown hawker with its glowing amber wings. The difference between dragonflies and the closely related damselflies is subtle. Dragonflies are fast and aggressive; they perch with their wings held wide open, and have extremely big eyes that meet in the middle to create a helmet-like effect (*see emerald dragonfly, top right*). Damselflies, on the other hand, are smaller and more delicate; they perch with their wings folded back, and their smaller, spherical eyes are widely separated (*see blue-tailed damselfly, left*). Several of the smaller dragonflies spend a lot of time perched – as do the less frenetic damselflies – and this permits more leisurely inspection, especially if you have equipped yourself with a pair of close-range binoculars. Even without them, the paths through the Dragonfly Sanctuary will give you plenty of close views.

Inset: The fairy-like blue-tailed damselfly.
Below (left to right): Golden-ringed dragonfly; a pair of migrant hawker dragonflies.

THROUGH THE YEAR
CORNMILL MEADOWS

In **autumn** the Lee Valley Park, in which Cornmill Meadows is situated, attracts bitterns. The water birds come to avoid icy conditions further north, and stay over the winter. They are very elusive, but are regularly seen from the bittern watchpoint near the Fisher's Green visitor centre (*see pp.26–27*).

Throughout the **winter** the lakes provide a home for large numbers of waterfowl, which are in splendid breeding plumage at this time of year. In late winter, herons start breeding in the trees overlooking Hooks Marsh, near the Dragonfly Sanctuary.

Spring is when dragonflies start hatching. Look for drab brown nymphs climbing the stems of emergent plants, and check for their empty skins. The emergence takes some time, but you may see different insects at different stages of the process.

WHERE ELSE TO SEE
DRAGONFLIES AND DAMSELFLIES

Dragonflies and damselflies breed in still or slow-flowing fresh water, so they are usually associated with ponds, lakes, and wetlands. Damselflies stay close to water, but dragonflies range much more widely. Some species have a restricted distribution, but many are widespread throughout Britain.

One of the best sites for these insects is **Thursley Common** in Surrey (*see pp.128–129*), a heathland and acid bog that supports 26 breeding species. [SE]

Another good place to look is Crockford Bridge in the **New Forest** (*see pp.174–175*) in Hampshire, where a wide variety of species can be seen on a relatively short stretch of stream. [SE]

Upton Fen in Norfolk is an excellent site, with a waymarked trail taking you through habitats including ditches and pools, open fen, and woodland. [SE]

Plantain Loch in **Dalbeattie Forest**, Scotland, is a good place to look for northern species. The Bridge of Grudie by **Loch Maree** is also a fine example of a bog habitat. [SC]

JAN

FEB

MAR

APR

MAY

JUN

JUL

AUG

SEP

OCT

NOV

DEC

Below: The broad-bodied chaser is found around ponds and lakes.

THE BEAUTY OF THE LAKES

FRIARS CRAG IS THE PERFECT PLACE FOR FANS OF LITERATURE AND NATURE. This promontory jutting out into the wide-open space of Derwentwater in the Lake District has breathtaking views. The writer John Ruskin claimed it was "one of the three most beautiful scenes in Europe", while another literary giant, Arthur Ransome, immortalized the crag as "Darien" in his most famous book: *Swallows and Amazons*.

Friars Crag is also brilliantly accessible: the short path from Keswick town centre is suitable for everyone, whether walking or in buggies or wheelchairs. If you wish, you can then continue along the nature trail for another 5.6 km (3 ½ miles). The area is wonderful in the summer – you can see right across the water towards the dramatic "Jaws of Borrowdale" and to Cat Bells, or watch the incredible skies reflected in Derwent's mirror-glass waters. On closer inspection of the crystal-clear water, you'll soon realize that it contains some interesting wildlife.

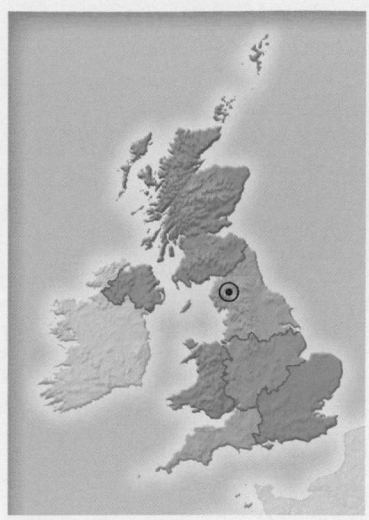

WHERE
Friars Crag, Derwentwater, Keswick, Cumbria, CA12 5DJ; www.lake-district.gov.uk

CONTACT
Lake District National Park Authority; tel: 01539 724555; hq@lake-district.gov.uk

GETTING THERE
To reach Keswick by car, take junction 40 off the M6, and then take the A66 to Keswick. By train, travel to Penrith, and then take a bus (nos. X4, X5, or X50) to Keswick. You can walk to Friars Crag from the centre of Keswick, or park at Derwentwater's lakeside car park and walk from there. Walk past the theatre by the Lake to the shore, then take the wide path, keeping the lake to your right.

ACCESS AND FACILITIES
There are toilets in the lake-side car park; the key is held at the National Trust shop and information centre (this is closed in winter). The path to Friars Crag is partially paved in places and is suitable for wheelchairs and pushchairs; there are no steep slopes. Plenty of facilities of all types can be found in the town of Keswick.

OPENING TIMES
Open all year round.

CHARGES
For car parking.

Crayfish wars

Cumbria remains one of the last strongholds for the native white-clawed crayfish, which has been decimated by the North American signal crayfish (*shown above*). These escaped from captivity into British waters in the late 1970s, carrying spores of a fungal disease that is harmless to itself, but deadly to the white-clawed crayfish. As a last resort, conservationists are transferring native white-clawed crayfish to extremely remote bodies of water around the UK in the hope of protecting the species.

Main: The still surface of Derwentwater acts as a mirror.

Left (left to right): Otters are shy, but can sometimes be seen at the water's edge; signs of otter activity: prints in the soft mud.

Right (left to right): An osprey "catch" from the water is fast and dramatic; a migrant hawker dragonfly.

Watch out for the native white-clawed crayfish that scuttle across the tea-coloured pebbles, and study the depths for a glimpse of the small and incredibly rare vendace fish, with its bluish-green back, white belly, and silvery flanks. Derwentwater and the adjacent Bassenthwaite Lake are the only two places in the UK where this fish occurs naturally. Otters are seen around the water's edge, although they quickly vanish on sensing human presence. In late summer, particularly August, you will be treated to a fantastic display of hawker dragonflies. Migrant and southern hawkers hover around the water, and if you're lucky, you might see a stunning golden-ringed dragonfly zoom by.

One of the most impressive birds you might spy over the water is the osprey. This rare, fish-eating bird of prey breeds nearby, and it hunts over the lake for fish below, snatching them from the water with its razor-sharp talons. From a distance ospreys are frequently mistaken for big seagulls, so it's worth taking a closer look at every large "gull" that flies close to the water.

WHERE ELSE TO SEE
LAKESIDE WALKS

There are lots of stunning places for gentle wildlife walks around water in Britain, both within nature reserves and around the countryside generally. Some are especially beautiful, tranquil, and teeming with wildlife.

The many other lakes of the **Lake District** offer wonderful views and a wide range of wildlife, often in very accessible settings. The gentle walk along the shores of Brotherswater from the Cow Bridge car park offers stunning views and hopefully a good collection of water birds, including a variety of duck species, grebes, and goosanders. [N]

Blashford Lakes Wildlife Reserve, in the New Forest (*see pp. 174–175*), has paths and a hide centred around flooded gravel pits. [SE]

The **Trentham Estate**, near Stoke on Trent, has a huge and beautiful lake, enlarged by Capability Brown in the 18th century, that is home to a large colony of herons. There are five walks around the park and woodlands. [M]

THROUGH THE YEAR
FRIARS CRAG

Although it's only a short walk to Friars Crag, it's surprising just how much wildlife you can see. In **autumn**, don't forget to look up into the trees by the shoreline, where tits form large feeding groups. Often, the first sign that they're around is their high-pitched call. Look out for Europe's smallest bird flying in with the flock; goldcrests are common here but are often hard to see.

During **winter**, you may see large flotillas of coots gathered on Derwentwater.

In **spring**, if you visit on a still, sunny spring day, you might be lucky enough to see the first emerging dragonflies and damselflies flying alongside the lake. The exquisite downy emerald dragonfly emerges in early May, but it is scarce. You're more likely to see the small, red common darter.

JAN
FEB
MAR
APR
MAY
JUN
JUL
AUG
SEP
OCT
NOV
DEC

Above: Derwentwater viewed from Cat Bells, which derives its name from the Middle English *cat bield* – the lair of the wildcat.

Below: Friars Crag provides spectacular views over Derwentwater and, in the distance, the hill country of the Lake District.

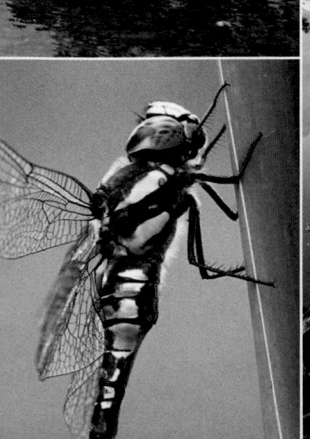

Below: Enjoying the Friars Crag walk in autumn.

SEAL-SPOTTING PARADISE

TWO SPECIES OF SEAL BREED IN BRITAIN: THE GREY AND THE COMMON SEAL. The common seal is not the commonest species in the UK, and its alternative name of harbour seal is certainly more appropriate in Scotland, where it is found along the west coast; but in eastern England it is more often found on estuaries and sand flats. Pupping takes place ashore. Common seals, which breed in summer, can use sand flats as the pups can swim almost as soon as they are born. Grey seals are born in winter and cannot swim until they shed their first white coat after two or three weeks, before which they must remain out of the water.

Both species spend much of their time when not feeding hauled out on beaches, often in mixed species groups. Blakeney Point on the north Norfolk Coast is one such haul-out spot, and some 500 seals of the two species can be found here during the summer. You can see them from seal-watching boat trips from Morston and

WHERE
Blakeney Point, Blakeney, North Norfolk, NR25 7NW; www.nationaltrust.org.uk

CONTACT
Norfolk Coast Office, tel: 01263 740241; blakeneypoint@nationaltrust.org.uk

GETTING THERE
Blakeney Point is 8km (5 miles) from Wells-next-the-sea on the North Norfolk coast. Park at Cley-next-the-sea and walk to the Point from Cley beach car park (5km/3 miles), or at Morston Quay and take a boat (times depending on tides). The nearest train station is Sheringham; from there take the Coasthopper bus to Cley or Morston. Both are on National Cycle Network Route 30.

ACCESS AND FACILITIES
Boat trips either make a round trip without disembarking, or allow for an hour or two exploring on the Point. The sand and shingle terrain is inaccessible by wheelchair. There are refreshments and toilets at Morston car park and at the Old Lifeboat Station on the Point (closed September–April). Some areas of the Point are out of bounds during the bird breeding season (April–August).

CHARGES
Car parking charges apply (NT members park free at Morston); the seal trip firms all charge the same or very similar rates.

Above: A common tern fiercely guards her chick.

Main: Both seal species bask sociably together on Blakeney Point.

Right panel (top to bottom): Low tide reveals wider stretches of sand and shallow pools inhabited by small marine creatures including the common starfish; a grey seal, with its long muzzle giving it an often mournful expression; a common or harbour seal looks perkier than a grey, with its rounder head and more cat-like, tip-tilted nose.

Below: Sea campion grows on the shingle bank.

Seeing seals up close

Seal-watching boat trips run from Morston and Blakeney quays from February until the end of October. This can be a wonderful way of seeing seals up close, and in their natural habitat – especially for children. You are likely to see seals basking on the sandbanks at the end of the Point, as well as some swimming through the sea – often up to the boat itself. You can identify the grey seals by their longer, more pointed heads, and their parallel nostrils; common seals have a more rounded face, and V-shaped nostrils.

Blakeney, or by making the energetic 5km- (3 mile-) trek west from Cley-next-the-sea. In the past, common seals predominated on the Point, but things are changing: it has now been more or less abandoned for pupping, and grey seals are on the increase. These two facts may not be unrelated, as grey seals tend to pack very tightly and could eventually displace the smaller common seals.

The Point also hosts important breeding colonies of water birds, especially terns. Sandwich, common, little, and a few Arctic terns wheel screechily around, plunge-diving and feeding their raucous chicks. Locally breeding ringed plovers and oystercatchers congregate at high tide, mingling with the returning Arctic waders, whose numbers increase daily at this time of year. If you go ashore, look out for the fading flowers of the shingle plants: yellow horned poppy, sea campion, and biting stonecrop. On the adjacent saltmarshes, look for the dense thickets of shrubby sea-blite, and several species of sea-lavender, including the rare matted sea-lavender.

The seals live here all year round, so close-up views from the seal boats are guaranteed.

WHERE ELSE TO SEE
SEAL COLONIES

Hauled-out grey seals can be seen in several parts of Britain, especially on northern and western coasts. Common seals, in contrast, tend to be more dispersed, especially around the Scottish west coast. Many of their locations are served by boat trips, and this can be a great way to see the seals at close range.

Boat trips also run from **Hunstanton** in Norfolk to Seal Island, in The Wash, to see a large common seal colony – around 7 per cent of the UK total. [SE]

Grey seals predominate in western Scotland on the **Isle of May** (the largest British pupping site), the **Monach Isles** (see pp.268–269), and **Treshnish Islands**. Scottish colonies of common seals live on **Dornoch Firth**, **Firth of Tay**, and **Skye**. [SC]

The **Farne Islands** (see pp.126–127) have one of Europe's largest grey seal populations. [N]

Donna Nook in Lincolnshire is one of the most accessible sites for seeing breeding seals. [M]

THROUGH THE YEAR
BLAKENEY POINT

Autumn brings seabirds close in to Blakeney Point. Skuas and shearwaters pass in numbers, together with a few Sabine's gulls and other scarce species. After easterly winds, the shrubby sea-blite can be teeming with smaller migrants, including Siberian rarities such as Richard's and olive-backed pipits.

In **midwinter**, the marshes behind the Point play host to hordes of wildfowl, including dark-bellied brent geese and wigeons, often in large flocks. Along the drift-line of the shingle bank, look out for flocks of snow buntings and smaller parties of shore larks, feeding unobtrusively among the debris.

The noisy arrival of the breeding terns is a sure sign that **spring** has sprung. When the winds come from the southeast, it can be a migrant hotspot, with wheatears and whinchats, and perhaps a gem of a bluethroat around the cover of the sea-blite scrub.

Below: The male sandwich tern offers fish to the female during courtship.

JAN

FEB

MAR

APR

MAY

JUN

JUL

AUG

SEP

OCT

NOV

DEC

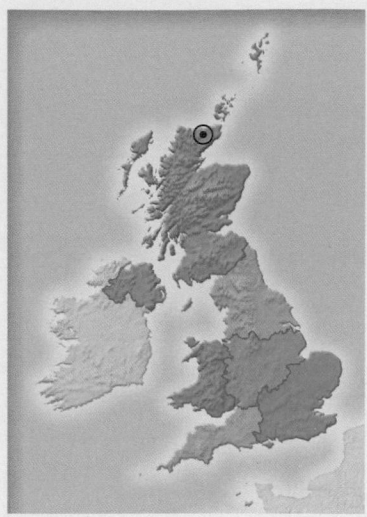

WHERE
RSPB Forsinard Flows, Forsinard, nr Thurso, Highland, KW13 6YT; www.rspb.co.uk

CONTACT
Tel: 01641 571225; forsinard@rspb.org.uk.

GETTING THERE
Forsinard lies on the A897, 38km (24 miles) north of Helmsdale. From Melvich on the north coast, turn south 3.2km (2 miles) east of Melvich on to the A897 for 22.5km (14 miles). There is no bus to Forsinard but Highland Council subsidize a taxi service from Thurso, Bettyhill, and Melvich; book in advance on 01641 541297.

ACCESS AND FACILITIES
The visitor centre at Forsinard railway station has car parking and cycle racks, and good access, with ramps. Toilet facilities accommodate all users' needs. The public road allows for observing the nearby countryside. The Dubh Lochan Trail is a 1.6km (1 mile) circular route on to the bog, with a stepping-stone-style flagstone surface, unsuitable for pushchairs and wheelchairs.

OPENING TIMES
The reserve is open at all times; the visitor centre is open daily from Easter to October, 9am–5.30pm.

Caught in a trap

One of the most interesting plants on British peat bogs is the insect-eating sundew plant. Its Latin name, *Drosera*, means "dewy", referring to the sticky droplets of mucilage that cling to its leaf hairs and never dry out. The plants rely on insects to supply vital nutrients that are not available from the ground. The sundew catches an unlucky insect with its sticky hairs, enfolds around it, then secretes enzymes to digest the insect and release the essential nutrients.

Left (left to right): Harriers hunt over the moorland; brown trout live in the peatland lochs and rivers.

Right (left to right): The peak of Morven dominates the peatlands; common butterwort flowers in August.

Below right: Golden plovers nest in large numbers around the peatlands of Forsinard.

Main: The lochs and lochans are an important feature of blanket bogs and esssential to their flora and fauna.

ANCIENT BOG LAND

WHEN THE PURPLE HEATHER BLOOMS IN AUGUST, and the sun glints on the small, still peatland pools, the vast prehistoric landscape of the Flow Country is a magnificent sight. This immense peatland blanket, lying between Caithness and Sutherland, is the largest area of blanket bog in the UK, and perhaps the world. If you love wild and remote places, this is undeniably the place for you.

The area came to ecological prominence in the 1980s when it became clear that government tax incentives had encouraged commercial conifer plantations on the irreplaceable peat bogs. This was stopped, and the challenging task of removing conifers and restoring the peatlands began. Thousands of ditches that had drained the life from these wet bogs were dammed, and thousands of alien trees uprooted. Gradually the sphagnum moss and the heather are reclaiming the land, and returning it to wildlife-rich peatland flows.

Above: Mountain hares can be seen around the bogs in winter.

THROUGH THE YEAR
FORSINARD FLOWS

In **autumn**, watch for flocks of redwings and fieldfares, and wild geese passing by on their way south. In September and October red deer roar across vast expanses of dramatic, chestnut-coloured deer grass; roe deer are frequent but elusive. The sphagnum mosses, inseparable from this world of wet peat, are at their most colourful in autumn, in rich clarets, apple greens, browns, and yellows.

There are hundreds of red deer in **winter**, and this is a good time of year to get close to them. Watch out for the mountain hare in its white winter coat, and check around the pools for otters. There are few birds in winter, apart from buzzards, red grouse, and ravens, but you might spot an occasional golden eagle.

Spring sees the return of most moorland birds, and you'll see golden plovers joining the greylag geese on the roadside fields, before they spread out on to the moors to breed. Look out for hen harriers displaying, and that rare treat: a golden eagle.

The peat blanket of the Flow Country is 9m (30ft) deep in parts, and took over 8,000 years to form.

WHERE ELSE TO SEE
PEAT BOGS

Such extensive peat bogs are rare, even on a world scale, but most of the wildlife of the bogs does live elsewhere in northern Scotland.

Inverpolly Nature Reserve in Wester Ross is a mixture of peat bogs, woodland, and moorland that attracts similar wildlife to Forsinard. Other sites worth visiting include the **Sleat peninsula** on **Skye**, and the Shetland Islands. **Lewis**, in the Western Isles, has the most important and most extensive peat bogs of the Scottish islands. [SC]

In North Wales there are areas of peat bog on the edges of Snowdonia, such as the **Migneint Moors**, but these are less productive than those in the far north. [W]

JAN   FEB   MAR   APR   MAY   JUN   JUL   **AUG**   SEP   OCT   NOV   DEC

The Dubh Lochan Trail from close to Forsinard Station takes you dry-shod into the world of the peat bog and the black pools, or "dubh lochans", which so characterize this area. The first thing you notice are the remarkable carnivorous plants – the sundew and butterwort – now in flower, jostling with the delicate blooms of bogbean, cotton grass, and bog asphodel. Great diving beetles share the pools with palmate newts, damselflies, and dragonflies, such as black darters and northern hawkers, which emerge from June to September.

But it's also the bird breeding season, and this is a birdwatcher's paradise: rare greenshanks and black-throated divers live among the golden plovers, sandpipers, dippers, teals, and greylag geese, the true native geese. If you're lucky, you might see one of Britain's rarest breeding birds, the common scoter, which nests on lochs in the area. Scan the moors for wheatears, stonechats, cuckoos, short-eared owls, merlins, and hen harriers, which hunt along the river corridor. The thin song of the dunlin whistles over the wet moors, while curlews trill among the glossy black pools. This is truly one of the last great wilderness areas in Britain.

GENTLY DOWN THE STREAM

A CHALK STREAM IS THE QUINTESSENTIAL BRITISH RIVER, with crystal clear, shallow waters tumbling over a gravel bed. Meandering through some of the UK's most beautiful countryside, the River Test is perhaps our most famous chalk stream, because it was here that flyfishing was perfected during the 19th century. Rising near Ashe, west of Basingstoke, the Test flows 65km (40 miles) via Stockbridge to Southampton Water.

Chalk streams owe their clarity to the fact that they filter rainwater for several months before it is released through springs, whereas other rivers are fed by silty rainwater running off the land. Their temperature is constant, so they feel cool in summer but warm in winter, which is ideal for the fish that swim and spawn in the river, and the voles and otters that live on the riverbank. The different environments created by carrier streams, sluices, and meadows allow a wide range of wildlife to grow and flourish.

WHERE
The Test rises from its source in the village of Ashe, in Hampshire, and travels through Whitchurch, Stockbridge, and Romsey to an estuary above Southampton Water.

FURTHER INFORMATION
The Environment Agency publishes a Fact File on the River Test, which is downloadable from its website; contact the Hampshire and IoW regional office, tel: 01962 713267, or visit www.environment-agency.gov.uk

Natural England's website contains details of all the National Nature Reserves and Sites of Special Scientific Interest along the Test: www.naturalengland.org.uk

In the village of Overton on the Upper Test, 12km (8 miles) west of Basingstoke, the Overton Biodiversity Society has developed nature trails that take in viewing points along the river. Leaflets are available from shops in the village, or from the Society's website: www.overton-biodiversity.org

The Hampshire and Isle of Wight Wildlife Trust manages the Lower Test reserve, Testwood Lakes, and several small chalk stream reserves along the nearby River Itchen; visit www.hwt.org.uk for details, or contact the Testwood Lakes Visitor Centre, tel: 02380 667929.

Furry menace

Introduced American mink have become a threat to native species in the River Test. Originally imported into the UK for fur-farming in the late 1920s, they escaped into the wild and began breeding. They feed on small riverside animals, such as frogs and rats, but are particularly good at catching water voles, because they can follow them into the water or into a burrow. The threat to the vole population is extremely serious: one female mink, with young, can decimate a river's entire water vole population in a single season.

Main and far right: The pure waters of the River Test; herons live all along the river.

Left (left to right): The native white-clawed crayfish, which is suffering from river pollution and the introduction of non-native species; the stone-sucking brook lamprey.

Right (left to right): Wild watercress grows on the River Test; water-crowfoot in flower.

Fish-watching is an underrated but hugely enjoyable wildlife experience. If you watch from a bridge in the right conditions you should see brown trout, sea trout (a migratory form of the brown trout), chub, graylings, dace, roach, and minnows. The valley of the River Test is full of clear watercourses, wonderful for kingfishers and grey wagtails, but in places a recent accumulation of silt has begun to affect the river life. Old-style river management has largely ceased, and silting of gravelly areas is a problem for spawning fish such as trout and salmon. It particularly affects the trout, as they lay their eggs in the gravel, and the hatchlings can be smothered by gathering silt.

The chalky water is high in calcium, which freshwater shrimps and snails need to build their external skeletons. The streams naturally support an abundance of insects and other invertebrates, and it's magical to watch the emergence of flies encouraging the trout to rise on a still, summer evening, sipping them from the surface or taking them with a sudden, noisy splash.

Fish dart through sparkling waters amidst some of England's most beautiful countryside.

WHERE ELSE TO SEE
CHALK STREAMS

Chalk streams occur in areas of chalk hills; rainwater falls on to the hills and filters through the chalk rock before being released into springs and streams. Areas of chalk rock include the Chilterns, in Buckinghamshire; the White Cliffs of Dover, in Kent; the Seven Sisters and the North and South Downs, in Sussex; and the Needles on the Isle of Wight.

The **River Itchen** flows close to the Test, running into the other side of Southampton Water and the upper reaches of the Avon around Salisbury. The **River Frome**, in Dorset, is the largest chalk stream in southwest England. [SW]

The **Great Stour** is Kent's largest chalk river, running for more than 80km (50 miles). It supports an interesting mix of wildlife, and travels through a National Nature Reserve at **Stodmarsh**. [SE]

The **Churnet** and **Dove** in Derbyshire and Staffordshire are not chalk streams but flow through limestone areas and share the characteristic clear water in which you can see brown trout and graylings and attract dippers and grey wagtails. [M]

THROUGH THE YEAR
THE RIVER TEST

Floods in **winter** encourage teals, shovelers, gadwalls, and mallards, with wigeons on the marshes downstream. Look out for little egrets.

Spring sees the arrival of sand martins, and you could be lucky enough to see a salmon. Pike can be spotted in the river in spring sometimes, when they are seeking out sites for spawning. As summer approaches, watch out for swallows and for house and sand martins, and listen for the song of Cetti's warblers.

Autumn is a good time to see dragonflies and hunting hobbies. Families of warblers live in the riverside bushes. Lapwing flocks often form in fields around the river.

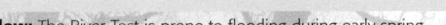

Below: The River Test is prone to flooding during early spring

JAN
FEB
MAR
APR
MAY
JUN
JUL
AUG
SEP
OCT
NOV
DEC

WHERE
Moray Firth, Ross-shire, Scotland, IV10 8SD; www.wdcs.org

CONTACT
North Kessock Dolphin and Seal Centre, tel: 01463 731866; Whale and Dolphin Conservation Society (WDCS), tel: 01343 820339; wildlifecentre@wdcs.org

GETTING THERE
The Dolphin and Seal Centre at Kessock Bridge is on the A9 from Inverness. For the WDCS Centre, take the A96 from Inverness, then the B9014 between Mosstodloch and Fochabers, and follow the brown tourist signs. The nearest train station is Elgin. For buses contact Traveline, tel: 0870 6082608; www.travelinescotland.co.uk

ACCESS AND FACILITIES
Good access for wheelchairs along the sea front, with facilities nearby. Both centres have cafes, information centres, and toilets.

OPENING TIMES
The Dolphin and Seal Centre is open daily June–September, the WDCS Centre is open daily April–October, and weekends only November–December.

CHARGES
None.

A unique population

Bottlenose dolphins are found in tropical and temperate seas around the globe. Those in the Moray Firth are one of only two or three resident groups in British waters, and the only group in the North Sea. Although vulnerable to a number of human threats, including pollution, collision with vessels, entanglement in fishing nets, and disturbance, they habituate to our presence well, with the result that they can thrive alongside regulated and responsible wildlife tourism.

Above (top and bottom): Chanonry Point lighthouse; the feet of black guillemots are red.

Below: Female bottlenose dolphins produce a single calf every 3–4 years, after a one-year gestation period.

Right panel (from top): Bottlenose dolphins playing; harbour porpoises reveal only their backs.

Inset: Bottlenose dolphin riding a boat's bow wave.

Main: The bottlenose dolphins in the Moray Firth constitute the most northerly resident population in the world.

DOLPHINS IN THE SURF

THERE ARE SEVERAL LOCATIONS AROUND THE BRITISH COAST where you can see inshore groups of bottlenose dolphins. The Moray Firth in northeast Scotland is one of the best – and easiest – places to watch these magnificent, inquisitive, playful animals. Present here all year round, your chances of seeing them are greatest in summer when salmon – one of their favoured foods – return to the Firth prior to entering the freshwater rivers for spawning. Although there are around 130 dolphins in this population, it is normal to see them in parties of less than 10 animals, mostly females with their calves.

The place to start is the Dolphin and Seal Centre near the Kessock Bridge. Here you can obtain information on where the dolphins have recently been seen, perhaps see them if they are in the area, or hear the noises they produce: strange clicks and squeaks that are picked up by hydrophone around the centre. The most reliable place

Frolicking close
inshore, the Moray
Firth bottlenose
dolphins seem
unafraid of humans –
in fact, they love
playing to an audience.

WHERE ELSE TO SEE
WHALES AND DOLPHINS

More than 20 species of cetacean have been recorded in British seas. Some, including minke whales, harbour porpoises, and bottlenose dolphins, can be seen at almost any time, while rarer visiting cetaceans, such as white-beaked dolphins, are only seen at specific times of year.

Just north of the Moray Firth, the **Cromarty Firth** is another regular haunt for the Moray Firth group of bottlenose dolphins. The **Isle of Mull** (*see pp.226–227*), off western Scotland, is one of Britain's best whale- and dolphin-watching localities. You can see bottlenose, common, and Risso's dolphins, and there's a chance of seeing orcas or killer whales. [SC]

A large resident group of dolphins is based around **Cardigan Bay**, Wales, where they are sometimes joined by Risso's dolphins and grey seals. [W]

The Lizard (*see pp.116–117*) and other headlands in Cornwall produce frequent sightings of dolphins. Lone individuals set up home on other parts of the coast, sometimes for several years, often associating with harbours. [SW]

THROUGH THE YEAR
MORAY FIRTH

In **autumn** the Moray Firth plays host to more than 100,000 water birds, including large numbers of sea ducks, such as common and velvet scoters, and red-breasted mergansers, as well as mute swans, and waders such as bar-tailed godwits. Purple sandpipers are numerous on the seaweed-covered shoreline.

Many birds stay on from autumn to **winter**, when it is a good time to look for birds of prey. Hen harriers can be seen, while the Black Isle has a reintroduced population of red kites. Findhorn Valley, to the south, is famed for golden and white-tailed eagles.

Spring brings large flocks of pink-footed geese as they head for Iceland, and seabirds such as black guillemots and cormorants returning to breeding colonies on the Cromarty Firth. The shingle habitat at Spey Bay bursts into flower as gorse scrub comes into bloom, and the first ospreys, fresh from migration, fish in the mouth of the river.

Above: Red-breasted mergansers frequent the Riff Bank of the Moray Firth.

to see them is in the narrows between the inner and outer Firth, from Chanonry Point on the north shore and Fort George on the south. With luck, dolphins will appear right in front of you, surfacing and leaping clear of the water, just a few metres out from the shore. If all is quiet, keep an eye on any passing ships, as bottlenose dolphins often ride the bow waves.

Look out too for other cetaceans. The smaller harbour porpoise is common but more difficult to see, as its small triangular fin barely breaks the surface. A few minke whales are often present in the outer Firth, especially in late summer.

Spey Bay, on the south shore, is another great place to visit. As well as the dolphins, you can see otters, seals, and ospreys feeding at the mouth of the Spey as it completes its journey from the highlands. You can visit the largest vegetated shingle complex in Scotland, and take advantage of the facilities at the Whale and Dolphin Conservation Society Wildlife (WDCS) Centre. Or, for an alternative viewpoint, take a boat trip from Inverness or Avoch – all the boat operators observe a code of conduct regarding dolphins, and you should get some great close-up views.

JAN
FEB
MAR
APR
MAY
JUN
JUL
AUG
SEP
OCT
NOV
DEC

WHERE
Aston Rowant National Nature Reserve,
The Chilterns, Oxfordshire OX49 5SG.

CONTACT
Thames and Chilterns Team,
Natural England, tel: 01844 351833;
enquiries@naturalengland.org.uk

GETTING THERE
Aston Rowant is 15km (9 miles) northwest
of High Wycombe; it straddles the M40
between junctions 5 and 6. By car, follow
signposts from the A40. The nearest train
stations are Saunderton (5km/3 miles) and
High Wycombe (15km/9 miles). Contact Red
Rose Travel for bus times and numbers.

ACCESS AND FACILITIES
The car park serving the reserve is at the end
of a minor road signposted off the A40 and
Christmas Common Road. There are no
facilities on site; the nearest refreshments
and full-access toilets are at Chinnor
(5km/3 miles away). There is a picnic
area in Cowleaze wood. Although there
are a number of marked trails, only one
of them is wheelchair friendly.

OPENING TIMES
Open all year round.

CHARGES
None.

Living light

The light of a glow worm is produced by a
chemical reaction in its light organs, which
contain a protein called luciferin and an enzyme
called luciferase. When the two are combined
they react with oxygen, and the reaction releases
light. The light organs have networks of air tubes
to make sure they get a good oxygen supply, and
by opening and closing the tubes the glow worm
can switch itself on and off. The chemical reaction
is extremely efficient, because 98 per cent of the
energy it produces is turned into light.

Above (left to right): Glow worm eggs; the more conventionally beetle-like male glow worm; male and female glow worms mating.
Main: At dusk, the female glow worm climbs the grass to display her "lamp".

GLOW WORMS AT NIGHT

PERCHED HIGH ON THE STEEP, WEST-FACING SLOPES of the Chilterns near Oxford, Aston Rowant National Nature Reserve is a precious survivor. It is an area of ancient downland turf that has not been cultivated or fertilized for centuries – if ever – yet has been kept closely grazed by sheep and rabbits. The combination of nutrient-poor soils and grazing has suppressed grass growth and encouraged a wealth of chalk-loving wild flowers. These in turn support several scarce grassland butterflies that make any daytime visit in early August a delight, but for a really memorable experience, stay until the light starts to fade at dusk. Then, if the conditions are right, you will be treated to one of the strangest of all courtship displays: the living light-show of glow worms.

A glow worm is actually a beetle, but you would not know this from looking at an adult female. She has no hard, shiny wing-cases – the beetle trademark – and no wings, so her segmented body looks more like that of a woodlouse. She has very small eyes and feeble mouthparts that barely function. But she does have one remarkable asset: a set of organs in the last three segments of her body that can produce an eerie, greenish-yellow light.

By day a female glow worm stays well hidden, but at dusk she climbs up to a vantage point and begins to glow. At Aston Rowant there may be dozens of glowing females dotted in the grass on a warm summer evening. Their aim is to attract males, who are smaller and look quite different. A male's role is to fly in search of females, so he is equipped with functioning wings and protective wing-cases, like a typical beetle. His big compound eyes are eight times more sensitive than the female's, enabling him to pinpoint her beacon from up to 10m (33ft) away and fly towards it. When he is directly above a signalling female he closes his wings to drop out of the air and land close beside her. They mate, and the female then switches off her light, lays her eggs, and dies soon afterwards.

The eggs hatch into mobile larvae that look very like adult females. However, unlike adult glow worms, which barely eat at all, the larvae live by preying on snails, injecting them with digestive juices that liquefy their tissues. The larvae glow very slightly, and only intermittently, for a few seconds at a time. After up to four years of this voracious lifestyle they begin their short careers as glowing or flying adults, for both sexes will die soon after breeding. Like the meteors that streak through the night sky above them, they burn most brightly just before the end.

Below (left to right): Voracious glow worm larvae feed on small slugs and snails; the chalk grasslands of Aston Rowant.

WHERE ELSE TO SEE
GLOW WORMS

Colonies of glow worms are scattered all over England and Wales, occurring mainly in the warmer south on chalk and limestone grasslands. This is because the larvae prey on snails, which need lime to make their shells and are therefore most common in regions with lime-rich soils.

One good place to look is on the chalk downs of the **Isle of Wight** (see pp.224–225), where there is still a lot of ancient grassland. There is also relatively little fast-moving traffic, which kills many of the flying male glow worms. [SE]

The grassy embankments of old railway lines are among the best places to look, forming ribbon-like sanctuaries of old grassland. The disused railway at **Tewkesbury**, Gloucestershire, supports a thriving glow worm colony, which is easy to visit as the line is now a cycle track and pathway. [M]

Parts of **Sherwood Forest**, Nottinghamshire (see pp.36 37), still have large numbers of glow worms, especially in the heaths around the ancient woodlands near Edwinstowe and Clipstone. [M]

THROUGH THE YEAR
ASTON ROWANT

The beech woodlands at Aston Rowant are a wonderful sight in **autumn** as the leaves change to coppery brown and float down from the trees. This is also the time to look for rare fungi that live on the woodland floor.

Winter can cause casualties among the rabbit population that are exploited by the local red kites. These magnificent birds of prey have become very common in the area, and can now be seen throughout the year.

In **spring** the extensive juniper scrub – itself a rare habitat – attracts a lot of insects that provide food for insectivorous breeding birds such as the wheatear, wood warbler, whitethroat, and blackcap. The grassland flowers provide nectar for butterflies including the Duke of Burgundy fritillary.

Below: The Duke of Burgundy fritillary butterfly appears at the site in spring.

JAN

FEB

MAR

APR

MAY

JUN

JUL

AUG

SEP

OCT

NOV

DEC

WHERE
Isle of Wight, English Channel.

CONTACT
Isle of Wight Tourism, tel: 01983 823031;
info@islandbreaks.co.uk or Hampshire & Isle
of Wight Wildlife Trust, tel: 01489 774446;
wildline@hwt.org.uk

GETTING THERE
You can reach the island by ferry from
Southampton, Lymington, Southsea, and
Portsmouth. Ferry routes connect directly
with road, rail, and coach links. Brook,
Compton, and Afton Downs, above
Freshwater Bay on the southern shore of
the western tip of the island, are among the
best places for immigrant butterflies at this
time of year. Arreton Down, managed by the
Hampshire & Isle of Wight Wildlife Trust, is
the island's premier reserve for butterflies
generally, lying southwest of Newport off
the A3056. The Trust's Ningwood Common
reserve at Cranmore, two miles east of
Yarmouth, also has butterfly-rich grassland.

ACCESS AND FACILITIES
Contact the Isle of Wight Tourism Authority
or the Hampshire & Isle of Wight Wildlife
Trust for information on individual sites.

Striking caterpillar

The two largest species of hawkmoth found in
Britain are both summer migrants from Africa:
the convolvulus hawkmoth, and the death's-head
hawkmoth. The death's-head is a long-winged
insect named for the sinister skull-like pattern
on its back. It is sometimes referred to as the
bee-robber, because it is known to raid hives
for honey. The adults are solitary, nocturnal,
and elusive, but since the moth lays its eggs
on potato foliage, its big caterpillars (*pictured
above*) are regularly found in gardens .

Above (left to right): Clouded yellow butterfly; silver-Y moth; newly arrived butterflies feed from wild flowers on Afton Down.
Main: A painted lady butterfly feeds from verbena by sipping nectar through its long, coiled tongue.

COLOURFUL MIGRANTS

STROLL ACROSS THE CHALK DOWNS OF THE ISLE OF WIGHT on a sunny, calm day in August, and you may witness something amazing: butterflies, dozens upon dozens of them, fluttering above the flower-rich turf on black-tipped, sulphur-yellow wings. These are the clouded yellows of continental Europe, which spill north across the Channel to feed on the clovers in old grasslands as their populations increase. Some arrive as early as May, but the main influx occurs in mid-August, when their numbers are boosted by the emerging offspring of the early arrivals. Very rarely – perhaps ten times in a century – they swarm over the downs in tens of thousands.

The fact that delicate butterflies migrate across broad stretches of sea may seem improbable, but clouded yellows are not unique. Most of the magnificent red admirals that appear in summer are migrants from mainland Europe, as are the closely related painted ladies. They move north throughout the summer, breeding and producing new generations. These second- or third-generation butterflies then move south in the autumn, and some make the return trip across the Channel. This ebb and flow means that the greatest numbers are always to be seen near southern coasts, like those of the Isle of Wight. They find life increasingly hard further north, and painted ladies in particular rarely survive a British winter. Red admirals are tougher and often manage to hibernate as adults, especially in mild years.

Migrant painted ladies are often accompanied by two day-flying moths: the frequently seen silver-Y moth, and the rarer hummingbird hawkmoth. These moths often appear in seaside parks and gardens with plenty of nectar-rich flowers such as buddleia and jasmine, which also attract painted ladies and red admirals. It can be a lovely sight, but never quite as memorable as the spectacle of a mass influx of clouded yellows on glorious, open downland rolling down to the glittering, sunlit sea.

Inset: A hummingbird hawkmoth extracts nectar with its long, tubular tongue.
Below (left to right): Queen of Spain fritillary; a bedstraw hawkmoth.

The hummingbird hawkmoth is an agile, fast-flying moth that darts from bloom to bloom on whirring wings almost exactly like a hummingbird.

WHERE ELSE TO SEE
IMMIGRANT BUTTERFLIES

Many immigrant butterflies and moths are regular migrants, while others, such the Camberwell beauty and the queen of Spain fritillary, are extremely rare "vagrants" – arrivals that have strayed from, or simply been blown off, their usual course.

One of the best sites for butterflies and moths on the south coast is **Dungeness** in Kent (*see pp.162–163*), an enormous shingle spit renowned for its wide variety of unusual insects. [SE]

Further west, the isolated headland of **Portland Bill** in Dorset (*see pp.90–91*) is often the first landfall of migrating butterflies and moths, which can be found resting among the vegetation near the shore. [SW]

The most southerly point of the British Isles, **The Lizard** in Cornwall (*see pp.116–117*), has an excellent record of rare migrant butterflies and moths from Europe. As it is so far west, it sometimes attracts stray fliers from across the Atlantic as well, such as the huge monarch butterfly. [SW]

THROUGH THE YEAR
THE ISLE OF WIGHT

The Isle of Wight benefits from its southerly location by staying sunny and warm well into **autumn**, allowing many butterflies and other insects to stay on the wing. The island is also a stopping-off point for many migrant birds on passage to southern Europe and Africa, including scarce raptors like the osprey.

Winter is a good time to go fossil hunting on the southern shores of the island, especially in Compton Bay, where dinosaur footprints are exposed at low tide. Winter storms may blow ocean birds onshore, such as the aptly named storm petrel.

Spring is the best time to look for wildflowers on the ancient downland turf, and in late spring these attract a wide variety of grassland butterflies. Breeding birds fill the air with birdsong as they claim and defend their nesting territories.

Below: The eroding chalk stacks of Freshwater Bay.

JAN
FEB
MAR
APR
MAY
JUN
JUL
AUG
SEP
OCT
NOV
DEC

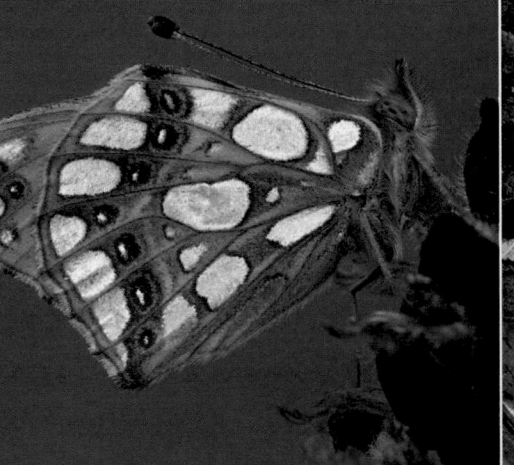

Left (left to right): Puffins can be seen on the Treshnish Isles; Fingal's Cave, Staffa, is the only sea cave in the world formed completely from hexagonally-jointed basalt.

Right (left to right): A female otter teaches its young to fish – they especially love butterfish; huge basking sharks are often seen swimming with their mouths open to sieve plankton from the water.

WHERE
Isle of Mull, Argyll and Bute, Scotland.

CONTACT
The Pier Head, Craignure, tel: 01680 812377; craignure@visitscotland.com
RSPB Mull sea eagle watch, tel: 01688 302038. The RSPB eagle-watching hide moves around Loch Frisa each year to gain the best views of the birds; more information can be found at www.rspb.org.uk/brilliant

GETTING THERE
The Isle of Mull is an island in the Inner Hebrides, and has no airports. The fastest and most exciting arrival option is to catch a seaplane from Glasgow (www.lochlomondseaplanes.com), which also gives you great views of the island from the air. Alternatively, you can catch a ferry from Oban to Craignure; Kilchoan to Tobermory; or Lochaline to Fishnish. They are all served by Caledonian MacBrayne (www.calmac.co.uk). There is a good bus service on the island, and you can rent cycles.

OPENING TIMES
Open all year round. RSPB Mull sea eagle watch is from July–September.

CHARGES
Ferry charges apply. There is no charge to use the RSPB eagle-watching hide.

Rocks at Staffa cave

While you're on Mull, don't miss the chance to visit the nearby island of Staffa. The uninhabited island is a national nature reserve teeming with birds, but is most famous for its columnar basalt formations, which gave rise to its name: "Staffa" is an Old Norse word meaning "wooden building staves". The lava-formed columns can be seen all around the island, but are most spectacular within the setting of Fingal's Cave, where they mirror those of the Giant's Causeway (see pp.208–209).

Main: The west-flowing Coladoir River on the Isle of Mull. **Far right:** The white-tailed eagle has a wingspan of over 2.7m (9ft).

SUMMER ON EAGLE ISLAND

LYING JUST OFF OBAN ON SCOTLAND'S WEST COAST, the Isle of Mull is a year-round destination for wildlife watching, both on land and at sea. It is rightly renowned for its eagles, otters, dolphins, and whales. Despite the midges, late summer is a good time to see them all, but you'll probably need a car to get around the best sites.

Mull really lives up to its nickname of "Eagle Island". The road from Craignure to Fionnport passes through Glen More, which is dominated by the imposing peak of Ben More, at 966m (3,170ft). The mountain forms the southern part of the island and holds several pairs of golden eagles. Take a drive through Glen More in good weather and you should see them swooping along the mountain slopes, their long-winged, long-tailed shapes altogether more elegant than the more compact buzzards. In contrast, the very rare white-tailed sea eagles, derived from the reintroduction scheme on Rum to the north, have much shorter tails and broad wings, giving

Above: Red deer stags can be seen baying on the hills in autumn.

JAN

FEB

MAR

APR

MAY

JUN

JUL

AUG

SEP

OCT

NOV

DEC

Eagles, peregrines, otters, and whales are just some of the animals that make Mull a wildlife-watching paradise.

THROUGH THE YEAR
THE ISLE OF MULL

Autumn is the rutting season for red deer, which range over the hills and moors of Mull, and also pupping time for grey seals in the Treshnish Isles – typically around 1,000 pups are produced each year. As the oakwood trees drop their leaves, sunlight illuminates a fantasy world of lichens, in all shapes and colours, dripping off the tree trunks: Aros Park near Tobermory has a spectacular array.

Winter birds usually include great northern divers, sometimes close inshore. There are a few wintering greenshanks around the sea-lochs, which are washed by warm oceanic currents.

Migrant birds return in **spring**, such as wheatears, whinchats, and redstarts, and at sea three species of divers moult into their spectacular breeding plumages. This is the time to take the short trip to nearby Iona, where you are almost certain to hear, if not see, several "singing" corncrakes, especially among fields with dense stands of yellow iris.

WHERE ELSE TO SEE
BASKING SHARKS

Basking sharks may be found during the summer months all around the British coast, but especially the western areas.

Cornish waters, such as off **The Lizard** (see pp.116–117), have produced groups of a hundred or more animals in recent years. [SW]

Lyme Bay (see pp.298–299), in Devon/Dorset, is a regular area for basking sharks. Its eel-grass beds draw birds, and are home to fish and seahorses. [SW]

Many fewer basking sharks enter the North Sea than southern waters, but there are regular sightings from the **Moray Firth** (see pp.220–221). [SC]

a distinctive "flying barn-door" silhouette. Sea eagles can be seen hunting over the lochs and rocky shores, or around their nesting site near Loch Frisa in early summer, which you can view from the established watchpoint.

You'll need a little more luck to find Mull's otters. They are sometimes spotted scrambling across seaweed-covered boulders, or feeding in the shallows – the shores of Loch na Keal or Calgary Bay are good places to look. You may also come across feeding groups of bottlenose dolphins here, but if you want to see dolphins close-up, take a boat trip from Tobermory or Ulva. A longer trip into deeper waters is very likely to produce a minke whale or two, together with basking sharks and perhaps an ocean sunfish; if you are really lucky, you could see a pod of killer whales, common dolphins, or other cetaceans (whales, dolphins, or porpoises). Some boat trips also offer the chance to visit the more remote islands, such as the Treshnish Isles, which holds one of the largest British colonies of grey seals, along with breeding puffins and storm petrels. These tiny petrels visit land only under the cover of night, although you may encounter them feeding at sea.

SEPTEMBER

Where to Go: September

Woodland and parkland begins to echo to the noise of red and fallow deer, roaring and grunting their magnificence during the annual ritual of the rut. Roe deer and muntjacs bark, which sounds surprisingly loud in the confines of a wood. This is a good time for seeing stoats and weasels on the prowl, and to see badgers, but their increased activity can mean danger: many are killed by traffic on our roads. Join up with a badger group to visit an organized watchpoint, if you want to see some of these fascinating animals. Birds are on the move everywhere: autumn is a time of great activity as young birds seek their own territories and migrants undertake their extraordinary wanderings around the world. On the coast you can see it all in action, but even

WOODLANDS

ARIUNDLE Roe deer hide among the trees of the ancient forest.

HEATH AND MOOR

NORTH YORK MOORS Purple heather dominates in September.

PARKS AND GRASSLANDS

BLAENAVON The colliery wasteland is now an important nature reserve.

WOOD OF CREE
DUMFRIES AND GALLOWAY [SC]

The largest ancient wood in southern Scotland is a good place to see breeding woodland birds, birds of prey, the rare Leisler's bat, otters, and roe deer.
See pp.234–235

This damp, moss-covered sessile oak forest is reminiscent of a time when dinosaurs hunted and pterosaurs soared in the skies.

KNAPDALE FOREST
LOCHGILPHEAD, ARGYLL [SC]

This ancient, hilly forest has great views across to the Isle of Jura. The wildlife here includes wildcats and pine martens.
See pp.238–239

GLEN NANT
OBAN, ARGYLL [SC]

This National Nature Reserve is a small remnant of the extensive native forests that at one time dominated the Highlands; its mammals include red deer and red squirrels.
See pp.238–239

ARIUNDLE FOREST
STRONTIAN, ARGYLL [SC]

These old Atlantic woodlands feel almost prehistoric – there are 500 species of moss and lichen covering just about every surface, while ferns hang from trees like rainforest epiphytes.
See pp.238–239

NORTH YORK MOORS
YORKSHIRE [N]

This rolling heather moorland is stunning in September, when the near-silence is only broken by the humming of bees and the cry of the meadow pipit.
See pp.232–233

GRIMSPOUND
DARTMOOR, DEVON [SW]

You can still see the outlines of the Bronze Age settlement here, and imagine the farmers' lives. The calls of skylarks, red grouse, and curlews add to the eeriness.
See pp.244–245

HATFIELD MOOR
YORKSHIRE [N]

Hatfield Moor is all that remains of the once-extensive bog and fen peatlands, and it's a good place to see nightjars, nightingales, merlins, hobbies, and long-eared owls.
See pp.242–243

BLEAKLOW
DERBYSHIRE [N]

This gritstone plateau has fantastically shaped, wind-carved and eroded stones that hide red grouse, golden plover, dunlin, and curlew.
See pp.242–243

BLAENAVON
TORFAEN, SOUTH WALES [W]

This World Heritage Site was dominated by the iron industry until the 1900s, but is now a stunning place filled with colourful waxcap fungi.
See pp.236–237

ARGYLL FOREST PARK
GLASGOW [SC]

These forests are famed for their rugged beauty. Red and roe deer, red squirrels, hares, and grouse live beneath the watchful eyes of birds of prey.
See pp.234–235

Blaenavon's rescued landscape has returned to upland grassland, heather moorland, blanket bog, ponds, streams, and woodland.

KNIGHTSHAYES COURT
TIVERTON, DEVON [SW]

This Gothic-style mansion is home to the Devon Wildlife Trust. See real birds in the woodlands, and huge topiary ones in the formal gardens.
See pp.236–237

CLUMBER PARK
NOTTINGHAMSHIRE [M]

The woodlands, heathland, and farmland of Clumber Park are a good place to see deer, foxes, and, if you're lucky, a badger. Listen out for nightjars as the light fades at the end of the day.
See pp.240–241

Previous page: A red deer stag at sunrise, Wester Ross, Scotland.

inland it is noticeable; stand on a hilltop early one morning in September and you'll be able to see the bird migration as it occurs – look out especially for larks, pipits, thrushes, and finches. The butterflies still hover around our flowers, and September is a particularly good month for migrant clouded yellows and painted ladies, while others, such as peacocks, red admirals, brimstones, and commas are also still with us. Silver-Y moths and hummingbird hawkmoths are both long-distance migrants, like the birds. Hornets – our biggest and most handsome wasps – are frequently more evident now, coming to drink at garden ponds, to feed on nectar, or to raid the stores of smaller nectar-loving insects.

ISLANDS

BIRSAY MOORS The unlikely refuge of the great yellow bumblebee.

UPLANDS

GALLOWAY FOREST PARK A vast, dramatic landscape.

VALLEYS AND DOWNLANDS

GLEN TANAR Look for the endangered Scottish crossbill in this forest.

BIRSAY MOORS
ORKNEY ISLANDS [SC]

The rough moorland here provides a home for thousands of birds, including large numbers of hen harriers.
See pp.242–243

ISLE OF MAN
IRISH SEA [N]

Watch hen harriers roost at Ballaugh, and pipistrelle bats over St Judes. Long-eared owls sometimes roost at Sulby.
See pp.232–233

GALLOWAY FOREST PARK
DUMFRIES AND GALLOWAY [SC]

There are more than 25 trails in this forest park, where you can see black grouse, roe deer, owls, and badgers. Scarce arctic-alpines grow on the mountains.
See pp.234–235

GLEN TANAR
ABOYNE, ABERDEENSHIRE [SC]

Much of the heather moorland here is managed for the red grouse. The River Dee runs through the reserve, its waters rich in salmon; dippers and grey wagtails abound.
See pp.246–247

Scan the skies for birds of prey, especially hen harriers, who quarter the moorland, their wings forming a perfect "V".

TRETHEVY QUOIT
ST CLEER, CORNWALL [SW]

This is a wonderful place to see interesting ruins in a wild space – wildlife now flourishes among the huge, intriguing stones that date back to the Bronze Age.
See pp.244–245

DOWN HOUSE
DOWNE, KENT [SE]

Charles Darwin's former house has a bee observatory. It also boasts large numbers of ballerina waxcaps, orchids, and carnivorous plants.
See pp.236–237

ISLE OF WIGHT
ENGLISH CHANNEL [SE]

Its southerly location keeps the island warm well into autumn, so you can still see many butterflies and insects here. Migrant birds, including the scarce osprey, use the island as a stopping-off point.
See pp.224–225

BLENCATHRA
KENDALL, CUMBRIA [N]

The most impressive of the Lake District's mountains, Blencathra's peaks include Hallsfell Top, Scale Tarns, and Sharp Edge.
See pp.236–237

DALBY FOREST
YORKSHIRE [N]

The vistor centre at Dalby Forest organizes badger-watching evening expeditions.
See pp.240–241

THE SLAD VALLEY
GLOUCESTERSHIRE [SE]

This part of the Cotswolds has a large number of badger setts: join up with a badger group for an exciting evening watch.
See pp.240–241

ISLE OF MULL
INNER HEBRIDES [SC]

This island is a wonderful place to see golden eagles, white-tailed sea eagles, otters, porpoises, hen harriers, and a whole host of Hebridean wildlife.
See pp.226–227

LOWTHER HILLS
DUMFRIES AND GALLOWAY [SC]

Lowther Hill itself marks the highest point of the Southern Upland Way. Adders and grass snakes may be seen on the trails.
See pp.232–233

Rugged mountains rise above moorland and grassland, divided by waterfalls that tumble down the rocky slopes into tranquil lochs.

GELTSDALE
BRAMPTON, CUMBRIA [N]

The wooded river valley of Geltsdale is a wonderful area to see birds of prey in autumn. Look for dippers and otters around the rivers.
See pp.232–233

HIGH ON THE HEATHER

THE LARGEST CONTINUOUS AREA OF UPLAND HEATHER MOORLAND in England, the North York Moors provide a spectacle in any season. But in September they are simply stunning: flowering heather casts a purple glow over the hills, with highlights of yellowing bracken, and all is illuminated by the soft, early-autumn sunlight. Even better, nearly all of the moorland is fully accessible under the UK's "right-to-roam" legislation.

Most of the breeding wading birds for which the Moors are so important have departed for lowlands by the end of the summer, though there may be a few lingering curlews or lapwings. Without their calls, a near-silence descends, broken only by the hum of nectaring bumblebees, the plaintive yet piercing "sip!" of meadow pipits, and the cackle of red grouse. These iconic moorland birds feed mostly on the tender shoots of heather. Reliant on their camouflaged plumage, they may allow close approach; but listen out too, for the whirring sound of a flock mid-air.

WHERE
North York Moors National Park, Yorkshire, England; www.visitnorthyorkshiremoors.co.uk

CONTACT
The Moors National Park Visitor Centre, tel: 01439 770657; info@northyorkmoors-npa.gov.uk

GETTING THERE
By car, head for one of the park's visitor centres: The Moors Centre (Lodge Lane, Danby, YO21 2NB); or Sutton Bank National Park Centre (Sutton Bank, Thirsk, YO7 2EH). By rail or coach, travel to one of the towns surrounding the National Park, such as York, Malton, Scarborough, Middlesbrough, Whitby, Northallerton, or Thirsk, which all have good bus links into the park. The Esk Valley railway runs between Middlesbrough and Whitby, and takes you right into the heart of the National Park. The Moorsbus Network serves North York Moors itself from April to October.

ACCESS AND FACILITIES
The National Park has a committed policy for the disabled traveller and there are good facilities at all the visitor centres.

OPENING TIMES
Open all year round.

CHARGES
None.

The trouble with bracken

Large (and increasing) tracts of the moors are covered in bracken. Few species are able to grow under its dense canopy, and so it is actively controlled by spraying or rolling. However, in moderation, some things quite like bracken: whinchats breed among it; adders bask on the leaf-litter; dwarf cornel and chickweed-wintergreen – two of the moor's special plants, near the southern edge of their ranges – shelter beneath it. Importantly, violets thrive under it, providing food for caterpillars of the dark green fritillary butterfly.

Main: The flowering purple heather of Commondale Moor acts as a colourful backdrop for the moor's ancient stone circle.

Left (left to right): Cotton grass; bog-rosemary flowers can be found among the mosses.

Right (left to right): Common heather; the sandstone outcrop known as The Bridestones; a red grouse in flight.

Above right: A merlin watches over the moors for prey.

Grouse numbers fluctuate according to parasite and predator cycles, and as a result of moorland management and shooting pressure. The major economic value of moorland lies in grouse shooting, and large swathes are burned or cut each year to produce the fresh new growth favoured by grouse, and by chance, the varied habitats favoured by breeding curlews and golden plovers. The older, leggier heather is favoured by merlins for nesting in the summer, but they disperse over the whole of the moors in search of prey – especially pipits and skylarks – during autumn. They are often joined by the much-larger hen harriers and short-eared owls, who effortlessly quarter the moors. Among the dry heather moorland, there are also wet heaths and bogs on areas of poor drainage. In early autumn, you can see the white fluffy seedheads of their cotton-grasses and the reddish mounds of some of the bog-mosses. If you don't mind getting your feet wet, a closer look may reveal sundew, bog-myrtle, bog asphodel, cloudberry, and bog-rosemary.

Above: The North York Moors have regular snow falls in winter.

THROUGH THE YEAR
NORTH YORK MOORS

Winter wildlife is rather sparse, though red grouse remain on the moors throughout the year, especially in the shelter of the valleys. Visit the landscape attractions, such as The Bridestones (*pictured below left*), while you have the moors to yourself.

Spring sees birdlife flooding back to the moors. Curlews, golden plovers, redshanks, lapwings, and snipes are on the moors and bogs; wheatears and ring ouzels fly around stone walls and rocky outcrops; while common sandpipers join the resident grey wagtails and dippers along the tumbling rivers.

The first two heathers of mid-**summer** – pale pink cross-leaved heath and bright purple bell heather – come into flower before the mass of common heather or ling. Redstarts and wood warblers inhabit the valley woods, while the meadows darken from the yellow of globe-flower and meadow-rue, to the blue and purple of devil's-bit scabious and betony.

The North York Moors are the largest block of upland heather in England, ablaze with colour in autumn.

WHERE ELSE TO SEE
HEATHER MOORLAND

All British uplands on acidic rocks support heather moorland, though those that are more westerly are usually wetter, and may have a higher proportion of wet heath and blanket bog.

The Scottish mountains, including those of the Southern Uplands, have vast areas of moorland, such as the high moors of the **Lowther Hills**. These areas support red grouse in large numbers, though they are more scattered. [SC]

The RSPB reserve of **Geltsdale** (*see pp.24–25*), in the Pennines, is an area of protected moorland where you can see black grouse, birds of prey, and breeding waders. A limited number of grouse live on the **Isle of Man** (*see pp.300–301*). [N]

In other areas, such as the uplands of north and mid Wales, grouse are more scattered and live at a lower density. **Ruabon Moors** (*see pp.102–103*) in Denbighshire is one of the best places to see the male black grouse "lekking" or displaying. [W]

JAN
FEB
MAR
APR
MAY
JUN
JUL
AUG
SEP
OCT
NOV
DEC

WHERE
Galloway Forest Park stretches over several Scottish counties; the nearest towns are: Newton Stewart, New Galloway, Gatehouse of Fleet, Dalmellington, and Castle Douglas. Visit www.forestry.gov.uk for more details.

CONTACT
The Recreation Ranger, Galloway Forest Park, tel: 01671 402420. Clatteringshaws Visitor Centre (Easter–end October), New Galloway DG7 3SQ; tel: 01644 420285.

GETTING THERE
By car from the south, take the M6 to Carlisle, then the A75 to Newton Stewart (signposted to Stranraer). From Glasgow: A77 to Girvan, then the A714 to Newton Stewart or the A713 to New Galloway. From Edinburgh: A702 to Abington services, then M74 to Beattock, A701 to Dumfries, and finally the A75 to Newton Stewart. The nearest bus services (nos. 520 and 521) are at Dalry and New Galloway. The nearest main railway stations at Ayr and Dumfries.

ACCESS AND FACILITIES
All of the trails have parking, and many have picnic sites and toilets. The park's three visitor centres – Glentrool, Clatteringshaws, and Kirroughtree – are open from Easter to the end of October; they offer a full range of facilities, and lots of information.

Robert the Bruce country
A popular landmark in Galloway Forest Park is Bruce's Stone, a huge boulder commemorating the Battle of Trool in 1307 – it is said that the Scottish king Robert the Bruce rested against it after defeating the English. The stone sits along the shores of Clatteringshaws Loch. Feral goats and roe deer run wild around this area – don't panic if you hear an explosive "hss!" – the goats make this noise when disturbed, and the sound carries for 1km (½ mile).

Above (top and bottom): Red deer stags roar during the autumn rutting season; pine martens show remarkable agility as they run through the trees.

Right panel (top and bottom): A stream flows through woodland close to the banks of Loch Trool; the Merrick is the highest hill in Scotland's Southern Uplands, at 843m (2,766ft).

Below: The rare Scotch argus butterfly.

Main: The rugged beauty of the park's scenery and its wealth of wildlife has led to it being dubbed "The Highlands of the Lowlands".

MOUNTAINS AND MOORLAND

GALLOWAY FOREST PARK IS A VAST, DRAMATIC LANDSCAPE that stretches over 780 sq km (300 sq miles). Its rugged mountains rise above moorland, wet heath, blanket bogs, and acid grassland, divided by the streams and waterfalls that tumble down the rocky slopes into tranquil lochs and rushing rivers. Remnants of ancient forests are alive with wildlife, while the newer conifer forests of the 1950s and 60s – such as Glen Trool – are being broken up to create light, wonderful views, and new homes for birds such as pied flycatchers and nightjars.

There are 27 walkers' trails around the park, and three visitor centres to help you decide where best to go. Carrick Forest, in the north, has black grouse, roe deer, and badgers. You can sometimes see barn owls here – Galloway offers shelter to around 10 per cent of the UK population, which is in serious decline. Look for the forest's artificial nestboxes, which provide homes for 70 pairs of owls. At the centre of the park, in the largest remaining

Above: Loch Trool lies just 5km (3 miles) beyond Glentrool Visitor Centre.

Galloway Forest Park stretches the full length of the Galloway Hills, from Loch Doon in the north, to Gatehouse of Fleet in the south.

THROUGH THE YEAR
GALLOWAY FOREST PARK

Galloway Forest Park and its surroundings provide great walking country and abundant opportunities for watching wildlife at all times of year. **Winter** is a great time to visit the red kite feeding station at Bellymack Farm, when the birds flock in to receive the food. Over 30 kites often come in together to feed on the chicken meat put out for them, along with ravens and buzzards.

Spring sees the height of songbird activity and spring flowers, such as snowdrops and drifts of bluebells in the mixed woodlands. From May to September the park is full of midges, so insect repellent is strongly recommended.

Visit Stroan Loch or one of the other lochs in **summer** to see many different species of dragonflies and damselflies. Surrounded by the forest park, Silver Flowe National Nature Reserve protects one of Europe's finest and most undisturbed systems of mires, and its mosaic of boggy hummocks and pools is a prime site for the rare azure hawker dragonfly. There are thousands of butterflies around the park, including the Scotch argus, which may be seen over the rough boggy grassland.

WHERE ELSE TO SEE
FOREST WILDLIFE

Britain's forests, packed with wildlife and historical intrigue, are great places to visit.

The **Wood of Cree**, just outside Galloway Forest Park, is the largest ancient semi-natural woodland in southern Scotland. Now an RPSB reserve, it has many breeding songbirds, including redstarts and pied flycatchers; butterflies include purple hairstreak and Scotch argus, and otters live on the River Cree. [SC]

Argyll Forest Park, to the northwest of Glasgow, is one of the UK's oldest forest parks, and it has a rich mix of wildlife. [SC]

Kielder Forest, Northumberland, is England's largest forest and surrounds the largest artificial lake in northern Europe. This is a great place for wildlife, including goshawks, red kites, and red squirrels, and it is also home to some 6,000 roe deer. [N]

unafforested area, the cluster of summits and glens radiate out like five fingers, earning them the colourful name of "Range of the Awful Hand". Climb to the summit of southern Scotland's highest mountain, The Merrick, and you will be rewarded by breathtaking views in all directions. Scarce Arctic-alpine flowers, such as starry saxifrage and dwarf juniper, flourish in this harsh environment, as do birds of prey. You are most likely to see buzzards and kestrels, but you may also encounter hen harriers, merlins, and peregrines. Golden eagles are more rarely seen, but are always thrilling to watch. Red kites were reintroduced to the park in 2001, and you can enjoy watching them from the Galloway Kite Trail on the southeastern edge of the park, or from the hide at Bellymack Hill Farm, a feeding station near Laurieston.

Mountain hares, red deer, and wild goats roam the hills. You may also see deer in the forests, and you can safely watch the drama of the autumn rut from close range at the Galloway Deer Range near Clatteringshaws Visitor Centre. You can also see the goats close up at the Wild Goat Park near Murray's Monument. But watch out: they come very close, and may try to steal your sandwiches.

JAN
FEB
MAR
APR
MAY
JUN
JUL
AUG
SEP
OCT
NOV
DEC

WAXCAP GRASSLANDS

FOR 200 YEARS, BLAENAVON IN WALES and its surrounding countryside was dominated by the iron industry. Mineral extraction ravaged the landscape, which had fragments of important wildlife habitats, such as acid and limestone upland grassland, heather moorland, blanket bog, ponds, streams, and woodland. Iron production ceased in the early 1900s and the land was rescued, to the extent that it is now a designated World Heritage Site.

Stand at one of the site's highest points today, and you'll have breathtaking views across the Black Mountains and the Brecon Beacons – but turn around and look west, and you'll see the area's industrial past carved into the scarred landscape. Amazingly, the mosaic of colliery waste and acid grassland has produced something special. It is renowned among mycologists (those who study fungi) for its rich variety of waxcap mushrooms, so colourful that they are called "the orchids of the fungus world".

WHERE
Blaenavon World Heritage Centre, Church Road, Blaenavon, Torfaen NP4 9AS, Wales; www.world-heritage-blaenavon.org.uk

CONTACT
Blaenavon Tourist Information Centre, tel: 01495 742333; blaenavon.tic@torfaen.gov.uk

GETTING THERE
Blaenavon lies at the head of the Avon Valley, on the slopes of the Coity and Blorenge mountains. From the M4, take junction 25A to Newport, then the A4042 as far as Pontypool. Take the turning (off a roundabout) to the A4043 to Blaenavon, following the brown Heritage signs.

ACCESS AND FACILITIES
There is information about the site and its history at the Church Road visitor centre. You can pick up a "walks pack" from here, containing details of eight walks around the site. The centre has full-access toilets, a café, shop, and car park.

OPENING TIMES
Open all year round.

CHARGES
None.

Above: Heather moorland vegetation at Blaenavon.

Main: Moor grass, rushes, and cotton grass grow in the boggy areas where ground water has been retained within the rich upland habitat of Coity mountain.

Right panel (top to bottom): Ballerina waxcap; parrot waxcap; vermilion waxcap.

Below (top and bottom): Longhorn beetles live in the woodland areas; scarce blue-tailed damselflies can be seen on the ponds.

Identifying waxcaps

Many waxcaps undergo colour changes, which complicates identification – even the weather can change a fungus's appearance. For example, the blackening waxcap (*above*) has a fruiting body, or "cap", of glistening amber when it first appears after rain in late summer or autumn; it then begins to turn black from the tip of the cap downwards. If possible, take a photo, note the date, and write a description including the colour, shape, height, and whether the fungus looks dry or sticky, smooth or fibrous in texture.

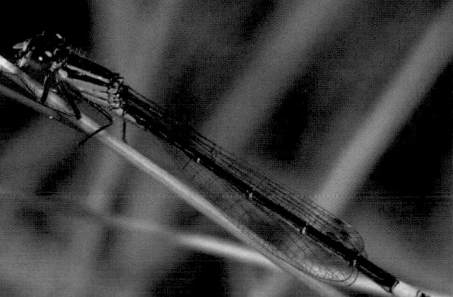

Waxcap fungi are named for the waxy surface of their caps, or fruiting bodies, although many are more sticky, greasy, or slimy to the touch. Some have an aroma of honey, while others are more acrid. Some waxcaps are dull-coloured, but most are bright red, orange, or yellow, or delicate shades of pink or violet. Their common names are almost as exotic as their colours, which they reflect: snowy waxcap, citrine waxcap, vermilion waxcap, and scarlet waxcap. The parrot waxcap gets its name from its feathered green and yellow coloration; the date waxcap is brown; while the ballerina (or pink) waxcap is a delicate pink, just like a classical ballerina's tutu.

There are over 40 different waxcap species in Britain, although many have become rare as the old, unspoilt grasslands that they need are left ungrazed – allowing tall vegetation to invade – or ploughed up, "improved" with artificial fertilizers, or built upon. But still the waxcaps persist, in small numbers, making an exciting find for those willing to search for their rainbow colours.

WHERE ELSE TO SEE
WAXCAP FUNGI

Look for waxcaps where the grass is kept short and contains plenty of moss. As well as areas of ancient grassland like Blaenavon, some of the best sites for waxcaps are old, unspoiled lawns, such as those surrounding ancient monuments and stately homes. Many old churchyards and cemeteries have good populations of waxcaps too.

Downe House, Kent, where Charles Darwin spent most of his life, has large numbers of ballerina waxcaps. [SE]

Windsor Great Park (*see pp.258–259*) is home to waxcaps and other scarce fungi, ancient trees, rare beetles, deer, and a wide variety of birds. [SE]

Waxcaps are generally more abundant in the wetter western parts of Britain. Good waxcap grasslands in southwest England include **Stonehenge**, Wiltshire, and **Knightshayes Court**, Devon. [SW]

Farther north, try the grasslands of **Blencathra**, Cumbria, an area rich in fungi. [N]

THROUGH THE YEAR
BLAENAVON

Sometimes the above-ground fruiting bodies of the waxcaps appear outside the traditional mushroom-hunting period of autumn. They may be seen as early as June, especially after an extensive period of rainfall, and can also linger for longer, even well into **winter**, in milder years. It is increasingly possible to find a display in late December.

In **spring**, look out for linnets, Dartford warblers, and red grouse on the heathland; lapwings, grey partridges, and yellowhammers in the grassland; and reed buntings in the blanket bog.

From late May to early August, a very local insect, the scarce blue-tailed damselfly, flies around the pools on the bogland. You should also look out for the rare great crested newts that breed in the ponds in spring and **summer**, and the otters that hide there.

JAN

FEB

MAR

APR

MAY

JUN

JUL

AUG

SEP

OCT

NOV

DEC

Below: The scarlet waxcap only grows in "unimproved" short grassland.

WHERE
Ariundle Nature Reserve, Strontian, Argyll, Scotland PH36; www.snh.org.uk

CONTACT
Reserve Manager, Scottish National Heritage, tel: 01397 704716; enquiries@snh.gov.uk

GETTING THERE
Heading north from Glasgow, take the A82 from Stirling to the Corran Ferry; turn left off the ferry on to the A861 towards the small village of Strontian. Follow the Forestry Commission signs to Airigh Fhionndail car park, 3.2km (2 miles) north of Strontian. Access the reserve via a track, which also forms part of the Strontian River Trail, leading to the reserve's nature trail.

ACCESS AND FACILITIES
There are no facilities other than information boards. The forest trail is 3km (5 miles) long and takes around two-and-a-half hours to walk. There is a teashop nearby, or you can find facilities in Strontian, the nearest town.

OPENING TIMES
Open all year round.

CHARGES
None.

The chequered skipper

The jewel in the crown of Ariundle is a small chocolate-brown butterfly called the chequered skipper. It used to occur throughout the British Isles, but now only survives in a few places in Scotland. Its favourite habitat is broad-leaved woodland next to grasslands rich with purple moor-grass, which is essential to successful breeding. The caterpillar pulls a tube of the moor-grass around itself, before hibernating in a tent of the grass's leaf blades. Look out for the butterfly's fast, darting flight.

Above (left to right): Small bonnet fungi grow through mosses on oak trunks; fruticose lichen; ferns grow from tree trunks and branches.
Main: The green carpeting over boulders and wood in Ariundle is made up of rare mosses and liverworts.

PREHISTORIC ADVENTURE

S TEPPING INTO THE ARIUNDLE FOREST is like taking a step back in time. This damp, moss-covered oak forest is reminiscent of a time when dinosaurs hunted and pterosaurs soared in the skies. Ariundle Nature Reserve is part of the larger Sunart woods, one of Britain's finest examples of ancient Atlantic oakwoods, and the last remnant of the native forest that once covered most of the west coast of Scotland. The prehistoric feel comes in part from the thick carpet of mosses, lichens, and liverworts that cling to almost every surface. As these plants don't have roots – they take in water and minerals through their leaves and stems instead – the clean sea air and damp climate present ideal conditions for them to thrive. Collectively they are called the "Lower Plants" and a staggering 500 species of moss, liverwort, and lichen have been recorded here. As you walk through you'll see ferns hanging, like epiphytes in tropical rainforests, from the mossy branches. And in the dwindling light, gnarled tree trunks take on magical shapes; you can almost convince yourself that you have, in fact, spotted a prehistoric creature.

The predominant trees in Ariundle are sessile oaks, but there are many other native trees scattered throughout the forest. Hazel, birch, and rowan are typical examples, whereas larch and beech have been introduced. It's not surprising that, with the impressive list of deciduous trees here, autumn is a good time to visit. As well as the myriad autumn colours throughout the forest, many trees are fruiting. Rowans are laden with berries, while hazels attract squirrels with their crop of nuts.

The best time to try to find Ariundle's shyest creatures is dawn and dusk. Listen out for the squeak of a shrew or pipistrelle bat. If you're very, very lucky you might chance upon a pine marten or a wildcat; but you're more likely to see the white rump of a roe deer as it vanishes like magic into the forest.

The cool, clean, clear, and wet environment of the Scottish Atlantic woodlands has led them to be described as temperate rainforests".

Inset: The distinctive leaves of the sessile oak in their autumn colours.
Below (left to right): Roe deer with fawn; wildcats live here but are rarely seen.

WHERE ELSE TO SEE
NATIVE FOREST

Scotland is thought to have lost 99 per cent of its native forests, but those that remain are testimony to the vital ecosystems they supported.

Knapdale Forest, Lochgilphead, is an ancient Caledonian forest situated in a National Scenic Area. It has an interesting mix of animals, including red squirrels, wildcats, pine martens, and otters. Its birds include black grouse, ospreys, peregrines, and golden eagles. [SC]

Glen Nant National Nature Reserve is a small remant of the extensive native forests that once dominated the Scottish Highlands. The mixed woodlands are mainly oak and birch, with ash, elm, and hazel in the more fertile, sheltered areas. [SC]

The sessile oaks of the **Wood of Cree** are intermixed with hazel, rowan, birch, ash, and willow. This RPSB reserve has many breeding songbirds, including redstarts and pied flycatchers; butterflies include purple hairstreak and Scotch argus, and there are otters along the river. [SC]

THROUGH THE YEAR
ARIUNDLE NATURE RESERVE

In **winter** you can clearly see the epiphytes and bryophytes (liverworts, lichens, mosses, and more) that grow on the ancient trees. The bare trees also give you a better chance of spotting some of Ariundle's mammals, especially badgers.

A walk around the looping forest track in early **spring** gives you a very different experience. Lesser celandine, wood anenome, and primrose are among some of the early flowerers. Overhead, many species of birds call out their territorial songs, especially the woodland specialists, such as wood and willow warblers.

Butterflies and moths abound in the forest in **summer** – there are over 200 species of moth here. Watch out especially for the chequered skipper butterfly (*see box, far left*) and the small pearl-bordered fritillary. The northern emerald dragonfly can be found around Sunart Loch.

Below: Willow warblers visit Ariundle in spring.

JAN
FEB
MAR
APR
MAY
JUN
JUL
AUG
SEP
OCT
NOV
DEC

BADGERS IN THE VALLEY

WITH LUSH, GENTLY UNDULATING PASTURES, STEEP HILLSIDES and stunning panoramic scenery, it's not surprising that many call the Cotswolds the most beautiful place in England. The whole of the Cotswolds is classed as an Area of Outstanding Natural Beauty (AONB), but there's one area in particular that stands out, especially for nature: the sumptuous Slad Valley, immortalized in Laurie Lee's *Cider with Rosie*. Of the five beautiful valleys that surround Stroud, the Slad Valley – a treasure trove of wildlife habitats – is probably the least spoilt, and as a consequence it is one of the best places in the UK to watch badgers.

Badger-watching trips run throughout the year in the Slad Valley, and they are certainly the best way to guarantee seeing these shy and elusive animals. Expect some strange requests from the trip organizers: you'll be asked to avoid wearing perfume or deodorant. Badgers live in family groups of around 14 animals, called clans,

WHERE
The Slad Valley is centred around Slad, near Stroud, Gloucestershire, GL6 7QA; www.visitthecotswolds.org.uk
www.gloucestershirewildlifetrust.co.uk

CONTACT
To find out how you can see the Slad Valley badgers, contact The Gloucestershire Badger Group: www.badgerland.co.uk
For everywhere else, contact The Badger Trust: www.badger.org.uk
Snows Farm nature reserve is run by the Gloucestershire Wildlife Trust.

GETTING THERE
By car, take the Stroud to Slad road (B4070). Stroud has a rail and bus station.

ACCESS AND FACILITIES
Trip organizers will supply details of meeting points, parking etc. For general visits to the area, the Slad Valley Wildlife Way is a five-hour walk that takes you right through the valley. The walk begins at the Bulls Cross layby on the B4070, near Frith Wood, where there is car parking. There are no facilities on the walk or in the valley outside of villages.

OPENING TIMES
Open all year round.

CHARGES
None.

Looking for badgers

Badger watching can be fantastically frustrating, but there are a few easy things you can do to increase your chances. Look for holes into the ground with D-shaped entrances that are at least 20cm (7½in) wide. Ignore any with bones nearby, as these are likely to be fox holes. Look for fresh muddy tracks from the sett entrances. Badger tracks are wider than dog or fox tracks, and have five small pads (with claw marks) on top of a larger, kidney-shaped pad, while fox tracks have four pads on top of a smaller pad.

Main: An adult badger foraging in the Slad Valley in autumn.

Left: The rolling landscape of the Cotswolds.

Right (left to right): Badgers playing; young badgers looking for worms, their favourite food.

Right panel (top and bottom): The badger sett hole is D-shaped, with the flat edge at the bottom; a badger drinking from a river.

that do a lot of rubbing and scratching. This is to cover each other and their territory in their own special clan scent or musk. For an animal whose primary sense is smell, these scents are vital. Any unusual smells will send the badgers into hiding. In September you'll see the badgers preparing for winter, dragging fresh bedding down into their tunnels. These animals are quite particular about where they make their underground homes – they need fairly soft soils for excavating setts, ample forest for cover, and rich feeding areas nearby – just the kind of habitat found around the Slad Valley. You'll notice that these opportunistic feeders seem to eat almost anything, from other mammals to insects, frogs, and fruit, although their favourite food is worms. Sometimes you can spot badgers feeding on more open areas with short grass, such as the nearby Snows Farm nature reserve, where the worms are easier to find. This reserve is well worth visiting for its 300 species of plants, especially in September, when you'll be able to see the late-flowering autumn gentian.

A walk in the woods at dusk is made magical by the sight of these charming creatures.

WHERE ELSE TO SEE
BADGERS

Badgers can be found in all of Britain's counties, although they are less common in East Anglia and most common around the southwest. The locations of badger setts are not publicized, to protect them from persecution.

The best way to see badgers is to join one of the 100 or so badger groups around the country, that are interested in studying and protecting badgers. They will know the places and times that are most likely to result in seeing badgers. Contact The Badger Trust, based in East Grinstead: www.badger.org.uk or your local wildlife trust via www.wildlifetrusts.org

The **Falls of Clyde** Scottish Wildlife Trust reserve in New Lanark [SC] organizes badger-watching evening expeditions, as does **Dalby Forest** visitor centre near Thornton-le-Vale in Yorkshire [N]. Visitors to **Clumber Park** in Cheshire [N] in search of nightjars at dusk (*see pp.118–119*) may also spot badgers.

THROUGH THE YEAR
THE SLAD VALLEY

Early **winter** is a great time to look for fungi. Frith Wood has over 100 species, including a variety of waxcaps. It's also a good time to go on night walks – the valley is home to one of the country's rarest bats: the greater horseshoe bat.

Spring is the best time of year to visit the valley if you want to see wild flowers. Badger cubs are born in January or February, but they don't leave the sett until around April. Watching cubs emerge nervously from the sett, then quickly losing themselves in the important business of play, is utterly enchanting.

Summer is the time to see the Slad Valley's orchid species. Visit Swifts Hill, also known as Elliott Reserve, in early June, and you're likely to see up to 11 species of orchid, including the bee orchid and the last orchid to appear in late August: the beautiful ladies tresses. The nationally scarce musk orchid flowers on Painswick Hill in July. Butterflies and grasshoppers abound; look out for the rare stripe-winged and rufous grasshoppers at Swifts Hill or the even rarer Adonis blue butterfly at Rodborough Common.

Below: Orchids grow wild on Swifts Hill in June.

JAN
FEB
MAR
APR
MAY
JUN
JUL
AUG
SEP
OCT
NOV
DEC

WHERE
RSPB Birsay Moors, Orkney Islands, Scotland; www.rspb.org.uk

CONTACT
RSPB Birsay Moors, tel: 01856 850176; orkney@rspb.org.uk

GETTING THERE
By road the reserve is west of Evie on the A966. The B9057 (Hillside Road), between Evie and Dounby, cuts right through the reserve. Buses stop at Evie, 3.2km (2 miles) to the east of the reserve, and also in Dounby, 4.8km (3 miles) to the west. Durkadale is to the west of Birsay Moors and extends to the southern shore of the Loch of Hundland.

ACCESS AND FACILITIES
The reserve has car parks and a picnic area, but no toilets or refreshments. The hide on Burgar Hill is accessible to the disabled and wheelchair users. Much of the reserve's best bird life can be easily viewed from a car on the hillside road (B9057) that runs between Evie and Dounby.

OPENING TIMES
Open all year round.

CHARGES
None.

Harrier displays

When they move to their nesting grounds in March, hen harriers perform a spectacular aerial display, known as skydancing. The male bird climbs steeply before somersaulting and diving straight down. Females also display, but less often. Another acrobatic behaviour is the food pass, in which the male approaches with food and the female flies beneath him, turning on to her back or side and catching the prey with a foot as he drops it.

Above (top to bottom): The remains of the Norse settlement on the Brough of Birsay; Ring of Brodgar – Orkney's neolithic standing stones.

Below: A group of feeding twite.

Right (top to bottom): A short-eared owl hunting; the view over moorland habitat at Birsay Moors; the Orkney vole was thought to have been introduced to the island by Neolithic man.

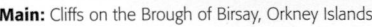

Main: Cliffs on the Brough of Birsay, Orkney Islands.

ORKNEY ODYSSEY

ORKNEY IS AN ARCHIPELAGO OF 70 ISLANDS just 16 km (10 miles) north of mainland Scotland, where the Atlantic Ocean swirls into the North Sea. A visit to this rugged wilderness, lashed by angry seas, always leaves a lasting impression, not only because of the archipelago's remarkable Neolithic and Viking ruins, which helped make Orkney a UNESCO World Heritage Site, but because of its outstanding landscape and wildlife.

There are few places in the UK that can boast such a mixture of bird habitats within such a small area as the Orkneys. The area is a stronghold for divers, waterfowl, seabirds, raptors, and owls. A staggering 385 species have been counted among the cliffs, moors, marshes, and heath, and even more remarkably, 116 are known to breed here. In the heart of the largest island, known as Mainland, lies one of the UK's most northerly moors, Birsay, which is a fabulous example of rough moorland teeming with wildlife.

Above: The flooded marshes of Orkney.

THROUGH THE YEAR
BIRSAY MOORS

Winter is a good time to see the communal roost of hen harriers at Durkadale, as well as visiting birds, such as great northern divers, long-tailed ducks, and Slavonian grebes.

Moorland nesting birds jostle and sing for territory in **spring**. Skylarks and meadow pipits perform their enthralling skyward display flights, while the eerie call of the curlews is never far away. Both Arctic and great skuas arrive back on territories and the red-throated divers return to the hill-top lochans to breed.

You need to take extra care if you're walking in **summer**. Great skuas – huge, dark birds that look like giant muddy seagulls – will dive bomb anything that gets too close. Also, from the Burgar Hill hide, you may be lucky enough to see red-throated diver chicks, which are present until the end of August.

WHERE ELSE TO SEE
NORTHERN MOORS

Northern moors are wondrous places of wild and windswept beauty.

Moine Mhor National Nature Reserve, Argyll, is one of the last wild, raised bogs left in Britain, where hen harriers and curlews can be seen hunting over the ancient hill fort of Dunadd. [SC]

Hatfield Moor, Yorkshire, is a remanant of the once-extensive Humberhead Levels; you're likely to see both hen and marsh harriers, and occasionally long-eared owls. [N]

Bleaklow, Derbyshire, is an eerie expanse of peat-covered moorland sitting about 600m (2,000ft) above sea level. Large eroded rocks sit among vast plateaus, divided by deep river valleys. Golden plovers, dunlins, and curlews live here, surrounded by cloudberry, hell heath, and the rare bog rosemary. [M]

Run by the RSPB, Birsay Moors reserve glitters with wildlife gems. Summer is a wonderful time to visit; the whole area is awash with wild flowers, including thrift and grass of Parnassus. If you're lucky, you may see the rare Scottish primrose still in flower in September, when male hen harriers are in their striking, pale-grey breeding plumage and the moor hums with insects, including the rare great yellow bumblebee. Towards the end of September, moorland berries, such as crowberry and bearberry, start to appear alongside the cheery purple flowers of devil's bit scabious.

In autumn, Orkney becomes a staging post for birds moving south from the Arctic; almost anything can turn up. Around 50,000 birds arrive on the shoreline, while whooper swans and greylag geese feed on open fields. This is a good time to see visitors such as the great northern diver, long-tailed duck, and Slavonian grebe. Durkadale in Birsay Moors – a sumptuous habitat of sedge meadows, reedbeds, willow scrub, and bog – is great place to watch raptors, especially hen harriers. By November you can see up to 25 harriers coming in to roost. Stand by the road at dawn or dusk, and be mesmerized as their dark silhouettes glide in silently.

JAN
FEB
MAR
APR
MAY
JUN
JUL
AUG
SEP
OCT
NOV
DEC

THE DARK HEART OF DARTMOOR

NESTLED IN THE MOUNTAIN PASS BETWEEN HOOKNEY and Hambledown Tor, amidst the rolling, windswept uplands of Dartmoor, Grimspound is one of the finest examples of a Bronze-Age settlement in the UK. At 450m (1,476ft) above sea level, it's easy to feel like you're part of the enormous skies; in fact, you're never far from the weather here. Mist, rain, fog, and snow can be upon you in minutes, sometimes all in the same day; the fickle weather and random areas of bog reinforce the exhilarating experience this lonely landscape offers.

Climb up Hookney Tor, from where you can look down on to the Grimspound remains: an enormous circular perimeter wall, at points 4.5m (15ft) thick, enclosing almost 1.6 hectares (4 acres) of land and the ruins of 24 dwellings. The ruins are so well preserved, it's possible to tell how the homes were constructed, and the outside wall – built either to keep predators out, or livestock in – seems to have used drystone-walling techniques.

WHERE
Grimspound, Dartmoor National Park, Newton Abbot, Devon TQ13 9JQ.

CONTACT
Dartmoor National Park Authority:
01626 832093; hq@dartmoor-npa.gov.uk

GETTING THERE
Grimspound hut circles and settlement are 9.6km (6 miles) southwest of Moretonhampstead; they are not signposted. By car, follow the B3212 for about 6km (4 miles) from Postbridge towards Moretonhampstead. When you reach Challacombe Cross, turn right into a road signposted "Widecombe In The Moor". Travel about 2km (1 mile) down this narrow road until you see a car-parking area to your right. By bus, take the Countybus no. 82. By rail, travel to Exeter, and take the no.82 Transmoor bus (this only runs on Sundays). If you are walking, follow the Two Moors Way.

ACCESS AND FACILITIES
There are no facilities on site. The path from the car park to the site is clear and well-worn, but not suitable for wheelchairs. There are facilities and an information centre at Postbridge, 6.4km (4 miles) away, including full-access toilets.

CHARGES
None.

Keeping the balance

Moorland can be deceptively fragile. Hazards such as overgrazing or irresponsible hiking can drastically upset the natural balance of the habitat. Dartmoor is an important breeding area for many birds, some of which are rare. Although fewer than 20 dunlin nest here, it is still the most southerly site in the whole world. Nationally important numbers of wheatears (*above*) also breed here, along with golden plovers and the rare ring ouzel. During the breeding season (March–July) it is essential to keep to the paths.

Main image: Granite rock outcrops at Grimspound.

Left: Dartmoor ponies were once used to haul tin mined on the moor.

Right (left to right): Red grouse amongst heather; acidic pools form within the ruins of the prehistoric hutments.

Right panel (top to bottom): Skylark; curlew; golden plover.

Most of the ruins of huts lie in the southern sector of the enclosure, and archaeologists believe that the outer huts were probably used for livestock and storage. Where once the Bronze Age farmers eked out a living on the moor, now a wonderful wildlife habitat abounds. Skylarks battle the winds, and low-flying red grouse skim the heather, calling – "go back, go back" – while our smallest raptor, the merlin, darts close to the ground to hunt for prey. In September many birds are "moulting" and hide themselves away, although you will see family groups of stonechats; some males develop sooty-black faces that cover their white cheeks. There are still some butterflies to be seen, such as speckled woods, large whites, brimstones, and the occasional small copper.

But still, it is the landscape that commands your attention. If you are on the moor as the swirling mists start to gather, as they often do, and the curlew utters its eerie call, it's all too easy to remember that the site inspired Sir Arthur Conan Doyle's terrifying *Hound of the Baskervilles*.

WHERE ELSE TO SEE
UPLAND HEATH

Dartmoor is one of the largest areas of upland heath in southwest England, and it is a unique combination of craggy tors, vast bogs, wild ponies, and massive tracts of colourful heathers. Other moors tend to offer a similarly interesting combination of habitat and history.

Exmoor (*see pp.44–45*), an old royal hunting forest, is home to threatened fritillary butterflies (including the heath, high brown, and marsh species), the rare whitebeam tree, and birds such as ring ouzels, curlews, stonechats, Dartford warblers, grasshopper warblers, and reed buntings. [SW]

If you're looking for a moorland walk with historical interest, **Bodmin Moor**, Cornwall is covered with interesting stone buildings, tombs, and memorials dating back 5,000 years. [SW]

For interesting ruins in wild spaces, visit King Arthur's Quoit – also known as **Trethevy Quoit** – near St Cleer, Cornwall. These huge, intriguing stones also date back to the Bronze Age. [SW]

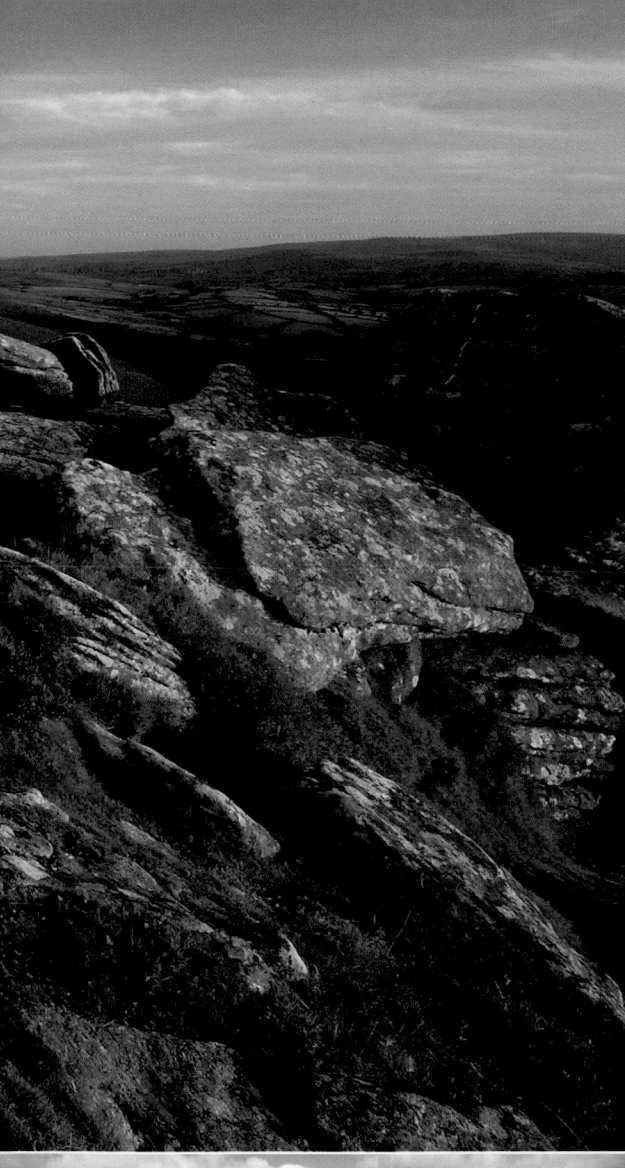

The curlew's haunting cry over Conan Doyle's "Grimspound Mire" sends a shiver down the spine.

THROUGH THE YEAR
GRIMSPOUND

In **winter**, the moors become difficult for animals – and walkers. Mist, rain, and even snow can come and go in minutes. The red grouse become increasingly territorial during winter. Lapwings and fieldfares brave the moors, under the watchful eyes of sparrowhawks, buzzards, and brown owls.

Heather and ling start to flower in **spring**, dominating the upland heath of the moor. You'll also notice bilberry, cross-leaved heath, and western gorse in the drier areas. The eggs of any breeding red grouse hatch in May and June, and the young fly after 12–13 days.

The Two Moors Way walking path becomes very busy in **summer**. Meadow pipits, stonechats, and skylarks chatter around the moor, while lizards bask in the sun. Foals of the Dartmoor ponies frolic on the grassland. Look out for the rare high brown fritillary butterfly, which lives in the bracken stands, and the green hairstreak butterfly.

Below: Dartmoor ponies enjoy the grassland just below the heath.

JAN
FEB
MAR
APR
MAY
JUN
JUL
AUG
SEP
OCT
NOV
DEC

Left: The brown, peaty Water of Tanar flows through the heathery moorland.

Right (left to right): Wild blaeberries are vital food for the capercaillie; funnel-tooth fungus; Glen Tanar supports the UK's largest population of Scottish crossbills.

Right below: The Scots pine was the main tree of the first wildwood to grow after the last Ice Age.

WHERE
Glen Tanar, Aboyne, Aberdeenshire
AB34 5EU, Scotland; www.glentanar.co.uk

CONTACT
Glen Tanar Ranger Service, tel: 01339 886072; ranger@glentanar.co.uk

GETTING THERE
The reserve is 4.8km (3miles) southwest of Aboyne, across the River Dee; it is signposted off the B976 from Aboyne. There are buses between the reserve and Aboyne, and the nearest rail stations are Stonehaven and Aberdeen. The reserve is around one hour's drive from Aberdeen airport.

ACCESS AND FACILITIES
The Glen Tanar Visitor Centre at Braeloine has full-access toilets, parking, and information displays. There are no refreshment facilities but there are picnic areas. All-ability trails radiate out from the visitor centre: the red trail takes visitors on a circular loop along the waterway, through the pine forest, and across farmland.

OPENING TIMES
The reserve is open all year round. The visitor centre is open from 10am to 5pm daily except Tuesdays. Times vary in winter.

CHARGES
Car-parking charges only.

Capercaillie watching

This is one of the best places in the Highlands to see capercaillie, but make sure you don't disturb them while they display or feed, as their numbers are now so low in the UK that they are in danger of extinction. Follow the capercaillie Code of Conduct (see pp.66–67). You may also see black grouse among the scattered pines or where the forest abuts the moorland; if you want to watch them safely, follow the black grouse Code of Conduct (see pp.102–103).

Main: Glen Tanar is a Caledonian forest with areas of dry and wet heath, blanket bogs, and lochans, where otters can sometimes be seen.

CALEDONIAN DELIGHT

GLEN TANAR NATIONAL NATURE RESERVE EXTENDS UPWARDS into the mountains from the wooded valley of the Dee, on the southeastern flanks of the vast brooding massif of the Cairngorm Mountains. The reserve contains one of the largest and finest remaining stands of ancient native Caledonian Scots pine forest, and careful management has helped to create the best possible environment for its special animals, including the capercaillie.

The area's royal connections date back to 1852, when Queen Victoria and Prince Albert bought nearby Balmoral castle. Much of the heather moorland is managed for red grouse: bracken and heather are thinned or cleared to encourage the growth of blaeberry, which the grouse relies upon for food, both as an adult and as a chick, when it eats the caterpillars and other insects associated with the plants. The estate staff at Glen Tanar have also created thickets and brushwood shelters where the grouse can find shelter from harsh weather and predators.

Above: The bare trees of winter open up the skies for birdwatching.

This is one of the best places to explore the wonders of an ancient Caledonian Scots pine forest: the huge capercaillie, the Scottish crossbill, red squirrels, and Highland plants.

THROUGH THE YEAR
GLEN TANAR

Winter brings harsh conditions to Glen Tanar, and you'll need to take extra care if you are venturing on to the moor and mountains. Wildlife is sparse, apart from ptarmigan – now in their all-white winter plumage – and the occasional golden eagle.

Goshawks perform soaring and diving display flights above the trees in **spring**. Migrant birds include wheatears and ring ouzels on the moorland and redstarts in the woods. Woodcocks perform their slow-flying "roding" displays – males fly over the treetops at dusk and dawn, patrolling their territories, uttering strange croaking and sneezing sounds.

In **summer** the many rare wildflowers include the delicate pink, drooping, bell-shaped blooms of twinflower, and the spirals of white flowers of an endangered wild orchid: creeping lady's tresses.

WHERE ELSE TO SEE
HIGHLAND BIRDS

The whole of the Upper Deeside region is a superb place to see the special birds of the Highlands.

The high tops of the mountains around **Lochnagar**, overlooking the royal forest of Balmoral, have the greatest breeding density of one of the Highland's most special birds, the dotterel, and a few pairs of nesting snow buntings. Be careful to avoid undue disturbance. The 21km (13 mile) walk to the summit and back is for experienced hill-walkers only. [SC]

Just north of the A93, the **Davan** and **Kinnord** lochs are worth a visit in late autumn or winter for the whooper swans and thousands of greylag and pink-footed geese that winter there. [SC]

On the other side of the Cairngorms National Park, **Rannoch** (see pp.66–67) has all the birds of Glen Tanar, plus crested tits. Visit in spring or autumn, when it is less crowded than in summer. [SC]

This part of Scotland is also salmon-fishing country, and Glen Tanar – which flanks the upper reaches of the Tanar river and the Dee – is one of the best places to see salmon spawn in late autumn. The river also draws birds into the area, and you'll often see dippers and grey wagtails on the water, while siskins and Scottish crossbills feed in the pines. This is one of the best of all sites for crossbills, which may even be seen from the car park of the visitor centre. Red deer remain for much of the year on the higher ground, while roe deer roam the valley woodlands. The forest is rich in rare fungi, such as the scaly-tooth and goblet-scented spine fungi, which favour pine forests.

At the head of the glen, the Mount Keen area is a good place to look for ptarmigan, those high-altitude relatives of the red grouse. Up on the open mountains above the forest, look out for buzzards; there is also a good chance of seeing a merlin or a peregrine flashing past, or perching, perfectly still, on a rock. Scan the skies for hen harriers quartering the heather moorland, their wings forming a perfect "V". This region is also home to majestic golden eagles; watching them glide alongside a ridge or soar high into the skies is one of nature's finest sights.

JAN
FEB
MAR
APR
MAY
JUN
JUL
AUG
SEP
OCT
NOV
DEC

OCTOBER

Where to Go: **October**

A month of storms, lashing rain, and days of the most beautiful peace and stillness, coupled with splendid autumn colours. October has everything: it is arguably one of the finest times of the year for anyone who enjoys wildlife and rural landscapes. While most summer birds have gone – except perhaps for a few lingering swallows and chiffchaffs – vast numbers of new arrivals

make up for their departure; we begin to see fieldfares, redwings, and the various geese and ducks of the coast. At Loch of Strathbeg, north of Aberdeen, more than 50,000 geese assemble, creating an awesome spectacle for people in the area, before moving further south, to Norfolk, just a few weeks later. This is a great month, too, for birds that simply pass through our islands, not

COAST

MOUNTAINS

INLETS AND ESTUARIES

CADER IDRIS A sublime and exhilarating landscape.

LOUGH FOYLE The vast mudflats provide rich pickings for birds.

FLAMBOROUGH HEAD A classic east-coast seawatching point.

FLAMBOROUGH HEAD
BRIDLINGTON, YORKSHIRE [N]

This is one of the best places in the UK to see small, perching birds in huge numbers on their migration. Exciting rarities may blow in, such as Pallas's warbler.
See pp.252–253

CADER IDRIS
GWYNEDD, NORTH WALES [W]

This majestic mountain rises abruptly from the land to give incredible views over the surrounding uplands. High glacial lakes are flanked by dizzying precipices.
See pp.254–255

LOUGH FOYLE
LONDONDERRY [NI]

Over 20,000 wildfowl visit this shallow sea inlet in October to take advantage of Ireland's milder weather. Threatened fish species such as allis shad swim in the lough's waters.
See pp.266–267

SHERINGHAM CLIFFS
NORTH NORFOLK [SE]

Soft, sandy material deposited during the last Ice Age makes up Sheringham's crumbly cliffs. This is an ideal place to watch for passing seabirds, and occasionally harbour porpoises.
See pp.252–253

Far below, you can see the U-shaped valleys of Snowdonia, carved by the massive weight of ice as the glaciers ground their way towards the sea.

SNOWDON
GWYNEDD, NORTH WALES [W]

Wales's highest mountain has everything, from dramatic views and a wide range of habitats and animals, to rare flowers, insects, and abandoned mines.
See pp.254–255

BANN ESTUARY
NORTH ANTRIM [NI]

This is a wonderful estuary for birds, especially wintering waders and wildfowl, with around 4,000 birds feeding on the mudflats in October.
See pp.266–267

SPURN POINT
KILNSEA, HUMBERSIDE [N]

There is a bird observatory at the Point to record the exceptional number of passage birds – but everyone can join in the fun, while sheltering in the dunes.
See pp.264–265

LOCH SPYNIE
ELGIN, MORAY [SC]

The special habitat surrounding this loch gives rise to rare aquatic flora. Its large roost of Icelandic greylag geese is astonishing to watch in October.
See pp.260–261

GLENCANISP FOREST
ASSYNT, SUTHERLAND [SC]

Canisp is an isolated mountain that rises out of the Glencanisp forest, close to the magnificent "pillar mountain" of Suilven, a renowned climbing challenge.
See pp.254–255

THAMES ESTUARY
KENT/ESSEX [SE]

This vast estuary is an important refuelling point for hungry migrating birds. Brent geese can be seen here in huge numbers.
See pp.252–253

The estuary is at its best at high tide, when waders roost on the saltmarsh close to shore, their outlines ghostly as the dusk deepens.

FILEY BAY
FILEY, EAST YORKSHIRE [N]

Walk along the seemingly endless sands of Filey Bay to the sheer cliffs of Filey Brigg, where you can join the bird observatory in watching large numbers of migrating birds.
See pp.264–265

THE LAKE DISTRICT
CUMBRIA [N]

The mountains and lakes of the Lake District are rich in wildlife in autumn, including red deer, golden eagles, red squirrels, and natterjack toads.
See pp.254–255

SLIMBRIDGE
GLOUCESTERSHIRE [SE]

Slimbridge is located on the edge of the Severn estuary, and it is a good place to see returning waders in autumn. Large flocks of starlings swirl in displays overhead.
See pp.256–257

Previous page: Autumn colour in Thetford Forest.

settling for the winter but hurrying on south; on the coast, especially, who knows what you might find in this annual rush – October is a time to see rarities from Siberia and even North America. It sees the real beginning, too, of the season for fungi enthusiasts: so many and so varied – mushrooms, toadstools, brackets, and puffballs appear everywhere, especially after rain.

They are a treat, but a challenge to your identification skills; find a good guide, and never eat any that you are unsure about. On the coast, the grey seals are giving birth to their white-coated pups. In Pembrokeshire, they give birth on secluded stony beaches, but in Lincolnshire, they can be seen on more accessible sandy shores. Be sure to give them respectful peace and quiet.

WOODLANDS

THE BIRKS OF ABERFELDY Red and orange leaves carpet the forest.

THE BIRKS OF ABERFELDY
PERTH AND KINROSS [SC]

Warm autumn colours are seen at their finest in this birch wood, which hugs the sides of the Moness Burn. Dippers dive for prey and fungi hide among fallen leaves.
See pp.262–263

EPPING FOREST
LONDON [SE]

Epping Forest is an ancient deciduous woodland that is designated a Site of Special Scientific Interest for its varied habitats and wildlife.
See pp.258–259

DENDLES WOOD
DARTMOOR, DEVON [SW]

A wonderful stretch of upland, this oak-beech woodland lies to the south of Dartmoor National Park. It is rich in ferns, mosses, and lichens, and home to the UK's rarest bat, the barbastelle.
See pp.262–263

WINDSOR GREAT PARK
BERKSHIRE [SE]

Cranbourne Chase is Windsor's oldest wood, dating back some 400 years. In October, the woodland floor is covered in fungi, including the delicate purple amethyst deceiver.
See pp.258–259

THE HERMITAGE
DUNKELD, PERTHSHIRE [SC]

The trail here leads you along the River Braan, through an ancient woodland rich in autumnal colour to a waterfall, gorge, and folly.
See pp.262–263

ISLANDS

MONACH ISLES Home to over 30,000 breeding grey seals.

THE MONACH ISLES
WESTERN ISLES [SC]

Grey seals can breed here without being disturbed by humans, and Monach's colony produces around 9,000 pups every year here in October.
See pp.268–269

STRANGFORD LOUGH
DOWNPATRICK, CO.DOWN [NI]

There are over 120 islands within the lough, including some that are important homes for wildlife. Bird island has 400 pairs of cormorants living on it in winter.
See pp.266–267

THE FARNE ISLANDS
NORTHUMBERLAND [N]

These rugged islands have a famous sea bird sanctuary and an internationally important colony of grey seals, with pups born every day in October.
See pp.268–269

As you approach the sandy beaches and dunes of the remote islands in October, a mass of bobbing seal heads rise to greet you.

PORTLAND BILL
DORSET [SW]

This is one of the best places in the UK to see the Balearic shearwater, a threatened bird, during the autumn migration.
See pp.252–253

WETLANDS

MARTIN MERE Huge flocks of pink-footed geese spend winter here.

MARTIN MERE
BURSCOUGH, LANCASHIRE [N]

This Wildfowl & Wetlands Trust site is famed for its overwintering wildfowl – by October it plays host to 1,000 whooper swans and 17,000 pink-footed geese.
See pp.256–257

During October thousands of geese, ducks, and swans converge on the low-lying marshes and lagoons of Martin Mere.

LOCH LEVEN
PERTH AND KINROSS [SC]

Lying just below the Lomond hills, the islands, lagoons, and reedbeds of this reserve fill with wild geese in October; the birds swoop in huge flocks as if choreographed.
See pp.260–261

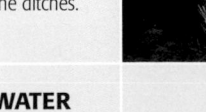

MARSHSIDE
SOUTHPORT, LANCASHIRE [N]

The RSPB reserve here lies on the edge of the famous Ribble estuary, and has large roosts of pink-footed geese at dusk and dawn. Migrant hawker dragonflies patrol the ditches.
See pp.256–257

COTSWOLD WATER PARK
GLOUCESTERSHIRE [SE]

Britain's largest water park is great in autumn; head for Coke's Pit Nature Reserve, where you can see water voles and Daubenton's bats.
See pp.261–262

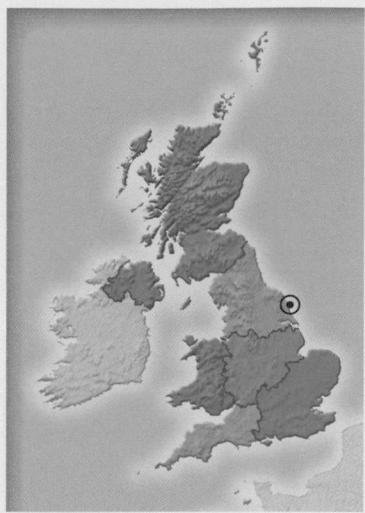

WHERE
Flamborough Head, Bridlington, Yorkshire
YO15 1AR; www.flamboroughuk.net

CONTACT
Bridlington Tourist Information, tel: 01262
673474; bridlington.tic@eastriding.gov.uk

GETTING THERE
By car, drive through Flamborough on the
B1255 and head out on the B1259. The
Head lies 3km (2 miles) east of the village.
By bus, catch the Bridlington–Speeton bus,
alighting at Flamborough. The nearest rail
stations are Bridlington and Bempton.

ACCESS AND FACILITIES
There are several car parks; the main
lighthouse car park has toilets, and a shop
and café with wheelchair access. The
headland terrain is difficult for wheelchair
users and pushchairs, but the Lighthouse,
North Landing, and South Landing car parks
all offer good viewpoints. Warning: stay well
clear of the crumbling cliff edges and under
no circumstances attempt to climb the cliffs
from the beaches below.

OPENING TIMES
Open all year round.

CHARGES
Yes, for the lighthouse car park. The
lighthouse is closed in the winter.

Getting your bearings

Seawatching needs patience, a comfortable
sitting position, shelter from the elements, and
a good deal of optimism. When you arrive, take
note of the main direction of bird movement,
then start scanning the sea with binoculars,
using a telescope if necessary when you spot
something. Be aware of the position of buoys,
ships, or other seamarks – these are essential to
point something out to fellow observers in the
vastness of the vista.

Above: The sooty shearwater's plumage is completely
dark, except for the pale flashes in its underwings.

Below: A pair of fulmars squabble on the cliffs.

Right panel (top to bottom): The cliffs of
Flamborough Head; little auks seem to have almost
no neck or beak, and endure the nickname of "flying
cotton bobbins".

Main: Flocks of sooty shearwaters and kittiwakes feeding off the coast of Flamborough Head.

SEAWATCHING OFF THE HEAD

SEAWATCHING IS AN ACQUIRED TASTE: IT MEANS AN AWFUL LOT of time doing just that – watching the
sea. But if birds are moving they can be in huge numbers, and the thrill lies in never quite knowing what will
come in with the wind. To give yourself the best chance of witnessing seabird movements, get out to sea on a boat
or visit one of our great coastal headlands, with an eye to the weather – onshore gales should blow birds towards
the land. Or wait until the wind has subsided and then watch as the displaced birds reorient themselves.

Flamborough Head is a classic east-coast seawatching point. Sightings of guillemots, kittiwakes, fulmars,
and gannets are guaranteed; with luck, there could be divers heading to their wintering grounds, and manx or
sooty shearwaters, not to mention a variety of other, rarer species sailing past or skimming the waves. Skuas
could be coasting south, especially in October, when storms often bring the rarest species, the long-tailed skua,

Above: Puffins breed on Flamborough Head in the spring.

Flamborough Head
is brilliantly placed
for seabird watching
– it juts out 10km
(6 miles) into the
North Sea, into the
path of passing birds.

THROUGH THE YEAR
FLAMBOROUGH HEAD

Seabirds are still moving through Flamborough in the **winter**. Divers are ever-present, often including a few great northern, and after an Arctic blast, the stream of little auks can number tens of thousands. The cliff-top stubble fields may hold a few snow and Lapland buntings among the skylarks.

Breeding seabirds return to the cliffs in **spring**, with guillemots and kittiwakes on the faces, and puffins in holes in the grassy slopes. Gannets are always offshore, moving to and from their nesting colony a few kilometres up the coast at Bempton Cliffs (*see pp.104–105*), in Yorkshire.

In high **summer**, with noisy nesting under way, the first shearwaters can appear as early as July. The cliff slopes are a riot of colour, with flowering red campion, kidney vetch, lady's bedstraw, and wild carrot, colourfully setting off the deep purple spikes of northern marsh orchid.

WHERE ELSE TO SEE
PASSING SEABIRDS

Go to any headland, and you have a good chance of seeing seabird movements. You will need binoculars or a telescope to see seabirds well; try to avoid looking into the light if you want to pick up any details of colour.

Classic sites include the numerous Cornish headlands, among them **Pendeen**, **Porthgwarra**, and **Lizard Point** (*see pp.116–117*). **Portland Bill** (*see pp.90–91*) in Dorset is one of the premier mainland sites to see the Balearic shearwater, a threatened bird. [SW]

Although lacking peninsulas, the north Norfolk coast can be productive for sightings of seabirds, especially the cliffs at **Sheringham**. [SE]

Southend Pier in Essex stretches 1.6km (1 mile) into the Thames Estuary and is well known for its terns and skuas. Seabirds also collect offshore around the cooling water outflows of the power stations at **Dungeness** (*see pp.162–163*) in Kent and **Sizewell** in Suffolk. [SE]

within sight. Watch out for the great skuas, too, who deploy their hit-and-run food-stealing tactics on victims as large as gannets. The first couple of hours of daylight often provide the most birds when you're seawatching, but the views are extraordinarily atmospheric in the evening, when the sunlight falls on the passing birds. Just beware of fog – the most convenient watchpoint is the cliff slopes below the foghorn, which can suddenly produce a deafening blast.

Scan the sea for groups of diving gannets – they gather when they have found a shoal of fish. This is a dramatic spectacle in its own right, but those same fish might also attract other predators, especially harbour porpoises, often in surprising numbers: 10, 20, or more.

In October Flamborough also welcomes migrating songbirds. The hedges and bushes in an otherwise windswept landscape become a magnet for birds that have just made landfall after crossing the North Sea. Hawthorn berries are greedily devoured by redwings and fieldfares, and perhaps a ring ouzel or two, while the more skulking warblers, deep in the gorse, could include anything from a barred warbler to that diminutive jewel of Siberia: the Pallas's warbler.

JAN
FEB
MAR
APR
MAY
JUN
JUL
AUG
SEP
OCT
NOV
DEC

THE GIANT'S THRONE

I T MAY NOT BE THE HIGHEST MOUNTAIN IN WALES, but Cader Idris is certainly one of the most impressive. Towering 893m (2930ft) above the Mawddach estuary on the mid-Wales coast, its long, rocky ridge is all the more spectacular for rising virtually from sea level. The majesty of its skyline is more than matched by the magnificence of the view from its summit, which on a clear day takes in the sea off Barmouth, the mountains of Snowdonia, and, nearer to hand, some of the most dramatic upland terrain in Britain.

This is a landscape carved by ice. During the last Ice Age, glaciers scooped away the slopes of the mountain to form crater-like corries or cwms, now occupied by high glacial lakes such as Llyn Cau and Llyn y Gadair. The cwms are divided by the narrow ridge that forms the long spine of Cader Idris, flanked by dizzying precipices. Far below can be seen the deep U-shaped valleys carved by the massive weight of ice as the glaciers ground their way

WHERE
Cader Idris National Nature Reserve, Dolgellau, Gwynedd, LL40 2HZ, Wales; www.snowdonia-npa.gov.uk

CONTACT
Snowdonia National Park Authority, tel: 01766 770274.

GETTING THERE
Cader Idris lies at the southern end of the Snowdonia National Park. Dolgellau is the nearest town. Travel out of Corris and Corris Uchaf on the A487 and take a left on to B4405 signposted Tywyn.

ACCESS AND FACILITIES
There is free parking, but no facilities, other than toilets and a visitor centre. Cader Idris is most easily climbed by the Pony Path, which starts 3.2km (2 miles) southwest of Dolgellau, from the car park at Ty-nant, near Llyn Gwernan. It leads to the highest point, Penygadair. There is a steeper route from Minffordd in the Tal-y-llyn valley, from the Dôl Idris car park near the junction of the A487 and the B4405 Dolgellau to Tywyn road.

OPENING TIMES
Open all year round. The visitor centre has a reduced service during winter.

CHARGES
None.

Mountain flora

The sheer cliffs and crags of Cader Idris provide refuges for specialized plants that flourish in the harsh conditions. They include purple saxifrage (*above*) and dwarf willow, both more commonly seen in the Arctic, as well as the dense green cushions of moss campion, with its small pink flowers. These "Arctic-alpines" are relics of the late Ice Age, when the ice sheets had retreated but the region was still half-frozen tundra. They are on the edge of their range in mid Wales and their survival may be threatened by climate change.

Above: The mountain slopes are said to form the *cader* (chair) from which the mythological giant Idris surveyed the land.

Left: Waterfall in Cwm Amarch on Cader Idris.

Right (left to right): Looking across the Llyn Cau lake; a hovering hen harrier.

Right panel (top to bottom): Meadow pipit; purple heather.

towards the sea some 20,000 years ago, now occupied by bright-green pastures, sinuous rivers, and the glittering Tal-y-llyn lake. Everywhere there are relics of the glaciation, with ice-scoured rocks and piles of rocky debris left by the ice when it finally melted away.

Above the valley floors, vivid-green farmland gives way to the darker hues of heather, moor grass, and bare rock, enriched in October by glowing autumn colour. Meadow pipits flushed from the grass flutter erratically into the air with thin, sharp cries of alarm, while overhead a deep croaking call may betray the dark, ragged form of a raven. If you are lucky you may see a merlin darting low in pursuit of a smaller bird – meadow pipits are among its favourite prey – or a hen harrier floating buoyantly over the rough grass as it searches for small animals. Many of these birds will move to more sheltered lower ground as autumn hardens into winter, but while the weather holds they stay on, as if reluctant to abandon this sublime and exhilarating landscape.

As summer's vegetation fades, the bare bones of a 20,000-year-old landscape are revealed.

WHERE ELSE TO SEE
GLACIATED LANDSCAPES

There are many other regions of Britain that offer a similar experience and equally graphic evidence of our Ice-Age past.

Elsewhere in the Snowdonia National Park in North Wales, the landscape around **Snowdon** (*see pp.172–173*) is equally spectacular, with similar mountain flora that includes the Snowdon lily, found nowhere else in Britain. [W]

The valleys of the Lake District, formed by glaciers that radiated from a central dome of ancient rock like the spokes of a wheel, now contain lakes of limpid beauty. [N]

The Scottish Highlands were so deeply buried by ice that only the highest peaks remained exposed. The rest was stripped of all soft rock, creating the largely barren terrain of regions like **Glencanisp Forest** in Wester Ross. [SC]

Strangford Lough in Northern Ireland (*see pp.288–289*) is dotted with low, rounded drumlins – islands shaped by the moving ice sheets. [NI]

THROUGH THE YEAR
CADER IDRIS

While the autumn often provides the clear skies essential to the most rewarding ascent of Cader Idris, this dramatic landscape retains its breathtaking beauty year-round.

Winter can be a dangerous time to climb any mountain, owing to the hazards of ice and exposure, but for the experienced it can provide a memorable insight into the elemental forces that shaped this landscape.

Spring is superb for both flowers and birds, with ravens frequently seen tumbling through the sky in their aerobatic courtship displays. Watch too for the ring ouzel, a summer visitor that resembles a blackbird with a white chest.

In **summer** the mountain can be surprisingly popular, but heading east away from the summit towards Mynydd Moel soon leaves the crowds behind.

Below: The summit of Cader Idris in winter.

JAN

FEB

MAR

APR

MAY

JUN

JUL

AUG

SEP

OCT

NOV

DEC

WHERE
Martin Mere Wetland Centre, Fish Lane, Burscough, Lancashire L40 0TA; www.wwt.org.uk

CONTACT
Martin Mere Wetland Centre, tel: 01704 895181; info.martinmere@wwt.org.uk

GETTING THERE
The Wetland Centre lies 9.5km (6 miles) from Ormskirk. It is signposted from junction 8 of the M61, junction 3 of the M58, and junction 27 of the M6. The nearest train stations are New Lane and Burscough Bridge; both are within walking distance, around 3km (2 miles) away along signposted paths. A bus service runs from Ormskirk bus station.

ACCESS AND FACILITIES
The visitor centre has a large viewing area, with a range of facilities. The reserve is very wheelchair-friendly: all trails and hides are accessible. There are 10 hides, four of which are multi-storey. The visitor centre has a restaurant, shop, and full-access toilets.

OPENING TIMES
Open all year round (except Christmas Day) from 9.30am–5.30pm (5pm in winter).

CHARGES
Yes, for non-WWT members. Essential helpers for disabled visitors are free.

The beaver returns

The Eurasian beaver used to live in Britain in large numbers, but it became extinct by the 1500s, and by the end of the 1800s there were only a few hundred left in Europe. It is now on the European Species Action List, which recommends reintroducing the animal into its former habitats, and in 2007, Martin Mere did just this, releasing four Eurasian beavers into a "natural-habitat" enclosure. The beavers are monogamous, family-oriented herbivores, who love to sink their teeth into woody, broadleaved plants.

Above (left to right): A male ruff; a brambling flock above the lagoon; look for redwings along the hedgerows.
Main: Whooper swans roosting at Martin Mere call to each other through the autumn dusk.

LANCASHIRE HOTSPOT

S ITUATED NORTH OF ORMSKIRK, THIS WILDFOWL & WETLANDS TRUST reserve is famed for its overwintering wildfowl. During October thousands of geese, ducks, and swans converge on the low-lying marshes and lagoons, and spectacular roosts of thousands of geese take place at dusk. Pink-footed geese migrate from Greenland and Iceland, whooper swans come from Iceland, while a handful of Bewicks's swans migrate from Russia. Dabbling ducks are attracted to the shallow lagoons and marshy fields, where the wigeons, pintails, teals, mallards, and a few shovelers can be seen tipping upside down in the water to feed on the aquatic plants.

Visit one of the various hides around the reserve to enjoy some wonderful views of the wildfowl. By late October there may be more than 1,000 whooper swans, and 17,000 pink-footed geese, often harbouring small numbers of other species, such as white-fronted, barnacle, and bean geese. The geese spend much of their day grazing on the fields, but you'll see these large birds take to the air as they commute between favourable feeding sites. Martin Mere is one of the country's most important wintering sites for ruffs, with more than 100 overwintering here. Look towards the wet fields to see these waders, together with huge flocks of lapwings and golden plovers – perhaps 1,000 or more of each. Snipe feed along the muddy margins, keeping a watchful eye on the sky for birds of prey such as merlins and peregrines. Marsh and hen harriers hunt over the area too.

Martin Mere Wetland Centre is home to a splendid range of endangered wildfowl, including more than 100 rare species of geese, swans, and ducks.

Martin Mere's other big attractions are a large captive collection of waterfowl – representing more than 100 species from around the world – and two pairs of the world's second-largest rodents, the European beavers. These animals are nature's engineers – they love excavating canals and building dams using branches and earth, so the reserve has installed a "beaver deceiver" to provide them with a water flow that constantly needs damming.

Inset: A pintail in flight at last light.
Below (left to right): A flock of bramblings tree-roosting; pink-footed geese.

WHERE ELSE TO SEE
WETLANDS

Wetland centres provide a mosaic of habitats and so attract a very diverse range of species. They are often particularly good for children, providing information, hides, observatories, and suggestions for exploration.

RSPB **Marshside** nature reserve is situated nearby, not far from Southport. Grazing marsh and lagoons attract plenty of wildfowl and waders. [N]

Holkham (see pp.18–19) in North Norfolk is a dramatic wetland reserve on the coast that hosts the largest concentration of wintering pink-footed geese in Britain. Go to Lady Ann's Drive an hour before dusk to see spectacular numbers. [SE]

The **London Wetland Centre** (see pp.16–17), Barnes, is a great urban reserve for watching wildlife, including bitterns, kingfishers, and water voles. [SE]

The Wildfowl & Wetlands Trust has a number of centres around the country that combine a captive collection with great birdwatching in winter. Try **Slimbridge** in Gloucestershire (see pp.34–35), their flagship reserve, for plenty of wildfowl. [M]

THROUGH THE YEAR
MARTIN MERE

Wildfowl swarm across the lagoons and marshes in **winter**. Pink-footed geese and whooper swans are joined by various dabbling ducks and wintering waders and raptors – a sighting of the lightning-fast peregrine falcon is almost guaranteed.

The winter visitors depart in **spring**. Migrants passing through Martin Mere may include spotted redshanks and whimbrels. Birds arriving to breed here include garganeys and yellow wagtails.

Breeding shelducks and avocets are among the highlights at the centre in **summer**. Returning autumn waders may include black-tailed godwits, green sandpipers, ruffs, and others. The centre runs a programme of interesting activities for children right through the summer, including pond dipping and interactive workshops on topics such as the mysteries of the food chain and how birds move.

Below: Shelduck family feeding in shallow water in summer.

JAN
FEB
MAR
APR
MAY
JUN
JUL
AUG
SEP
OCT
NOV
DEC

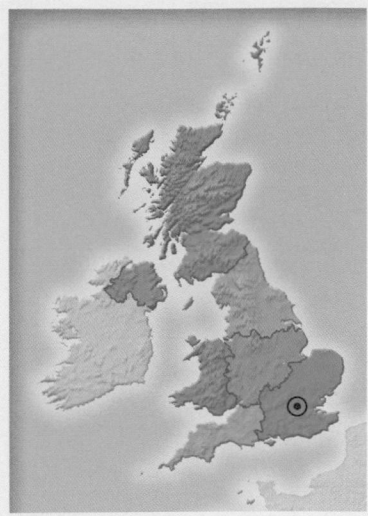

Left: The rich colours of the woodland in autumn.

Right (left to right): Poisonous fly agaric toadstools; common stinkhorns have a vile-smelling sticky spore mass when fresh; the stems of amethyst deceiver are covered in tiny white hairs; the highly-prized *Boletus edulis* – the cep or porcini mushroom.

WHERE
Windsor Great Park, Windsor, Berkshire
SL4 2HT; www.thecrownestate.co.uk

CONTACT
The Crown Estate Office, tel: 01753 860222.

GETTING THERE
The A332 runs directly through the centre of Windsor Great Park. By train, travel to Windsor Central or Windsor Riverside. By bus, take White Bus Services no.1 bus to Windsor Great Park Post Office. National Cycle Network route no. 4 runs through the park.

ACCESS AND FACILITIES
Car parks are located along the A332, which runs through the park. Roads and paths through the park are suitable for pushchairs and wheelchairs, and wheelchairs are available at Savill Garden.

OPENING TIMES
Open all year, from 7am to 5pm. Savill Garden is open from 10am until around dusk (4pm November–February, 6pm March–October).

CHARGES
Entry to the park is free, but there is a charge to enter Savill Garden.

Common earth-star

This extraordinary soil fungus is part of the Gasteromycetes ("stomach fungi") group, members of which all feature a stomach-shaped sac filled with spores. It is called an "earth-star" because when it rains, the outer walls split open into sections, widening flat out into the shape of a star, pushing the spore-filled inner sac up above any surrounding leaves. As raindrops hit the thin-walled spore sac, the spores puff out of the pore at the top of the sac.

Main: The fruiting bodies of honey fungus. **Far right:** Sulphur polypore on bark.

WOODLAND FUNGI AT WINDSOR

THE REMNANT OF AN ANCIENT FOREST AT THE EASTERN EDGE of Cranbourne Chase was incorporated into Windsor Great Park in the 1790s. It is celebrated for its ancient trees, many of them oaks over 400 years old. Dotted among them on October mornings you can find organisms that are here one day and gone the next – fungi.

Fungi are famous for the way they spring up overnight and vanish almost as fast. Some are culinary delicacies, while others are notoriously deadly. Many have a slightly sinister beauty. They seem like alien life forms, which is not far from the truth, because although most people think of them as plants, they comprise a separate kingdom of life that has a lot in common with animals. Instead of making food, as plants do, they consume it, usually in the form of dead wood and other plant material. In the process they break down dead organic matter and release nutrients that are vital to living plants. Without them, many plants could not grow at all.

JAN

FEB

MAR

APR

MAY

JUN

JUL

AUG

SEP

OCT

NOV

DEC

WHERE ELSE TO SEE
WOODLAND FUNGI

Almost any wood in Britain will sprout a variety of fungi in the damp, yet still quite warm, weeks of autumn. Most species have associations with certain trees, such as the well-known partnership of fly agaric with birch. This means that different types of woodland support different types of fungi, and the more diverse the habitat, the greater the variety.

One of the best places to look is the **New Forest** in Hampshire (*see pp.174–175*). It has a wide range of woodland habitats, from ancient oakwoods to conifer plantations, as well as grasslands and heaths that support distinctive fungi of their own. [SE]

Epping Forest in London is a well-known hunting ground for fungi enthusiasts, with large areas of oak, beech, hornbeam, and birch, and plenty of dead wood left to rot on the forest floor. [SE]

Some of the older parts of **Sherwood Forest** in Nottinghamshire (*see pp.36–37*) are also excellent places to search for fungi. Check inside old hollow trees as well as on the ground around them. [M]

THROUGH THE YEAR
WINDSOR GREAT PARK

The woodlands have their own stark beauty in **winter** when the dark tracery of branches is revealed by the fallen leaves. Look for woodpeckers, nuthatches, and treecreepers searching for food on the tree bark; if you search hard you may spot a tawny owl roosting on a branch close to a tree trunk.

Spring sees the trees burst into leaf, an event that triggers a mass hatching of leaf-eating insects. These in turn are gathered in their thousands by the breeding woodland birds whose songs fill the air.

In **summer**, look for woodland butterflies such as the purple emperor and white admiral, as well as visitors like the painted lady. Look up to check for hobbies – fast-flying falcons that pluck dragonflies out of the air and eat them on the wing.

Scientists believe there may be over a million species of fungi, only 10 per cent of which have been officially described.

As you walk among the old trees near Forest Gate, you will find all kinds of fungi pushing up through the autumn leaf litter at your feet. Some are conspicuous, like the bright red russulas and white-spotted fly agaric. Others are easy to overlook, like the delicate purple amethyst deceiver. But the more you look, the more you see, both on the ground and sprouting from trees and old stumps. You might even find the rare bearded tooth fungus, a species that is only found here and a few other places in Britain. You can smell the fungi too – the delicious mushroomy fragrance of ceps and the disgusting smell of the stinkhorn that attracts flies to carry away its spores.

Spore dispersal is the function of all these fungi. They are the seasonal "fruiting bodies" of much larger organisms that form complex networks in the soil and dead timber. These networks enmesh tree roots, supplying them with nutrients while absorbing sugars from the trees' root sap. They occupy hollow trees and convert the dead heartwood into substances that help nourish the living parts of the tree. As old parts of the network die off, new stems grow, so the organism is effectively immortal. The trees of the forest are old, but many of its fungi may be even older.

Below: Rhododendrons bloom in late spring in the Park's Savill Garden.

AUTUMN BY THE LOCH

LOCH LEVEN NATIONAL NATURE RESERVE LIES BELOW THE LOMOND HILLS, where its vast, tranquil loch spreads over 16 sq km (6 sq miles). The loch encompasses islands, lagoons, reedbeds, and grazing marshes, which provide food and shelter for thousands of birds in the autumn and winter. The best place to appreciate the wildlife, especially close up, is the RSPB reserve at Vane Farm, which has excellent views across the main loch, specially created shallow lagoons, and nature trails on nearby wooded hillsides.

In October, it is one of the best places in the UK to see vast numbers of wild geese. These iconic birds are closely associated with the romance and mystery of migration and the changing of the seasons. In England, the increase of semi-wild Canada and greylag geese has devalued them somewhat, but the real thing – the truly wild birds that annually cross the seas from the north to spend the winter with us – are magnificent.

WHERE
Loch Leven, Perth and Kinross KY13 7LX, Scotland.

CONTACT
RSPB Vane Farm Nature Reserve, tel: 01577 862355; vanefarm@rspb.org.uk

GETTING THERE
By car, take the M90 to Junction 5, then follow signs to the reserve. The nearest train station is Cowdenbeath, 11km (7 miles) away, but there is no onward public transport. A bus runs from Kinross on Wednesdays and Saturdays. Vane Farm lies 7km (4 miles) off Route 1 of the National Cycle Network.

ACCESS AND FACILITIES
There are three hides at Vane Farm, all with good access. The visitor centre has a café, trail and bird information, car park, full-access toilets, and good facilities for wheelchair users. Some of the trails are difficult for wheelchairs.

OPENING TIMES
Loch Leven is accessible at all times. Vane Farm visitor centre is open 10am–5pm daily, but the trails and hides are open 24 hours a day all year, except for Christmas Day, Boxing Day, New Year's Day and 2 January.

CHARGES
A small charge applies, except for RSPB and Wildlife Explorer members.

Above: The first sight of pink-footed geese in flight is symbolic of the changing seasons.

Below (top and bottom): Vane Farm Nature Reserve from above; the reserve lies along the south shore of Loch Leven, and includes a trail up to the top of Vane Hill, from where you can gain spectacular views.

Bilberry lover

The bilberry bumblebee, which is found at Loch Leven, is particularly fond of bilberry – a wild, wiry shrub that grows best on the heathlands and high grounds of northern Britain – hence the bee's other name, the mountain bumblebee, or "humble-bee". This heart-shaped, red-tailed bee emerges in early spring as the bilberry flowers. Deer grazing, dense forest canopies, and an inability to compete successfully against the fiercer heathers has led to a decrease in plants, and a serious decline in numbers of the bee.

They are at their best in large, flying flocks, when they make the familiar V-shapes, chevrons, and wavy lines and the air fills with their ringing, clanging, and clattering calls. You can distinguish the greylag geese by their harsher, more rattling notes; the pink-footed geese form a more musical chorus – deep calls interspersed with high, sharp "win-wink" notes. On the ground, the geese march steadily along in tightly packed groups, often squabbling and calling, making them always interesting to watch.

With the geese, or nearby, will be hordes of ducks: the wigeons like to patrol the grass, while pintails, teals, and mallards stay close to the water. Look for lapwings and golden plovers; these are the signalling birds, who will suddenly take flight, and noisily sound the alarm if birds of prey appear in the skies overhead. Groups of whooper swans may be hiding a few rarer Bewick's; smaller wading birds can be found at the edges of the water.

WHERE ELSE TO SEE
FRESHWATER WILDFOWL

Loch Leven is Scotland's largest lowland freshwater loch. This kind of natural standing water habitat is imitated by man-made waters such as reservoirs, and provides a perfect habitat for wintering birds.

Lochs Oire, **na Bo**, and **Spynie**, in Moray, Scotland, are all freshwater lochs with winter wildfowl. Loch Spynie is a large loch with reedbeds, fen, and woodlands, famous for the huge numbers of greylag and pink-footed geese that roost there in winter. [SC]

Pink-footed geese can be seen at **Marshside** and **Martin Mere** (see pp.256–257) in Lancashire, where they come to feed on crop waste. [N]

At **Holkham**, Norfolk (see pp.18–19), and the **Sevenoaks Wildlife Reserve**, Kent, you can see geese aplenty. [SE]

The Cotswold Water Park, near Cirencester in Gloucestershire, has 147 lakes that were formerly gravel pits and now provide a winter home for thousands of wintering waterbirds and gulls. [M]

THROUGH THE YEAR
LOCH LEVEN

In **winter**, look for birds of prey over the hill, and roe deer, which seek shelter in the woods. Finches and tits visit bird feeders, while geese live around the loch.

Spring sees toads emerging from the loch, just as the last geese leave for Iceland. The birchwoods come back to life, and begin to fill with visiting summer birds. Look out especially for great spotted woodpeckers and lesser redpolls.

In **summer** it's worth staying until dusk, when you can see Daubenton's and pipistrelle bats emerging. Ospreys hover over the loch in the early morning and late afternoon, while damselflies enjoy the water during the heat of the day. A beautiful flowery meadow has recently been created as a bumblebee sanctuary (see box, facing page), and it is a great place to see a wide variety of insects, including bees and butterflies.

Main: Loch Leven was formed by retreating glaciers.

Above: Greylag geese are the largest of the UK's geese; whooper swans' bills have long triangles of yellow.

Below: A redshank preens itself.

Below: The common toad emerges from the loch during spring.

JAN
FEB
MAR
APR
MAY
JUN
JUL
AUG
SEP
OCT
NOV
DEC

Left: Yellow chanterelle thrives among moss in the beech woodland of the Birks.

Right (left to right): Common yellow russula loves the cool dampness of the gorge; ferns thrive in the Birks; the Birks of Aberfeldy Walking Trail.

Right panel: The walking trail leads you past many small waterfalls, up to the bridge overlooking the Upper Falls.

WHERE
The Birks of Aberfeldy, Aberfeldy, Perthshire, Scotland; www.perthshire.co.uk

CONTACT
Aberfeldy Tourist Information Centre, The Square, Aberfeldy, PH15 2DD, tel: 01887 820276 or Visit Scotland, tel: 01738 627958; info@visitscotland.com

GETTING THERE
From Perth, take the A9 north towards Pitlochry, then turn left onto the A827 at Ballinluig towards Aberfeldy.

ACCESS AND FACILITIES
The nearest facilities are in Aberfeldy town. The 4km (2½ mile) circular walk is accessible from the centre of Aberfeldy or from the Birks car park, reached by following the A826 south and following the signs. There are seats and viewpoints along the walk. For those not so mobile, there is a picnic area at the car park that gives a good flavour of the walk. There is also a short tree trail identifying a large number of tree species for people unable to climb the main path.

OPENING HOURS
Open all year round.

CHARGES
None.

Map lichen

Lichens are ancient, slow-growing plants that can survive in harsh environments, including extreme temperatures or seemingly nutrient-free areas. They do not have roots and do not need water, so they can live on bare rock or sand. They also grow at a uniform rate, and are now often used to reveal the age of the exposed rock surface on which they live. Map lichen (*below*) is particularly useful for this, as it grows less than 1mm (¹⁄₃₂ inch) each year, allowing for finely tuned dating.

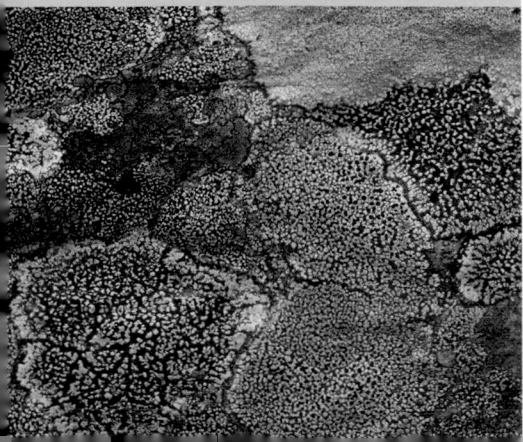

Main: The woodland path through the Birks of Aberfeldy is most atmospheric in autumn.

AUTUMN FIRE IN THE FOREST

TUCKED AWAY IN THE FOLDS OF THE PERTHSHIRE HILLS LIES an enchanting, steep-sided wooded glen, with magical mosses, stunning waterfalls, and breathtaking views. The wild, ancient woodlands that once covered the entire landscape have all but disappeared, and while there are a few remnants of the Caledonian forest tucked away in the most inaccessible parts of this glen, the predominant trees now are the "birks" – the Scottish gaelic word for "birch trees". These elegant, silver-barked species hug the upper slopes either side of the rushing, tumbling white waters of the Moness Burn, a tributary of the Tay – itself the longest river in Britain. The looping 3.2km (2 mile) nature trail takes you up to the wooden bridge that runs right over the top of the impressive waterfall, called the Falls of Moness. Once at the top, the views are incredible. The Falls tumble some 150m (492ft) down the ancient gorge, where bright red and orange leaves carpet the dark-green, mossy forest; some fall

Above: Ramsons, or wild garlic, grows in the damper woodland in spring.

JAN

FEB

MAR

APR

MAY

JUN

JUL

AUG

SEP

OCT

NOV

DEC

THROUGH THE YEAR
THE BIRKS OF ABERFELDY

Winter is a great time to study the multitude of mosses around the gorge, after the trees have died back. Take an identification guide with you, and don't miss the very fine hair moss, fork moss, and tamarisk-leaved feather moss.

In **spring**, forest buds and blossom attract early-flying insects, which is encouraging for one of the Birks' most important breeding birds, the attractive pied flycatcher. Woodland plants light up the forest floor, as wild flowers like the yellow pimpernel, bugle, and sweet woodruff give way to creamy white carpets of wild garlic, also known as ramsons.

Red campion and wood crane's bill grow around the gorge in **summer**. You may see yellow and grey wagtails flit up and down the streams with bills crammed full of insects. The forest acts as a crèche for the many woodland birds that breed here, and young birds, such as woodpeckers and warblers, can be seen learning life skills from their parents. The pinkish-white bell-like flowers of wintergreen and the white flowers of wood vetch, finely lined with blue or purple, flourish between **June** and **August**.

WHERE ELSE TO SEE
AUTUMN COLOUR

Oak, ash, beech, birch, and maple woodland produces spectacular colours in autumn. For more suggestions of colourful displays near you, visit the Woodland Trust website (www.woodland-trust.org.uk).

The Hermitage, at Dunkeld in Perthshire, is a grove of giant oak, rowan, and Douglas and Scot's pine growing beside the dramatic waterfalls, rapids, and swirling pools of the river Braan. [SC]

Dendles Wood in Devon has barely been managed during its long history and is home to the rare barbastelle bat. [SW]

Dunkery and Horner Wood, in Somerset is an ancient sessile oakwood where you can see tawny owls, green woodpeckers, stoats, slow-worms, weasels, and squirrels. Heath fritillary butterflies breed there. Look out for red deer in October. [SW]

The myriad colours of this wildwood of birch, oak, and ash trees make autumn the perfect time to visit.

onto the dark, water-washed rocks, while others get carried away downstream by the frothing white water. Birch might be the predominant species here, but other trees cloak the steep edges, including ashes, oaks, and willows. As the path winds its way through the overhanging trees, the sheer power of the roaring falls can be felt, especially if you visit after heavy rain. In sheltered pools beside the cascading waters, dippers bob up and down on rocks; their white bibs are usually the first thing to catch your eye. Remarkably, these water-loving birds not only dive for their underwater prey – they also run along the bottom of the riverbed to catch it. Look for interesting fungi among the fallen leaves; russulas are probably the most common, but you should also see the unusual shapes of helvellas, otherwise known as "elfin saddles".

An amazing collection of ferns, liverworts, and mosses – feather, fork, and hair – prosper in the constant water spray of the gorge's cool depths. Almost the whole gorge has been designated a Site of Special Scientific Interest – but you might be happy just sitting on the same stone seat on which the poet Robert Burns sat in 1787, soaking up the magical atmosphere of the Birks.

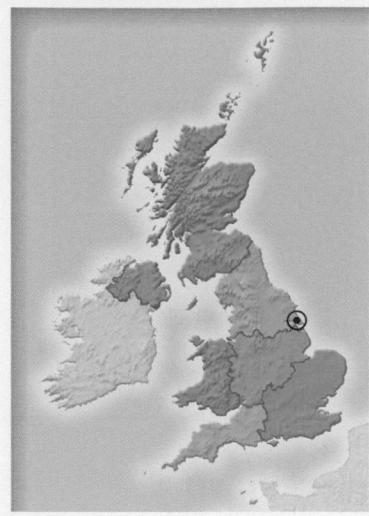

WHERE
Spurn Point, Spurn, near Kilnsea, Humberside
HU12 0UB; www.ywt.org.uk

CONTACT
Tel: 01964 650533 or 01904 659570;
info@yorkshirewt.cix.co.uk

GETTING THERE
The reserve is located at the extreme
southeastern tip of the Yorkshire coast, 32km
(20 miles) from Hull. By car, take the A1033
east towards Withernsea; then the B1445
from Patrington towards Easington village.
From Easington follow the brown tourist signs
to Spurn Point. The nearest train station is
Hull. By bus, take "The Spurn Ranger" (nos.
71 and 73) which runs from Withernsea
through Patrington to Spurn Point.

ACCESS AND FACILITIES
Wheelchair access is limited due to the
terrain, however there is disabled parking in
the car park at the end of the Point, with
toilets and a café. The are good viewpoints
from paths around the Point car park, plus
two viewing hides.

CHARGES
There is a charge to drive to the Point, but
once there, parking is free.

Beware buckthorn!

Spurn's dunes are dominated by sea buckthorn.
This invasive plant is native to the UK, and it
produces nutritious berries in winter that are a
vital food source for migrating birds. But be
careful around these bushes – brown-tail moth
has become established in them, and in autumn
you can see their silken tents in the branches.
The caterpillars (*above*) are covered in irritant
hairs that can trigger a severe reaction if you
touch them or breathe them in. Cuckoos have a
very tolerant digestion and feed on the caterpillars.

Above (left to right): Sea-buckthorn (*see feature box, below left*); the UK's smallest songbird, the goldcrest; fieldfare feeding on berries. **Main:** A landmark lighthouse sits above the dunes at Spurn Point.

MIGRATION IN ACTION

BIRD MIGRATION CAN PRODUCE SIGHTS AND SURPRISES throughout the country, especially in autumn. For the greatest chance of catching up with autumn migrants, it's best to head to a place with a good track record at a time when the winds are in the right direction. Spurn Point is one of Britain's classic birdwatching locations – especially in October. This fragile finger of sand stretches 5km (3 miles) south from Yorkshire into the Humber estuary, and it is best visited after easterlies. However, some migrants are likely to appear whatever the wind, which is why it is home to one of the UK's Bird Observatories. These are located around the coastline at strategic locations to record bird movements through ringing and observation.

Some birds typically migrate under the cover of night, such as warblers, flycatchers, and most of the chats. For a chance of seeing these, you'll need to be up at first light, examining all the available bushes and perches for anything that might have dropped in overnight. But for most people, the excitement lies in actually seeing the birds fly by – a phenomenon known as "visible migration". Spurn is spectacularly good for this, because its funnel shape helps to concentrate the birds as they fly southwards.

All you need to do is to find some shelter on the dunes, and then wait. The visible migration of swifts, swallows, and martins happens in July and August; as autumn sets in, they are replaced by pipits, larks, finches, thrushes, and pigeons – often as many as tens of thousands of birds per day. Identify them through a combination of flight action, silhouette, and particularly their call. If in doubt, remember that most of the birds you see will be common birds, rather than the hoped-for rarities. But stay a while, and be patient; you might just hear a chirping Richard's pipit among the "teezing" tree pipits, or a late honey buzzard – giving a tantalizing glimpse of the raptor migration within Europe.

In a landscape dominated by sea and sky, Spurn's narrow strip of sand and shrubs is a beacon for birds looking for food and rest on their long journey.

Inset: Spurn Point's sea buckthorn bushes provide food for a hungry blackcap. **Below (left to right):** Northern wheatear; snow buntings.

WHERE ELSE TO SEE
VISIBLE MIGRATION

Migration is something you can witness anywhere, from your office window or your garden, or indeed wherever you can see the sky. Even inland can be excellent – the heights of Parliament Hill on **Hampstead Heath** (*see pp110–111*) in London are renowned for it and anywhere within the great cross-country flyways, such as the Humber–Trent–Severn, or the Wash–Great Ouse–Lee Valley–Thames has a great chance of producing migrants.

For migrant birds, try any of the British Bird Observatories (www.birdobscouncil.org.uk), but note that many of them are not open all the time – always call to arrange a visit with the warden.

Landguard is an exposed sand and shingle peninsula in Suffolk that sees a breathtaking number of migrating birds, as does **Sandwich Bay** in Kent. Both locations also have bird observatories. [SE]

Further north, **Filey** in Yorkshire is good for watching birds moving south from the near continent and our own birds departing. [N]

THROUGH THE YEAR
SPURN POINT

Water birds flock to the sheltered mudflats of the Humber estuary, visible from the Point, during **winter**. You should see good numbers of shelducks and dark-bellied brent geese; when the tide is out, they will be joined by curlews, lapwings, dunlins, bar-tailed godwits, and a host of others.

In **spring**, the migrants start to reappear, usually in smaller numbers but some in much brighter plumage than during the autumn. Wheatears and black redstarts may well be the first, arriving usually from mid-March. Surprisingly, visible migration of birds such as swallows is often in a southerly direction.

The dunes are covered in flowers in **summer**: sea-holly, sea bindweed, and viper's-bugloss nestle among the sea-buckthorn bushes and clumps of marram grass. Little terns nest on the beach, hopefully within the protected fenced area. Keep an eye open for basking common lizards.

JAN
FEB
MAR
APR
MAY
JUN
JUL
AUG
SEP
OCT
NOV
DEC

Below: Sea bindweed grows on the dunes during the summer.

WHERE
Lough Foyle, Londonderry, Northern Ireland;
www.rspb.org.uk

CONTACT
RSPB Lough Foyle, tel: 028 9049 1547;
rspb.nireland@rspb.org.uk

GETTING THERE
By car, you can take any of a small number
of minor roads off the A2 between Limavady
and Londonderry. The site is 12.8km
(8 miles) from Londonderry. The RSPB
reserve is 6.4km (4 miles) from Route 93
of the National Cycle Network.

ACCESS AND FACILITIES
This is a remote site with no facilities, and
unimproved paths and trails. However, there
are good vantage points on the minor roads
off the A2 between Londonderry and
Limavady – either of these nearby towns
also have facilities.

OPENING TIMES
Open all year round.

CHARGES
None.

What lies beneath

Look out across the mud around Lough Foyle,
and you may wonder why it is so attractive to so
many birds. The answer is food. The light-bellied
Brent geese like grazing on the extensive beds of
eelgrass that grows on the mud in the autumn.
There are also plenty of lugworms (*below*) and
ragworms, shrimps, periwinkles, and vast mussel
beds concealed in the mud – all foods that the
clever waders can find by probing in the mud
with their different-shaped bills.

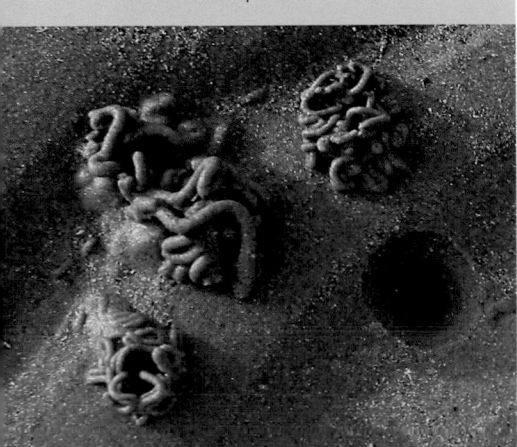

Above: Whooper swans arrive in large groups on the
mud banks of Lough Foyle.

Below (top and bottom): Dunlins probe for molluscs,
worms, and crustaceans along the lough; wigeons enjoy
the lough's shallow waters.

Right (top and bottom): A flock of oystercatchers; the
light-bellied Brent goose has a smudgy-white half collar.

Main: The mudflats and mussel beds of Lough Foyle, looking towards Donegal.

FLOCKING TO THE LOUGH

LOUGH FOYLE IS A LARGE SHALLOW SEA LOUGH OR INLET that combines with the river estuaries of the
Roe, Foyle, and Faughan to support an internationally important number of birds. The lough separates
County Londonderry from County Donegal, and it is the Londonderry side of the lough that is richest for birds.

A late-October visit should provide some wonderful birdwatching. Over 20,000 waterfowl arrive here in
autumn from Iceland, Greenland, and the Canadian Arctic to take advantage of Ireland's milder weather. Huge
flocks of of whooper swans and light-bellied Brent geese arrive, along with smaller flocks of Bewick's swans. The
later-arriving wigeons make the most of the lough's abundance of food, spending a few days – or sometimes a few
weeks – before dispersing to sites around Ireland. At low tide the mud and sand flats throng with waders: bar-
tailed godwits, oystercatchers, grey plovers, and curlews are easy to see, but look around too, at the river estuaries

JAN

FEB

MAR

APR

MAY

JUN

JUL

AUG

SEP

OCT

NOV

DEC

Across this vast intertidal lough, seagrass and mussel beds provide a feasting ground for waterfowl.

Above: Summer wild flowers on the banks of Lough Foyle.

THROUGH THE YEAR
LOUGH FOYLE

Look out for divers and grebes at high tide in **winter**, especially the great northern diver. Wildfowl and waders dominate the lough, especially whooper swans and light-bellied Brent geese. Winter stubble provides food for flocks of finches, larks, and buntings – and so, in turn, attracts raptors, including buzzards, kestrels, merlins, peregrines, and sparrowhawks.

In **spring**, there are still a few lingering winter visitors, while whimbrels visit on passage. The damp coastal pastures are home to breeding waders, especially lapwings. You'll hear the hedgerows begin to fill with birds, and may see linnets, song thrushes, reed buntings, bullfinches, yellowhammers, spotted flycatchers, and skylarks.

Terns and skuas can be seen off Magilligan Point in **summer**, and waders return from their breeding grounds by July. Check the sand dunes – they support interesting plants at this time of year, including the pyramidal orchid and creeping thyme. Inside the railway bridge is an area of saltmarsh vegetation, where you can watch the lapwings' aerobatic displays in early summer.

WHERE ELSE TO SEE
ESTUARY WILDLIFE

The intermingling of ocean salt water and river freshwater gives rise to a very productive ecosystem in estuaries and coastal loughs, providing vital plant material on the marshes for visiting birds. These areas are always great places to see winter wildlife.

The **Bann Estuary** on the North Antrim coast is good for wader watching in autumn. [NI]

Strangford Lough, County Down (see pp.288–289) is joined to the sea by a narrow strait, and has a number of small "islands" along its western shores. Huge numbers of Brent geese and grey seals spend the winter here. [NI]

Belfast Lough, Belfast (see pp.38–39), is an intertidal lough known for its flourishing mussel beds. It is home to an RSPB reserve, where the mudflats welcome significant numbers of winter waders. [NI]

where plentiful mud provides good feeding for dunlins, redshanks, and small numbers of wintering greenshanks. At high tide the lough attracts wintering divers and grebes, and the deeper water off Magilligan Point is a good place to look for them, especially the rarer Slavonian grebe. Magilligan Point is one of the largest sand-dune systems in the British Isles, and groups of sanderlings really make the most of it, scurrying to and fro on the shore as the waves wash in and out.

South of the point lies the Roe Estuary, the legendary roaming grounds of the very last Irish wolf. The Roe is at its best at high tide, when waders roost on the saltmarsh close to shore, their outlines ghostly as the dusk deepens. Peregrines and other raptors hunt overhead.

The lough has a rich and varied fish population including Atlantic salmon – which pass through the lough as they head for, or leave, their spawning grounds. Several species found here are listed as Red Data Book, or threatened, species, including allis shad, twaite shad, European smelt, and sea lamprey. The saltmarsh area inside the railway bridge is home to Lough Foyle's otters, which feed on the fish and crabs of the shallow pools, but are quick to hide.

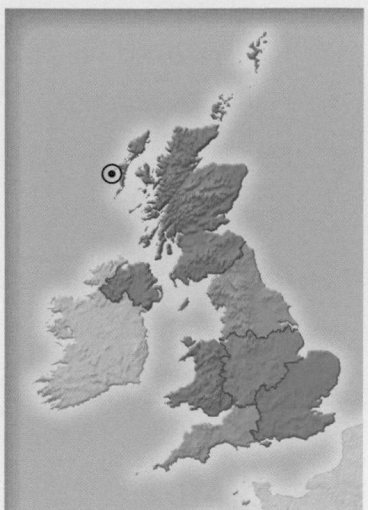

Left (left to right): The lighthouse on Sillay, or *Siolaigh*, westernmost of the Monachs; the beaches consist of calcium-rich shell-sand.

Right (left to right): Bulls and immature males gather on "bachelor beaches" during pupping; a seal pup shortly after losing its birth coat of white fur; the bulls return within weeks to mate.

WHERE
The Monach Isles, Western Isles, Scotland.

CONTACT
Scottish Natural Heritage, Stilligarry, Isle of South Uist, tel: 01870 620238.
The Uist Outdoor Centre, Loch Maddy, North Uist HS6 5AE is the main organizer of local trips to the islands, tel: 01876 500480 or visit www.uistoutdoorcentre.co.uk

GETTING THERE
The islands lie about 8km (5 miles) west of North Uist, and are visible from both North Uist and Benbecula. To see the seals, you need to take a local charter trip by boat from North Uist. Some wildlife-watching sea trips from Oban on the Scottish mainland include the Monach Isles.

ACCESS AND FACILITIES
Trips from North Uist outside the summer tourist season usually need to be chartered in advance and are weather-dependent; the Uist Outdoor Centre is a good source of information. This remote location is not easily accessible for wheelchair users, but boat trips are manageable by prior arrangement. The islands have no facilities of any sort, and trips do not normally include landing.

CHARGES
Charges vary for the boat trips.

Fattening up the pups
During the first few weeks, seal pups rely on their mother's milk, which is 60 per cent fat – during early life a pup can double its weight in one week. It is building a layer of blubber that will protect it from the cold, and sustain it while it refines its hunting skills. The mother fasts during the lactating period, but is finally forced to return to the sea to feed. The pup remains at the breeding ground for around two more weeks, before heading out to sea to fend for itself.

Main and far right: A pup cuddles up to its mother; male grey seals sparring in the surf around the island.

PUPPING GREY SEALS

AS YOU APPROACH THE SANDY BEACHES AND DUNES OF THE remote Monach Isles in October, a mass of bobbing heads rise to greet you. There are no people living here, the islands were abandoned in 1948 – these nodding heads belong to the largest colony of grey seals in Europe. The five low-lying isles are part of the Outer Hebrides; they lie 8km (5 miles) off the west coast of North Uist, and three of them are linked by shell-sand tombolos, or sandbars. Rocky reefs line the shores, and the shell content of the sandy beaches is reflected in the machair habitat (*see pp.108–109*) around the sand dunes, stabilized by the interweaving roots of marram grass.

The remoteness of these islands means the seals are rarely disturbed by humans during the breeding season. Estimates put the number of pups born in autumn at a staggering 9,000, and the total number of seals on the islands in the breeding season at around 30,000 animals – more than 25 per cent of the UK's entire grey seal

Above: A grey seal pup in the soft white coat in which it is born.

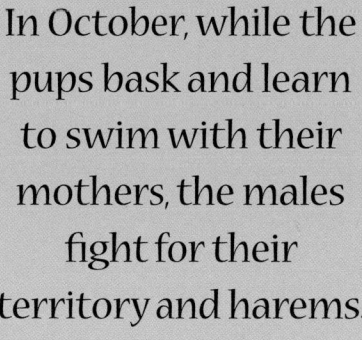
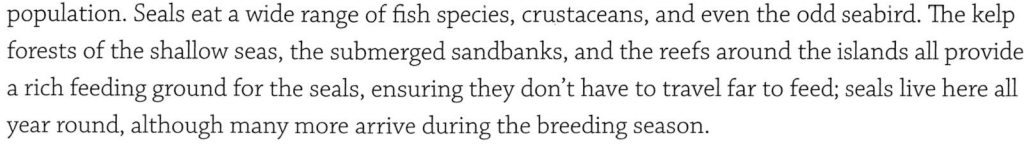

In October, while the pups bask and learn to swim with their mothers, the males fight for their territory and harems.

THROUGH THE YEAR
THE MONACH ISLANDS

The five Monach Islands – Ceann Ear, Shivinish, Ceann Iar, Sillay, and Stogay – are difficult to reach in **winter**, a time when the seals are joined by a wintering flock of around 500 barnacle geese.

The machair dune system starts to bloom in **spring**. This calcium-rich soil supports around 200 flowers, including stone-crop, kidney-vetch, thyme, heartsease, and bird's-foot trefoil. Oyster plant, a rare sub-Arctic plant of shingle beaches, can be seen growing on the shoreline of Stockay island.

The lack of cliff shelter on the islands means there are few seabirds in **summer**, but those that do come to the islands to breed include common, Arctic, and little terns (which make their nests in scoops in the sand); and a scattering of black guillemots, fulmars, shags, eiders, and dunlins.

WHERE ELSE TO SEE
SEALS PUPS

Seals produce their pups in the colder months of the year. In the UK, the pupping season runs between September and the end of December.

One of Britain's most accessible grey seal colonies can be found at **Donna Nook** in Lincolnshire. Visit from early November through to Christmas to see pups up close from special viewing areas. [M]

Blakeney Point in Norfolk (see pp.214–215) is home to a large colony of common seals, which produces hundreds of pups. Boats run regularly from Morston. [SE]

The **Farne Islands** (see pp.126–127) has a large grey seal colony that can be reached on boat trips from Seahouses in Northumberland. [N]

population. Seals eat a wide range of fish species, crustaceans, and even the odd seabird. The kelp forests of the shallow seas, the submerged sandbanks, and the reefs around the islands all provide a rich feeding ground for the seals, ensuring they don't have to travel far to feed; seals live here all year round, although many more arrive during the breeding season.

The grey seal's gestation period is just over 11 months, so the mating season follows close behind the pupping: the females give birth to the pups in October, and when they have finished suckling the pups, some three or four weeks later, they mate once more with the dominant males – known as "beach masters". These big male seals herd the females into harems of up to 10, which they defend aggressively from the amorous advances of rival males. After mating, the female seals can at last return to the sea to feed – they have been fasting during lactation.

If you can drag your eyes away from the seals, check offshore for divers and black guillemots, which can be seen around the islands throughout the year. Barnacle geese arrive during the autumn to graze; some using the islands for a short stop, others staying for the whole of the long winter.

JAN
FEB
MAR
APR
MAY
JUN
JUL
AUG
SEP
OCT
NOV
DEC

NOVEMBER

Where to Go: **November**

The clocks have changed: wrap up warm, and head for November, a month of stormy weather, but blessed with a wealth of colour and clarity that enduces a marvellous sense of tranquillity in those of us lucky enough to be outside. Birds are around in thrilling numbers; the marshes and grasslands on the coast welcome geese, ducks, and waders by the thousand. These birds are fresh from the Arctic, and have survived challenging journeys. The flocks of brent geese arriving at the southern estuaries have flown from far-off Siberia, while avocets are pausing before heading to their final winter refuges. This is a peak time for seeing estuary birds, which have come from all around the northern hemisphere. Even the towns feel the effect of the seasonal change;

ISLANDS

LINDISFARNE The wide-open shores of Holy Island.

PARKLAND AND GRASSLAND

RICHMOND PARK Around 350 fallow deer roam within the park.

WOODLANDS

CHURCH WOOD Flocks of bramblings forage and roost here.

LINDISFARNE
NORTHUMBERLAND [N]

This island, with its amazing lava rock shapes and complexity of habitats, is always worth visiting, but especially so in November, when the rockpools are fun and the birdwatching is outstanding.
See pp.274–275

RICHMOND PARK
RICHMOND, SURREY [SE]

The huge grounds of Richmond Park, so close to central London, are a great place to watch the rituals of the red deer rut, as the stags fight for supremacy.
See pp.276–277

SALTWELLS RESERVE
DUDLEY, WEST MIDLANDS [M]

Saltwells Wood lies at the heart of this reserve, its oak and beech trees sheltering many woodland birds. The incredible cliffs of Douton Claypit are well worth a visit.
See pp.282–283

CHURCH WOOD
HEDGERLEY, BUCKS [SE]

The beech mast attracts lots of birds in late autumn, including the hawfinch. An abundance of fungi grows among the fallen leaves.
See pp.280–281

HAVERGATE ISLAND
ALDEBURGH, SUFFOLK [SE]

This island is a winter haven for large numbers of ducks and wading birds. Birds of prey such as short-eared owls and marsh harriers hunt over the island.
See pp.286–287

The grass is crisp with frost, and all is quiet, until the silence is suddenly shattered by a fearsome, drawn-out roar – the rutting season has begun.

BEDGEBURY ARBORETUM
GOUDHURST, KENT [SE]

Part of Bedgebury forest, the arboretum has one of the world's best collections of rare conifers. Goldcrests and migrant firecrests shelter here in winter.
See pp.280–281

ISLE OF RUM
WEST HIGHLANDS [SC]

The Isle of Rum on the west coast of Scotland is a National Nature Reserve, with red deer, feral goats, and spectacular birds, incuding sea eagles and golden eagles.
See pp.276–277

ASHTON COURT
LONG ASHTON, BRISTOL [SW]

This country house has vast grasslands and woods, and a 600-year-old deer park, where you can see red and fallow deer.
See pp.276–277

FOREST OF DEAN
GLOUCESTERSHIRE [SE]

Stunning countryside and woodland coincide here. Deer and wild boar wander within the forest, and you can watch peregrines and goshawks diving for fun and for prey.
See pp.280–281

ISLE OF MULL
ARGYLL AND BUTE [SC]

One of Scotland's most stunning islands on the west coast, here you can see a staggering array of wildlife from otters and puffins to basking sharks and whales.
See pp.288–289

The Isle of Mull off the west coast of Scotland is a year-round destination for wildlife watching, both on land and at sea.

THETFORD FOREST
THETFORD, NORFOLK [SE]

The largest lowland forest in Britain never disappoints. Visit the arboretum for wonderful autumn colour.
See pp.276–277

Previous page: Strangford Lough estuary, Northern Ireland, at low tide.

any large suburban park is stunning when mists clear to reveal the glory of an autumn wood. In a few ancient parklands, the sound of roaring red deer carries your imagination straight to the Highlands. Wilder and more rural woodlands offer smaller, more subtle treasures: berries and fungi of many shapes and colours, and wandering flocks of feeding birds. In the rivers, November offers the chance to experience the truly magical migration of the salmon. returning from the sea, driven by the irresistible urge to spawn at their birthplace. The crystal clear waters of chalkstreams repay our attention with sightings of brown trout and graceful graylings. Foxes are often active by day, and badgers not long after dark. The natural world is preparing for winter.

LAKES AND WATERWAYS

ETTRICK WEIR Watch the salmon from underwater, via cameras.

WETLANDS

CONWY The fairytale turrets of the castle, seen from Conwy reserve.

INLETS AND ESTUARIES

EXE ESTUARY The RSPB reserve sits alongside the estuary.

ETTRICK WEIR
PHILIPHAUGH, SELKIRK [SC]

No one really understands the mysteries of salmon migration, but this is one of the best places to see salmon leaping, as they try to conquer the almost impossible height of the weir.
See pp.284–285

CENARTH FALLS
NEWCASTLE EMLYN, CEREDIGION [W]

The River Teifi tumbles down the Cenarth falls, where moss-covered rocks puncture the white water and dippers dive while salmon bravely leap.
See pp.284–285

TITCHWELL MARSH
HUNSTANTON, NORFOLK [SE]

This RSPB reserve has a maze of shallow lagoons surrounded by reedbeds that hide bearded reedlings and up to 20 different species of wader.
See pp.278–279

EXE ESTUARY
EXETER, DEVON [SW]

Whether you walk along the shore or travel the estuary by boat, you're likely to see ducks and geese, but especially avocets, sweeping their curved beaks through the water.
See pp.286–287

> The avocets, despite their inky-black wingtips, catch the eye because of their remarkable whiteness, and their curiously curved beaks.

BUCHANTY SPOUT
RIVER ALMOND, PERTHSHIRE [SC]

This powerful waterfall is one of the best places in Scotland to watch leaping salmon.
See pp.284–285

> The reserve is a breath of fresh air, hiding a rich mix of lakes, reedbeds, grassy meadows, and thickets. In winter it is a great place for ducks.

CONWY
CONWY [W]

A wetland reserve lies here between a busy road and the fast-flowing estuary. The views of nearby Conwy Castle are enhanced by the duck-watching to be had so close to the town.
See pp.278–279

FIRTH OF FORTH
FIFE/EAST LOTHIAN [SC]

This massive estuary is one of the best places in Britain to see migrating waders, bottlenose dolphins, porpoises, and grey seals, whose young are born in November.
See pp.274–275

FALLS OF SHIN
LAIRG, SUTHERLAND [SC]

Enjoy wonderful highland scenery and dramatic waterfalls, and experience the drama of leaping salmon trying to make their way home.
See pp.284–285

SANDWELL VALLEY
GREAT BARR, BIRMINGHAM [M]

Lying just outside West Bromich, this reclaimed land has become a renowned reserve. Its lakes and streams hold many attractions, including the nationally scarce goosander.
See pp.282–283

SNETTISHAM
HUNSTANTON, NORFOLK [SE]

Sit in the hides by the lagoons just behind the beach to see knots and goldeneyes. Huge numbers of waterfowl begin to gather for the oncoming winter.
See pp.308–309

STRANGFORD LOUGH
DOWNPATRICK, COUNTY DOWN [NI]

This huge sea lough near Belfast is known for its Ice-Age islands, marine life, winter birds, and grey seal colony – which will have pups in November.
See pp.288–289

MINSMERE
SUFFOLK [SE]

Nature trails at this RSPB reserve take you through woodland, heathland, and reedbeds. Red deer gather on the heath in late autumn, and Bewick's swans start to arrive for winter.
See pp.276–277

BURRY INLET
GOWER PENINSULA [W]

Large numbers of wintering wildfowl begin to gather on these huge sand and mudflats in November, perhaps because the tide regularly reveals the site's prodigious cockle beds.
See pp.288–289

WHERE
Lindisfarne (Holy Island), Berwick-upon-Tweed, Northumberland TD15 2SH; www.lindisfarne.org.uk

CONTACT
Berwick Tourist Information Office, tel: 01289 330733; lindisfarne-centre@uk2.net

GETTING THERE
By car, turn off the A1 towards Beal and Holy Island/Lindisfarne. As the metalled causeway linking Lindisfarne to the mainland floods at high tide, check tide times before departure at www.lindisfarne.org.uk. The nearest train and coach station is Berwick-upon-Tweed. On certain days a local bus service, no. 477, runs between Lindisfarne and Berwick.

ACCESS AND FACILITIES
Access around the island is tricky for wheelchairs due to the uneven terrain. Many of the attractions are wheelchair friendly; check beforehand. There are car parks, refreshments, and toilets in Holy Island village. The island also runs a minibus park-and-ride facility.

CHARGES
There are no charges for access to the island, but there are fees for individual attractions and car parking.

Be aware of the tides

This eerie line of posts marks the traditional route to the island from the mainland, known as the Pilgrims' Way. It is strongly recommended that you do not attempt this ancient route across the mudflats unless accompanied by someone with local knowledge, and above all never start to cross on a rising tide, or at dusk. The metalled causeway to the island used by traffic, while less atmospheric, is far safer for pedestrians; it has refuge stations for those who have left it too late to successfully complete the crossing.

Above (left to right): Shore crabs and beadlet anemones hide in rock pools; the extraordinary rocks of Lindisfarne's shores.
Main: Lindisfarne Castle sits above the igneous formation of Beblowe Crag.

ON HOLY ISLAND

T HE FIRST THING THAT STRIKES YOU ABOUT LINDISFARNE – or Holy Island – is the extraordinary variety of rock types. The island is low-lying, with shore-line coal seams that withstood igneous activity over 300 million years ago, as molten rock squeezed through the seams and solidified into resistant bands. This was how the striking forms of the Whin Sill and the shapely Beblowe Crag – a cone-shaped eminence supporting Lindisfarne Castle – were created.

Sand dunes cover the northern parts of Lindisfarne, with open sea to the east, and sheltered mudflats and saltmarsh to the west. This complexity of habitat creates a wonderful area for the naturalist and geologist, all on an exposed part of the northeast coast that makes it a natural landfall for tired migrant birds from across the North Sea. Stay over while the tide is high and you experience the remoteness and quiet of this extraordinarily historic island, just as the monks did 1,300 years ago. With its castle, ruined monastery, history and legends, and hosts of birds, Holy Island is a truly memorable place.

This ancient place
of religious pilgrimage,
cut off from the
mainland twice a day by
the rising tide, now
draws nature-lovers
to its shores.

In summer, Lindisfarne is renowned for its plants, but in winter people visit for the birds. The island is great for wigeons, teals, pintails, dunlins, oystercatchers, and bar-tailed godwits, but the star birds are the pale-bellied brent geese. You can get quite close as they grunt and forage in the shallow water, or potter about on the mud, to the sounds of the ringing notes of redshanks and curlews, and the haunting, triple whistles of grey plovers.

When the tide falls, head for the rockpools. Have fun watching shellfish such as limpets, mussels, whelks, and periwinkles; and trace the darting shapes of gobies and the sideways-scuttling shore crabs. In deeper pools, under the shade of rocks, look for the dark red of beadlet anemones, waving their spindly arms, or closed up, like little red blobs of jelly. Deeper still are the jewels: the 15-spined sticklebacks, wrasse, and northern octopuses.

Inset: Lindisfarne, looking towards Emmanuel Head.
Below (left to right): A curlew feeds; the saltmarsh and mudflats of the west.

WHERE ELSE TO SEE
ROCKPOOLS

Rockpooling is a fascinating pastime, and keeps both children and adults amused for hours. Rock pools can be found on any coast with rocky ledges, as the sea retreats at low tide.

Enjoy rock pools on rocky shores around Aberdeen, around the **Firth of Forth** (see pp.296–297), and on the deeply indented western shores of Argyll. [SC]

The Gower Peninsula (see pp.122–123) has excellent rock pools from Mumbles to Worm's Head. Look carefully, as some of the potential finds are miniature, such as the tiny feather star. The rock pools under **Mumbles Pier** at low tide have very interesting inhabitants. [W]

Rockpooling and fossil-hunting vie as the main attraction at **Lyme Bay** (see pp.298–299), a glorious sweep of Jurassic and Triassic rock formations on the Devon and Dorset coast, in the south of England. [SW]

THROUGH THE YEAR
LINDISFARNE

The birds build in number in **winter**: the pale-bellied brent geese are joined by thousands of wigeon and other wildfowl and increasing numbers of pink-footed geese, pintails and shelducks. Numbers of wildfowl and waders rise to around 50,000 birds.

Spring sees migrant birds arriving, such as red-backed shrikes and bluethroats, and occasionally marsh harriers, ospreys, honey buzzards, white storks, and icterine and subalpine warblers.

Lindisfarne is famously rich in flowers during the **summer**, including orchids such as marsh helleborines, common spotted, northern and early marsh orchids, and the Lindisfarne helleborine, a unique species closely related to the dune helleborine, protected by an enclosure on the dunes. Grey seals and common seals can be seen between the island and the mainland.

Below: Swallows nest on the island in spring.

JAN
FEB
MAR
APR
MAY
JUN
JUL
AUG
SEP
OCT
NOV
DEC

RUTTING RED DEER

A STILL, LATE-AUTUMN DAWN, THE GRASS CRISP WITH FROST. All is quiet, until the silence is suddenly shattered by a fearsome, drawn-out roar. It is a red deer stag, Britain's largest land mammal, advertising his presence, his power, and his control over a harem of females to any potential rivals. And what an impressive sight he is, his magnificent branched antlers held high, his hot breath condensing around him in the cool autumn air.

The rutting season lasts for a couple of months, and for much of the time such posturing is the limit of his display. But at its peak, and when rivals cannot be separated on roars alone, the rut turns physical. Heads down, antlers locked, the stags push at each other

In Richmond Park you can see the "Monarch of the Glen" in all his glory, just 15km (9 miles) from St Paul's Cathedral. Virtually unchanged since its creation in the 17th century, this royal park is also home to badgers, foxes, and tawny owls.

WHERE
Richmond Park, Richmond on Thames, Surrey TW10 5HS; www.royalparks.org.uk

CONTACT
Richmond Park Office, tel: 020 8948 3209; richmond@royalparks.gsi.gov.uk

GETTING THERE
Richmond Park is only about 20 minutes from central London. Richmond Station is served both by overground and underground trains. By bus, catch the 371 or 65 to the pedestrian gate at Petersham.

ACCESS AND FACILITIES
There are six free car parks within the park. There are also cafés, restaurants, and refreshment points throughout the park. There is a car park reserved for disabled-badge-holders only, near the Isabella Plantation.

OPENING TIMES
The park is open all year round, from 7.00am in summer and 7.30am in winter, closing at dusk. Specific opening and closing times can be found on the Royal Parks website.

CHARGES
None.

powerfully, each trying to force the other to give ground. The risks are evident: those sharp points can inflict serious, or even mortal, wounds. The rewards though are great – the dominant male wins the chance to father all of the next year's offspring from the harem.

One great place to witness this annual trial of strength is Richmond Park, one of London's "green lungs", which has around 300 red deer. Gates open at 7.30am, so by the end of the month there is plenty of time to get into the heart of the action before the sun rises. There are also some 350 fallow deer, and these too have a rut, albeit a little less noisy and dramatic. Take care not to disturb the deer with your appearance or scent – keep your distance, and remain downwind wherever possible.

The Park was first enclosed in 1637, as a royal hunting park. The ancient trees, many of which pre-date the enclosure, have been managed as pollards, so that succulent new growth is produced above the reach of the deer. This has left the trunks to grow thick and old; healthy – but hollow, or full of dead wood. Perfect, in fact, for wood-dwelling beetles. This superlative site has more than 1,350 species of beetles – over a quarter of the total British list. No wonder, then, that it is given the highest level of nature conservation protection.

Main: A majestic red deer stag lifts his head to roar.
Below (left to right): Dawn is a wonderful time to watch the deer; there are around 350 fallow deer in the park.
Inset: Red deer stags clash antlers during rutting.

Hybrid deer

Truly native populations of red deer are now rather localized, mostly in Scotland, Exmoor, and the Quantock Hills, but for centuries they have been kept in semi-domestication in deer parks, such as Richmond. Much of the UK now has free-roaming populations, but almost all now show signs of "genetic pollution". This is often the result of interbreeding with a smaller, introduced Asian species, the sika deer (*below*), which has a distinctive white rump patch.

Above: Fallow deer males – called "bucks" – fight in the rutting season.

WHERE ELSE TO SEE
RUTTING RED DEER

Free-roaming red deer populations can today be found in many parts of the country, especially where there are commercial forestry plantations or other extensive woodlands.

The forested areas of **Thetford Forest**, on the Norfolk/Suffolk border, and the **Suffolk Sandlings** have large deer populations; catch up with the rut by joining an RSPB safari from **Minsmere** nature reserve (*see pp.100–101*). [SE]

Given the extent of available habitat in Scotland, you can see deer in many places, though they are particularly wonderful to see on the islands of **Rum** and **Mull** (*see pp.226–227*). Otherwise, try the Forestry Commission's **Galloway Forest Park** (*see pp.234–235*), which at 780 sq km (300 sq miles) is the largest forest park in Britain. [SC]

For outstanding photo-opportunities, the semi-wild red and fallow deer within the Repton landscape of **Ashton Court**, Bristol, are hard to beat. [SW]

THROUGH THE YEAR
RICHMOND PARK

As the rut dies down, the park seems to slumber. But **winter** is still a great time to visit – with the leaves off, it is possible to really see the trees, their individual unique shapes formed by centuries of human management and deer browsing.

As **spring** approaches, birds start to become more vocal, including those that use the park's dead-wood resource: three species of woodpecker, each with a distinctive drumming; stock doves, little and tawny owls, and, increasingly, ring-necked parakeets.

Early **summer** sees the emergence of the most impressive, and internationally protected, of the park's beetles: the stag beetle. And while most of the park's huge range of fungi appear in the autumn, one of the rarest – the oak polypore – fruits in high summer. At the same time, the acidic grasslands are in full flower; carpets of harebells contrasting beautifully with white heath bedstraw and yellow tormentil.

JAN
FEB
MAR
APR
MAY
JUN
JUL
AUG
SEP
OCT
NOV
DEC

WHERE
Conwy RSPB Nature Reserve, Llandudno Junction, Conwy LL31 9XZ, North Wales.

CONTACT
RSPB Nature Reserve, tel: 01492 584091; conwy@rspb.org.uk

GETTING THERE
The reserve lies off junction 18 of the A55, and is signposted from there. The nearest train station is Llandudno Junction, which is a 10-minute walk away from the reserve. By bus, catch the no.27 bus from Llandudno to the large A55 roundabout – the reserve lies on the south side of the roundabout, and is signposted. By bicycle, follow National Cycle Network Route no. 5.

ACCESS AND FACILITIES
The visitor centre is wheelchair-friendly and has parking, toilets, a café, and picnic area. Along the trails there are three viewing hides and two nature trails, totalling 4.8km (3 miles), which are accessible by wheelchairs and pushchairs. There is a childrens' activities table, and two childrens' activity trails.

OPENING TIMES
The visitor centre is open every day (except Christmas Day) from 9.30am to 5pm.

CHARGES
A small charge for non-RSPB members.

Strong beaks

Wildfowl are web-footed water birds, adapted to a variety of lifestyles. Swans graze on dry land, and browse on underwater plants by upending and using their long necks. Geese (like the greylag shown below) eat grass and roots; they have thick, strong beaks with a stout "nail" at the tip. Dabbling ducks eat grain, grass, shoots, and roots on dry land, and sieve seeds from shallow water. Diving ducks catch aquatic invertebrates and eat shellfish and aquatic plants.

Left: Conwy Castle sits on a rock above the estuary.

Right (left to right): The teal has a distinctive black stripe on its head; the yellow-foreheaded wigeon; a mallard in flight; the sharp-billed red-breasted merganser.

Right, below: The chunky shelduck lives in large numbers on the estuary.

Main: The sheltered coastal lagoons of the RSPB reserve sit beside the Conwy Estuary.

DUCKS OF CONWY CASTLE

THE NORTH WALES COAST IS A SERIES OF WONDERFUL SANDY BAYS. You can really appreciate the changing nature of the land if you travel by train from Chester to Holyhead, which takes you past the wide sweeps of Liverpool Bay and the broad shoulders of the Great Orme, before diving into a tunnel alongside the wonderful bulk of Conwy Castle, just as you're straining to see the beautiful estuary that has appeared on your left, snaking towards the magnificent hills of Snowdonia.

It's here that a rather incongruous nature reserve has been created, based on lagoons that were scooped out to provide foundations for the road. Positioned between the busy road and the full, fast-flowing estuary – which turns into a vast mudflat at low tide – the reserve is a breath of fresh air, hiding a rich mix of lakes, reedbeds, grassy meadows, and hawthorn thickets. In winter it is a great place for ducks, which are such

THROUGH THE YEAR
CONWY

In **spring**, you can see all the birds at Conwy in their bright breeding colours. Look for migrants such as little egrets, sandpipers, wheatears, whitethroats, and sedge warblers. Lapwings also nest here.

In **summer** the reserve really comes to life, as the grasslands become covered in wild flowers, attracting many of the commoner butterflies. You might see a stoat or weasel; polecats live here too, but they are much harder to find.

Large numbers of waders pass through here in the **autumn**, and many remain for the winter. Watch the skies above the nearby woods for buzzards, and don't miss the spectacular roosts of the starlings, which gather in the reedbeds.

WHERE ELSE TO SEE
WINTER WILDFOWL

Coastlines and estuaries around the country are often rich in wildfowl, especially during the winter, but there also some good inland sites.

The **Burry Inlet** at the other end of Wales is good for wildfowl, including Penclacwydd near Llanelli. The saltmarshes here have little egrets and offer a chance of seeing hen harriers and peregrines. [W]

You may see good numbers of ducks on the lagoons beside Morecambe Bay at **Leighton Moss** (*see pp.78–79*), Lancashire. [N]

Slimbridge (*see pp.34–35*), on the Severn estuary, is excellent for wild ducks, swans, and geese. [M]

In Norfolk, **Titchwell Marsh** is excellent for close views of shovelers, teals, pintails, and other ducks. Lady Ann's Drive, at **Holkham** (*see pp.18–19*), can be great for geese. [SE]

Vane Farm on **Loch Leven**, Perth & Kinross (*see pp.260–261*), is a fine wildfowl site, as is **Loch of Strathbeg**, north of Aberdeen. [SC]

JAN
FEB
MAR
APR
MAY
JUN
JUL
AUG
SEP
OCT
NOV
DEC

Situated on the banks of the Conwy estuary, with views of Snowdonia and Conwy Castle, this a true wildlife haven.

a delight to watch: nothing is so relaxing and so good for relieving the stress and rush of modern living. The large green-headed mallards potter about in a familiar way on their distinctive bright-orange legs, while the smaller wigeons waddle forwards on their short, dark legs, in dense packs, looking for food. Teals are the smallest of the ducks, and look rather dark, but the males are intensely coloured when seen well in good light; visit one of Conwy's spacious hides for some great close-up views. You might also see a few pintails, shovelers, tufted ducks, and pochards.

Perhaps the most spirited and sharply dressed duck is the red-breasted merganser: the drake has a terrific spiky crest and a long, bright-red, serrated beak, which is ideal for catching fish when it dives under the water. Its glossy green head resembles a mallard's, but it is a sleeker bird, designed for underwater living. The shelduck, on the other hand, is massively built – almost a goose – as you'll notice when it appears on the mud or lagoons, or flies overhead, its wings whistling. Its striking whiteness – set off by touches of black, a broad chestnut band around the chest, and the brightest red bill in the bird world – make it entirely unmistakable.

Above: Stoats can be seen around the reserve in summer.

Left: The colourful but poisonous fly agaric toadstool grows in Church Wood.

Right (left to right): A bullfinch enjoying guelder rose berries; the great tit, a strident woodland songster; the colourful greenfinch; the nuthatch likes to scurry up and down tree trunks.

WHERE
Church Wood RSPB reserve, Hedgerley, Gerrards Cross, Buckinghamshire SL2 3UY; www.rspb.org.uk

CONTACT
RSPB Church Wood, tel: 01865 351163.

GETTING THERE
Church Wood lies in Hedgerley village, about 5km (3 miles) from junction 2 of the M40. Walk down the private track to the right of the village pond, then follow the footpath for 200m (660ft). The reserve entrance is on the left, through a kissing gate. The nearest train station is Gerrards Cross. By bus, take the no. 40 bus from Slough to Hedgerley.

ACCESS AND FACILITIES
Park in Hedgerley village. There are no facilities at the site. The wood's paths are unimproved and therefore not suitable for wheelchairs, although they are negotiable with a pushchair. There is one marked trail of 2km (1¼ miles) on sloping ground accessed by a kissing gate; the ground here gets muddy when wet.

CHARGES
None, but donations to RSPB are welcomed.

The powerful hawfinch

Hawfinches are notoriously elusive. They love hornbeams, so stand at a little distance from one and scan the treetops against the sky – the birds often sit, upright and thickset, on the topmost perches. Sometimes you see them on the ground, hard to spot in the leaf litter. If you accidentally get too close, they fly off, with a flash of broad white wingbars and an eye-catching pure-white tip to the tail. Then you might hear their characteristic sharp, explosive ticking notes.

Main: The orange shoulders of the male bramblings make for a dazzling flock in flight. **Right panel:** A sapling beech grows from a seed dropped by its parent.

FLIGHTS OF FINCHES

FINCHES ARE SMALL, COMPACT, TRIANGULAR-BILLED BIRDS with distinctive calls. Some, such as siskins, are acrobatic and can swing upside-down to feed at the tips of the smallest twigs, while others, such as chaffinches, are comparatively heavy, short-legged, and nowhere near so agile, so they have to feed mostly on the ground. All of the finches' beaks are to some extent adapted to their foods: the goldfinch's thin, tweezer-like bill can take seeds from thistle heads and teasels; the greenfinch's thick, sharp-edged beak deals easily with tough-skinned berries and can peel husks from large seeds. The bull-headed hawfinch (*see picture, left*) has several adaptations: a conical bill, strong tongue, and muscular cheeks; it can crack the hardest stones of wild cherries, and extract the seeds of beech and hornbeam trees. The bullfinch has a round, stubby beak, for nibbling fleshy berries and young, soft buds – making it very unpopular among gardeners.

JAN

FEB

MAR

APR

MAY

JUN

JUL

AUG

SEP

OCT

NOV

DEC

THROUGH THE YEAR
CHURCH WOOD

A good beech wood such as Church Wood is an all-year venue for the wildlife enthusiast. The finches stay for the **winter**, still singing on warmer days. Goldcrests, redpolls, and treecreepers flit among the trees. Keep an eye on the sky for buzzards and red kites, and be ready for a glimpse of a roe deer or muntjac.

In **spring**, arrive early for the incredible dawn chorus and enjoy the swathes of bluebells, as well as wood anemone, wood sorrel, and primroses. Great stitchwort grows along the southern path. The honeysuckle and butcher's broom are buzzing with bumblebees.

In **summer** look for white admiral butterflies in the open areas and red admiral, marbled white, comma, and peacock butterflies along the woodland edges. The birds are busy feeding their young, while centaury, lady's smock, and fleabane add colour to the meadow area.

WHERE ELSE TO SEE
FINCHES

Warmer winters have led to increased numbers of finches in Britain, with larger numbers visiting from Scandinavia. You may be able to spot goldfinches and yellow and black siskins in your own garden; if not, head south to see these pretty birds.

Blashford Lakes, north of Ringwood on the Hampshire/Dorset border, can be brilliant for finches on the feeders around the visitor centre. [SE]

You have a good chance of seeing finches, and even hawfinches, at **Virginia Water** in Surrey and **Bedgebury Arboretum** in Kent. **Blean Woods** near Canterbury, in Kent, can also be excellent. [SE]

The Forest of Dean in the **Wye Valley** (*see pp.80–81*), Gloucestershire, is home to the rare hawfinch. [M]

The fruit of the beech tree used to be called a "buck" – the county of Buckinghamshire takes its name from its beech woods.

Most bird populations fluctuate from year to year, and in winter, they must have seeds: a poor crop combined with harsh weather can lead to a very low breeding population of birds the following spring. Church Wood is a wonderful larder: its beech trees produce an abundance of seed in good years, and "beech mast" – the small, spiny-cased nuts of this lovely tree – is the perfect take-away for this group of birds. The beech mast ripens in November, making this a great time to visit the wood – finches visit in large numbers, along with chaffinches, great tits, and nuthatches.

In November you will also see bramblings, from continental Europe. These are close relatives of the chaffinch, with yellow beaks, whiter bellies, and orange wing patches. They forage beneath the trees in groups with the chaffinches, dashing up into the treetops if you get too close. As you walk around Church Wood, listen for their short "chup" calls, then watch for the flash of the chaffinches' white wingbars and the bramblings' white rumps as they fly. Then back off a little, be patient and let them drift back, to see them on the ground. There you can appreciate their rich colours and patterns, and the subtle differences between these two gregarious birds.

Below: Bluebells cover the ground in spring.

WHERE
RSPB Sandwell Valley, 20 Tanhouse Avenue, Great Barr, Birmingham, West Midlands B43 5AG.

CONTACT
Tel: 0121 3577395;
sandwellvalley@rspb.org.uk

GETTING THERE
From Birmingham, take the A34 to Scott Arms; turn left into A4041 (Newton Road); then take the B4167 (Hamstead Road); and follow the RSPB signs. You can walk to the reserve from Hampstead train station, and there are regular buses from Birmingham. The reserve lies on the Sustrans National Cycle Network route 5.

ACCESS AND FACILITIES
The visitor centre is wheelchair friendly and has parking, toilets, baby-changing facilities, and refreshments. There are good walking trails and viewing areas easily accessible for all abilities.

OPENING TIMES
The reserve is open at all times but the visitor centre opening times vary, opening at either 9am or 10am and closing at 5pm. Check before arrival.

CHARGES
None.

The worm-detector

In late autumn, numbers of snipe (*pictured*) build up. These striped brown birds probe soft mud with their long, straight beaks. The bill tip is sensitive and flexible enough to detect and grasp a worm underground. If disturbed, snipe fly up with loud calls, like the tearing of cloth, and zigzag high into the sky. Jack snipes are smaller, shorter-billed, and always much scarcer: they sit tight until almost trodden on, then flutter quietly away before dropping again, out of sight.

Above (top to bottom): The distinctive crest of the lapwing can be seen even when the bird is in flight; a little ringed plover, easily identified by its yellow eye ring.

Below: Sandwell Valley Country Park abuts the RSPB reserve and offers wonderful walks.

Right panel: Little grebes on the waters of the reserve.

Inset: A goldfinch perches on teasel, its favourite food.

Main: A flock of wigeons approaching land as they arrive in the Sandwell Valley.

RESTORED GLORIES

YOU MIGHT NOT EXPECT TO FIND AN AREA OF GREEN LANDSCAPES, shimmering blue pools, and plentiful wildlife in the wedge of land between the M6 and M5 motorways, a mile from the middle of West Bromwich. Here, though, is the Sandwell Valley, part of the Tame Valley and formerly woodland, farmland, and, in the peak of the coal mining era, the busy Hamstead and Jubilee Collieries. After the mines closed and the motorways were built, the area was landscaped into 8sq km (3 sq miles) of open space, with nine protected nature reserves. Its lakes, ponds, streams, and bogs attract resident and migratory wildfowl, including geese, swans, and ducks.

Forge Mill Lake in the RSPB nature reserve, and Swan Pool in the adjoining country park, lie to the east of the M5 motorway and offer the best possibilities for water birds. On Forge Mill Lake during the winter, there may be as many as 80 goosanders, which is extraordinary, as this large and beautiful fish-eating duck is generally scarce

Above: Sandwell Valley's lagoons in spring.

The brightly coloured goldfinch is a sociable bird, twittering loudly as it eases out tricky teasel seeds using its long, fine beak.

THROUGH THE YEAR
SANDWELL VALLEY

Many of the birds that arrive in autumn stay for the **winter,** including the wigeons, teals, pochards, and goosanders. Occasional goldeneyes pass through. Grey herons can be seen feeding on the lake and marsh pool. In January, listen out for the singing of an early great tit, hinting at the coming spring.

In **spring**, lapwings and plovers display and sing. Sedge and reed warblers, whitethroats, and garden warblers arrive, while sand martins pass through. Reed buntings and dunnocks sing their hearts out, as the willow tits begin nesting in standing deadwood around the RSPB reserve.

In **summer**, swifts, swallows, and house martins hunt over the lakes. Dragonflies fly erratically over the water. Light blue flowers of wild chicory make a stunning display, while teasel grows tall and spiky in readiness for hungry hordes of colourful goldfinches seeking food later in the year.

WHERE ELSE TO SEE
RESCUED LAND

Old quarries and mining sites represent unique challenges, but are worth the trouble: they have the potential to return huge areas of land back to nature.

Ifton Meadows nature reserve at St Martins, Shropshire, formerly a coal-mining area, is now a peaceful wildlife haven noted for its 300-year-old woodland – Price's Dingle – and its skylarks. [M]

The land at **Saltwells Nature Reserve**, near Dudley, has been used for many things, including a colliery and clay pit. The old clay pit is now a Site of Special Scientific Interest, and is home to hundreds of orchids, and a large population of reptiles. [M]

Cwmllwyd Wood, on the southern slope of Cockett Valley, Swansea, was a coal mining area from the 17th–20th centuries. The site includes 100-year-old oak trees and lots of apple trees – believed to have grown from the discarded apple-cores of miners. [W]

in lowland Britain. A big flock simply dominates the water, sailing like a fleet of small ships: the males, especially, in their clean salmon-pink with green-black heads and long, plum-red beaks, are very impressive. Up to 60 wigeons may be grazing on the shore, while a scattering of teals, shovelers, mallards, tufted ducks, and pochards sit on the open water. On a sunny day, especially, it is worth looking closely at all of these, for ducks are amongst the most richly colourful birds in Britain.

Look carefully amongst the ducks and coots and you'll find small numbers of both great crested and little grebes, which spend about as much time under water as on top of it. The great crested grebes have elegant, slender necks and silky-white fronts, while the little grebes are round, dumpy, and dark brown. Cormorants – those great divers, whose powers of diving to 35m (115ft) are hardly tested here – are also found on the water, while handsome Canada and greylag geese strut around the grassy surrounds. In winter, large numbers of lapwings come to the reserve from the cold north-east and mainland Europe. Fieldfares and redwings gather in the poplar trees before going off to roost as the skies begin to darken at the end of the day.

JAN
FEB
MAR
APR
MAY
JUN
JUL
AUG
SEP
OCT
NOV
DEC

LEAPING SALMON

FOR THOUSANDS OF YEARS THE HEADWATERS of British rivers have been used as breeding sites by the magnificent Atlantic salmon. Having spent most of their adult lives in the ocean, the salmon somehow return to the rivers where they were born, perhaps by following some distinctive trace in the river water as it flows out to sea. This achievement alone is miraculous, but the fish then swim upriver to spawn in the upland reaches – a journey that involves leaping rapids, waterfalls, and even artificial barrages. One of the most spectacular of these runs takes place on the River Ettrick, where the obstacle of Ettrick Weir forces the fish to put on the performance of their lives.

The salmon make their way upstream in autumn when heavy rain has swollen the river, so November is one of the best times to watch them. They congregate in the deep, well-oxygenated pools below the weir, waiting for the ideal time to make their attempt. If you visit the nearby Philiphaugh Salmon Viewing Centre you can watch them

WHERE
Ettrick Weir, on the River Ettrick, Philiphaugh, Selkirk, Selkirkshire TD7 5LX, Scotland; salmonviewingcentre.com

CONTACT
Philiphaugh Salmon Viewing Centre, tel: 01750 21766; mss@philiphaugh.com

GETTING THERE
By car, take the A7 to Selkirk, then take the Moffat Road (A708) out of the village, for approximately 2km (1 mile), following signs to the viewing centre at Philiphaugh Farm.

ACCESS AND FACILITIES
The viewing centre has live footage relayed from the river onto a big screen, on which a short film showing underwater highlights is shown if no fish are leaping at the time of your visit. The centre is accessed across a bridge with slats, which can prove tricky for wheelchairs. There is free car parking, and toilets; wheelchair users may use the disabled-access toilets in the Waterwheel Restaurant, within the centre's car park.

OPENING TIMES
The viewing centre opens 9am–5pm daily.

CHARGES
None.

A helping hand home

Two centuries ago salmon even migrated up the Thames to spawn. But pollution and the proliferation of locks and weirs eventually made the journey impossible. The same problem afflicted many other British rivers, and for decades you had to visit the unpolluted, free-flowing rivers of Scotland and Ireland to see salmon on their annual migration. But many rivers have now been cleaned up, and "fish ladders" (as above) built to enable the fish to bypass artificial barriers are helping salmon recolonize their ancestral waters.

Main: The spectacular leaping of salmon at Ettrick Weir.

Left: The salmon leap waterfall on the River Ettrick.

Right (left to right): Atlantic salmon resting in calm waters before attempting their jump; the young of Atlantic salmon, in the same birthplace as their parents.

Right panel (top and bottom): An otter feeding on fish from the river; a grey heron spies out prey.

underwater, thanks to live images relayed from up to five submerged cameras. The big fish power up through the water and into the air as they try to clear the torrent flowing over the weir. The task looks impossible, and many fish fail. But others succeed, landing above the falls and driving themselves forward against the flow in a last desperate effort to reach calmer water. You feel like applauding. These fish are not like the silvery salmon raised in fish farms. They are in full breeding condition, with dark backs and reddish flanks. Once above the weir, the determined fish keep moving upstream until they reach the shallow, gravel-bedded headwaters. Here the females shed their eggs, which are then fertilized by the males. Exhausted by the effort, most then make easy prey for herons, otters, and other predators. But deep in the gravel their eggs develop into young fish that, after about three years, head out to sea to feed. Then one day they, too, will instinctively make their way back to leap the rushing waters of Ettrick Weir.

The spectacular leap of a salmon here is the last stage of a journey that started 4,000km (2,500 miles) away.

WHERE ELSE TO SEE
SALMON LEAPING

The best places to see leaping migrant salmon are all in the north and west. This is because salmon are more numerous here, and the rivers are more dramatic, with waterfalls and rapids tumbling over hard rock. This poses a real challenge to the salmon, and ensures some spectacular action as they attempt to leap the white water.

Buchanty Spout, on the River Almond in Perthshire, is a powerful waterfall and one of the best places in Scotland to watch leaping salmon. Another excellent site in the area is the **Linn of Tummel**, just north of Pitlochry. [SC]

The **Falls of Shin**, near Lairg in Sutherland, is a truly spectacular salmon leap, with good viewing facilities and a nearby visitor centre. [SC]

The **Cenarth Falls**, on the river Teifi near Newcastle Emlyn, are famous for their leaping salmon. Viewing areas and pathways allow easy access for everyone and provide wonderful views of the falls. [W]

THROUGH THE YEAR
ETTRICK WEIR

In **winter** the river near the weir is a good place to look for dippers, small wren-like birds that hunt for insects underwater by walking along the riverbed against the waterflow. You may also see grey wagtails, herons, and fish-hunting goosanders. Arrive early enough, and you may spot an otter.

Kingfishers nest in holes in the riverbank in **spring**, and can be seen flashing up and down the river as they carry fish back to their young. Check overhanging trees for perched birds, and you may see one catch a fish. Swallows also nest in the barns around the Philiphaugh Salmon Viewing Centre.

In **summer**, watch for buzzards soaring on thermals, and hunting kestrels, merlins, and peregrines. Further afield in nearby woodlands, look out for red squirrels.

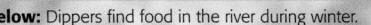
Below: Dippers find food in the river during winter.

JAN FEB MAR APR MAY JUN JUL AUG SEP OCT **NOV** DEC

Left (left to right): A brent goose taking off; the RSPB reserve on the Exe Estuary.

Below left (top and bottom): A ringed plover; thousands of birds winter on the estuary.

Right (left to right): An avocet foraging in the mud; avocets take to the skies; a shelduck and an avocet squabble for territory.

WHERE
Exe Estuary, Exeter, Devon; www.rspb.org.uk

CONTACT
RSPB Visitor Centre, Darts Farm Village, Topsham, Devon EX3 0QH, tel: 01392 879438; info@rspb.org.uk

GETTING THERE
The reserve is two areas of coastal grazing marsh – Exminster Marshes and Bowling Green Marsh. Both are 8km (5 miles) south of Exeter on either side of the Exe Estuary. The RSPB Visitor Centre is located at Darts Farm Village, off the A376 Exmouth road, 5 minutes from junction 30 (Exeter Services) of the M5. Topsham Station is 1.6km (1 mile) away. Route 2 of the National Cycle Network links both sides of the estuary.

ACCESS AND FACILITIES
Darts Farm Village, where the RSPB visitor centre is located, has a restaurant, picnic area, shop, and disabled toilets. There's a car park at Exminster Marshes but not at Bowling Green Marsh; park in Topsham, a 15-minute walk away.

OPENING TIMES
Reserve and visitor centre is open all year.

CHARGES
None, but the RSPB welcomes donations.

RSPB avocet cruises
The Exe is internationally important for its birds, with up to 25,000 wildfowl and wading birds attracted to the estuary in winter by the mild climate and abundant food in the estuary silt. Up to 40 species of bird can be seen on the RSPB's avocet cruises, which run on the estuary between November and March. Unsurprisingly, the trips, which last up to four hours, are extremely popular and advance booking is essential. For more details, visit www.rspb.org.uk.

Main: Nearly half of the UK population of avocets spend the winter on the Exe Estuary.

FLOCKS OF AVOCETS

ESTUARIES ARE BRILLIANT PLACES, BUZZING WITH WILDLIFE – and the Exe Estuary, between Exeter and Exmouth, is big enough to be really wild and wonderful. It is a vast open space, with magnificent skies, but it's accessible enough to be seen easily from roads and footpaths. In November you can walk on the shore or go along the estuary by boat – always a wonderful experience – to get even closer to the birds. This is a famous site for avocets, because many of those that breed along the English east coast come to shallow, muddy southern estuaries like this one for the winter. And the Exe suits them well: you are likely to see scores of them together.

Far out on the mud an avocet might be overlooked, because you've taken it for a gull, or just another white spot on the dark mud. But look again; these birds are favourites with artists for good reason. Try to get close enough to see their delicate black patterns, long, grey legs, and remarkable beaks, curving upwards to a sharp,

Above: The marshes on either side of the estuary are now an RSPB reserve.

JAN

FEB

MAR

APR

MAY

JUN

JUL

AUG

SEP

OCT

NOV

DEC

THROUGH THE YEAR
EXE ESTUARY

Lapwings and redshanks display over fields on Exminster and Powderham Marshes during the **spring**, when shelducks display on the estuary and ravens fly overhead. Listen for rare Cetti's warblers.

In **summer**, damselflies and dragonflies skim over the ditches, where yellow iris blooms. By July, black-tailed godwits – many still in breeding plumage – ringed plovers, little stints, ruffs, and sandpipers are already heading south from their northern breeding grounds.

Ospreys are regularly seen each **autumn**, hunting over the estuary or roosting on trees. The avocets arrive in late autumn. Head for Bowling Green Marsh to see large flocks of wading birds, and whimbrels on their way to Africa.

WHERE ELSE TO SEE
FLOCKING AVOCETS

Avocets disappeared from Britain in the 1840s, driven to extinction by hunters, egg-collectors, and land drainage. They returned in 1947, when the East Anglian coasts were flooded to prevent invasion during World War II, incidentally creating the ideal habitat for avocets. They are now seen regularly around the south and east coasts.

Other southwestern estuaries near the Exe have avocets, including the **Tamar** in Devon, and **Poole Harbour**, Dorset (*see pp.48–49*), where large numbers roost on lagoons at the eastern end of Brownsea Island. [SW]

Some avocets remain in the estuaries along the Suffolk coast, such as **Minsmere** (*see pp.100–101*) and **Havergate Island** on the Ore Estuary. [SE]

Many southern estuaries have mixed flocks of ducks, waders, and brent geese, including those of the **Medway**, in Kent, and the Thames, in Essex. [SE]

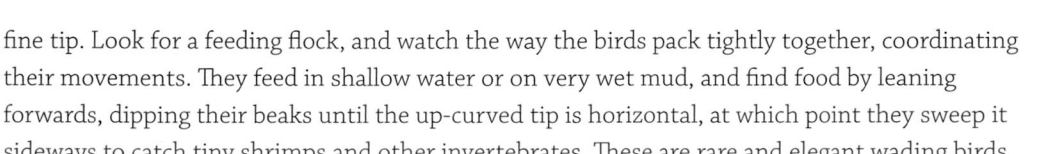

fine tip. Look for a feeding flock, and watch the way the birds pack tightly together, coordinating their movements. They feed in shallow water or on very wet mud, and find food by leaning forwards, dipping their beaks until the up-curved tip is horizontal, at which point they sweep it sideways to catch tiny shrimps and other invertebrates. These are rare and elegant wading birds.

Winter birds on the Exe, from the top of the estuary near Topsham to the mouth at Dawlish Warren, number many thousands. Ducks include wigeons, teals, pintails, and shovelers on the marshes, while red-breasted mergansers dive for fish in the open water. Go to one of the roost sites such as Bowling Green Marsh at high tide, when the birds are forced off the mud for an hour or two, and you may see hundreds of avocets, black-tailed godwits, and golden plovers, as well as a fine selection of ducks and brent geese. Should a hunting peregrine appear, they all fly up at once and separate, species by species, in the air. The avocets, despite their inky-black wingtips, catch the eye because of their remarkable whiteness. Their calls are wonderful, too: liquid, but ringing "quilp quilp" or "klute klute" notes, adding to the chorus of alarm notes from the panicking birds.

STRANGFORD LOUGH IS ONE OF BRITAIN'S LARGEST and most wildlife-rich sea loughs, and it lies just outside the large city of Belfast. After stretching for nearly 30km (18 miles), the lough narrows right down to just 500m (550 yards) close to its mouth, forming strong currents – each tide brings a staggering 350 million litres (77 million gallons) of water streaming through the narrows, bringing with it microscopic life that supports millions of filter-feeding animals. The area is dotted with drumlins – rounded hills formed by glacial deposits during the last Ice Age – and some of these help make up the hundred or so islands found largely along the west side.

Around half of the lough comprises intertidal mudflats, and these attract thousands of birds in early winter, especially light-bellied brent geese. The geese prefer the northern end of the lough, as do many other species of wildfowl and waders, because this is where the huge beds of eel-grass grow. Once this food source has

WHERE
Strangford Lough, County Down, Northern Ireland; www.strangfordlough.org

CONTACT
The Strangford Wildlife Centre, Downpatrick Rd, Strangford BT30 7LS, tel: 02844 881411; strangford@nationaltrust.org.uk
WWT Castle Espie Wetland Centre, 78 Ballydrain Road, Comber, BT23 6EA, tel: 028 9187 4146;
info.castleespie@wwt.org.uk

GETTING THERE
Strangford Lough lies 21km (13 miles) southeast of Belfast. From Belfast by car, take the A23 south, towards Ballgowan, then Balloo; turn right on the A22 at Balloo, and follow signs to the lough. There are no public transport links to the site.

ACCESS AND FACILITIES
The two visitor centres detailed above both have full facilities. There are other wildlife centres around the lough, most of which have good facilities. Maps and brochures are available at the Tourist Information Centre at Portaferry Castle, which overlooks the lough at the southern end, or downloadable from www.ards-council.gov.uk/visitor-information

CHARGES
Entry charge for non-National Trust/WWT members at the centres mentioned above.

Above: The rounded humps of drumlins breach the water along the south and western shores of the lough.

Below: Five types of sea urchin can be found under low shore boulders, where redshanks and turnstones feed; the variegated scallop is a speciality here.

Below the surface

Few people get a chance to explore Strangford Lough's wild riches below the water surface, but it has a number of wrecks that are popular with divers, and these harbour menacing-looking conger eels. The many holes, pipes, and cracks of the wrecks make a perfect habitat for the eels, some of which grow to exceed 1m (39in), and tend to be exceptionally shy. The wrecks are also home to spider crabs, velvet swimming crabs, porcelain crabs, oysters, flat worms, sea-mice, and starfish, scallops, and sea-squirts.

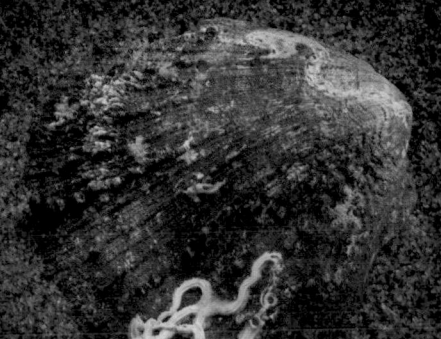

been depleted, many of the geese depart for other sites in Ireland, but the whooper swans stay on for winter, as do many of the waders, including the black-tailed godwits and greenshanks. Try to time your visit for the two hours either side of high tide to get the best views. The northern shore also hosts a Wildfowl & Wetlands Trust reserve – Castle Espie – which has a bounty of wild birds and an impressive captive collection too, making it a great family destination.

There are two types of seal in Strangford Lough – grey seals and common seals. The colony of common seals here is the largest breeding population within Ireland, but it is the grey seals that are pupping in November. These gentle animals, larger than the common seals, and recognizable by their grey coats, flatter heads, and parallel nostrils, give birth to their pups between September and November. They stay on land until they lose their white furry birth coats, and if you take a boat trip around the lough, you should see them lying around the rocks and islands.

Above: Huge flocks of golden plovers and dunlins gather over the lough in November.

Main: Swans wintering on the lough.

Below: The lough at low tide.

WHERE ELSE TO SEE
SEA INLETS

Strangford Lough is the UK's largest sea inlet, with huge numbers of wintering birds, some of which can be found on other sea inlets around the UK.

The **Isle of Mull** (see pp.226–227) has many sheltered sea lochs and estuaries, which welcome wintering ducks, divers, barnacle geese, and Greenland white-fronted geese. Otters breed here in winter, taking advantage of the warmer waters of the Gulf Stream. [SC]

Burry Inlet on the Gower Peninsula (see pp.122–123) supports a huge number of birds on its mudflats and saltmarshes, and the mouth of the estuary has an interesting sand-dune system. Little egrets, great crested grebes, herons, and dark-bellied brent geese can all be seen here in winter. [W]

The Fleet lagoon of **Chesil Beach** (see pp.180–181) is a good place to see mute swans, wigeons, pochards, brent geese, and coots in winter. [SW]

THROUGH THE YEAR
STRANGFORD LOUGH

Many of the birds that arrive in November stay for the **winter**, and thousands of plovers, godwits, and knots perform spectacular aerobatic displays over the water. The sediment of the mudflats is full of lugworms, catworms, and burrowing shrimp-like creatures that make up most of the diet for the 45,000 overwintering waders. Sandhoppers, which look like tiny jumping jellybeans, emerge from under cobbles in the evenings.

In **spring**, large numbers of waders pass through the lough, including whimbrels and common sandpipers. Garganeys may also be seen. Around 40,000 birds, including common, Arctic, and sandwich terns, arrive to nest on the lough's islands.

Peregrine falcons often breed in **summer** at Scrabo Tower, at the northern end of the lough – when this happens, a special watchpoint is erected. The colony of common seals is pupping in June and July, and the pups take to the water immediately.

Below: The green-winged orchid flowers around the lough in summer.

JAN

FEB

MAR

APR

MAY

JUN

JUL

AUG

SEP

OCT

NOV

DEC

DECEMBER

Where to Go: December

If you head to the coast at just the right moment – an hour or two before high tide – and at just the right place, where the wading birds come to roost while the mudflats are underwater, you're in a good position to enjoy one of the great spectacles of British wildlife. Tens of thousands of knots, dunlins, oystercatchers, and godwits fly in to settle in dense packs, rising, falling, twisting, and turning like smoke in the wind. The same experience is almost replicated by starlings coming to roost in a wood or reedbed, and even cities have their share of roosts. Inland reservoirs welcome flocks of gulls that arrive each evening, bringing with them the chance of an exciting northern rarity, which you might see if you are patient, persistent, and dressed

COAST

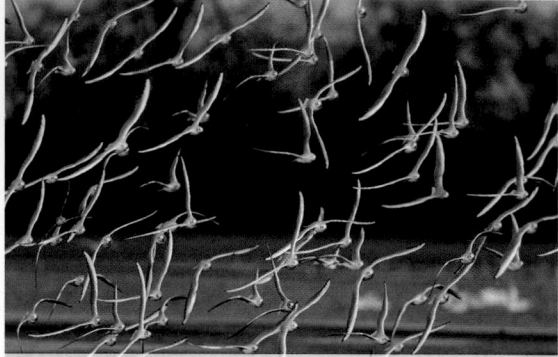

SNETTISHAM Huge flocks of birds twist and turn above the sea.

LAKES AND WATERWAYS

GRAFHAM WATER Watch the extraordinary aeronautical skills of gulls.

WOODLANDS

KINGLEY VALE The oldest and largest yew forest in western Europe.

SNETTISHAM
HUNSTANTON, NORFOLK [SE]

The most spectacular winter roost takes place here, as hundreds of thousands of birds are forced into the air by the incoming tides.
See pp.308–309

GRAFHAM WATER
CAMBRIDGESHIRE [SE]

Black-headed and herring gulls pack into tight groups here, as thousands roost upon the water.
See pp.302–303

DRAYCOTE WATER
RUGBY, WARWICKSHIRE [M]

This huge reservoir is a great place to see scarce gulls, grebes, divers, and sea-ducks in December.
See pp.302–303

KINGLEY VALE
CHICHESTER,
WEST SUSSEX [SW]

This is a magical place in winter, as birds look for berries among the ancient, gnarled trees.
See pp.310–311

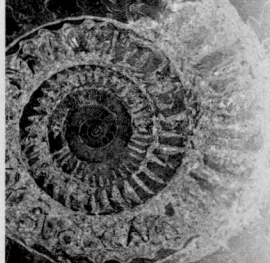

LYME BAY
PORTLAND, DORSET [SW]

A fossil-hunter's delight, this bay offers a glimpse of life over the last 250 million years in its rocks and fossils.
See pp.298–299

ABBERTON RESERVOIR
COLCHESTER, ESSEX [SE]

Canada geese and wigeons graze around this reservoir in winter, which is also host to large gull roosts.
See pp.302–303

BOX HILL
TADWORTH, SURREY [SE]

Box Hill gets its name from the box trees that grow so abundantly here, but wild yew trees also thrive on its chalk soil.
See pp.310–311

CROM CASTLE
COUNTY FERMANAGH [NI]

A romantic landscape of ancient woodland, lakes, and islands, which is also a great place to go bat-watching.
See pp.310–311

ROBIN HOOD'S BAY
WHITBY, YORKSHIRE [N]

The cliffs that cradle the bay here have amazing views on to the rock pavements below, which date back to the Jurassic period.
See pp.298–299

History is displayed in the cliffs and foreshore exposures – simply walk along the beach to find fossil ammonites, sea-lilies, and belemnites.

ELMLEY MARSHES
SHEERNESS, KENT [SE]

This vast area of coastal grazing marsh is filled with birds of prey in December, including rough-legged buzzards, and marsh and hen harriers.
See pp.306–307

Woodlands are quiet places in winter, but the atmosphere is magical, and the forms of the trees seem almost sculptural.

ST ABBS HEAD
BERWICKSHIRE [SC]

The spectacular geology of this exposed, rocky headland is complemented by plenty of seabirds, especially gannets.
See pp.298–299

NORFOLK BROADS
NORFOLK [SE]

The Broads are rich in winter birds, and see nightly roosts of around 20 hen harriers in December.
See pp.300–301

FORTINGALL
ABERFELDY, PERTH AND KINROSS [SC]

This small village is home to the oldest living thing in Britain – the Fortingall yew.
See pp.310–311

Previous page: A frosty sunrise at Elmley Marshes, Kent.

warmly enough to brave the cold. Gull roost watching is not for the faint-hearted! On the coast, gulls are often the main feature of sandy beaches, harbours, and promenades, but something interesting can usually be found even in these unpromising places, such as turnstones or even purple sandpipers. The British woods are quiet places in December, often deeply secluded and

undisturbed. There is little movement, unless a flock of small birds passes through, but the atmosphere is magical, and the tree shapes seem almost sculptural. At dusk you might see a woodcock flying off to feed, or hear the glorious hoot of a tawny owl. Grey squirrels are constantly on the move, smelling out the nuts and acorns they stored below ground during the autumn.

ISLANDS

ISLE OF MAN Look for cheeky choughs along the cliffs.

INLETS AND ESTUARIES

FIRTH OF FORTH Grey seals give birth to their pups in winter.

WILD IN THE CITY

NORWICH Pied wagtails are happy to be urban birds in December.

ISLE OF MAN
IRISH SEA [N]

Wander the boardwalks of the Ballaugh Curragh wetland in search of the rare corncrake, and you might be surprised by a wallaby.
See pp.300–301

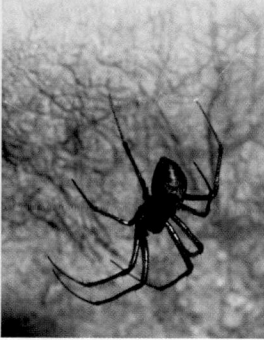

LUNDY ISLAND
BRISTOL CHANNEL [SW]

This island has a huge seabird colony in winter, and you can see porpoises, dolphins, seals, and basking sharks offshore.
See pp.126–127

FIRTH OF FORTH
FIFE/EAST LOTHIAN [SC]

Seals bask on the rocks and thousands of wintering waterbirds from more northerly climes seek refuge here in December.
See pp.296–297

SEAL SANDS
TEESSIDE [N]

This nature reserve supports common and grey seals, and is visited in winter by thousands of migrating birds.
See pp.304–305

CITY OF NORWICH
NORWICH, NORFOLK [SE]

Around 2,000 pied wagtails gather in the city centre at night to keep warm, calling out to Christmas shoppers.
See pp.294–295

PARLIAMENT SQUARE
YORK, YORKSHIRE [N]

Parliament Square sees large wagtail roosts of around 400 birds. Song thrushes and mistle thrushes have also been heard singing at York Science Park in December.
See pp.294–295

LINDISFARNE
NORTHUMBERLAND [N]

In winter Lindisfarne's mudflats provide food for around 50,000 birds that visit the island. Short-eared owls and merlins hunt among the waders.
See pp.306–307

Merlins chase their prey low and with speed, until the final dashing, twisting, and turning pursuit that decides the outcome of the encounter.

THAMES ESTUARY
ESSEX/KENT [SE]

The outer estuary has an enormous number of seabirds, including red-throated divers, which can be seen following shoals of sprats.
See pp.296–297

ADDENBROOKE'S HOSPITAL
CAMBRIDGE [SE]

This hospital is regularly treated to pied wagtail roosts of more than 400 birds.
See pp.294–295

ALUM BAY
ISLE OF WIGHT

Alum Bay is famous for its coloured sands, packed with interesting fossils, and the steep chalk cliffs of The Needles.
See pp.298–299

MINSMERE
SUFFOLK [SE]

Hen and marsh harriers join owls and peregrines in hunts across the heathland and reedbed. Great spotted woodpeckers start drumming on milder days.
See pp.306–307

Birds will roost on supermarkets, commercial greenhouses, power station cooling towers, and even sewage farms.

WINTER CITY ROOSTS

BIRDS FORM FLOCKS FOR A VARIETY OF REASONS. Feeding flocks of geese or waders may be gathering around a patchy food resource, or relying on safety in numbers – more pairs of eyes increase the chance of spotting predators, and extra wings can create confusion if one strikes. For roosting flocks, safety is again a factor, but there are others too: warmth on a cold night may be one, and social functions another – the birds might share information about good feeding areas, for example. The need for warmth, to conserve energy, also helps explain one of the more surprising roost phenomena – the aggregation of wild birds in the most unnatural of situations, in our towns and cities, where the urban "heat island" effect can

Many birds seek safety and warmth in numbers at night, from the hundreds of rooks and jackdaws that gather in farmland woods to the energetic little wagtails that come to roost in our city centres.

WHERE
Norwich City Hall, St Peter's Street, Norwich, Norfolk NR2 1NH; www.norwich.gov.uk

CONTACT
Norwich City Council, tel: 08449 803333; info@norwich.gov.uk

GETTING THERE
By car, travel to the centre of Norwich; the most convenient car parks for City Hall are St Giles and St Andrews car parks. By train, travel to Norwich station; it is only a 15-minute walk to City Hall via Prince of Wales Road. By bus, catch any bus within the area – all will stop within the city centre. By bicycle, take the National Cycle Network Route no.1, which passes right through the city centre.

ACCESS AND FACILITIES
Norwich is a large city with superb facilities for everyone. For online information about access to shops, pubs, restaurants, and offices in Norwich for people with hearing, vision, or mobility impairments, go to www.disabledgo.info

OPENING TIMES
Open all year round.

CHARGES
None, except to park in the city.

lift winter night-time temperatures well above that of the surrounding countryside. Pied wagtails are a case in point. Normally rather solitary, these birds form winter roosts, often on buildings in the heart of a city. Such roosts are notoriously unpredictable from year to year, but Norwich city centre is one place where large numbers are often present. In some years more than 2,000 birds gather here: listen out for their high-pitched "chissick, chissick" calls while you are doing your last-minute Christmas shopping, and keep an eye on the local media, who often feature them. The birds like to cluster together on the Christmas trees outside City Hall, and they attract attention whenever they are in residence.

But city centre buildings are not the pied wagtail's only roosting choice: out-of-town supermarkets, commercial greenhouses, power station cooling towers, and even sewage farms attract them, as do more natural habitats, such as reedbeds. In Devon, Slapton Ley has a reedbed roost of up to 1,000, and remarkably up to 60 per cent of the birds there in the autumn and early winter have been shown to be continental and Icelandic white wagtails, not pied wagtails. If other roosts had similar in-depth studies, we might find that white wagtails are a widespread migrant and wintering phenomenon.

Main: Pied wagtails roosting in the trees of Norwich city centre at Christmas.
Below (left to right): The pied wagtail adopts a more urban lifestyle in winter; the female pied wagtail in winter plumage.
Inset: Norwich marketplace, a Christmas destination for both shoppers and pied wagtails in December.

Predators on the prowl

Like other flocking birds, pied wagtail roosts attract their share of predators. Arriving as darkness falls, they try to avoid diurnal dangers, although sparrowhawks remain active at very low light levels when potential food is around. The darkness of night brings further dangers – some wagtail roosts have become favoured hunting grounds for little owls. The city roosts are also at risk from ground predators: domestic cats are known to cause significant mortalities.

JAN

FEB

MAR

APR

MAY

JUN

JUL

AUG

SEP

OCT

NOV

DEC

THROUGH THE YEAR
NATURE IN NORWICH

In **spring**, the ancient woods of Norwich are in full bloom, and some, such as Lion Wood, are especially good for bluebells. Several of the parks have adopted sympathetic mowing regimes, allowing a range of attractive flowers such as cowslips to bloom freely.

Summer is the time to head for Sweet Briar Marsh, and its array of orchids, marsh marigolds, purple loosestrife, and other attractive plants, while brown hawkers and other dragonflies and damselflies patrol for their insect prey. Around the city, watch the road verges and waste ground for the impressive, nationally scarce woolly mullein plant, and keep an eye on the rooftops for the black redstart, a tiny population of which may just survive in the area.

As an **autumn** destination, try Mousehold Heath – it is the largest open space in the city and has wonderful views. The heather turns purple, the bracken starts to brown, and that archetypal toadstool, the "red-with-white-spots" fly agaric, appears in force under the birch trees.

WHERE ELSE TO SEE
CITY ROOSTS

Urban birdwatching can be done at any time – even in your lunch break. Green spaces are good, but look out, too, for birds using high-rise buildings or any open area, such as a playground or sports club.

Urban wagtail roosts have been recorded in many British towns, some of the most reliable being in **Parliament Square**, York. [N]

Addenbrooke's Hospital, Cambridge, regularly sees pied wagtail roosts of around 400 birds. [SE]

Other surprising winter bird roosts worth searching out include the pied wagtails in Plymouth city centre. [SW]

If crows are more to your taste, visit **Buckenham** in Norfolk to witness 40,000 or more rooks and jackdaws that roost in nearby woodlands. [SE]

Below: Pied wagtails "decorating" a street tree in Loughborough.

WHERE
The Firth of Forth, between Fife and East Lothian, Scotland.

CONTACT
The Scottish Seabird Centre, The Harbour, North Berwick, Scotland EH39 4SS; tel: 01620 890202; info@seabird.org

GETTING THERE
The Firth of Forth estuary flows into the North Sea, north of Edinburgh. The Scottish Seabird Centre overlooks the islands of the Firth of Forth – travel there by train to North Berwick station, from which it is a 10-minute walk. By car, take the A1 towards Berwick and follow signs to the centre.

ACCESS AND FACILITIES
The Seabird Centre has a range of interactive cameras. The centre is fully accessible, with a lift to the Discovery Centre, a café, and full-access toilets. The RSPB offers guided birdwatching tours around the Firth of Forth; contact them via: www.rspb.org.uk

OPENING TIMES
The Seabird Centre is open all year, except Christmas day, opening at 10am and closing between 4pm and 6pm (check opening times before visiting).

CHARGES
The Seabird Centre has a small entry charge.

The red-necked grebe

A rarer bird often seen in the Forth is the red-necked grebe. Its winter plumage is a pale shadow of the rich chestnut of its breeding dress. Remarkably, this plumage can be seen here in late summer and early autumn, when Gosford Bay in particular hosts more than 40 moulting birds. Once out of breeding plumage and after the flight feathers have regrown, red-necked grebes then disperse, both within the Firth of Forth and more widely round the coastline.

Left (left to right): The nutrient-rich sands of Gosford Bay are popular with wading birds; there is a grey seal colony at Inchcolm Island.

Right (left to right): Velvet scoters prefer the areas of Musselburgh and Largo Bay; look for neat little long-tailed ducks in the deeper waters.

Main: A flock of greater scaup flies in to winter at Largo Bay. **Far right:** An eider shakes off the cold sea water – more than 3,000 spend the winter here.

DIVERS BY THE DOZEN

THE SHALLOW SEAS AROUND THE BRITISH COASTLINE are home to huge numbers of wintering water birds, especially ducks, divers, and grebes – mostly birds that have bred in more northerly climes. Many lie out of sight of land, but where the food supplies are good, the birds are undisturbed, and there is plenty of shelter, it becomes possible to see quite large concentrations from land, especially with the help of a telescope.

One such place is the Firth of Forth, that great gash in the eastern flanks of Scotland between Lothian and Fife. The south shore is best, if only because viewing is easiest with the low winter sunlight behind you, and access is provided along the John Muir Way, which runs east from Musselburgh, much of it next to the Firth. The car parks around Gosford Bay make excellent viewing points. Try and pick a calm day, especially if you want to count the birds: their habit of diving for food makes counting tricky in fine weather – impossible in windy conditions.

Above: Shags nest around the Firth of Forth in July.

> These stretches of open water, shores, and mudflats attract around 90,000 water birds to the area each winter.

THROUGH THE YEAR
THE FIRTH OF FORTH

In **spring**, eiders become even more vocal and engage in courtship displays. Similarly, goldeneyes form small rafts to watch the head-tossing male display, especially on calm, sunny days.

Summer is the time to visit the dunes of Aberlady Bay, one of the best sand-dune systems in Scotland. The RSPB lays on seabird cruises around the Firth of Forth in summer to watch gannets, puffins, terns, and whatever else is breeding in the vicinity. After midsummer, the red-necked grebes and common scoters start to return, seeking the sanctuary of the area for their post-breeding moult. The very scarce sand dart moth and the northern brown argus butterfly are sometimes seen in summer.

Most of the water birds, from ducks to waders, arrive in **autumn**. But also look out for smaller migrants: the extensive patches of sea-buckthorn on the Gullane Bay dune system provide both food and shelter.

WHERE ELSE TO SEE
WATER BIRDS

Water birds can be seen at any coastal reserve and estuary; try these for sea ducks and divers.

Farther up the Scottish coast, the **Moray Firth** (*see pp.220–221*) holds a similar range of birds, including an even larger number of common scoters. [SC]

Liverpool Bay, Merseyside, has important numbers of waterbirds, especially common scoters. [N]

The outer **Thames Estuary**, Essex, has a huge population of waterbirds, including red-throated divers, but they are often a very long way from the shore, except when following shoals of sprats. [SE]

The North Norfolk coast supports a range of sea ducks and divers, including great northern divers, often lingering into late spring. The chalk cliffs of **Hunstanton** can give a grandstand view. [SE]

Eiders favour rocky stretches with mussel beds, so they are always closest to shore. Their wedge-shaped beaks and thick-set necks supply the force to wrench mussels off the rocks while diving, which they then swallow whole, to be crushed in the gizzard. In winter, the eider males are unmistakeable – black and white, with a hint of peach and apple. Their quizzical cooing signals the onset of courtship; listen for the more guttural croaking of the females in reply.

Farther out, any "oily black patch" on the water might well turn out to be a raft of scoters. Most will be common scoters, but there are likely to be velvet scoters among them; look out for the tell-tale white wing-patch of the velvets when they fly. You should also see goldeneyes, scaups, red-breasted mergansers, and all sorts of grebes, together with large numbers of long-tailed ducks, which love the deep water and can dive to around 30m (100ft). If you want to experience a different side of the Forth's water bird populations, head to sheltered inlets such as Aberlady Bay when the mud is exposed. There you'll find waders – including curlews, redshanks, and knots – and sometimes pink-footed geese along with genuine wild Icelandic greylags.

JAN FEB MAR APR MAY JUN JUL AUG SEP OCT NOV DEC

WHERE
Lyme Bay lies on the south coast of England, running from Torbay, Devon, in the west to Portland, Dorset in the east.

CONTACT
www.jurassiccoast.com has details of all tourist and visitor centres along the bay, or contact Devon Wildlife Trust, tel: 01392 279244; contactus@devonwildlifetrust.org

GETTING THERE
Lyme Bay is 14.4km (9 miles) from Sidmouth and 12.8km (8 miles) from Lyme Regis with good access from the M5, A303, and A35. By bus from Lyme Regis, catch the Jurassic Coast Bus Service, Coastline X53. If you want to walk, the South West Coast Path runs along the entire length of the Jurassic Coast.

ACCESS AND FACILITIES
There are no facilities on the beach itself, but Lyme Regis, Seaton, and Beer all have good facilities, including accessible restaurants and public toilets. Warning: exceptional care is needed on eroding coasts. Do not climb on the cliffs; beware of crumbling cliff-edges; and don't get caught out by the tides.

OPENING TIMES
Open all year round.

CHARGES
None.

Honeycomb reefs
Some of the formations along Lyme Bay are created by the honeycomb worm. The worms, which live in large colonies, construct tubes from sand or shell fragments to form large hummocks, sheets, or uneven boulder-type blocks with a unique "honeycomb" structure. These structures are, strictly speaking, "reefs", and they are mainly found in the bottom third of the shore, which has a guaranteed saline environment. The worms are found along the southwest coast of England, and the coasts of Northern Ireland.

Above (left to right): Some of the many rock pools at Lyme Bay; sea lettuce wilts on the lower shore; lobsters hide in the seawater.
Main: Lyme Bay is one of the most famous fossil locations in the world, with fossils over 190 million years old on the beach.

FOSSIL FANTASY

THE JURASSIC COAST OF DORSET AND DEVON IS internationally recognized for its geological features, which offer a window into the past going back 250 million years. In Lyme Bay, a portion of that story is displayed in the cliffs and foreshore exposures – simply walking along the beach you will find fossil ammonites, belemnites, Devil's toe-nails, and sea-lilies, the remnants of long-extinct species that abounded in the Jurassic seas. In Monmouth Bay to the west there are huge ammonites still embedded in the rocks, some almost 1 m (3ft) across.

Those same rocks, moulded and pitted by the action of the sea, are also home to modern forms of wildlife. Limpets, winkles, and top-shells cling to the rocks; a myriad of seaweeds blanket the shore: leathery kelps, knotted wrack, sea-lettuce, coral weed, and thongweed and many more. Turnstones and rock pipits poke their way through the weed, uncovering the invertebrate morsels on which they feed. And then there are the rock pools. Sheltered, and filled with water even at low tide, these provide a refuge for plants and animals less tolerant of exposure. The shore clingfish, with its odd, "duck-billed" appearance, can be found attached to rocky overhangs by its thoracic sucker; equally unusual is the peacock's-tail, a small chalky seaweed with funnel-shaped fronds, a species that is more characteristic of the Mediterranean. Blobs of red or green "jelly" on the rocks are the beadlet anemone with its feeding tentacles withdrawn; while the beautiful green snakelocks anemone remains open even when the tide is out.

Of course, the intertidal zone is only the tip of the iceberg. In the clear waters of Lyme Bay, the scuba diver can find much more, from scallops to lobsters and rare species like the pink sea-fan and sunset coral, an underwater cornucopia now thankfully protected against the damaging effects of scallop dredging.

Lying at the heart of England's first natural World Heritage Site, Lyme Bay attracts divers and fossil-hunters from all over the globe to witness its treasures.

Inset: A fossil ammonite found on the Jurassic coast of Lyme Regis dates back to the time of the dinosaurs.
Below (left to right): A beadlet sea anemone in a shallow rock pool, with tentacles out; the beautiful purple-tipped, green anemone.

WHERE ELSE TO SEE
ROCKS AND FOSSILS

Coastal erosion is disastrous on many levels, but it is great for exposing rocks and fossils. Rock pools and their associated wildlife are found around the British coast wherever rocks meet the sea. Any coastal area is worth combing for fascinating relics of our past.

Some of the cliffs around the coast that are similarly celebrated for their geology are at **Robin Hood's Bay**, North Yorkshire, where Jurassic rocks similar to those in Dorset are exposed. **St Mary's Island**, Tyneside, and **Flamborough Head**, (see pp.252–253) Yorkshire, are good for rockpooling. [N]

You can find interesting rocks among the limestones and coloured sands of **Alum Bay**, on the Isle of Wight (see pp.224–225), and the fossil-rich London clay and red crag cliffs at **The Naze**, Essex. There are good rock pools at **Samphire Hoe**, Kent. [SE]

In Scotland, visit **St Abbs Head**, Berwickshire, for spectacular cliffs and rocks. [SC]

THROUGH THE YEAR
LYME BAY

Running west from Lyme Regis, the slipping cliff slopes have become colonized by ash, hazel, and sycamore woodland. **Spring** flowers include dog's-mercury, herb-robert, pendulous sedge, and the beautiful but rare purple gromwell. Ravens and peregrines may be seen displaying over the cliffs.

In **summer**, any patch of bare sand will be riddled with the holes of solitary bees and wasps, including numerous rare species, while metallic green tiger-beetles scurry around in search of their insect prey. The cliff-top has displays of pyramidal orchids and other grassland flowers, and carpets of ivy harbour the parasitic plant, ivy broomrape.

Autumn brings Atlantic storms, and the chance for some beachcombing. Among the human detritus and seaweed, you might find goose-barnacles, their egg-shaped shells attached to driftwood with an extendable stalk, or the transparent blue floats of the by-the-wind sailor, a jellyfish-like animal .

Below: Tiger-beetles scuttle over the cliffs of Lyme Bay in summer.

JAN
FEB
MAR
APR
MAY
JUN
JUL
AUG
SEP
OCT
NOV
DEC

WHERE
Isle of Man, Irish Sea;
www.gov.im/wildlife and www.manxwt.org.uk

CONTACT
Manx Wildlife Trust, tel: 01624 801985;
enquiries@manxwt.org.uk

GETTING THERE
The island's ferry services are provided
by the Isle of Man Steam Packet Company
(www.steam-packet.com) and depart
from Heysham, Liverpool, Dublin, Belfast,
and Fleetwood.

ACCESS AND FACILITIES
The Curraghs Wildlife Park lies at the edge of
the Ballaugh Curraghs, and has a boardwalk
nature trail with good access and facilities.
The are two visitor centres with facilites at
Ayres and Scarlett.

OPENING TIMES
Contact individual reserves for opening times.

CHARGES
Curraghs Wildlife Park charges a small
admission fee; Ayres and Scarlett visitor
centres are free.

The Isle of Man cabbage

The Isle of Man cabbage still grows on the island,
including the same beach on which it was first
recorded and described by the English botanist,
John Ray, in 1660. This wild flower is scarce
within the British Isles, and its numbers have
declined even on the island, where it used to
grow all along the north coast dunes. In 2005
the cabbage was growing wild at ony two sites
on the island, but numbers have increased
since conservationists added propagated plants.

Above: More than 80 hen harriers roost in winter on
the Isle of Man.

Below (top to bottom): The island has vast areas
of unspoilt wilderness; the elusive cave spider.

Right: Hooded crows stalk the sandy shorelines.

Main: The coast at Douglas, on the Isle of Man. **Inset:** A large population of choughs live on the island.

WINTER WONDERLAND

RIGHT IN THE MIDDLE OF THE IRISH SEA, BETWEEN IRELAND and Britain, lies a beautiful island that is rich
in wildlife and steeped in ancient history. At only 53km (33 miles) long and 21km (13 miles) wide, the Isle of
Man is relatively small, but it offers wildlife a wide range of enticing habitats, from cliff edges and woodland glens,
to mountains and wide, open moors, all spread out among the ancient Celtic and Viking ruins and monuments.

One of the most important habitats on the island is the Ballaugh Curragh wetland. This reserve has a
network of boarded walks. As you wander through areas of bog myrtle, willow scrub ("curragh"), bog pools,
marshy grasslands, and birch woodland, keep an eye out for that elusive bird, the corncrake, which likes to hide
under the abundant royal fern. Another reclusive creature lives beneath you, deep in the heart of the island – the
cave spider, one of Britain's largest, yet notoriously difficult to find. You may, though, see a red-necked wallaby:

The island's rocky coastline is lined by fields, making the area idyllic for the noisy chough, which lives on cliffs and feeds in grassland.

Above: The greater butterfly orchid flowers on the island in summer.

THROUGH THE YEAR
THE ISLE OF MAN

Ballaglass Glen is an ancient woodland that is full of bluebells during **spring**. The wild red-necked wallabies breed in the spring, and you can often see the "joeys", or young, poking their heads out of their mother's pouch.

During the **summer**, enormous basking sharks – around 10m (35ft) long – visit Manx waters; you can see them from The Sound or take a boat trip for a closer view. The best months are June and July. Common dolphins swim offshore in the summer, and Langness is a beautiful setting to watch out for passing Risso's dolphins. Close Sartfield reserve organizes an orchid walk in June to witness the thousands of spotted and butterfly orchids in flower.

In **autumn**, especially during October and November, the stretch of sea between Baldrine and Maughold is the best place to see minke whales, which visit to feast on the spawning herring. Killer whales have also been seen here. Autumn is also a good time to get close up views of grey seal pups around Port Mooar and The Sound, and watch the lizards basking in the sun at Ayres.

WHERE ELSE TO SEE
HEN HARRIER ROOSTS

The Isle of Man is famous for its large hen harrier roosts. These birds winter mainly around the south and east coasts of Britain, but some do remain farther north, on the Scottish moors. They tend to roost in wetlands, such as marshes and reedbeds.

Wicken Fen (*see pp.204–205*) in Cambridgeshire is an important roosting site for hen harriers in autumn and winter around dusk; earlier in the day you may spot bitterns, long-eared and barn owls, woodcocks, jays, and woodpeckers. Reptiles, including grass snakes and common lizards, laze on the boardwalks. [SE]

The **Norfolk Broads** (*see Strumpshaw Fen, pp.152–153*), has nightly roosts of around 20 hen harriers in winter. [SE]

20–30 of them escaped from captivity many years ago, and now run wild in the Curragh. Gorse, and especially yellow ragwort – the island's national flower – grows everywhere. But it's the amazing number of hen harriers that makes this site so special. Visit Close Sartfield nature reserve, within the Ballaugh Curragh, and you'll see the largest hen harrier roosting site in Western Europe, with up to 80 hen harriers coming in to roost.

Another Manx star is the chough, which can be seen around the cliffs to the south and west of the island, or foraging along the tideline. These handsome, shiny black birds are very sociable; in winter, you can watch groups of up to 40 sweep in, noisily calling to each other. Along the shore of the mainland, the mid-shore pools are full of delights, especially for children: the red blobs of beadlet anemones sit among limpets and periwinkles. Check the low-tide pools for sea urchins and starfish. Take a boat to the Calf of Man to see seabirds: the bird observatory there has recorded Manx shearwaters, razorbills, cormorants, fulmars, and puffins. Harbour porpoises swim in the waters around the islands, joined by bottlenose dolphins in winter.

JAN

FEB

MAR

APR

MAY

JUN

JUL

AUG

SEP

OCT

NOV

DEC

INLAND GULL ROOST

THE SIGHT OF THOUSANDS OF GULLS flying in to roost is associated with coastal habitats, but it is a spectacle that can be enjoyed inland too. Grafham Water, the third largest area of inland water in England, is so huge that, at times, you feel that you are by the sea rather than on the shores of a reservoir. On winter afternoons, you will see gulls arriving to spend the night on the grey, cold water. They pour in by the thousand, beginning quite early and still arriving after dark. A small flock forms first, to act as a necessary focus for later arrivals. If this is disturbed, perhaps by boats, the whole roost may fail to form that night and moves elsewhere.

Most roosts have a large majority of black-headed gulls, often packing tightly together in an obvious pale, pearly-grey patch in the fading light. Depending on the time of year, you might find the rest are mainly herring gulls, or evenly split between herring, lesser black-backed, and common gulls, with a scattering of big, burly great

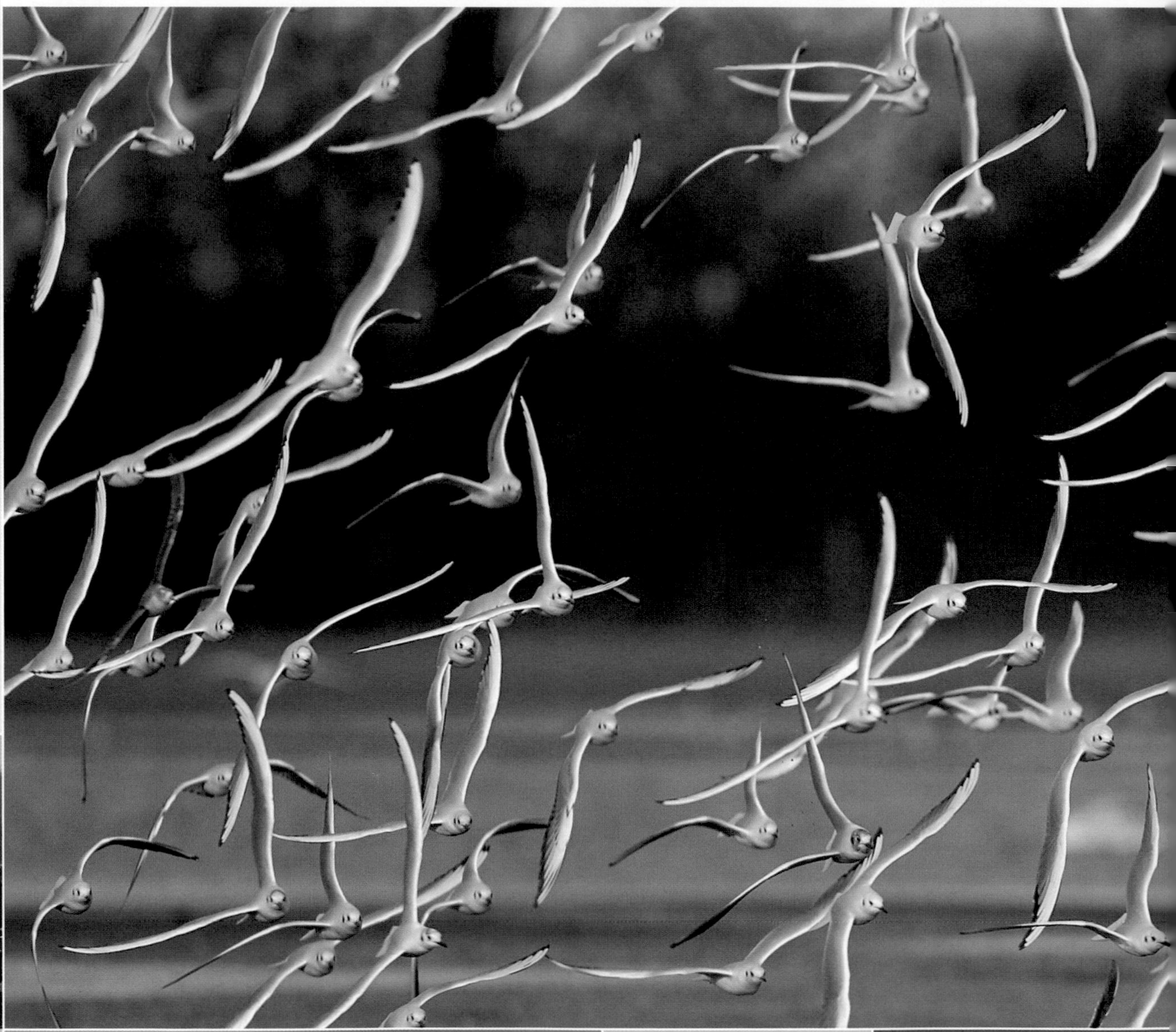

WHERE
Grafham Water, West Perry, Huntingdon, Cambridgeshire PE28 0BX;
www.wildlifebcnp.org

CONTACT
The Mander Park Visitor Centre,
tel: 01480 811075;
www.anglianwater.co.uk
grafham@wildlifebcnp.org

GETTING THERE
By car, leave the A1 at the Buckden roundabout taking the B661 signposted to Kimbolton and Grafham Water. Go through Perry until you see the right hand turn to the Mander Car Park. For bus information contact www.travelineeastanglia.org.uk

ACCESS AND FACILITIES
There are five bird hides around the Grafham Water but there's also good viewing from the three car parks around the site. Maps showing these are available from the visitor centre, which has a range of facilities, including full-access toilets and refreshments.

OPENING TIMES
Open all year round.

CHARGES
Parking charges only.

Following the plough

Grafham Water lies within a largely agricultural area, and as you pass the fields, you're likely to see – and hear – noisy clouds of white gulls avidly following the tractor and plough. Gulls are great scavengers and are always on the look out for easy, opportunistic feeding situations. When the plough churns up the soil, it uncovers an incredible variety of animal food for the gulls to feast on. Almost all of our gull species will take advantage of this easy food. Frogs, grubs, pupae, earthworms, and even rodents are snapped up.

Main: A wheeling flight of black-headed gulls.

Left: The shoreline of Grafham Water is more than 14km (9 miles) in length.

Right (left to right): A herring gull in flight; a fawn-mottled juvenile Iceland gull.

Right panel (top and bottom): Gulls facing into the wind; a glaucous gull from the far north.

black-backed gulls. If there are buoys and rafts, they are often claimed by young great black-backs, but on the water, the dense flocks typically arrange themselves so that the adults are safe and sheltered in the centre, while the young are exposed on the outer edges.

On one level, this is a fascinating and beautiful sight, punctuated by the ringing calls of gulls piercing the gloom. On another, for the more advanced watcher, it is a race against time, to identify the birds before it gets too dark – perhaps also to count them and record the varying proportions of one-year-old, two-year-old, and adult birds, or to find any unusual ones that may be hidden among the more common birds. These roosts are great places for discovering examples of two white-winged visitors from the Arctic – glaucous and Iceland gulls – and there's always the chance of seeing Mediterranean gulls, or a rare visitor from North America. Wrap up warm, set up your telescope and off you go; or just sit back and enjoy the view.

> Gulls eat whatever they can find on refuse tips and farmland and then retreat to their reservoir roost.

WHERE ELSE TO SEE
GULL ROOSTS

Many undisturbed beaches witness gulls roosting every evening in winter, but remember that their movements are also complicated by the tides. There are great gull roosts at many reservoirs too.

Blithfield Reservoir and **Chasewater** in Staffordshire both have gull roosts in winter, as do the meres around **Ellesmere** in Shropshire. [M]

Draycote Water, a huge reservoir in Warwickshire, is a great place to see scarce gulls, grebes, divers, and sea-ducks in winter. [M]

Several of the Greater London reservoirs, including **Staines** and **Abberton Reservoir** in Essex, have large gull roosts. Check the surrounding pylons for peregrine falcons, too. [SE]

The beach and mudflats at **Blackpill**, near Swansea, has a huge gull roost. It is also where the ring-billed gull was first seen in the UK. [W]

THROUGH THE YEAR
GRAFHAM WATER

Grafham Water is a big reservoir with sanctuary areas in the western bays, but birds can be seen anywhere around its shores. Other areas around the reservoir include ancient woodlands, grasslands, reedbeds, and open water – home to many species of wildlife.

In **spring** watch for migrant waders, including dunlins, ruffs, common sandpipers, and greenshanks. The western woodland has nightingales in spring, singing above carpets of bluebells and primroses.

Short grass close to the southern car parks can be good for bee orchids in **summer**. Look out for common spotted orchids too. The meadows are alive with dragonflies, butterflies, voles, and grass snakes. Juvenile birds, including shags, terns, flycatchers, shovelers, and little egrets can be seen.

Autumn gales may bring storm-blown seabird rarities. As water levels in the reservoir drop, sandpipers are attracted to the site.

Below: In autumn, look for rare visitors like the Leach's storm petrel.

JAN
FEB
MAR
APR
MAY
JUN
JUL
AUG
SEP
OCT
NOV
DEC

A TRIUMPH OF NATURE

DESPITE BEING SURROUNDED BY THE INDUSTRIAL LANDSCAPE of one of Britain's major centres of heavy industry, with views in various directions of oil refineries, steelworks, a nuclear power station, and one of Europe's largest chemical plants, this unusual nature reserve is a haven for wildlife. The contrast between the great expanses of sea, mud, sand, and sky and the calls of waders within the apparently unsalubrious surroundings actually emphasizes the wildness of the place. And the presence of industry brings some surprising benefits: limited human access ensures minimal disturbance, and waders can feed round the clock thanks to artificial lighting.

Seal Sands forms the southern part of the Teesmouth National Nature Reserve, a huge area of intertidal mud and sand flats that also encompasses a brackish lagoon and a reedbed. It supports common seals and a few grey seals, and you can usually see them lounging on the sandbanks, even in the coldest weather. If you approach

WHERE
Seal Sands, Teesmouth National Nature Reserve, Middlesbrough, Cleveland.

CONTACT
Countryside Wardens, tel: 01429 853325; northumbria@english-nature.org.uk
Teesmouth Field Centre, Hartlepool Power Station, Tees Road, Hartlepool TS25 2BZ; tel: 01429 264912; fieldcentre@teesmouth.freeserve.co.uk

GETTING THERE
Seal Sands is part of the Teesmouth reserve, between Hartlepool and Middlesbrough, just off the A178. The closest train station is Seaton Carew. The no.1 bus runs from Hartlepool and Middlesbrough to the reserve.

ACCESS AND FACILITIES
There are no facilities on site; the nearest are at Seaton Carew 8km (5 miles) away. There are several car parks, including North Gare and Cowpen Marsh (on the A178). The Greatham Creek car park has a solid path to a viewing hide. The Teesmouth Field Centre, next to North Gare, provides a range of educational activities. Book in advance.

OPENING TIMES
Open all year round.

CHARGES
None.

The seals and birds of this extraordinary reserve seem oblivious to the busy industrial activity around them, but are happy to enjoy its unique benefits.

The seals' return

The seals for which the sands are named include both common (*pictured*) and grey seals. During the 19th century they succumbed to the triple effects of hunting, disturbance, and industrial pollution. By about 1860, they had become extinct in the Tees Estuary, but in the late 20th century, following the cleaning-up of much of the pollution, these fascinating sea mammals returned. The common seals started breeding, and today there are about 70 adults. A few grey seals can also be seen, but do not breed here.

too close on foot, though, they are likely to slip back into the water. By November they are joined by a large number of migrating winter birds – over 20,000 waterfowl visit Teesmouth each year. Waders include oystercatchers, dunlins, ringed plovers, redshanks, knots, sanderlings, and turnstones, while wildfowl include several hundred shelducks. Wintering songbirds may include occasional twites, snow buntings, and Lapland buntings feeding on seeds while trying to avoid the raptors – peregrines, merlins, and kestrels – that perch on the old industrial chimneys.

Seal Sands is hugely important for wintering ducks – look closely among the gatherings of mallards, teals, and wigeons, and you'll find a small number of other dabbling ducks, including gadwalls, shovelers, and pintails. For close-up views of the rarer birds, visit the hide; with luck, you'll spot goldeneyes, pochards, and scaups. The divers – including common and velvet scoters, eiders, goosanders, and long-tailed ducks, like to swim and dive in the waters of Greatham Creek.

Above: A petrochemical refinery lies just beyond the reedbeds at the Teesside Nature Reserve.

Main image: The unlikely setting of Seal Sands.

Left (top to bottom): Grey seals; wigeons foraging in the shallows; a knot in winter plumage.

Below: The Lapland bunting is a rare and elusive visitor to rough pasture.

WHERE ELSE TO SEE
POST-INDUSTRIAL WETLANDS

Although nowhere else has such a massive concentration of major industry next to prime wildlife habitats, other sites that may at first glance seem unsuitable, do bring rich rewards for the naturalist.

Rainham Marshes, Purfleet, Essex, has recently become an RSPB reserve. These medieval marshes were for many years used as a military firing range and the land was disfigured by a huge refuse dump, car-breakers' yards, and derelict factories. The wealth of birds includes avocets, little egrets, peregrines, and kingfishers, and there are butterflies, dragonflies, weasels, and foxes. [SE]

Dungeness (*see pp.162–163*), Kent, is a bleak stretch of coast overlooked by two nuclear power stations – but it is ideally situated to attract migrant birds and insects, from cuckoos and hobbies to painted lady butterflies and migrant hawker dragonflies. [SE]

The **London Wetland Centre** in Barnes, London, provides a haven for an amazing range of wildlife within the nation's capital, including little ringed plovers, bitterns, scarce insects, and water voles. [SE]

THROUGH THE YEAR
SEAL SANDS

Spring sees many migrant birds passing through, and you may see handsome little garganey drakes, ospreys, or marsh harriers among the commoner wheatears, whinchats, and yellow wagtails. The saltmarsh, dunes, and grassland are studded with wildflowers, as the skylarks and meadow pipits get busy for the breeding season.

In **summer**, noisy "kirrick" calls announce the presence of sandwich terns. Shelducks shepherd their young to feed on the mudflats, while sedge and reed warblers sing in the reedbeds.

The approach of **autumn** brings more migrant birds. Passage waders include regular species, such as whimbrels, black-tailed godwits, little stints, and curlew sandpipers, and some rarities – such as a great snipe or Terek sandpiper from eastern Europe, or, from North America, a white-rumped or Baird's sandpiper, or a Wilson's phalarope.

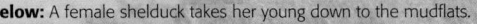
Below: A female shelduck takes her young down to the mudflats.

JAN

FEB

MAR

APR

MAY

JUN

JUL

AUG

SEP

OCT

NOV

DEC

HUNTING OVER THE MARSH

WHERE
RSPB Elmley Marshes, Kingshill Farm, Sheerness, Kent, ME12 3RW; www.rspb.org.uk

CONTACT
RSPB Elmley Marshes, tel: 01795 665969; northkentmarshes@rspb.org.uk

GETTING THERE
By car, at junction 5 on the M2, follow the A249 on to the Isle of Sheppey, heading for Sheerness. After 2km (1¼ miles), turn right following the RSPB sign. Follow the rough track for 3km (2 miles) to Kingshill Farm. The nearest train station is Swale Halt, 4.8km (3 miles) from the reserve's car park. The nearest bus stop is Queensborough, 6.4km (4 miles) away.

ACCESS AND FACILITIES
There are five bird-watching hides, including two with disabled access. Paths are largely suitable for electric scooters. The first hide is 0.6km (1 mile) from the reserve's car park, but elderly and disabled visitors can drive closer by arrangement. The trails are natural, and can be difficult to negotiate for people with mobility problems.

OPENING TIMES
Open 9am to sunset (closed Tuesdays).

CHARGES
Yes, for non-RSPB members.

ELMLEY MARSHES IS AS CLOSE AS YOU CAN GET TO WILDERNESS in south east England. It is a vast area of coastal grazing marsh, with some saltmarsh, fleets, and brackish water pools. But it's not the landscape here that thrills – it's the birds, and most especially, the awesome birds of prey that wheel and soar in the skies above the marshes. In December the marshes can be bleak, with cold winds off the North Sea penetrating the Thames estuary, but on a clear day the sheer wildness of the area, and the sense of isolation, can become sublime.

Watch the flocks of starlings and small wading birds for clues to the raptors' positions. The sharp "tik tik" alarm of the starlings is a real giveaway, and if a merlin, hen harrier, marsh harrier, or short-eared owl is close, the birds will get up and fly around in a panic until the danger passes. Sometimes a rough-legged buzzard flies in, a rarely-seen migrant from Scandinavia that has become almost a regular on the Isle of Sheppey. Only in

Identifying the kestrel

The most common falcon is the kestrel. Don't mistake one for a merlin, even though its colouring is relatively close to the smaller, browner female merlin. Kestrels are more gingery, with distinctively two-toned, black-ended wings. They are the only ones that hover in the air, hanging as if tied on a string, until diving headlong into the grass after a tiny vole or mouse. At other times, they watch patiently for prey from a perch; they are also active remarkably late, even as dusk turns gently into night.

Left: A birdwatcher scans the skies from the bridge between reedbeds at Elmley Marshes.

Right (left to right): Wigeons winter at Elmley Marshes in huge numbers – look for them on the water; hares are mainly solitary, but can often be seen in pairs or groups in the winter, as the courtship season begins.

occasional "invasion" years do more than a handful reach the UK in autumn. The marsh and hen harriers are older friends that sail low over the ground, travelling much more quickly than you might think. Watch the extraordinary skill with which they bank over on raised wings, trying to scare up a pipit or disturb a vole – always watching, always in control. The bigger, heavier marsh harrier is also a sight to see, as it hones in on a moorhen or coot, or perhaps even a water vole.

Merlins tend to sit inconspicuously on a clod of earth or low post, keeping a low profile until they see a pipit or a finch flock – and then they suddenly take off, in fast pursuit of a possible meal. These small falcons – with a wingspan of only 53–68cm (21–27 in), chase their prey low and with speed, until the final dashing, twisting, and turning pursuit that decides the outcome of the encounter. Often the intended prey gets away and the merlin gives up and peels away, until the next time.

WHERE ELSE TO SEE
BIRDS OF PREY

There are few sights to beat seeing these majestic birds swooping over an icy winter landscape.

The whole Solway Firth region, along the Cumbrian/Scottish border, is excellent for winter birds of prey. [SC]

Winter birds of prey can be seen at **Titchwell Marsh**, Hunstanton, on the North Norfolk coast, and **Minsmere** (*see pp.100–101*) in Suffolk. [SE]

You might be successful at other estuaries, including **Lindisfarne** (*see pp.274–275*) in Northumberland, the **Dee** (*see pp.14–15*), Wirral, and the **Ribble** in Lancashire. [N]

Several of the English south coast estuaries have winter birds of prey. Inland, the wetland centre at **Slimbridge**, near Dursley, Gloucestershire (*see pp.34–35*), is always worth a visit. [M]

THROUGH THE YEAR
ELMLEY MARSHES

In **spring**, look for breeding lapwings and redshanks, even from the car park; avocets should be in front of the first hide. Shovelers, pochards, tufted ducks, and shelducks all nest here. You should also see marsh harriers, the males displaying in steep undulations high in the sky. Yellow wagtails add colour in summer, as do dragonflies, damselflies, and butterflies of many species.

By late **summer**, migrant waders are returning, including green sandpipers and spotted redshanks, and little egrets can be numerous. Look for family parties of marsh harriers around the general area.

The number of ducks soars in **winter** to include around 20,000 wigeons and 5,000 teals. The wader roost at high tide can include several hundred grey plovers and black-tailed godwits, and several thousand dunlins.

Main: Elmley Marshes is a place of eerie wilderness in winter, yet lies so close to major towns and cities.

Above: A female marsh harrier flying up from the reedbed, where it both breeds and winters.

Below: The male merlins have a slate-blue upper plumage, in contrast to the female's brown feathers. Both birds are extremely agile, using quick, shallow wingbeats to give them enormous but controlled speed.

Below: This is one of the few places to see a rough-legged buzzard.

JAN
FEB
MAR
APR
MAY
JUN
JUL
AUG
SEP
OCT
NOV
DEC

Left: Knots display in huge groups, with birds so tightly distributed that the flock resembles a swarm.

Right (left to right): During low tide, birds feed out on the mud and sand flats; a dunlin at rest; oystercatchers roosting on a gravel pit at Snettisham; a Eurasian oystercatcher feeds on the mud.

WHERE
Snettisham RSPB Reserve, Snettisham, Hunstanton, Norfolk PE36 6LQ

CONTACT
RSPB Snettisham, tel: 01485 542689; snettisham@rspb.org.uk

GETTING THERE
By car, take the A149 from King's Lynn towards Hunstanton, and follow the brown signs to the RSPB reserve. The nearest station is King's Lynn; regular buses run between King's Lynn and Snettisham village – the reserve is a 3.2-km (2-mile) walk from there.

ACCESS AND FACILITIES
Snettisham does not have any facilities. There are facilities in the local villages, and at nearby RSPB Titchwell Marsh, which is just north of Hunstanton, and around 20 minutes away by car.

OPENING TIMES
Open all year round.

CHARGES
None.

Snettisham's star species

The knots (*pictured*) that fly together so spectacularly and in such great numbers at Snettisham are dumpy, short-legged wading birds, driven from the mudflats by the rising tide. They forage on mud and sand, using their tapered beaks to find hidden invertebrates. The red knot is a champion amongst migrating birds, with some flying from the top of North America to the southern-most tip of South America. Those in the UK come from Canada and Greenland.

Main: The heady sight of hundreds of thousands of birds taking flight at high tide. **Right panel:** A knot flock in winter plumage.

AERIAL DISPLAYS

WRAP UP WARM AGAINST THE WINTER WINDS, because Snettisham reserve is a truly wild place and very cold in December, and in order to witness its most amazing sight, you'll need to walk across the wide beaches of The Wash for about 20 minutes before the main event. Check the times of the tide before you go; for this to work, you need to be there on a rising tide and, best of all, a big spring tide, when the whole estuary is submerged.

Out on the mud and sand flats of The Wash, you'll see tens or even hundreds of thousands of wading birds feeding at low tide. As the tide rises, the mud and sand flats disappear underwater, and the birds are suddenly forced to move by the incoming sea. They take off, and fly in vast and awesome flocks towards you at Snettisham, which provides one of the safe refuges at which they can rest until the falling tide allows them back onto the reinvigorated tidal flats. Some of the birds, such as the redshanks, curlews, bar-tailed godwits, oystercatchers, and

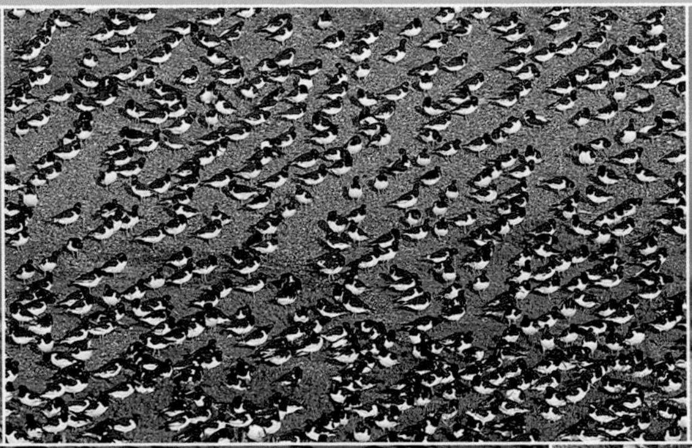

JAN
FEB
MAR
APR
MAY
JUN
JUL
AUG
SEP
OCT
NOV
DEC

WHERE ELSE TO SEE
FLOCKS OF WADERS

You can enjoy epic displays of wading birds at many estuaries, although usually in smaller numbers.

Hest Bank on Morecambe Bay in Lancashire is excellent for waders, as is nearby **Southport Pier**. **Hilbre Island** in the Dee Estuary (*see pp.14–15*) on the Wirral attracts huge numbers of birds. [N]

In the southeast, try **Titchwell Marsh** RSPB Reserve or **Breydon Water**, close to Great Yarmouth, both in Norfolk; **Leigh-on-sea** in Essex; or the Medway complex of north Kent. [SE]

There are large numbers of waders on many south-coast estuaries, including Dawlish Warren on the **Exe Estuary** (*see pp.286–287*). [SW]

Langstone Harbour in Hampshire, a sheltered harbour situated between Portsmouth and Chichester harbours, is a good site for waders. [SE]

THROUGH THE YEAR
SNETTISHAM

Spring sees migrants such as wheatears and sand martins return from Africa. Common terns and hundreds of black-headed gulls nest on the lagoons. Many of the wading birds have transformed into their colourful breeding plumage by the spring, and are waiting until the time is right to head for the Arctic.

In **summer**, watch for barn owls at dawn and dusk over the saltmarsh and surrounding fields, and nesting avocets. Butterflies such as peacocks and painted ladies are frequently seen over the mass of colourful wild flowers on the shingle, including yellow-horned poppies and viper's bugloss.

Thrushes and finches migrate overhead by day in **autumn**, and tens of thousands of waders return. Wigeon and brent geese arrive from breeding grounds, too. Check the skies for birds of prey, including peregrines and hen harriers.

As the tide draws in, thousands of birds are chased by the waters of The Wash and forced to fly straight towards you.

grey plovers, are wonderful to watch because of the sheer size of the flocks. But others, particularly the smaller waders, such as the dunlins and knots, really steal the show. They perform to their admiring public, gathering in great, dense packs and lines – almost like bee swarms – rising, falling, twisting and turning, stretching and contracting, in great rhythmic sweeps and stalls, before pouring in like hailstones to the roost site. Then, as if they have not quite decided it is safe, or they really want to be just a little farther one way or another, up they get and do it all over again, to land once more, close to where they were in the first place.

They fly almost as one, now dark, now flashing silvery-white, as all turn their dark backs to you, then their pale undersides, at once, in a show of coordination that is second to none: and all, it seems, without a signal or mishap. Never, so far as you can tell, do two birds ever make contact, except when on the ground, where they hustle and bustle shoulder to shoulder in front of the rising tide. The return to the mudflats as they are slowly exposed is a less coordinated affair; but if you can't resist staying to watch, the smaller flocks will still reward you with some fine performances.

Above: The birds return in large numbers to roost in autumn.

WHERE
Kingley Vale, West Stoke, Chichester, West
Sussex PO18; www.naturalengland.org.uk

CONTACT
Natural England, tel: 01273 476595;
sussex.surrey@naturalengland.org.uk

GETTING THERE
Kingley Vale lies 5km (3 miles) northwest
of Chichester. By car, take the A286 from
Chichester, leaving it at Mid Lavant to
continue towards West Stoke. You'll see
a signpost to the reserve's car park on the
west side of the village. The visitor centre
is signposted from there and is about a
15-minute walk along a footpath leading
to the main entrance. By rail, travel to
Chichester; bus sevice no. 54 runs
from Chichester to West Stoke Farm.

ACCESS AND FACILITIES
The visitor centre is unmanned with no
toilets or facilities. The track from the car park
to the centre is manageable for wheelchairs
but after that the terrain is uneven.

OPENING TIMES
Open all year round.

CHARGES
None.

Toxic temptation

Yew seeds are notoriously toxic, yet the bright
red berries are eaten with relish by birds such
as thrushes and finches. If they were to crack
the seeds inside they would die, but since they
swallow them whole, the seeds pass through
their bodies intact, to sprout into seedlings where
they fall. In this way the tree has, over the course
of evolution, encouraged animals that spread its
seeds while eliminating any that destroy them.
The foliage is poisonous too, but the toxins are
the basis of a drug that is effective against cancer.

ANCIENT YEW FOREST

I N THE COLD DAYS OF DECEMBER, when the branches of most native trees are bare and low-growing plants
have been beaten down by winter rain and frost, one tree remains almost unnaturally glossy and vigorous – the
yew. This tough survivor is one of only three needle-leaved evergreen trees native to Britain, along with the Scots
pine and the juniper. We usually associate the yew with churchyards and formal gardens, but it is widespread in
the wild on lime-rich soils, where it tends to grow in mixed woodland. But the Kingley Vale reserve in West Sussex
contains the largest and oldest yew forest in western Europe; some of these trees are the oldest living things in Britain.

As you approach the forest from the south along the main path, you get little inkling of the sight that
awaits you. Once past the small field centre, the path leads you to the left of the trees in the bottom of the valley,
and eventually through a dark gap into the very heart of the yew forest. The scene that greets you seems to have

Main: These venerable yew
trees have witnessed countless
generations of human activity.

Left: A Bronze Age burial mound
– the reserve has 14 monuments.

Right (left to right): Brain fungi
grow on dead wood; roe deer.

Right panel (top and bottom):
A coal tit feasting on berries;
slippery Jack fungus grows under
the yews.

sprung from one of the more alarming fairy tales. As you thread your way between a succession of huge, gnarled trees – centuries or possibly thousands of years old – your feet crunch on the scattered fragments of dead branches on the ground. The forest floor is otherwise bare, because few plants can grow in the intense shade beneath a yew tree, let alone a whole forest of them. Massive trunks surround you; many split and hollow, some entirely horizontal – uprooted by storms.

At the northern end of the valley is the biggest yew of all: a leviathan with branches that have arched down to the ground and taken root to create a whole grove of trees. Yet the parent still lives, with fresh new growth sprouting from its ancient trunk. The yews produce berries that attract birds, who have spread the seed to create the younger forest of yews on the surrounding slopes. The path takes you up to Bronze Age burial mounds at the the top of the hill, and far-reaching views. This landscape has been special for a very long time.

WHERE ELSE TO SEE
ANCIENT YEWS

Yew trees are widespread throughout Britain. In the wild they favour the free-draining, lime-rich soils that develop on chalk or limestone, but many have been planted in churchyards and have thrived for hundreds of years. Some are as old as the yews growing in the core of Kingley Vale.

Box Hill in Tadworth, Surrey, is a chalk down with many wild yew trees, some quite old. The county also has several ancient churchyard yews, including those at **Tandridge** and nearby **Crowhurst.** [SE]

The churchyard yew at **Much Marcle**, Herefordshire, is estimated to be at least 1,000 years old. [M]

The yew in the churchyard at **Fortingall**, Perth and Kinross in Scotland, is reputed to be the oldest in Britain, at anything up to 5,000 years old. [SC]

The **Castle of Crom** in County Fermanagh, Northern Ireland, has two extraordinary yews. Planted in the 17th century, both have grown into bizarre tangles of branches. [NI]

THROUGH THE YEAR
KINGLEY VALE

The old grasslands between the yew groves of Kingley Vale burst into flower in **spring**. There may be up to 50 species of plants in each square metre of the ancient turf, including salad burnet, wild thyme, common rock-rose, and many others that flower later in summer. Nightingales sing from the deciduous scrub fringing the yew forest.

Summer is the season for butterflies, with 39 of Britain's 58 breeding species recorded here. Many are residents, such as the boldly marked marbled white and the delicate chalkhill blue. Bolder residents include birds of prey, including hobbies, tawny owls, and sparrowhawks.

In **autumn**, migrant flocks of redwings and fieldfares – relatives of thrushes – arrive from Scandinavia to feast on the berries of the yews and other trees. This is also the season of the roe and fallow deer ruts, when the bucks of the vale compete over females.

Estimated at anything from 500 to 2,000 years old, the ancient yews of Kingley Vale are among the national monuments of Britain.

Below: The brown argus butterfly.

JAN
FEB
MAR
APR
MAY
JUN
JUL
AUG
SEP
OCT
NOV
DEC

REGIONAL DIRECTORY

REGIONAL DIRECTORY

The information in this Directory is intended to help you find out more about the sites listed in this book. Some, being natural features of the landscape, lack familiar reference points such as postcodes and visitor centres, but even small, local wildlife trusts and societies are generally only too happy to advise real enthusiasts. Even when going out locally or to popular visitor destinations, it's best to get the latest information about where and when you can go. For example, your rights to go onto some areas of open land may be restricted while work is carried out, for safety reasons, or during breeding seasons. If you're visiting wild places, check weather conditions before you leave, and don't be afraid to turn back if conditions change. Remember that much of what we generally think of as "the countryside" is privately owned, so always respect private property. Follow the countryside code, at www.countrysideaccess.gov.uk, which is designed to help everyone respect, protect, and enjoy the countryside.

SCOTLAND

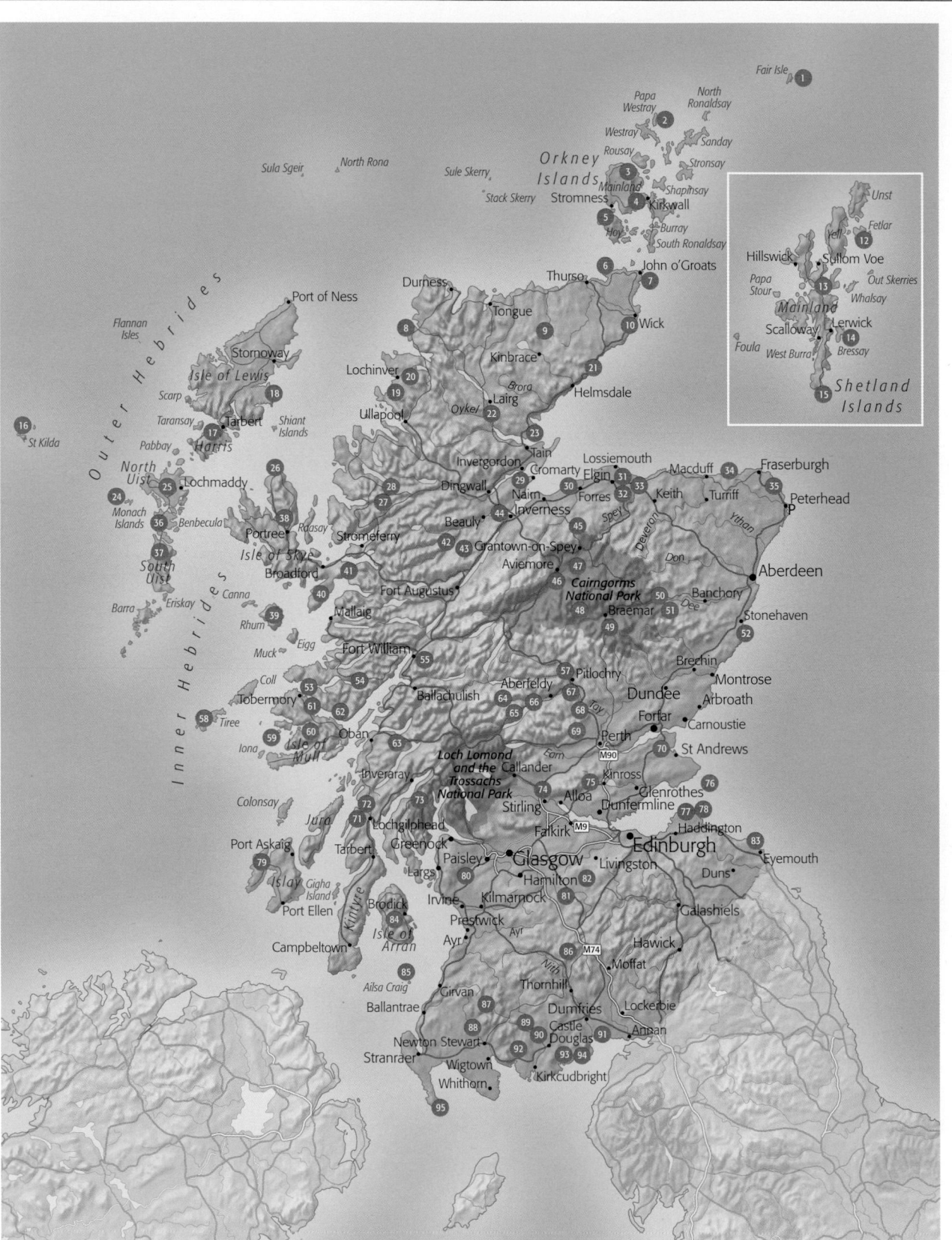

Ardtornish (pp.206–207) 62
Ardtornish Estate, Morvern, near Oban, Argyll PA34 5UZ; contact: The Ardtornish Estate Office; tel: 01967 421288; tourism@ardtornish.co.uk
www.ardtornish.co.uk

Argyll Forest Park 73
Dunoon, Argyll and Bute G83 7AR; Recreation team; tel: 01877 382383; cowal.trossachs.fd@forestry.gsi.gov.uk
www.forestry.gov.uk/argyllforestpark

Ailsa Craig 85
RSPB Ailsa Craig Reserve, near Girvan, South Ayrshire; tel: 0141 3310993; glasgow@rspb.org.uk
www.rspb.org.uk

Ariundle Forest (pp.238–239) 54
Ariundle Nature Reserve, Strontian, Argyll, Scotland PH36 4JA; contact: The Reserve Manager, Scottish National Heritage; tel: 01397 704716; enquiries@snh.gov.uk
www.nnr-scotland.org.uk

Bass Rock (pp. 168–169) 78
Firth of Forth, North Berwick, Scotland; contact: The Scottish Seabird Centre, The Harbour, North Berwick EH39 4SS, Scotland; tel: 01620 890202.
www.seabird.org

Beinn Eighe (pp.202–203) 27
Beinn Eighe National Nature Reserve, Torridon Mountains, Kinlochewe, Highland, Scotland; contact: Beinn Eighe Visitor Centre; tel: 01445 760254; Scottish National Heritage, Kinlochewe Office; tel: 01445 760254.
www.snh.org.uk

Ben Lawers 65
Loch Tay, Killin, Perthshire; contact: NTS Ranger Service, Main Street, Killin FK21 8UW; tel: 01567 820988, or the NTS Mountain Visitor Centre; tel: 01567 820397
www.nnr-scotland.org.uk

Ben Nevis 55
Glen Nevis, Fort William PH33 6PF;
contact: Glen Nevis Visitor Centre;
tel: 01397 705922;
glen.nevis@highland.gov.uk
www.highland.gov.uk

Benbecula 36
Outer Hebrides; contact: The Scottish
Tourist Board; tel: 0150 6832121
www.isle-of-benbecula.co.uk

Berriedale 21
Between Wick and Helmdale, Highland
www.undiscoveredscotland.co.uk

Birks of Aberfeldy (pp.262–263) 67
The Birks of Aberfeldy, Aberfeldy,
Perthshire, Scotland; contact: Aberfeldy
Tourist Information Centre, The Square,
Aberfeldy, PH15 2DD; tel: 01887 820276,
or Visit Scotland; tel: 01738 627958;
info@visitscotland.com
www.perthshire.co.uk

Birsay Moors (pp.242–243) 3
RSPB Birsay Moors Reserve, Orkney
Islands, Scotland; tel: 01856 850176;
orkney@rspb.org.uk
www.rspb.org.uk

Black Wood of Rannoch (pp.66–67) 64
Kinloch Rannoch, Perth and Kinross,
Scotland; contact: Rannoch Moor Visitor
Centre, Rannoch Station PH17 2QA;
tel: 01796 472215.
www.perthshire.co.uk

Braehead Moss 82
Braehead Moss National Nature Reserve,
near Carnwath, Lanarkshire ML11 8EY;
contact: Falls of Clyde Scottish Wildlife
Trust Reserve (*see below*).

Buchanty Spout 69
River Almond, Easter Glenalmond,
Buchanty, near Crieff, Perthshire
www.perthshire.co.uk

Caerlaverock 91
WWT Caerlaverock Wetland Centre,
Eastpark Farm, Caerlaverock, Dumfries and
Galloway DG1 4RS; tel: 01387 770200;
info.caerlaverock@wwt.org.uk
www.wwt.org.uk

The Cairngorms (pp.178–179) 48
The Cairngorms National Park, Aviemore,
Scottish Highlands; contact: Cairngorms
National Park Authority; tel: 01479
873535; enquiries@cairngorms.co.uk
www.cairngorms.co.uk
Glenmore Visitor Centre,
Glenmore Forest Park, Aviemore,
Highland PH22 1QU, Scotland;
tel: 01479 861220

Carstramon Wood 92
Carstramon Wood Scottish Wildlife
Trust Reserve, Gatehouse of Fleet,
Dumfries and Galloway DG7;
contact: Scottish Wildlife Trust;
tel: 0131 312 7765
www.swt.org.uk

Corrimony 43
RSPB Corrimony Reserve, Loch Ness,
Cannich, Highland IV63 6;
tel: 01463 715000; nsro@rspb.org.uk
www.rspb.org.uk

Cromarty Firth 29
RSPB Nigg Bay Reserve, Cromarty Firth,
Nigg, Highland IV18 0; tel: 01463 715000
www.rspb.org.uk

Culbin Sands 30
RSPB Culbin Sands Reserve, Nairn,
Highland IV36 2; tel: 01463 715000
www.rspb.org.uk

Dalbeattie Forest 93
Dalbeattie, Dumfries & Galloway DG5 4;
contact: The Recreation Ranger; tel: 01387
860247; feae@forestry.gsi.gov.uk
www.forestry.gov.uk

Dornoch Firth 23
Loch Fleet National National Reserve,
Dornoch Firth, Golspie, Sutherland
KW10 6TG; contact: the Reserve
Manager; tel: 01408 633602,
or the Scottish Wildlife Trust;
tel: 0131 3127765
www.snh.org.uk

Duncansby Head 7
Nr John O'Groats, Caithness, Highland
www.undiscoveredscotland.co.uk

Dunnet Head 6
Nr Castleton, Pentland Firth, Caithness,
Highland KW14 8XD
www.undiscoveredscotland.co.uk

Fair Isle 1
Fair Isle Bird Observatory,
Shetland ZE2 9JU, tel: 01595 760258;
fairisle.birdobs@zetnet.co.uk
www.fairislebirdobs.co.uk

Falls of Clyde 81
Falls of Clyde Scottish Wildlife Trust
Reserve, New Lanark ML11 9DB;
Visitor Centre; tel: 01555 665262;
fallsofclyde@swt.org.uk
www.swt.org.uk

Falls of Shin 22
Achany Glen, Lairg, Sutherland IV27 4EE;
tel: 01549 402231;
info@fallsofshin.co.uk
www.fallsofshin.co.uk

Fetlar 12
Fetlar Interpretive Centre, Beach of Houbie,
Fetlar, Shetland ZE2 9DJ; contact:
Tourist Information; tel: 01957 733206;
info@fetlar.com
www.fetlar.com

Fingal's Cave 59
Staffa, west of Mull, Inner Hebrides, Argyll
and Bute PA73 6; contact: National Trust
for Scotland; tel: 01463 232034.
www.nts.org.uk

Firth of Forth (pp.296–297) 77
Between Fife and East Lothian, Scotland;
contact: The Scottish Seabird Centre, The
Harbour, North Berwick, Scotland EH39
4SS; tel: 01620 890202; info@seabird.org
www.seabird.org

Firth of Tay 70
Firth of Tay and Eden Estuary Reserve,
Dundee DD6 8; tel: 01463 72500;
enquiries@snh.gov.uk
www.snh.org.uk

Forsinard Flows (pp.216–217) 9
RSPB Forsinard Flows Reserve, Forsinard,
nr Thurso, Highland, KW13 6YT; tel: 01641
571225; forsinard@rspb.org.uk
www.rspb.org.uk

Fortingall Church 66
Fortingall, Aberfeldy, Perthshire PH15 2NQ;
contact: Forestry Commission Scotland;
tel: 0845 3673787;
fcscotland@forestry.gsi.gov.uk
www.forestry.gov.uk

Fowlsheugh 52
RSPB Fowlsheugh Reserve, Stonehaven,
Crawton, Aberdeenshire AB39; tel: 01346
532017; strathbeg@rspb.org.uk
www.rspb.org.uk

Galloway Forest Park (pp.234–235) 87
Contact: The Recreation Ranger,
Galloway Forest Park,
tel: 01671 402420; Clatteringshaws Visitor
Centre, New Galloway DG7 3SQ; tel:
01644 420285
www.forestry.gov.uk

Glen Affric 42
Cannich, Beauly IV47 7ND; contact: the
Reserve Manager; tel: 01479 810477, or
Forestry Commission Scotland;
tel: 01320 366322
www.forestry.gov.uk/glenaffric

Glen Nant 65
Glen Nant National Nature Reserve, Argyll
and Bute PA35 1; contact: the Reserve
Manager; tel: 01546 603611, or Forestry
Commission Scotland; tel: 01631 566155
www.snh.gov.uk

Glen Tanar (pp.246–247) 51
Glen Tanar, Aboyne, Aberdeenshire
AB34 5EU, Scotland; contact
Glen Tanar Ranger Service; tel: 01339
886072; ranger@glentanar.co.uk
www.glentanar.co.uk

Glencanisp Forest 20
Lochinvir, Wester Ross; contact: The Assynt
Foundation, Glencanisp, Lochinver,
Sutherland; tel: 01571 844100
www.assyntfoundation.org

Handa Island 8
Ferries to the island leave from Tarbet,
Argyll and Bute; contact: Scottish Wildlife
Trust; tel: 0131 3127765;
northernenquiries@swt.org.uk
www.swt.org.uk

Harris 17
Western Isles HS3 3UA; contact
Tourist Information; tel: 01851 703088
www.explore-harris.com

Hermaness 13
Hermaness National Nature Reserve,
The Visitor Centre, Muckle Flugga,
Hermaness, Unst, Shetland;
tel: 01595 693345
www.nature-shetland.co.uk

The Hermitage 68
Dunkeld, Perthshire PH8 0HX; contact: The
National Trust for Scotland; tel: 0844
4932100; information@nts.org.uk
www.nts.org.uk

Hoy 5
RSPB Hoy Reserve, Orkney KW16 3NS;
tel: 01856 850176; orkney@rspb.org.uk
www.rspb.org.uk

Inverpolly 19
Inverpolly National Nature Reserve,
Coigach, Wester Ross;
contact: Polly Estates, Inverpolly, Ullapool,
Ross-Shire IV26 2YB; tel: 01854 622452
www.inverpolly.com

Islay (pp.12–13) 79
Isle of Islay, Argyll and Bute, Scotland;
contact: RSPB Loch Gruinart Reserve,
Bushmills Cottage, Gruinart, Bridgend,
Isle of Islay, Argyll and Bute PA44 7PR,
Scotland; tel: 01496 850505;
loch.gruinart@rspb.org.uk
www.rspb.org.uk

Isle of Arran (pp.42–43) 84
Contact: Countryside Ranger Service,
Brodick Castle and Country Park, Isle of
Arran; tel: 01770 302462; Ayrshire and
Arran Tourist Board; tel: 0845 2255121;
info@ayrshire-arran.com
www.ayrshire-arran.com

Isle Of May 76
East of Anstruther KY10 3; contact: the Reserve Manager; tel: 01334 654038.
www.snh.org.uk
www.isleofmayferry.com

Isle of Mull (pp.226–227) 60
Isle of Mull, Argyll and Bute, Scotland; contact: The Pier Head, Craignure; tel: 01680 812377; craignure@visitscotland.com; RSPB Mull sea eagle watch, Loch Frisa; tel: 01688 302038
www.rspb.org.uk/brilliant

Isle of Rum 39
By Mallaig, Inverness-shire PH43 4RR; contact: the Reserve Office; tel: 01687 462026
www.snh.org.uk; www.isleofrum.com

Isle of Skye (seabirds) 26
Rubha Hunish seabird watchpoint, Trotternish Peninsula, Uig, Isle of Skye
www.skye-birds.com

Isle of Skye (otters) 41
The Eilean Bàn Trust, The Pier, Kyleakin, Isle of Skye, IV41 8PL; tel: 01599 530040
www.eileanban.org

Isle of Skye (sea eagles) 38
RSPB sea eagle watchpoint; contact: The Aros Centre, Viewfield Road, Portree, Isle of Skye IV51 9EU; tel: 01478 613649 or the RSPB; tel: 01471 822882
www.rspb.org.uk

Ken-Dee Marshes 90
RSPB Ken-Dee Marshes, Castle Douglas, Dumfries & Galloway DG7 2; tel: 01556 670464.
www.rspb.org.uk

Knapdale Forest 71
Lochgilphead PA31 8; contact: the Beat Forester; tel: 01546 602518.
www.forestry.gov.uk

Lewis 18
Western Isles; contact: Tourist information; tel: 01851 703088
www.isle-of-lewis.com

Linn of Tummel 57
Nr Killiecrankie, Pitlochry PH16 5LG; contact: The National Trust for Scotland; tel: 01796 473233.
www.nts.org.uk

Loch an Eilean 46
Rothiemurchus, Aviemore PH22 1QH; contact: The Visitor Centre; tel: 01479 811085.
www.rothiemurchus.net

Loch Davan 45
Dinnet, Aberdeenshire AB34 5LU; contact: Cairngorms National Park Authority; tel: 01479 873535; enquiries@cairngorms.co.uk
www.cairngorms.co.uk

Loch Garten (pp.86–87) 47
RSPB Loch Garten Reserve, Tulloch, Nethy Bridge, Highland PH25 3EF, Scotland; tel: 01479 831476; abernethy@rspb.org.uk
www.rspb.org.uk

Loch Ken 89
Castle Douglas DG7 3NQ; contact: the Recreation Ranger; tel: 01671 402420
www.forestry.gov.uk

Loch Kinnord 50
Dinnet, Aberdeenshire AB34 5JY; contact: Cairngorms National Park Authority; tel: 01479 873535; enquiries@cairngorms.co.uk
www.cairngorms.co.uk

Loch Leven (pp.260–261) 75
RSPB Vane Farm Nature Reserve, Perth and Kinross KY13 7LX, Scotland; tel: 01577 862355; vanefarm@rspb.org.uk
www.rspb.org.uk

Loch Maree 28
Ross-shire IV22 2HL; contact: the Reserve Manager; tel: 01445 760254
www.nnr-scotland.org.uk

Loch na Bo 33
Loch Oire 32
Loch Spynie 31
Near Elgin, Moray; contact: the Tourist Information Centre, 17 High St, Elgin IV30 1EG; tel: 01343 542666

Loch of Strathbeg 35
RSPB Loch of Strathbeg Reserve, Fraserburgh, Aberdeenshire AB43 8QN; tel: 01346 532017; strathbeg@rspb.org.uk
www.rspb.org.uk

Lochnagar 49
Balmoral, Aberdeenshire AB35 5; contact: the Ranger Service, Loch Muick Visitor Centre; tel: 013397 55059; info@balmoralcastle.com
www.balmoralcastle.com

Lochwinnoch (pp.82–83) 80
RSPB Lochwinnoch Reserve, nr Paisley, Renfrewshire, Scotland PA12 4JF; tel: 01505 842663; lochwinnoch@rspb.org.uk
www.rspb.org.uk

Lowther Hills 86
South Lanarkshire, Dumfries and Galloway; contact: The Museum of Lead Mining, Wanlockhead, Lanarkshire ML12 6UT; tel: 01659 74387.
www.visitdumfriesandgalloway.co.uk

Mersehead 94
RSPB Mersehead Reserve, Southwick, Dumfries and Galloway DG2 8AH; tel: 01387 780579; mersehead@rspb.org.uk
www.rspb.org.uk

Moine Mhor 72
Moinhe Moor National Nature Reserve, Kilmichael Glassery, Lochgilphead, Argyll and Bute PA31 8; contact: the Reserve Manager; tel: 01546 603611
www.snh.org.uk

Monach Isles (pp.268–269) 24
The Monach Isles, Western Isles, Scotland; contact: Scottish Natural Heritage, Stilligarry, Isle of South Uist, tel: 01870 620238, or for trips to the islands, The Uist Outdoor Centre, Loch Maddy, North Uist HS6 5AE; tel: 01876 500480.
www.uistoutdoorcentre.co.uk

Moray Firth (pp.220–221) 44
Ross-shire, Scotland, IV10 8SD; contact: North Kessock Dolphin and Seal Centre; tel: 01463 731866
www.wdcs.org

Mull of Galloway 95
RSPB Mull of Galloway Reserve, Dumfries and Galloway DG9 0; tel: 01556 670464
www.rspb.org.uk

North Uist (pp.108–109) 25
North Uist, Outer Hebrides, Scotland; contact: RSPB Balranald Reserve; tel: 01463 715000; nsro@rspb.org.uk
rspb.co.uk

Noss 14
Noss, off Bressay, Shetland; contact: the Tourist Centre, Market Cross, Lerwick; tel: 01595 693434
visitshetland.com

Orkney 4
Contact: Kirkwall Visitor Centre, 6 Broad Street, Kirkwall KW15 1DH; tel: 01856 872856; info@visitorkney.com
www.visitorkney.com

Papa Westray (pp.112–113) 2
Papa Westray, Orkney Islands, Scotland; contact: RSPB North Hill Reserve; tel: 01856 850176; orkney@rspb.org.uk
www.papawestray.co.uk

Queen Elizabeth Forest Park 74
Contact: The Visitor Centre, Trossachs Road, Aberfoyle, Stirling, Scotland FK8 3UX; tel: 01877 38225890

Sleat Peninsula 40
Isle of Skye, Inner Hebrides; contact: Clan Donald Visitor Centre, Isle of Skye IV45 8RS; tel: 01471 844305
www.sleat.f9.co.uk

St Abbs Head 83
St Abbs, Eyemouth TD14 5QF; contact The Ranger's Cottage; tel: 01890 771443
www.snh.org.uk

St Kilda 16
Outer Hebrides; contact: The National Trust for Scotland; tel: 0844 493 2100; information@nts.org.uk
www.kilda.org.uk

South Uist 37
Loch Druidibeg Nature Reserve, Stilligarry, South Uist HS8 5RS; contact: the Reserve Manager; tel: 01870 620238
www.snh.org.uk

Sumburgh Head 15
RSPB Sumburgh Head Reserve, Lerwick, Shetland ZE3 9; tel: 01950 460800.
www.rspb.org.uk

Tiree 58
Inner Hebrides, Argyll and Bute PA77 6UH; contact: the Visitor Information Helpline; tel: 01879 220510; info@isleoftiree.com
www.isleoftiree.com

Tobermory 53
Isle of Mull, Argyll and Bute; contact: Tourist information; tel: 01688 302182
www.tobermory.co.uk

Treshnish Islands 61
Inner Hebrides, Argyll and Bute; contact: The Hebridean Trust; tel: 01865 311468
www.hebrideantrust.org

Troup Head 34
RSPB Troup Head, Fraserburgh, Aberdeenshire AB45 3; tel: 01346 532017; strathbeg@rspb.org.uk
www.rspb.org.uk

Wick 10
Caithness, Highland, KW1 4NG; contact: Tourist information; tel: 0845 2255121
www.visithighlands.com

Wood of Cree 88
RSPB Wood of Cree Reserve, Newton Stewart, Dumfries and Galloway DG8 6; tel: 01556 670464
www.rspb.org.uk

NORTHERN ENGLAND

Ainsdale Dunes (pp.88–89) 59
Ainsdale Dunes, Sefton Sands, Formby, Liverpool L37 1LJ; www.seftoncoast.org.uk; contact: the Natural England site manager; tel: 01704 578774; northwest@naturalengland.org.uk

Arnside Knott 36
Between Silverdale and Arnside, Cumbria; contact: Morecambe Bay Properties Office, Bank House Farm, Silverdale, Carnforth, Lancashire LA5 0RE; tel: 01524 702815 (Warden's Office), or 01524 701178 (General enquiries)

Bempton Cliffs (pp.104–105) 33
RSPB Bempton Cliffs, Cliff Lane, Bempton, Bridlington, East Yorkshire YO15 1JD; tel: 01262 851179; bempton.cliffs@rspb.org.uk
www.rspb.org.uk

Blacktoft Sands (pp.158–159) 57
RSPB Blacktoft Sands Reserve, nr Goole, East Yorkshire; tel: 01405 704665; blacktoftsands@rspb.org.uk
www.rspb.org.uk

Bleasdale 49
Forest of Bowland, Lancashire; contact: Bowland Countryside Ranger Service
www.lancswt.org.uk

Blencathra 14
Blencathra Field Centre, Threlkeld, Keswick, Cumbria CA12 4SG; tel: 017687 79601
www.field-studies-council.org/ blencathra

Calf of Man 35
The Sound Visitor Centre, Port St Mary, nr Cregneash, Isle of Man; tel: 01624 648000; enquiries@mnh.gov.im; contact: The Manx Wildlife Trust, Tynwald Mills, St Johns; tel: 01624 801985
www.manxwt.org.uk

Coquet Islands 6
RSPB Coquet Island Reserve, off Amble, Northumberland NE65 0; contact: Amble Tourist Information; tel: 01665 712313
www.rspb.org.uk

Dalby Forest 30
Dalby Forest Visitor Centre, nr Thornton-le-Dale, Yorkshire YO18 7LT; tel: 01751 460295
www.forestry.gov.uk

Dee Estuary 69
RSPB Parkgate Reserve, Neston, Cheshire CH64 6; tel: 0151 3367681
www.rspb.org.uk

Druridge Bay (pp.20–21) 7
Druridge Bay Country Park Visitor Centre, Red Row, Morpeth, Northumberland NE61 5BX; tel: 01670 760968; druridgebay@northumberland.gov.uk; Northumberland Wildlife Trust; tel: 0191 2846884; mail@northwt.org.uk
www.northumberland.gov.uk

Ettrick Weir (pp.284–285) 1
Philiphaugh, Selkirk, Selkirkshire TD7 5LX, Scotland; contact: Philiphaugh Salmon Viewing Centre; tel: 01750 21766; mss@philiphaugh.com
salmonviewingcentre.com

East Fleetham ④
Northumberland NE68 7UX;
contact: Northumberland Wildlife Trust;
mail@northwt.org.uk
www.nwt.org.uk

Fairburn Ings ⑤⑤
RSPB Fairburn Ings Reserve,
Newton Lane, Ledston, Castleford,
Yorkshire WF10 2BH;
tel: 01977 628191;
fairburnings@rspb.org.uk
www.rspb.org.uk

Far Ings ⑤⑧
Far Ings Visitor Centre, Far Ings Road,
Barton-on-Humber DN18 5RG;
tel: 01652 637055
www.lincstrust.org.uk

Farndale Moor (pp.58–59) ㉘
Hutton le Hole, North Yorkshire;
contact: Natural England;
tel: 01904 435500;
York@naturalengland.org.uk
www.naturalengland.org.uk

The Farne Islands (pp.126–127) ③
Off Seahouses, Northumberland; contact:
The National Trust; tel: 01665 720651
(general enquiries); for boat trips,
tel: 01665 721099 (Infoline);
enquiries@farne-islands.com
www.farne-islands.com

Filey ㉜
The Country Park Café, North Cliff,
Filey, North Yorkshire, YO14 9HG
(open Easter–Nov) is excellent for
seawatching, with bird log and key
to hide; off season, contact Filey Brigg
Ornithological Group
www.fbog.co.uk

Flamborough Head (pp.252–253) ㉞
Bridlington, Yorkshire YO15 1AR;
contact: Bridlington Tourist Information;
tel: 01262 673474;
bridlington.tic@eastriding.gov.uk
www.flamboroughuk.net

Formby Pinewoods ⑤⑨
Formby Pinewoods and Red Squirrel
Reserve, Victoria Road, Freshfield,
Formby L37 1LJ;
tel: 01704 878591;
formby@nationaltrust.org.uk
www.nationaltrust.org.uk

Friars Crag (pp.212–213) ⑬
Derwentwater, Keswick, Cumbria CA12
5DJ; contact: the Lake District National
Park Authority;
tel: 01539 724555;
hq@lake-district.gov.uk
www.lake-district.gov.uk

Gait Barrows ㉛
Gait Barrows National Nature Reserve,
nr Morecambe Bay LA5 0;
tel: 01539 531604;
northwest@naturalengland.org.uk
www.naturalengland.org.uk

Geltsdale (pp.24–25) ⑩
RSPB Geltsdale Reserve, Stagsike
Cottages, Hallbankgate, Brampton,
Cumbria CA8 2PW;
contact: The Reserve Information Point,
tel: 01697 746717;
northernengland@rspb.org.uk
www.rspb.org.uk

Gordale Scar ㊹
Malham, Skipton, North Yorkshire
BD23 4DL; enquiries@malhamdale.com
www.malhamdale.com

Grasmere ㉒
Lake District National Park, Cumbria;
contact: Grasmere Tourist Information
Centre, Red Bank Road, The Lake District
LA22 9SW; tel: 015394 35245
www.grasmere.com

Hatfield Moor ㉢
Doncaster, South Yorkshire DN9 1;
tel: 01924 334500;
humber.pennines@englishnature.org.uk
www.naturalengland.org.uk

Hest Bank ㊴
RSPB Morecambe Bay Reserve, Hest
Bank, 3km (2 miles) northeast of
Morecambe on the A5105; tel: 01524
701601 or contact nearby RSPB Leighton
Moss Reserve (*see below*).

Hilbre Island ㉘
Off West Kirby, The Wirral CH48 8;
contact: the Ranger; tel: 0151 632 4455;
hilbre@wirral.gov.uk
www.deeestuary.co.uk/hilbre

Humberhead Peatlands ㉕
Moorends, DN8 5; tel: 01924 334500;
humber.pennines@englishnature.org.uk
www.naturalengland.org.uk

Ingleton ㊵
Yorkshire Dales Ingleton Limestone Walk;
contact: the Site Manager, English Nature,
Chapel-le-Dale, Carnforth LA6 3JF;
tel: 015242 42021, or download the
walking guide from:
www.naturalengland.org.uk

Isle of Man (pp.300–301) ⑲
Isle of Man, Irish Sea;
contact: the Manx Wildlife Trust;
tel: 01624 801985;
enquiries@manxwt.org.uk
www.manxwt.org.uk

Kielder Forest ⑤
Hexham, Northumberland NE48 1ER;
contact: Kielder Castle Visitor Centre;
tel: 01434 250209;
kieldercastle@forestry.gsi.gov.uk
www.forestry.gov.uk

Leighton Moss (pp.78–79) ㊳
RSPB Leighton Moss Reserve, Storrs Lane,
Silverdale, Carnforth, Lancashire LA5 0SW;
tel: 01524 701601;
leighton.moss@rspb.org.uk
www.rspb.org.uk

Lindisfarne (pp.274–275) ②
Berwick-upon-Tweed, Northumberland
TD15 2SH; contact: Berwick Tourist
Information Office; tel: 01289 330733;
lindisfarne-centre@uk2.net
www.lindisfarne.org.uk

Liverpool Bay ㊿⑦
See Dee Estuary (*p.317*); also visit
www.deeestuary.co.uk

Lower Derwent Valley ⑫
Red Kite Trail starts and finishes at
Derwenthaugh Park car park at Winlaton
Mill on the A694
www.northernkites.org.uk

Malham Cove ㊸
Malham, North Yorkshire, BD23 4;
contact: Malham Tourist Information
Centre; tel: 01729 830363
www.malhamdale.org.uk

Manchester (peregrines) ㉒
RSPB peregrine viewing point,
Exchange Square, Manchester M3 1BD;
tel: 01484 861148
www.rspb.org.uk

Marshside ㊶
RSPB Marshside Reserve, Southport,
Lancashire PR9 9; tel: 01704 226190
www.rspb.org.uk

Martin Mere (pp.256–257) ㊾
Martin Mere Wetland Centre, Fish Lane,
Burscough, Lancashire L40 0TA;
contact: Martin Mere Wetland Centre;
tel: 01704 895181;
info.martinmere@wwt.org.uk
www.wwt.org.uk

Millington Pastures ㊽
East Riding, Yorkshire YO42 1TZ;
contact: Hull Tourist Information Centre;
tel: 01482 223559
www.yorkshirewoldsheritage.org.uk

Mount Grace Priory ㉗
Staddle Bridge, Northallerton, North
Yorkshire DL6 3JG; tel: 01609 883494
www.nationaltrust.org.uk

Muker Meadows ㉕
Yorkshire DL11 6; contact: Yorkshire
Dales National Park Authority;
tel: 0300 4560030
www.yorkshiredales.org.uk

Muncaster Castle ㉑
Ravenglass, Cumbria CA18 1RQ;
tel: 01229 717614
www.muncaster.co.uk

Nob End ㉛
Wildlife Trust for Lancashire Nob End
Reserve, Bolton, BL3 1;
tel: 01772 324129;
info@lancswt.org.uk
www.lancswt.org.uk

North York Moors (pp.232–233) ㉙
North York Moors National Park, Yorkshire;
contact: The Moors National Park Visitor
Centre; tel: 01439 770657;
info@northyorkmoors-npa.gov.uk
www.visitnorthyorkshiremoors.co.uk

Old Moor ㉓
RSPB Dearne Valley Reserve, Old Moor
Lane, Wombwell, Barnsley S73 0YF;
tel: 01226 751593;
old.moor@rspb.org.uk
www.rspb.org.uk

Orton Fells ㉔
Cumbria CA10 3;
contact: Natural England, Cumbria;
tel: 01539 792800;
northwest@naturalengland.org.uk
www.naturalengland.org.uk

Pennines ㊷
North Pennines AONB and Geopark
www.northpennines.org.uk

Ravenglass Estuary ⑳
Lake District National Park, Cumbria
CA18 1; contact: the Lake District National
Park Authority; tel: 01539 724555
www.lake-district.gov.uk

Ribble Estuary ㊿
RSPB Ribble Discovery Centre, Fairhaven
Lake, Inner Promenade, Lytham St Annes,
Lancashire FY8 1BD; tel: 01253 796292
www.rspb.org.uk

Robin Hood's Bay ㉛
Whitby YO22 4SJ; contact: Old Coastguard
Station visitor centre; tel: 01947 885900
www.robin-hoods-bay.co.uk

Salford Forest Park ㉛
Salford, Manchester M5 4; contact Peel
Holdings Limited, Peel Dome, The Trafford
Centre, Manchester M17 8PL;
tel: 0161 6298200
www.salfordforestpark.co.uk

Saltholme 🄦
RSPB Saltholme Reserve, Tees Valley
TS1 5; tel: 0191 2334300;
northernengland@rspb.org.uk
www.rspb.org.uk

Scales Moor 🄬
Ingleton, North Yorkshire LA6 3; contact:
Yorkshire Dales National Park Authority;
tel: 0300 4560030
www.yorkshiredales.org.uk

Seal Sands (pp.304–305) 🄮
Teesmouth National Nature Reserve,
Middlesbrough, Cleveland;
contact: The Countryside Wardens;
tel: 01429 853325;
northumbria@english-nature.org.uk;
Teesmouth Field Centre, Hartlepool Power
Station, Tees Road, Hartlepool TS25 2BZ;
tel: 01429 264912;
fieldcentre@teesmouth.freeserve.co.uk

Solway Firth 🄨
RSPB Campfield Marsh Reserve,
Bowness-on Solway
www.rspb.org.uk

Southport Pier 🄲
The Promenade, Southport, Merseyside
PR8 1QX; tel: 01704 533333
www.southportpier.com

Spurn Point (pp.264–265) 🄶
Spurn, near Kilnsea, Humberside HU12
0UB; tel: 01964 650533 or
01904 659570;
info@yorkshirewt.cix.co.uk
www.ywt.org.uk

St Mary's Island 🄶
Whitley Bay NE26 4RS; contact: St Mary's
Lighthouse & Visitor Centre;
tel: 0191 2008650
info@friendsofstmarysisland.co.uk
www.friendsofstmarysisland.co.uk

Strid Wood 🄶
Bolton Abbey, Yorkshire Dales BD23 6AN;
tel: 01756 718009
www.boltonabbey.com

Swinefleet 🄶
East Yorkshire; contact nearby RSPB
Blacktoft Sands Reserve (*see p.317*)

Upper Teesdale (pp.114–115) 🄖
Moor House Upper Teesdale National
Nature Reserve, Widdybank Farm,
Langdon Beck, Forest in Teesdale,
Barnard Castle, Co Durham;
contact: Natural England;
tel: 0845 6003078;
enquiries@naturalengland.org.uk
www.naturalengland.org.uk

Waterton Countryside Discovery Centre 🄴
Anglers Country Park, Haw Park Lane,
Wintersett, Wakefield WF4 2EB;
tel: 01924 303980;
countrysideinterp@wakefield.gov.uk
www.wakefield.gov.uk

Weardale 🄦
Irehopesburn, County Durham

Wensleydale 🄶
Yorkshire Dales; contact: Dales Countryside
Museum, Station Yard, Hawes, North
Yorkshire DL8 3NT;
tel: 01969 666220;
Yorkshire Dales National Park Authority;
tel: 0300 456 0030
www.wensleydale.org

Wharfedale 🄵
Yorkshire Dales; contact: the National Park
Centre, Grassington, nr Skipton;
tel: 01756 751690;
grassington@yorkshiredales.org.uk;
Yorkshire Dales National Park Authority;
tel: 0300 4560030
www.yorkshiredales.org.uk

Whitbarrow 🄶
Howe, near Kendal, Cumbria; contact
Natural England; tel: 0845 600 3078;
enquiries@naturalengland.org.uk;
Cumbria Wildlife Trust; tel: 01539 816300;
mail@cumbriawildlifetrust.org.uk
naturalengland.org.uk

York (peregrines) 🄷
Parliament Square, York YO1 8SG; contact:
Tourist information; tel: 01904 550099;
info@visityork.org
www.visityork.org

The Yorkshire Dales (pp.184–185) 🄶 🄵
Yorkshire Dales National Park Authority;
tel: 01756 751600;
info@yorkshiredales.org.uk
www.yorkshiredales.org.uk

NORTHERN IRELAND

Bann Estuary ❷
Castlerock Strand, Castlerock, near
Coleraine, Londonderry; contact: National
Trust Portstewart Strand Visitor Centre, 118
Strand Road, Portstewart, Londonderry
T55 7PG; tel: 028 70836396
portstewart@nationaltrust.org.uk
www.nationaltrust.org.uk

Belfast Lough (pp.38–39) ❼
RSPB Belfast Lough Reserve, Belvoir
Park Forest, Belfast, Antrim, Northern
Ireland BT8 7QT; tel: 02891 479009;
belfast.lough@rspb.org.uk
www.rspb.org.uk

Crom Castle ⓫
Upper Lough Erne, Newtownbutler, County
Fermanagh BT92 8AP; contact: National
Trust Visitor Centre; tel: 028 6773 8118;
crom@nationaltrust.org.uk
www.nationaltrust.org.uk

Giant's Causeway (pp.208–209) ❸
Bushmills, County Antrim; contact: Giant's
Causeway Visitor Centre, 44 Causeway
Road, Bushmills, Co. Antrim, BT57 8SU;
tel: 028 20731855
www.giantscausewaycentre.com
giantscauseway@nationaltrust.org.uk

Killykeeghan and Crossmurrin ❿
Killykeeghan and Crossmurrin Nature
Reserve, Marlbank, Florence Court,
County Fermanagh
www.ni-environment.gov.uk

Lough Foyle (pp.266–267) ❺
RSPB Lough Foyle Reserve, Lough Foyle,
Londonderry, Northern Ireland; tel: 028
90491547; rspb.nireland@rspb.org.uk
www.rspb.org.uk

Magilligan Dunes ❶
Magilligan Point Nature Reserve, Point
Road, Downhill Strand, Londonderry BT49
www.ni-environment.gov.uk

Peatlands Park ❻
Peatlands Country Park, 33 Derryhubbert
Road, Dungannon, Co Tyrone; tel: 028
38851102; peatland@doeni.gov.uk
www.ni-environment.gov.uk/peatlands

Rathlin Island ❹
RSPB Rathlin Island Seabird Centre,
Ballycastle, County Antrim;
tel: 028 20760062
www.rspb.org.uk

Ross Lough ❾
Ross Lough nature reserve, just west of
Monea off the B81, nr Enniskillen, County
Fermanagh; tel: 028 68621588
www.ni-environment.gov.uk

Strangford Lough (pp.288–289) ❽
County Down, Northern Ireland;
contact: Portaferry Tourist Information
Centre, The Stables, Castle Street,
Portaferry BT22 1NZ; tel: 028 42729882
www.strangfordlough.org

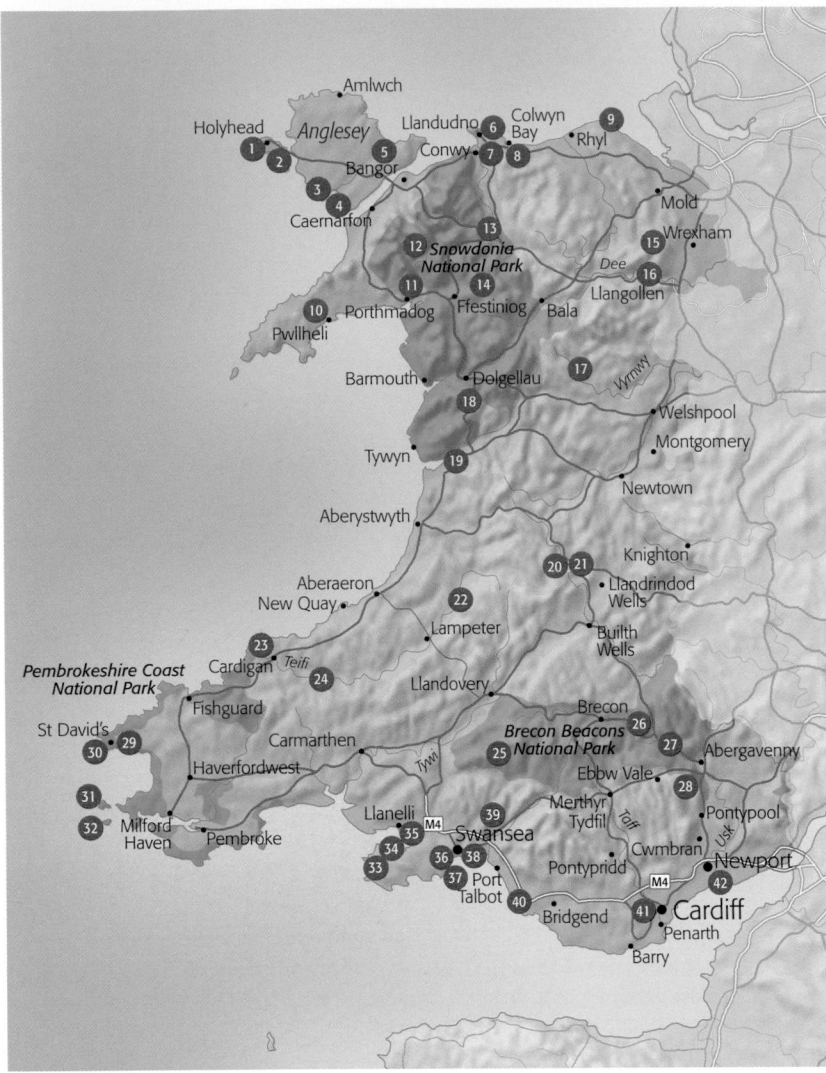

WALES

Abberffraw Dunes ❸
Llys Llewelyn Countryside Centre
ABERFFRAW, Isle of Anglesey
LL63 5AQ; tel: 01248 725700;
info@llys-llewelyn.com

Anglesey ❺
Mynydd Llwydiarth Forest near
Pentraeth Village; contact: Countryside
Council for Wales enquiry line,
tel: 0845 1306229
www.ccw.gov.uk

Black Mountain ㉕
The Mountain Centre, Libanus, Brecon,
Powys LD3 7DP; tel: 01874 623366

Blackpill Beach ㊱
Mumbles Tourist Information Centre,
Mumbles Rd, Mumbles, Swansea, West
Glamorgan SA3 4BU; tel: 01792 361302

Blaenavon (pp.236–237) ㉘
Blaenavon World Heritage Centre, Church
Road, Blaenavon, Torfaen NP4 9AS, Wales
www.world-heritage-blaenavon.org.uk

Burry Inlet ㉞
Gower Peninsula, Carmarthenshire,
Swansea SA3 7; contact: WWT National
Wetland Centre Wales, Llwynhendy,
Llanelli, Carmarthenshire SA14 9SH;
tel: 01554 741087;
info.llanelli@wwt.org.uk

Cader Idris (pp.254–255) ⑱
Cader Idris National Nature Reserve,
Dolgellau, Gwynedd, LL40 2HZ, Wales
www.snowdonia-npa.gov.uk

Cardiff ㊶
Clock Tower, Castle Street, Cardiff,
South Wales CF10 3RB.
Roath Park, 170 City Rd Cardiff
CF24 3JE; tel: 029 20311049;
parks@cardiff.gov.uk
Bute Park, Cardiff City Centre CF10;
parks@cardiff.gov.uk

Cardigan Bay ㉓
Cardigan, Wales; contact: Cardigan Bay
Marine Wildlife Centre, Patent Slip Building,
New Quay, Ceredigion SA45 9PS;
tel: 01545 560032; info@cbmwc.orgj

Cenarth Falls ㉔
River Teifi, Newcastle Emlyn,
Carmarthenshire SA38 9JL;
tel: 01239 710980
www.coracle-centre.co.uk

Conwy (pp.278–279) ❼
RSPB Conwy Reserve, Llandudno Junction,
Conwy LL31 9XZ, North Wales;
tel: 01492 584091; conwy@rspb.org.uk
www.rspb.org.uk

Cors Caron (pp.190–191) ㉒
Cors Caron National Nature Reserve,
Tregaron, Ceredigion SY25 6AN, Wales;
tel: 0845 1306229; info@wales.info

Craig-y-Cilau ㉗
Craig-y-Cilau National Nature Reserve,
Crickhowell, Powys NP7 7NA

Cwm Clydach ㊴
RSPB Cwm Clydach Reserve,
Craigcefnparc, Swansea, Swansea County
SA6 5TL; tel: 01792 842927
www.rspb.org.uk

Cwmllwyd Wood Reserve ㊳
Cockett Valley, Cockett, Swansea SA2 0FG;
tel: 01792 635749;
nature.conservation@swansea.gov.uk
www.swansea.gov.uk

Dee Estuary (pp.14–15) ❾
RSPB Point of Ayr Reserve, Talacre,
Holywell, Flintshire, North Wales
CH8 9SA
www.rspb.org.uk

Elan Valley ⑳
Elan Valley Visitor Centre, Elan Valley,
Rhayader, Powys LD6 5HP;
tel: 01597 810898
www.elanvalley.org.uk

Fairy Glen Nature Reserve ❽
Betws y Coed LL24 0HF;
tel: 01402 512740

Gigrin Farm (pp.32–33) ㉑
South Street, Rhayader, Powys LD6 5BL,
Wales; tel: 01597 810243

Glaslyn ⑪
RSPB Osprey viewing point, Pont Croesor,
near Prenteg, Porthmadog;
tel: 01248 363800; cymru@rspb.org.uk
www.rspb.org.uk/wales

Gower Peninsula (pp.122–123) ㉝
Swansea, South Wales;
contact: Wildlife Trust of South and West
Wales; tel: 01656 724100;
info@welshwildlife.org
www.welshwildlife.org

Great Ormes Head ❻
Llandudno, Conwy County LL32 8QB;
tel: 01492 874151
www.conwy.gov.uk/countryside

Kenfig Burrows ㊵
Port Talbot;
contact: Kenfig National Nature Reserve,
Ton Kenfig, Pyle CF33 4PT;
tel: 01656 743386

Lake Vyrnwy (pp.154–155) ⑰
Bryn Awel, Llanwddyn, Powys, Wales
SY10 0LZ;
contact: RSPB Lake Vyrnwy Reserve;
tel: 01691 870278; vyrnwy@rspb.org.uk
www.rspb.org.uk

Llanelli Wetland Centre ㉟
WWT National Wetland Centre Wales,
Llwynhendy, Llanelli, Carmarthenshire
SA14 9SH; tel: 01554 741087;
info.llanelli@wwt.org.uk
www.wwt.org.uk

Llangollen Canal ⑯
Llangollen, Wales LL20;
contact: British Waterways;
tel: 01606 723800;
enquiries.wbc@britishwaterways.co.uk

Llangorse Lake ㉖
Brecon Beacons National Park Authority,
Plas y Ffynnon, Cambrian Way, Brecon,
Powys LD3 7HP; tel: 01874 624437
www.breconbeacons.org

Lleyn Peninsula ⑩
National Heritage Coastline
www.llyn.info

Migneint Moors ⑭
Snowdonia;
contact: Snowdonia National Park
Authority, National Park Office,
Penrhyndeudraeth, Gwynedd LL48 6LF;
tel: 01766 770274;
parc@snowdonia-npa.gov.uk

Mumbles Pier ㊲
Mumbles Rd, Mumbles, Swansea
SA3 4EN; tel: 01792 365200
www.mumbles-pier.co.uk

Newborough Warren (pp.142–143) ❹
Isle of Anglesey, LL61, Wales;
tel: 01248 672500 (warden) or
0845 1306229 (Countryside Council for
Wales enquiry line); info@wales.info

Newport Wetlands ㊷
West Nash Road, Newport NP18 2BZ;
tel: (01633) 636350
www.rspb.org.uk/wales

Penrhos Feilw ❷
Anglesey LL65 2LT;
contact: Tourist Information Centre,
Llanfairpwll; tel: 01248 713177;
Llanfairpwll@nwtic.com

Ramsey Island (pp.182–183) ❸⓿
Pembrokeshire, West Wales;
RSPB Ramsey Island; tel: 07836 535733;
ramsey.island@rspb.org.uk
www.rspb.org.uk

Ruabon Moors (pp.102–103) ⓯
Visitor Centre, Ruthin Rd, Wrexham;
tel: 01978 751656;
info@oneplanetadventure.co.uk
www.oneplanetadventure.co.uk

Skokholm ❸❷
The Wildlife Trust South and West Wales;
tel: 01656 724100; info@welshwildlife.org
www.welshwildlife.org

Skomer (pp.150–151) ❸❶
South West Wales, SA62 3BE;
contact: The Wildlife Trust South and West
Wales, tel: 01656 724100;
info@welshwildlife.org
www.welshwildlife.org

Snowdon (pp.172–173) ⓬
Snowdonia National Park Authority,
National Park Offices, Penrhyndeudraeth,
Gwynedd LL48 6LF; tel: 01766 770274;
parc@eryri-npa.gov.uk

Snowdonia National Park ⓭
Snowdonia National Park Authority,
National Park Offices, Penrhyndeudraeth,
Gwynedd LL48 6LF; tel: 01766 770274;
parc@eryri-npa.gov.uk

South Stack ❶
Ellin's Tower RSPB Seabird Centre, Plas
Nico, South Stack, Holyhead, Anglesey
LL65 1YH; tel: 01407 764973
www.rspb.org.uk

St David's Head ❷❾
Ysgubor Fawr, Mathry, Haverfordwest,
Pembrokeshire SA62 5HE; tel: 01348
837860; stdavids@nationaltrust.org.uk
www.nationaltrust.org.uk

Ynis-hir (pp.106–107) ⓳
RSPB Ynys-hir Reserve, Eglwys-fach,
Machynlleth, Powys, Wales SY20 8TA;
tel: 01654 700222; ynys-hir@rspb.org.uk
www.rspb.org.uk

MIDLANDS

Chasewater Country Park ❷❺
Pool Road, Brownhills,
Staffordshire WS8 7AL; contact:
Lichfield District Council;
tel: 01543 308860
www.chasewater.org.uk
www.visitlichfield.co.uk

Churnet Valley ⓳
Churnet Valley Wildlife Sanctuary
and Nature Reserve, Spink Lane,
Stoke upon Trent, Staffordshire
ST10 2BX;
tel: 01538 756702

Clumber Park (pp.118–119) ❽
Worksop, Nottinghamshire S80 3AZ;
tel: 01909 544917 or infoline
01909 476592;
clumberpark@nationaltrust.org.uk

**Coombes and Churnet Valley
RSPB Reserve** ⓲
RSPB Coombes and Churnet Valley
Reserve, Six Oaks Farm, Bradnop,
Leek, Staffordshire ST13 7EU;
tel: 01538 384017
www.rspb.org.uk

Cotswold Water Park ❹❷
Gateway Centre, Spine Road,
South Cerney GL7 5TL;
tel: 01793 752413;
info@waterpark.org
www.waterpark.org

Cromford Canal ❷❶
Cromford Canal Reserve, Belpher,
Derbyshire DE4;
tel: 01773 881188
www.derbyshirewildlifetrust.org.uk

Dole Wood ❸❷
Thurley, Lincolnshire, PE10;
tel: 01507 526667
www.lincstrust.org.uk

Attenborough Gravel Pits ❷❷
Attenborough Nature Centre, Barton Lane
Attenborough, Nottingham NG9 6DY;
tel: 0115 972 1777
enquiries@attenboroughnaturecentre.co.uk
www.attenboroughnaturecentre.co.uk

Birklands Woods ❾
Sherwood Forest, Edwinstowe, Mansfield,
Nottinghamshire NG21 9HN
Recreation rangers, tel: 01623 822447
www.forestry.gov.uk

Bleaklow ❹
High Peak Estate, Edale End,
Hope Valley, Derbyshire S33 6RF;
contact: estate office,
tel: 01433 670368
www.nationaltrust.org.uk

Blithfield Reservoir ❷❸
Dapple Heath, Admaston, Rugeley,
Staffordshire WS15 3PH;
tel: 01889 500541
www.blithfieldeducationcentre.co.uk

Dee Estuary ❶
RSPB Inner Marsh Reserve, Burton Point
Farm, Station Road, Burton CH64 5SB;
tel: 0151 3367681
www.rspb.org.uk

Cannock Chase Country Park ❷❹
Cannock Chase Visitor Centre, Marquis
Drive, Cannock Chase, Hednesford,
Cannock, Staffordshire WS12 4PW;
tel: 01543 876741
www.cannockchasedc.gov.uk

Donna Nook 12
Louth, Lincolnshire, LN11;
tel: 01507 526667
www.lincstrust.org.uk

Dovedale 20
South Peak Estate Office, Home Farm,
Ilam, Ashbourne, Derbyshire DE6 2AZ;
tel: 01335 350503;
southpeakestate@nationaltrust.org.uk
www.nationaltrust.org.uk

Draycote Water Country Park 29
Dunchurch nr Rugby, Warwickshire
CV23 8AB;
contact: Draycote Water Visitor Centre;
tel: 01788 811107
www.moretoexperience.co.uk

Ellesmere Meres 15
The Mereside, Ellesmere, Shropshire
SY12 0PA;
tel: 01691 622981;
ellesmere.tourism@shropshire-cc.gov.uk

Forest of Dean 38
Gloucestershire GL15;
contact: tourist information;
tel: 01594 812388
www.visitforestofdean.co.uk

Ifton Meadows 14
St Martins, Shropshire SY11;
adminmartin@btinternet.com
www.stmartins-online.org.uk

Longshaw Estate 7
Sheffield, Derbyshire S11 7TZ;
tel: 01433 637904
www.nationaltrust.org.uk

Lyme Park (pp.62–63) 3
Disley, Stockport, Cheshire SK12 2NR;
tel: 01663 766492 (Infoline)
www.nationaltrust.org.uk

Much Marcle 34
St Bartholomew's Church, Much Marcle,
Ledbury, Herefordshire HR8;
contact: church office;
tel: 01531 631531
www.muchmarcle.net

Newent 35
Tourist information office, 7 Church Street,
Newent, Gloucestershire GL18 1PU;
tel: 01531 822468
www.visitforestofdean.co.uk

Red Hill 11
Red Hill Nature Reserve, nr Goulceby,
Lincolnshire LN11;
tel: 01507 526667
www.lincstrust.org.uk

Rockingham Forest (pp.140–141) 30
Rockingham, near Corby,
Northamptonshire NN17 3BB;
contact: Forestry Commission Northants;
tel: 01780 444920;
northants@forestry.gsi.gov.uk
www.forestrycommission.gov.uk

Rodborough Common 40
Stroud, Gloucestershire GL5 5;
tel: 01452 814213 (general enquiries)
www.nationaltrust.org.uk

Ross-on-Wye 36
Tourist Information Centre; Swan House;
Edde Cross St; Ross-on-Wye HR9 7BZ;
tel: 01989 562768
www.herefordshire.gov.uk

Rutland Water 31
Rutland Water Nature Reserve, Egleton,
Oakham, Rutland LE15 8BT;
Anglian Water Birdwatching Centre;
tel: 01572 770651
www.rutlandwater.org.uk

Ryton Wood 28
Ryton on Dunsmore, Warwickshire
CV8 3; tel: 024 76302912
www.warwickshire-wildlife-trust.org.uk

Saltfleetby-Theddlethorpe Dunes 13
Between Saltfleet and Mablethorpe,
Lincolnshire; contact: reserve office;
tel: 01507 338611
www.naturalengland.org.uk

Saltwells Nature Reserve 27
Saltwells Lane, Quarry Bank, Dudley,
West Midlands DY5 1TF;
tel: 01384 812795
www.dudley.gov.uk

Sandwell Valley (pp.282–283) 26
RSPB Sandwell Valley Reserve,
20 Tanhouse Avenue, Great Barr,
Birmingham, West Midlands B43 5AG;
tel: 0121 3577395;
sandwellvalley@rspb.org.uk
www.rspb.org.uk

Sherwood Forest (pp.36–37) 10
Sherwood Pines Forest Park, Edwinstowe,
Nottinghamshire NG21 9JL;
tel: 01623 822447;
enquiries.sherwood@forestry.gsi.gov.uk
www.forestry.gov.uk

Slad Valley (pp.240–241) 41
Near Stroud, Gloucestershire GL6 7QA;
contact: The Gloucestershire Badger Group
www.badgerland.co.uk

Slimbridge (pp.34–35) 39
The Wildfowl & Wetlands Trust, Slimbridge,
Gloucestershire, GL2 7BT;
tel: 01453 891900;
enquiries@wwt.org.uk
www.wwt.org.uk

Symonds Yat (pp.80–81) 37
The Wye Valley, Herefordshire; contact:
Forestry Commission; tel: 0845 3673787;
or Symonds Yat information assistant;
tel: 07736 792511
www.visitwyevalley.com

Tewkesbury 33
Tourist Information, 100 Church Street,
Tewkesbury, Gloucestershire GL20 5AB;
tel: 01684 855040;
tewkesburytic@tewkesbury.gov.uk
www.tewkesbury.gov.uk

Trentham Estate 17
Stone Road, Trentham, Stoke-on-Trent,
Staffordshire ST4 8AX;
tel: 01782 657341
www.trenthamleisure.co.uk

Whixall Moss 16
Nr Whixall, Whitchurch, Shropshire
SY13; tel: 0845 6003078
www.naturalengland.org.uk

Winnat's Pass 5
Castleton, Derbyshire S33
Tel: 0844 800 1895
www.nationaltrust.org.uk

Woolston Eyes (pp.76–77) 2
Weir Lane, Woolston, Warrington,
Cheshire WA1 4QQ
www.woolstoneyes.co.uk

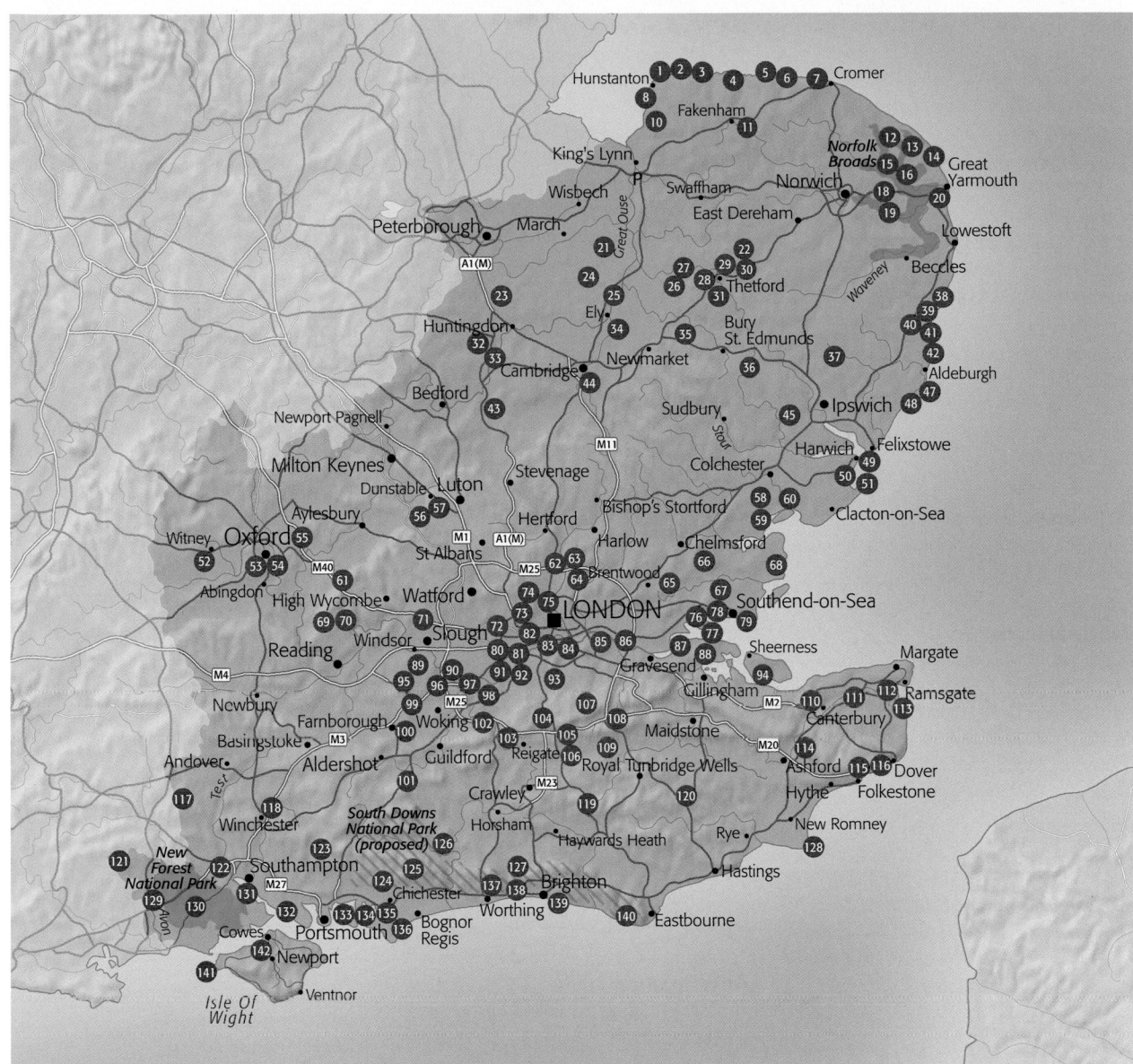

SOUTHEAST ENGLAND

Abberton reservoir ❺❽
Visitor Centre, Church Rd, Layer-de-la-
Haye, Colchester, Essex CO2 0EU;
tel: 01206 738172;
abberton@essexwt.org.uk
www.essexwt.org.uk

Abbott's Hall (pp.192–193) ❺❾
Great Wigborough, Colchester, Essex
CO5 7RZ; contact: Essex Wildlife Trust;
tel: 01621 862960; admin@essexwt.org.uk
www.essexwt.org.uk

Addenbrookes Hospital ❹❹
Cambridge University Hospitals NHS
Foundation Trust, Hills Road, Cambridge,
Cambridgeshire CB2 0QQ;
tel: 01223 245151
www.addenbrookes.org.uk

Alum Bay, Isle of Wight ⓵④①
Islandwide Leisure Ltd, 5 Cotton Close,
Cowes, Isle of Wight P031 7UG;
tel: 01983 292746

Ashdown Forest ⓵①⑨
The Ashdown Forest Centre,
Wych Cross, Forest Row,
East Sussex RH18 5JP;
tel: 01342 823583
conservators@ashdownforest.org
www.ashdownforest.org

Aston Rowant (pp.222–223) ❻①
Aston Rowant National Nature
Reserve, The Chilterns, Oxfordshire
OX49 5SG; contact: Thames and Chilterns
Team, Natural England;
tel: 01844 351833;
enquiries@naturalengland.org.uk
www.naturalengland.org.uk

Barnham Cross Common ❸①
Brecks Countryside Project,
Kings House, Kings Street, Thetford,
Norfolk IP24 2AT;
tel: 01842 754247
www.naturalengland.gov.uk

Basingstoke Canal ⓵⓪⓪
Basingstoke Canal Authority,
Canal Centre, Mytchett Place Road,
Mytchett, Surrey GU16 6DD;
tel: 01252 370073;
info@basingstoke-canal.co.uk
www.basingstoke-canal.co.uk

Bedgebury Arboretum ⓵②⓪
Bedgebury National Pinetum,
Park Lane, Goudhurst,
Kent TN17 2SL;
tel: 01580 879820;
friends@bedgebury.fsnet.co.uk
www.forestry.gov.uk/bedgebury

Bernwood Forest ❺❺
Bernwood Forest Nature Reserve,
Between Oakley and Stanton St. John,
Oakley, Buckinghamshire;
tel: 01865 775476;
countryside@aylesburyvaledc.gov.uk
www.aylesburyvaledc.gov.uk

Blakeney Point (pp.214–215) ❺
Norfolk Coast Office, Friary Farm,
Cley Road, Blakeney, Holt,
Norfolk NR25 7NW;
tel: 01263 740241;
blakeneypoint@nationaltrust.org.uk

Blashford Lakes ⓵②⑨
Blashford Lakes Study Centre,
Ellingham, Ringwood BH24 3PJ;
tel: 01425 472760
www.hwt.org.uk

Blean Woods ⓵①⓪
Canterbury TIC, Blean Woods,
12/13 Sun Street, Canterbury,
Kent CT1 2HX;
tel: 01227 378100
www.theblean.co.uk

Bookham Commons (pp.170–171) ⓵⓪②
The Common, Bookham, Leatherhead,
KT23; contact: The National Trust North
Downs Countryside Office;
tel: 01372 220641;
bookham@nationaltrust.org.uk
www.nationaltrust.org.uk

Bough Beech reservoir ⓵⓪⑨
Kent Wildlife Trust, Bough Beech Visitor
Centre, Winkhurst Green, Ide Hill,
Sevenoaks, Kent TN14 6LD;
tel: 01732 453880
www.kentwildlifetrust.org.uk

Box Hill ⓵⓪❸
The Old Fort, Box Hill Rd, Box Hill,
Tadworth, Surrey KT20 7LB;
tel: 01306 885502;
boxhill@nationaltrust.org.uk

Bradfield Woods ❸❻
Bradfield Woods, Bury St Edmunds,
Suffolk IP30 0AQ;
tel: 01473 890089;
info@suffolkwildlife.cix.co.uk

Breckland ❷⑨
Norfolk Wildlife Trust, Bewick House,
22 Thorpe Road, Norwich NR11RY;
tel: 01603 625540
www.norfolkwildlifetrust.org.uk

Brettenham Heath ❸⓪
Brettenham Heath, High
Bridgham Road,
Thetford IP25 6BQ;
info@brettenham.com
www.english-nature.org.uk

Breydon Water ❷⓪
Great Yarmouth, Norfolk NR30 1SF;
tel: 01493 700645;
berney.marshes@rspb.org.uk
www.rspb.org.uk

Brighton Pier 139
West Pier, Kings Rd, Brighton BN1 2FL

Buckenham, Norfolk 19
Norfolk Wildlife Trust, Bewick House,
22 Thorpe Road, Norwich NR1 1RY;
tel: 01603 625540
www.norfolkwildlifetrust.org.uk.

Canvey Wick (pp.156–157) 77
Canvey Wick, Canvey Island,
Essex SS8 0PT; contact: Natural England;
tel: 0845 6003078;
enquiries@naturalengland.org.uk
www.naturalengland.org.uk

Cavenham Heath 35
Nr Icklingham, Suffolk IP28 6QD;
tel: 01284 762218
www.naturalengland.org.uk

Chichester Cathedral (pp.134–135) 135
St. Richards Walk, Chichester,
West Sussex, PO19 1QB;
tel: 01243 782595
www.chichestercathedral.org.uk

Chichester harbour 134
The Harbour Office, Itchenor, Chichester,
West Sussex PO20 7AW;
tel: 01243 512301;
harbourmaster@conservancy.co.uk
www.conservancy.co.uk

The Chilterns 69
Chilterns Conservation Board, The Lodge,
Station Road, Chinnor, Oxfordshire
OX39 4HA; tel: 01844 355500
www.chilternsaonb.org

Chobham Common 97
Chobham, KT16 0ED;
contact: Surrey Wildlife Trust, Surrey
Wildlife Trust, School Lane, Pirbright,
Woking, Surrey GU24 0JN;
tel: 01276 858291;
info@surreywt.org.uk
www.surreywildlifetrust.co.uk

Church Wood (pp.280–281) 71
RSPB Church Wood Reserve, Hedgerley,
Gerrards Cross, Buckinghamshire SL2 3UY;
tel: 01865 351163
www.rspb.org.uk

Cissbury Ring, Sussex 137
tel: 01903 740233 (warden)
www.nationaltrust.org.uk

Cley-next-the-sea 6
Cley Marsh Visitor Centre, Cley next the
Sea, Norfolk NR25 7SA;
Tel: 01263 740008
www.norfolkwildlifetrust.org.uk

Cliffe Pools 87
RSPB Cliffe Pools, Rochester, Kent ME3;
tel: 01634 222480;
northkentmarshes@rspb.org.uk

Cornmill Meadows (pp.210–211) 63
Cornmill Meadows Dragonfly Sanctuary,
Abbey Gardens, Waltham Abbey,
Essex EN9 1XQ; tel: 01992 717711;
info@leevalleypark.org.uk
www.leevalleypark.org.uk

**Creekside Nature Conservation
Centre** 84
14 Creekside, Deptford, London, SE8 4SA;
creeksidecentre@yahoo.co.uk;
www.lewisham.gov.uk

Crowhurst Church 106
Crowhurst Lane, Crowhurst, Surrey RH7 6LR;
tel: 01342 833843

Dengie Marshes 68
Essex CM0 7JG; contact: Essex Wildlife
Trust, Abbotts Hall Farm, Gt Wigborough,
Colchester, Essex CO5 7RZ;
tel: 01621 862960
www.essexwt.org.uk

Down House 107
Luxted Road, Downe, Orpington, Kent
BR6 7JT; tel: 01689 859119
www.english-heritage.org.uk

Ducklington 52
Witney, Oxfordshire OX28 6HL
www.witney.net

Dungeness (pp.162–163) 128
Dungeness Bird Observatory, 11 RNSSS
Cottages, Dungeness, Romney Marsh,
Kent TN29 9NA; tel: 01797 321309
www.dungenessbirdobs.org.uk

Dunstable Downs 57
Dunstable Road, Whipsnade, Bedfordshire
LU6 2GY; tel: 01582 500920;
www.nationaltrust.org.uk

Dunwich 39
Dunwich, Saxmundham, Suffolk IP17 3DJ;
tel: 01728 648501
www.nationaltrust.org.uk

East Wretham 22
NWT East Wretham Heath, Wretham,
Norfolk IP24 1RL; tel: 01603 625540
www.norfolkwildlifetrust.org.uk

Elmley Marshes (pp.306–307) 94
RSPB Elmley Marshes Reserve, Kingshill
Farm, Sheerness, Kent, ME12 3RW;
tel: 01795 665969;
northkentmarshes@rspb.org.uk
www.rspb.org.uk

Ely Pits and Meadows 25
Contact: Natural England, Bedfordshire and
Cambridgeshire Land Management Team,
Ham Lane House, Ham Lane,
Orton Waterville, Peterborough,
Cambridgeshire PE2 5UR;
tel: 01733 405850;
beds.cambs@naturalengland.org.uk
www.naturalengland.org.uk

Epping Forest 64
Epping Forest Visitor Centre, Loughton,
Essex IG10 3RY;
tel: 020 8508028
www.cityoflondon.gov.uk/epping

Esher Rugby Club 98
Pillar Data Arena, 369 Molesey Road,
Hersham, Surrey KT12 3PF;
tel: 01932 220295
www.esherrugby.com

**Farthing Downs and Happy Valley
(pp.176–177)** 104
Ditches Lane, Coulsdon, Surrey CR5 3EA;
contact: Merlewood Estate Office;
tel: 020 8660 8533
www.croydon.gov.uk

Fingringhoe Wick (pp.124–125) 60
Fingringhoe Wick Visitor Centre, South
Green Road, Fingringhoe, Essex CR5 3EA;
tel: 01206 729678
www.essexwt.org.uk

Folkestone Warren 115
The Warren Campsite, Folkestone, Kent
CT19 6NQ; contact: Kent Wildlife Trust,
Romney Marsh Visitor Centre, Dymchurch
Road, New Romney, Kent TN28 8AY;
tel: 01797 369487

Fox Meadow 37
Nr Debenham, Suffolk; contact: Suffolk
Wildlife Trust, Brooke House, Ashbocking,
Ipswich, Suffolk IP6 9JY;
tel: 01473 890089 (viewing by
appointment only);
info@suffolkwildlifetrust.org
www.suffolkwildlife.co.uk

Grafham Water (pp.302–303) 32
West Perry, Huntingdon, Cambridgeshire
PE28 0BX; contact: The Mander Park
Visitor Centre; tel: 01480 811075
www.grafham.org

Great Stour, Kent river 112
Grove Ferry Road, Upstreet,
nr. Canterbury, Kent CT3 4BP;
contact: The Kentish Stour Countryside
Project, Sidelands Farm, Wye, Ashford,
Kent TN25 5DQ;
tel: 01233 813307;
kentishstour@kent.gov.uk

Hamford Water 50
Nr Walton-on-the-Naze, Essex CO14 8DM;
tel: 0845 6003078
www.naturalengland.org.uk

Hampstead Heath (pp.110–111) 73
London, NW3; contact: Hampstead Heath
Superintendents Office, Heathfield House,
432 Archway Road, London N6 4JH;
tel: 020 7332 3322/3977
www.cityoflondon.gov.uk/hampstead

Havergate Island 48
RSPB, Ore Estuary, nr Aldeburgh, Suffolk;
tel: 01394 450732; or to book boat trip,
tel: 01728 648281;
havergate.island@rspb.org.uk
www.rspb.org.uk

Hickling Broad (pp.46–47) 13
Hickling Broad National Nature Reserve,
Stubb Road, Hickling, Norfolk NR12 0BW;
tel: 01692 598276
www.norfolkwildlifetrust.org.uk

Highgate Wood 74
Highgate Wood and Queen's Wood,
Muswell Hill Road, Haringey,
London N10 3JN;
tel: 020 84446129

Hockley Woods 67
Main Road, Hockley, Rayleigh,
Essex SS5 4RN; tel: 01702 203078
www.rochford.gov.uk

Holkham (pp.18–19) 4
Holkham Nature Reserve,
Wells-next-the-Sea, Norfolk NR23 1RG;
tel: 01328 710227;
enquiries@holkham.co.uk
www.holkham.co.uk/naturereserve

Holme next the Sea 1
NWT Holme Dunes, Broadwater Road,
Holme-next-the-Sea, Hunstanton,
Norfolk PE36 6LQ; contact: Holme Bird
Observatory; tel: 01485 525406;
info@noa.org.uk

Hunstanton, Norfolk 8
Contact: Hunstanton Tourist Information
Centre, The Town Hall, The Green,
Hunstanton, Norfolk PE36 6BQ;
tel: 01485 532610

Iffley, Oxford 54
Iffley Meadows, Donnington Bridge Road,
Oxfordshire OX1 4UP; contact: Berks,
Bucks and Oxon Naturalists' Trust, The
Lodge, 1 Armstrong Road, Littlemore,
Oxford OX4 4XT; tel: 01865 775476;
info@bbowt.org.uk
www.bbowt.org.uk

Isle of Wight (pp.224–225) 142
Isle of Wight, English Channel; contact:
Isle of Wight Tourism; tel: 01983 823031;
info@islandbreaks.co.uk; or Hampshire &
Isle of Wight Wildlife Trust; tel: 01489
774446; wildline@hwt.org.uk

Itchen, Hampshire 131
Itchen Valley Country Park, Allington Lane,
West End, Southampton SO30 3HQ;
tel: 023 8046 6091;
ivcp@eastleigh.gov.uk
www.eastleigh.gov.uk

Ivinghoe Beacon 56
Chiltern Hills, Buckinghamshire;
contact: Ashridge Estate Visitor Centre,
Moneybury Hill, Berkhamsted,
Hertfordshire HP4 1LX;
tel: 01442 851227;
ashridge@nationaltrust.org.uk
www.nationaltrust.org.uk

Kew Gardens 80
Royal Botanic Gardens, Kew, Richmond,
Surrey TW9 3AB; tel: 020 8332 5655;
info@kew.org
www.kew.org

Kingley Vale (pp.310–311) 124
Kingley Vale National Nature Reserve,
West Stoke House Farm, Downs Road,
West Stoke, Chichester PO18 9BN;
tel: 01273 575353;
sussex.surrey@naturalengland.org.uk
www.naturalengland.org.uk

Landguard, Suffolk 49
Landguard Bird Observatory, View Point
Road, Felixstowe, Suffolk IP11 3TW;
tel: 01394 673782, enquiries@lbo.org.uk
www.lbo.org.uk

Langstone Harbour 133
Langstone Harbour Board, Harbour Office,
Ferry Road, Hayling Island,
Hampshire PO11 0DG;
tel: 02392 463419;
harbourmaster@langstoneharbour.org.uk
www.langstoneharbour.org.uk

Lee Valley Park (pp.26–27) 62
Lee Valley Regional Park Authority,
Myddelton House, Bulls Cross,
Enfield, Middlesex EN2 9HG;
tel: 01992 702200;
info@leevalleypark.org.uk
www.leevalleypark.org.uk

Leigh-on-Sea, Essex 78
Belfairs Nature Reserve and Golf Course,
Eastwood Road North, Leigh-on-Sea,
Essex SS9 4LR;
tel: 01702 520202;
info@leigh-on-sea.com

Lesnes Abbey Woods 85
Abbey Road, Belvedere, London, SE2 9RH;
tel: 0208 3037777;
worksdirect@bexley.gov.uk

Little Paxton 33
Little Paxton Nature Reserve, Huntingdon,
Cambridgeshire PE19 4ET;
tel: 01480 406795;
paxtonpits@btconnect.com
www.paxton-pits.org.uk

The Lodge 43
RSPB The Lodge Reserve, Sandy,
Bedfordshire SG19 2DL;
tel: 01767 680541
www.rspb.org.uk

London Wetland Centre (pp.16–17) 81
Queen Elizabeth's Walk, Barnes, London
SW13 9WT; tel: 020 8409 4400;
info.london@wwt.org.uk
www.wwt.org.uk

Magdalen College 53
Oxford OX1 4AU; tel: 01865 276000
www.magd.ox.ac.uk

Maids Cross Hill, Norfolk 26
Lakenheath, Brandon, Suffolk IP27 9EJ;
brecks.project@et.suffolkcc.gov.uk
www.brecks.org

Martin Down, Salisbury 121
Martin Down National Nature Reserve,
Sillens Lane, Martin, Hampshire SP6 3LB;
tel: 01392 457400
www.naturalengland.org.uk

Medway Estuary 95
Riverside Country Park, Lower Rainham
Road, Gillingham, Kent ME7 2XH;
tel: 01634 333333;
riversidecp@medway.gov.uk
www.medway.gov.uk

Minsmere (pp.100–101) 41
RSPB Minsmere Reserve, Westleton,
Saxmundham, Suffolk IP17 3BY;
tel: 01728 648281; minsmere@rspb.org.uk
www.rspb.org.uk

The Naze 51
John Weston Nature Reserve, The Naze,
Walton on the Naze, Essex CO14 8LE;
contact: Essex Wildlife Trust;
tel: 01621 862960
www.essexwt.org.uk

The New Forest (pp.174–175) 130
Lyndhurst Visitor Information Centre,
Lyndhurst, Hampshire SO43 7NY;
tel: 023 8028 2269;
information@nfdc.gov.uk
www.thenewforest.co.uk

Norfolk Broads 12
Contact: Broads Authority, 18 Colegate,
Norwich, Norfolk NR3 1BQ;
tel: 01603 610734
www.broads-authority.gov.uk

Norsey Wood (pp.84–85) 65
Norsey Wood Nature Reserve, Outwood
Common Road, Billericay, Essex
CM11 1HA; contact: Norsey Wood
Information Centre; tel: 01277 624553
www.norseywood.org.uk

Northward Hill (pp.54–55) 88
RSPB Northward Hill Reserve,
High Halstow, Kent ME3 8DS;
tel: 01634 222480;
northkentmarshes@rspb.org.uk or
info@kentwildlife.org.uk
www.rspb.org.uk

Old Winchester Hill 123
Warnford, Hampshire SO1 1HX;
contact: Old Winchester Hill National
Nature Reserve, Natural England,
1 Southampton Road, Lyndhurst,
Hampshire SO43 7BU;
tel: 023 8028 6410
www.naturalengland.org.uk

Orford Ness 47
Orford Ness National Nature Reserve,
Quay Office, Orford Quay, Orford,
Woodbridge, Suffolk IP12 2NU;
tel: 01728 648024;
orfordness@nationaltrust.org.uk
www.nationaltrust.org.uk

Ouse Washes (pp.22–23) 24
RSPB Ouse Washes, Welches Dam,
Manea, March, Cambridgeshire PE15 0NF;
tel: 01354 680212;
ouse.washes@rspb.org.uk
www.rspb.org.uk

Pagham Harbour 136
The Visitors Centre, Pagham Harbour Local
Nature Reserve, Selsey Road, Sidlesham,
Chichester PO20 7NE; tel: 01243 641508;
pagham.nr@westsussex.gov.uk
www.foph.org.uk

Parkhurst Forest 142
Forest Road, Newport, Isle of Wight,
PO30 5UH; tel: 0845 3673787
www.forestry.gov.uk

Penthorpe 11
Penthorpe, Fakenham, Norfolk NR21 0LN;
info@pensthorpe.com
www.pensthorpe.com

Perivale Wood 72
Perivale Wood Local Nature Reserve,
Greenford, Middlesex UB6 7FH

Petworth House 126
National Trust, Petworth, West Sussex
GU28 0AE; tel: 01798 343929
www.nationaltrust.org.uk

Porton Down 117
Defence Science and Technology
Laboratory, CBDE Porton, Porton Down,
Salisbury, Wiltshire, SP4 0JQ
www.ecn.ac.uk

Queen's Wood 75
Muswell Hill Road, Haringey,
London N10 3JN
www.fqw.org.uk

Rainham Marshes RSPB 86
Aveley, Essex RM13 9UT;
tel: 01708 899840;
rainham.marshes@rspb.org.uk
www.rspb.org.uk

Ranworth Broad 15
Ranworth, Norfolk NR13 6HS;
tel: 01603 270479
www.norfolkwildlifetrust.org.uk

Regents Park, London 82
Inner Circle, Regents Park,
London NW1 4NR; tel: 020 7298 2000;
hq@royalparks.gsi.gov.uk
www.royalparks.org.uk

Richmond Park (pp.276–277) 91
Richmond on Thames, Surrey TW10 5HS;
tel: 020 8948 3209;
richmond@royalparks.gsi.gov.uk
www.royalparks.org.uk

River Test (pp.218–219) 122
From Ashe in Hampshire, through
Whitchurch, Stockbridge, and Romsey to
an estuary above Southampton Water.

Samphire Hoe 116
Cambridge Terrace, Dover, Kent
CT16 1JT; tel: 01304 225649;
mail@whitecliffscountryside.org.uk
www.whitecliffscountryside.org.uk

Sandwich Bay bird observatory 113
Guilford Rd, Sandwich Bay, Sandwich,
Kent CT13 9PF; tel: 01304 617341
www.sbbot.co.uk

Scolt Head 3
Burnham Overy Staithe, Norfolk PE31 8JE;
tel: 01603 674926
www.naturalengland.org.uk

Seven Sisters Country Park 140
South Downs Joint Committee, Exceat,
Seaford, East Sussex BN25 4AD;
tel: 01323 870280;
sevensisters@southdowns-aonb.gov.uk

Sevenoaks Wildlife Reserve [108]
Bradbourne Vale Rd, Sevenoaks,
Kent TN13 3DH; tel: 01732 456407;
info@kentwildlife.org.uk
www.kentwildlifetrust.org.uk/reserves

Sheringham [7]
The lifeboat station is a popular seabird-
watching spot: Sheringham Promenade,
Norfolk NR26 8

Sizewell [42]
Sizewell B power station, nr Leiston,
Suffolk IP16 4UR

Snettisham (pp.308–309) [10]
RSPB Snettisham Reserve, Snettisham,
Hunstanton, Norfolk PE36 6LQ;
tel: 01485 542689;
snettisham@rspb.org.uk
www.rspb.org.uk

South Downs [125]
Contact: Midhurst Tourist Information
Centre, North St, Midhurst GU29 9DW;
tel: 01730 817322
www.visitsouthdowns.com

South Norwood Country Park [93]
Albert Road, London SE25 4QL;
tel: 020 8726 6900;
parks@croydon.gov.uk
www.croydon.gov.uk

Southend Pier [79]
Marine Parade, Southend-on-Sea,
Essex SS1 1EE
www.sarfend.co.uk

Staines reservoirs [90]
Wraysbury, Middlesex TW18 4

Stodmarsh [111]
Stodmarsh National Nature Reserve,
Kent CT3 4BJ;
contact: English Nature Kent Team,
Coldharbour Farm, Wye, Ashford,
Kent TN25 5DB;
tel: 01233 812525
www.naturalengland.org.uk

Strumpshaw Fen (pp.152–153) [18]
RSPB Strumpshaw Fen, Brundall, Norfolk
NR13 4HS; tel: 01603 715191;
strumpshaw@rspb.org.uk
www.rspb.org.uk

Suffolk Sandlings [40]
Hollesley, nr Woodbridge, Suffolk,
IP12 3RR; contact: The Sandlings Project
Manager, Suffolk Wildlife Trust, Foxburrow
Farm, Saddlemakers Lane, Melton,
Suffolk IP12 1NA
www.wildlifetrust.org.uk/suffolk

Surrey Heaths [99]
Contact Centre, Floor 3, Conquest House,
Wood Street, Kingston upon Thames,
Surrey KT1 1AB;
contact.centre@surreycc.gov.uk
www.surreycc.gov.uk/heathland

Tandridge Church [105]
Tandridge St Peter, Tandridge Lane,
Tandridge, Surrey RH8 9NJ
*www.achurchnearyou.com/tandridge-
st-peter*

Tate Modern [83]
Bankside, London SE1 9TG;
tel: 020 7887 8888
www.rspb.org.uk/brilliant

Thames Estuary [76]
Contact: Kent Wildlife Trust;
tel: 01622 662012;
info@kentwildlife.org.uk
www.kentwildlifetrust.org.uk

Thetford Forest [28]
High Lodge Forest Centre, Brandon,
Suffolk IP27 0AF;
tel: 01842 810090;
enquiries.anglia@forestry.gsi.gov.uk

Thrift Wood [66]
Bicknacre, Chelmsford, Essex CM3 4HD;
contact: Essex Wildlife Trust, Abbotts Hall
Farm, Gt Wigborough, Colchester,
Essex CO5 7RZ;
tel: 01621 862960
www.essexwt.org.uk

Thursley Common (pp.128–129) [101]
Near Godalming, Surrey GU8 6LW;
contact: Natural England Sussex;
tel: 01273 476595;
sussex.surrey@naturalengland.org.uk
www.naturalengland.org.uk

Titchfield Haven [132]
Titchfield Haven National Nature Reserve,
Haven Cottage, Cliff Rd, Fareham,
Hampshire PO14 3JT;
tel: 01329 662145
www3.hants.gov.uk/titchfield

Titchwell Marsh [2]
RSPB Titchwell, Main Rd, Titchwell,
King's Lynn, Norfolk PE31 8BB;
tel: 01485 210432
www.rspb.org.uk/reserves

Upton Broad [16]
Acle, Norfolk NR13 6ER;
contact: NWT Upton Broad and Marshes,
Norfolk Wildlife Trust, Bewick House,
22 Thorpe Road, Norwich NR1 1RY;
tel: 01603 625540
www.norfolkwildlifetrust.org.uk

Virginia Water [96]
Surrey, SL5 7RX;
contact: The Crown Estate Office,
The Great Park, Windsor,
Berkshire SL4 2HT;
tel: 01753 860222
*www.theroyallandscape.co.uk/
landscape/virginiawater/index.cfm*

Walberswick [38]
Ferry Road, Walberswick, Southwold,
Suffolk IP18 6TN
www.explorewalberswick.co.uk

Warburg Nature Reserve [70]
Bix Bottam, Bix, Henley-on-Thames,
Oxfordshire RG9 6BL;
tel: 01491 642001;
warburg@bbowt.org.uk
www.bbowt.org.uk

Weeting Heath (pp.92–93) [27]
Hockwold Road, Weeting, nr Brandon,
Thetford, IP26 4NQ;
tel: 01842 827615
www.norfolkwildlifetrust.org.uk

Welney [21]
Welney Wetland Centre, Hundred Foot
Bank, Welney, nr Wisbech,
Cambridgeshire PE14 9TN;
tel: 01353 860711;
info.welney@wwt.org.uk15

Wicken Fen (pp.204–205) [34]
Wicken Fen, Lode Lane, Wicken, Ely,
Cambridgeshire CB7 5XP; tel: 01353
720274; wickenfen@nationaltrust.org.uk
www.wicken.org.uk

Widewater Lagoon [138]
Lancing, West Sussex BN99 8
www.widewaterlagoon.org.uk

Wimbledon Common (pp.188–189) [92]
London SW19 5NR;
contact: The Ranger's Office, Manor
Cottage, Windmill Road, Wimbledon
Common;
tel: 020 8788 7655;
rangersoffice@wpcc.org.uk
www.wpcc.org.uk

Windsor Great Park (pp.258–259) [89]
Windsor, Berkshire SL4 2HT; contact: The
Crown Estate Office; tel: 01753 860222
www.thecrownestate.co.uk

Winnall Moors [118]
North Walls Recreation Ground, Gordon
Road, Winchester SO23 7DD;
tel: Reserves Officer 07831 692963;
*www.hwt.org.uk/pages/winnall-moors.
html*

Winterton Dunes NNR [14]
Beach Rd, Winterton-on-Sea,
Great Yarmouth, NR29 4AJ;
tel: 01603 674926
www.naturalengland.org.uk

Wolves Wood [45]
RSPB Wolves Wood Reserve, Hadleigh,
Suffolk IP7 6QG;
tel: 01473 328006;
stourestuary@rspb.org.uk
www.rspb.org.uk

Woods Mill [127]
Henfield, West Sussex BN5 9SD;
tel: 01273 492630
www.sussexwt.org.uk

Woodwalton Fen [23]
Woodwalton Fen National Nature Reserve,
Chapel Rd, Ramsey Heights, Huntingdon,
Cambridgeshire PE26 2RS;
tel: 01487 812363
www.naturalengland.org.uk

Wye Downs (pp.148–149) [114]
Wye Downs National Nature Reserve,
Wye, Ashford, Kent TN25 5HE;
contact Natural England, Kent;
tel: 01233 812525
www.naturalengland.org.uk

SOUTHWEST ENGLAND

RSPB Arne (pp.138–139) ③③
RSPB Arne Reserve, Arne Road, Arne,
Wareham, Dorset BH20 5BJ;
tel: 01929 553360;
arne@rspb.org.uk
www.rspb.org.uk

Ashton Court ⑧
Ashton Court Estate, Long Ashton,
Bristol, Somerset BS41 9JN
Tel: 0117 973 8508
www.ashtoncourtestate.co.uk

Avon Gorge ⑦
Peregrine watch point, Circular Road,
Seawalls, Bristol BS8 4LD
www.avongorge.org.uk
www.avonwildlifetrust.org.uk

Berry Head ㊻
Berry Head National Nature Reserve,
The Bungalow, Berry Head Country Park,
Brixham, Devon TQ5 9AL;
tel: 01803 882619;
berryhead@countryside-trust.org.uk
www.naturesouthwest.co.uk

Black Tor Copse ⑳
Black-a-Tor Copse National Nature Reserve,
Meldon Reservoir, nr Okehampton,
Dartmoor EX20 4LU
www.dartmoor-npa.gov.uk

Bodmin Moor ㊶
Bodmin Tourist Information Centre,
The Shire Hall, Mount Folly Square,
PL31 2DQ; tel: 01208 76616

Braunton Burrows (pp.68–69) ②
Heddon Mill, Braunton, Devon EX33 2NQ;
contact: Braunton Tourist Information
Centre, The Bakehouse Centre, Caen
Street, Braunton, Devon EX33 1AA;
tel: 01271 816400

Brownsea Island (pp.56–57) ㉟
Poole Harbour, Dorset BH13 7EE;
contact: National Trust; tel: 01202 707744;
brownseaisland@nationaltrust.org.uk
www.nationaltrust.org.uk

Camel Valley ㊵
Bodmin PL30 5LG; tel: 01208 77959;
contact: Cornwall Wildlife Trust, Allet,
Truro, Cornwall TR4 9DJ; tel: 01872 273939
www.cornwallwildlifetrust.org.uk

Catcott Lows ⑫
Nr Catcott, Somerset TA7;
tel: 01823 652400;
enquiries@somersetwildlife.org
www.somersetwildlife.org

Cheddar Gorge (pp.186–187) ⑩
Cheddar, Somerset, BS27 3QF;
contact: Cheddar Caves;
tel: 01934 742343
www.cheddarcaves.co.uk

Chesil Beach (pp.180–181) ㉙
Chesil Bank and Fleet Nature Reserve,
Portland Beach Road, Portland,
Dorset DT4 9XE; tel: 01305 760579;
reserve@chesil.fsworld.co.uk
www.chesilbeach.org

Chew Valley Lake ❾
Contact: visitor centre, Woodford Lodge, Chew Stoke, Bristol BS40 8XH; tel: 01275 332339
www.bristolwater.co.uk
www.avonwildlifetrust.org.uk

Cricklade Meadow (pp.74–75) ⓲
Cricklade National Nature Reserve, Cricklade, Wiltshire SN6 6HA; tel: 01380 726344; wiltshire@naturalengland.org.uk
www.naturalengland.org.uk

Dartmoor ㉑
High Moorland Visitor Centre, Old Duchy Hotel, Princetown, Devon PL20 6QF; tel: 01822 890414; hmvc@dartmoor-npa.gov.uk

Dawlish Warren ㉖
Dawlish Warren National Nature Reserve, Dawlish Warren, Devon EX7 0NF; tel: 01626 863980

Dendles Wood ㊹
Contact: Yarner Wood, Bovey Tracey, Devon, TQ13 9LJ; tel: 01626 832093; hq@dartmoor-npa.gov.uk
www.dartmoor-npa.gov.uk

Dunkery & Horner Woods ❸
Dunkery & Horner Woods National Nature Reserve, Horner Vale, Porlock, Exmoor National Park, Somerset TA24 8HY; tel: 01392 457400
www.naturalengland.org.uk

Durlston Head ㊳
Durlston Country Park, Lighthouse Road, Swanage, Dorset BH19 2JL; tel: 01929 424443; info@durlston.co.uk
www.durlston.co.uk

Exe Estuary (pp.286–287) ㉕
Exeter, Devon; contact: RSPB Visitor Centre, Darts Farm Village, Topsham, Devon EX3 0QH; tel: 01392 879438; info@rspb.org.uk
www.rspb.org.uk

Exmoor (pp.44–45) ❹
Exmoor National Park, Devon/Somerset; contact: National Park Authority, Exmoor House, Dulverton TA22 9HL; tel: 01398 323665; info@exmoor-nationalpark.gov.uk
www.exmoor-nationalpark.gov.uk

Fal Estuary ㊿
Falmouth Tourist Information Centre, 28 Killigrew Street, Falmouth, Cornwall TR11 3PN; tel: 01326 312300

Frome ⓰
Contact: Gloucestershire Wildlife Trust Conservation Centre, Robinswood Hill Farm, Reservoir Rd, Gloucester GL4 6SX; Tel: 01452 383333
www.gloucestershirewildlifetrust.co.uk

Grimspound (pp.244–245) ㉓
Dartmoor National Park, Newton Abbot, Devon TQ13 9JQ; contact: Dartmoor National Park Authority; tel: 01626 832093; hq@dartmoor-npa.gov.uk.

Haldon Forest (pp.144–145) ㉔
Haldon Forest Park, Kennford, Exeter EX6 7XR; tel: 01392 834251; haldon.rangers@forestry.gsi.gov.uk.
www.forestry.gov.uk/haldonforestpark

RSPB Ham Wall ⓭
Nr Glastonbury, Somerset BA6 9SX; tel: 01458 860494; ham.wall@rspb.org.uk
www.rspb.org.uk

Hengistbury Head ㊱
Dorset BH6 4EW
www.hengistbury-head.co.uk

Hope's Nose ㊺
Isham Marine Drive, Torquay, Devon TQ1 2

Jersey (pp.64–65) ㊻
Channel Islands
www.nationaltrustjersey.org.je

King Arthur's Quoit ㊷
St Cleer, Bossiney, Cornwall PL14 5

Knightshayes Court ❺
Bolham, Tiverton, Devon EX16 7RQ; tel: 01884 254665
www.nationaltrust.org.uk

Land's End ㊾
Land's End, Sennen, Penzance, Cornwall, TR19 7AA; tel: 0870 458 0099; info@landsend-landmark.co.uk
www.landsendswebsite.co.uk

Lodmoor ㉚
RSPB Lodmoor Reserve, Near Weymouth, Dorset DT4 7SX; tel: 01305 778313
www.rspb.org.uk

Lizard Point (pp.116–117) ㊺
The Lizard, Cornwall, TR12 7NT; contact: Lizard Countryside Office; tel: 01326 561407; lizard@nationaltrust.org.uk
www.lizard-peninsula.co.uk

Lundy Island ❶
Bristol Channel, Devon EX39 2LY; tel: 01271 863636 (National Trust Infoline)
www.nationaltrust.org.uk

Lyme Bay (pp.298–299) ㉗
From Torbay, Devon, in the west to Portland, Dorset, in the east; contact: Devon Wildlife Trust; tel: 01392 279244; contactus@devonwildlifetrust.org
www.devonwildlifetrust.org

Maiden Castle ㉘
Dorchester, Dorset DT2 7AW
www.english-heritage.org.uk
www.dorsetforyou.com

Marazion Marsh ㊿
Nr Longrock, Cornwall TR17 0DA; tel: 01736 711682
marazion.marsh@rspb.org.uk

Pendeen ㊾
Pendeen Lighthouse, Cornwall TR19 7SE
www.trinityhouse.co.uk

Poole Harbour (pp.48–49) ㉞
Poole Harbour, Dorset; contact: Poole Welcome Centre, Poole Quay, Poole, Dorset, BH15 1HJ; tel: 01202 253253; info@pooletourism.com

Porthgwarra Cove ㊸
Porthgwarra, St. Leven, Cornwall TR19 6JR
www.sennen-cove.com/pg.htm

Portland Bill (pp.90–91) ㉜
Portland, Dorset DT5 2JT; contact: Portland Bird Observatory and Field Centre; tel: 01305 820553; obs@btinternet.com

Prawle Point ㊽
Nr. Kingsbridge, Devon TQ7 2BY; contact: Devon Wildlife Trust Tel: 01392 279244
www.devonwildlifetrust.org

Radipole Lake (pp.60–61) ㉛
RSPB Radipole Lake Reserve, Weymouth, Dorset DT4 7TZ; tel: 01305 778313; weymouth.reserves@rspb.org.uk
www.rspb.org.uk

Salisbury Plain ⓱
Wiltshire, BA12 0; contact: Salisbury Plain LIFE Project, Westdown camp (Bldg 21) Tilshead, Wiltshire SP3 4RS; tel: 01380 737016
www.english-nature.org.uk/salisbury

Scilly Isles ㉜
Contact: Tourist Information Centre, Hugh Street, St. Mary's, Isles of Scilly TR21 0LL; tel: 01720 424031
www.simplyscilly.co.uk/

Shapwick Heath (pp.120–121) ⓮
Shapwick, nr Glastonbury, Somerset BA6 9TT; contact: Natural England; tel: 01458 860120; somerset@naturalengland.org.uk
www.naturalengland.org.uk

Slapton Ley (pp.40–41) ㊼
Slapton Ley National Nature Reserve, Slapton, Kingsbridge, Devon TQ7 2QP; contact: Slapton Ley Field Centre; tel: 01548 580466; enquiries.sl@field-studies-council.org

Somerset Levels ❻
See West Sedgemoor, below.

Stonehenge ⓳
Nr Amesbury, Wiltshire SP4 7DE
info@stonehenge.co.uk
www.stonehenge.co.uk

Studland ㊲
Studland Beach and Nature Reserve, Purbeck Estate Office, Studland, Swanage, Dorset BH19 3AX; tel: 01929 450259; studlandbeach@nationaltrust.org.uk
www.nationaltrust.org.uk

Tamar Estuary Reserve ㊸
Cargreen, near Saltash, Cornwall PL12 6LJ; contact: Cornwall Wildlife Trust; tel: 01872 273939; info@cornwt.demon.co.uk
www.cornwallwildlifetrust.org.uk

West Pentire (pp.136–137) ㊴
Crantock, Cornwall TR7 1PJ; contact: Cornwall Wildlife Trust; tel: 01872 273939; info@cornwt.demon.co.uk
www.cornwallwildlifetrust.org.uk

West Sedgemoor and Swell Wood ⓯
Curry Rivel, Langport, Somerset TA10 0HD; tel: 01458 252805; west.sedgemoor@rspb.org.uk
www.rspb.org.uk

Westhay Moor ⓫
Westhay Moor National Nature Reserve, Westhay, Glastonbury BA6 9TN; contact: Somerset Wildlife Trust; tel: 01823 652400; enquiries@somersetwildlife.org
www.somersetwildlife.org

Wistman's Wood (pp.160–161) ㉒
Wistman's Wood National Nature Reserve, Two Bridges, Devon PL20 6SW; contact: Natural England Devon; tel: 0300 0601110; devon@english-nature.org.uk
www.naturalengland.org.uk

Index

Page numbers in **bold** indicate main references; *italic* numbers refer to the illustrations.

Acknowledgments

The publisher would like to thank the following for their kind permission to reproduce their photographs:

KEY: a–above; b–below/bottom; c–centre; f–far; l–left; r–right; t–top

Alamy: A ROOM WITH VIEWS 154–155; AAD Worldwide Travel Images 111bc; Adam Burton 48–49, 174c, 244bc; Adrian Davies 247tl; Alain Le Garsmeur 288c, 288–289, 289tc; Alan Curtis 156br, 264–265; Alan Novelli 312–313c; Alistair Laming 204c; Andrew Darrington 105tr, 124–125; Andrew Holt 186bc; Andy Sutton 255br; Anna Sherwin 26cr; Apex News and Pictures Agency 132cra, 144tc; Arco Images GmbH 55bl, 237bc, 245c, 305br; Ashley Cooper 295br; ASP Norfolk Images 214–215; Beata Moore 175bl; Bernd Mellmann 202–203; Bill Coster PL 72tl, 84–85; Bill Coster Z 31cl, 44tl; BL Images Ltd 220tc, 251tl, 262–263, 263c; blickwinkel 6–7c, 14bl, 64bl, 83c, 89tr, 177c, 237c, 283tc, 297tr, 239cl; BlueSkyStock 240bc; Bob Gibbons 140–141, 161tl; Brian Crossley Photography 109bc; Cath Evans 275tr; Chris Gomersall 308bl; Cliff Hunt 149bc; Colin Palmer Photography 185br, 300cla; Cotswolds Photo Library 241br; D.G.Farquhar 199tr, 226–227; Daniel Bridge 85tc; Danita Delimont 180fbl; Dave Bevan 309tl; Dave Watts 144bl; David Boag 43tr; David Chapman 65cb, 95br, 99tc, 120–121, 137br, 221ca, 241bl, 299tc; David Cordner Main 4 38–39; David Gowans 268tl; DAVID NEWHAM 168–169; DAVID NOBLE PHOTOGRAPHY 245br; David Noton Photography 5br, 202bl; David Paterson 52tr, 67bl; David Robertson 109tr, 206tc; David Tipling 96–97c, 275bl; David Whitaker 260bl; Derek Croucher 293tl, 300–301; edo loi 288bc; Ewan Stevenson 198tr, 216–217; FLPA 98cb, 128–129; fotolincs 253c; Frank Blackburn 128tr, 145bc, 219br, 258tl; Gareth McCormack 208–209; Gary Cook 226tr, 233tr, 234bl; Gary John 32clb; Gary Stones 213bc; Genevieve Vallee 34–35; Graeme Peacock 11tl, 20–21; Graham Uney 24–25, 178–179, 254bc; I4images – Birmingham – 1 282clb; Ian West 149cl; imagebroker 132bl, 156cr, 248–249; ImageState 126–127; International Photobank 213br; James Davis Photography 45tl; James Hughes 186–187; Jan Smith Photography 198tl, 202tc; Jason Friend 235tc; Jason Gallier 258–259; Jeremy Inglis 122br; Jim Henderson 246tc,

247tr; Joan Gravel 56tr; John Barratt 72tr, 74–75; John Martin 225tr; Jon Arnold Images Ltd 273tc, 278tl; Jon Gibbs 46–47; Julia Gavin 188tc; Juniors Bildarchiv 221br; katewarn images 20clb, 272tl, 275cl; Keith Burdett 106tr; Keith M Law 47br, 214c; Krystyna Szulecka 158–159; Les Gibbon 98bl, 127bl, 146–147, 242tc, 242–243, 284bc; Leslie Garland Picture Library 53tc, 58–59, 305tc; Liam Grant 285bc; Lucy Levenson 259bl; Lynne Evans 20cla, 108bl; Marc Bedingfield 30tl, 42–43; Marc Hill 180–181; Mark Boulton 202ca, 202cb, 203tc; Mark Heywood 306bl; MARK HICKEN 234cb; Martin Fowler 120tl; Matthew Doggett 226tc; Michael Arthur Thompson 199tc, 212–213; Michael Howell 122br, 163c, 180cr; Michael Sayles 28–29; Michael Willis 230tc, 232–233; Mike Kipling Photography 59tr, 167tl, 184tc, 184–185, 233bl; Mike McEnnerney 56tl; Mirjana Nociar 189br; nagelestock.com 141br; Nature Photographers Ltd/PAUL R. STERRY 189c; Neil Hardwick 69c; Neil McAllister 62clb, 52ca; Niall Benvie 11tr, 13cl, 203c, 299bl; Nick Turner 35bc; Nigel Hicks 145br; Norsworthy Photography 30tc, 40bc; Organics image library/Nic Miller 292tr, 310bc; Organics image library/Veronica Carter 310–311; Pat Bennett 10tl, 10cl, 14tl, 14–15, 15tc, 15c, 102–103, 240br; Paul Brough 257tc; Paul Glendell 136–137; Paul Mogford 246–247, 247c; Paul Thompson Images 32tl, 33tc; PCL 111br; Peter Barritt 160–161; Phil Robinson/PjrFoto 172tc; Phil Wills 195br; picturesbyrob 250tl, 253tc; Ray Liversidge 284bl; Ray Wilson 183ca; Realimage 278–279; Renee Morris 20bl, 215ca, 269ftl, 276bl, 294bl, 305bc; Richard Becker 237br; Richard Childs Photography 42br, 238c; Richard Murph 208c; Robert Canis 11cl, 19tc, 306bc; Robert Estall photo agency 30tr, 36cr, 124tr; Robert Harding Picture Library Ltd 11br, 13tr, 53tl, 68tl, 245bl; Robert Morris 137tl, 274–275; Rod Edwards 270–271c; Scenics & Science 73clb, 88tl, 88–89; Scottish Viewpoint 231tc, 234–235; Sean Bolton 256–257, 304tc; Sean Burke 81tr; Shorelark 16tl; Simon Stirrup 170fbl, 240bl; South West Images Scotland 235tr, 235c; Springfield Photography 110bc; Stephen Bond 40c, 49tl; Stephen Dorey – Gloucestershire 81bl; Susan & Allan Parker 275br; tbkmedia.de 230tl, 239bl; Terry Mathews 218–219; Terry Wall 124bl; Terry Whittaker 221cb; The National Trust Photolibrary/Joe Cornish 288ca; The

Photolibrary Wales 99tr, 106–107, 254br; The Photolibrary Wales/Jeremy Moore 164–165; The Photolibrary Wales/Peter Lane 172cb; Thomas Dobner 2008 143bc; Tim Graham 18–19; Tom Mackie 263tr; Tony Cortazzi 264bl; Tony Lilley 162–163; Tony Pleavin 289bc; travelib europe 98tc, 102bc; Trevor Smithers ARPS 116cla; UK Alan King 63tr; Veronica Carter 310br; Vincent Lowe 217tl; WILDLIFE GmbH 280tr; WildPictures 210bl; wildpik 260c; Wildscotphotos 66bl; WilliamRobinson 62tl; willridge images 301c; Woodbridge Wildlife Images 293tc, 296tr.

Chris Gibson: 26–27, 53cl, 58cr, 63c, 64tc, 65tc, 68tc, 69tl, 69tc, 84bl, 98tr, 104–105, 109tc, 114bl, 114bc, 114–115, 116clb, 117tc, 124tl, 126bl, 128tl, 129tl, 129tc, 142bl, 143br, 156bc, 156–157, 176c, 176–177, 186bl, 209c, 209bc, 211tl, 211br, 214bc, 223bc, 265br, 266bl, 296bl, 299bc, 300bl.

Chris Gomersall: 22bl, 49tc, 52tc, 55cl, 61c, 63tc, 67tc, 83tl, 93tc, 98cla, 99ca, 112bc, 115bl, 125cr, 127tr, 146bl, 151tl, 166tl, 178bl, 192tc, 192bl, 192–193, 200bl, 201bl, 221tc, 226bl, 227tc, 272tc, 276br, 297c, 308tr, 309c.

Corbis: Andrew Parkinson 240–241; Barry Lewis 99tl, 110–111; Bryn Colton 294cr; Jeffrey L. Rotman 220cb; Kevin Fleming 273tl, 284–285; Mike McQueen 263tc; Owaki – Kulla 246tr; Paul Thompson 133tr, 142–143; Ralph A. Clevenger 48bl.

Darren Bland: 274bl.

David Shaw: 132tl, 134tl, 134cla, 134–135, 135t.

David Tipling: 2–3c, 13tl, 17ftl, 17cr, 22bc, 23bc, 26fbl, 35c, 38bl, 49tr, 49cl, 55tl, 66–67, 73cra, 79br, 86bl, 86br, 86cr, 87tr, 98tl, 99bl, 101tl, 105tc, 105bc, 105br, 108–109, 110br, 118tc, 118bc, 118–119, 122bl, 127tc, 127bc, 132tr, 133c, 136bl, 138bl, 141tl, 143tc, 149br, 150bl, 151tc, 153tc, 158bc, 158br, 167bl, 169c, 179br, 187br, 191cl, 201c, 207tc, 217c, 220ca, 227c, 233bc, 234tc, 250bl, 251tr, 253tr, 257bc, 265bl, 280bl, 281tr, 286tc, 286ca, 287tl, 302bc, 303bl, 308–309, 309tc, 309br.

Douglas Buchanan: 76–77.

FLPA: Alan & Linda Detrick 58fbl; Andrew Bailey 41bl, 41bc, 272clb, 275tl; Arthur Christiansen 119tc; B. Borrell Casals 88bl, 89tc, 125tc, 223tc, 223tr; Bill Baston 11tc, 24tl, 118bl, 154br, 205tc; Bjorn Ullhagen 205br; Bob Gibbons 36–37, 44bl, 109c,

138bc, 142br, 163bl, 163bc, 176tc, 178bc, 188bl, 191tl, 208bl, 219bc, 225br, 232br, 233fbl, 262bl, 275bc; Chris Mattison 89tl, 147tr, 236c; D P Wilson 53tr, 64c, 64bc, 160bl, 288bl, 298bl; David Burton 31tr, 49bc, 198tc, 214bl; David Hosking 35bl, 79tc, 91bl, 104bl, 125tl, 137bl, 149tl, 149tc, 172bl, 173tc, 176bl, 190bl, 195bc, 218bl, 232bl, 257tl, 293cla, 300clb, 310bl; David T. Grewcock 285bl; Derek Middleton 24bl, 33br, 58bc, 85br, 89cr, 108tc, 128bl, 152bl, 153tl, 175tc, 188tr, 216tr; Dickie Duckett 13br, 127tl, 155fbl, 159br, 169tr, 279tc; Dieter Hopf 17tr; Elliott Neep 30cl, 42bc, 50–51c, 79bl, 84bc, 121c, 141tr, 205bc, 227tr, 285ca; Foto Natura Stock 215bc; Foto Natura/Cisca Castelijns 198cr, 205cl, 211bl, 213bl, 225bl; Foto Natura/Flip de Nooyer 22c, 105bl, 231tr, 247tc; Foto Natura/Frits van Daalen 65bc, 67cl, 192cb; Foto Natura/Hans Leijense 299tr; Foto Natura/Hans Schouten 282cla; Foto Natura/Jaap Luijendijk 25tl; Foto Natura/Jan van Arkel 216bl; Foto Natura/Jan Vermeer 311bl; Foto Natura/Jef Meul 211cl; Foto Natura/Martin Woike 116tl, 178br; Foto Natura/Minden Pictures/Ingo Arndt 224bl; Foto Natura/Peter Verhoog 34br; Foto Natura/Rene Krekels 205bl, 211tc, 211bc; Foto Natura/Rob Reijnen 95bc; Foto Natura/Wil Meinderts 256bl; Foto Natura/Wim Weenink 55tc; Foto Natura/Piet Munsterman 296–297; Francois Merlet 236–237bc; Frans Lanting 127cl; Gary K Smith 12bl, 20tl, 21tr, 22ca, 40br, 60bl, 78bl, 82tc, 110bl, 185tl, 265tl; Gianpiero Ferrari 177tr; Hans Dieter Brandl 55bc; Hugh Clark 36bl, 39ftl, 62cla, 140bl, 170br, 218bc; Ian Rose 143bl, 184tr, 189tc; Imagebroker/Anton Luhr 168bl, 285br; Imagebroker/Bernd Zoller 62bl, 137bc, 185tc, 185c, 251tc, 268bl, 268–269; Imagebroker/Birgit Koch 75c; Imagebroker/Franz Waldhäusl 278bl; Imagebroker/Gerhard Zwerger-Schoner 167br, 179c; Imagebroker/Horst Jegen 309tr; Imagebroker/Karlheinz Irlmeier 130–131c; Imagebroker/Marko König 174bl, 205tl; Imagebroker/Martin Siepmann 80bl; Imagebroker/Michael Dietrich 31tc, 32–33; Imagebroker/Michael Krabs 219c; Imagebroker/Stefan Wackerhagen 179bl; Imagebroker/Winfried Schäfer 44tr; Jean Hall 187bc; Jeremy Early 82–83, 194bl; Joan Hutchings 163fbl; John Eveson 239tc; John Hawkins 10bc, 26bl, 77tl, 90br, 134clb, 141bl; John Watkins 26br, 278tr; Malcolm Schuyl 25c, 117tr, 141tc, 153bl, 191tr, 193c, 212bl;

FLPA (continued): Marcus Siebert 17ftr; Mark Newman 19bc; Mark Sisson 121tl; Martin B Withers 106tl, 149tr, 231cla, 238bl, 243bc, 298–299; Maurice Nimmo 161tr; Michael Callan 103br, 179bc, 203br; Michael Gore 199cr, 225cl; Mike J Thomas 142fbl; Mike Lane 26bc, 36br, 42fbl, 42cr, 89br, 103bl, 103tc, 129tr, 150tr, 215cb; Minden Pictures/Flip Nicklin 198bc, 201bc; Minden Pictures/Hiroya Minakuchi 200br; Minden Pictures/John Eastcott/Yva Momatiuk 144bc; Minden Pictures/Konrad Wothe 111tc, 122fbr, 252bl; Minden Pictures/Michael & Patricia Fogden 191bc; Minden Pictures/ Thomas Mangelsen 134bl; Neil Bowman 205cr, 269tl; Nicholas and Sherry Lu Aldridge 132tc, 139bl, 166cla, 180bc; Nigel Cattlin 65br, 91fbl; Paul Hobson 39tl, 49bl, 67tr, 72ca, 76tl, 85bc, 142bc, 148bl, 157tr, 159bl, 161tc, 162bc, 199bc, 218br, 230cb, 232bc, 233c, 244br; Peter Entwistle 75bl, 167ca, 170–171, 224c, 311br; Peter Reynolds 231tl, 242cb, 243c; Peter Wilson 112fbl, 115br, 146fbl, 152–153, 190c; Phil McLean 57tl, 81tl, 144c, 206tr, 259tl, 262tl, 263tl; R.Dirscherl 14clb, 47bc; Richard Becker 137tr, 166cra, 177tc, 194c, 195bl, 236cl, 239tl, 258tr, 311bc; Richard Brooks 47c, 60tl, 193tc, 265cl; Robert Canis 151br, 290–291c, 306br, 306–307, 307bl, 307c; Robin Chittenden 90bl, 92clb, 121tr, 153br, 170cr, 225tc, 303bc; Roger Tidman 21c, 42bl, 47tc, 67tl, 120bl, 137cl, 158bl, 186c, 252tc, 252c, 260tc, 302bl; Roger Wilmshurst 13bl, 95tl, 108c, 122fbl, 125tr, 133tl, 146bc, 163br, 193tr, 215br, 223br, 239br, 279tl, 293tr, 294bc; Silvestris Fotoservice 33c, 175tr; Simon Litten 276cr; Steve Young 273bl, 283c; Sunset 76tr, 77c; Terry Whittaker 10tr, 16tr, 34bl, 73tr, 81bc, 106bl, 181tr, 183cal, 199tl, 220bl, 220–221, 269cr; Tom and Pam Gardner 296bl; Tony Hamblin 23br, 38tl, 54bl, 195tl, 212br, 258bl, 269tr, 299br, 300tl; Tony Wharton 195tc, 225bc; Walter Rohdich 88tr; Wayne Hutchinson 57tc, 184bl; Winfried Wisniewski 159bc, 192ca, 247bl; Yossi Eshbol 180bl.

Getty Images: Cyril Ruoso 166tr, 188–189; Frank Siteman 292cla, 299cl;

Minden Pictures/Foto Natura/Danny Ellinger 83tc; Panoramic Images 168ca; Paul Wakefield 228–229; Sam Abell 31tl, 44–45; Travel Ink 80–81.

Gordon Allison: 55tr.

Harlequin Pictures: Robin Chittenden 14cla, 77tr, 239tr, 244bl, 245bc.

iStockphoto.com: Ai-Lan Lee 260–261; Alan Crawford 204bl; ALFIO FERLITO 242ca; Andrew Howe 36bc, 81cl, 255tc, 287ftl; anja frost 137tc; AtWaG 173c, 239bc; AVTG 281cr; Bartosz Budrewicz 57c; Black Beck Photographic 73tl, 90–91, 91fbr, 299tl; David Hughes 68bl; Dmitry Maslov 175tl; Douglas McGilviray 260bc; Eugenia Garcia-Valdecasas 41br; Gary Martin 122bl; Graeme Purdy 25tc ; Graham Taylor 212bc; hazel proudlove 95tl; Henk Bentlage 207tr; Ian Webb 155cr; John Williams 116–117; Joseph Gareri 307br; Karel Broz 120tr; Marco Rosario Venturini Autieri 167tc, 175cl; Mark Doyle 19br; Mark Wilson 61tr; Matt Norris 45c; Oleg Rubik 36fbl; Paul Mckeown 45tr; Piotr Peszko 255bc; Ralph Loesche 121ftl; Steve Geer 135c; Steve McWilliam 170bl; stevo112 303c; Tom Curtis 133br, 151c; Vladimir Chernyanskiy 91cr.

Kris Roberts: 230tr, 230cra.

Mike Read: 15tr, 30bc, 34bc, 37tr, 46tc, 46bc, 58bl, 58br, 68–69, 74bl, 74bc, 74br, 76bl, 81br, 82bl, 92bl, 99br, 101tc, 101tr, 107tl, 107tc, 112bl, 112br, 112cr, 114br, 114fbr, 116bl, 121ftr, 129c, 132cb, 135cb, 139c, 146cr, 148–149, 149bl, 150tl, 156fbl, 156bl, 160tl, 160tr, 161c, 168cb, 170bc, 173tr, 189tl, 191br, 195tb, 195cl, 200bc, 206bl, 213c, 216tc, 217tc, 219bl, 225tl, 227tl, 250tc, 250cra, 251bl, 254–255, 259tc, 259tr, 259c, 261tc, 261c, 261bc, 262tr, 265tc, 265tr, 265bc, 266cla, 279cr, 281tl, 293ca, 301tr, 304bl, 304c, 304bc.

Natural England: Peter Wakely 304–305.

naturepl.com: Adrian Davies 223bl; Andy Sands 279br; Artur Tabor 144–145; Dave Watts 35br; David Kjaer 277tr, 282–283; Dietmar Nill 16bl, 55br; Doug Perrine 200–201; Gary K. Smith 62–63; Geoff Simpson 18ct;

Hans Christoph Kappel 150–151; John Cancalosi 276–277; Laurent Geslin 38tr; Michael Durham 222bl; Michel Roggo 284br; Ross Hoddinott 244–245; Sue Flood 252–253; Todd Pusser 201br; Tony Heald 18cb; Torsten Brehm 77tc.

NHPA: A.N.T. Photo Library 92–93; Alan Williams 100–101; Alberto Nardi 45tc; Andy Rouse 241bc; Bill Coster 102bl; David Tipling 281br; James Warwick 16–17; Jari Peltomaki 178fbl; Jordi Bas Casas 32bl; Marie Read 243bl; Michael Leach and Meriel Lland 172ca; Robert Thompson 273br, 289br; Roger Tidman 297tl; Stephen Dalton 198bl, 222c, 223tl.

Northern Light Charters: Graham Savage 268tr; Michael McKee 269ftr.

NTPL: Joe Cornish 171tr.

Pat Rolph: 92cla, 93c.

Paul Reid: 73tc, 92tl.

Photolibrary: age fotostock/Morales Morales 67br; Dennis Green 182clb; Ian West 210c; Oxford Scientific (OSF)/ David Clapp 70–71c; Oxford Scientific (OSF)/Elliott Neep 8–9c; Oxford Scientific (OSF)/Iain Sarjeant 86–87; Robert Harding Travel/Julian Pottage 64–65; Robert Harding Travel/Neale Clark 119br.

rspb-images.com: Andrew Parkinson 52bl, 54–55, 72tc, 79cl, 199cl, 206–207; Andy Hay 12c, 13tc, 13bc, 24tr, 25tr, 39tr, 52tl, 60tr, 60–61, 61tl, 72cb, 73br, 79tr, 82tl, 82tr, 86bc, 95bl, 112–113, 117c, 133tc, 153tr, 153cl, 166tc, 166bc, 168tc, 169tc, 182cra, 183tr, 191bl, 243tr, 250tr, 251br, 255bl, 266clb, 266–267, 267tr, 273tr, 283tr, 286bl, 286cb, 286tr, 286–287, 287ftr; Ben Hall 1c, 17tl, 79tl, 139br, 162br, 182ca, 182bc, 257cl; Bob Glover 40bl, 40–41; Chris Gomersall 39cr, 46bl, 91br, 100tl, 122tc, 175bc, 182–183, 266tl; Chris Knights 53br, 56–57, 93tr, 257br, 287tr, 294–295; Chris Lloyd 56bl; Danny Green 243tc, 261bl; David Kjaer 138fbl, 138–139, 139bc, 209br, 257tr, 257bl, 272tr, 280–281, 292tc, 301tc, 302bc, 302–303; David Norton 127br, 276bc; David Osborn 292bc, 307bc; David Tipling 75br, 100tr, 101c, 196–197, 245tc, 292tl, 308tl; David Wootton 182cb; Ernie Janes 155br; Genevieve Leaper 113tr, 294br; Gerald

Downey 297tc; Graham Eaton 267tc; Jackie Cooper 162bl; Jan Halady 94bl, 94–95; Jodie Randall 23bl, 272cra, 280tl; John Markham 153bc; Laurie Campbell 231br, 241c; Mark Hamblin 103bc, 145tc, 207c, 282bl, 311c; Mike Lane 155fbr, 213fbl, 267c, 282tl; Mike Read 21tc, 107tr; Mike Richards 83br, 105tl, 138btr; Nigel Blake 107c; Peter Cairns 57tr, 135tr, 141bc, 234ca; Ray Kennedy 49br, 115bc, 119bc, 281tc; Richard Brooks 31br, 78–79, 159tc; Richard Revels 122bc, 139tc; Robert Horne 167tr, 172–173; RSPB 10tc, 22–23; Stanley Porter 119c; Steve Round 154bc, 279tr, 303br; Sue Kennedy 115c; Sue Tranter 18bl, 27tr, 61cb, 90bc, 111bl, 133bl, 154bl, 155bl; Tom Marshall 217tr; Tony Hamblin 32cla, 39ftr.

Science Photo Library: Dr Keith Wheeler 69tr.

Steve Williams: 236tc, 236, 237tc.

Tim Callaghan: 187c.

All other images © Dorling Kindersley For further information, see www.dkimages.com

Every effort has been made to trace the copyright holders. The publisher apologizes for any unintentional omission and would be pleased, in such cases, to place an acknowledgement in future editions of this book.

Cobalt id would like to thank Sarah Whittley and Neil Mason for additional material and editorial assistance, Dr Mark Boyd at the RSPB, and Hilary Bird for the index. Special thanks are also due to the following individuals who helped source images for this book: Fiona Ford, Kris Roberts, Steve Williams, and all the staff of Torfaen County Borough Council; Douglas Buchanan, Steve Oakes, and Alan Patterson at Woollston Eyes; Gordon Allison, RSPB North Kent Marshes; Andy Wakelin; and Hannah Thompson of Northern Light Charters for images of the Monach Isles (find out more at www. northernlight-uk.com).